Arabesques
Arabesken
Arabescos

L'Aventurine

• Contents • Sommaire • Inhalt • Índice •

Foreword

It is to Italian art that we are endebted for those magnificent designs called arabesques. Directly inspired by Arabic art which arrived massively in the port city of Venise, Renaissance artists continually used interlacing and foliated scrolls for decoration in architecture, garden design, textiles, typography, armour, vases and other objects from everyday life. Their sinuous lines became the attributes of luxury languidly covering stone, metal, ceramics, glass or leather in limitless variations.

Calligraphy also took possession of the arabesque, and soon ornamental letters were lost in a maze of embellishments which raised decorative writing to an art form.

The vogue was to such an extent that embroidery pattern books circulated throughout Europe. *Patrons de broderie façon arabique et ytalique,* by the Italian Francisque Pellegrin (1530) was copied by numerous artists and craftsmen. Leonardo da Vinci himself was extremely fond of interlacing. The gown worn by Mona Lisa is decorated with them as are the walls and ceiling of the Sala delle Asse in the Castello Sforzesco. The Italian master was copied by Albrecht Dürer who created a series of *Six knot designs* after Leonardo's etchings.

The works of other German artists – notably Virgile Solis, Peter Flötner, Theodore de Bry – enjoyed wide success. In a spirit of reciprocity soon the Italian masters were copying their German counterparts !

France was not to be left out, where the art of engraving was particularly brillant combining simplicity, clearness and elegance. The work of Androuet du Cerceau was a definite source of pride and glory. He engraved innumerable niellos, marquetry and flower bed patterns as well as textile designs. Intended for use by different trades, embroidery pattern books with their special flavor were in fashion there also, as were Moorish pattern books.

The finest examples of this art form have been brought together for your pleasure in this encyclopedia.

Avant-propos

C'est à l'art italien que nous devons ces magnifiques ornements que sont les arabesques. Directement inspirés par l'art arabe dont les productions arrivaient massivement dans le port de Venise, les artistes de la Renaissance n'eurent de cesse d'orner l'architecture, les jardins, les tissus, les livres, les armures, les vases et autres objets de la vie courante d'entrelacs et de rinceaux. Leurs lignes sinueuses devinrent l'apanage du luxe, s'étalèrent avec langueur en d'infinies variations sur la pierre, le métal, la céramique, le verre ou le cuir.

L'écriture elle-même s'empara de l'arabesque, noyant les lettres calligraphiées dans un dédale de fioritures qui la hissèrent au rang de véritable ornement.

L'engouement fut tel que des recueils de « patrons de broderies » circulaient à travers toute l'Europe. Ainsi celui de l'Italien Francisque Pellegrin, *Patrons de broderie façon arabique et ytalique,* fut-il copié par de nombreux artistes et artisans. Leonardo da Vinci lui-même avait un goût prononcé pour les entrelacs. La robe de la Joconde en est parée et elles figurent sur les fresques du plafond de la Sala delle Asse au Castello Sforzesco. Il fut lui-même copié par Albrecht Dürer qui exécuta une série de *Six nœuds* d'après les gravures de Leonardo.

Les œuvres des artistes allemands – il faut, entre autres, citer Virgile Solis, Peter Flötner, Theodore de Bry – eurent une très grande vogue. Bientôt, les maîtres italiens, usant de réciprocité, les copièrent à leur tour !

La France, quant à elle, ne fut pas en reste et vit s'épanouir un art de la gravure brillant par la simplicité et la clarté unies à l'élégance. Ce pays put se glorifier de posséder un artiste tel que Androuet du Cerceau qui grava une multitude de « nielles », de dessins destinés à la marqueterie aussi bien qu'aux broderies des jardins de son temps, ou encore au textile. Les « livres de broderies », à la saveur toute particulière, destinés à être utilisés par différents corps de métiers, firent florès, tout comme les recueils de moresques.

Ce sont ici les plus beaux exemples de cet art que nous vous donnons à admirer.

Vorwort

Die Arabesken, diese wundervollen Ornamente, verdanken wir den Künstlern der italienischen Renaissance. Sie wurden von arabischen Kunstwerken inspiriert, die in großer Zahl im Hafen von Venedig ausgeschifft wurden. Sie zögerten nicht alle Gegenstände des täglichen Lebens mit Flechtwerk sowie Laub- und Rankenwerken zu schmücken, in der Architektur und im Garten, Stoffe, Bücher, Vasen, Rüstungen, einfach alles. Die gewundenen Linien wurden das Symbol des Luxus und fanden sich in endlosen Variationen auf Stein, Metall, Keramik, Glas oder Leder. Auch die Schreibkunst bemächtigte sich der Arabesken, indem sie die kalligrafischen Lettern in einem wahren Wirrwarr von Verzierungen erstickte, um sie so zu eigenen, neuen Ornamenten umzugestalten.

Die Begeisterung ging so weit, daß umfangreiche Sammlungen mit Stickmuster in ganz Europa zirkulierten. So die des Italieners Francisque Pellegrin, „Patrons de broderie façon arabique et ytalique", die von vielen Künstlern und Handwerkern kopiert wurden. Selbst Leonardo da Vinci hatte einen ausgeprägten Sinn für die Schnörkel. Das Kleid der Monna Lisa ist übersäht damit ebenso wie die Fresken an der Decke der Sala delle Asse im Castello Sforzesco. Er wurde sogar von Albrecht Dürer kopiert, der eine Serie „die sechs Knoten" nach Werken von Leonardo schuf. Deutsche Künstler – u.a. Virgil Solis, Peter Flötner oder Theodor von Bry – hatten ihre große Zeit. Bald wurden sie sogar kopiert, sozusagen im Umkehrschluß, von den Italienern.

Auch Frankreich schloß sich nicht aus und erlebte die Blüte einer klaren stringenten und gleichwohl eleganten Kunstrichtung. Das Land ist stolz auf einen Androuet du Cerceau, der eine Vielzahl „Niellos" schuf, Zeichnungen für die Einlegearbeiten in den zeitgenössischen Gärten oder auch für textile Stickereien. Die „Bücher der Stickerei", mit ihrem ganz besonderen Reiz, sind Blumen geschmückt ganz wie die maurischen Sammlungen und dienten den verschiedensten Meistern.

Wir zeigen die schönsten Beispiele dieser Kunst, bewundern, bestaunen Sie sie.

Prólogo

Es al arte italiano a quien debemos los magníficos ornamentos que son los arabescos. Directamente inspirados en el arte árabe, donde las producciones llegaron masivamente al puerto de Venecia, los artistas del Renacimiento trabajaron sin interrupción en el adorno de la arquitectura, los jardines, los libros, las armaduras, los vasos y otros objetos de la vida corriente, con trazos y ornamentos. En sus sinuosas líneas se adivina un patrimonio de unidad de luz, exponiendo con languidez infinitas variaciones sobre la piedra, el metal, la céramica y el cuero.

Es la misma escritura quien se adueña del arabesco, estableciendo las letras caligráficas en un dédalo de florituras que la sube al rango de verdadero ornamento.

El capricho por semejante armazón, a partir de colecciones de "patrones de bordado", circularía a través de toda Europa. Así, los del italiano Francisque Pellegrin, titulados *Patrons de broderie façon arabique et ytalique,* fueron copiados por numerosos artistas y artesanos. El mismo Leonardo da Vinci tuvo el gusto de pronunciarse por los citados rasgos. De ese modo se adorna el vestido de la Gioconda, y ellos, los arabescos, figuran en los frescos del techo de la *Sala delle Asse* en el castillo Sforzesco. Esto fue copiado por Alberto Durero, quien ejecutó une serie de *Seis nudos* según los grabados de Leonardo.

La obras de los artistas alemanes – cabe citar, entre otros, a Virgile Solís, Peter Flötner y Theodore de Bry – estuvieron muy de moda. ¡Pronto a los maestros italianos se la jugaron, compiándoles en uso de una clara reciprocidad! En cuanto a Francia, no fue menos y vio desarollarse un arte de grabado brillante, por la simplicidad y la claridad añadidas a la elegancia. Este país puedo vanagloriarse de tener un artista tal como Androuet du Cerceau, que grabaría una multitud de añublados de diseño destinados a la marquetería y también a bordados de los jardines de sus tiempos, o todavía en textil. Los "libros de bordados" son el salvador de cualquier particular, destinados a ser utilizados por diferentes gremios de oficios on diversos floreados, todo como colecciones de moriscos.

Estos son los más bellos ejemplos de ese arte que nosotros les podemos ofrecer para admirar.

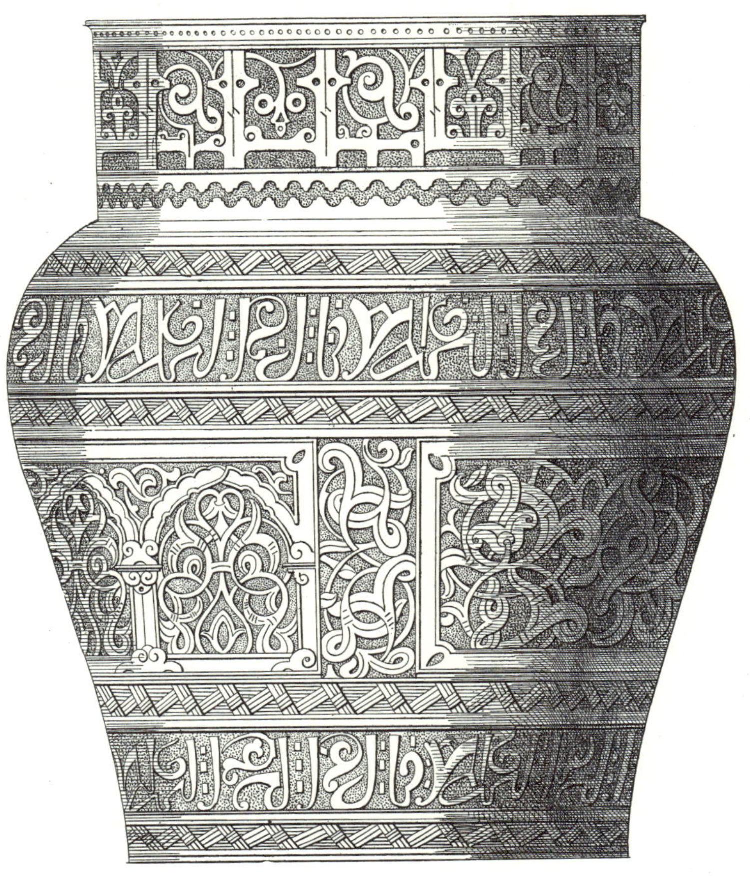

• Sources •

• Les sources •

• Quellen •

• Las fuentes •

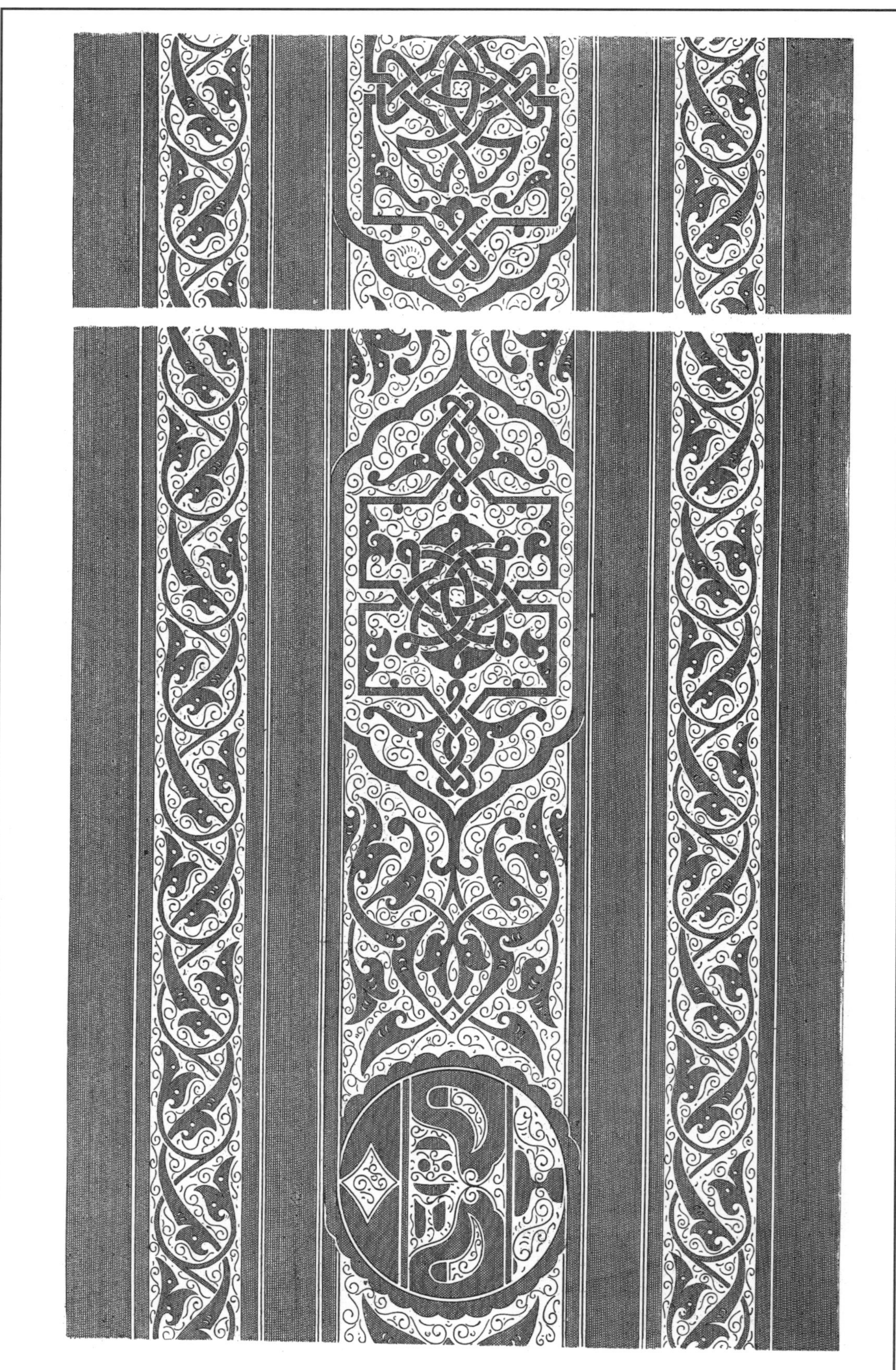

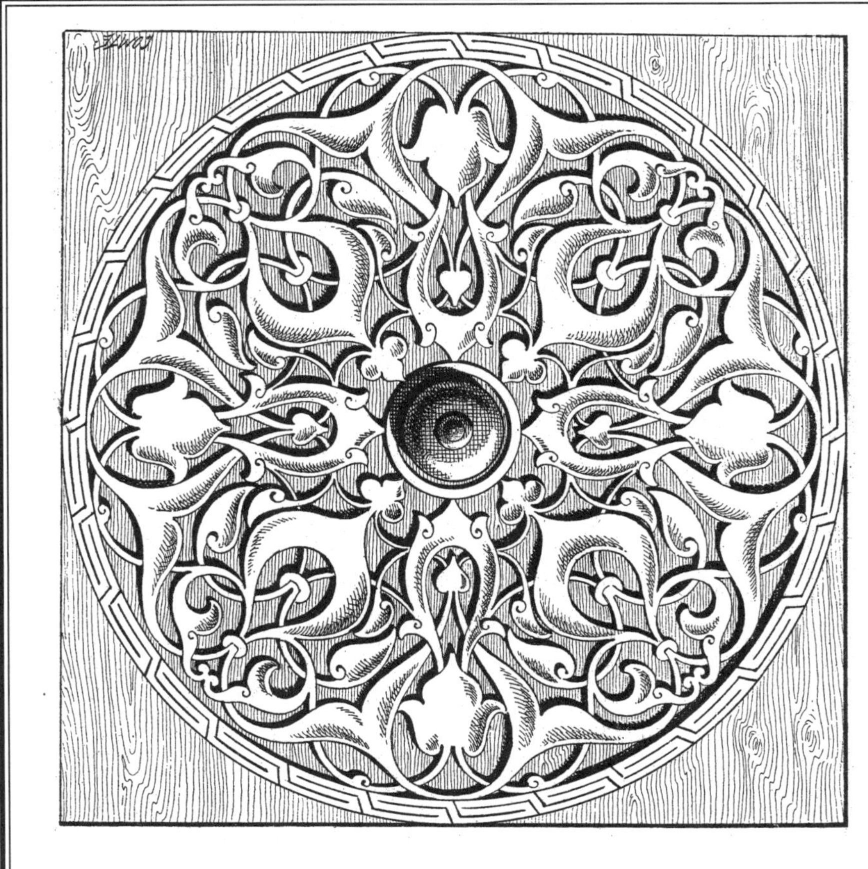

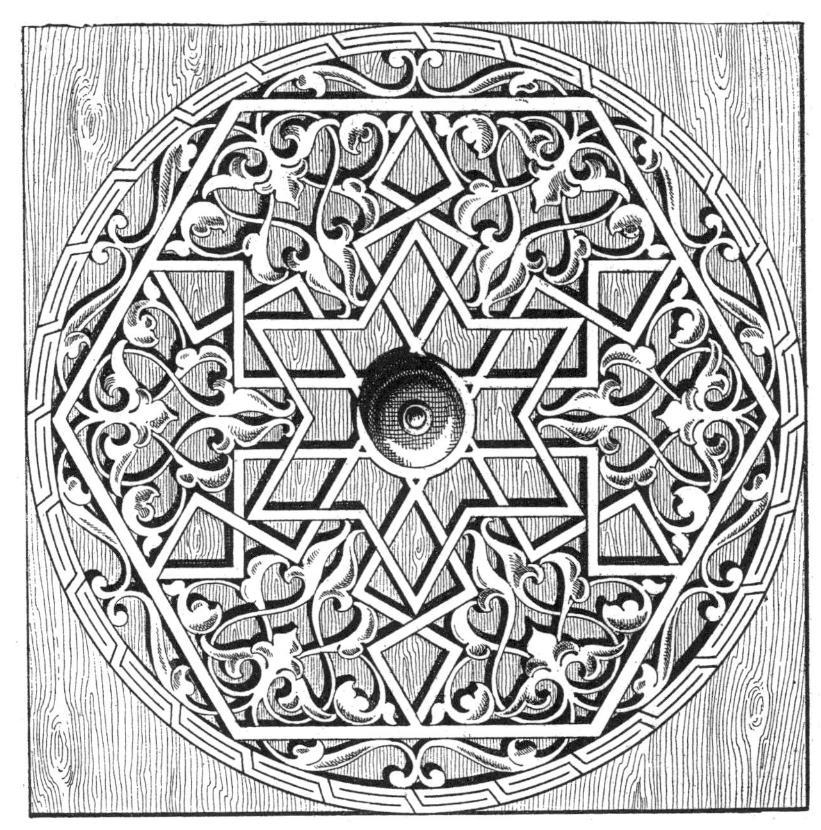

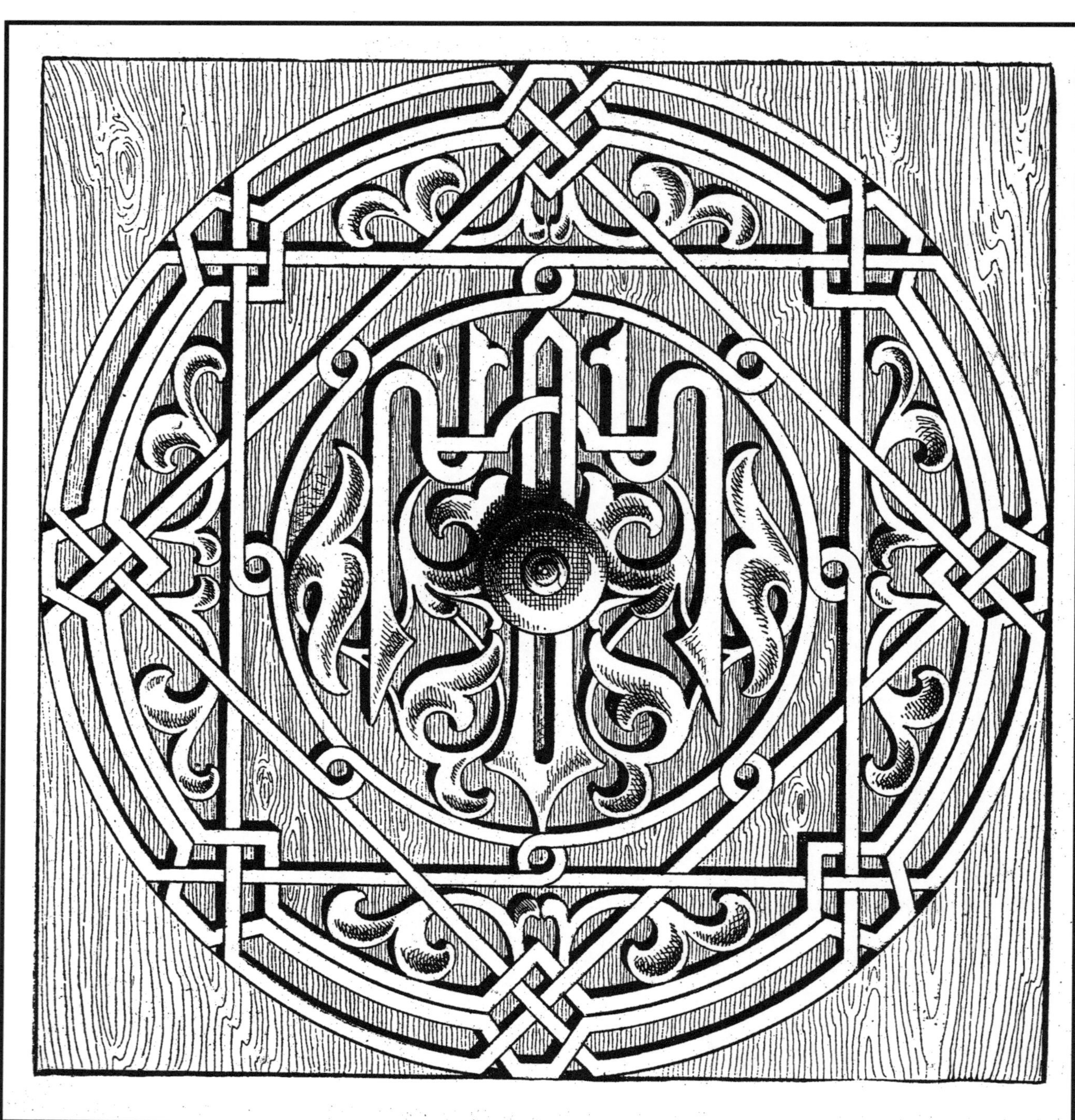

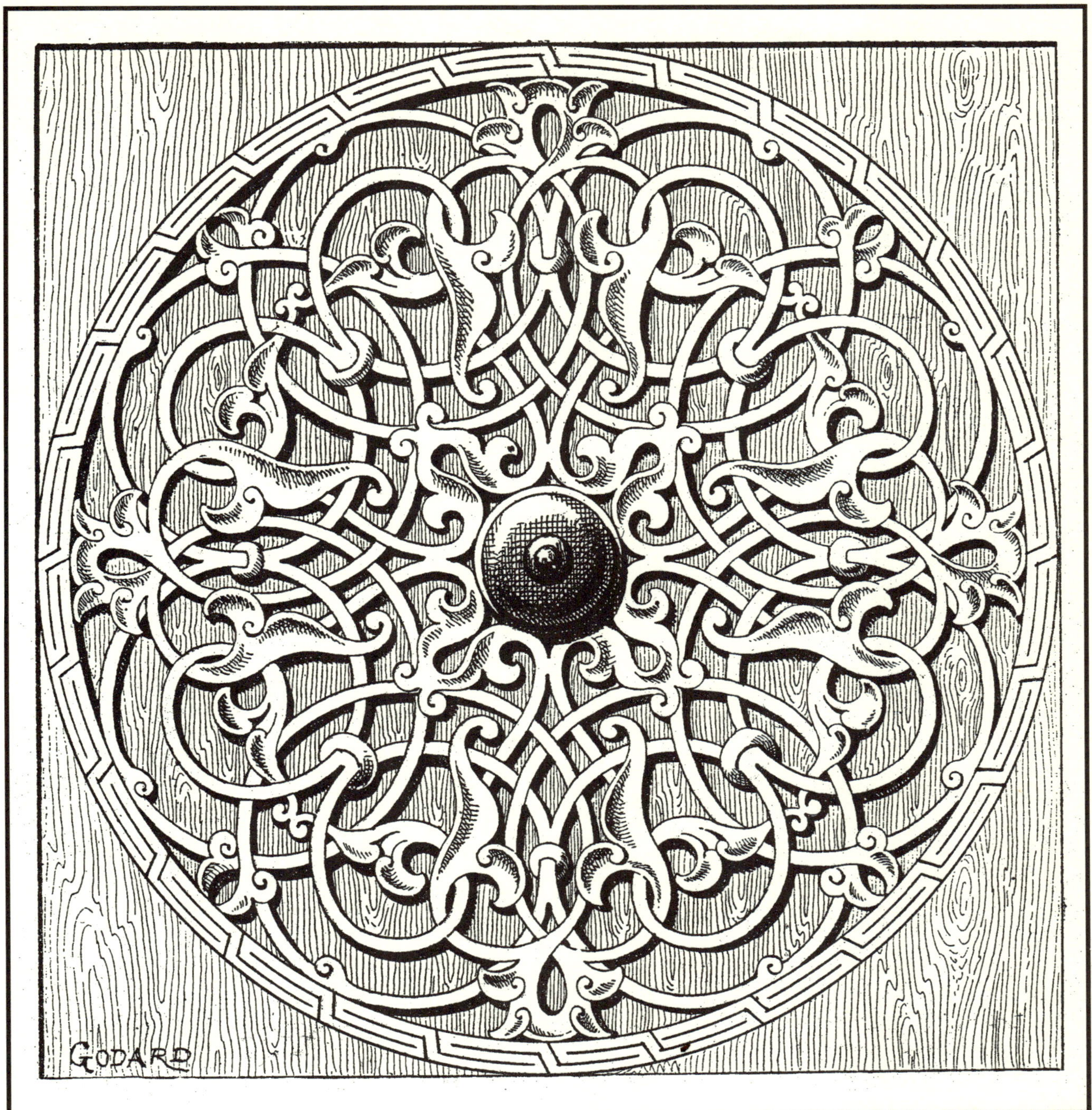

GODARD

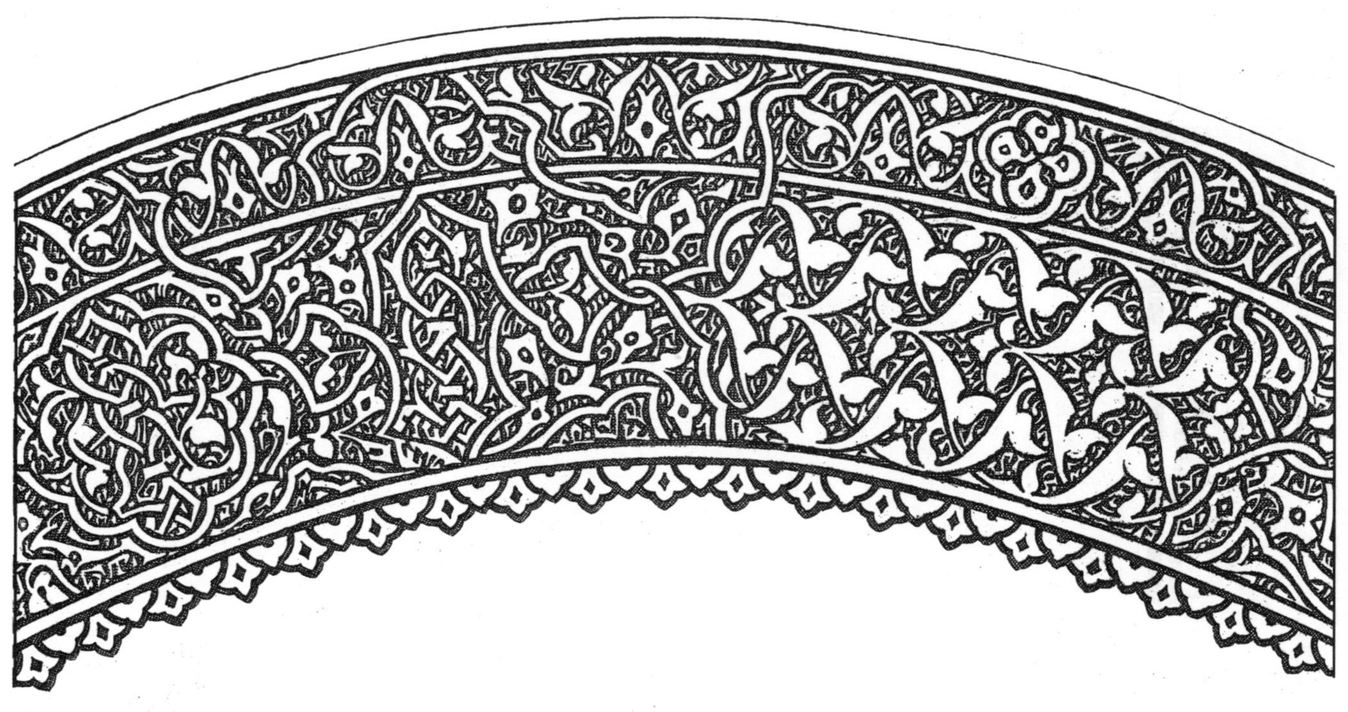

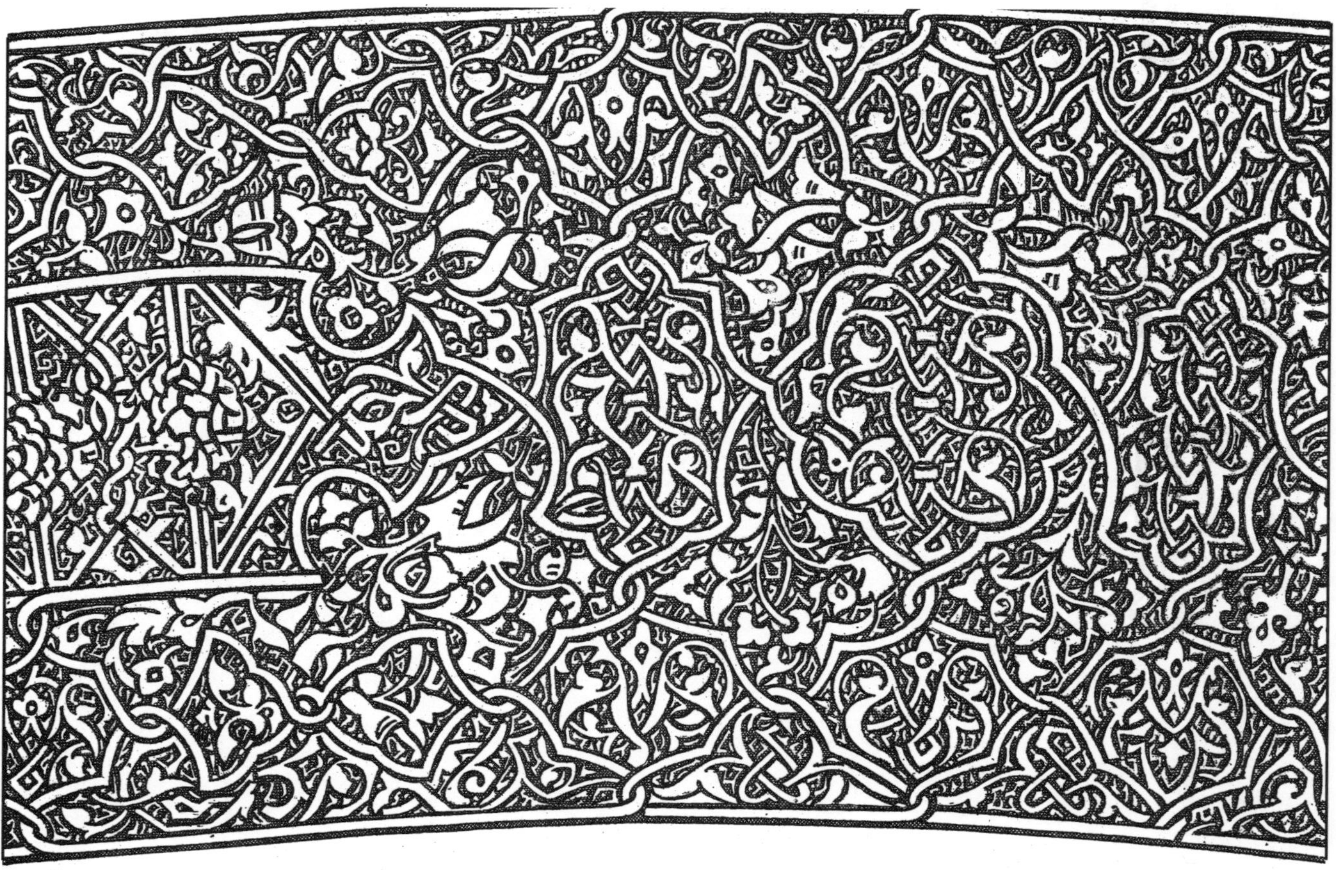

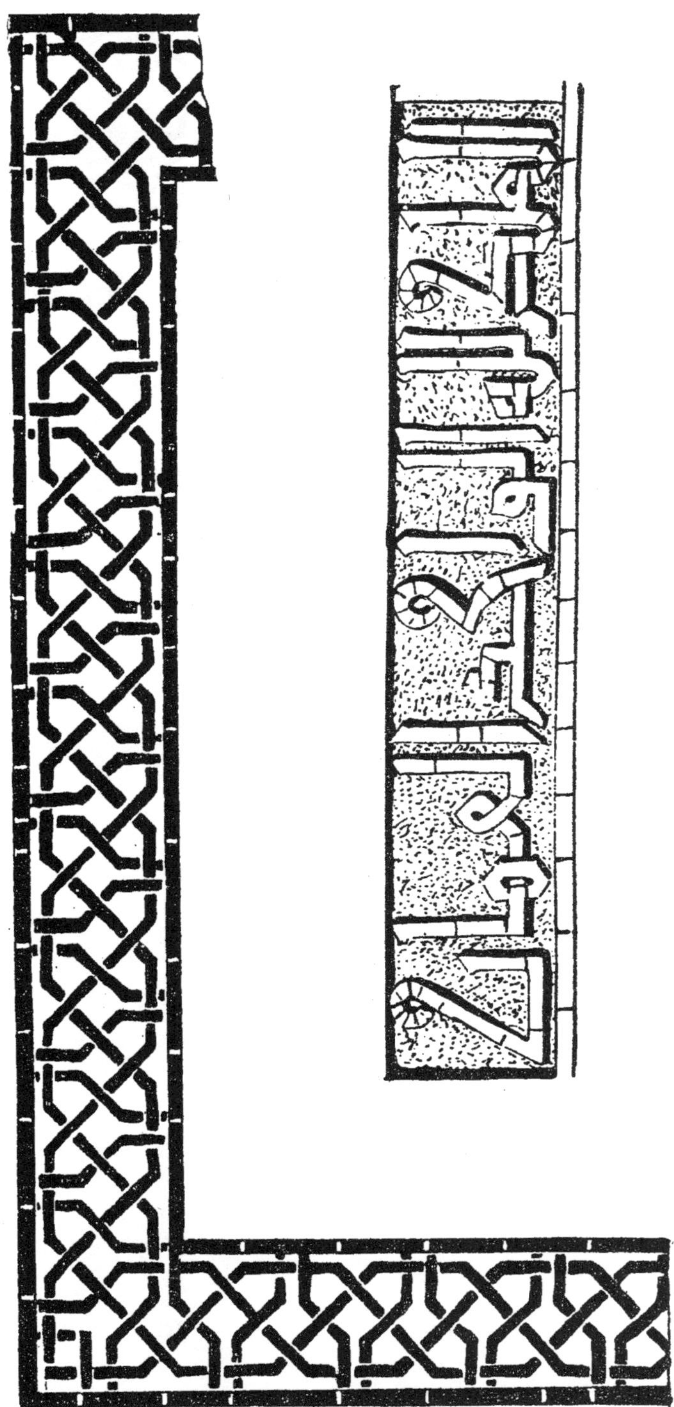

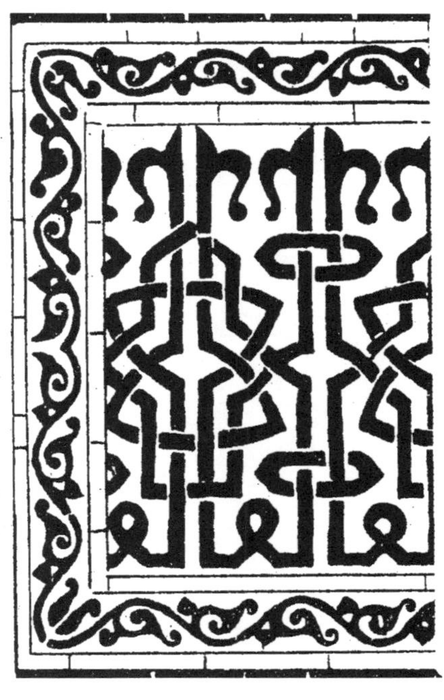

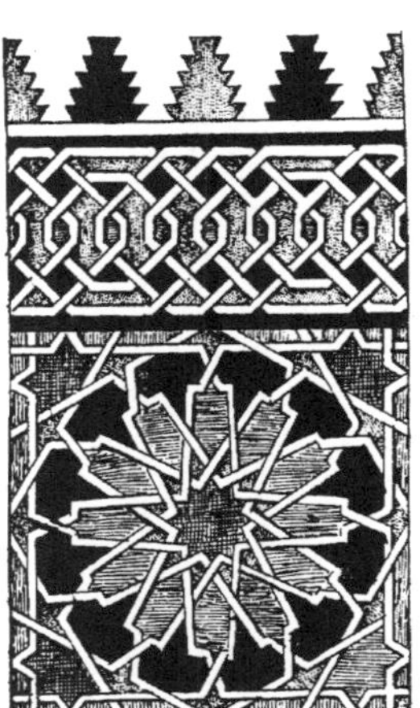

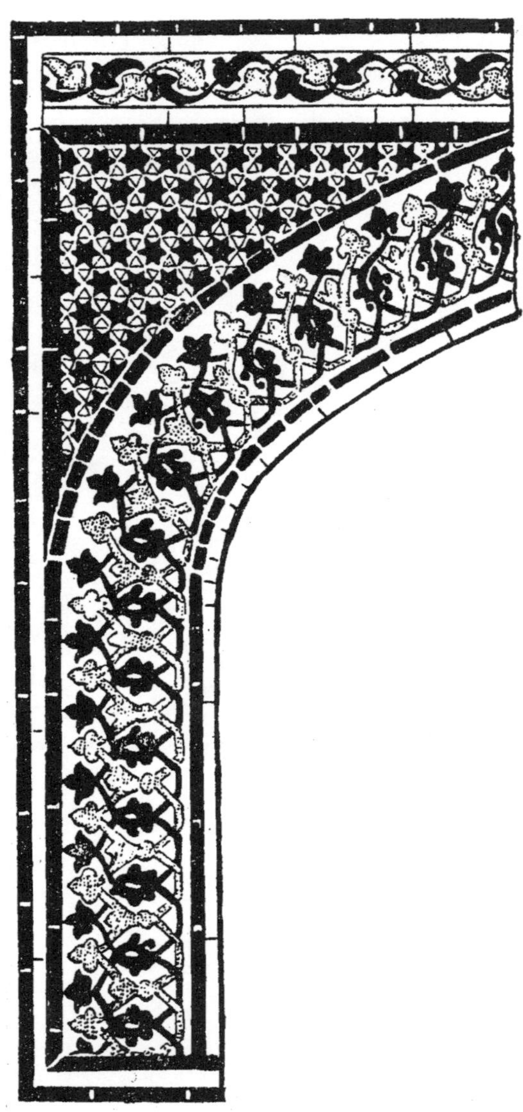

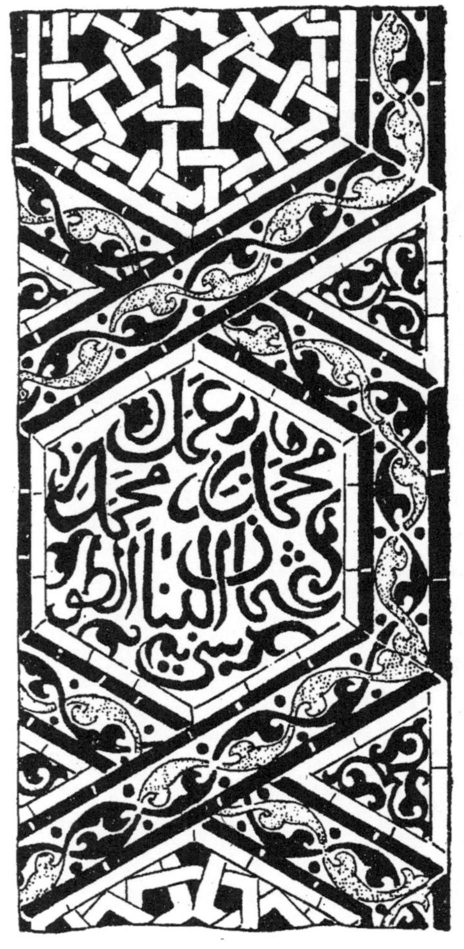

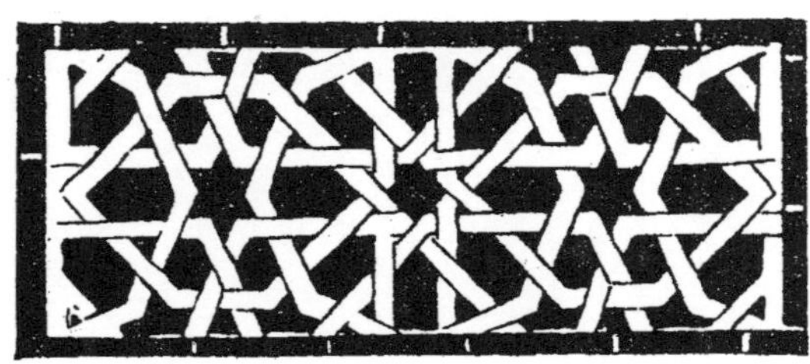

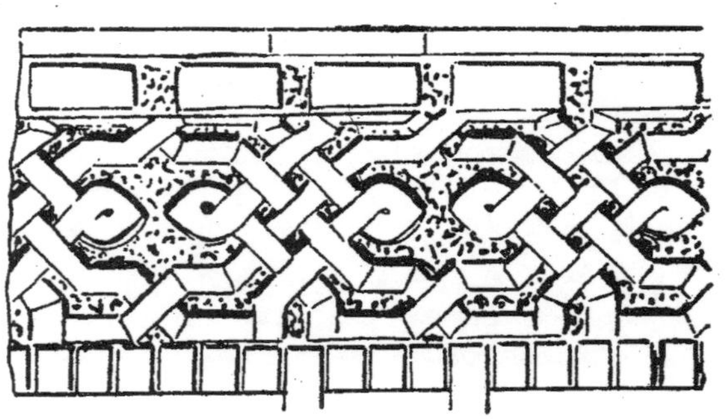

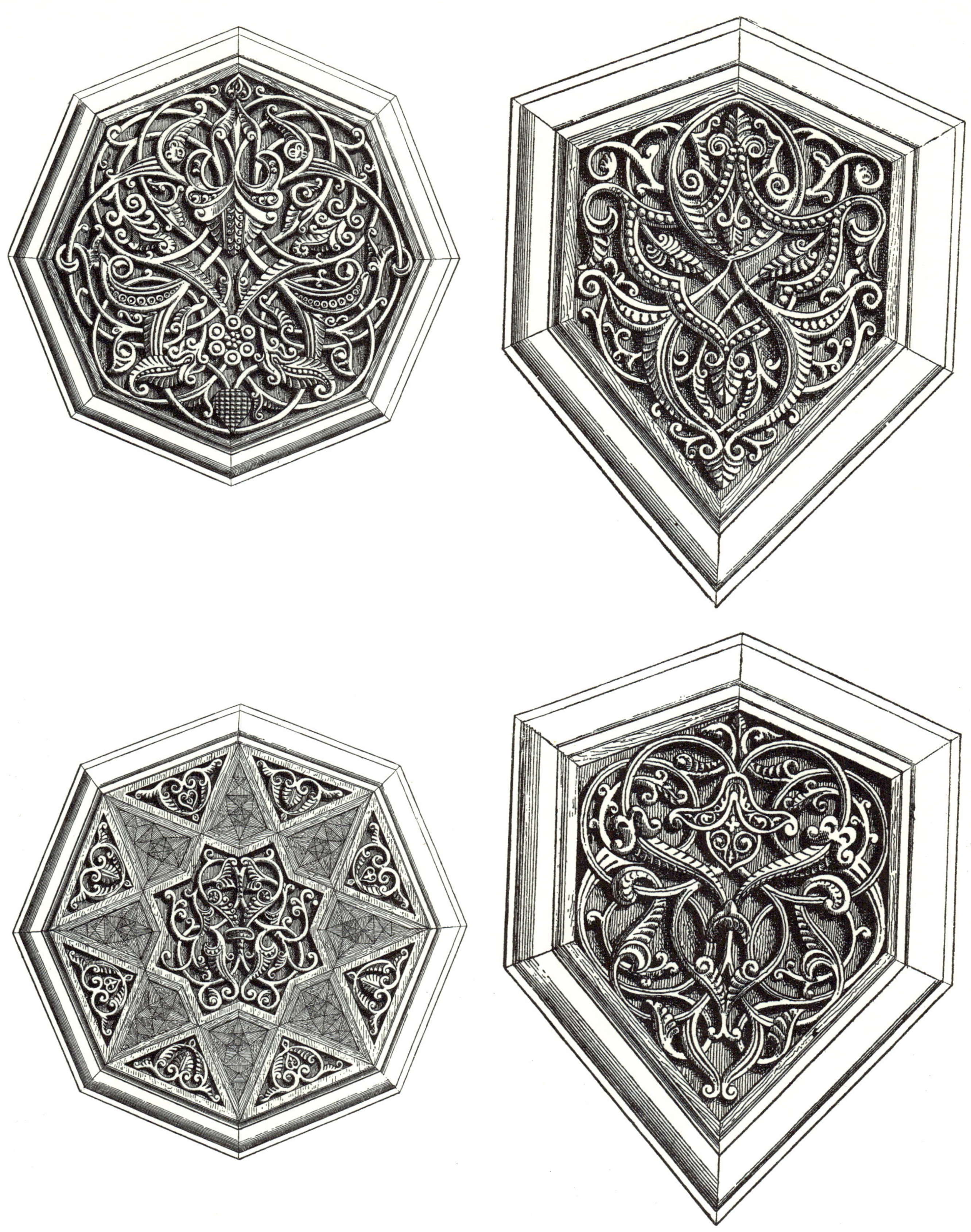

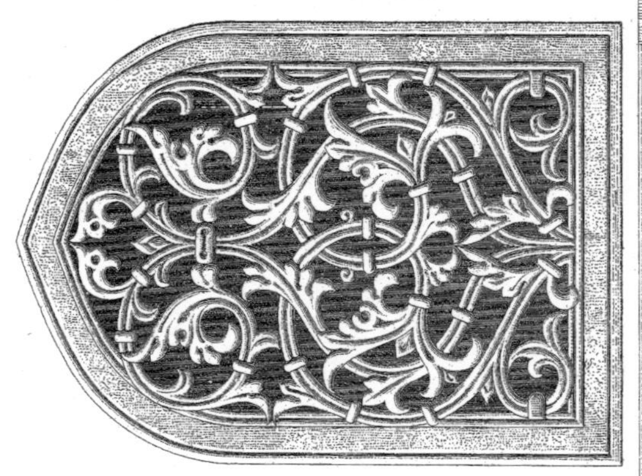

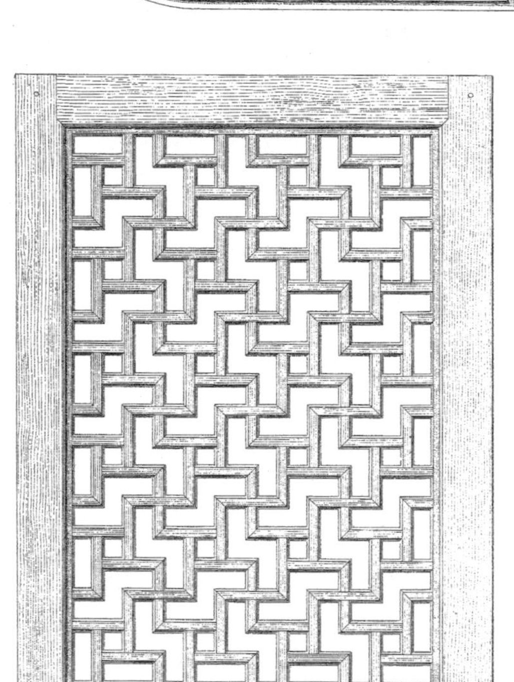

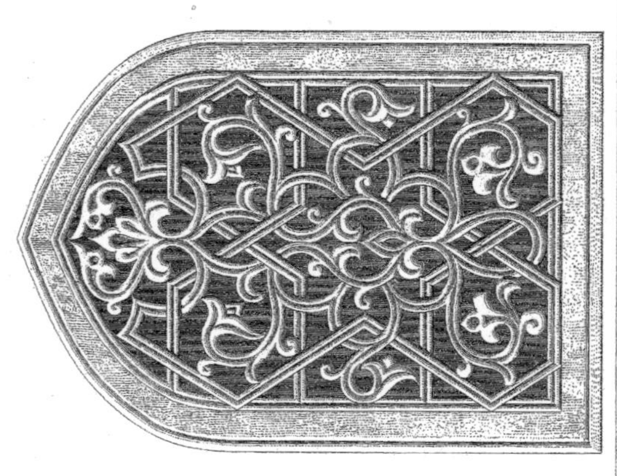

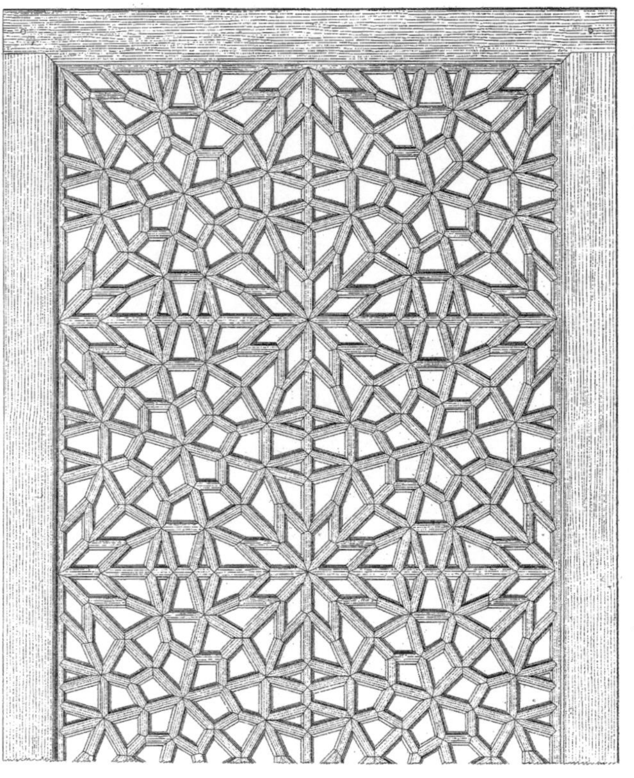

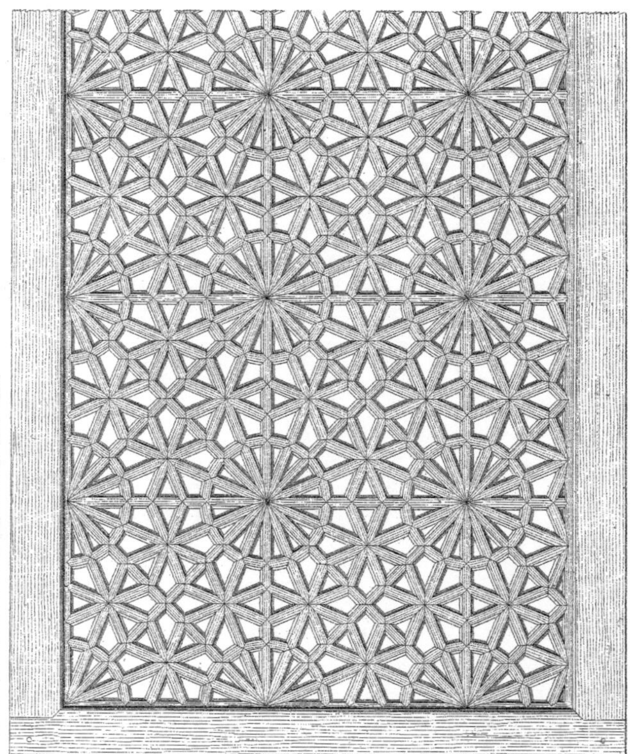

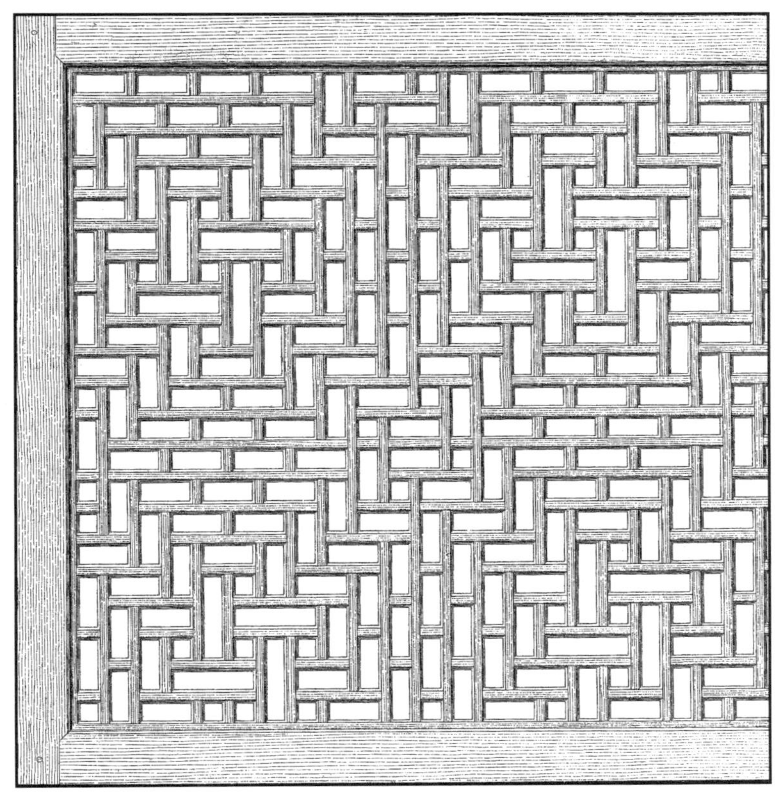

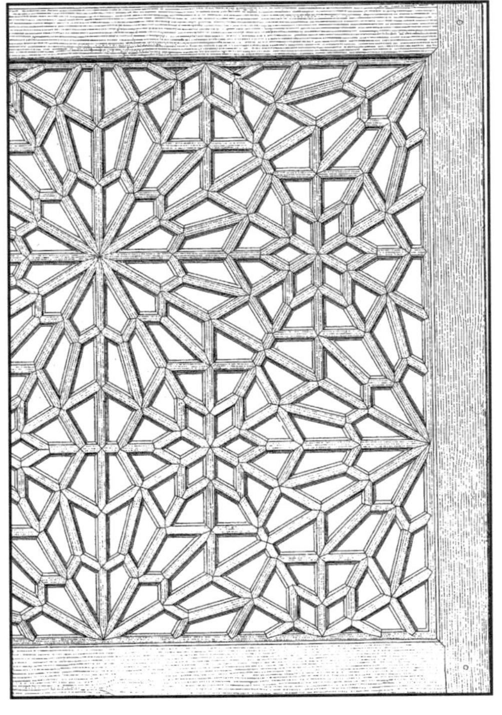

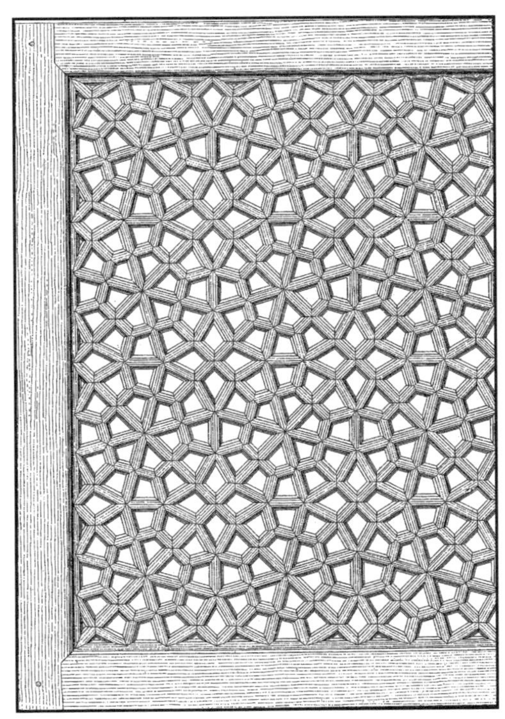

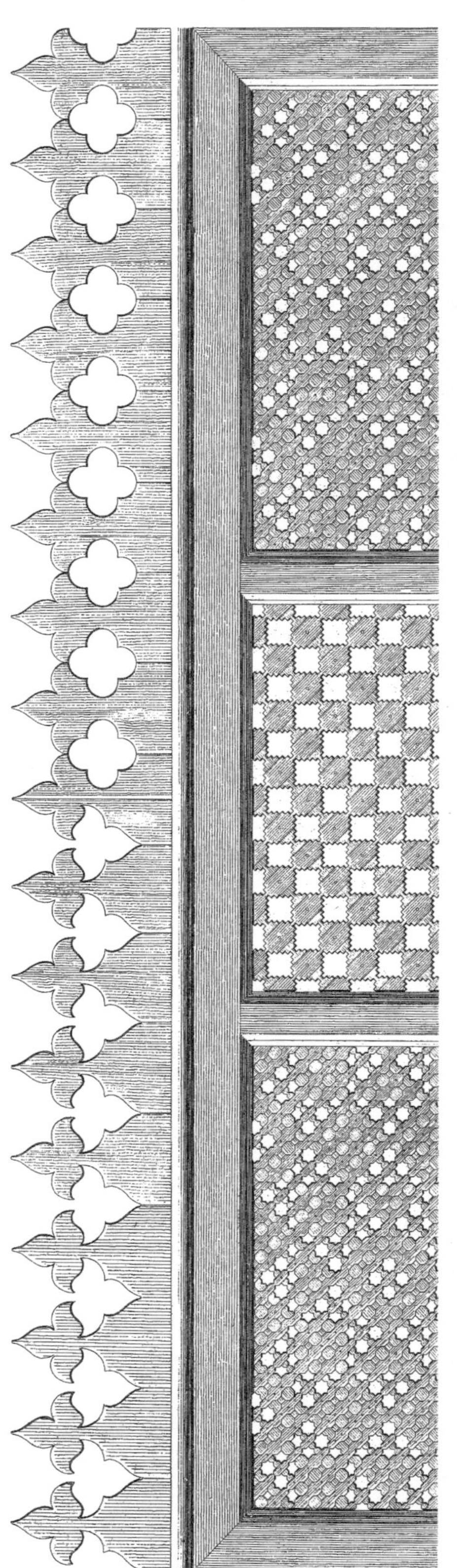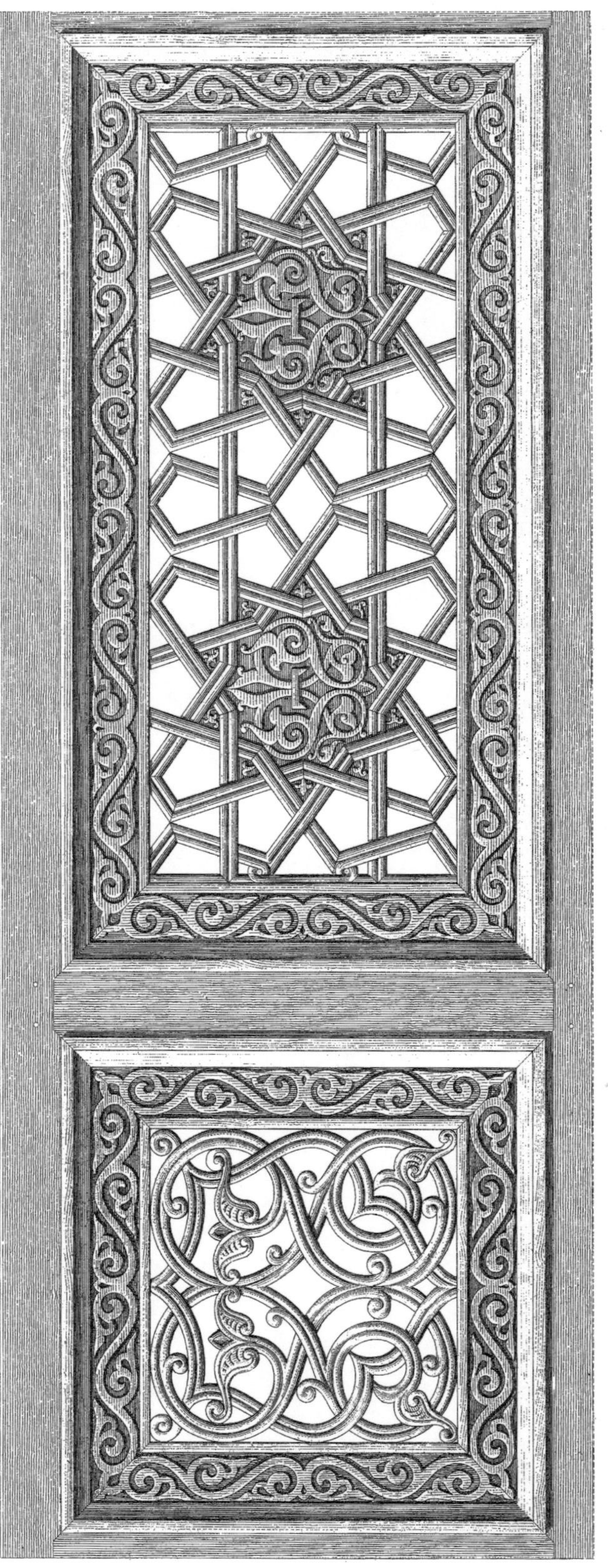

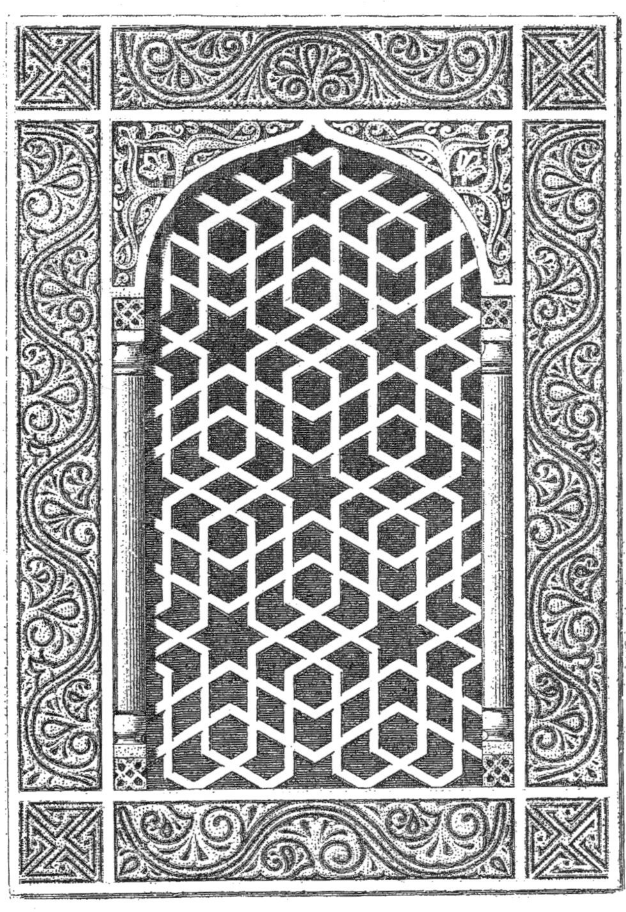
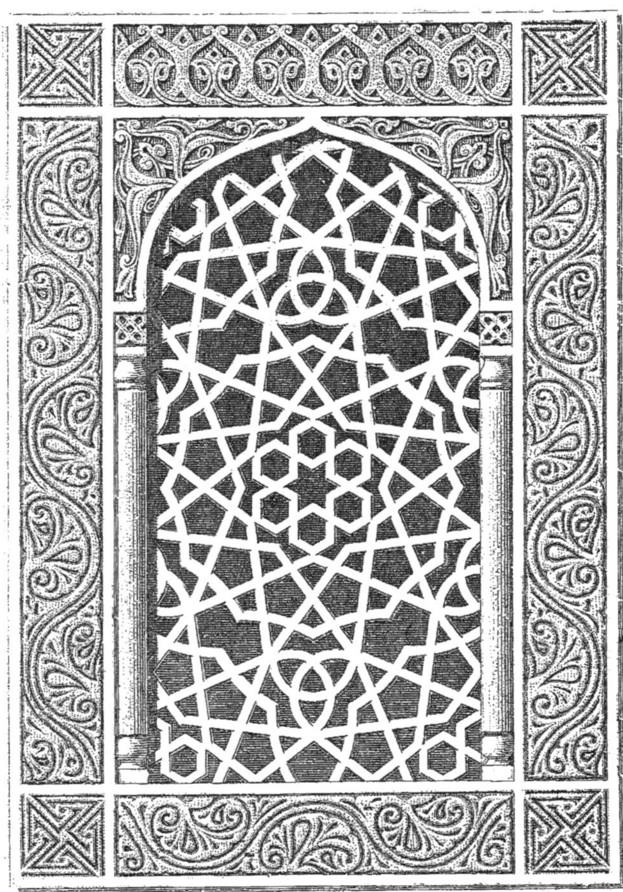
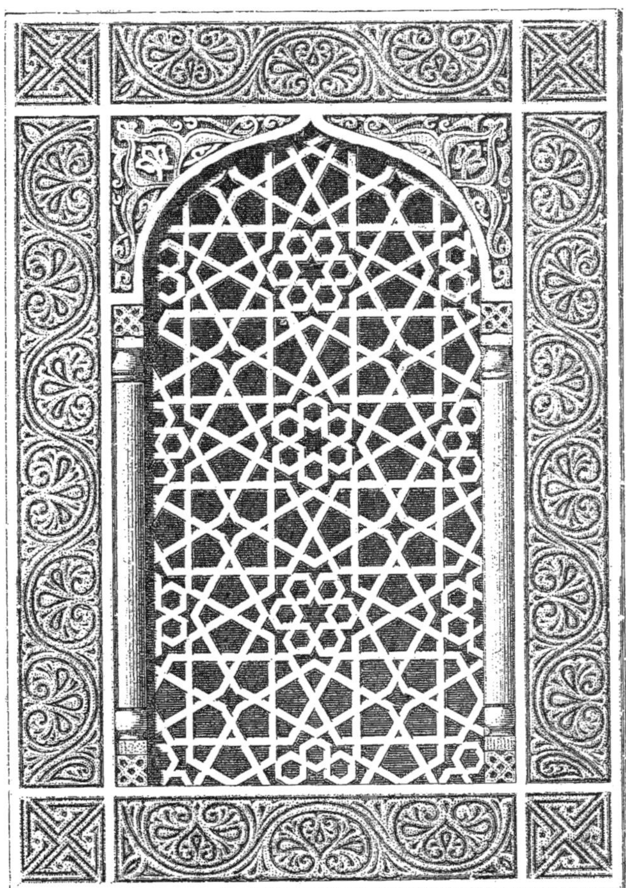
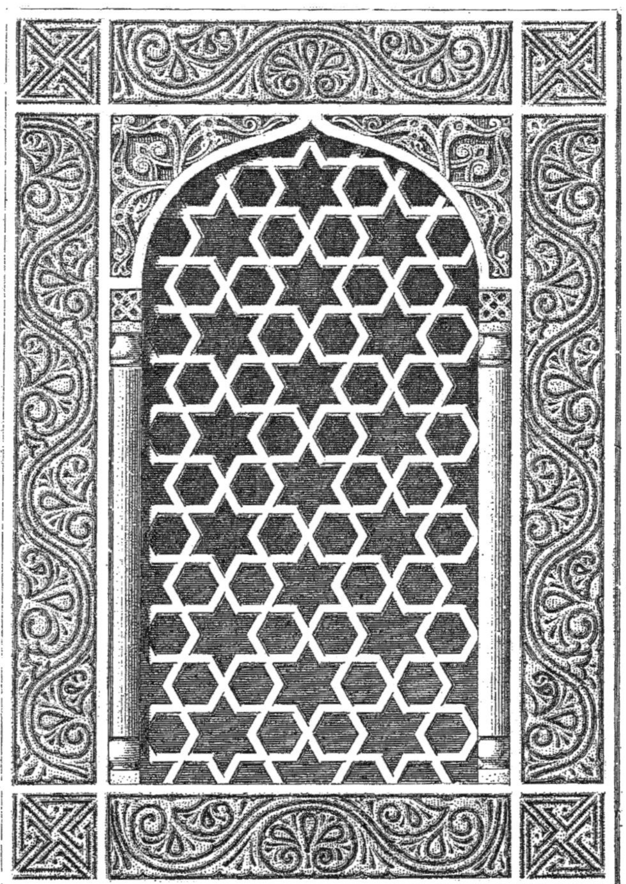

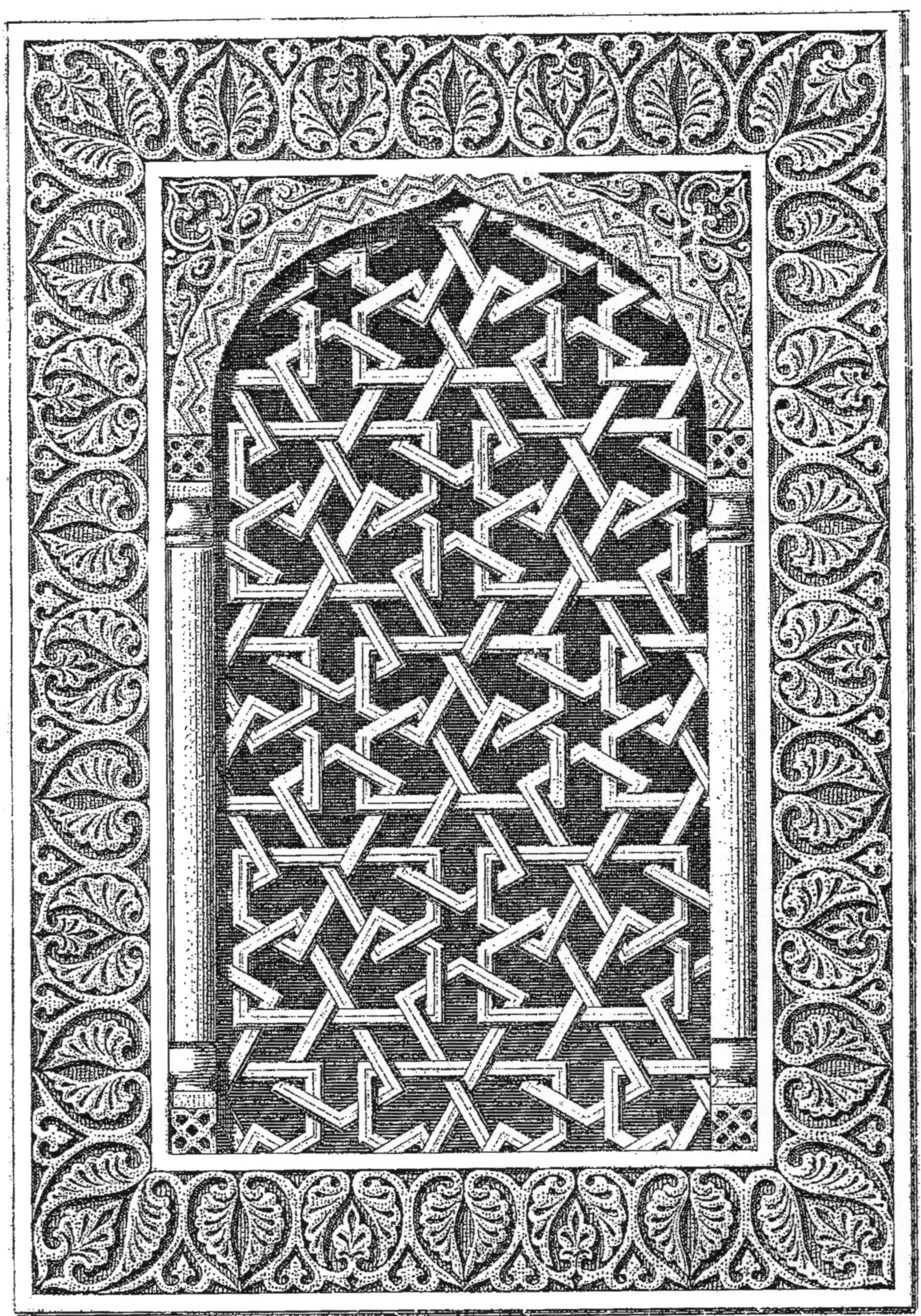

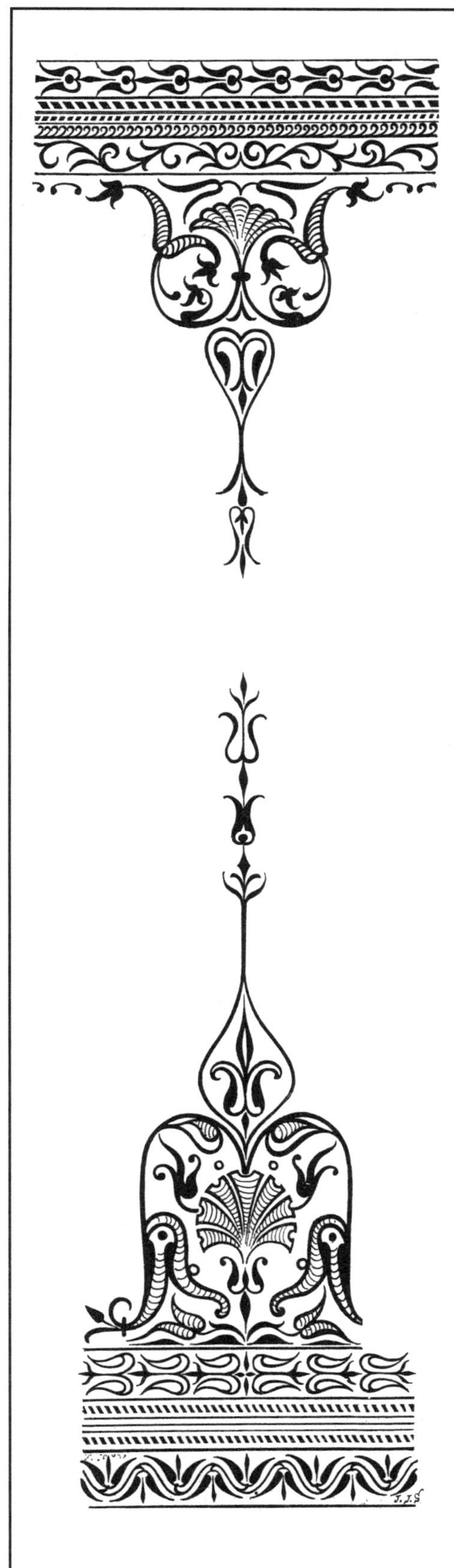

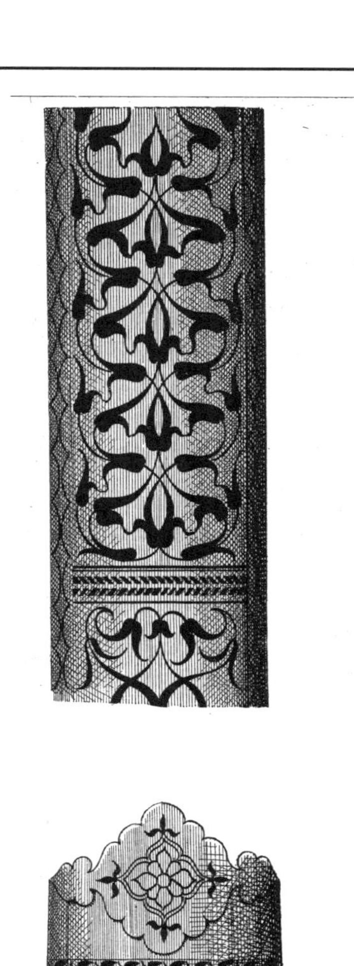

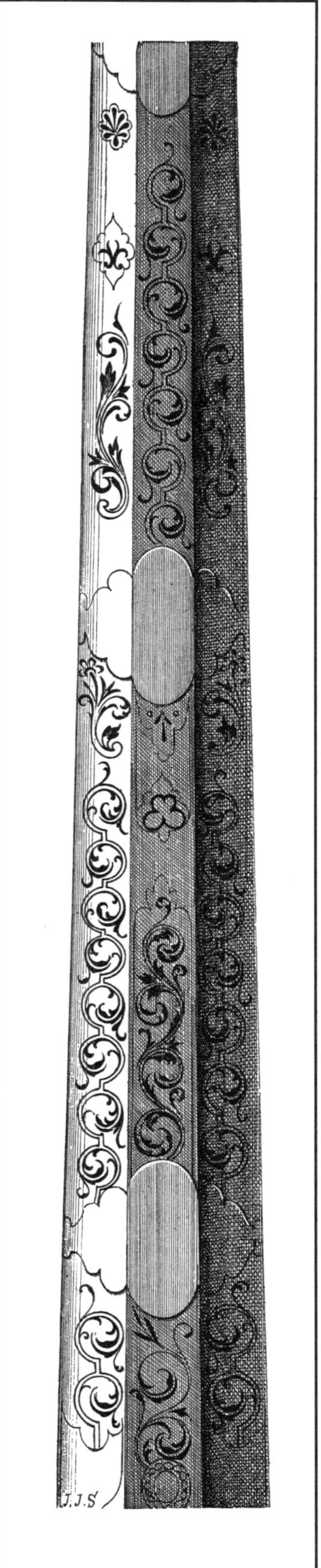

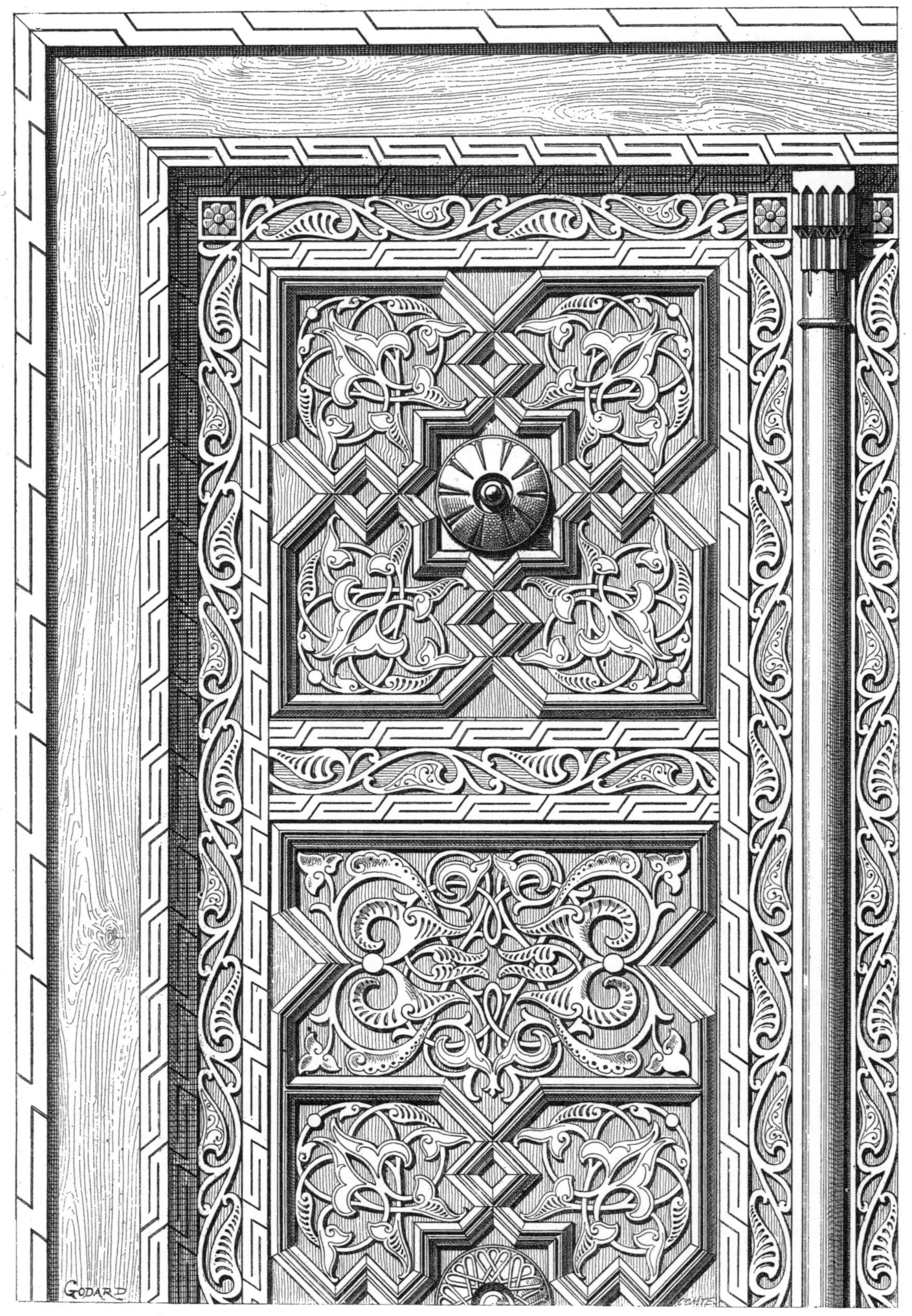

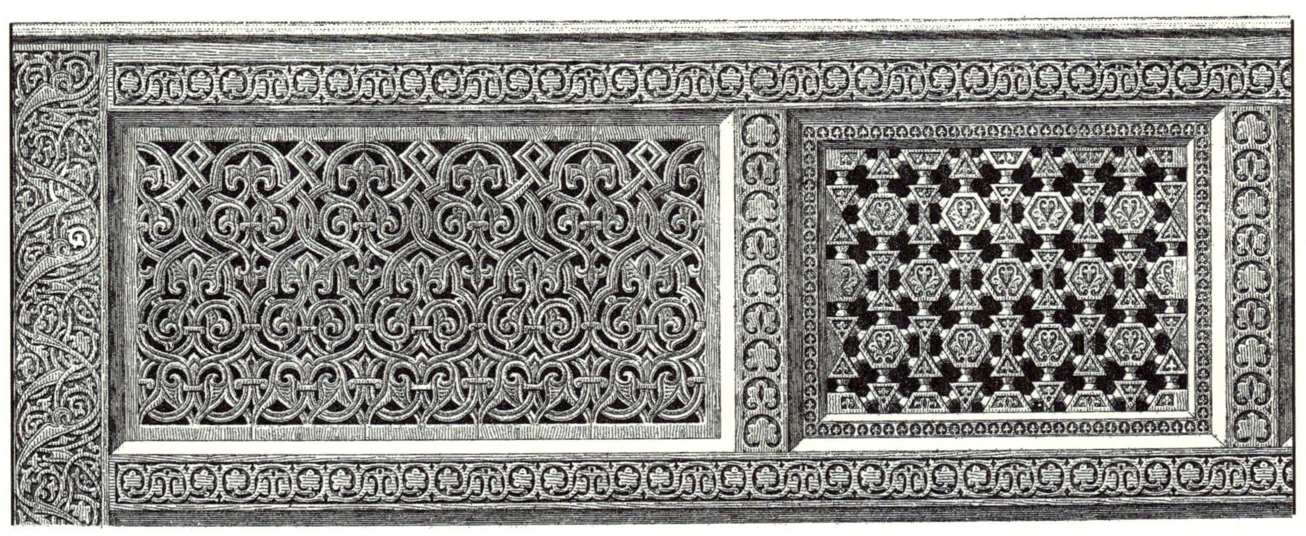

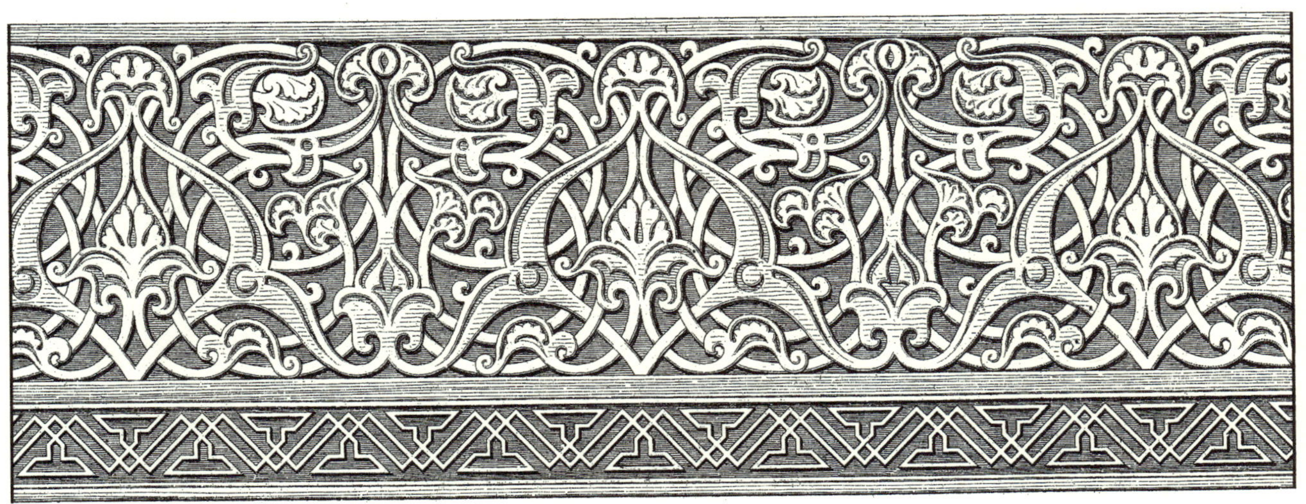

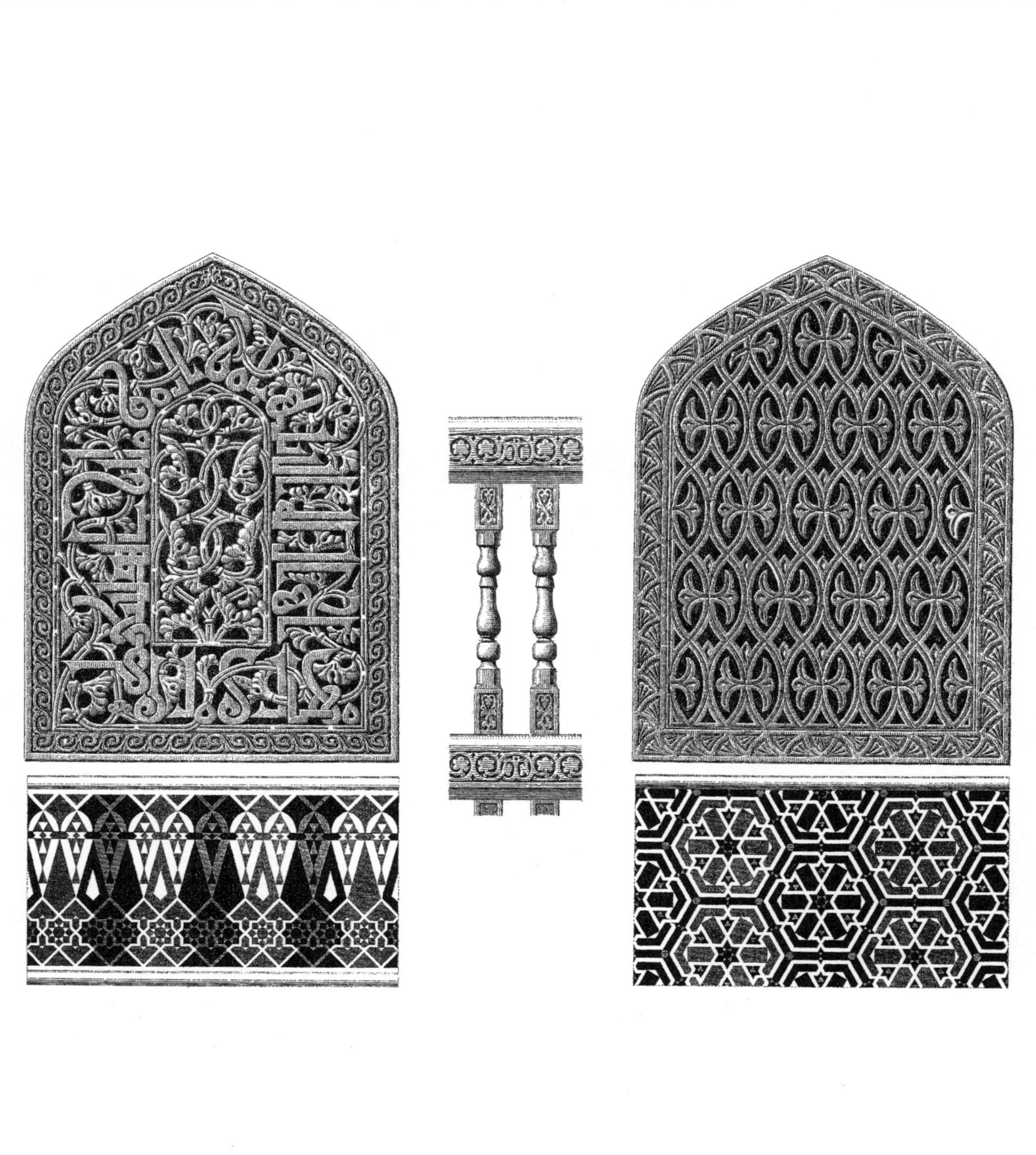

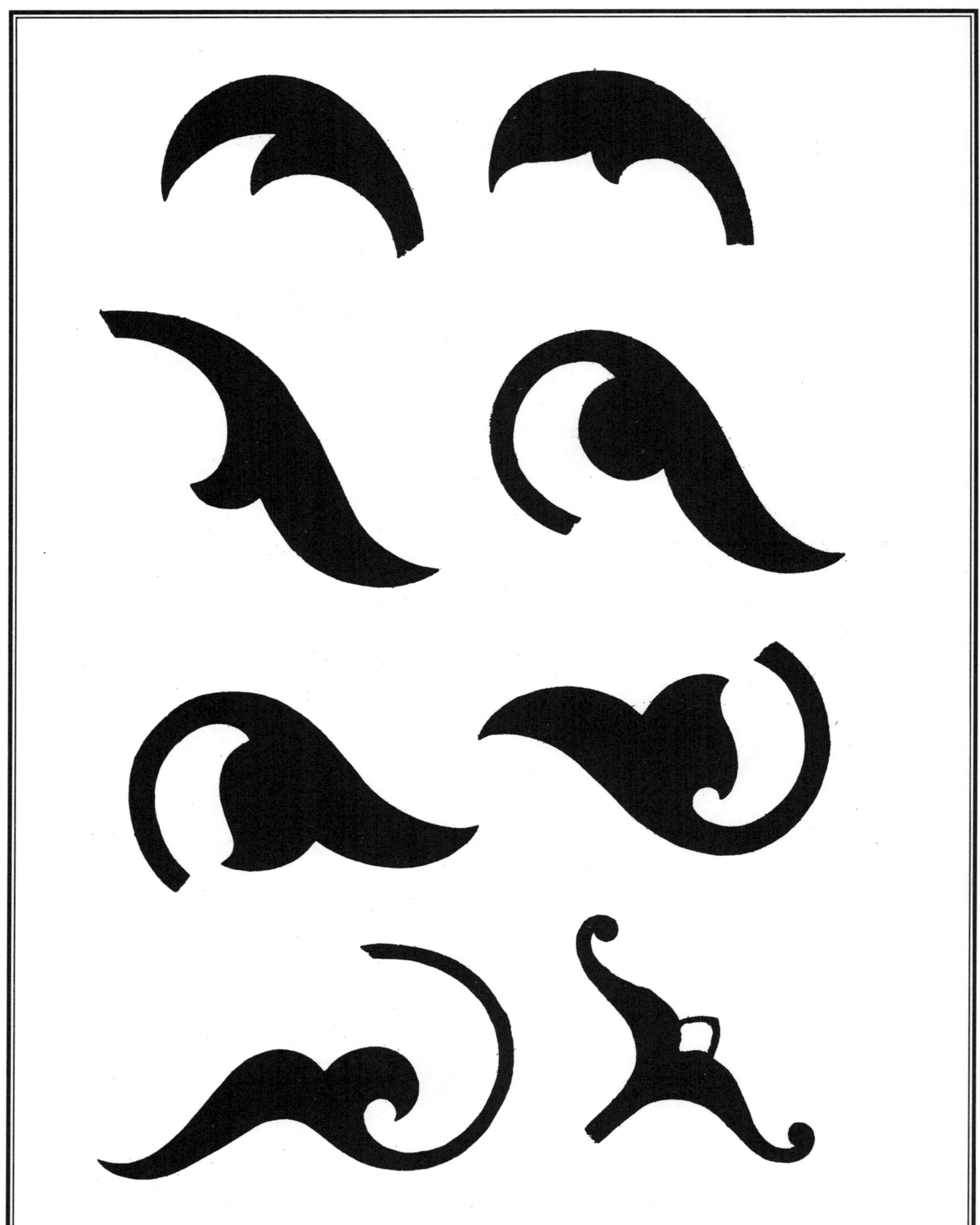

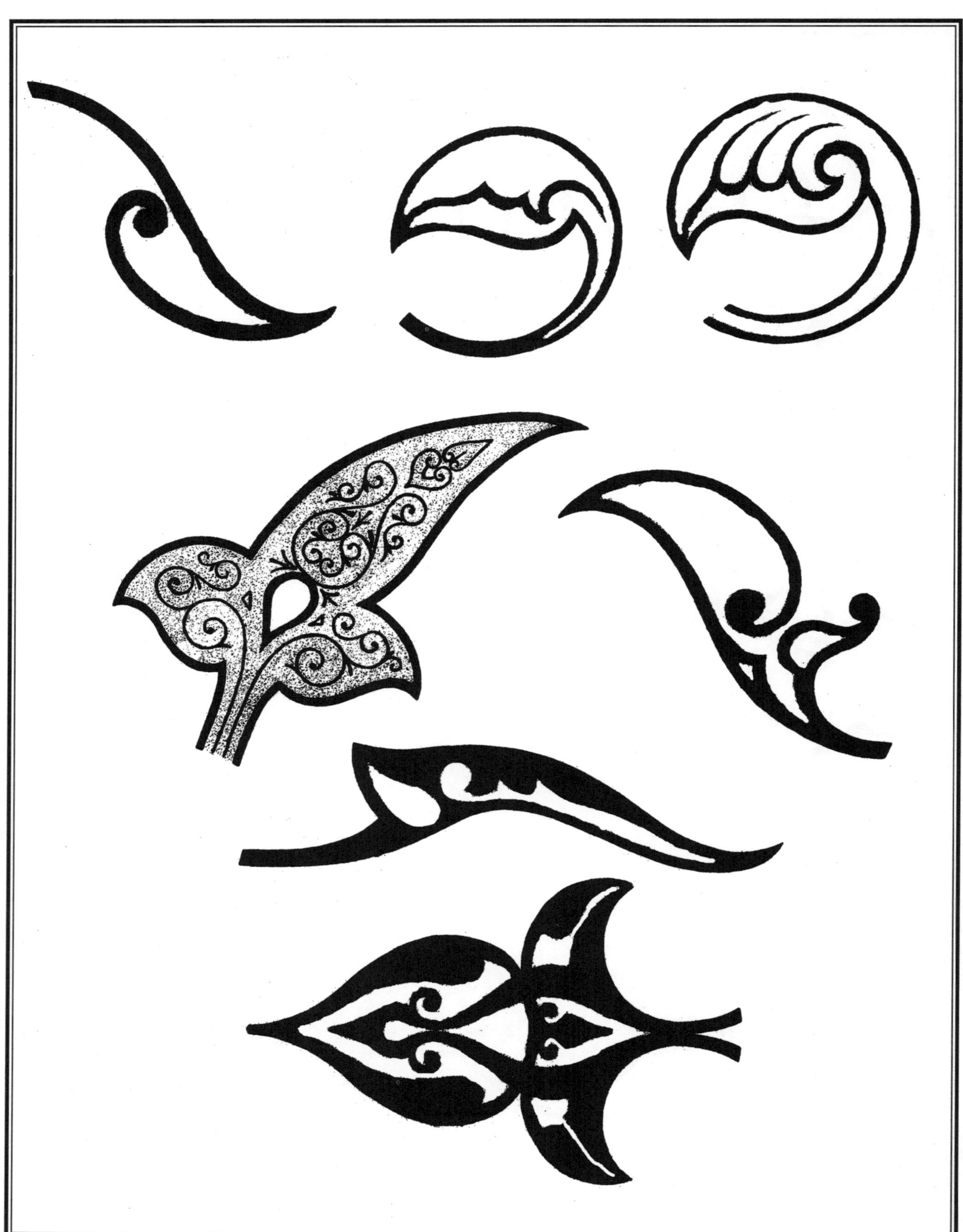

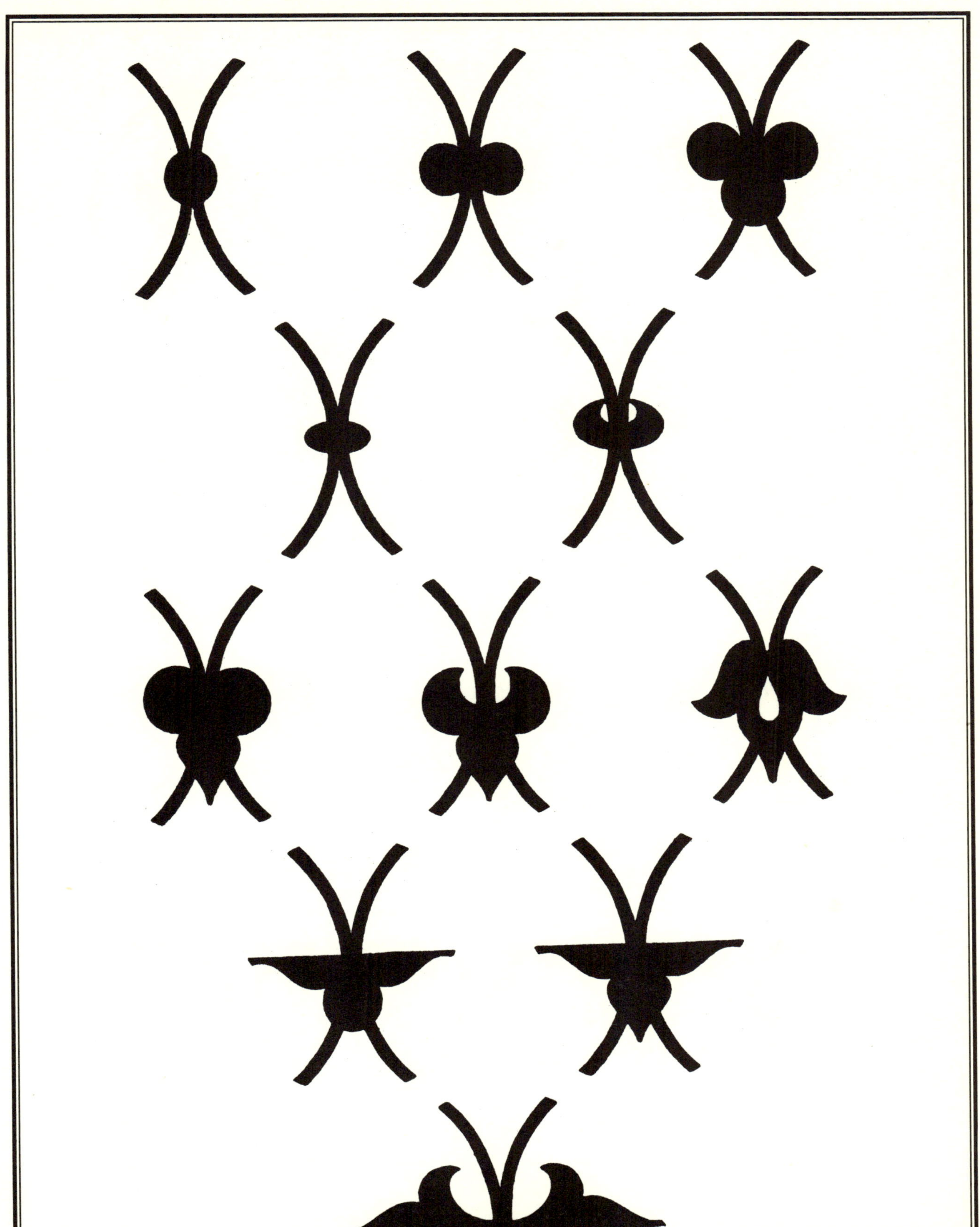

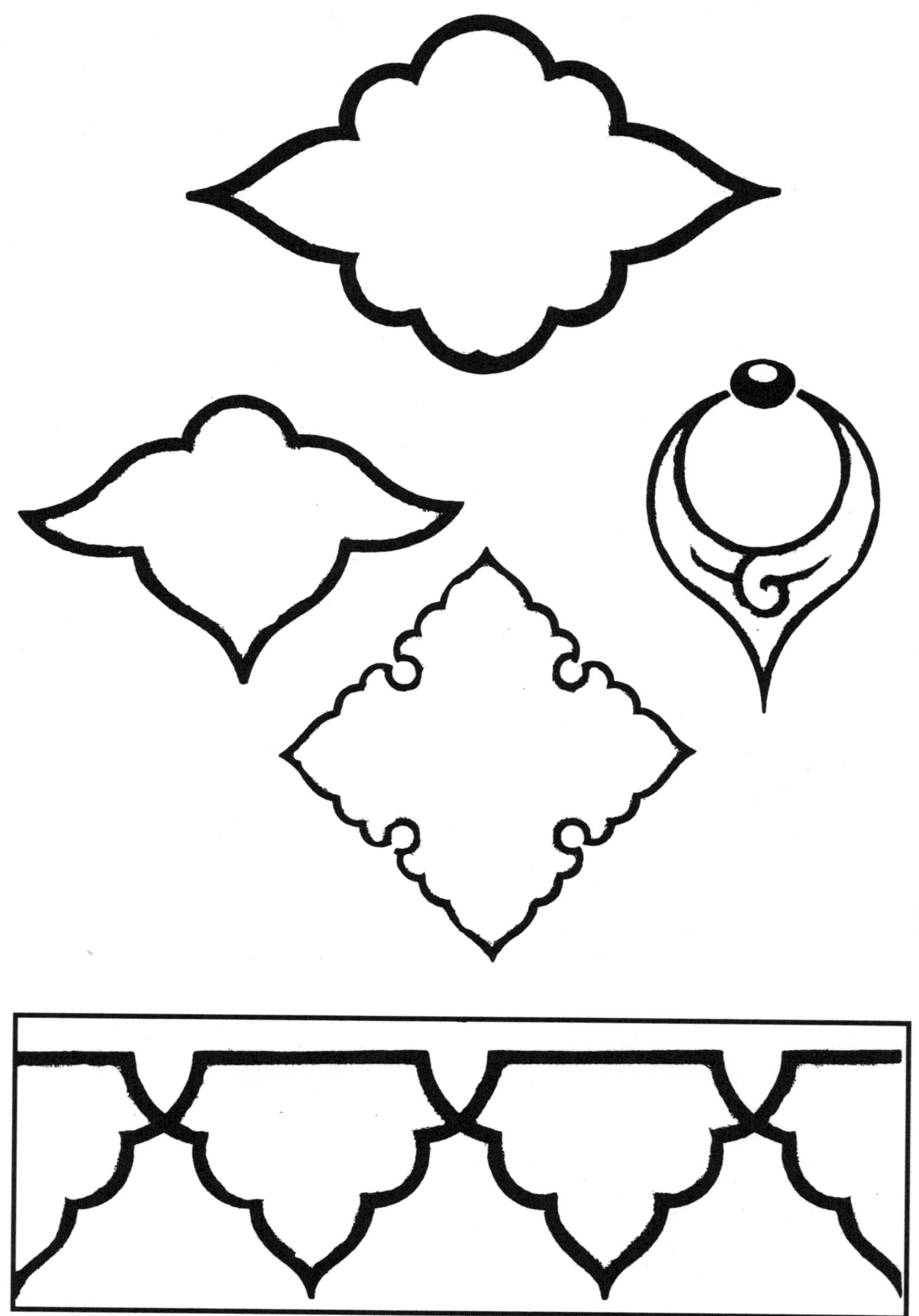

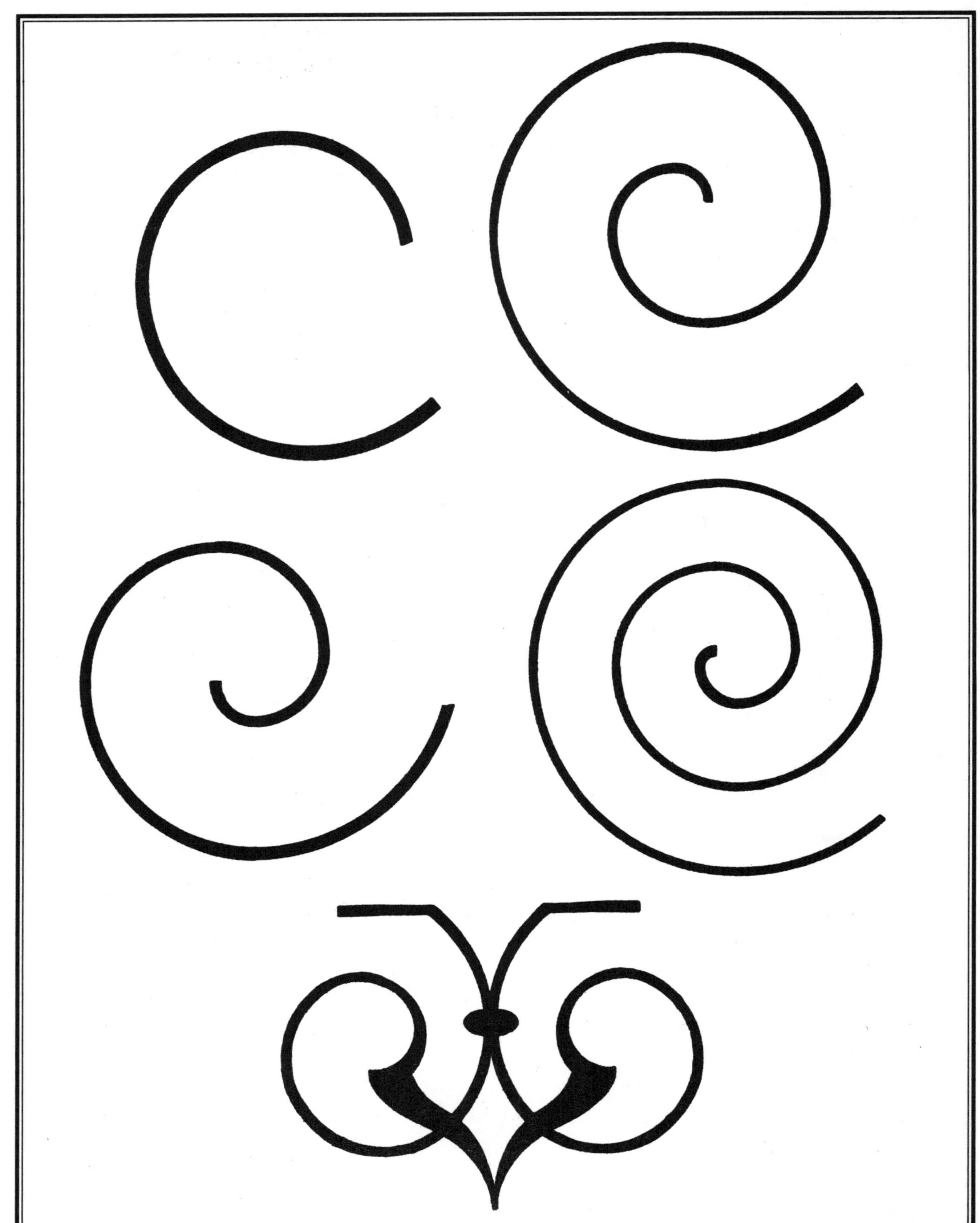

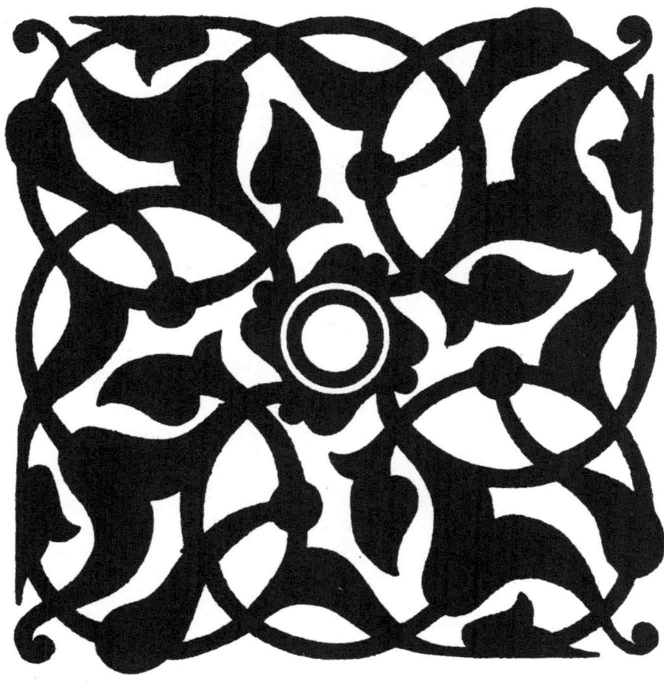

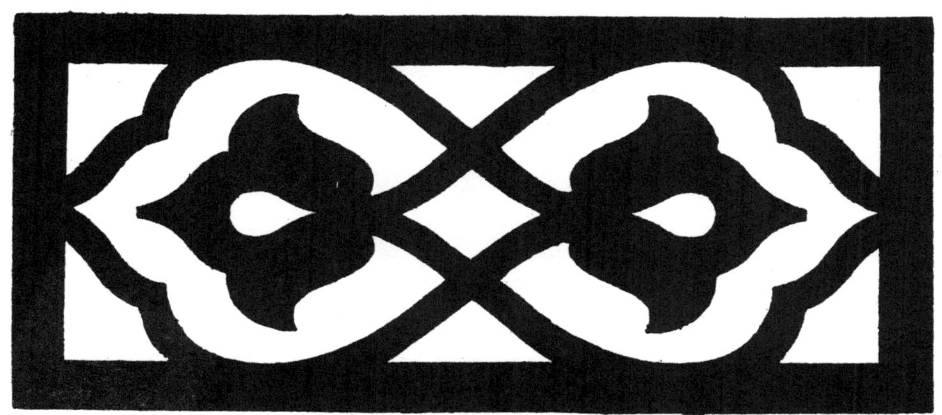

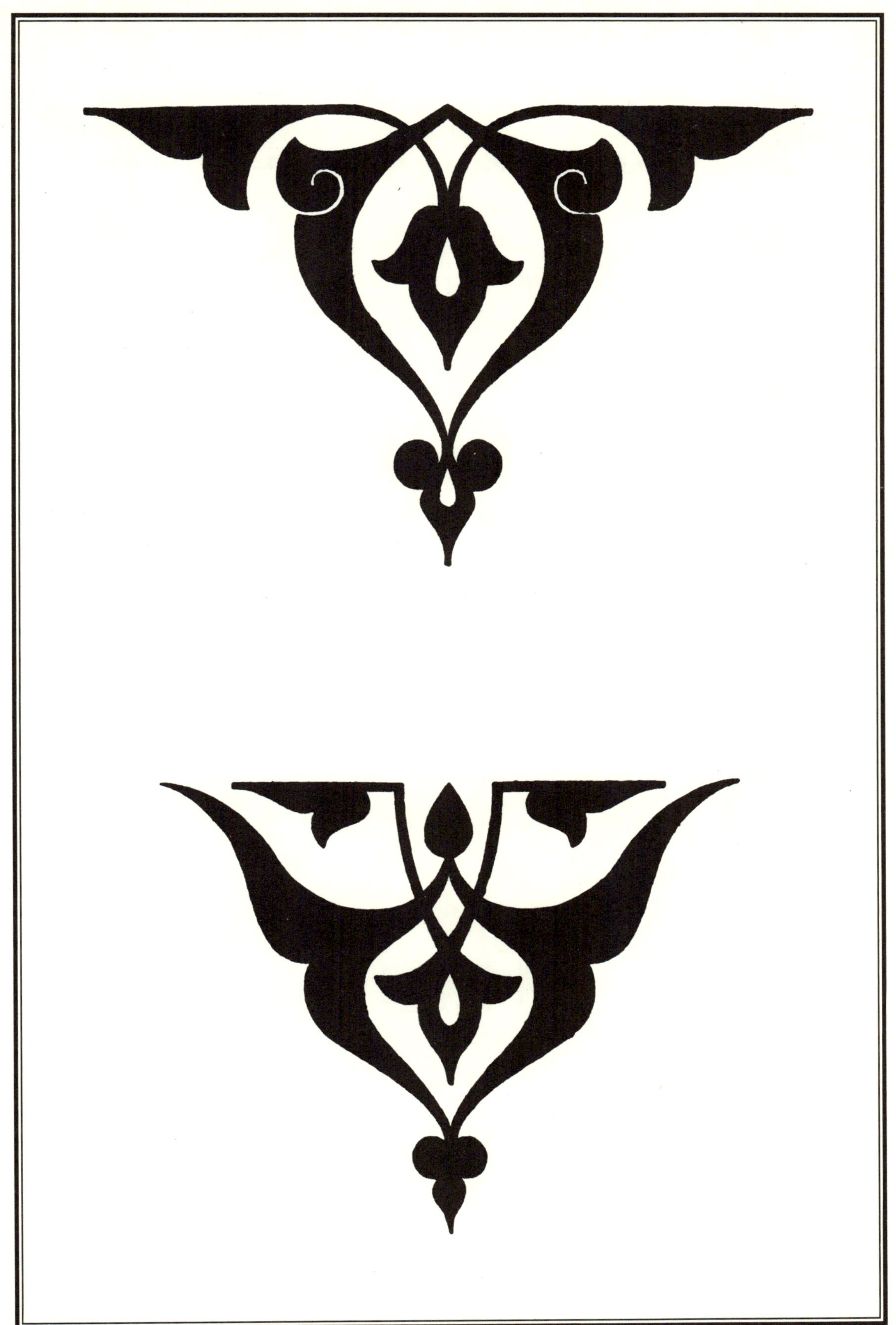

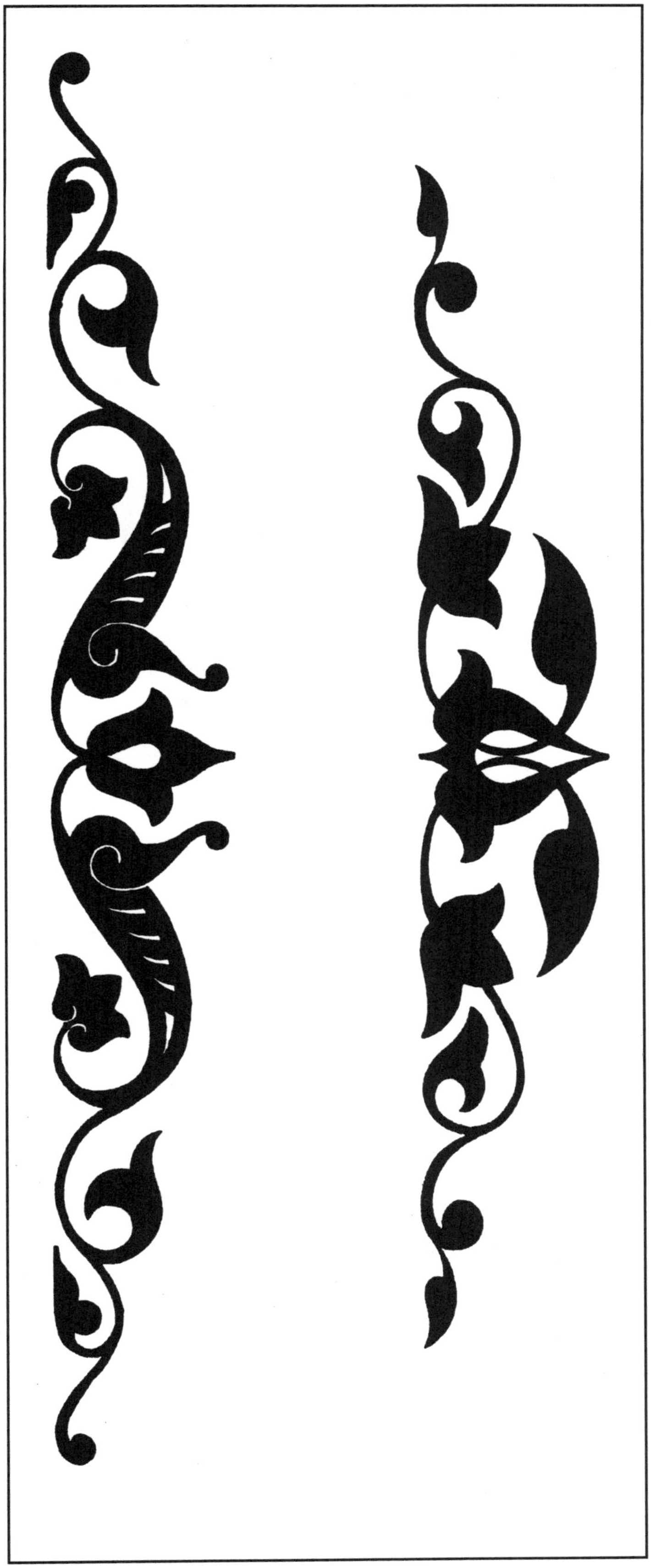

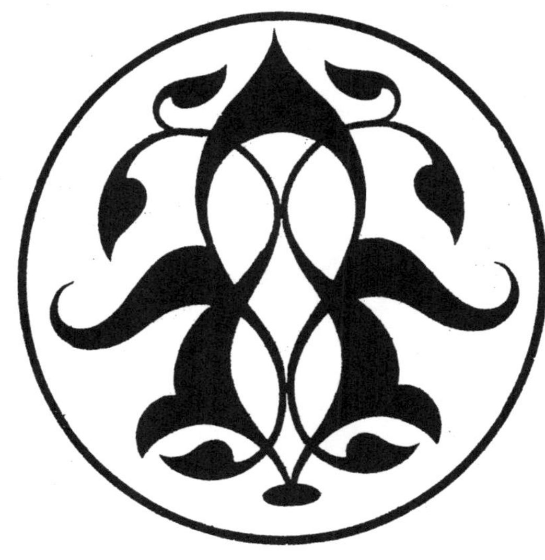

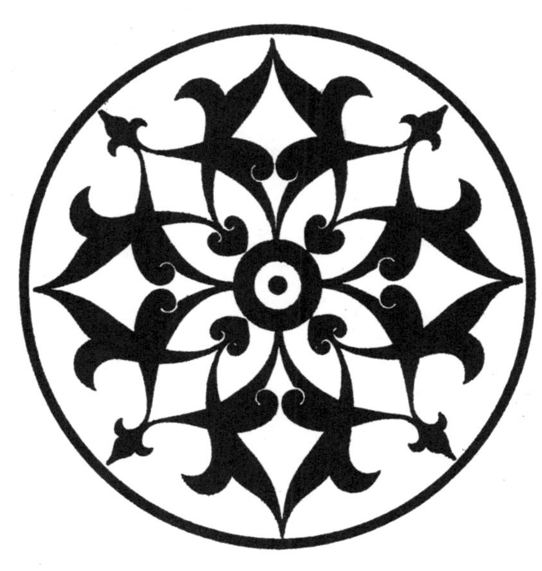

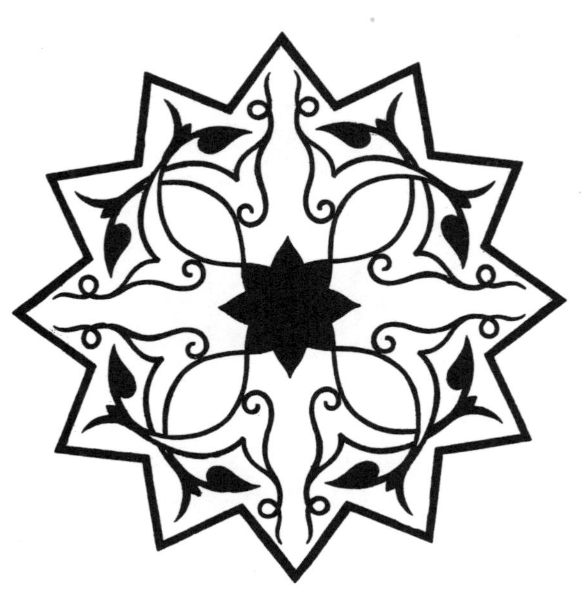

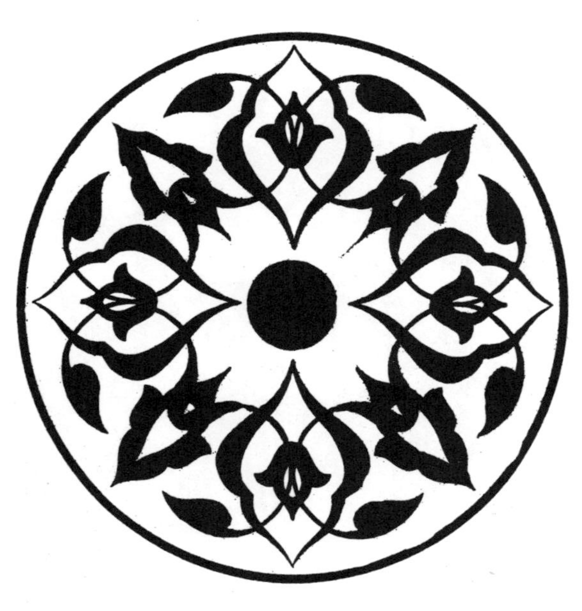

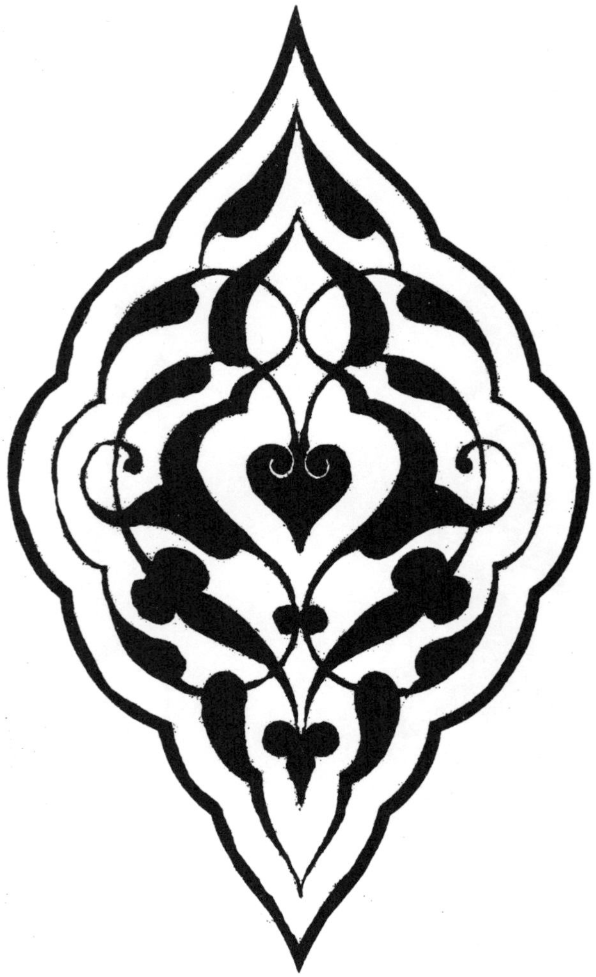

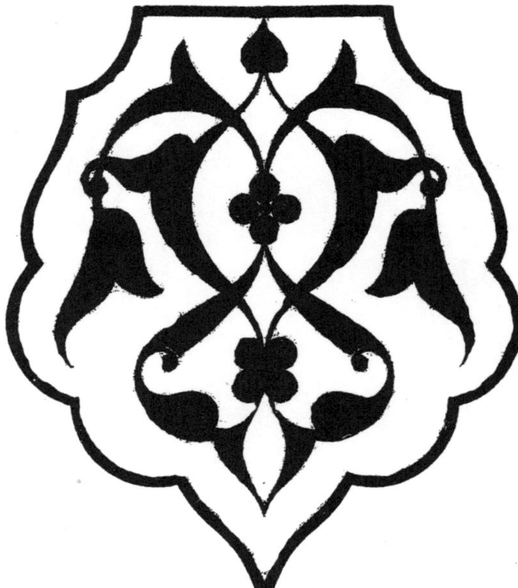

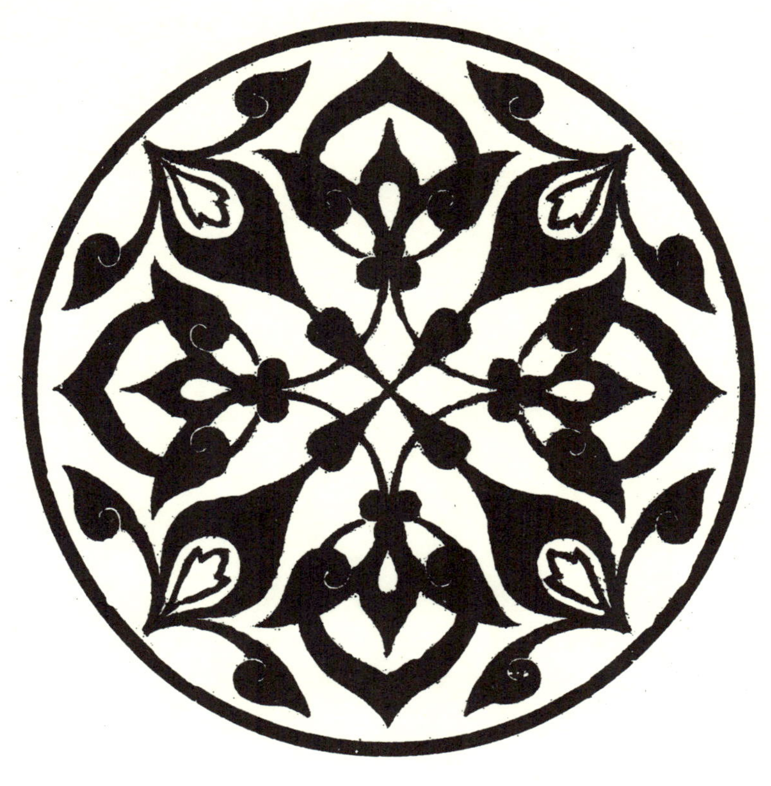

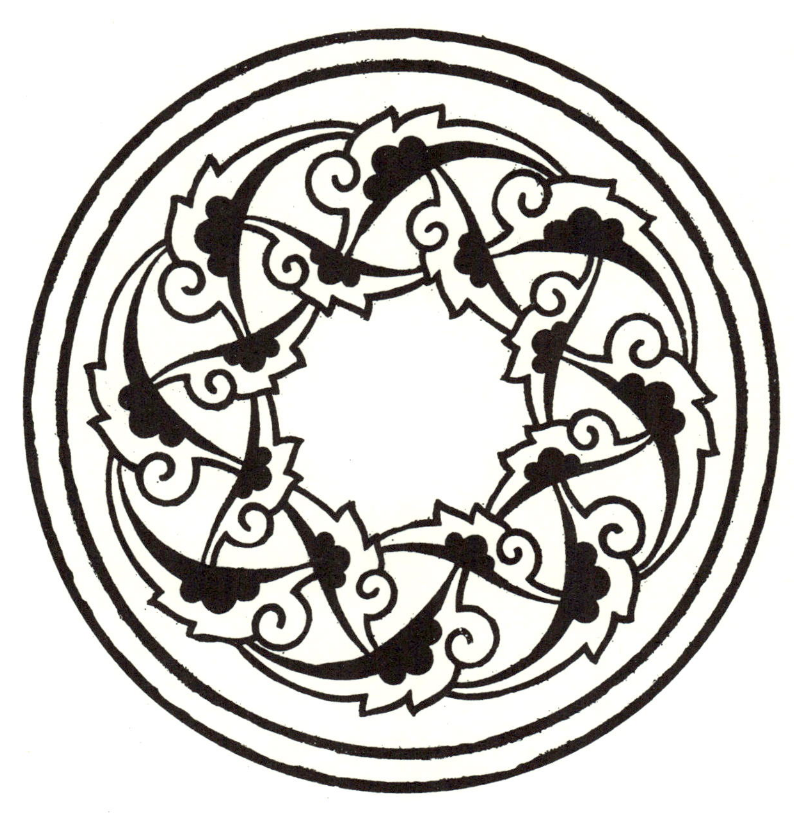

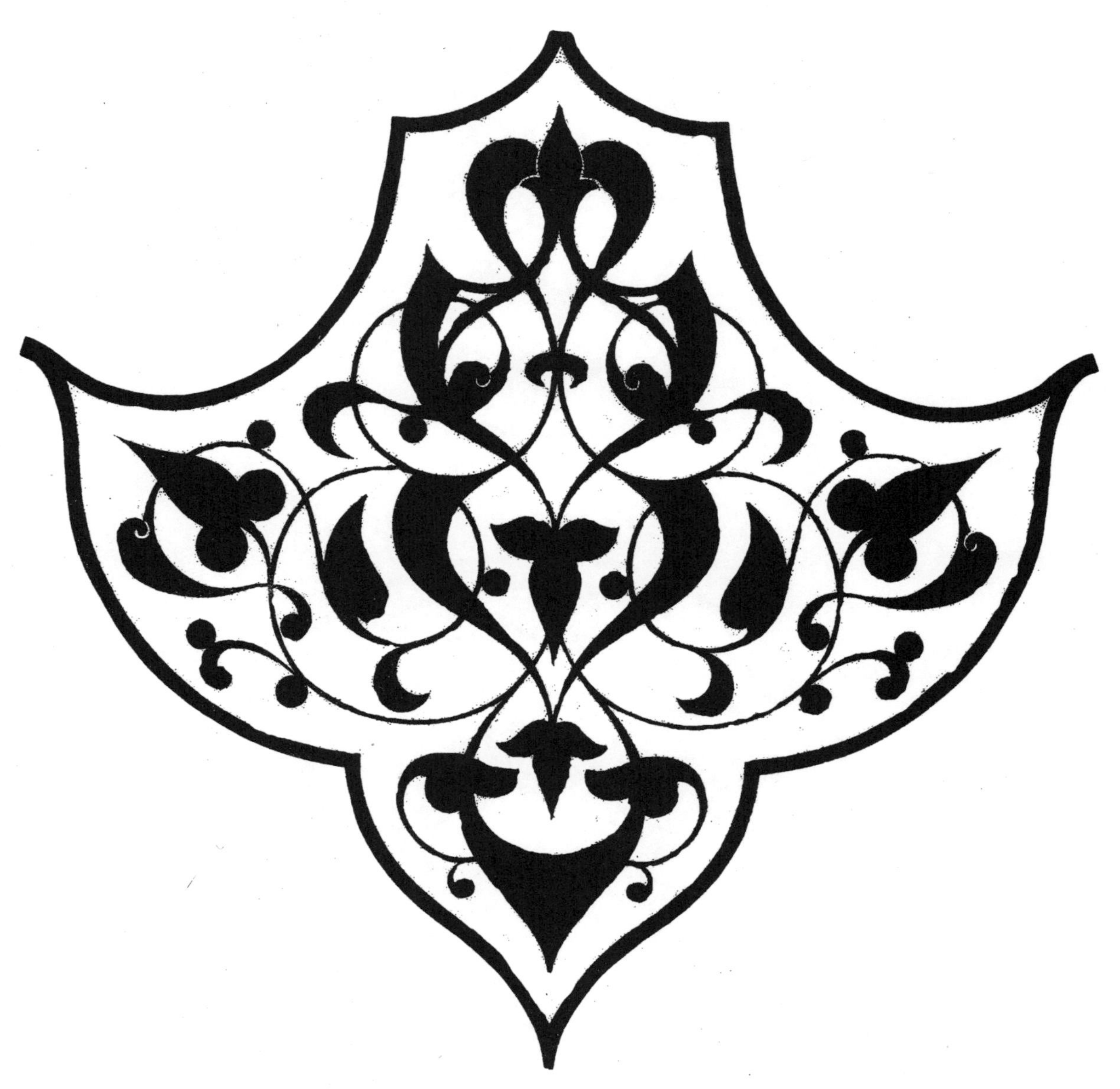

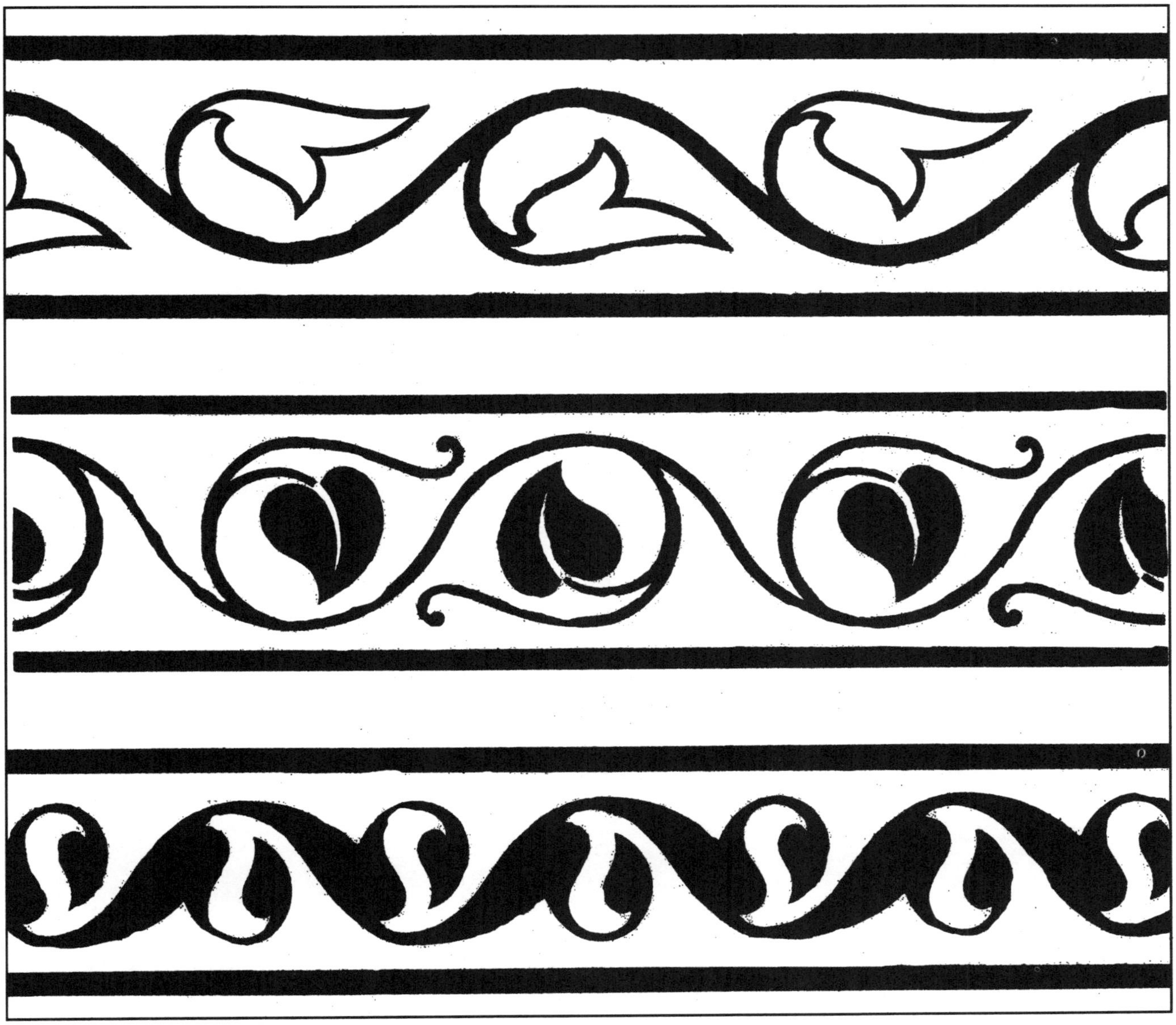

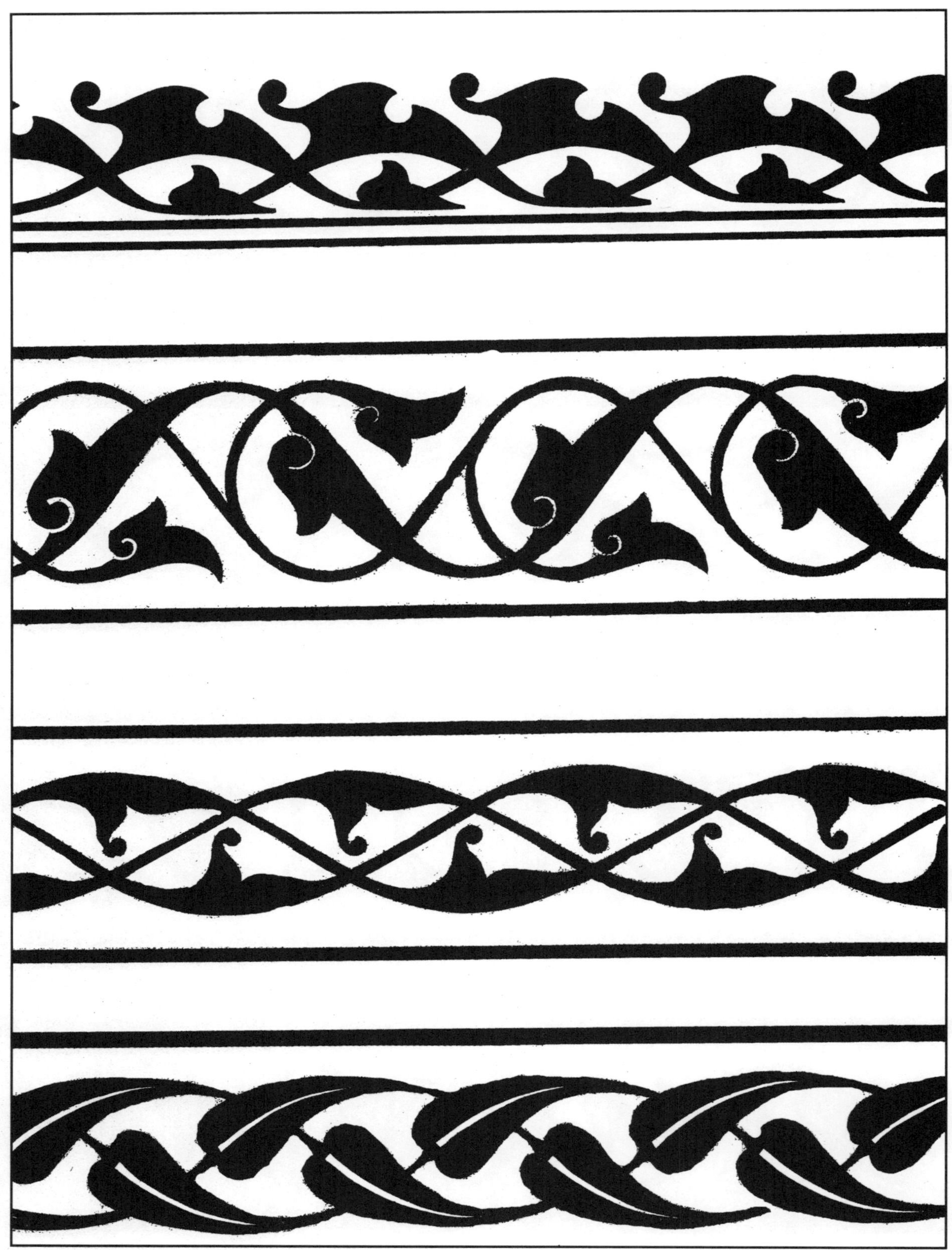

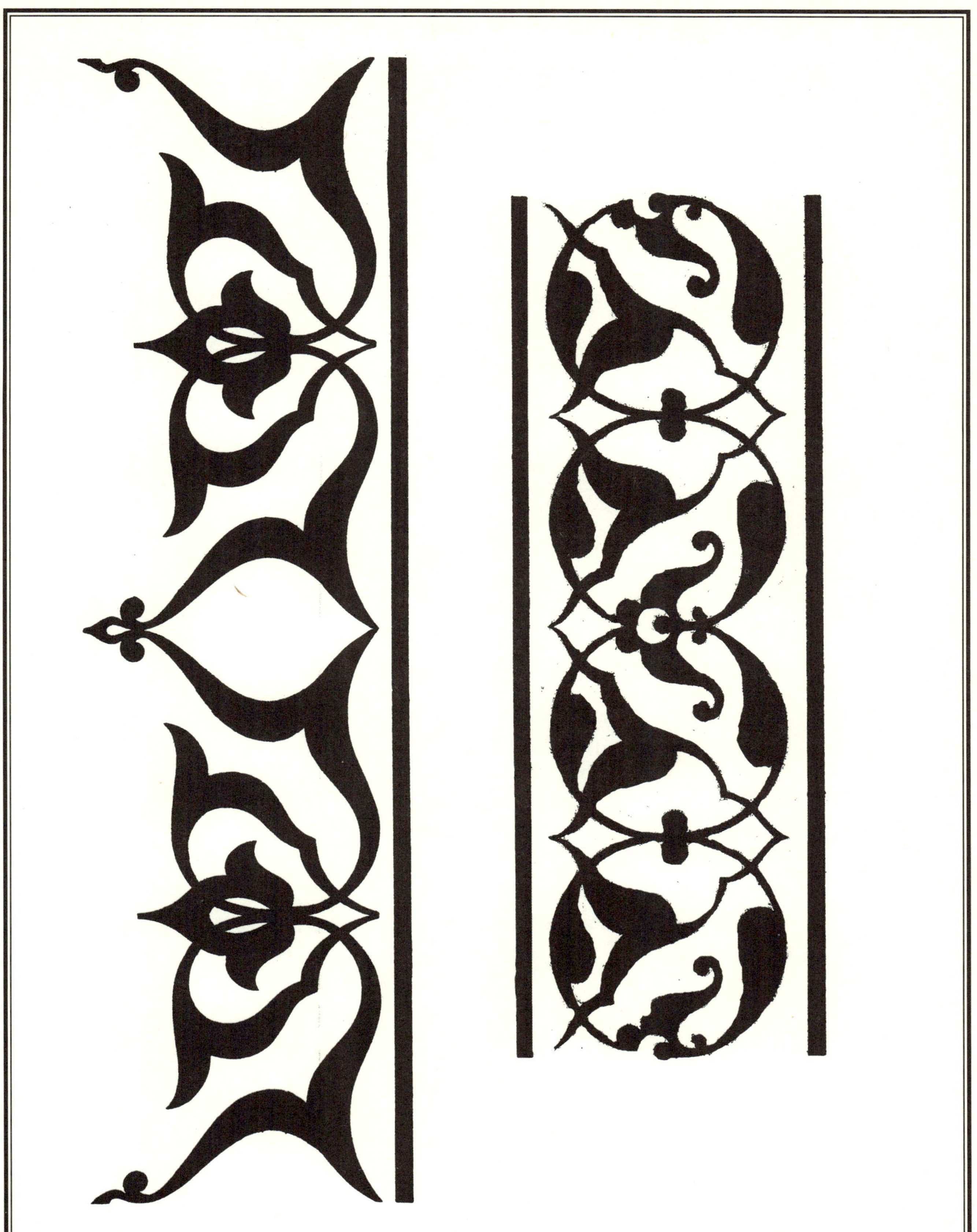

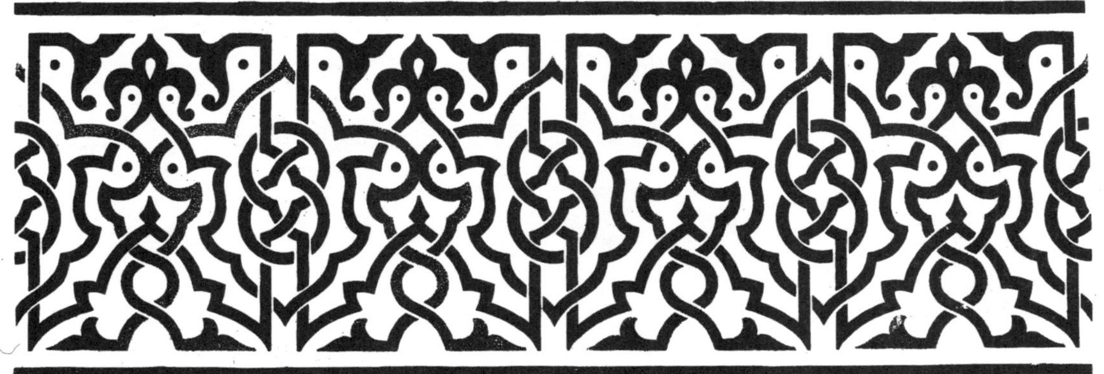

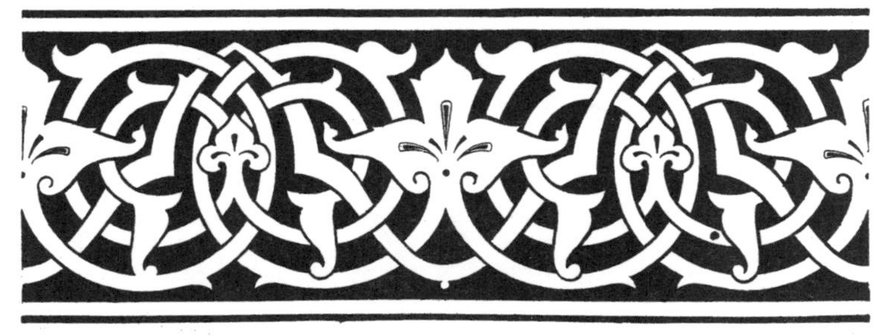

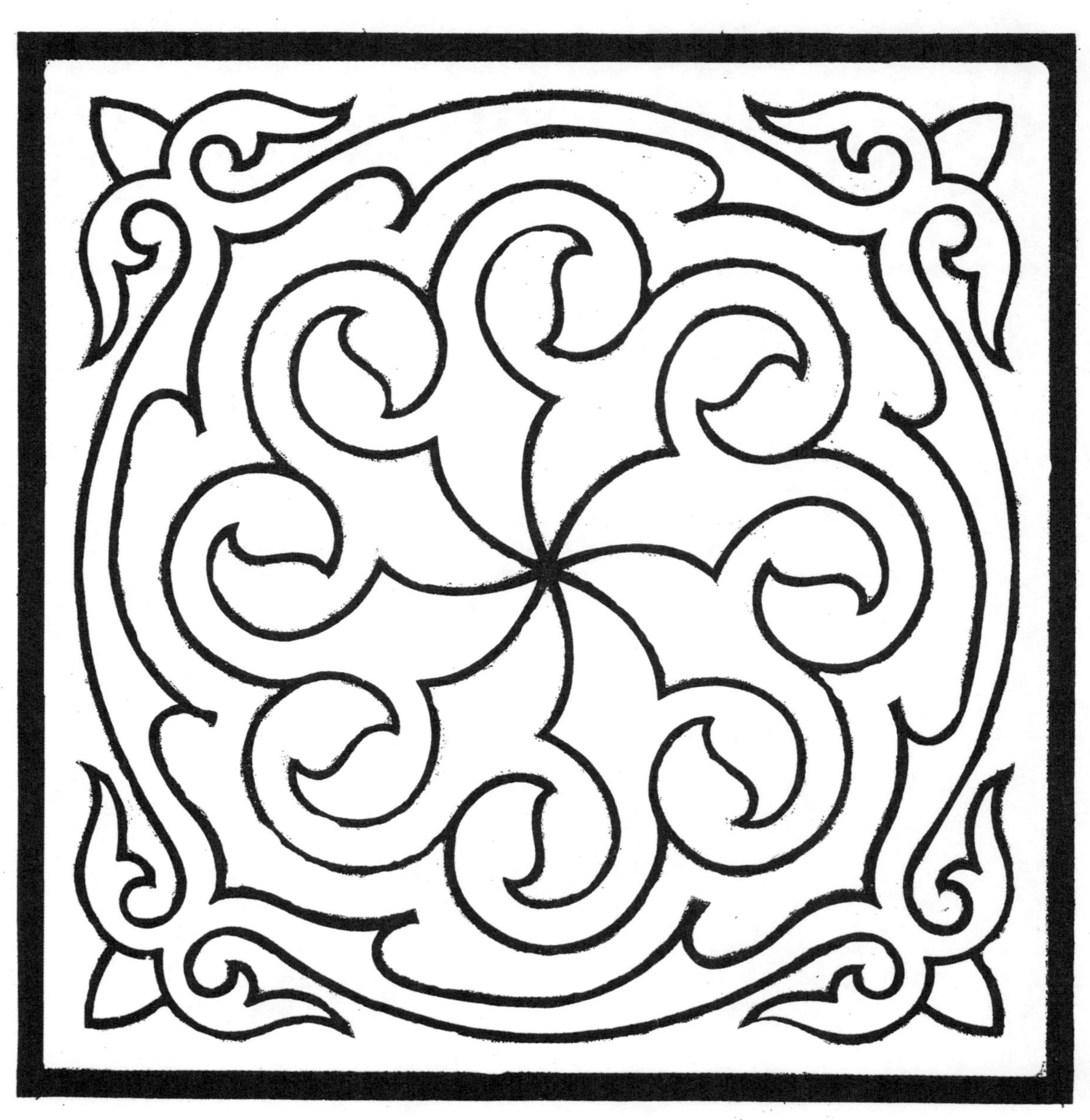

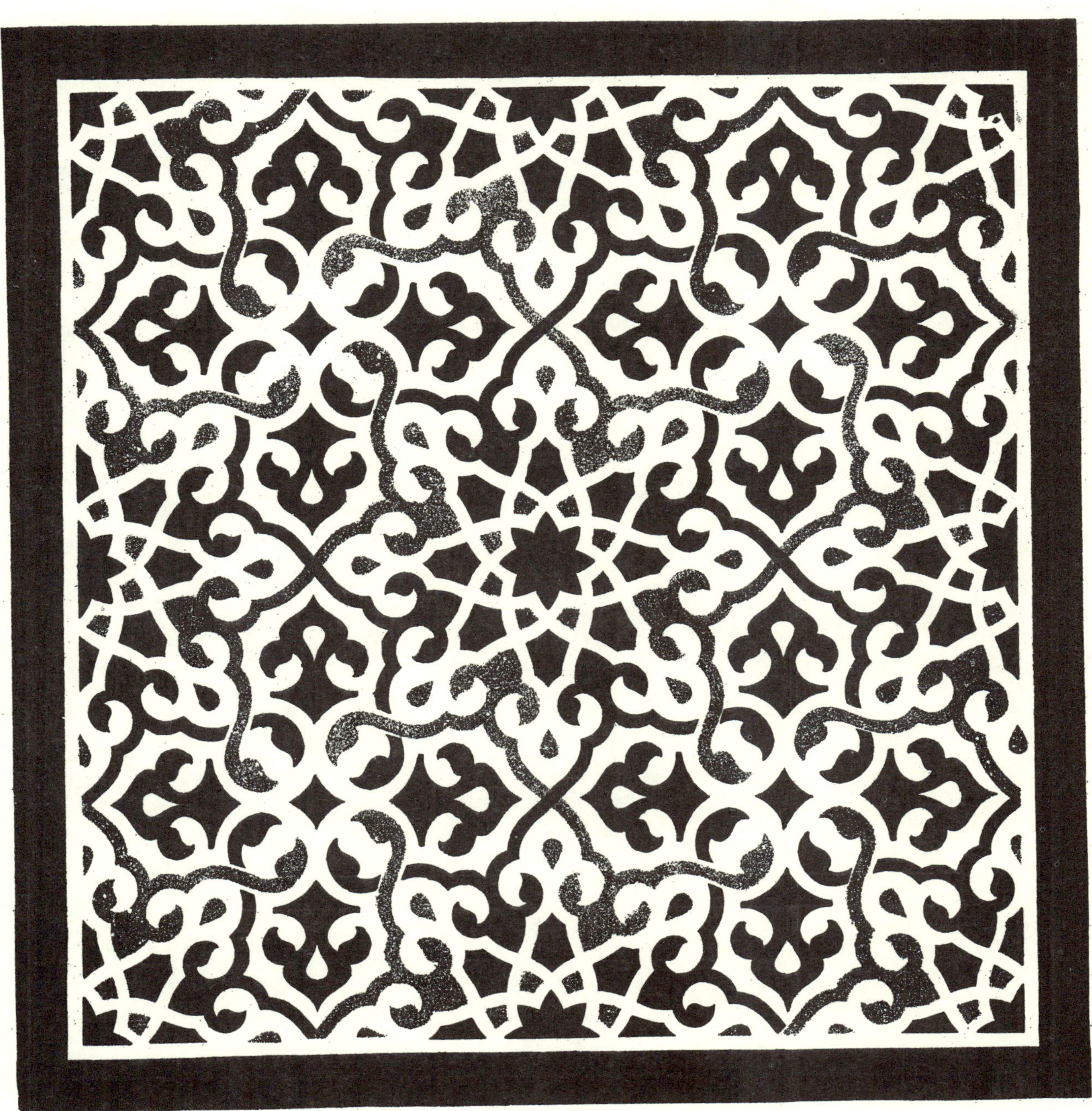

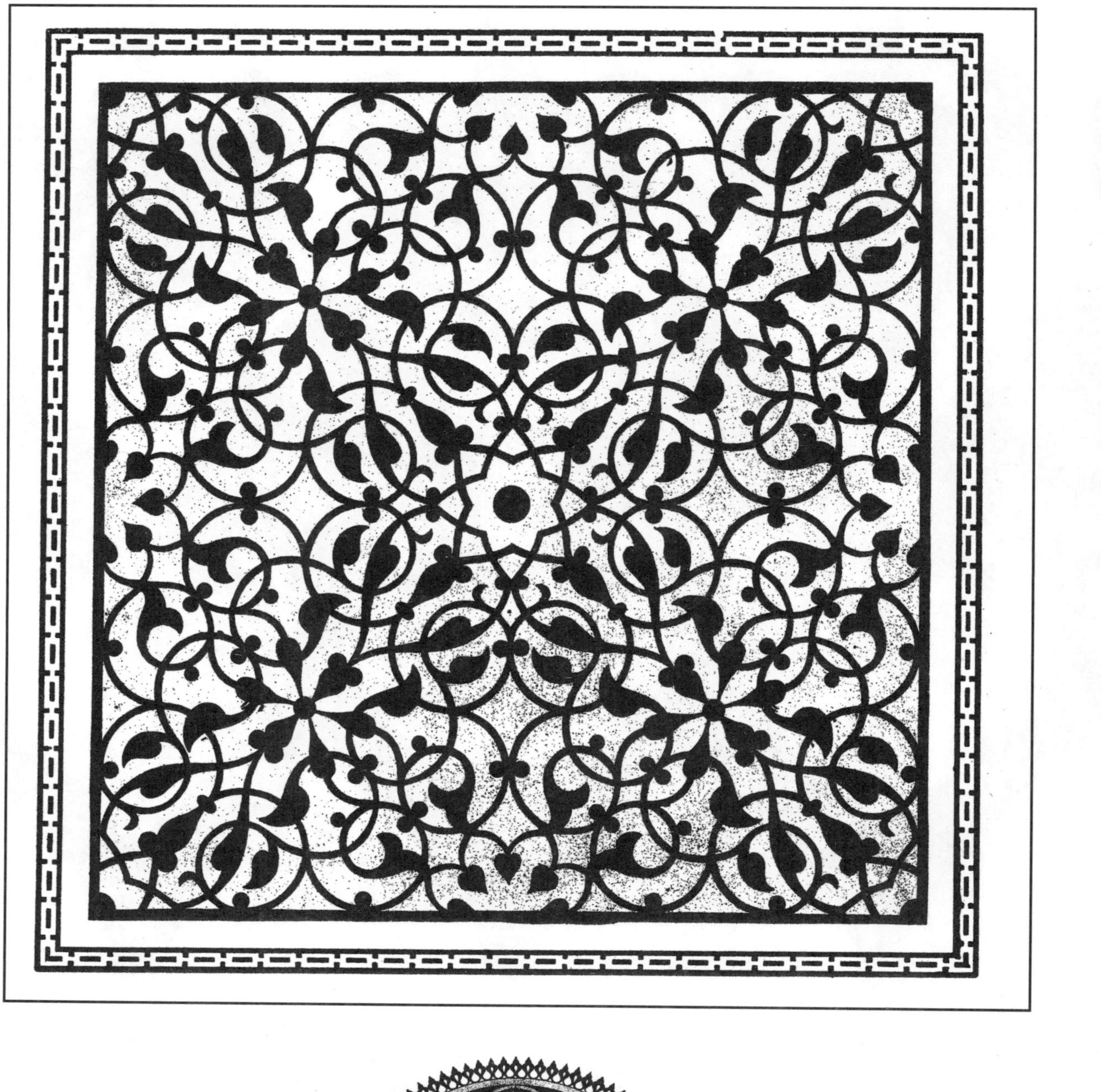

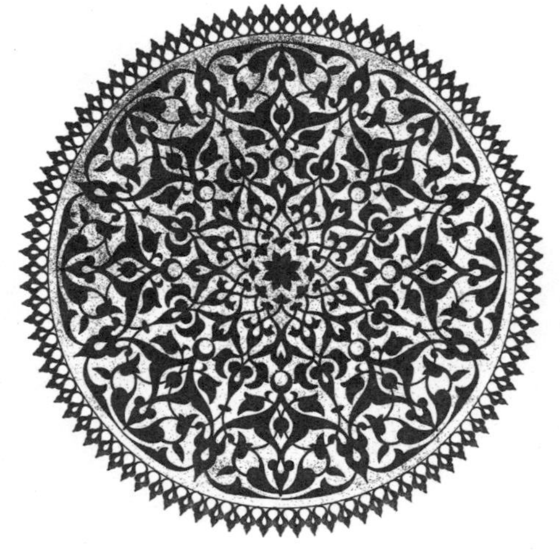

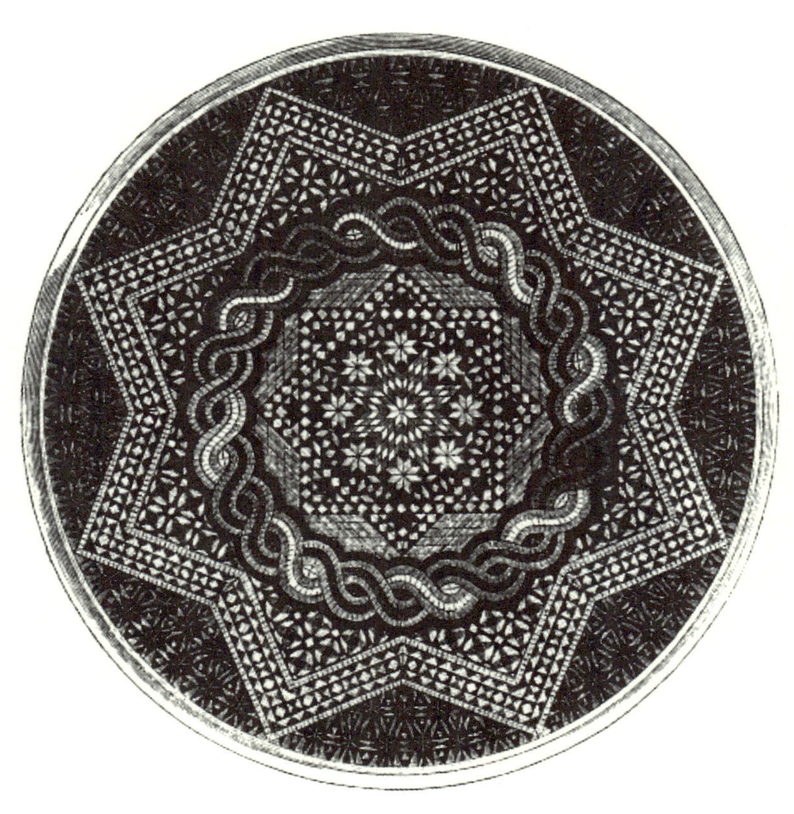

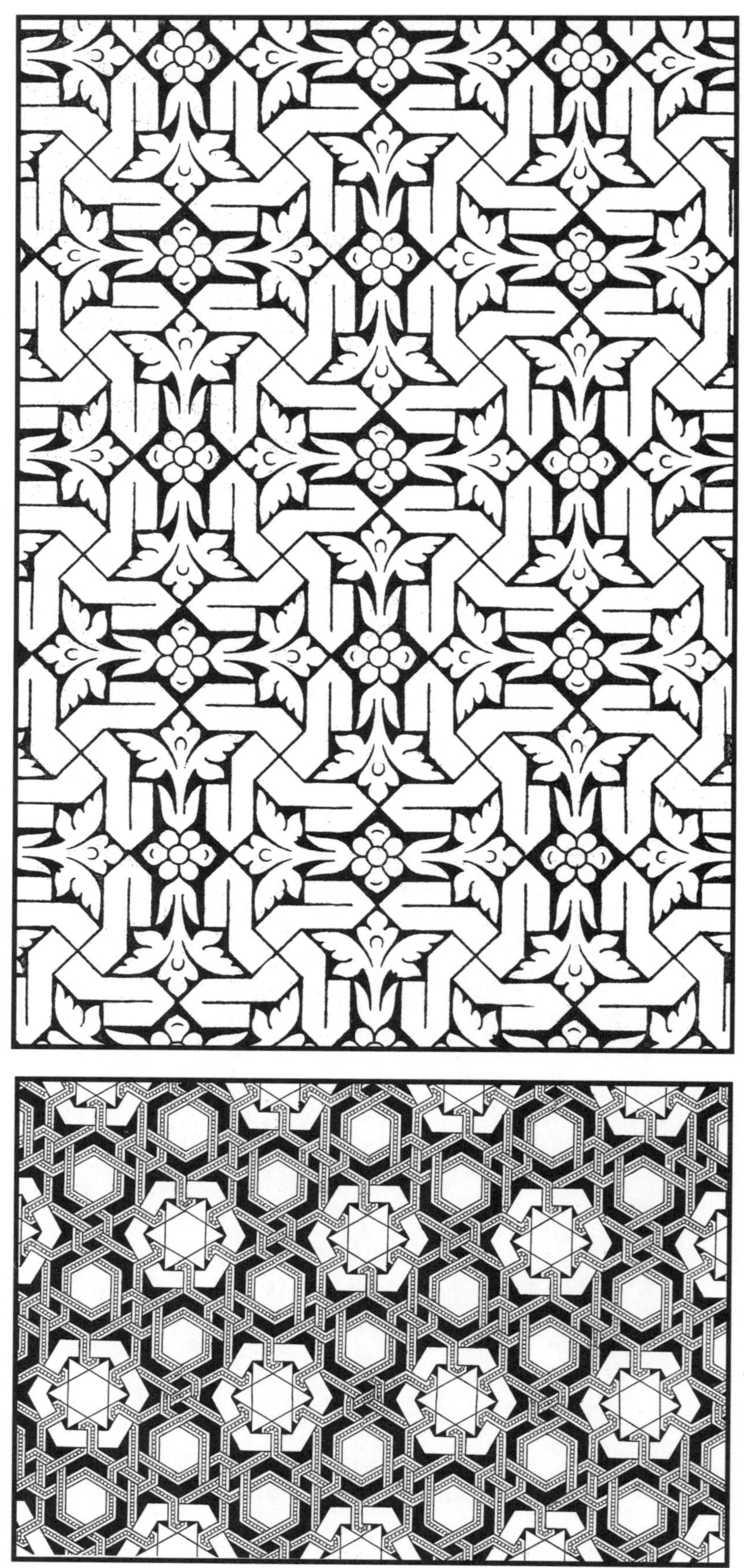

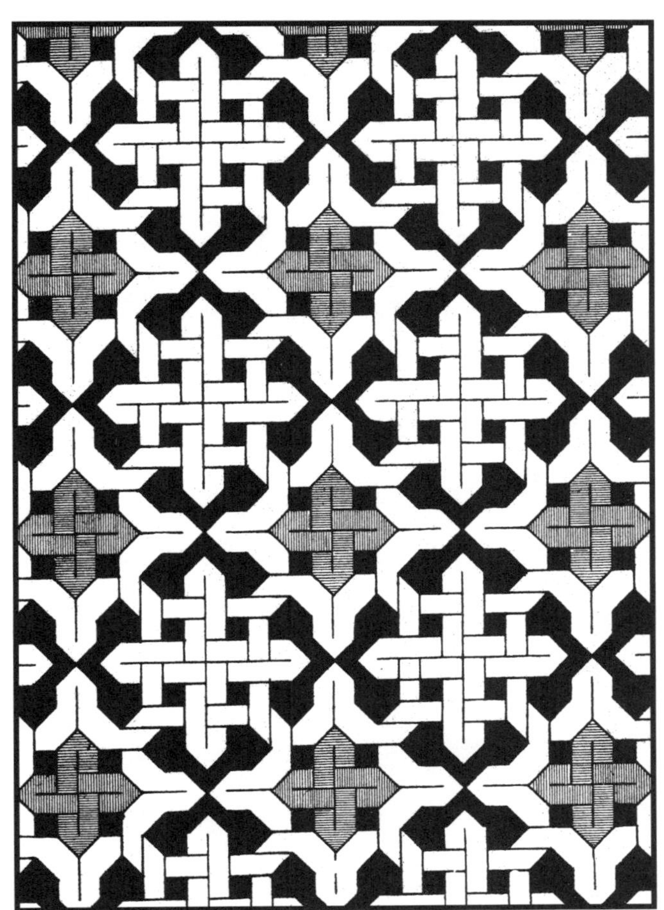

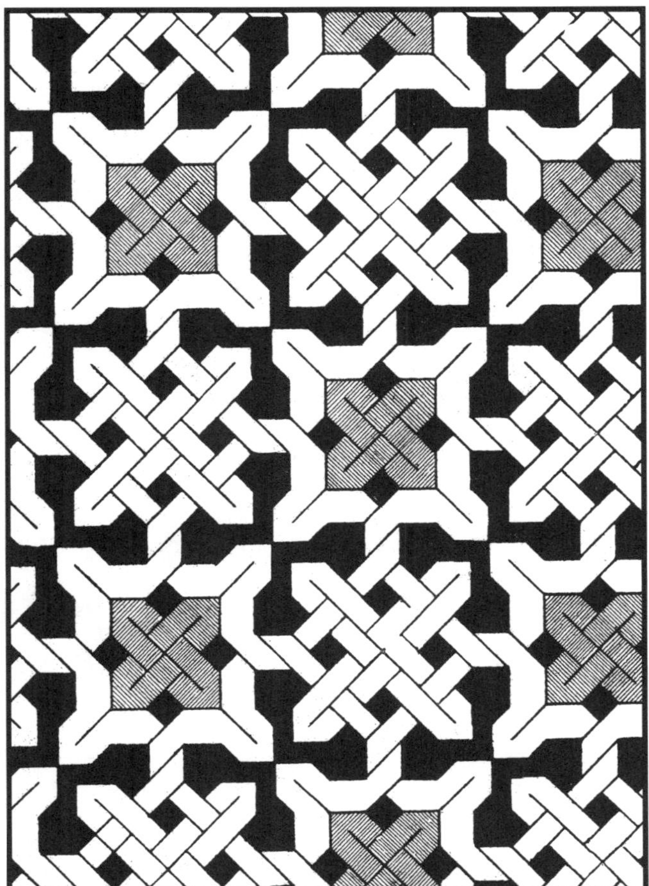

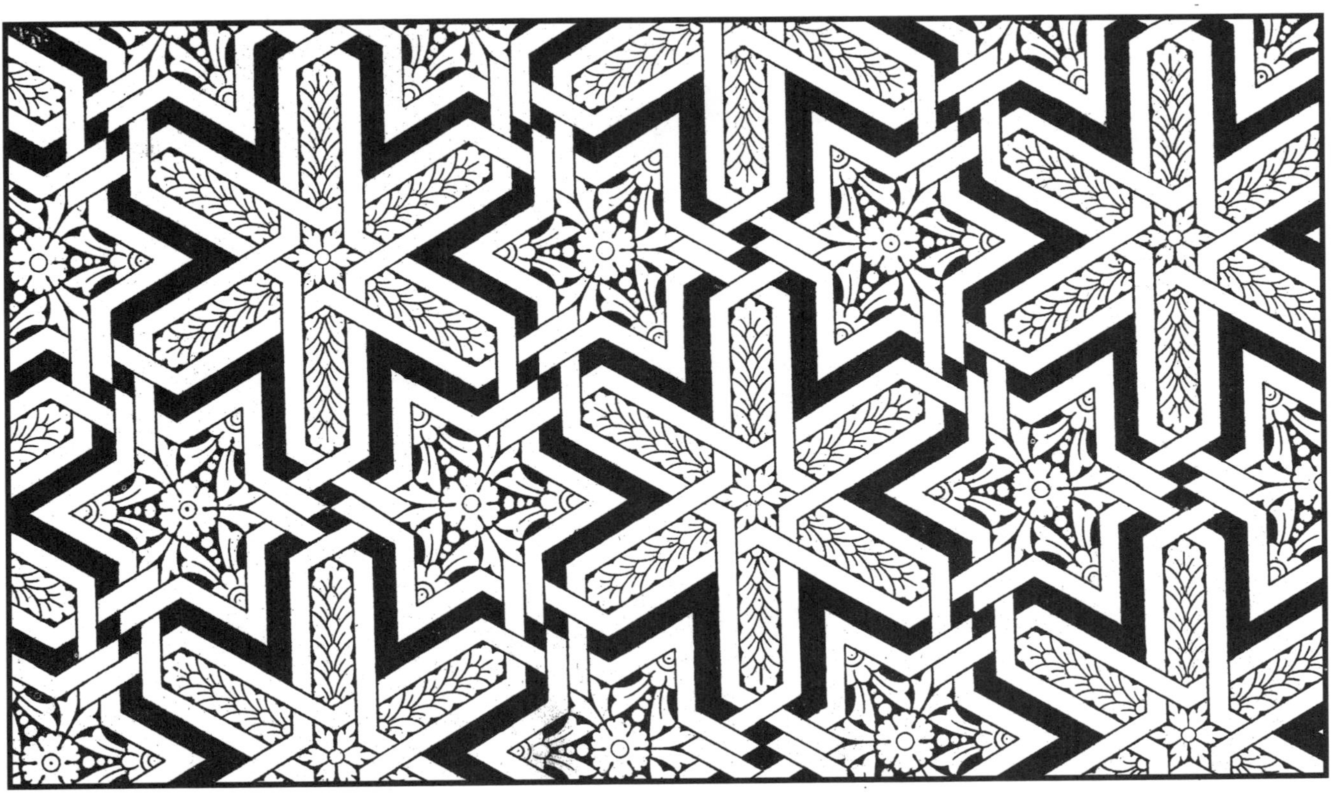

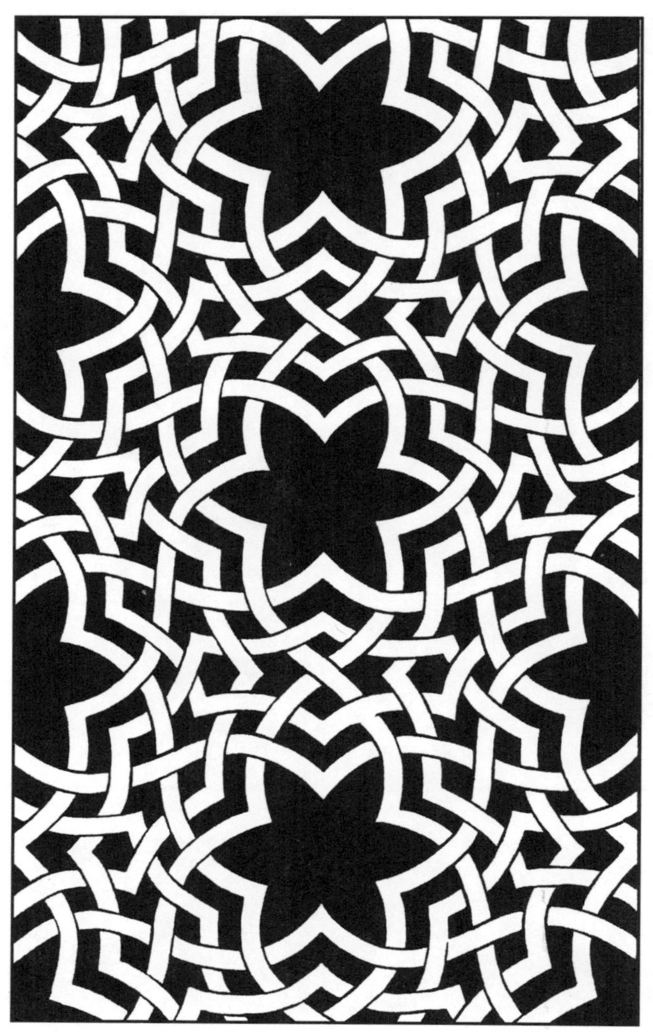

• Masters •

• Les Maîtres •

• Meister •

• Los maestros •

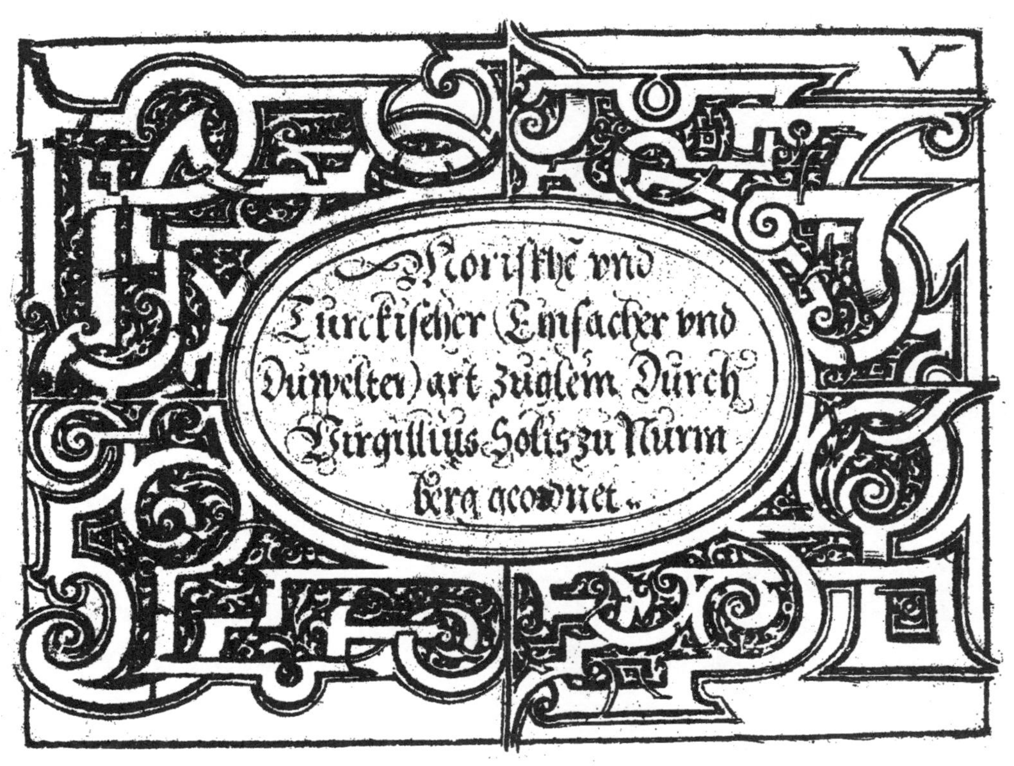
Morische vnd
Türckischer (Einfacher vnd
Duppelter) art zuglein Durch
Virgillius Solis zu Nurm
berg geordnet.

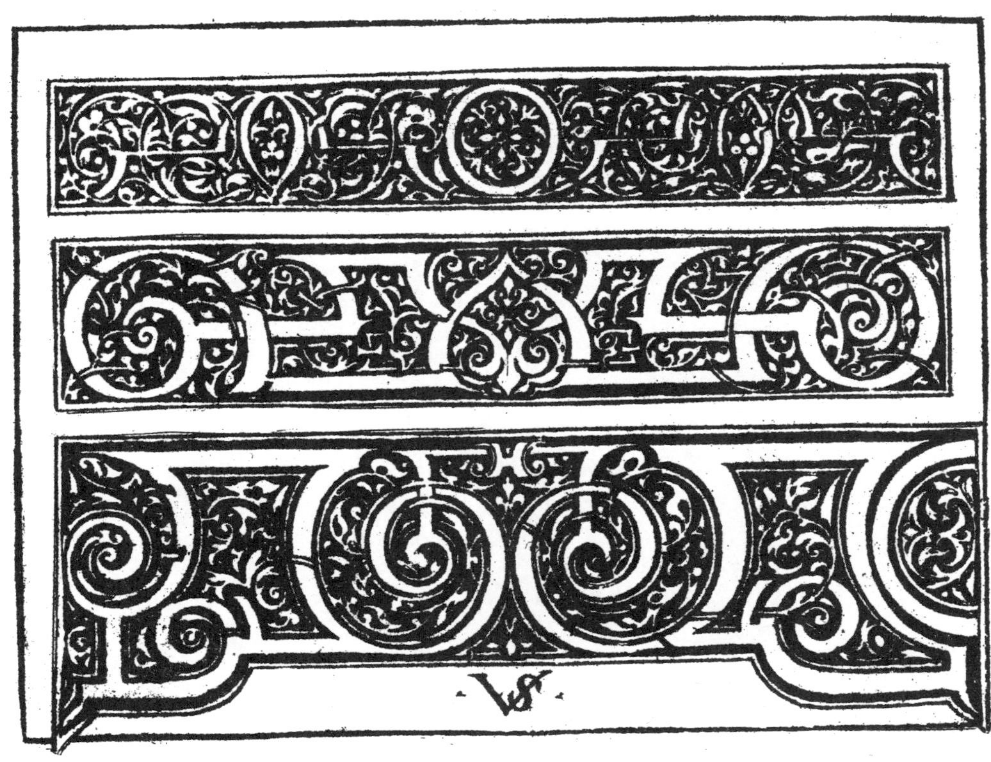

61

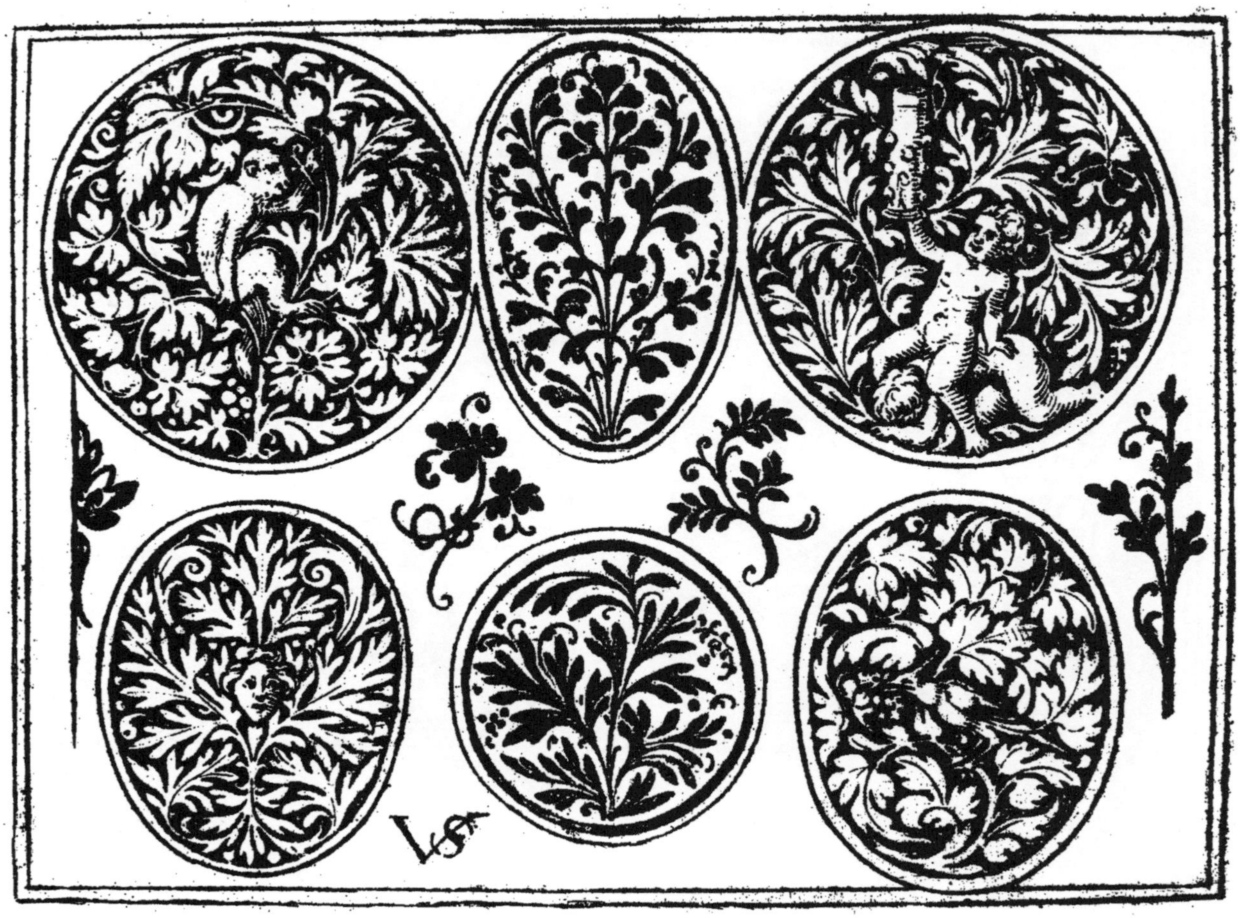

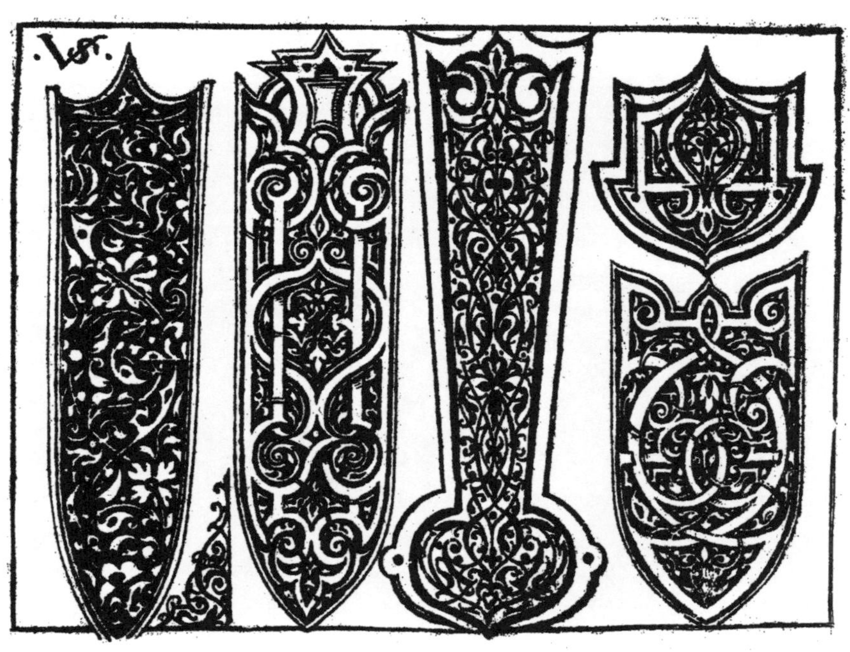

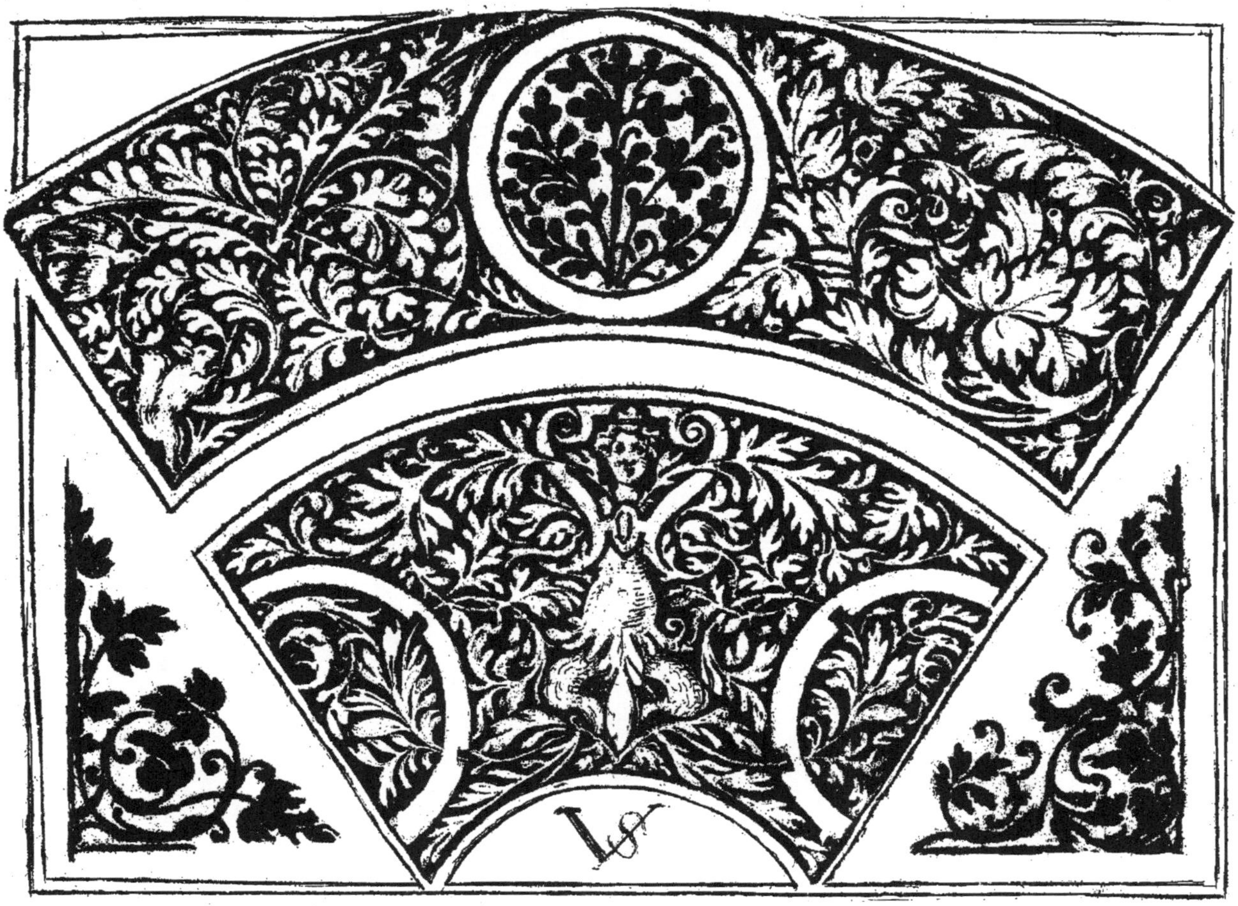

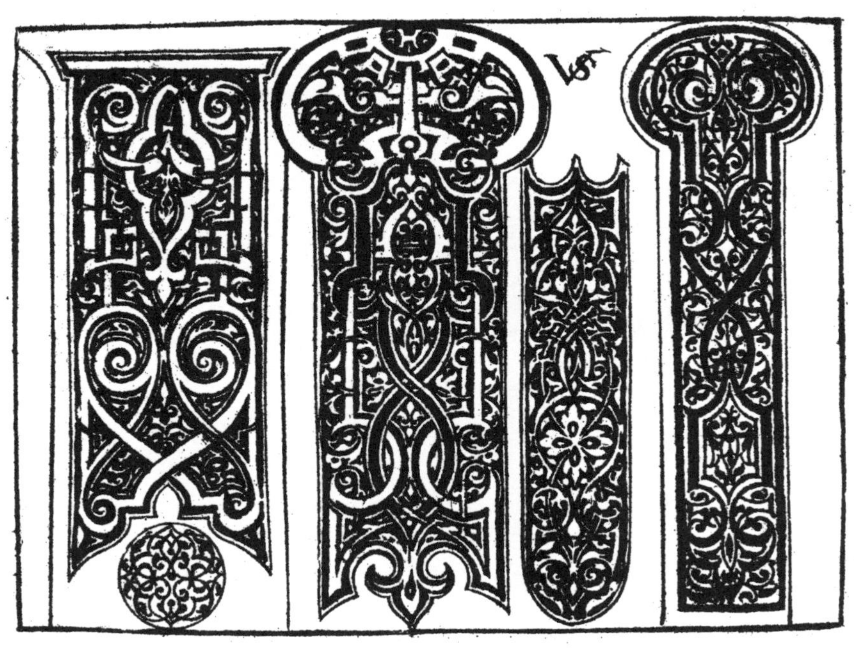

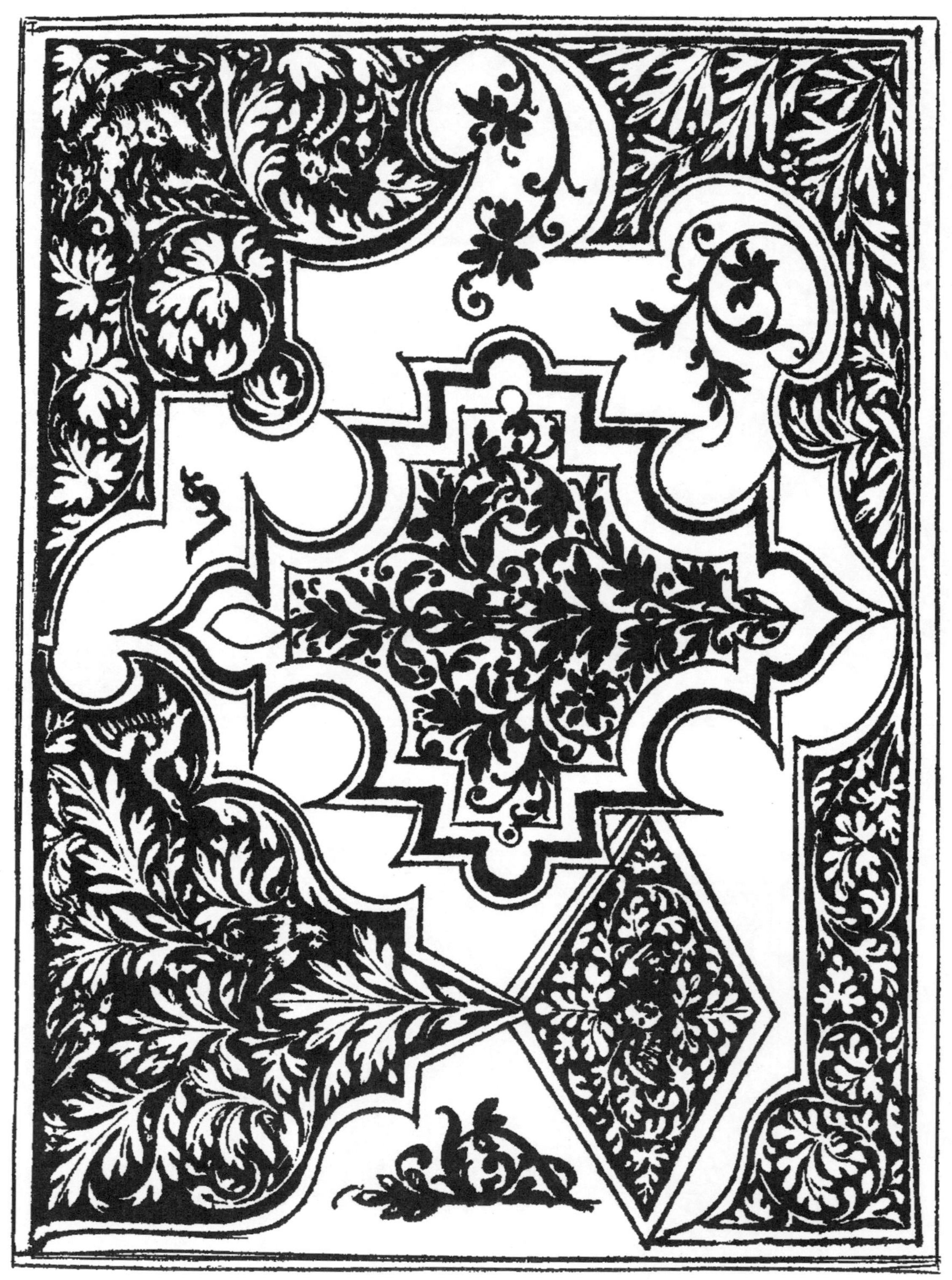

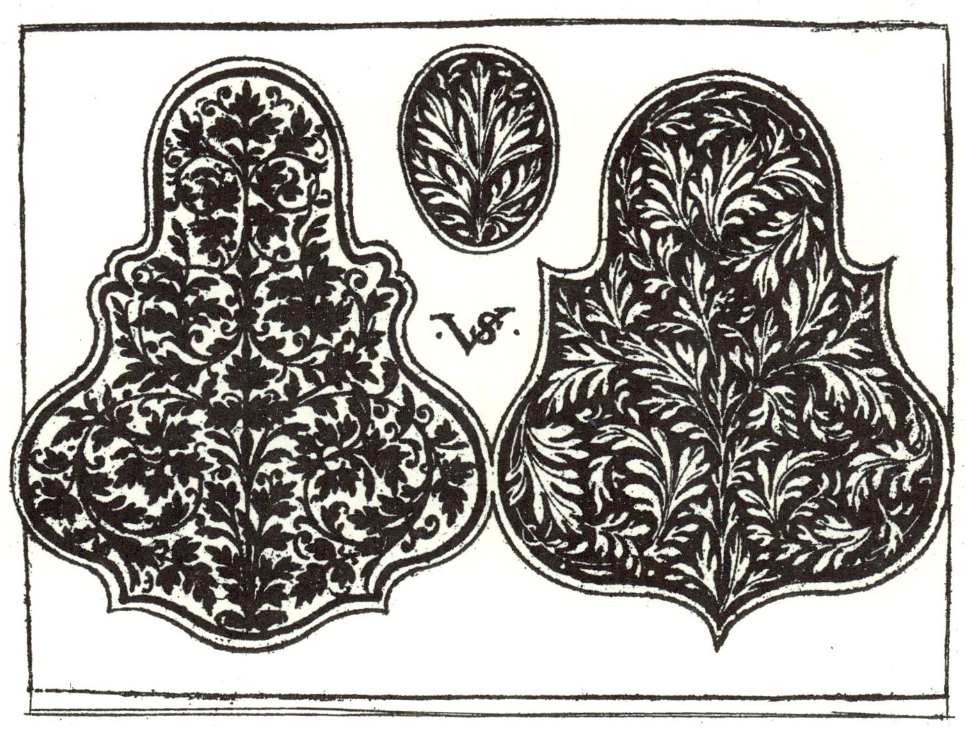

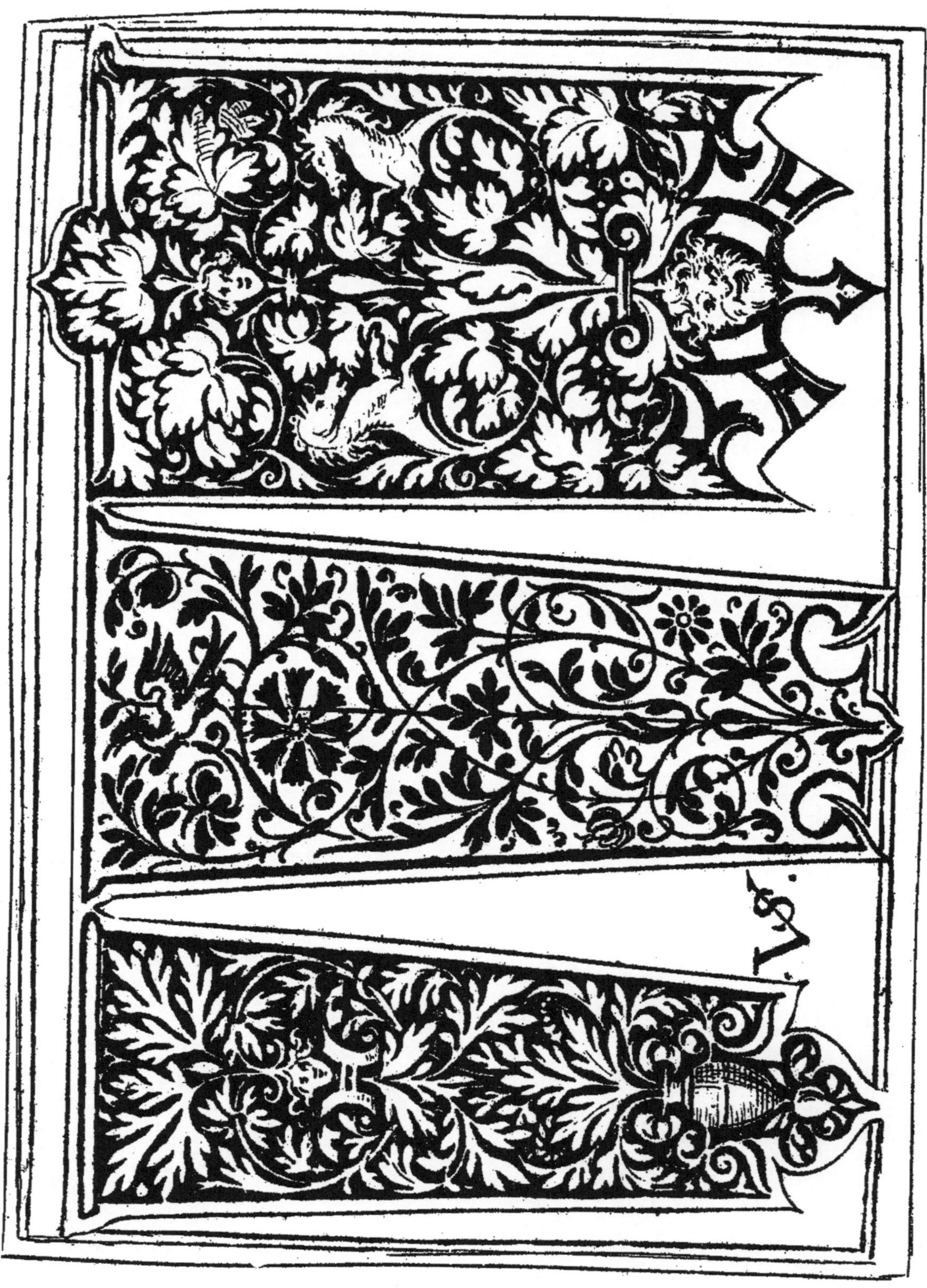

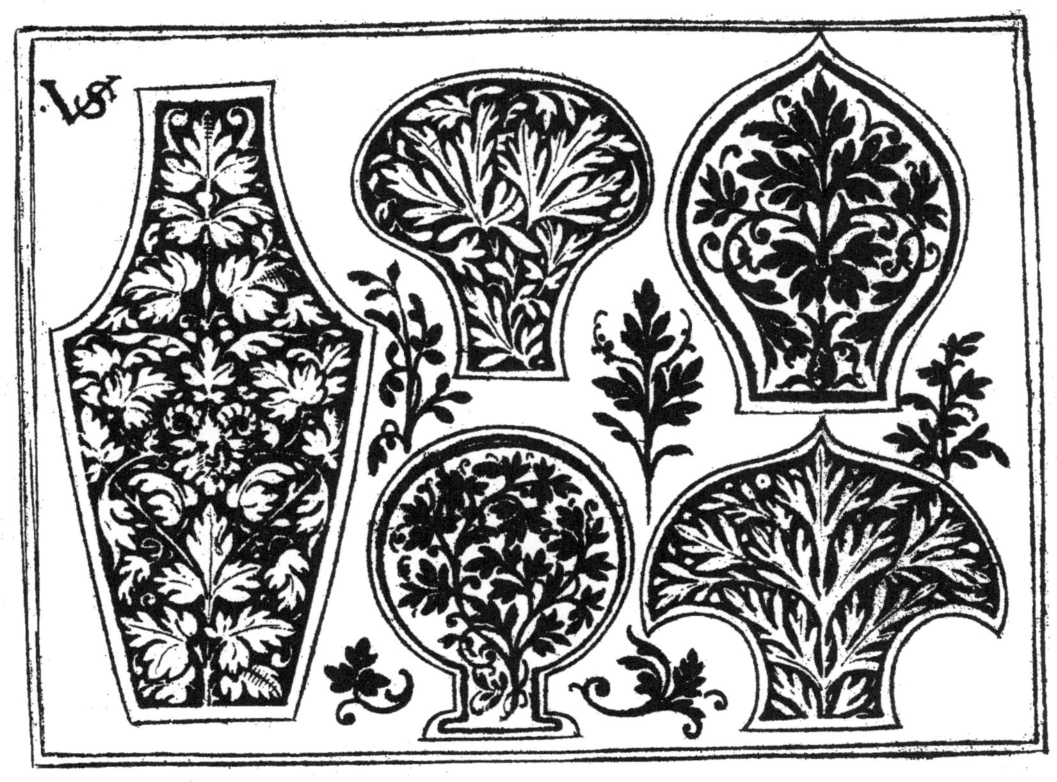

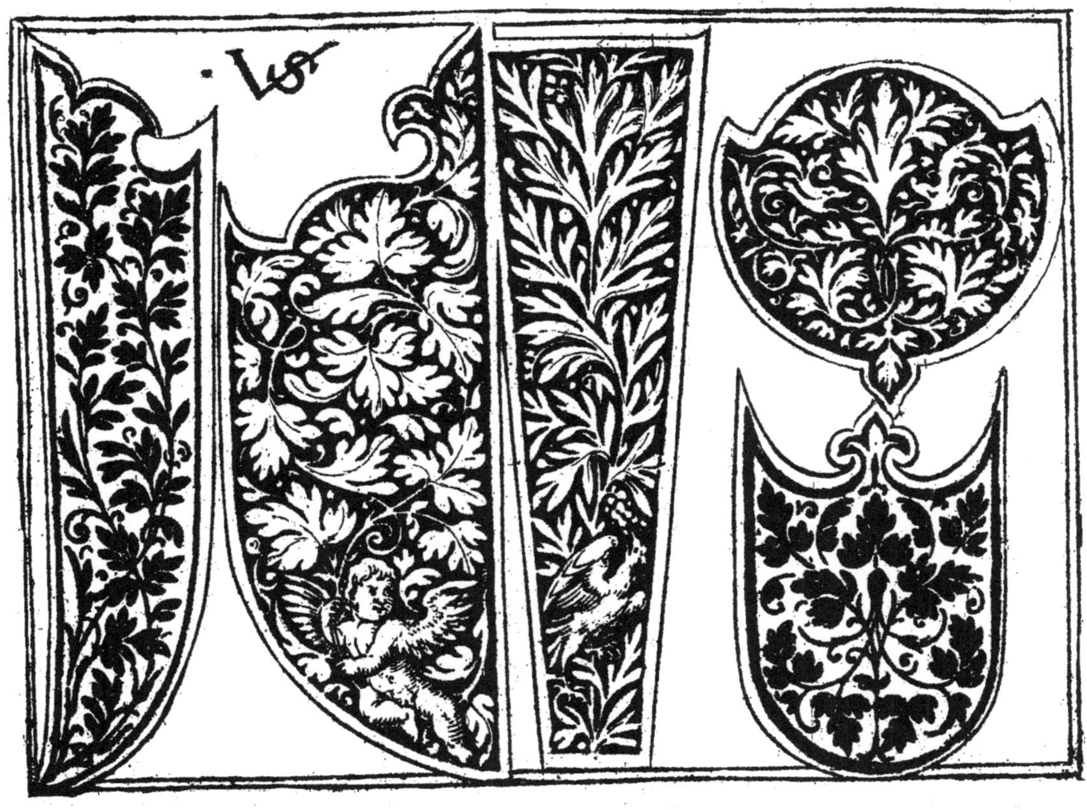

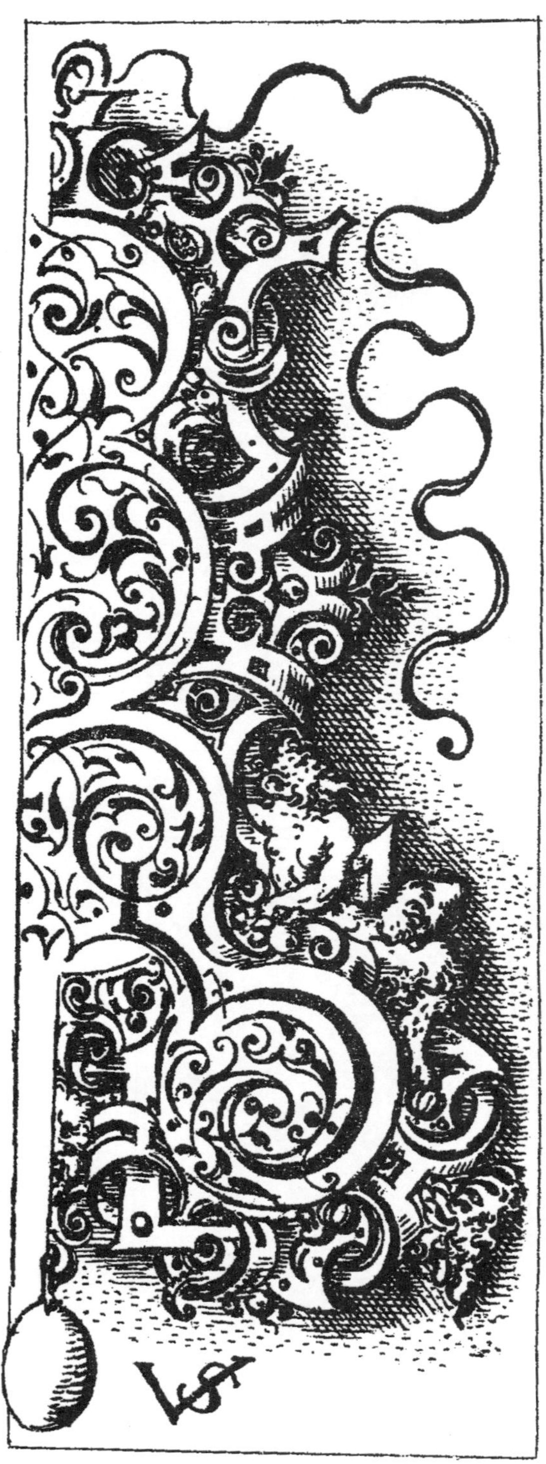

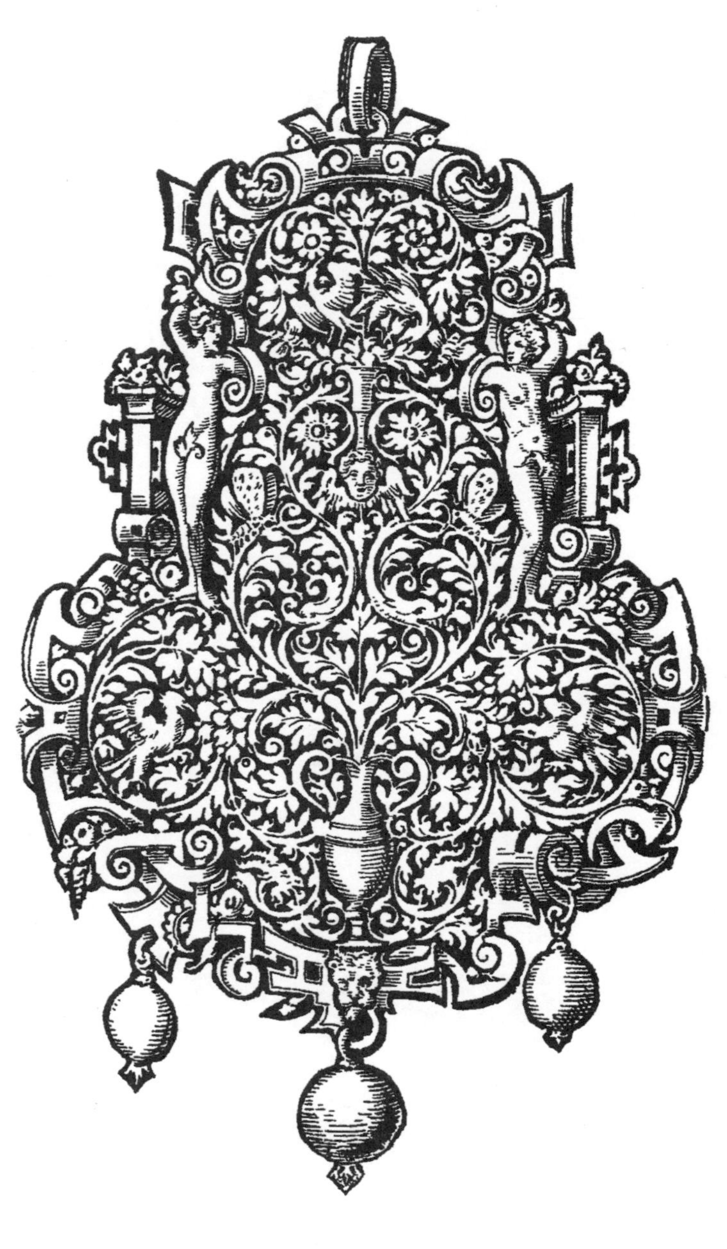

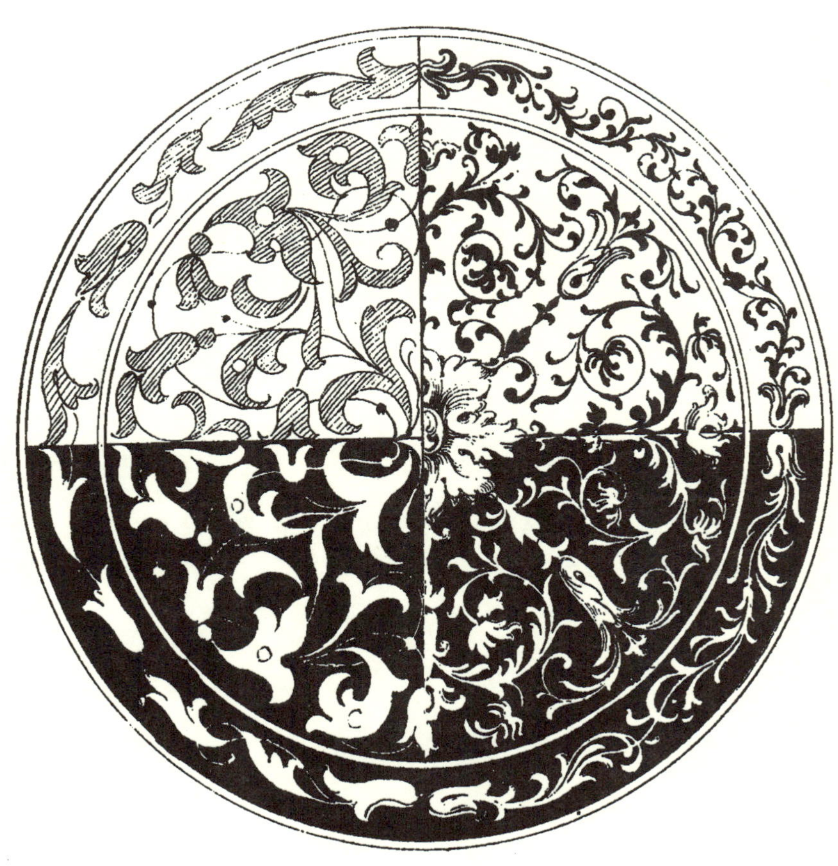

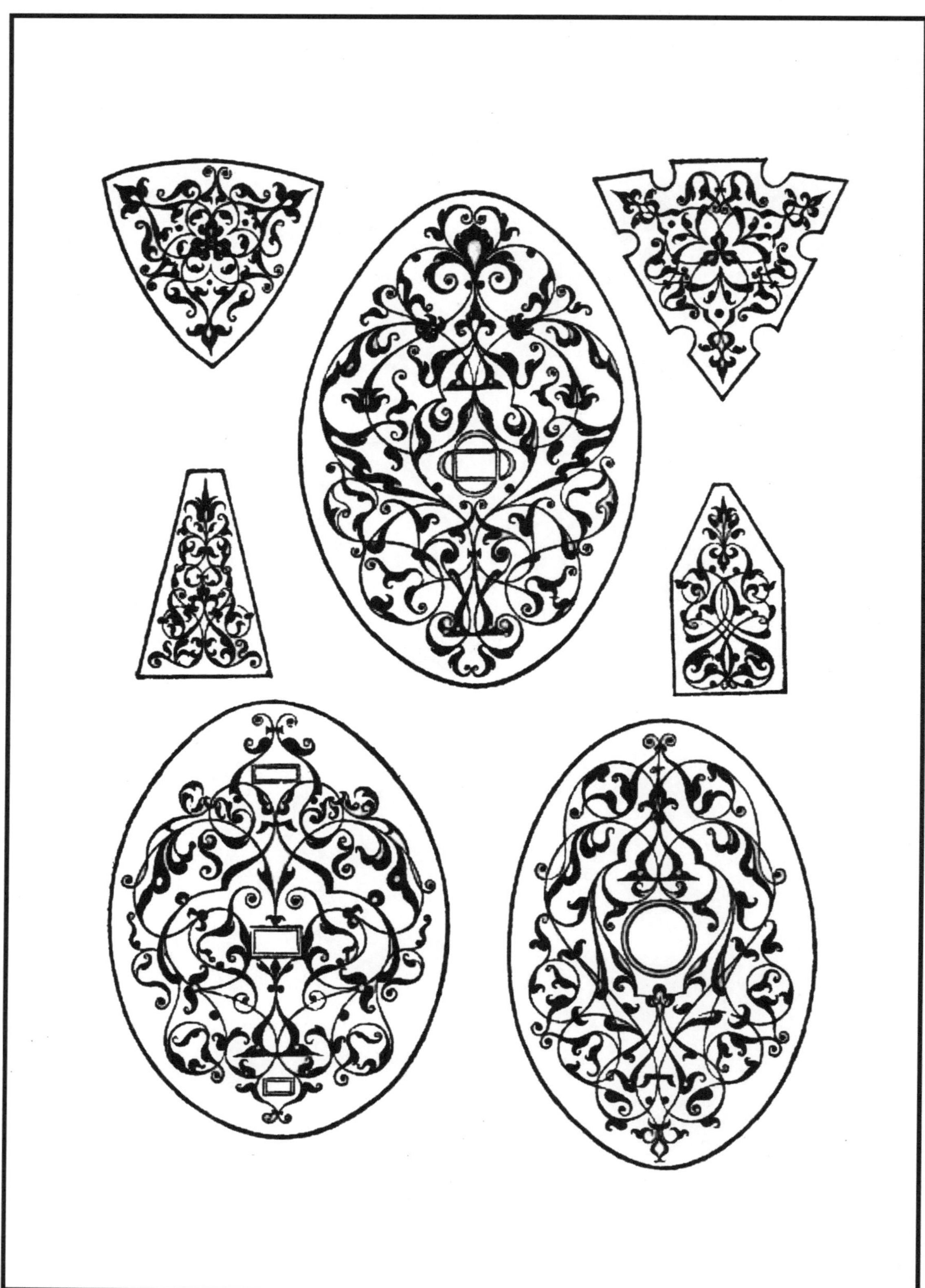

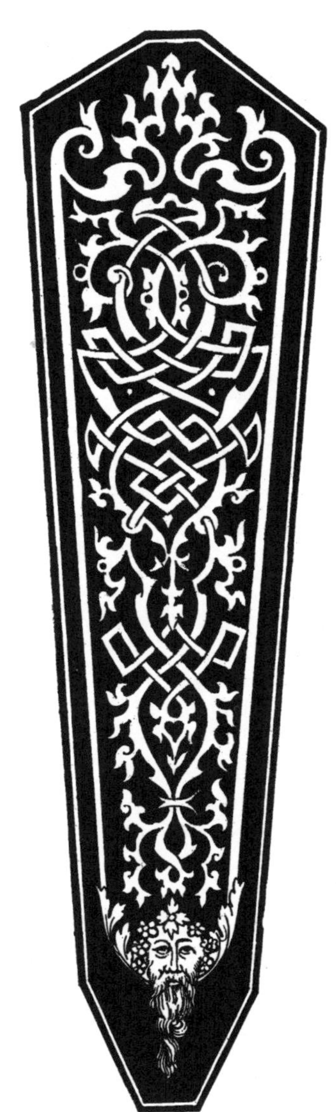
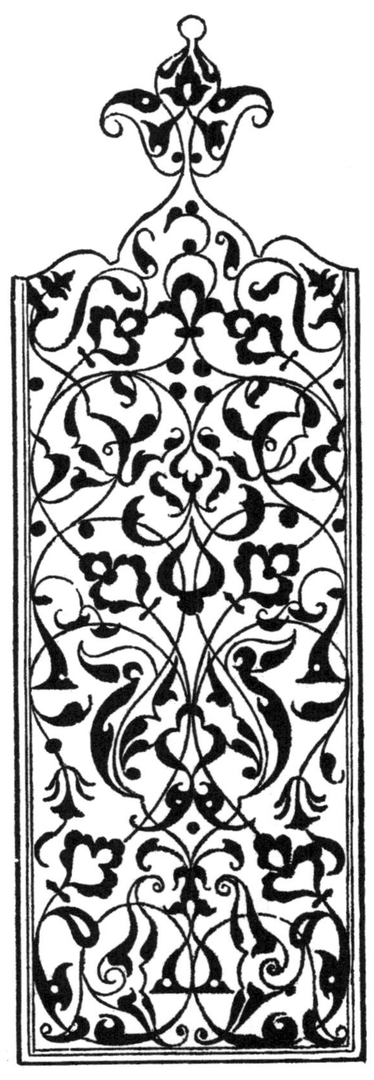

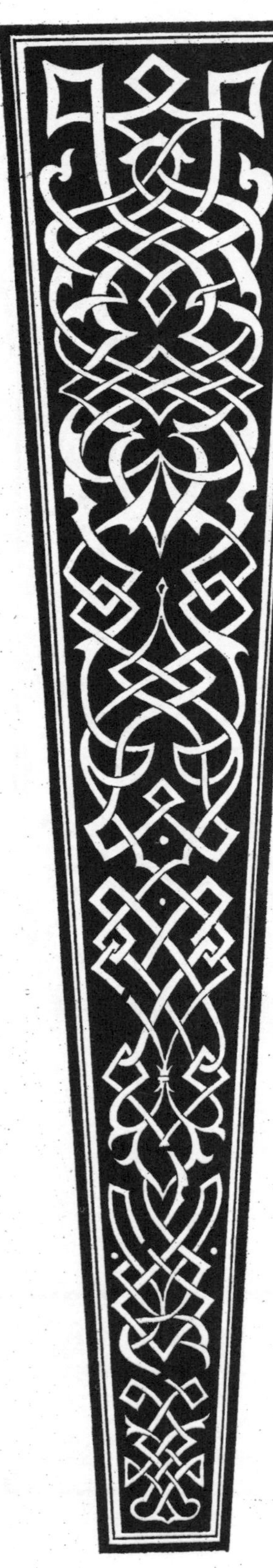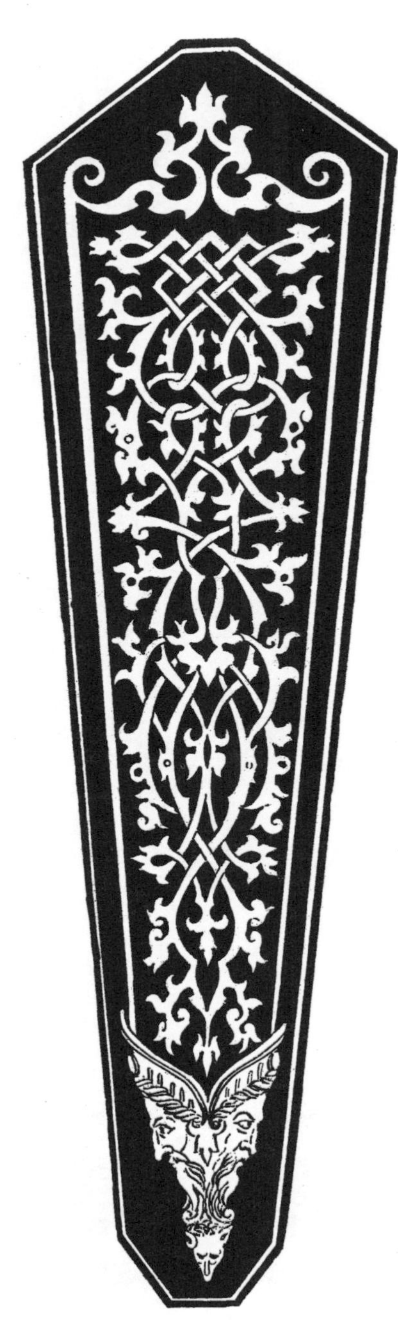

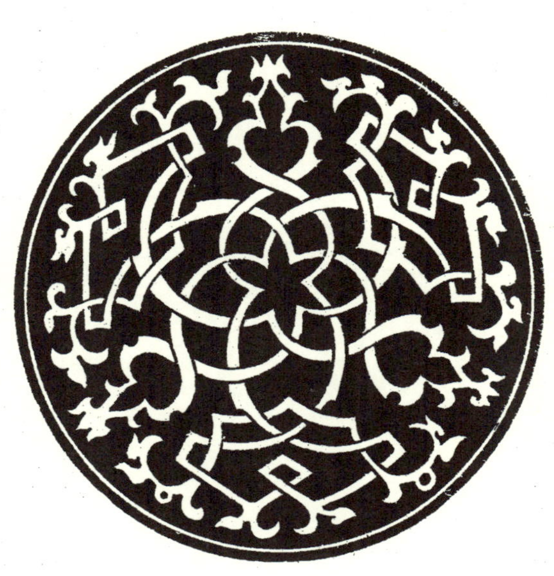

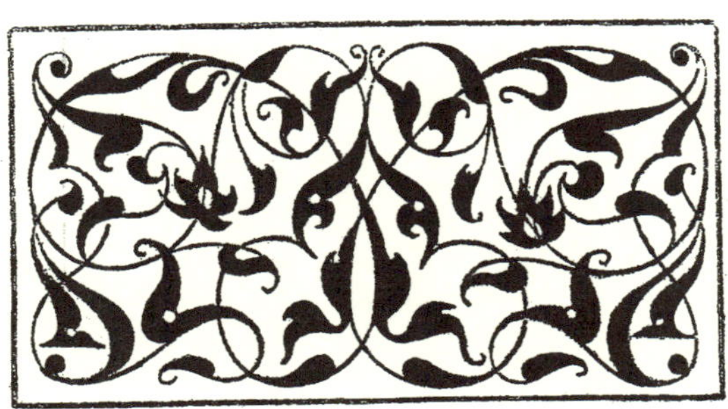

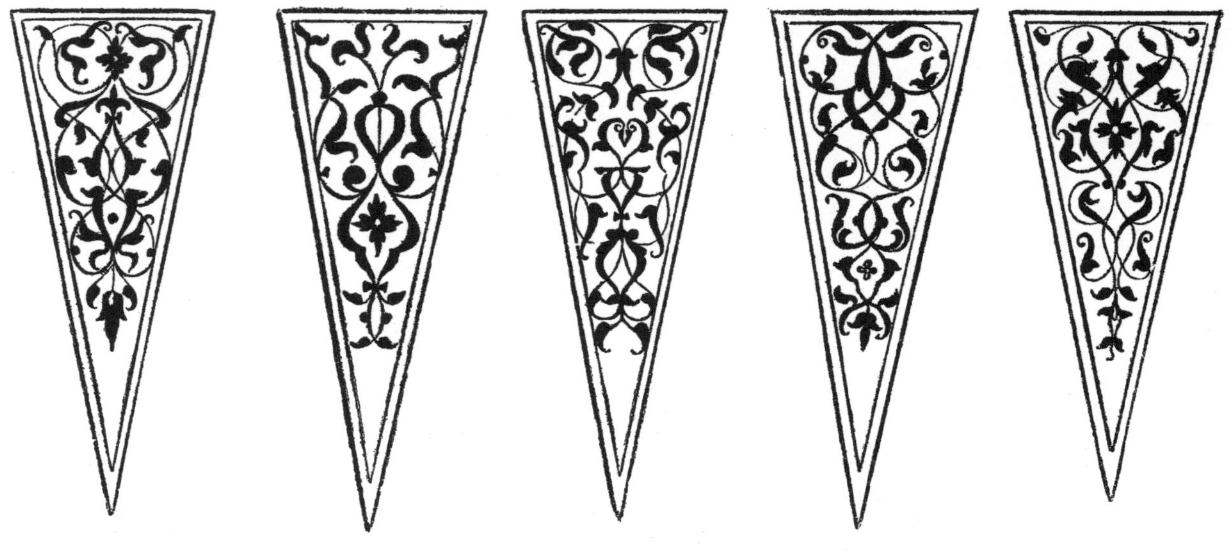

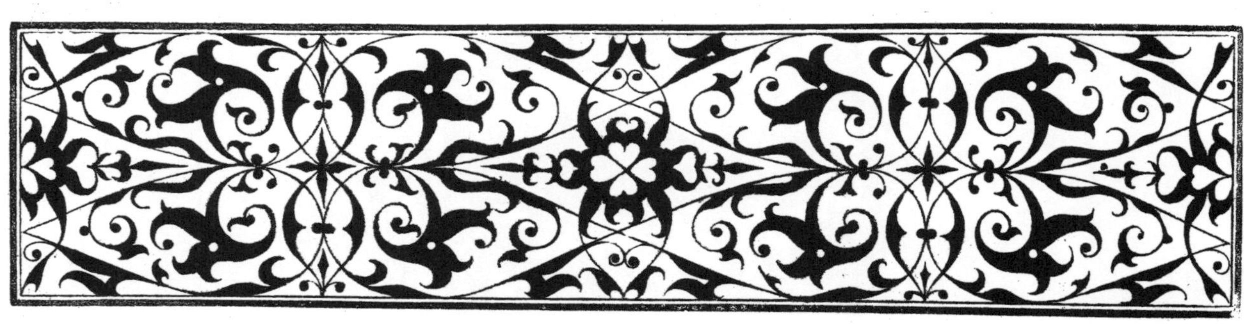

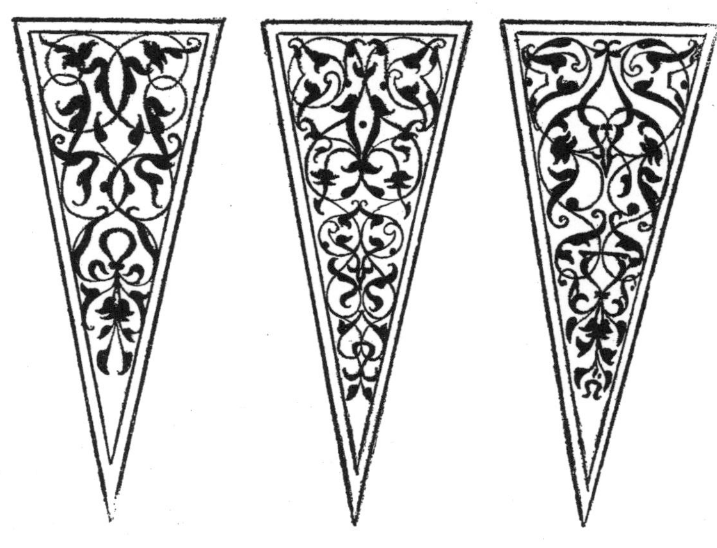

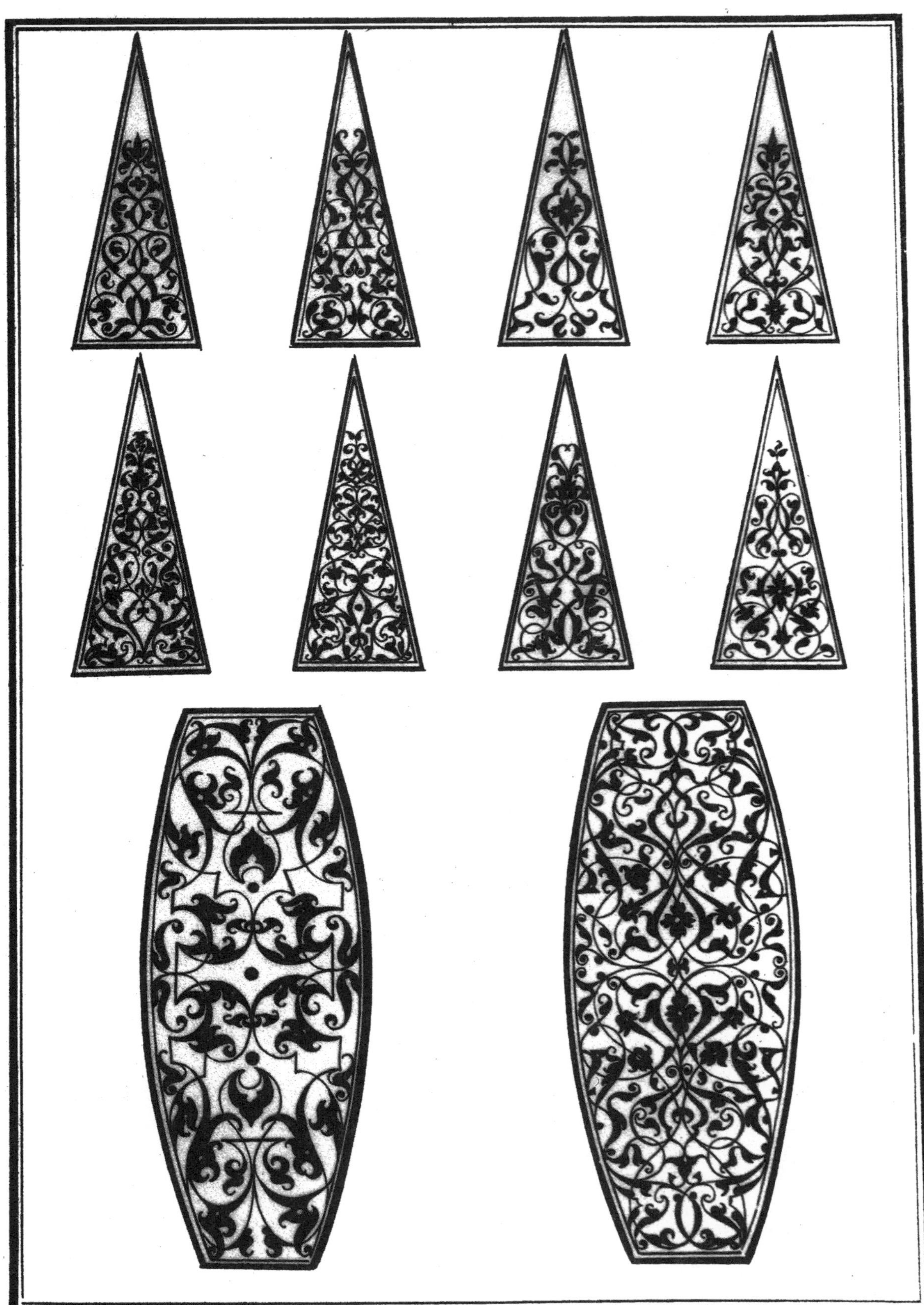

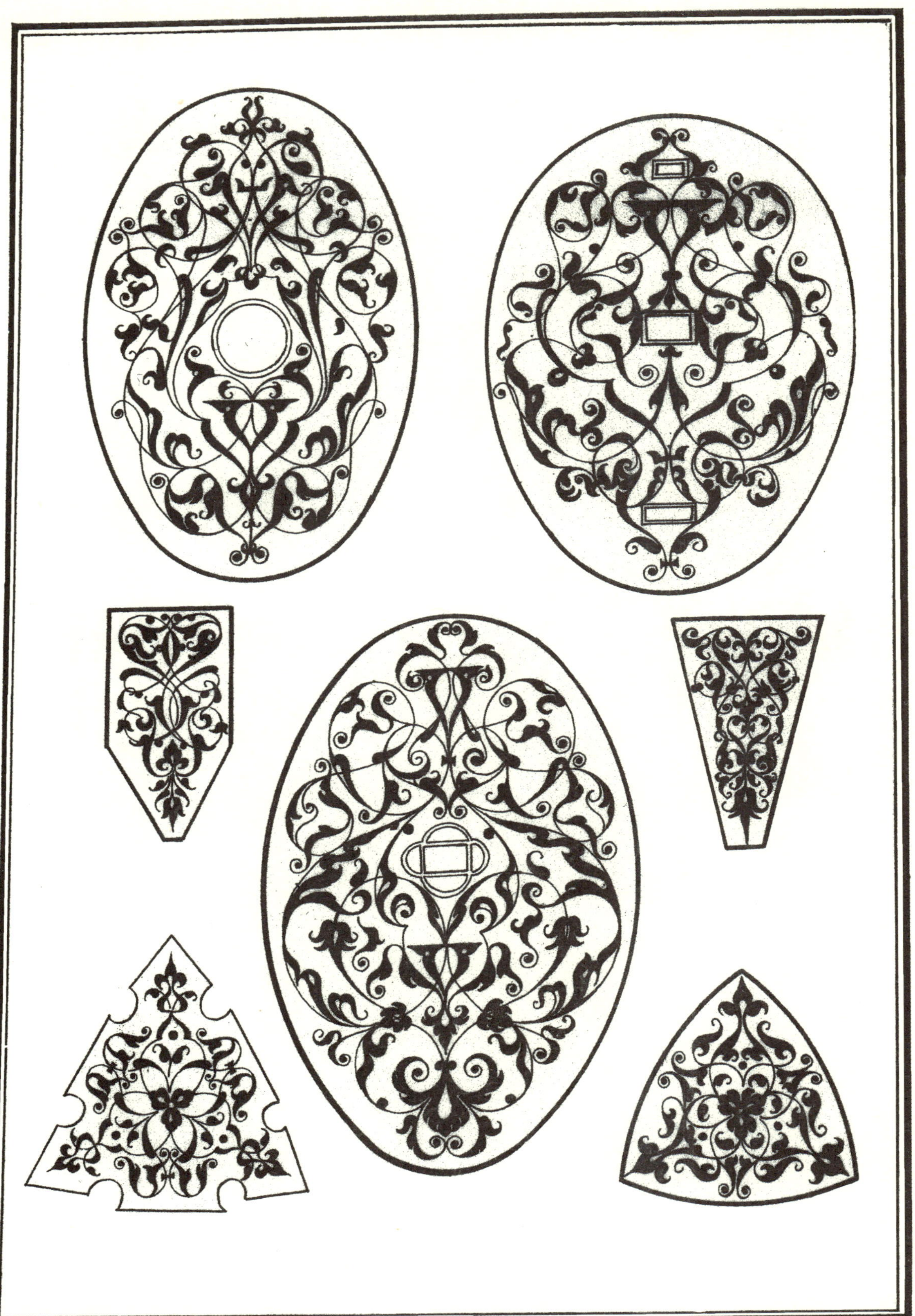

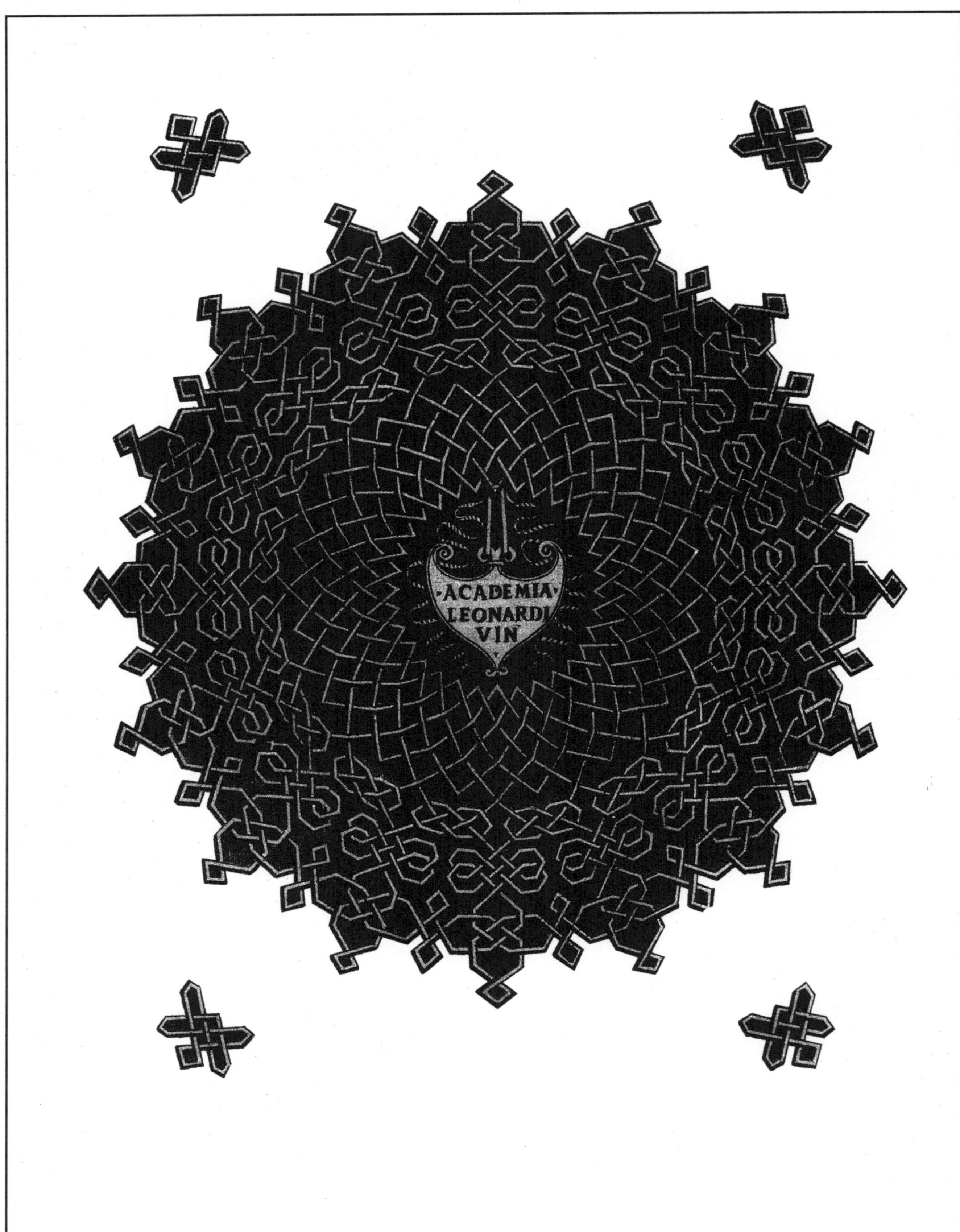

·ACADEMIA·
LEONARDI
VIN

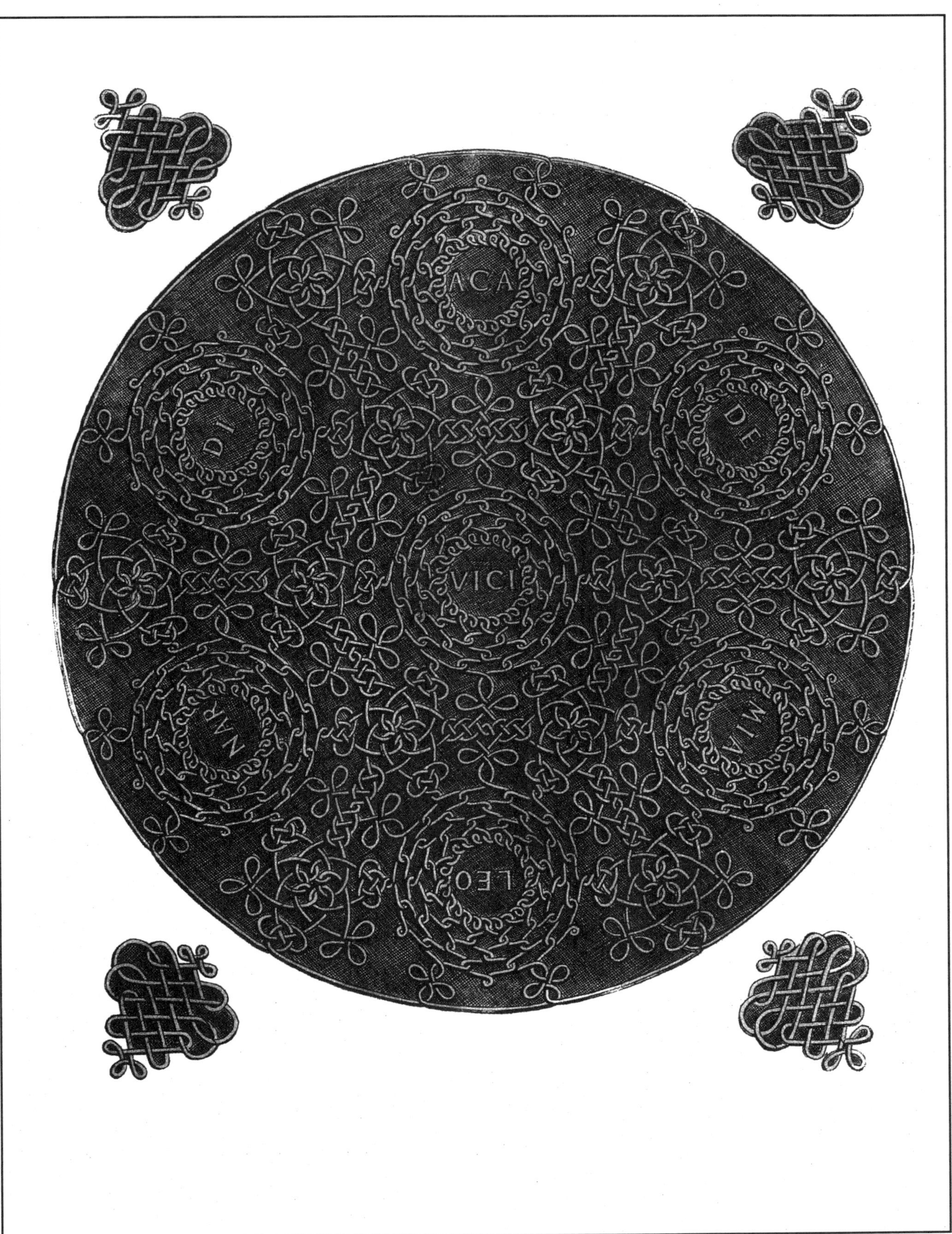

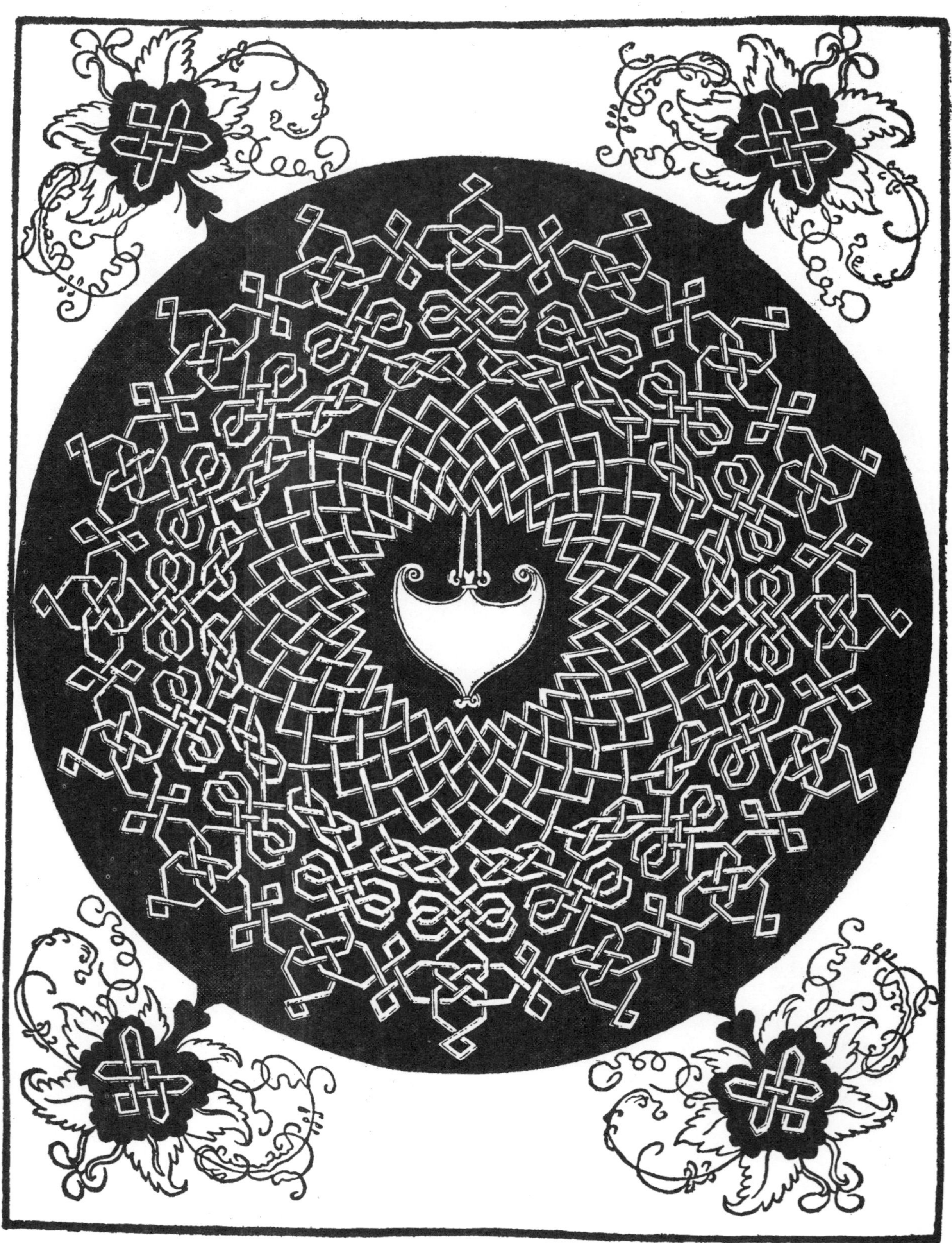

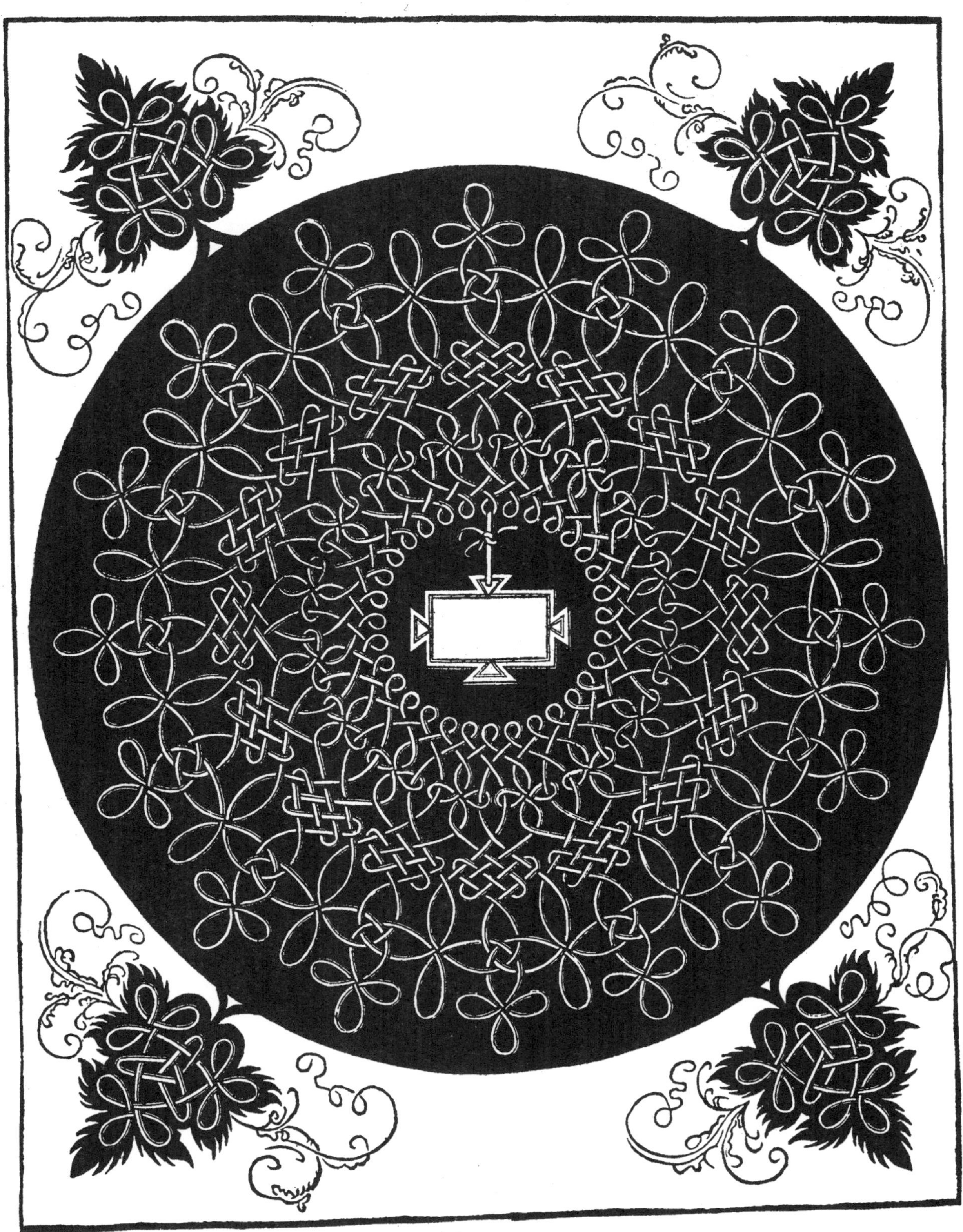

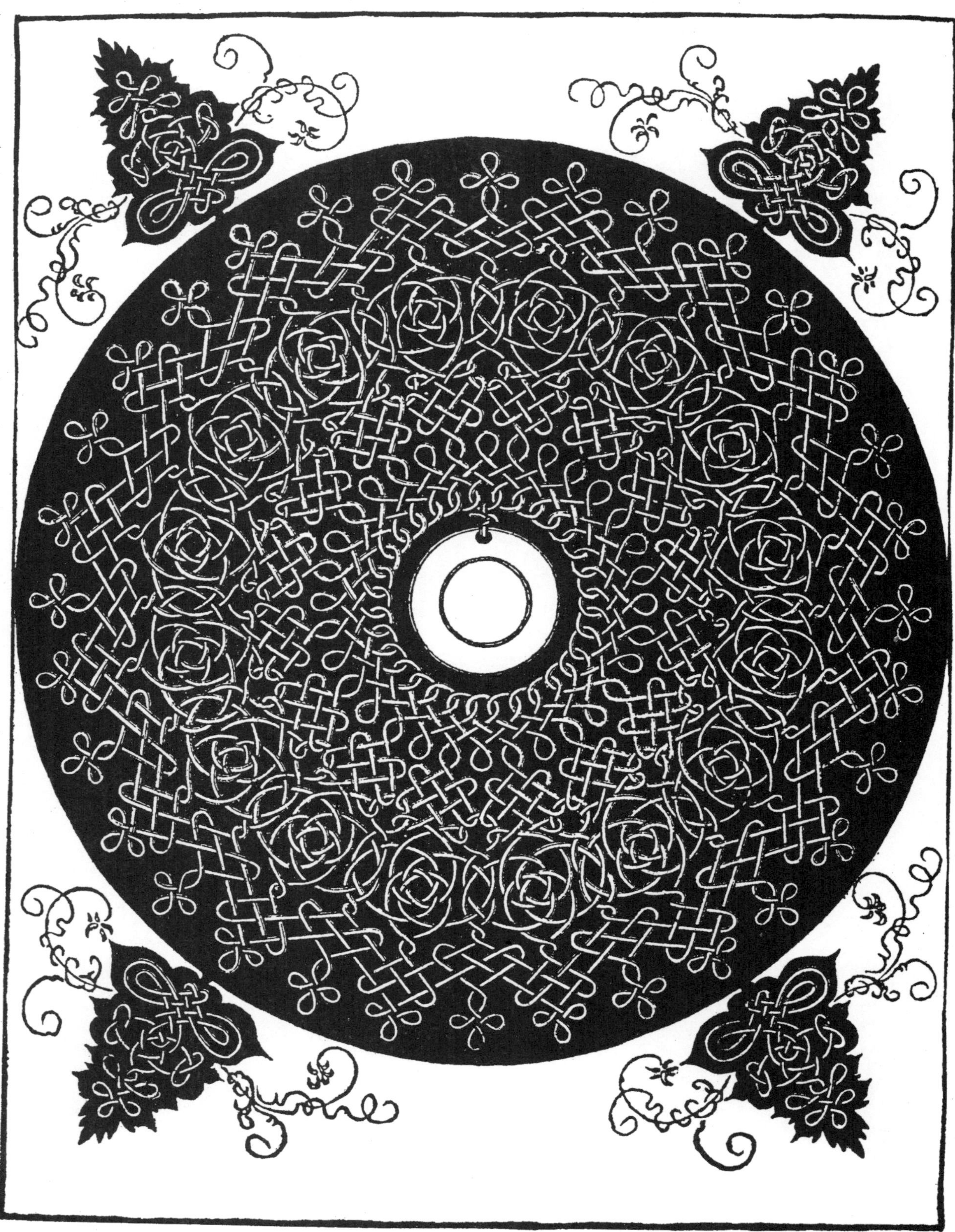

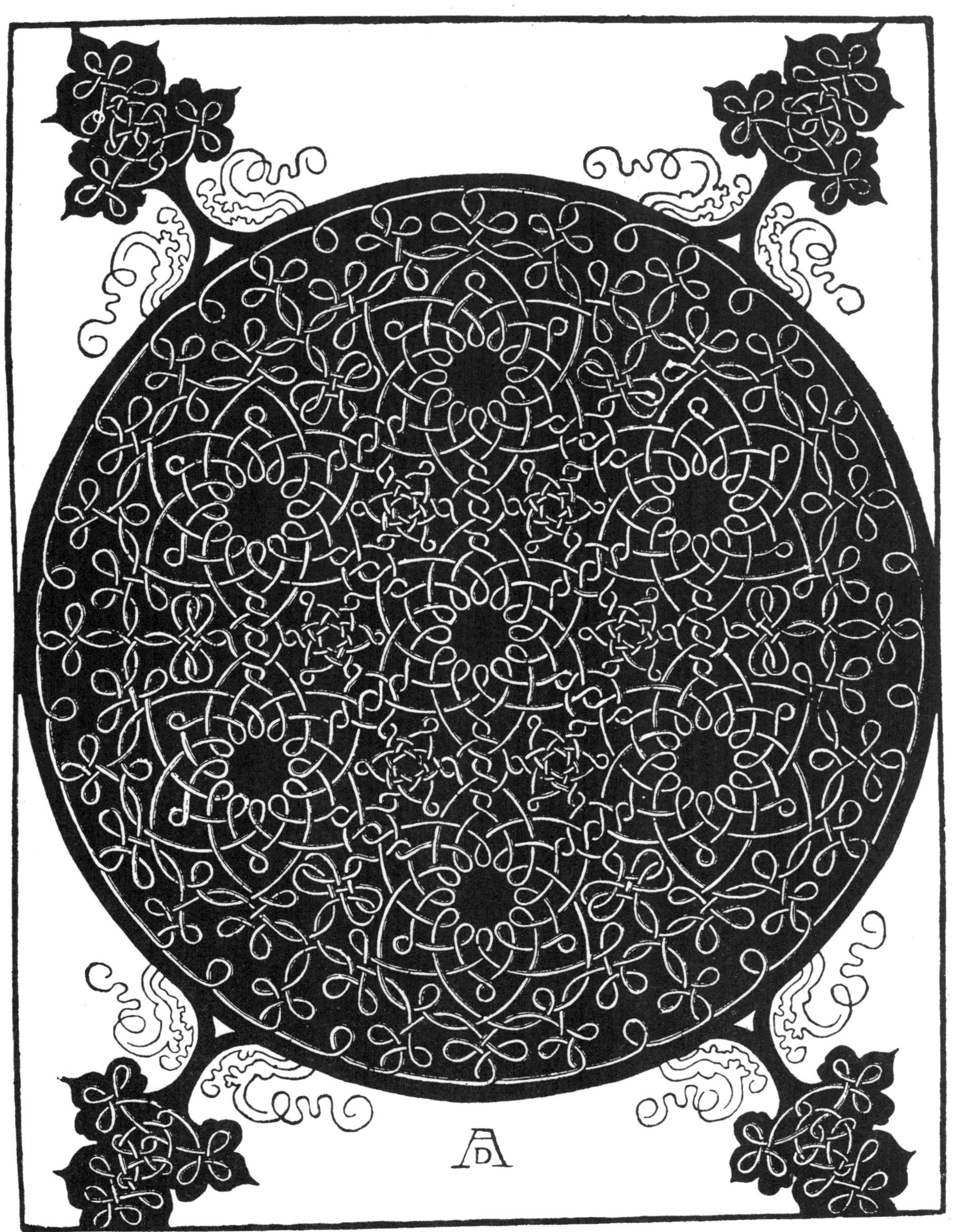

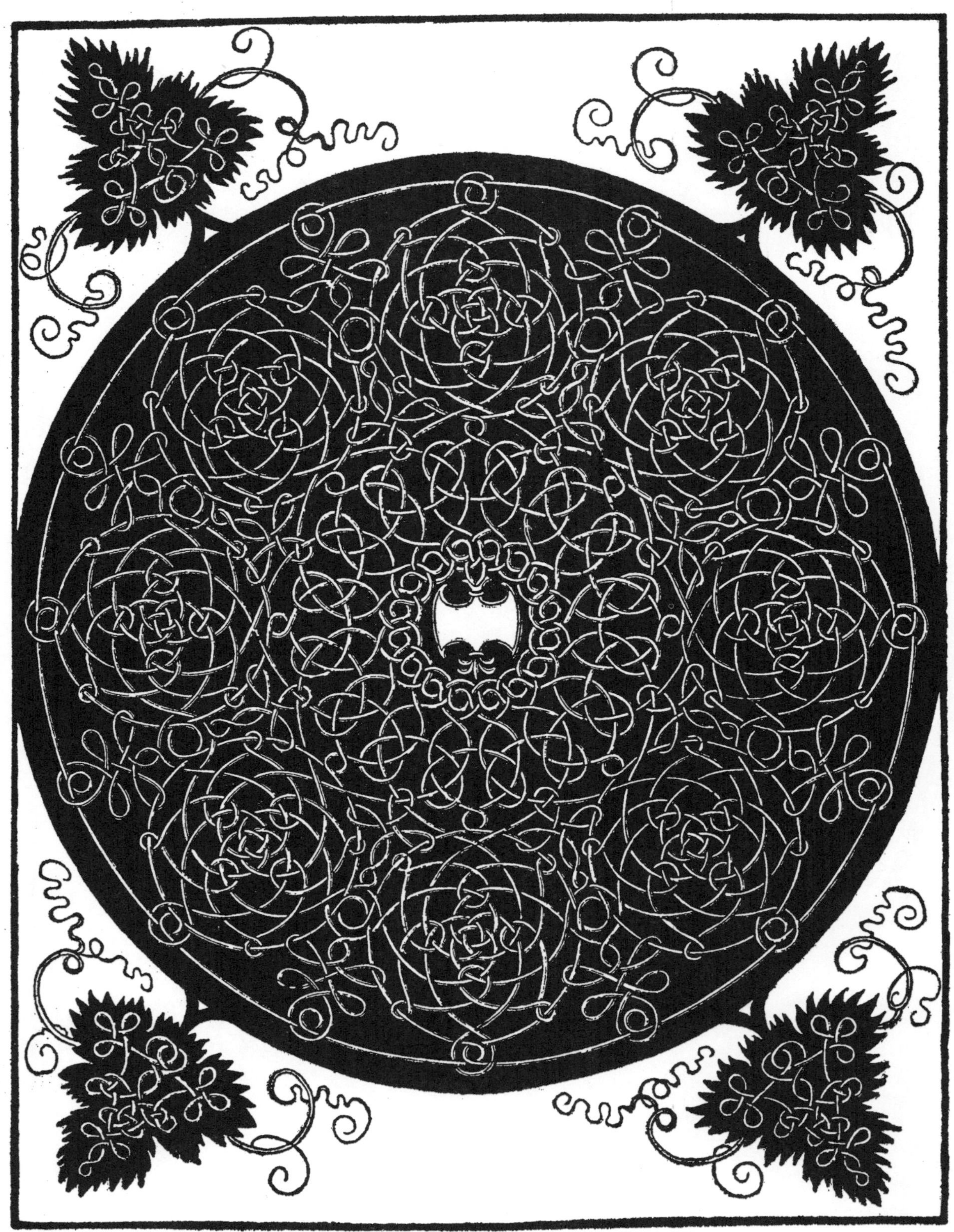

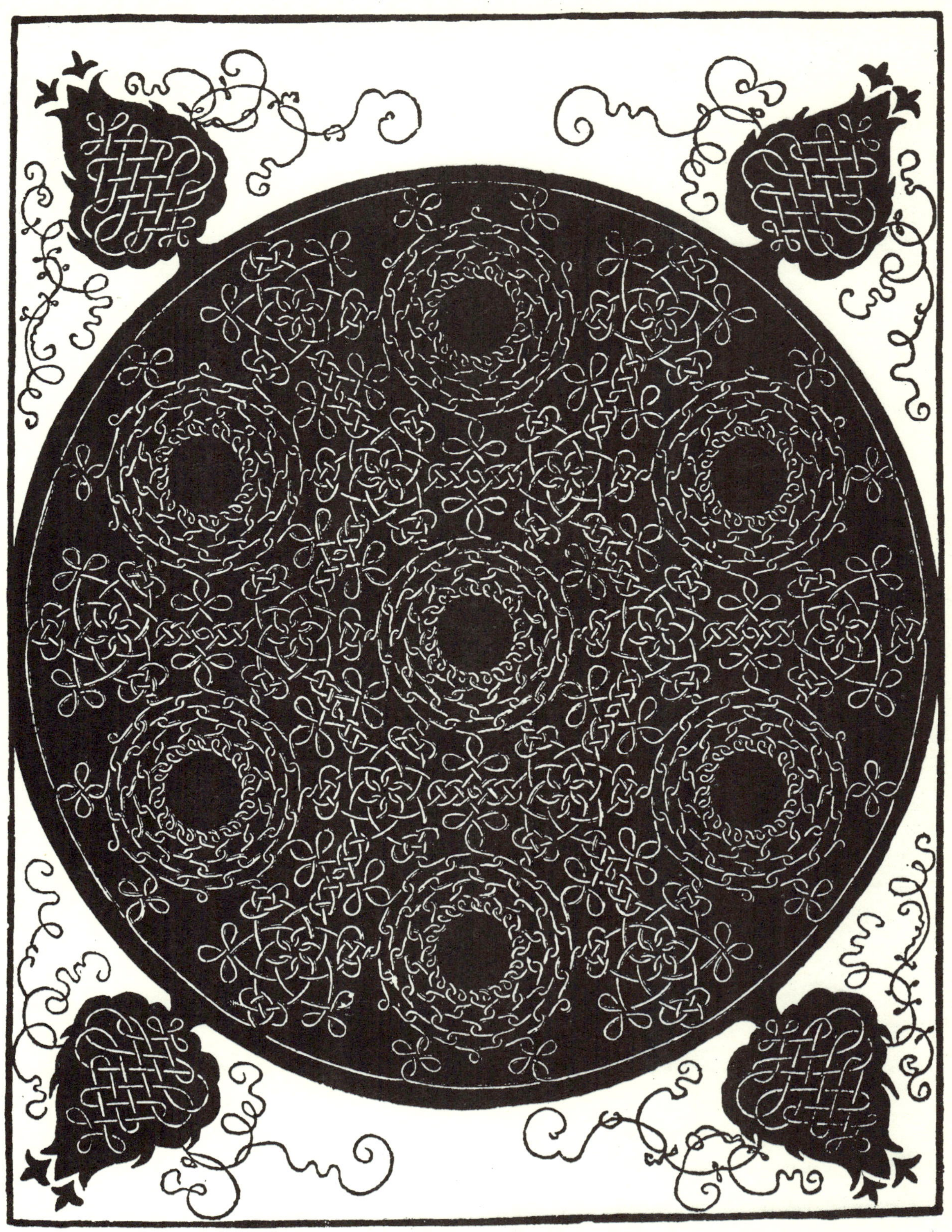

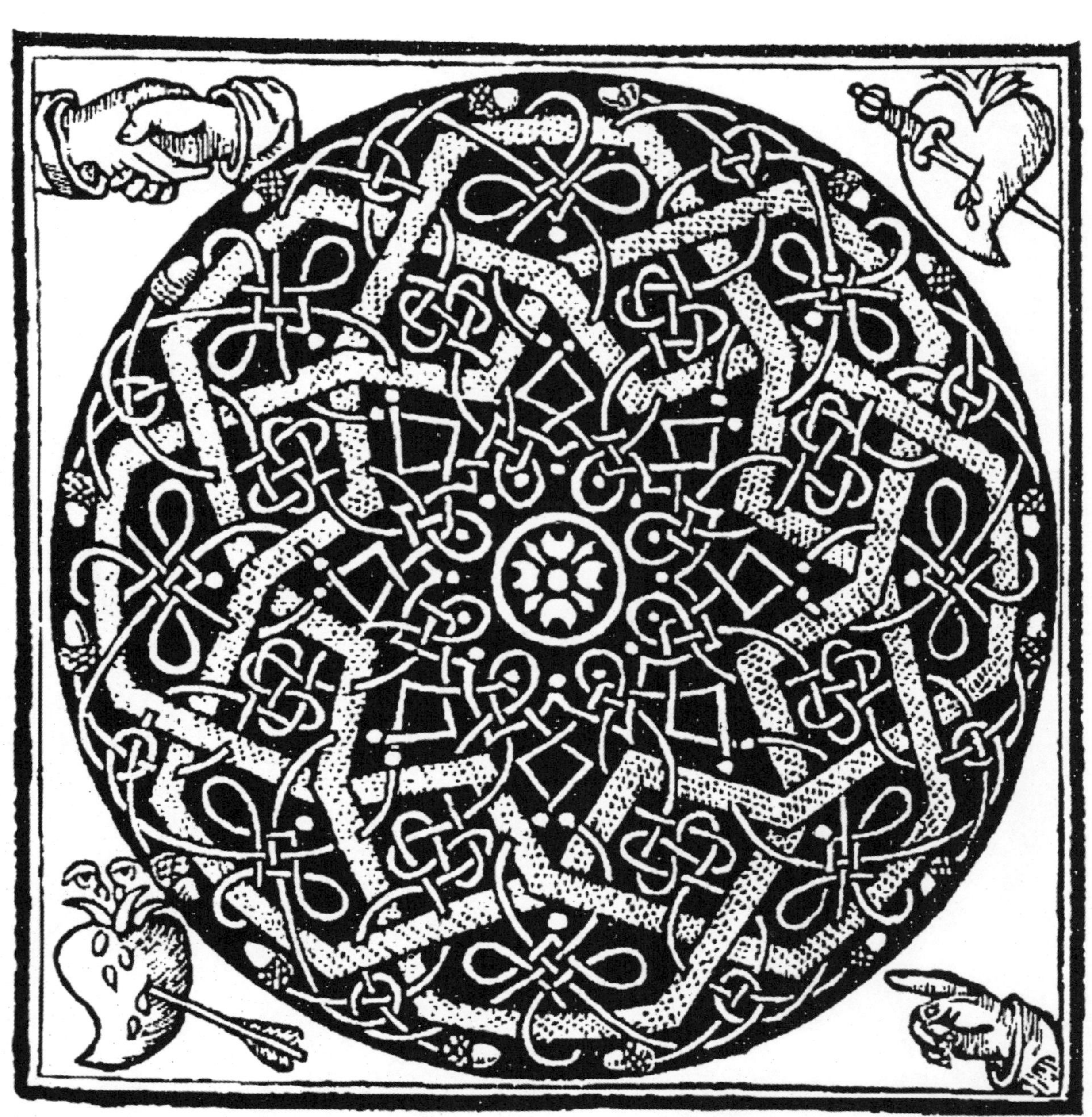

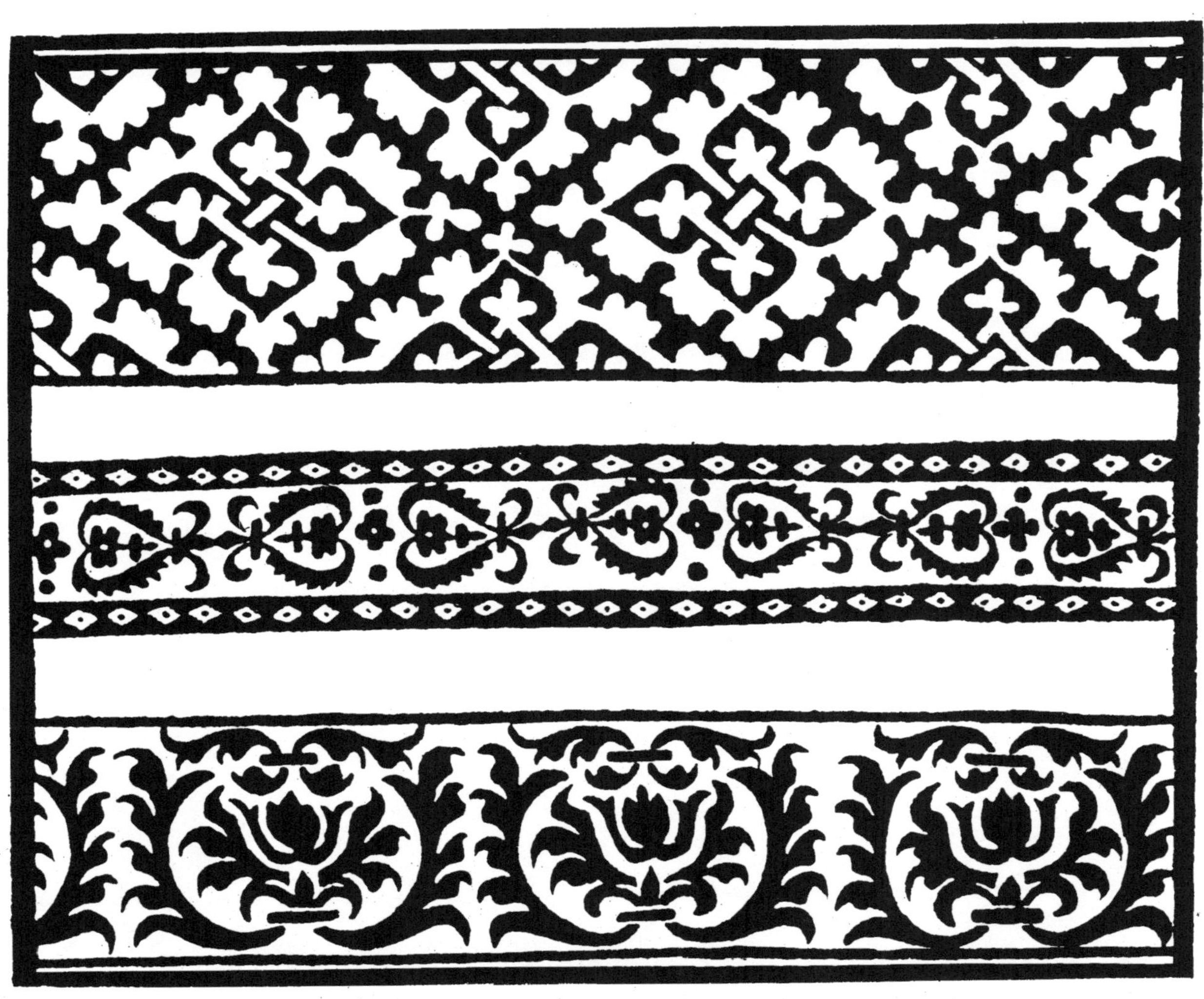

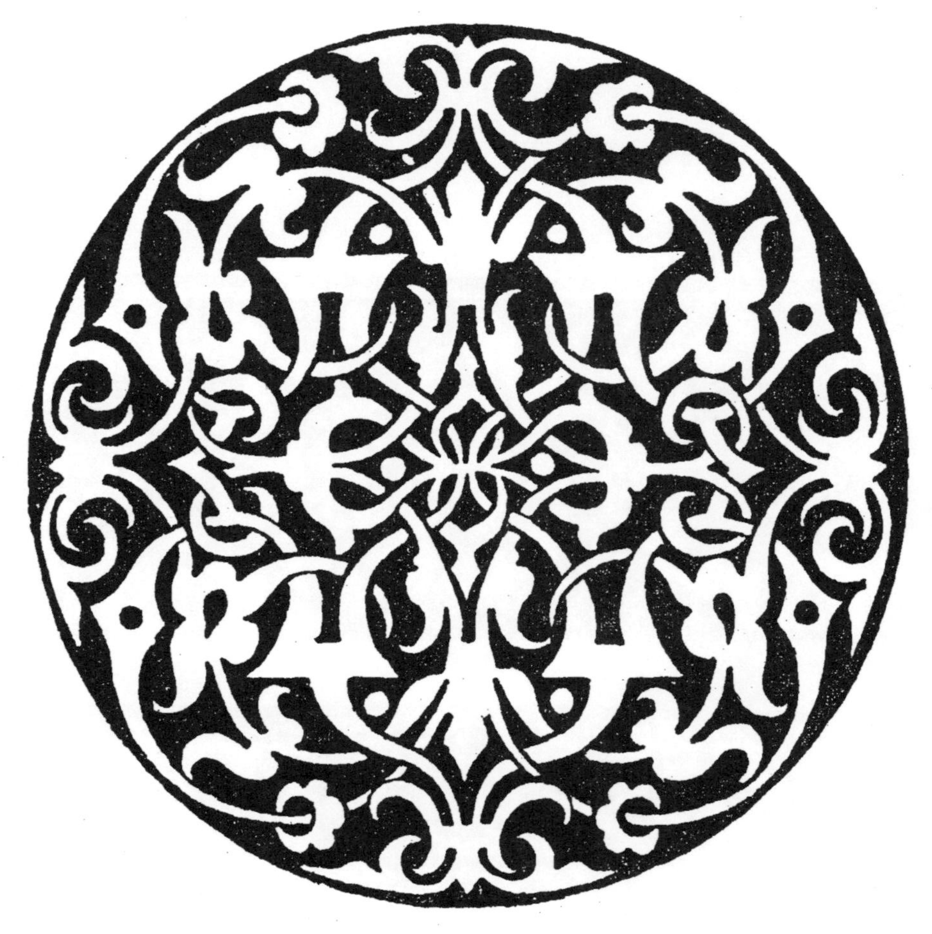

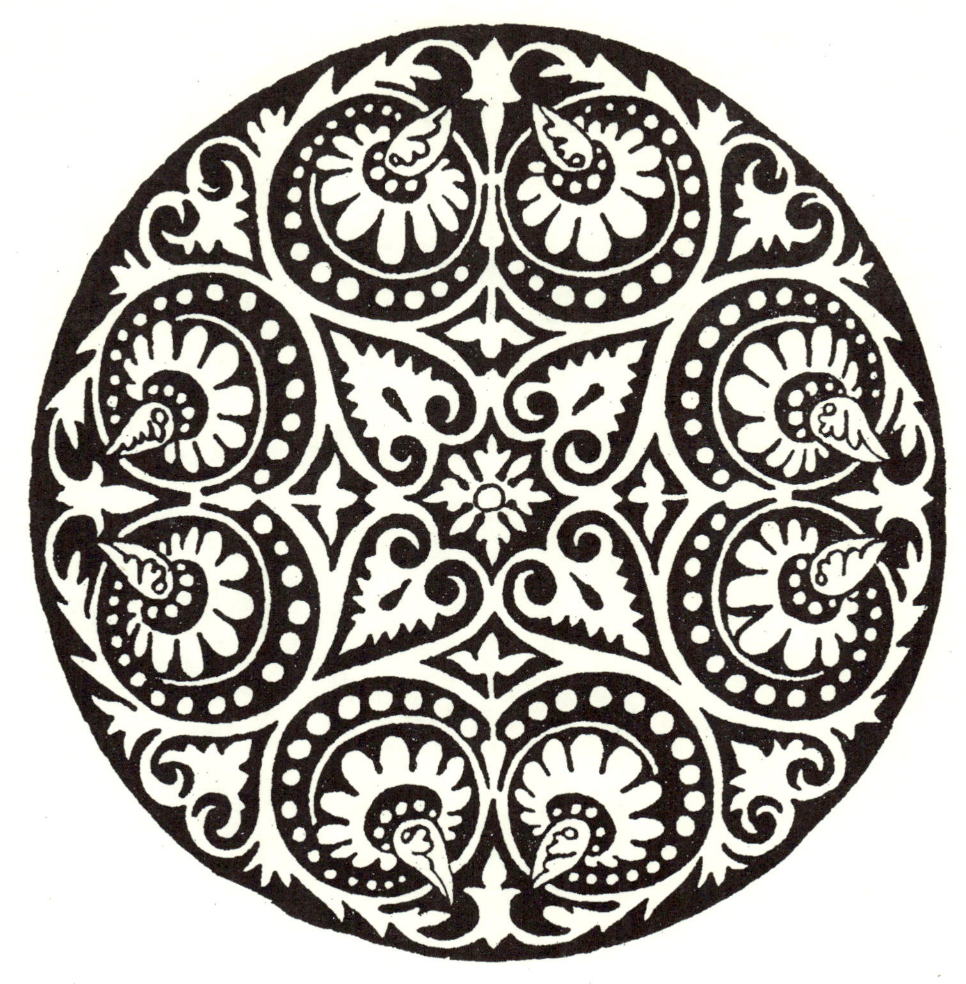

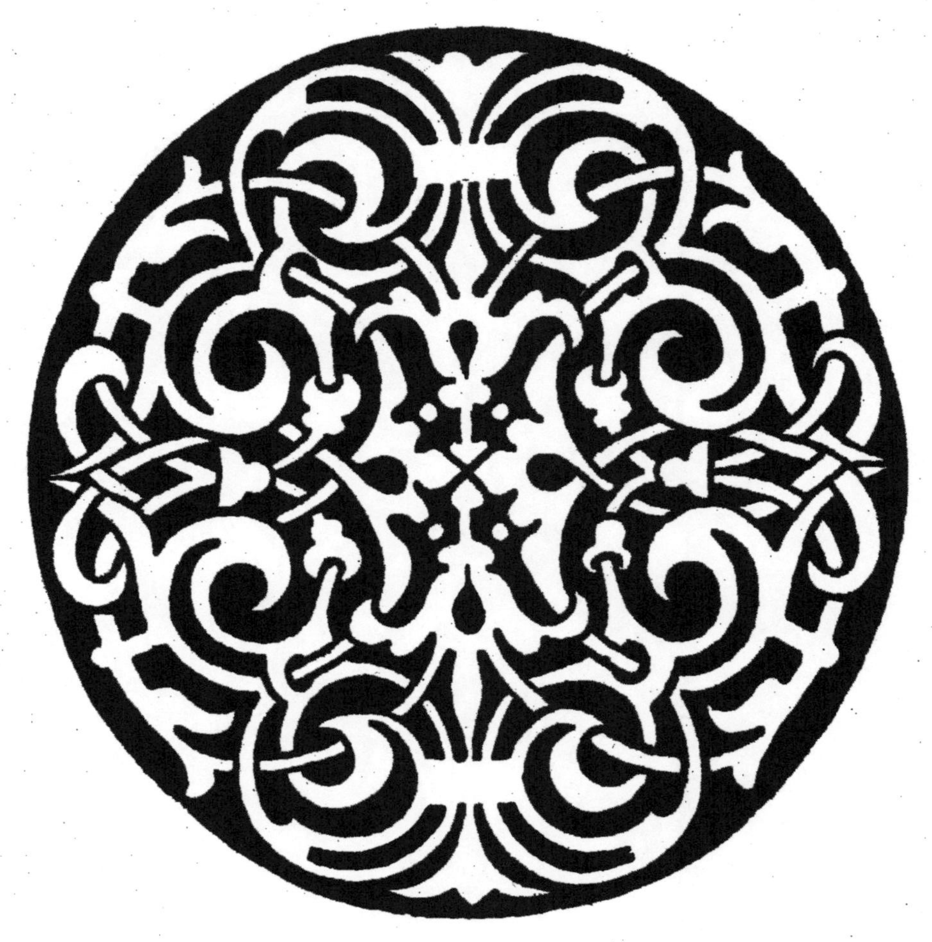

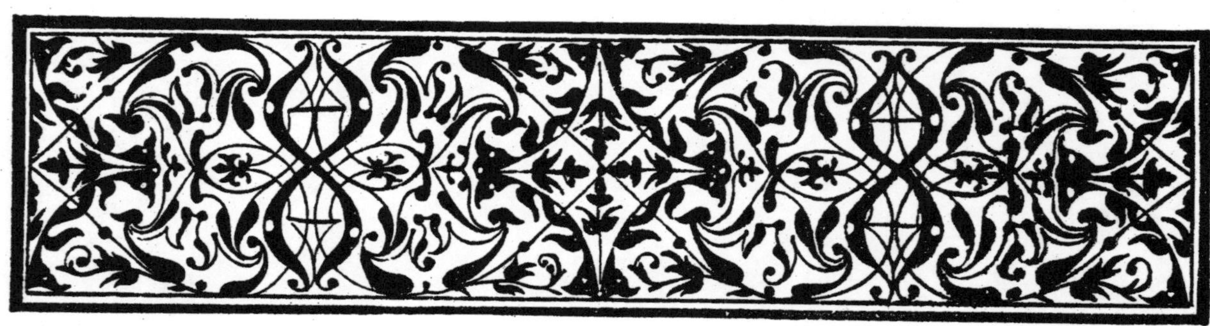

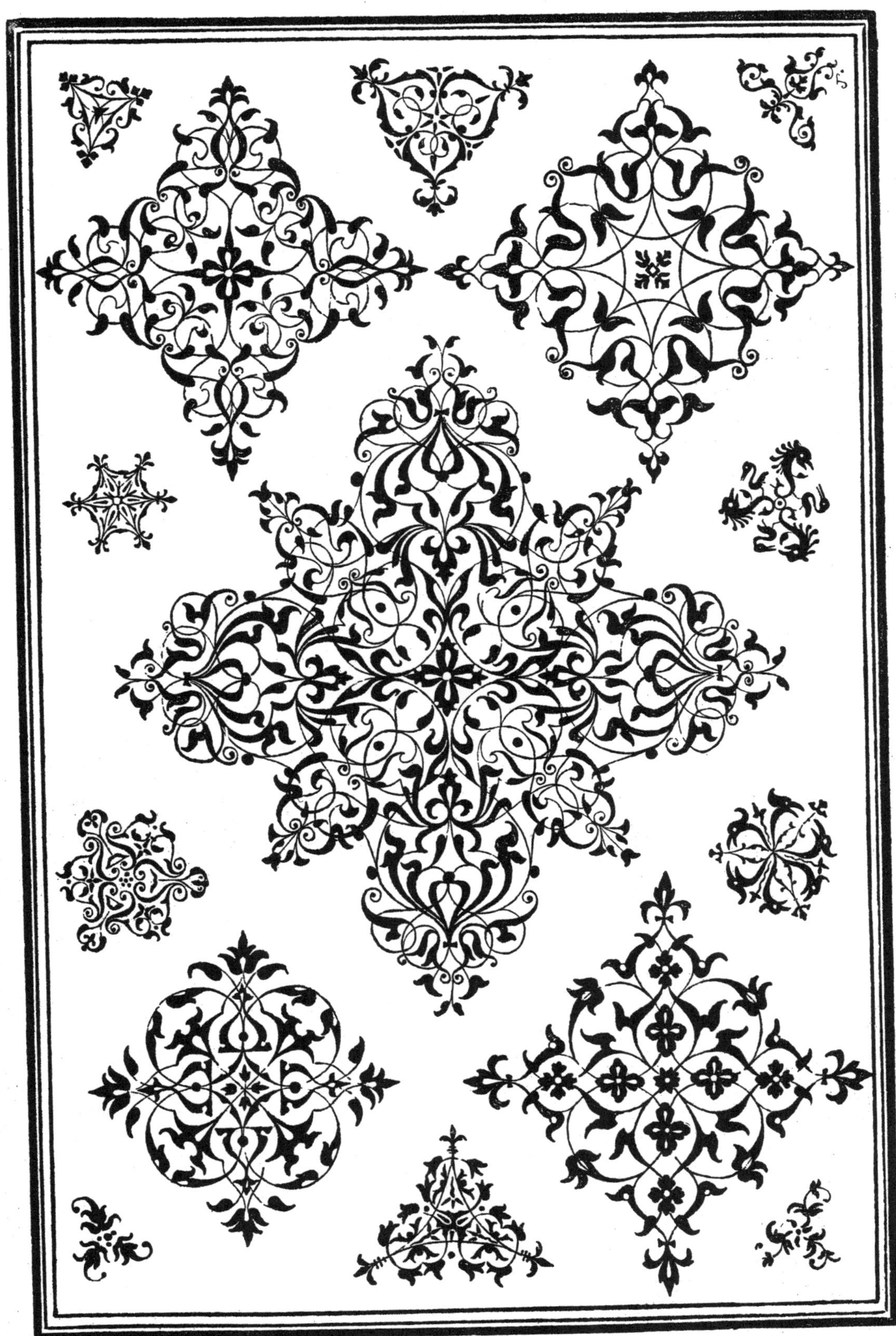

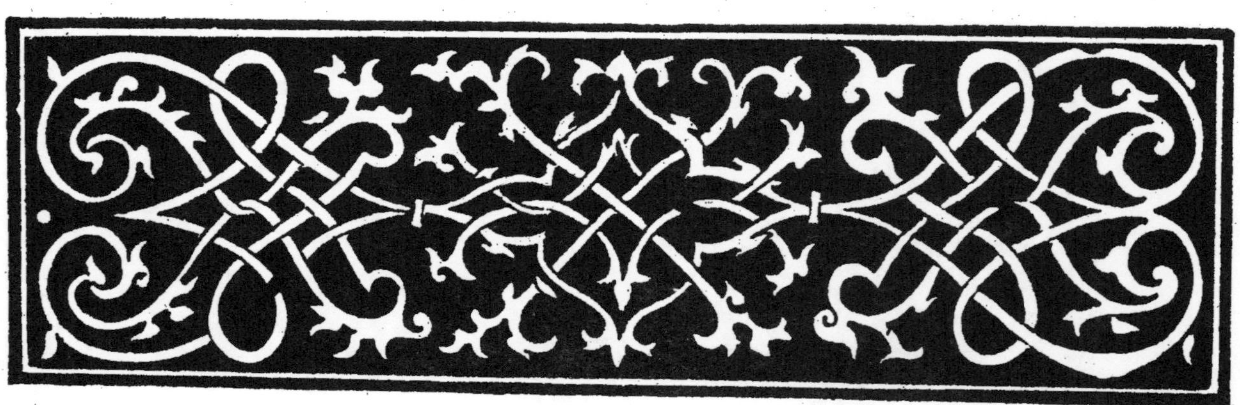

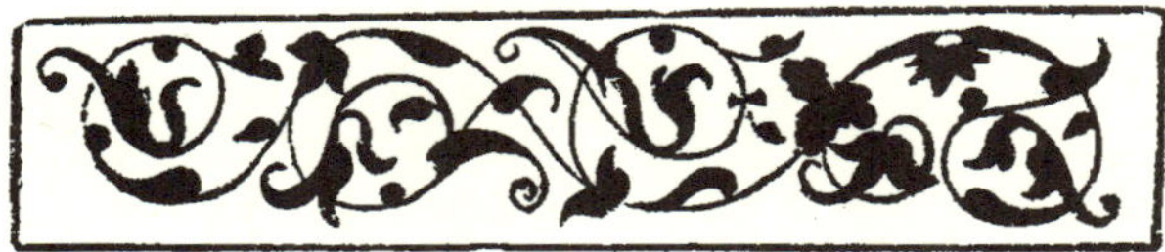

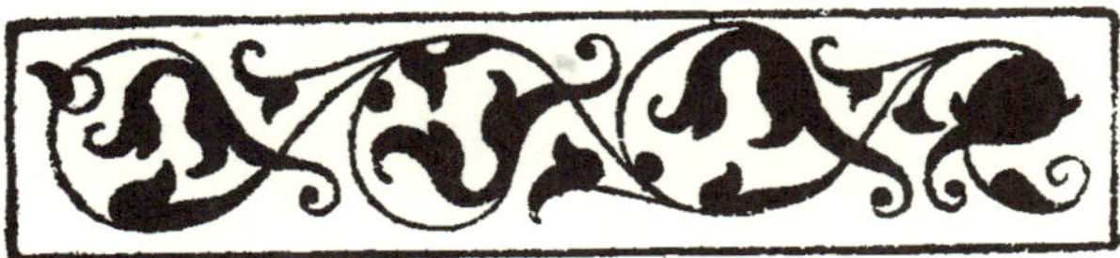

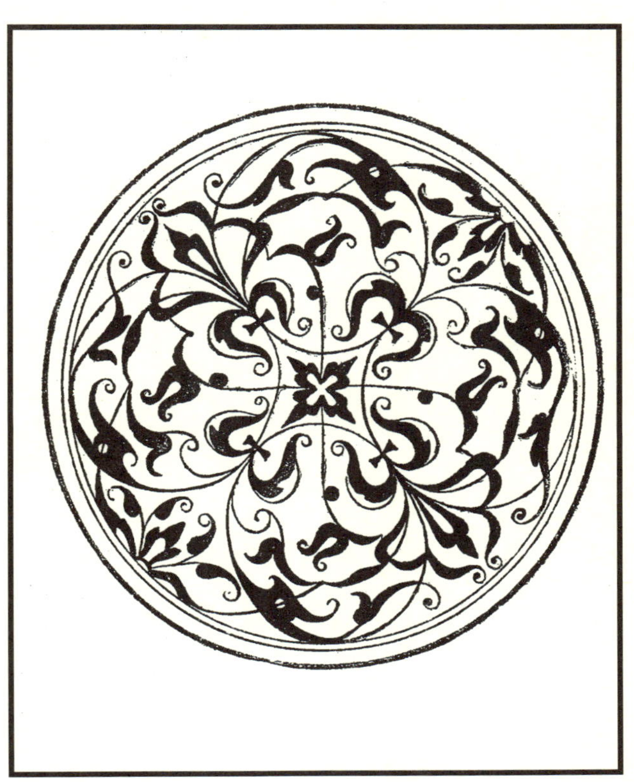

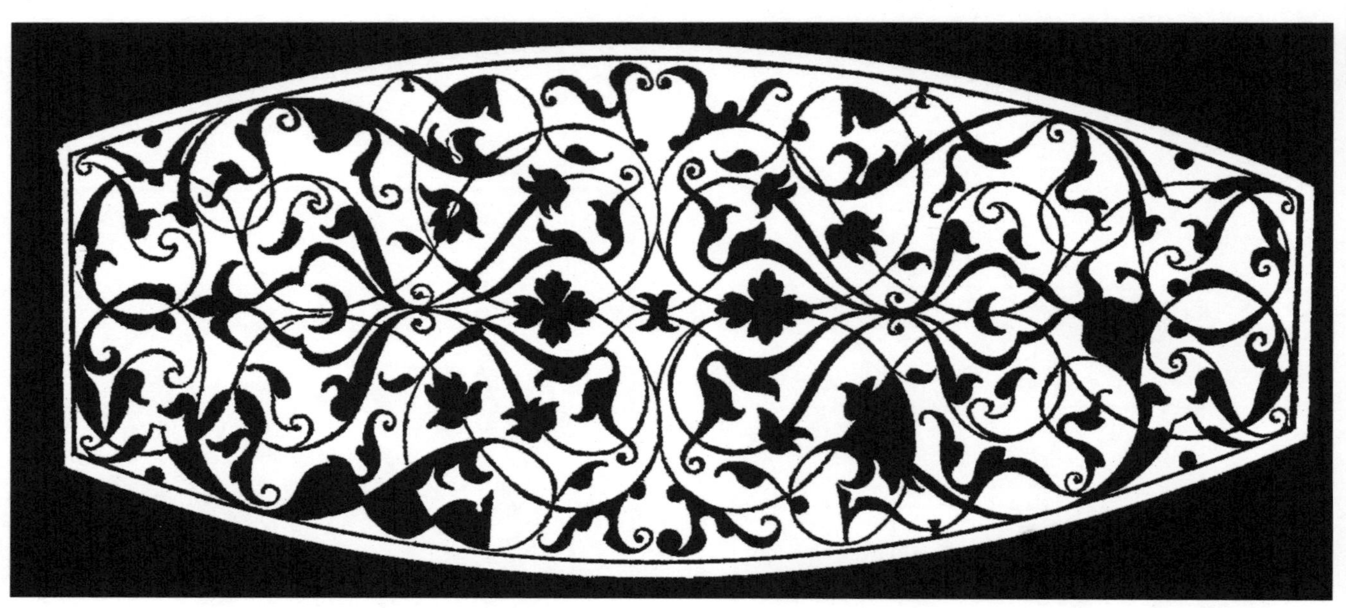

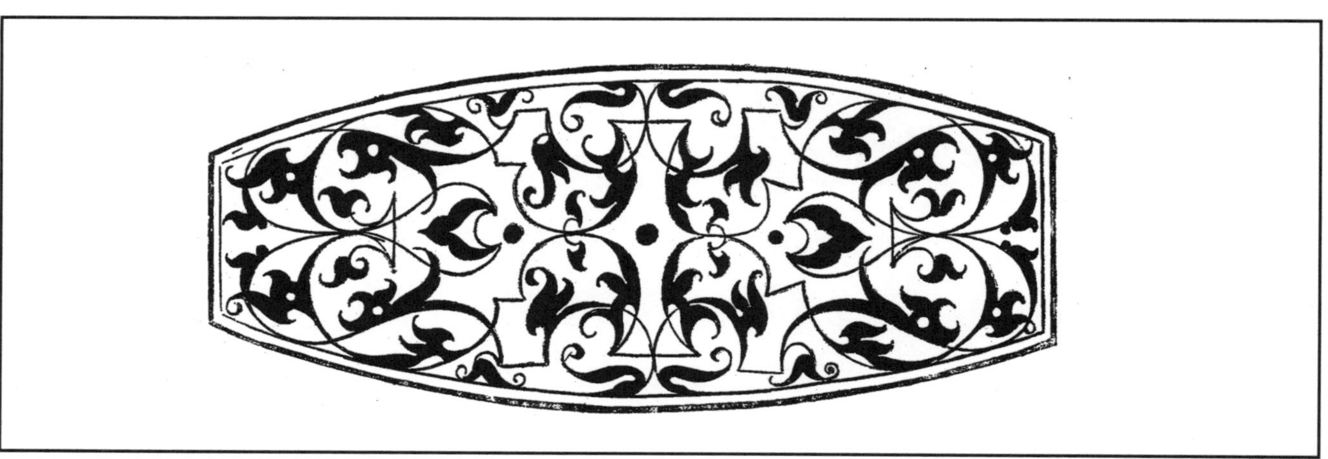

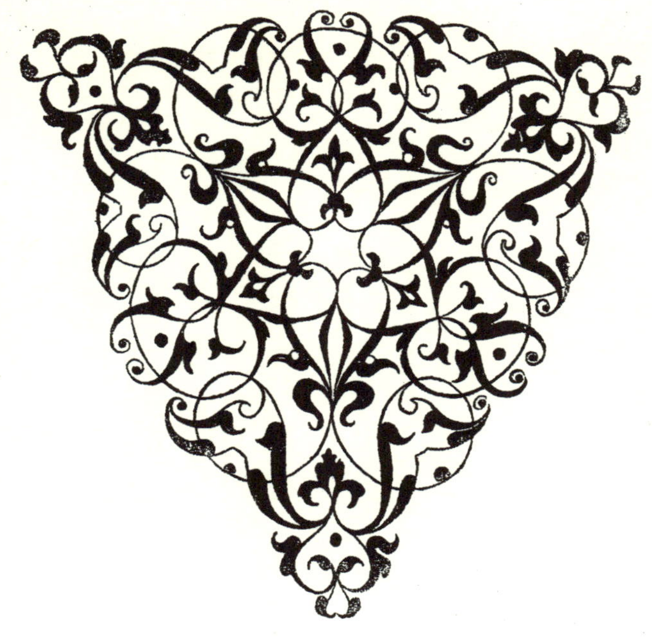
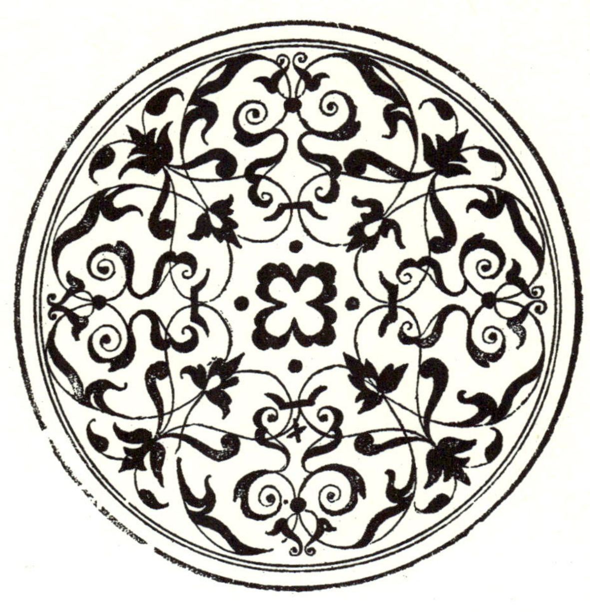

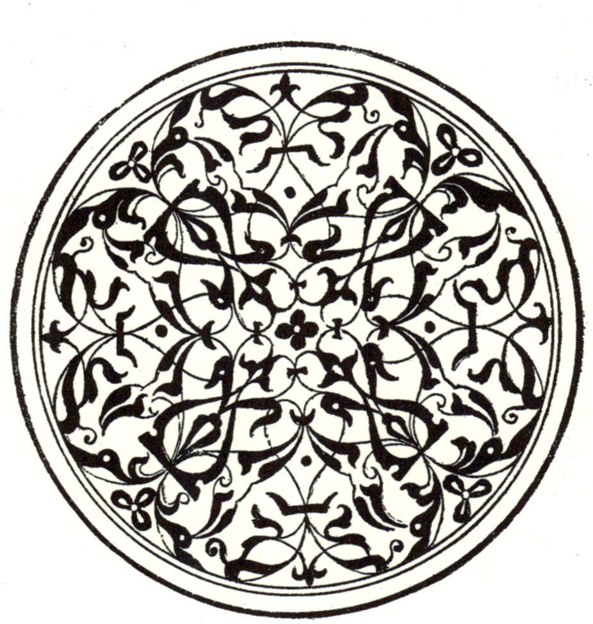

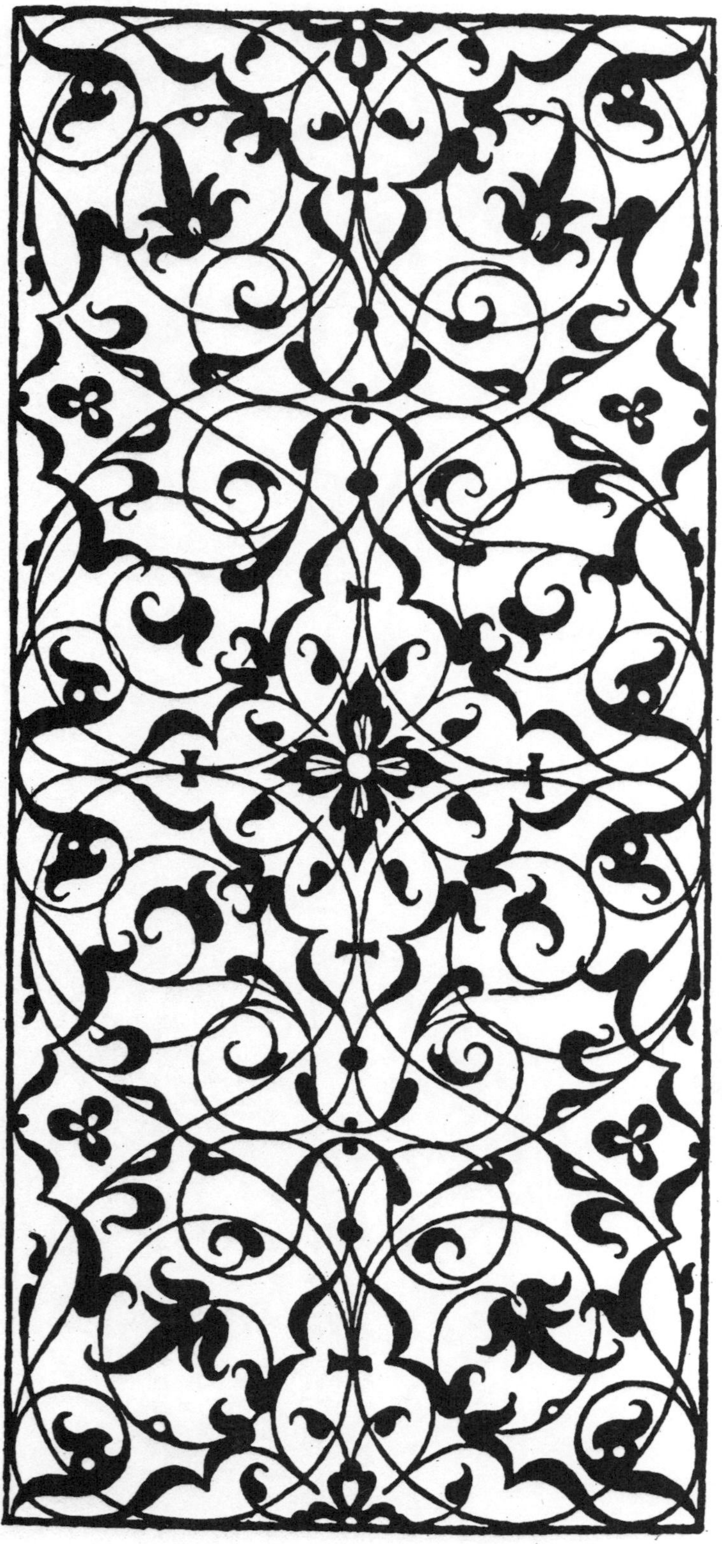

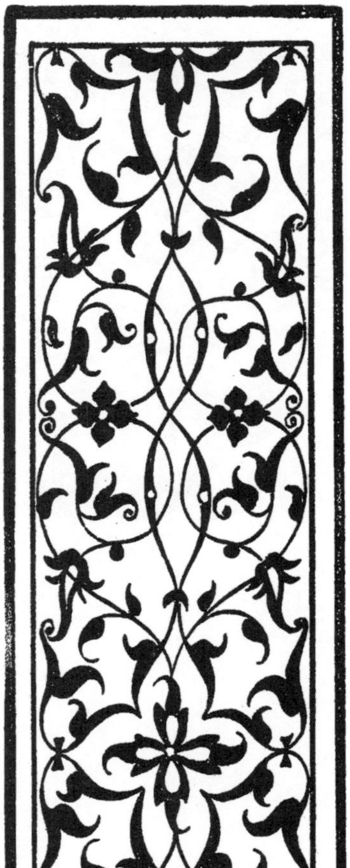

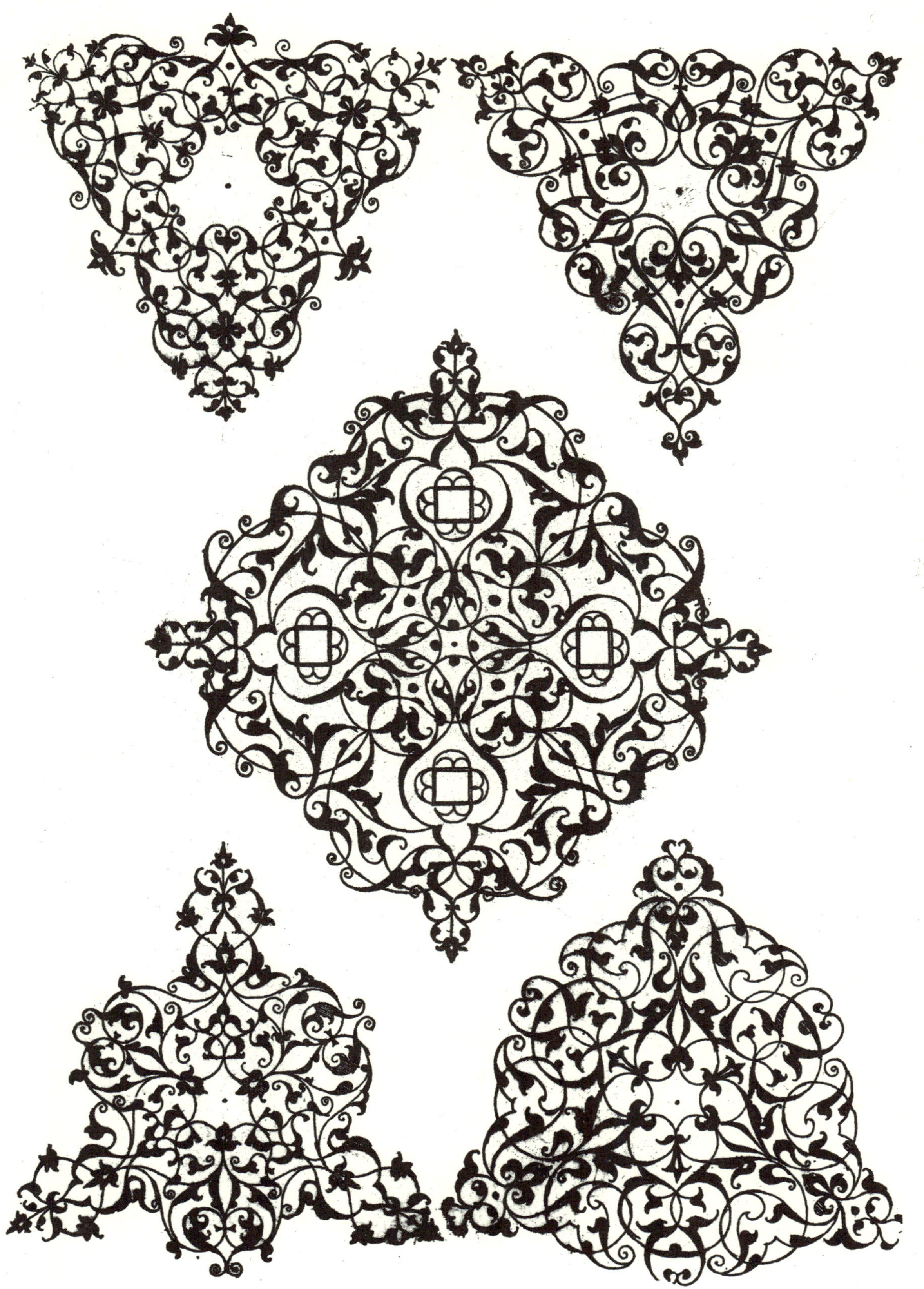

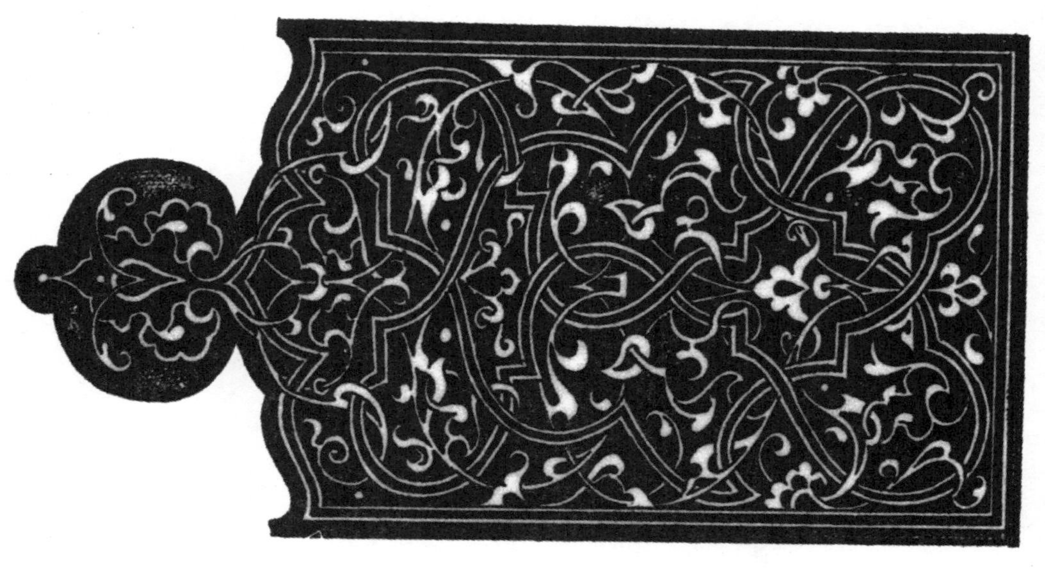

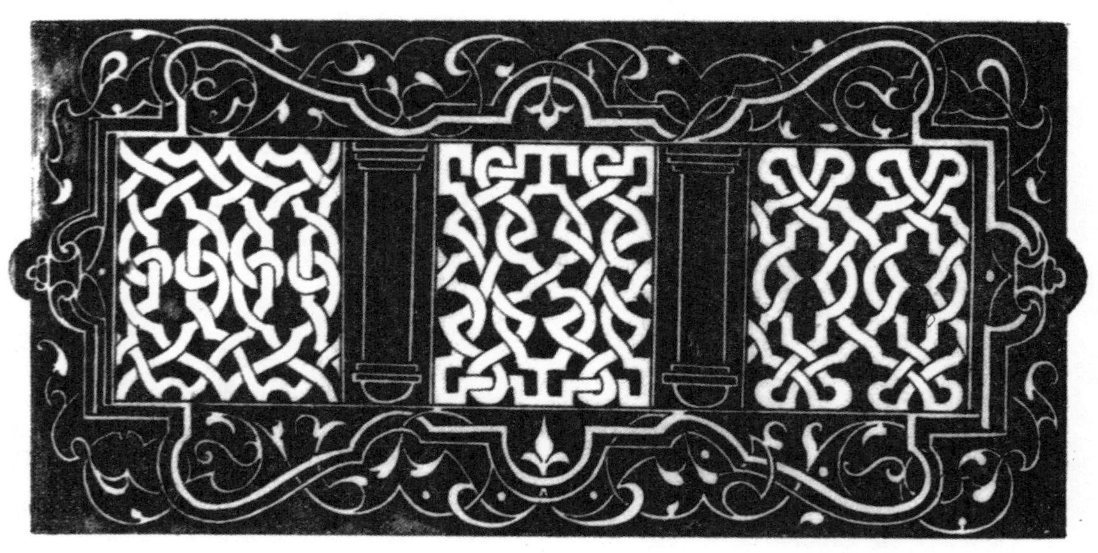

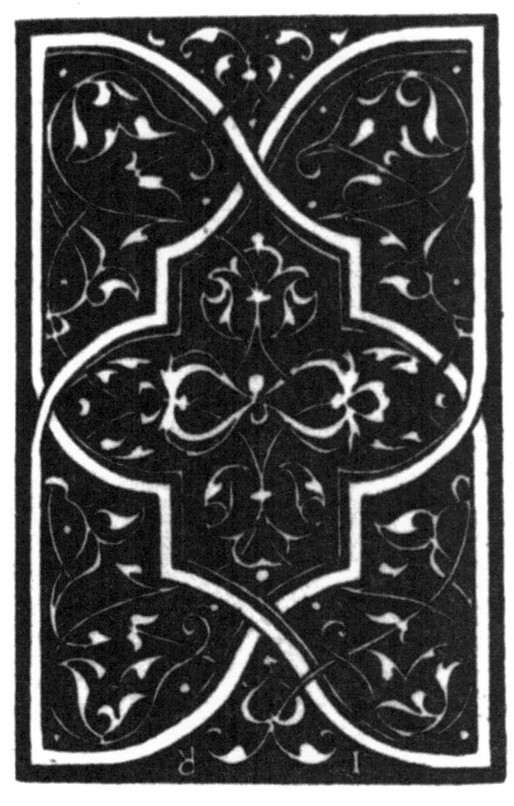

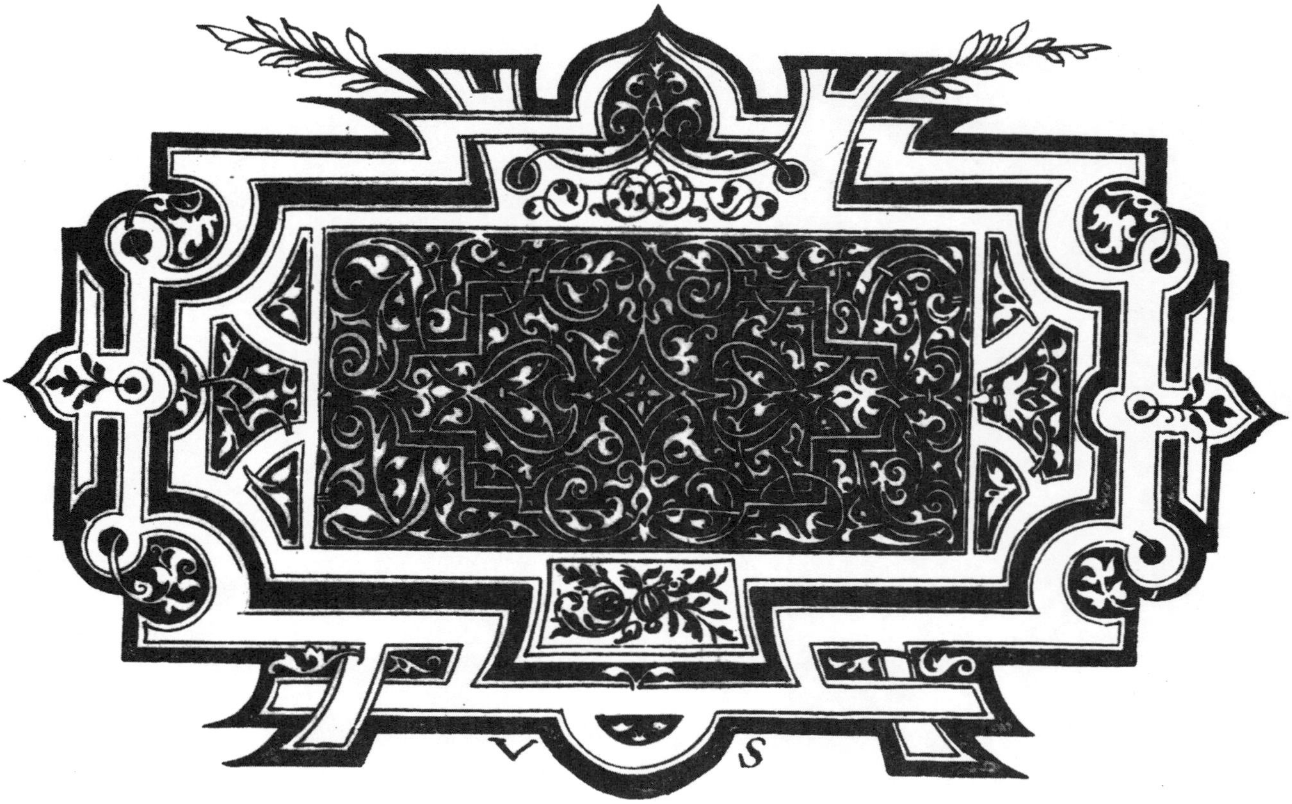

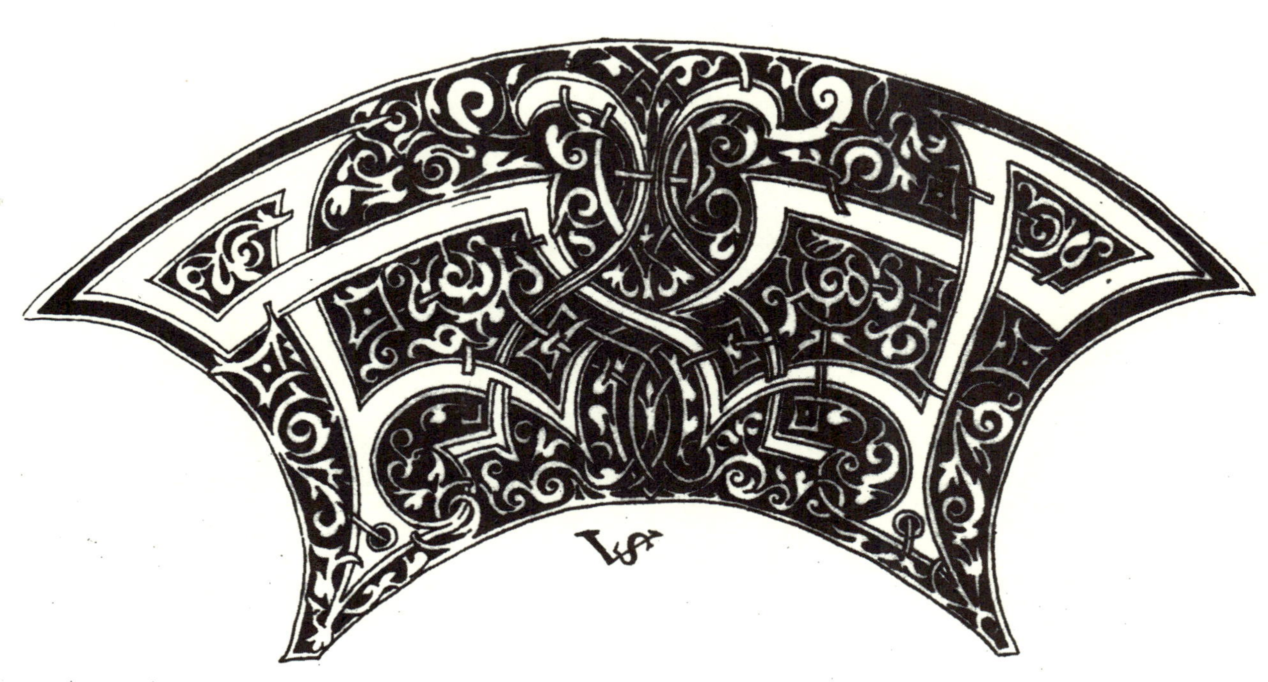

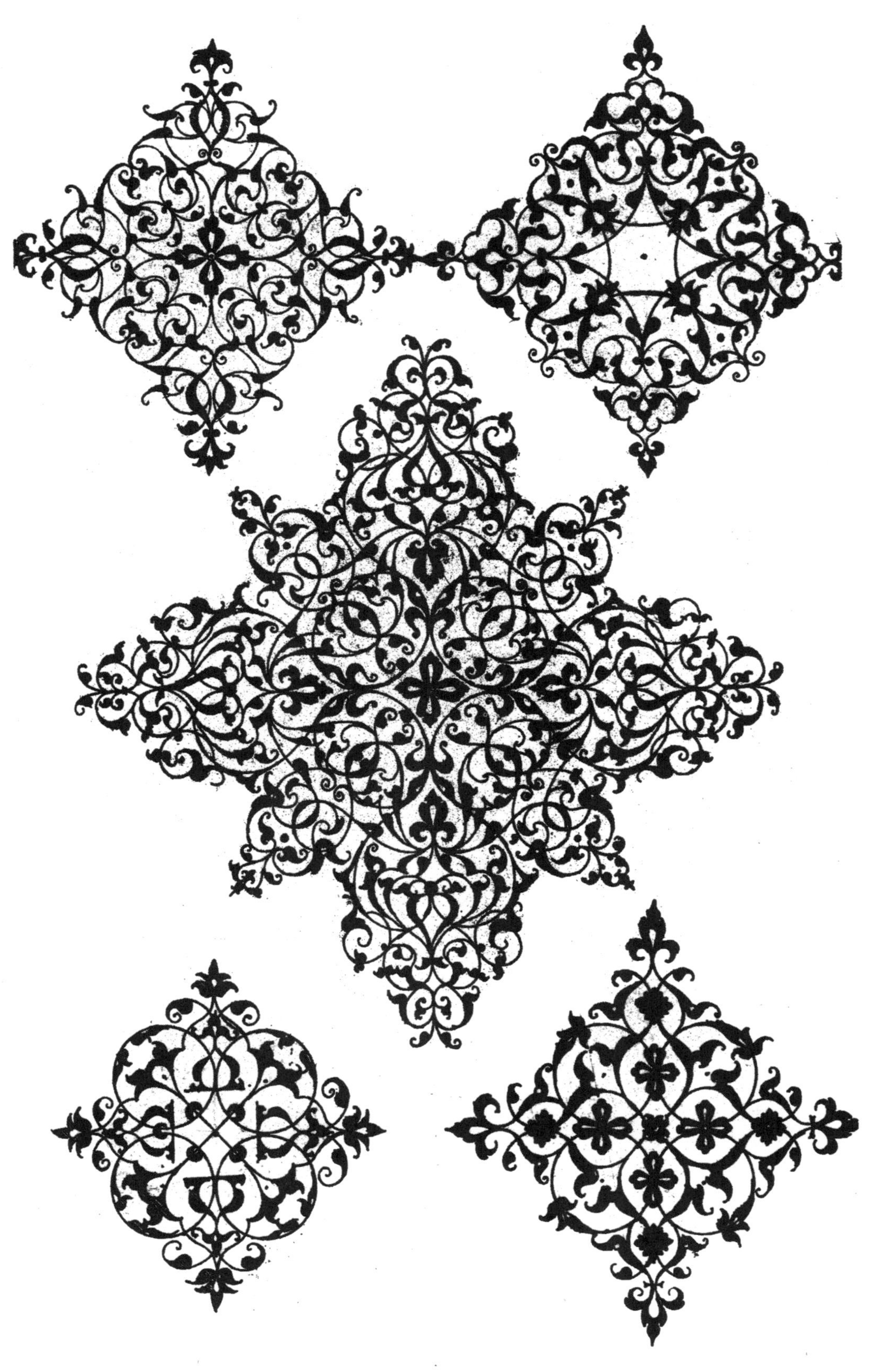

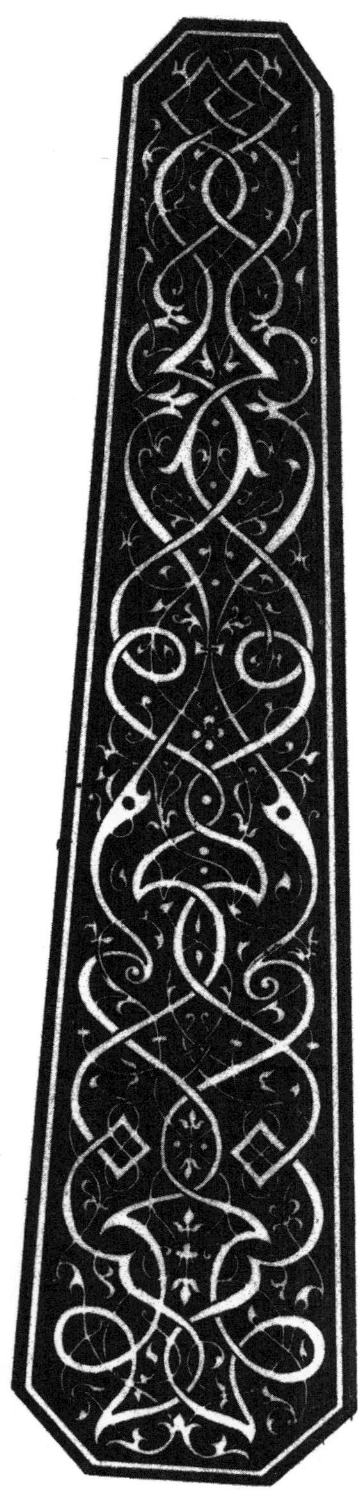

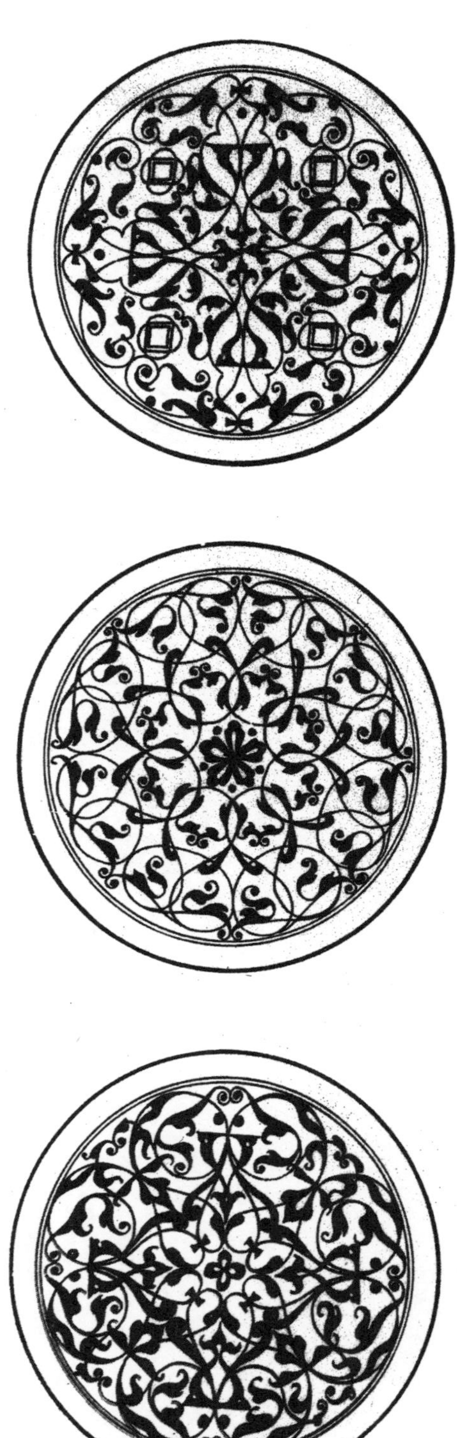

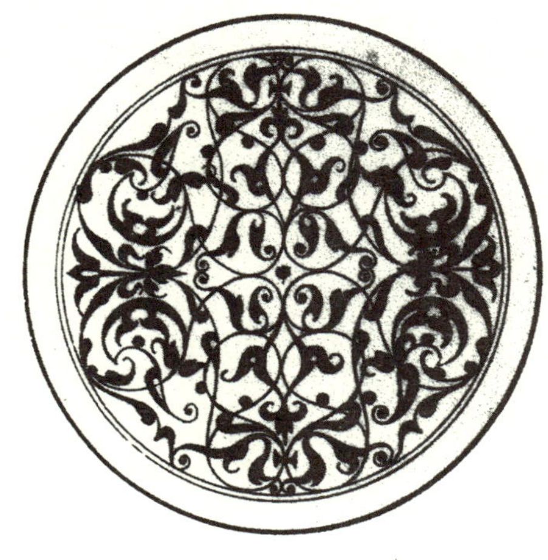

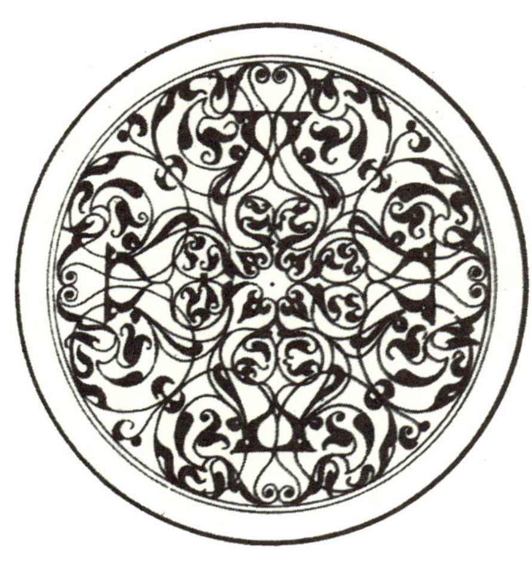

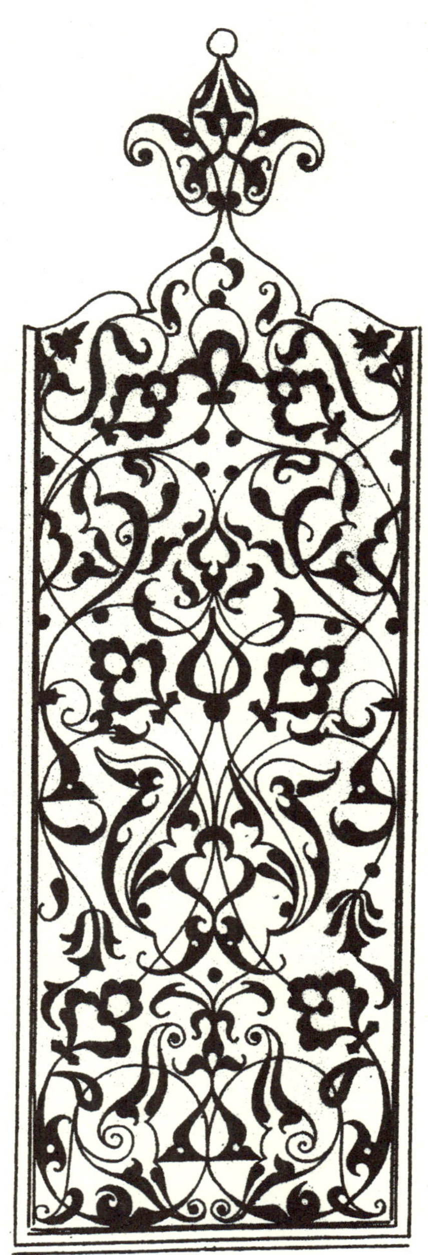

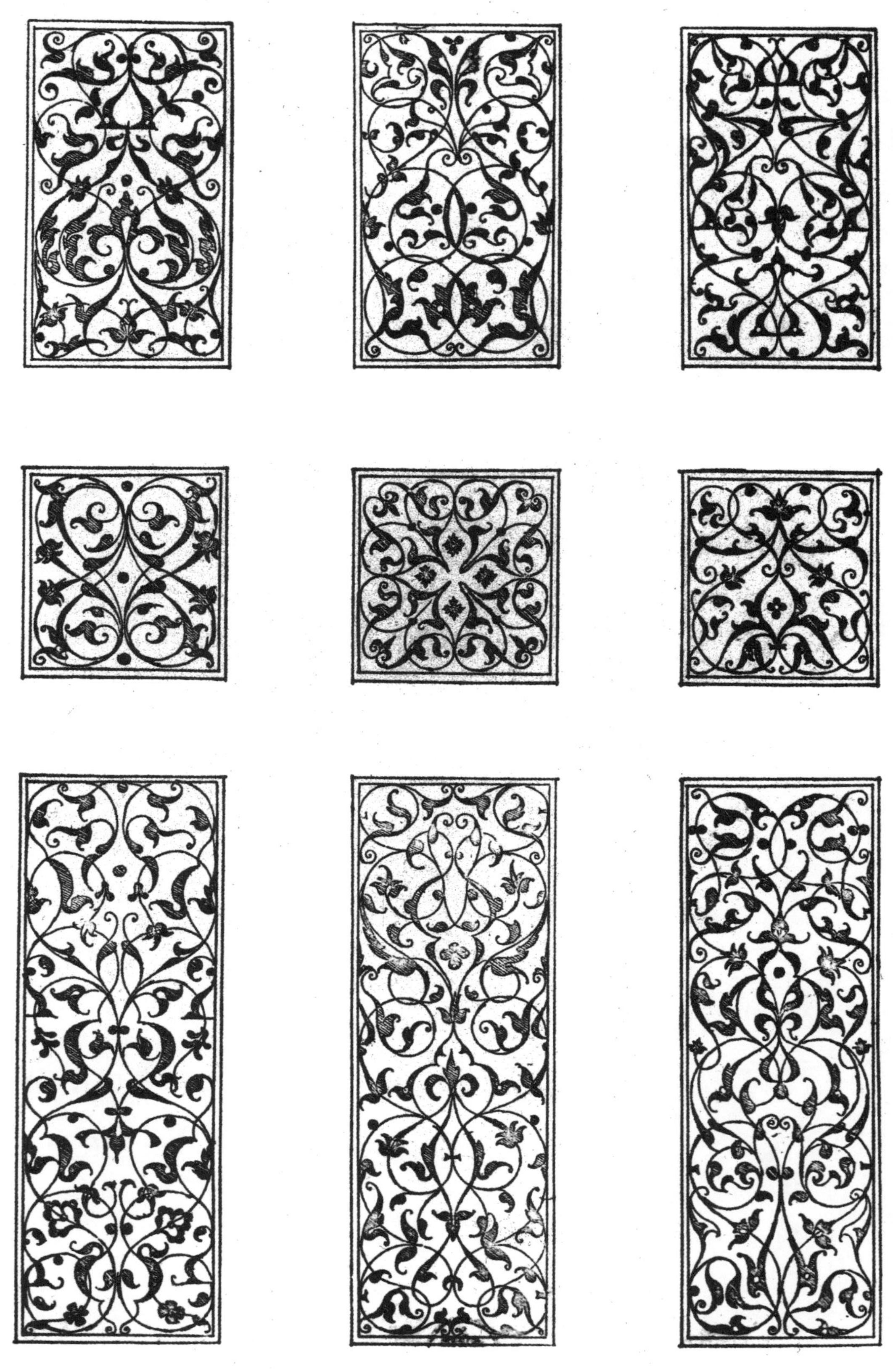

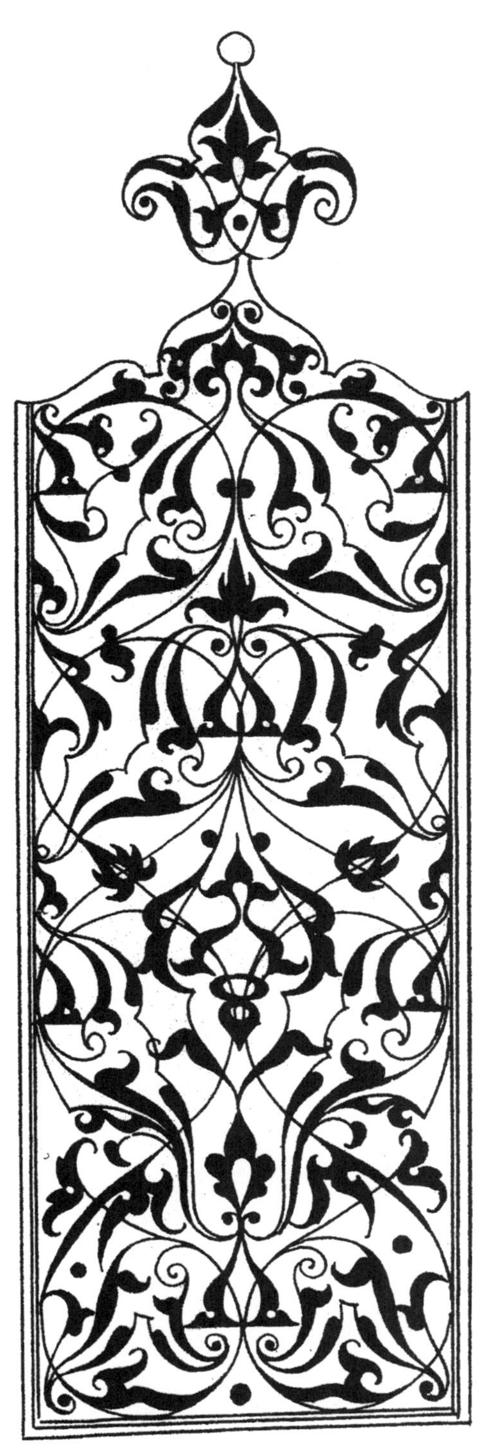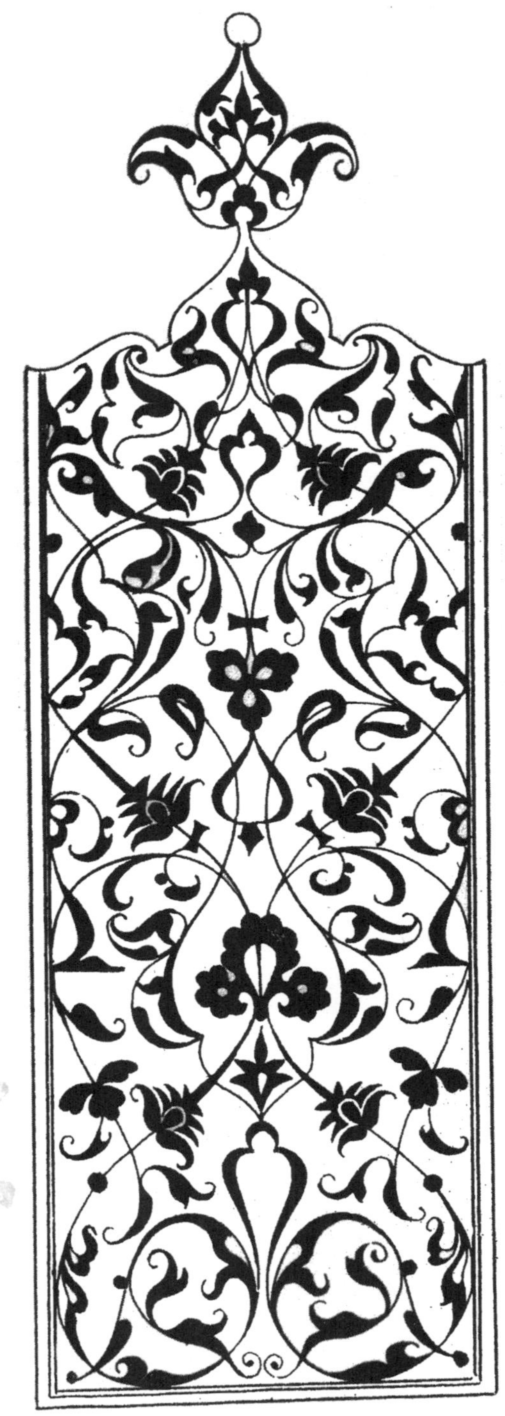

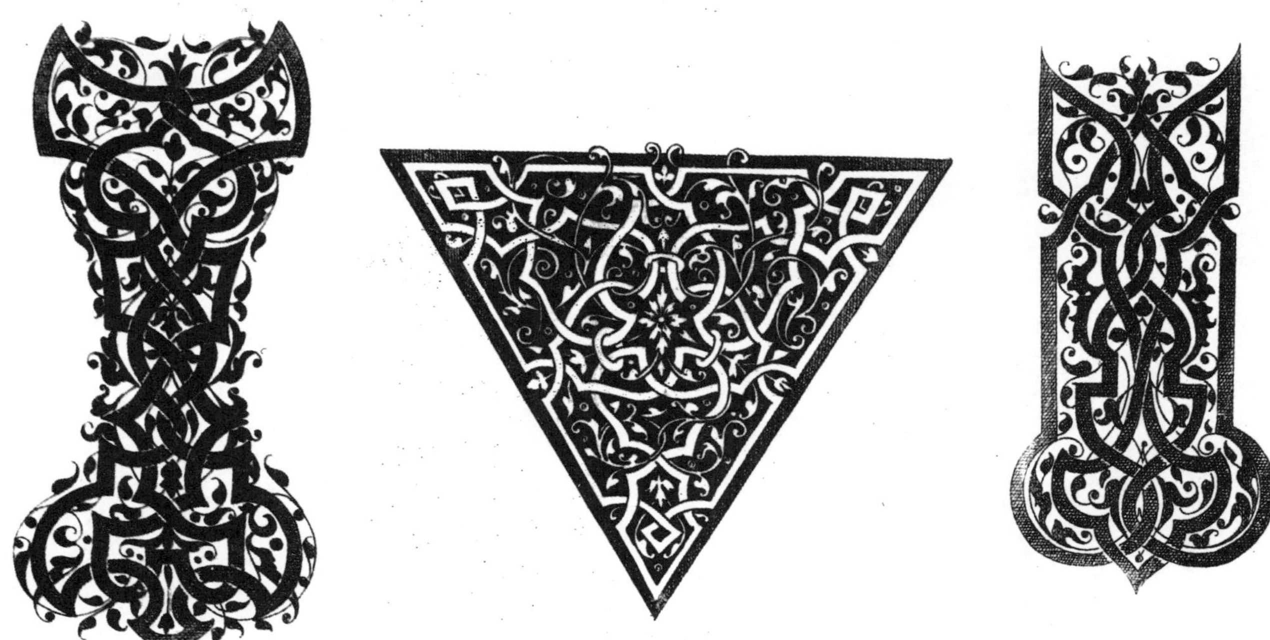

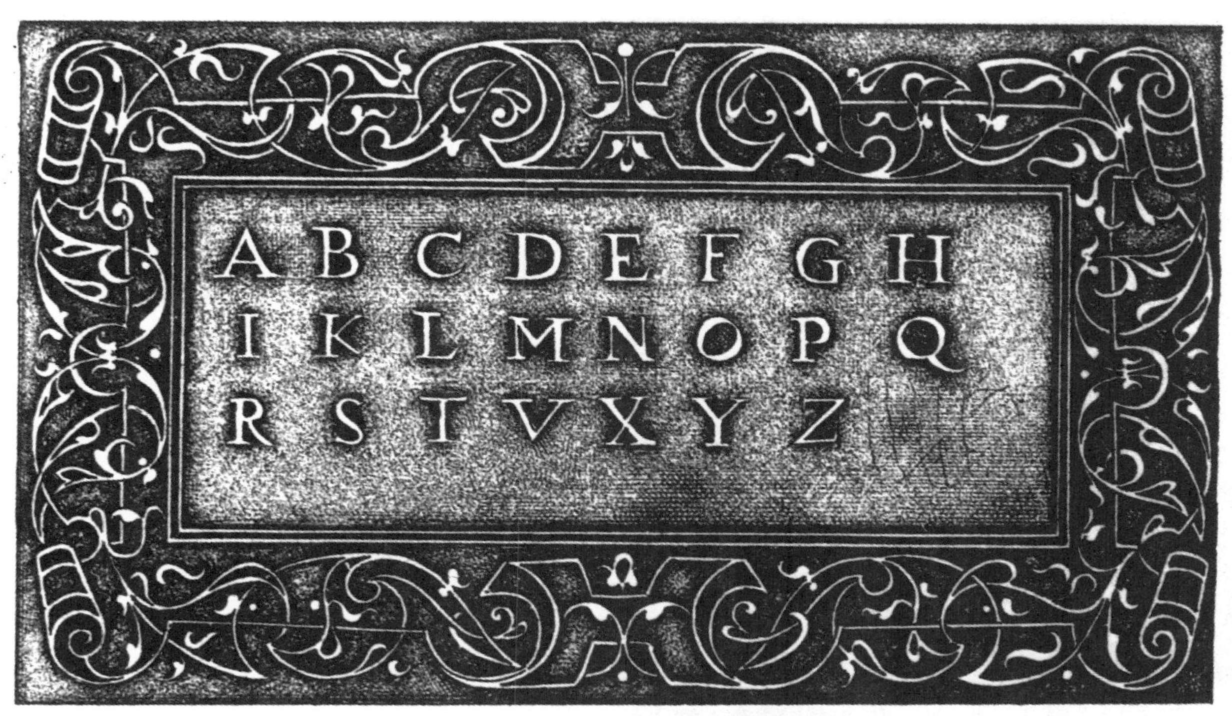
ABCDEFGH
IKLMNOPQ
RSTVXYZ

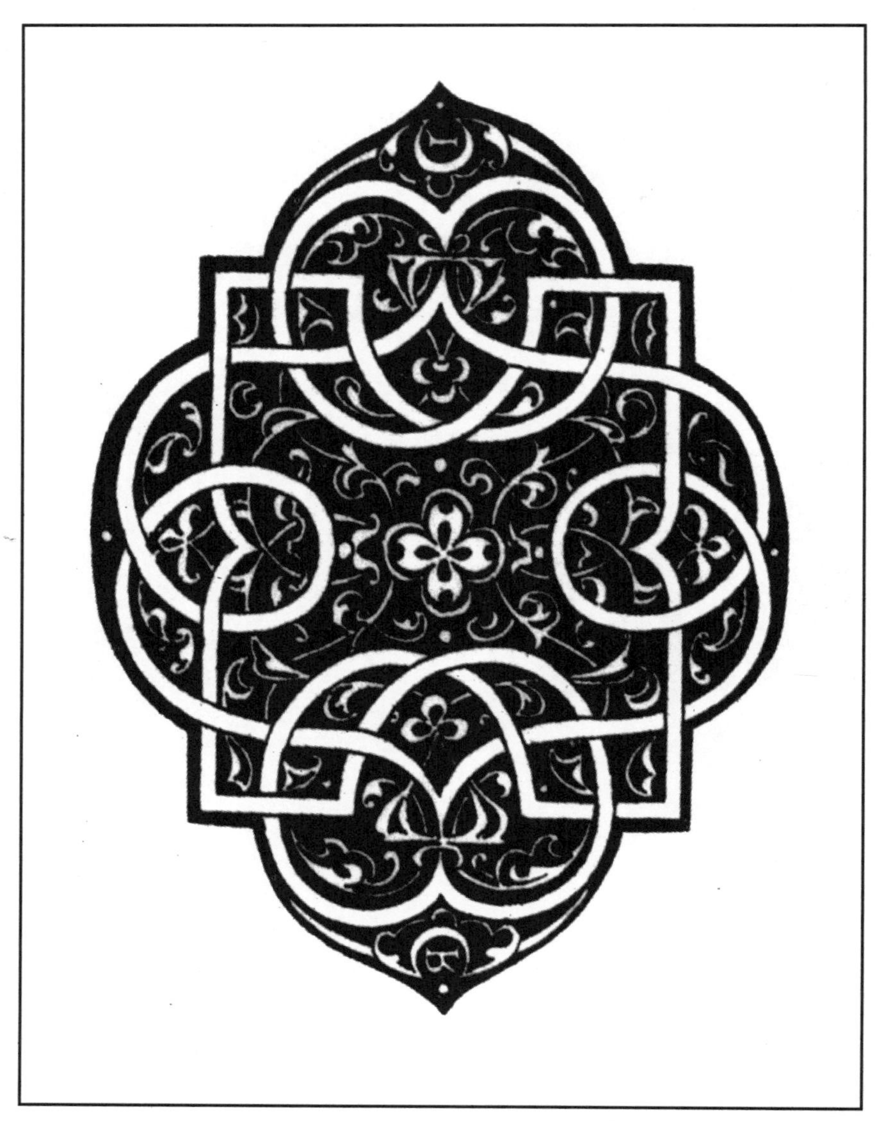

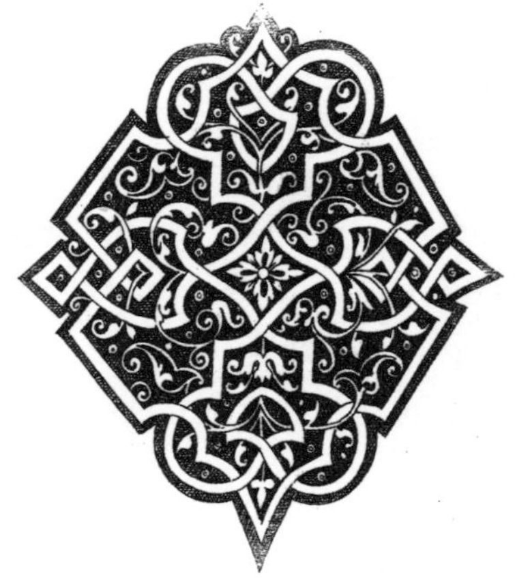

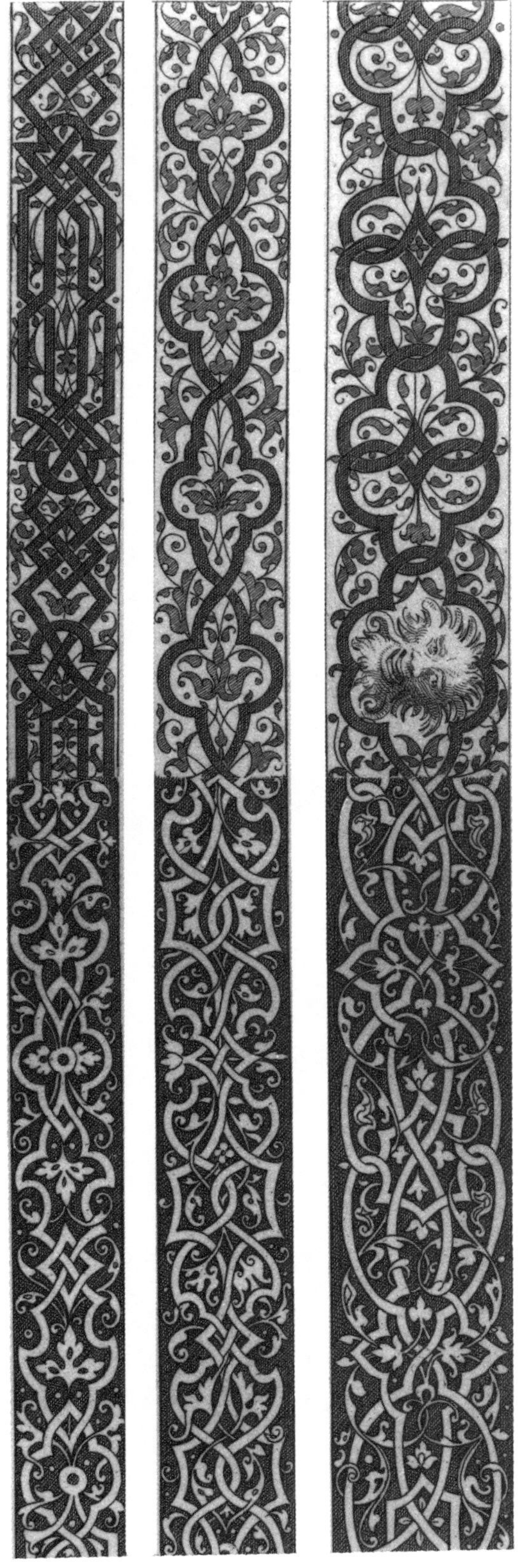

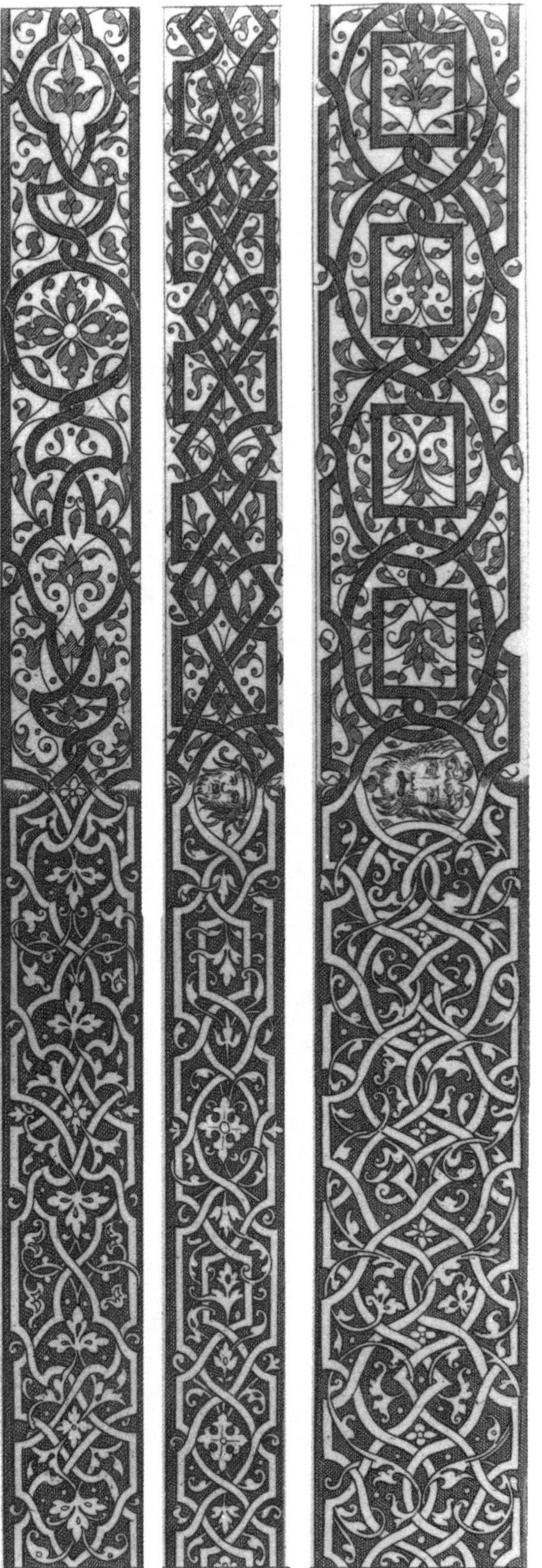

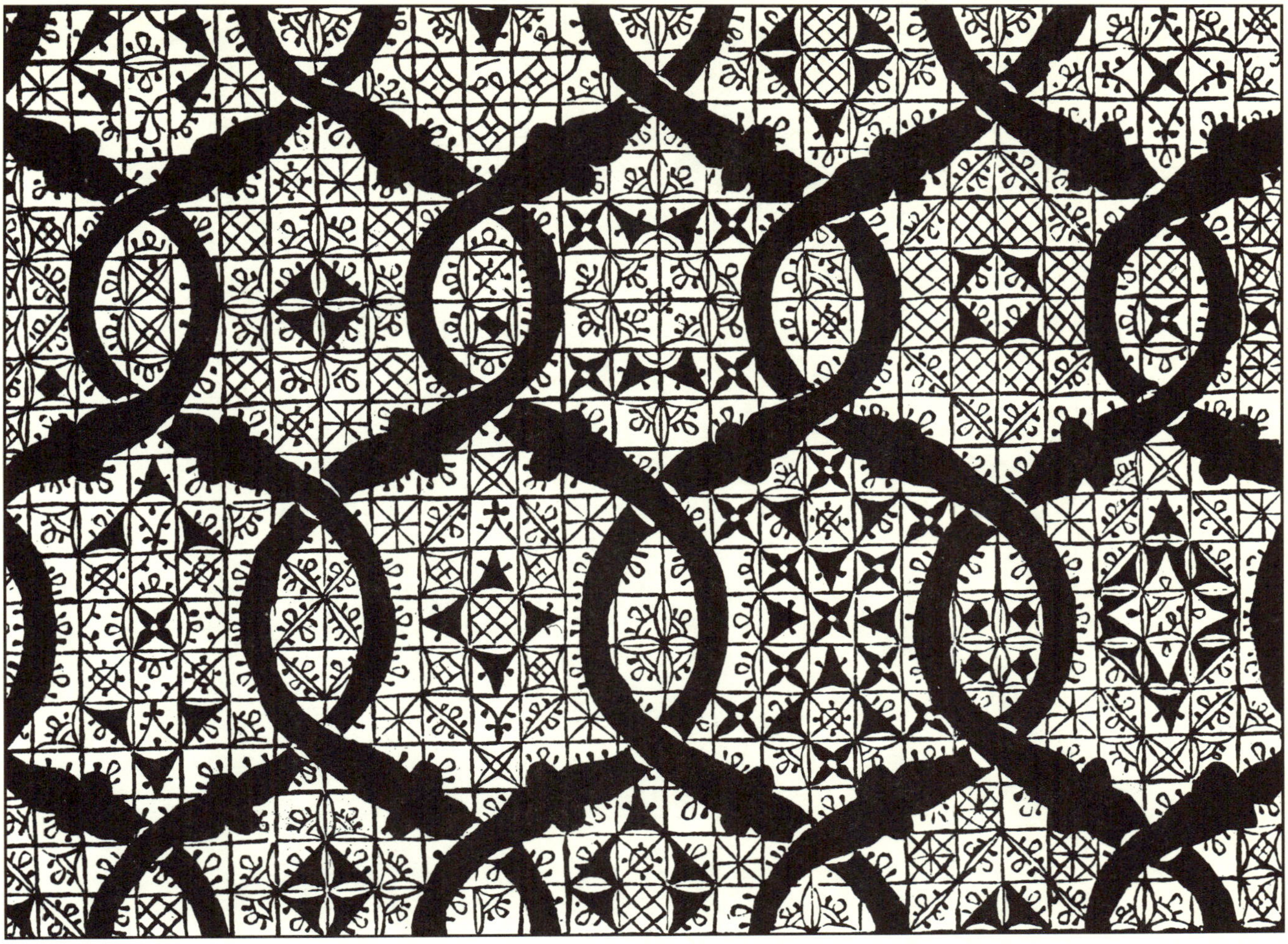

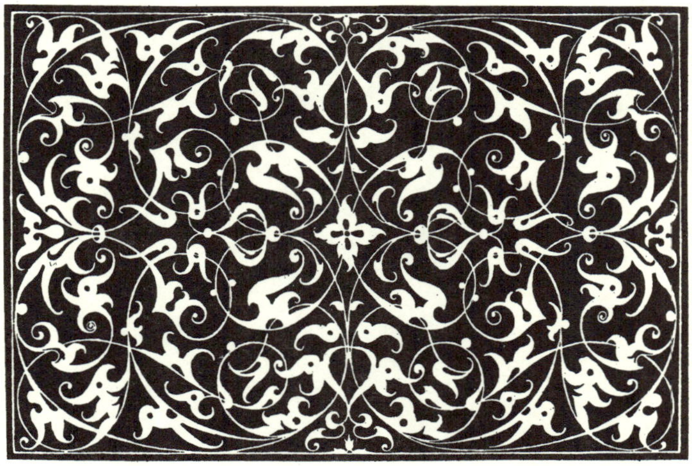

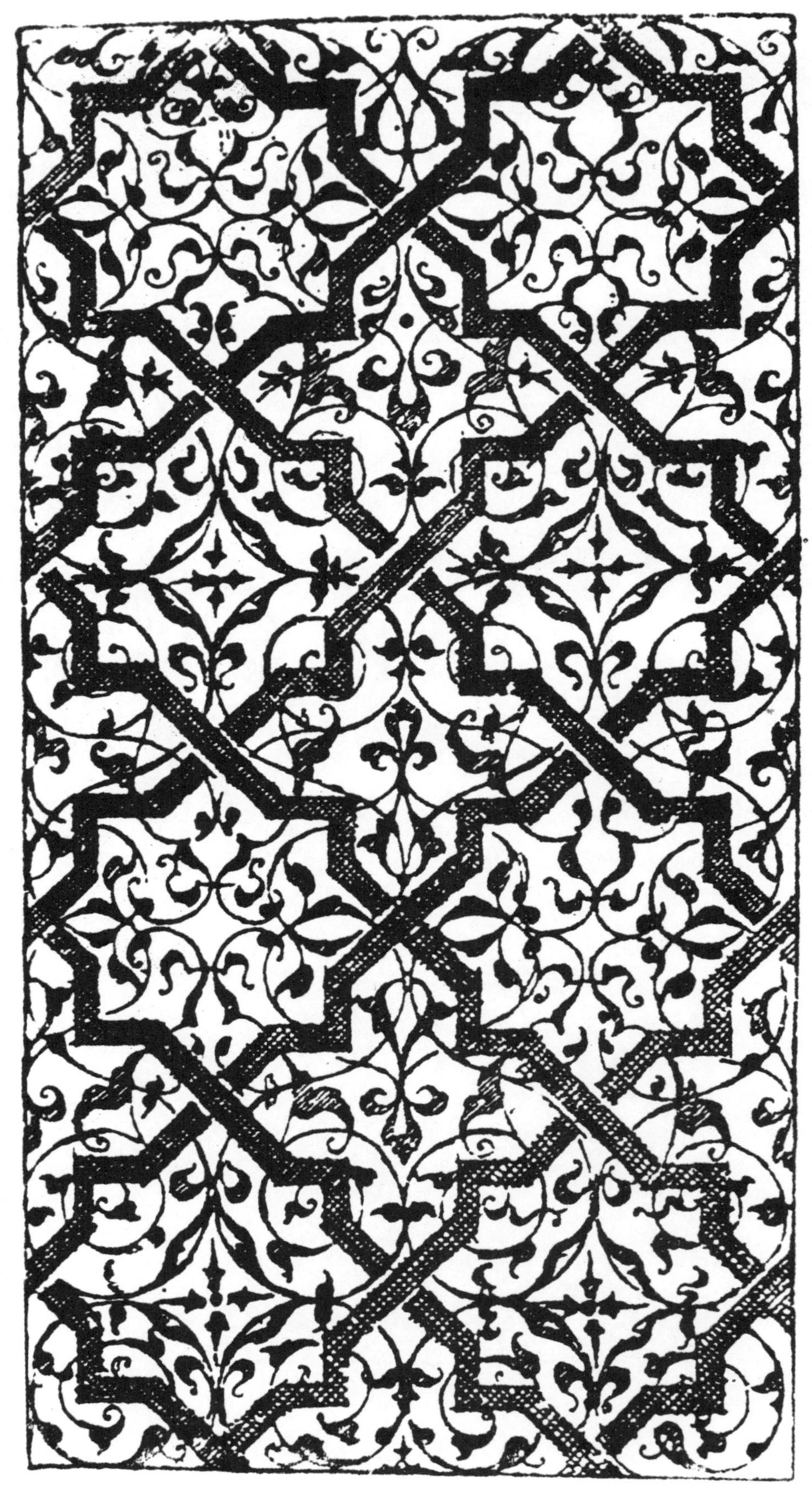

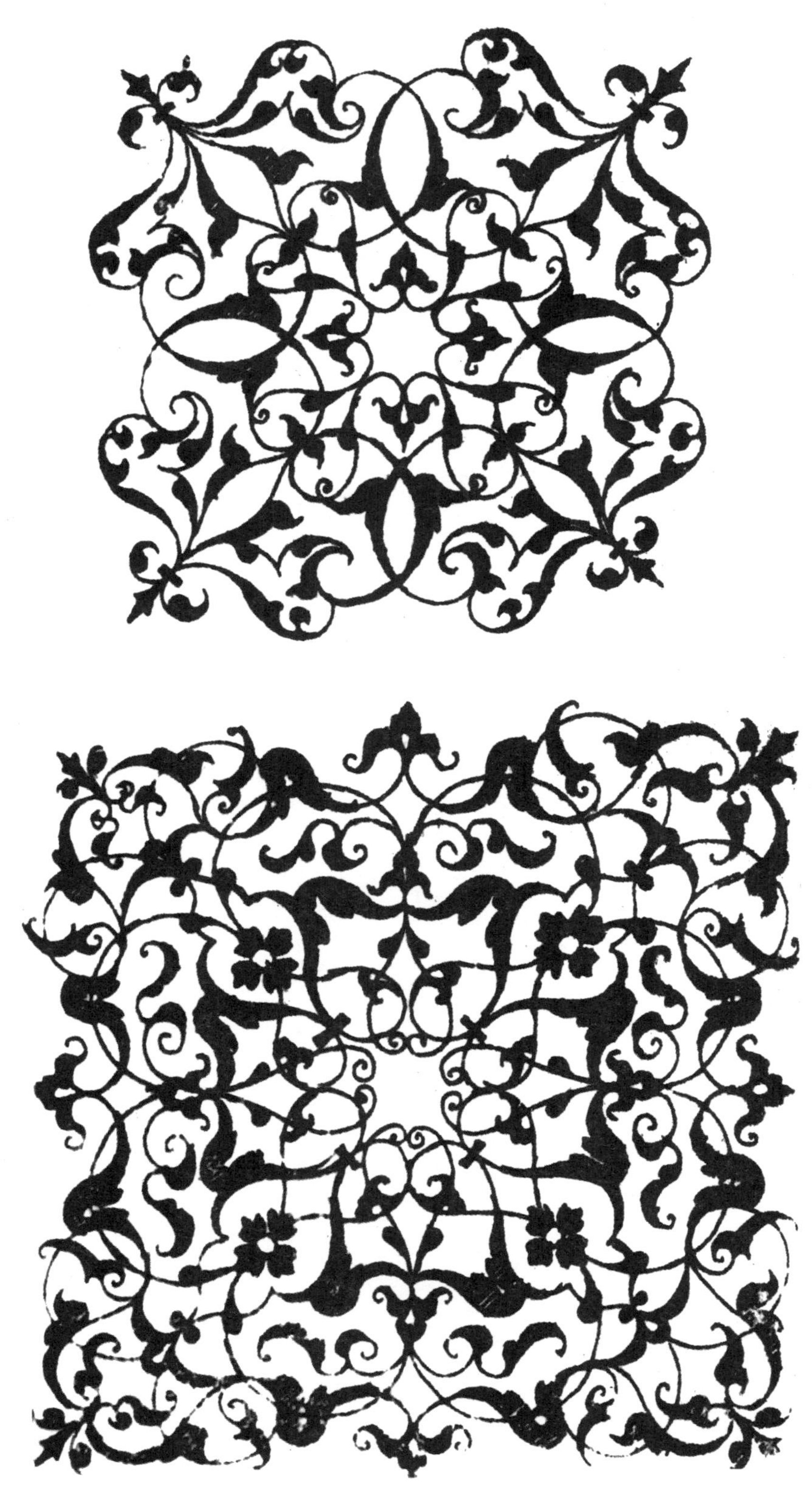

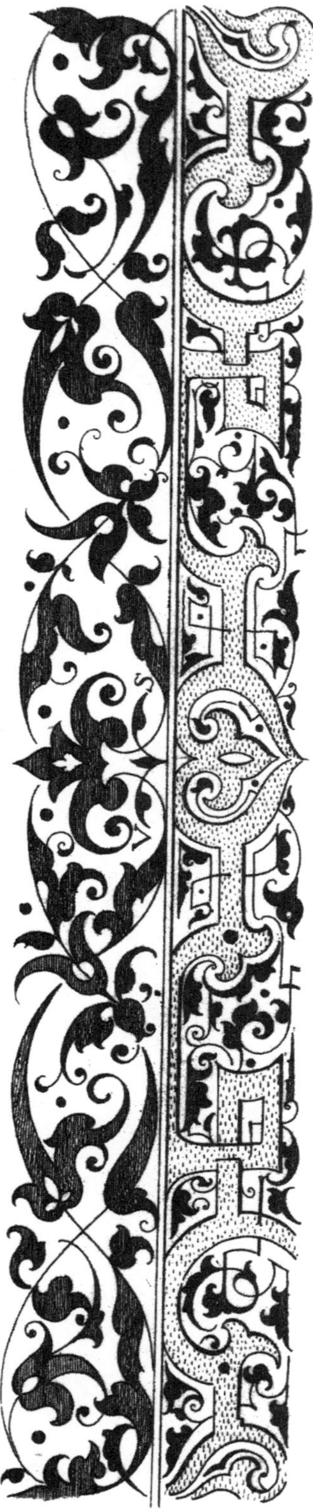
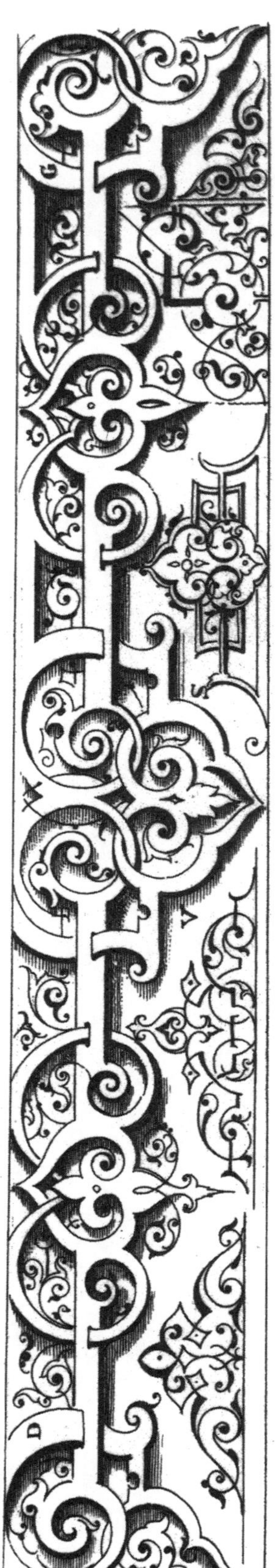
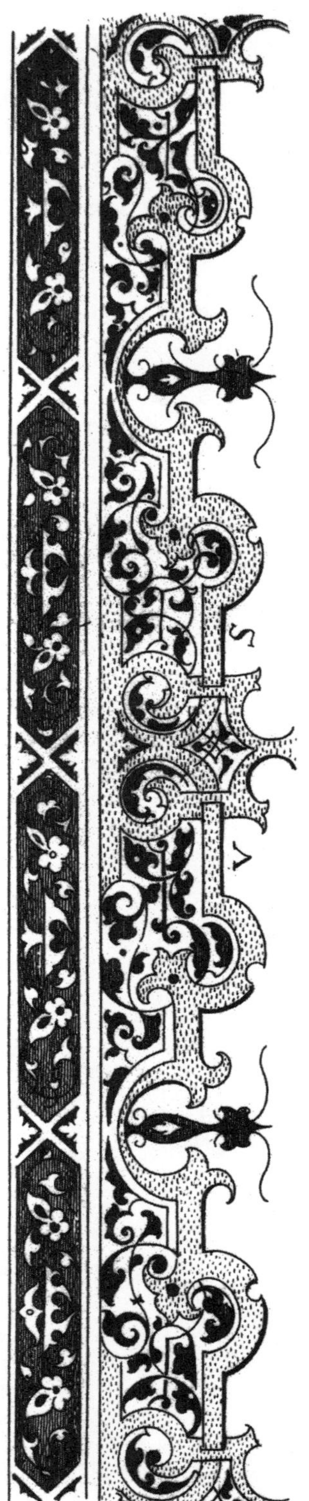

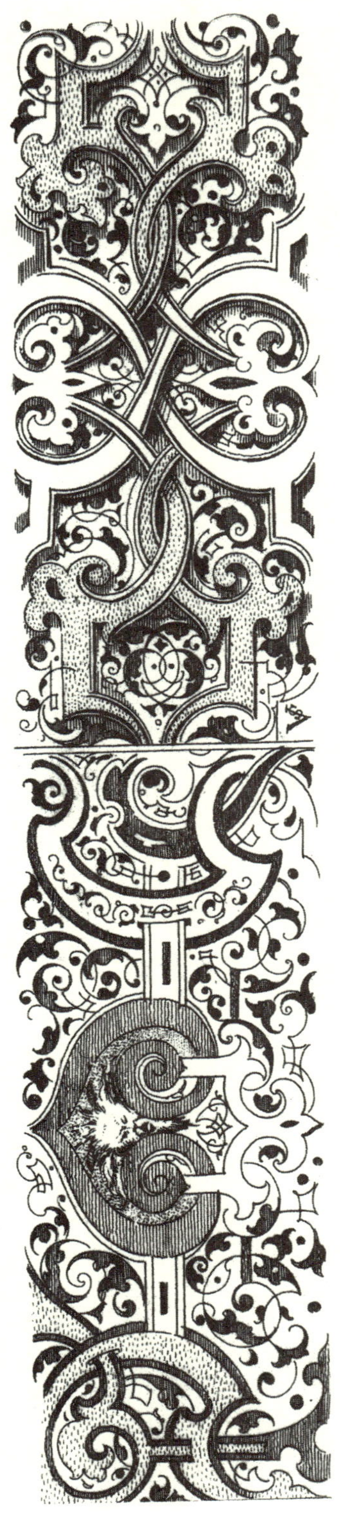 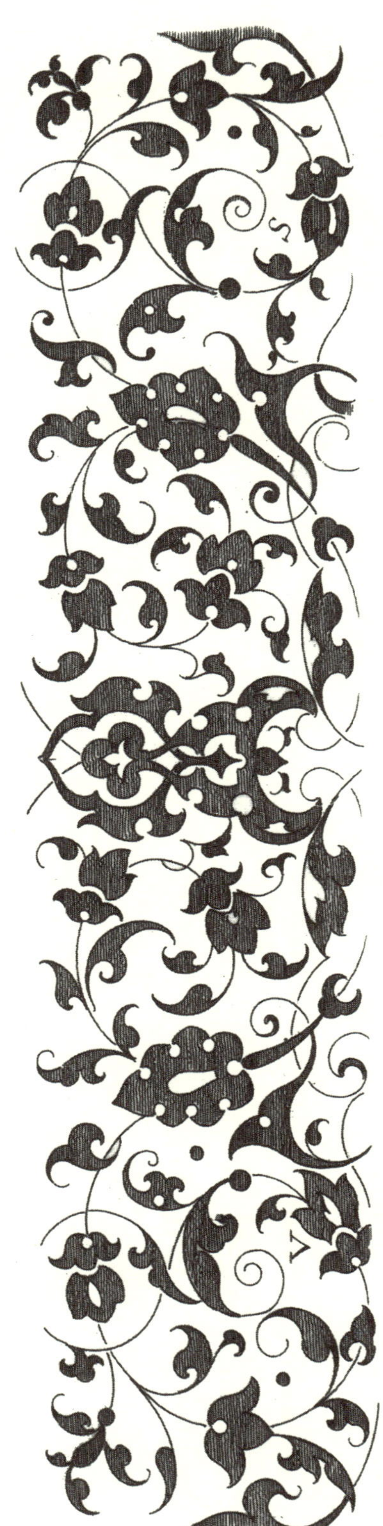 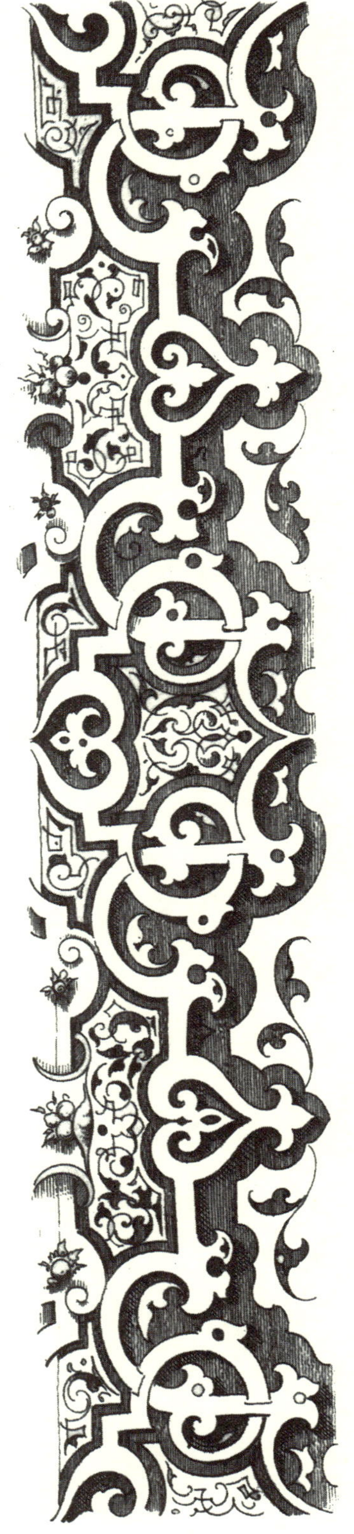

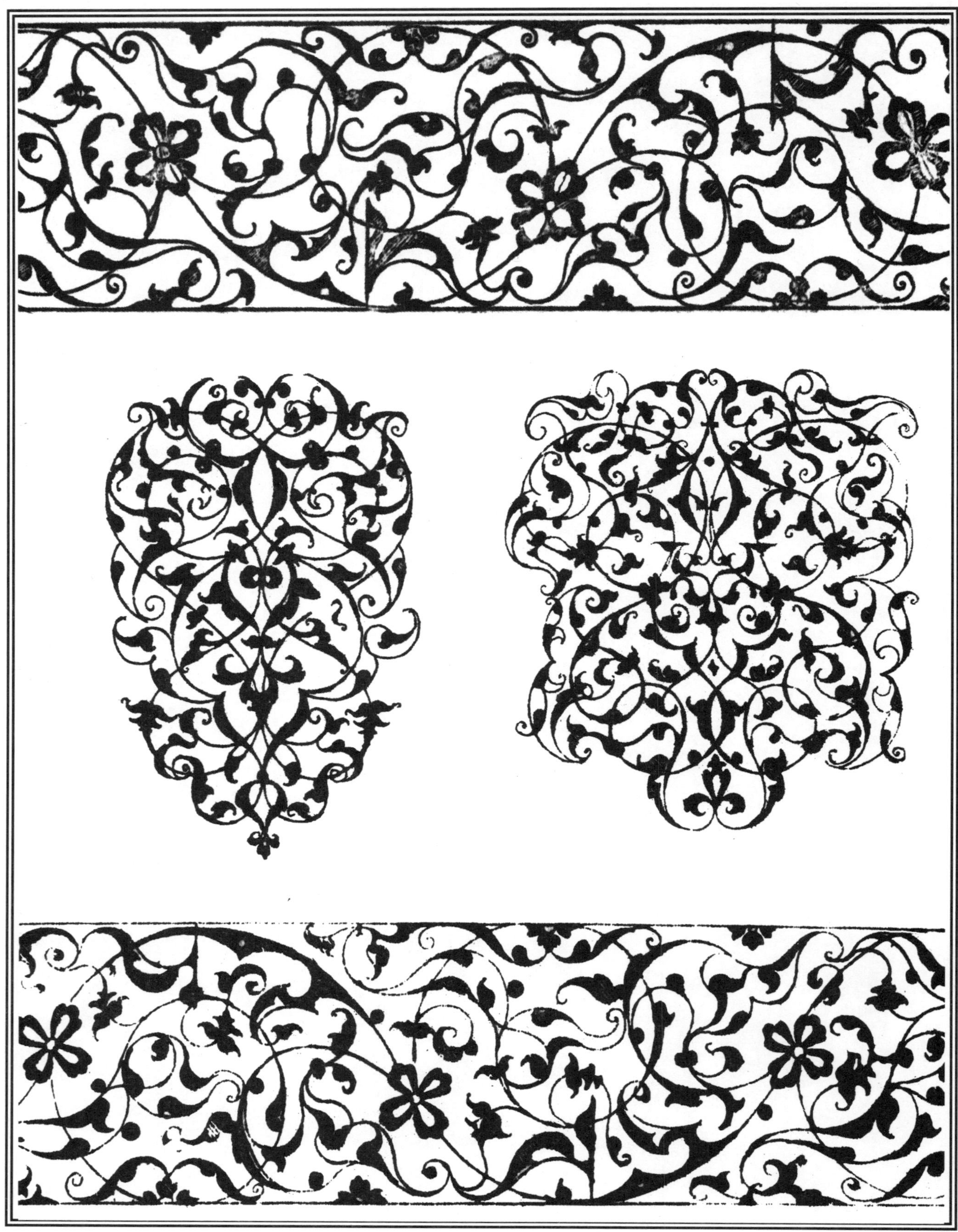

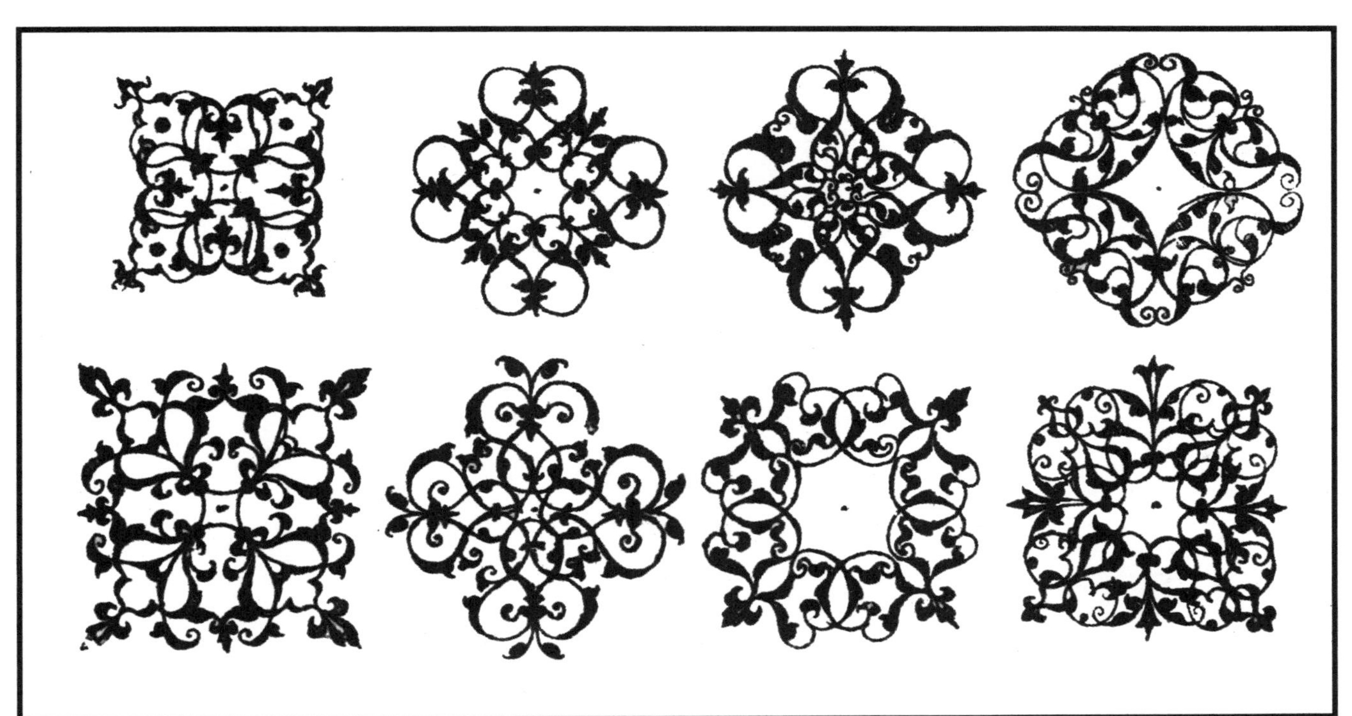

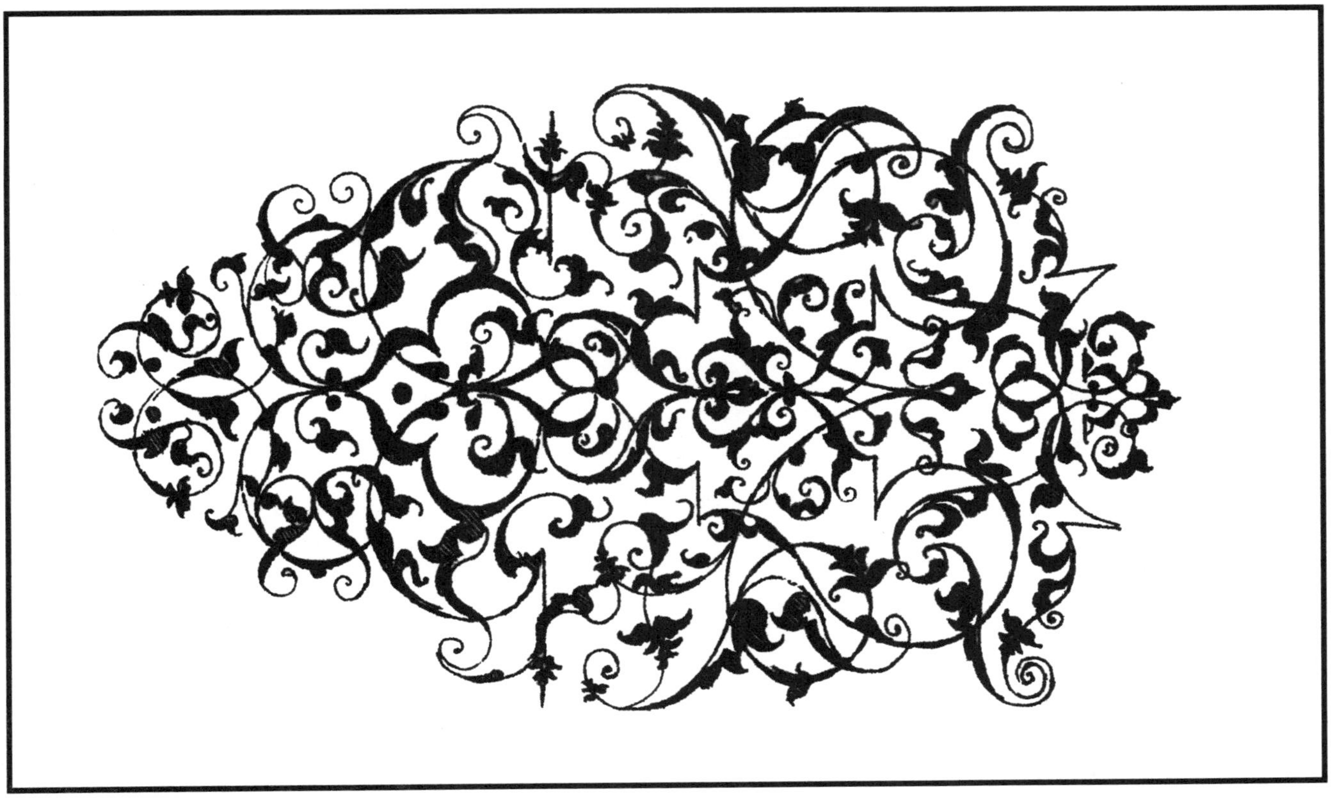

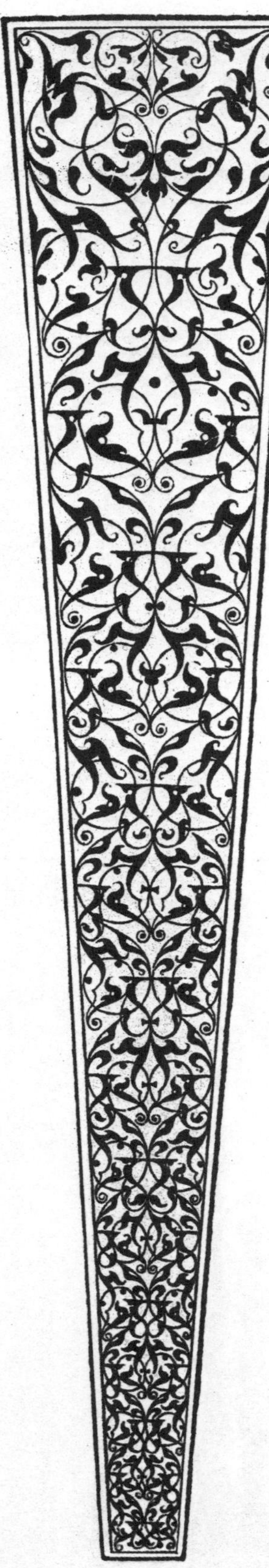
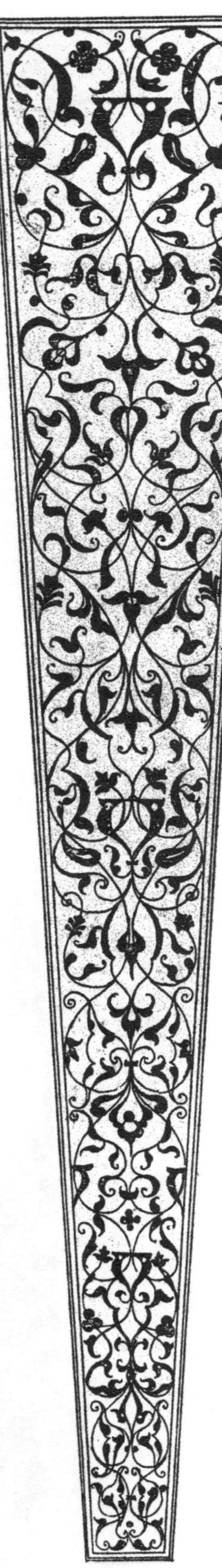
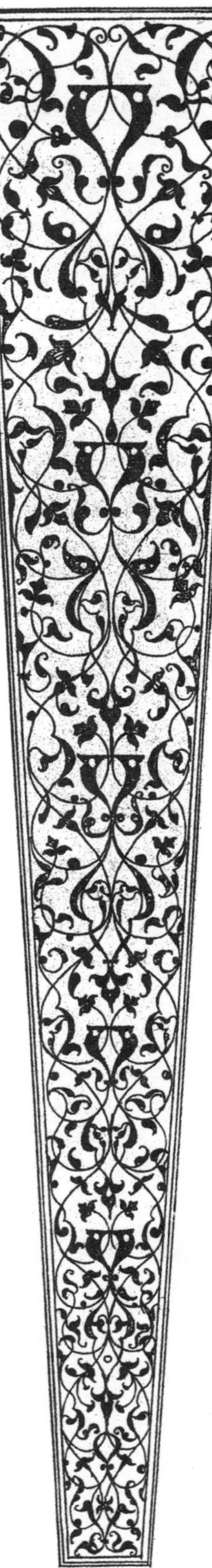

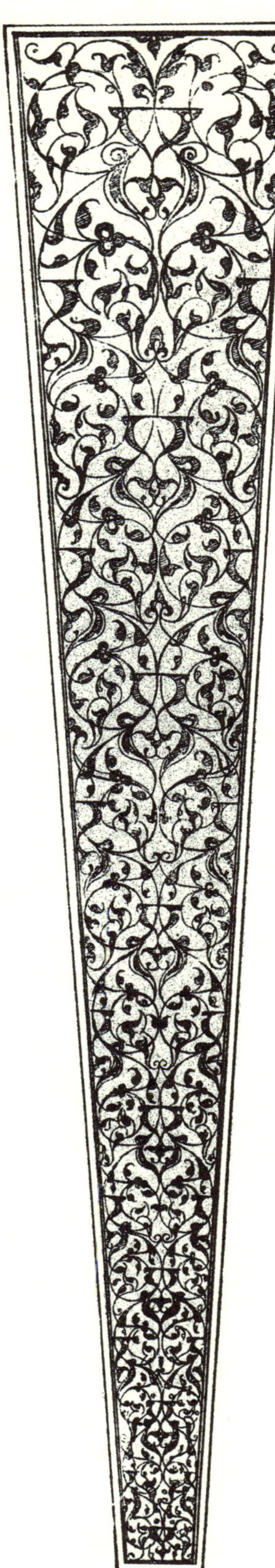
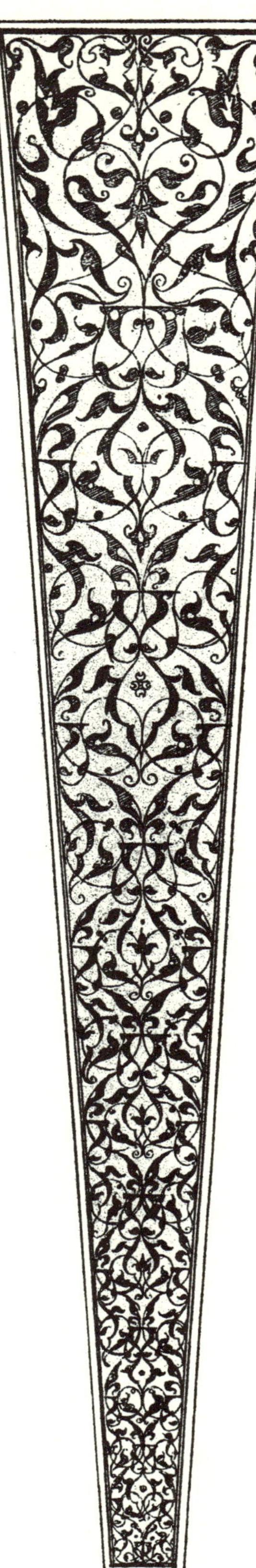
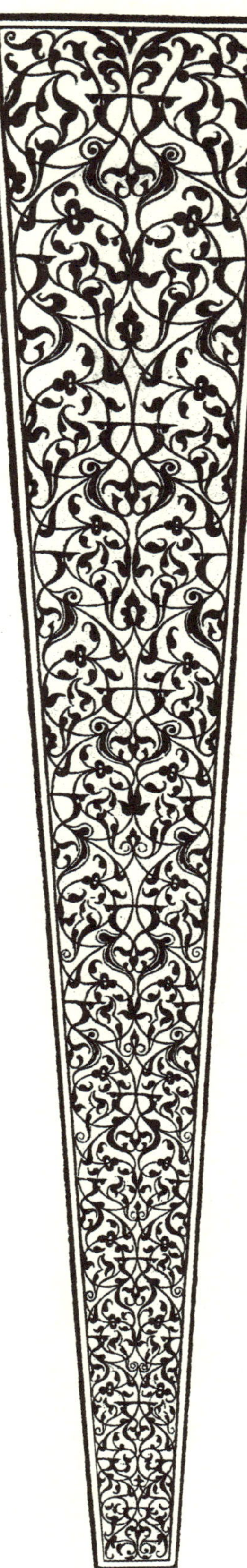

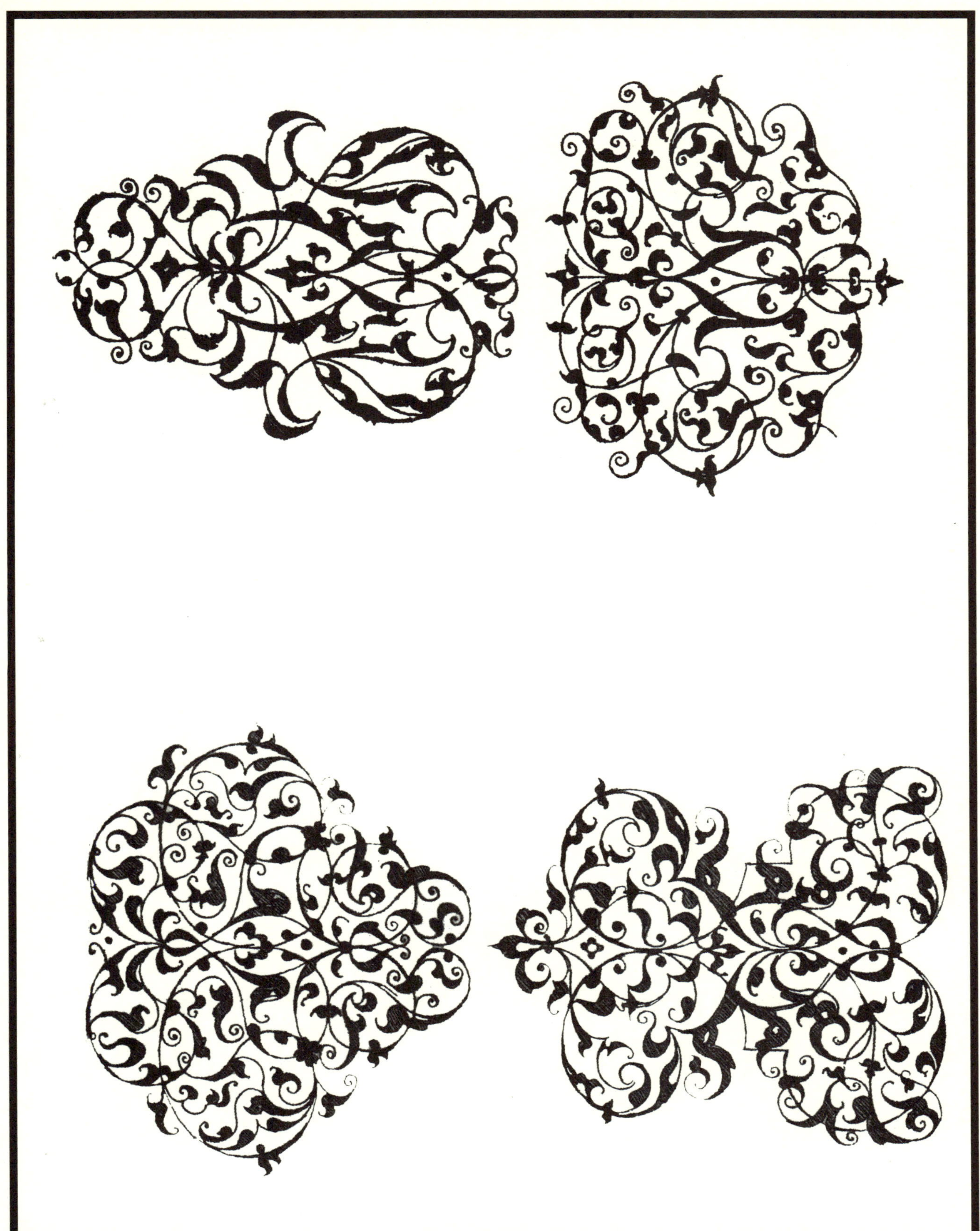

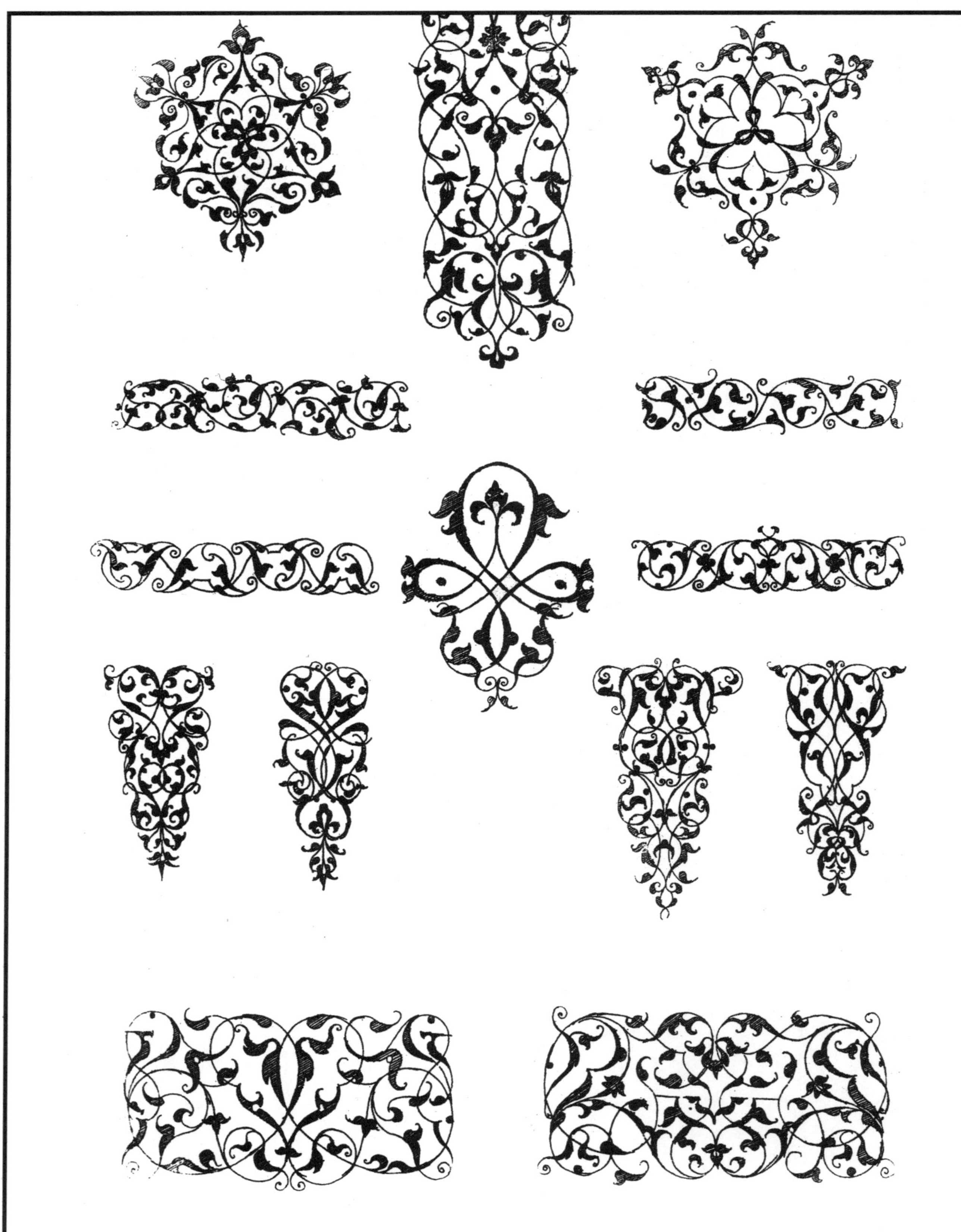

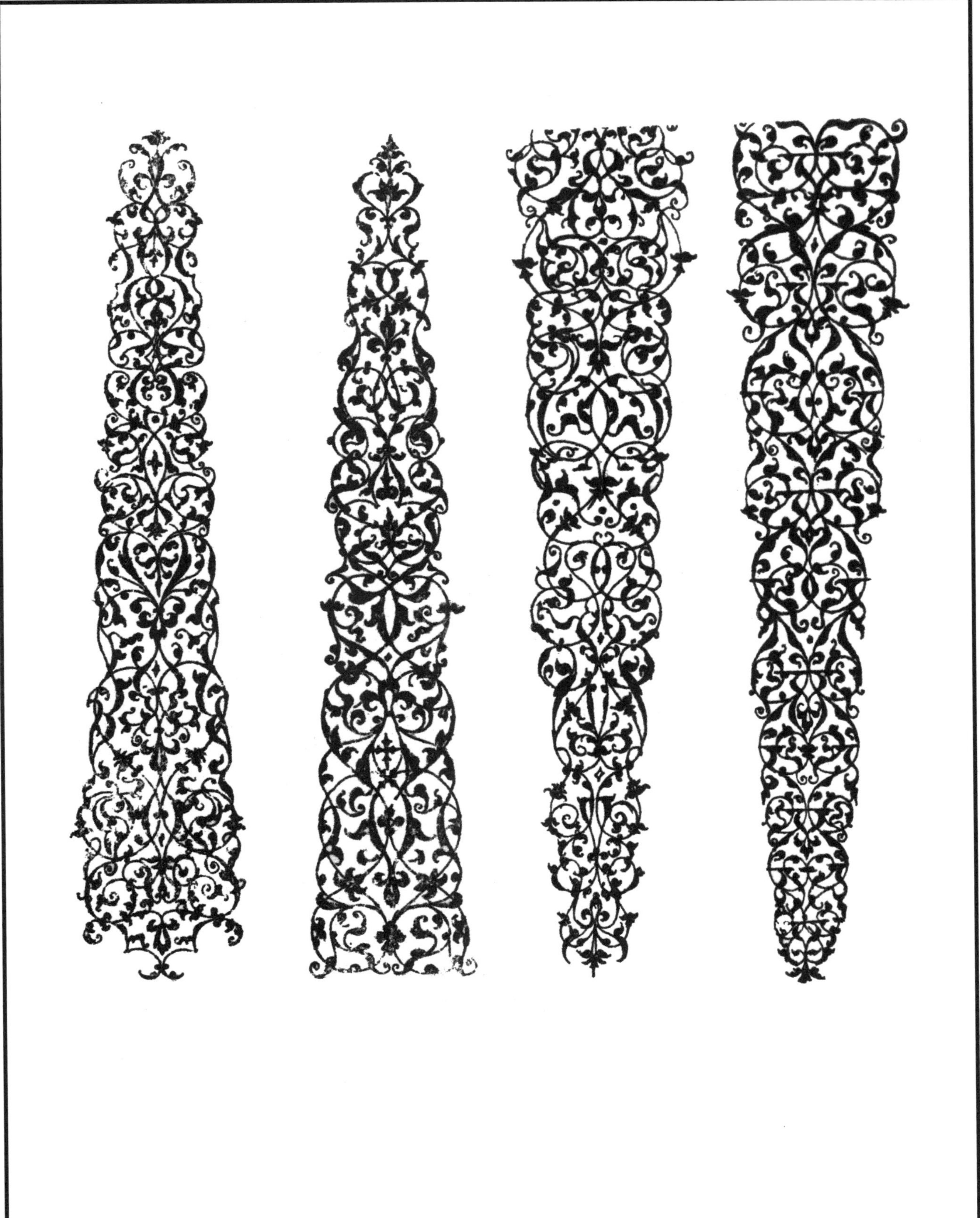

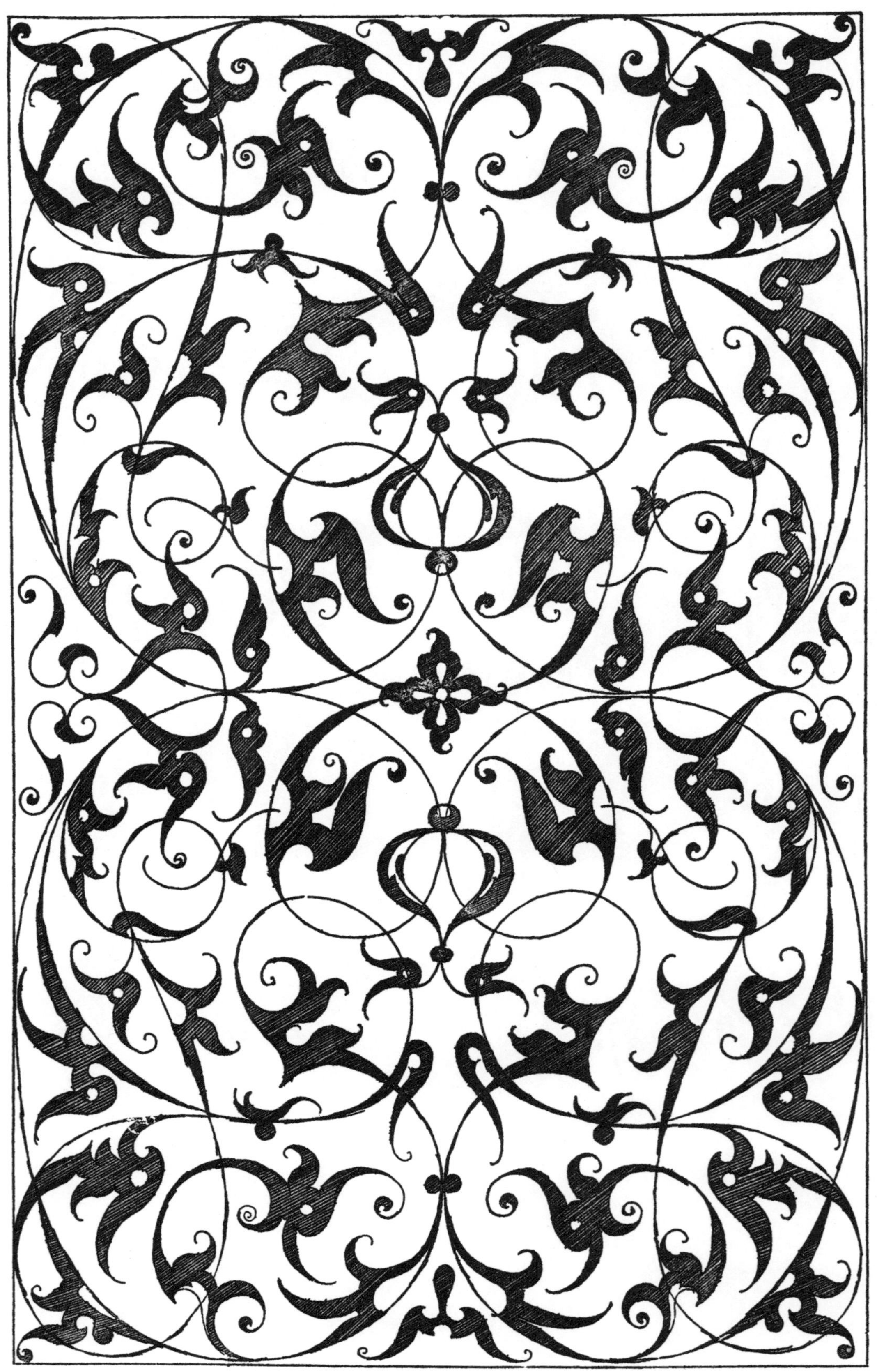

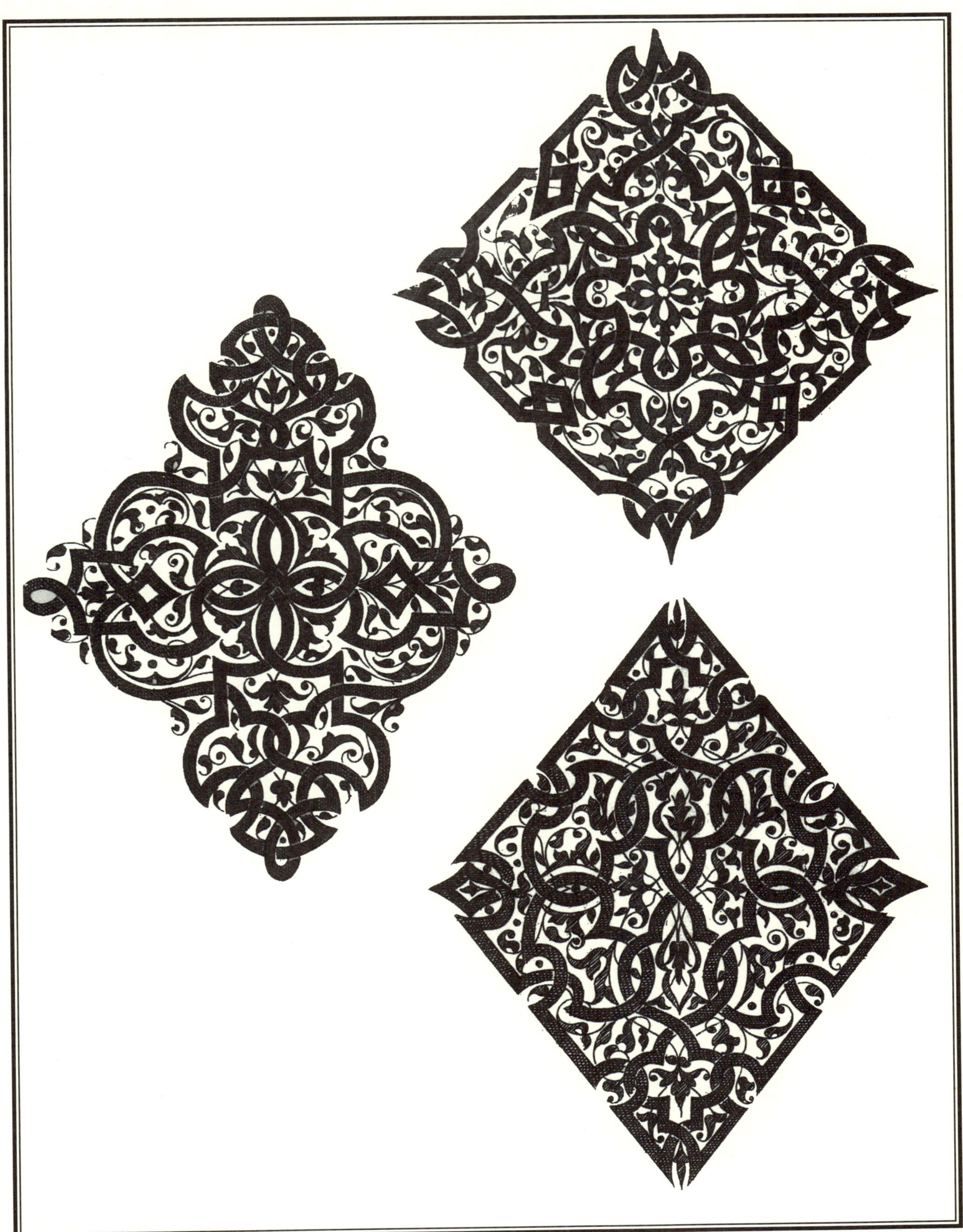

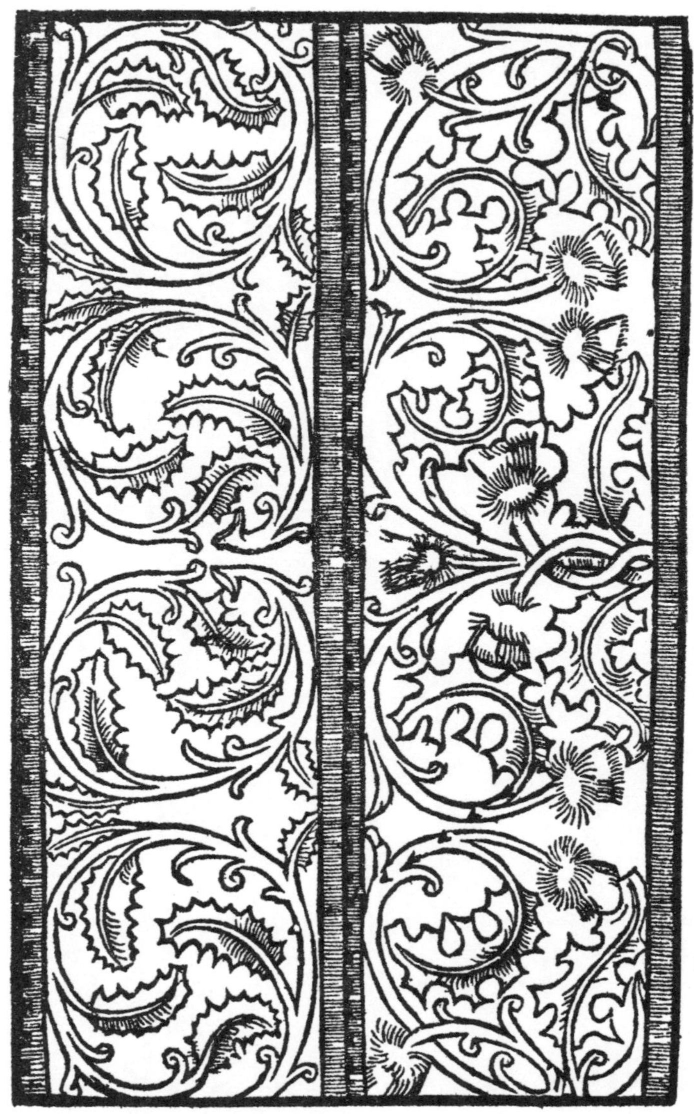

• Textile •

• Le textile •

• Textil •

• El textil •

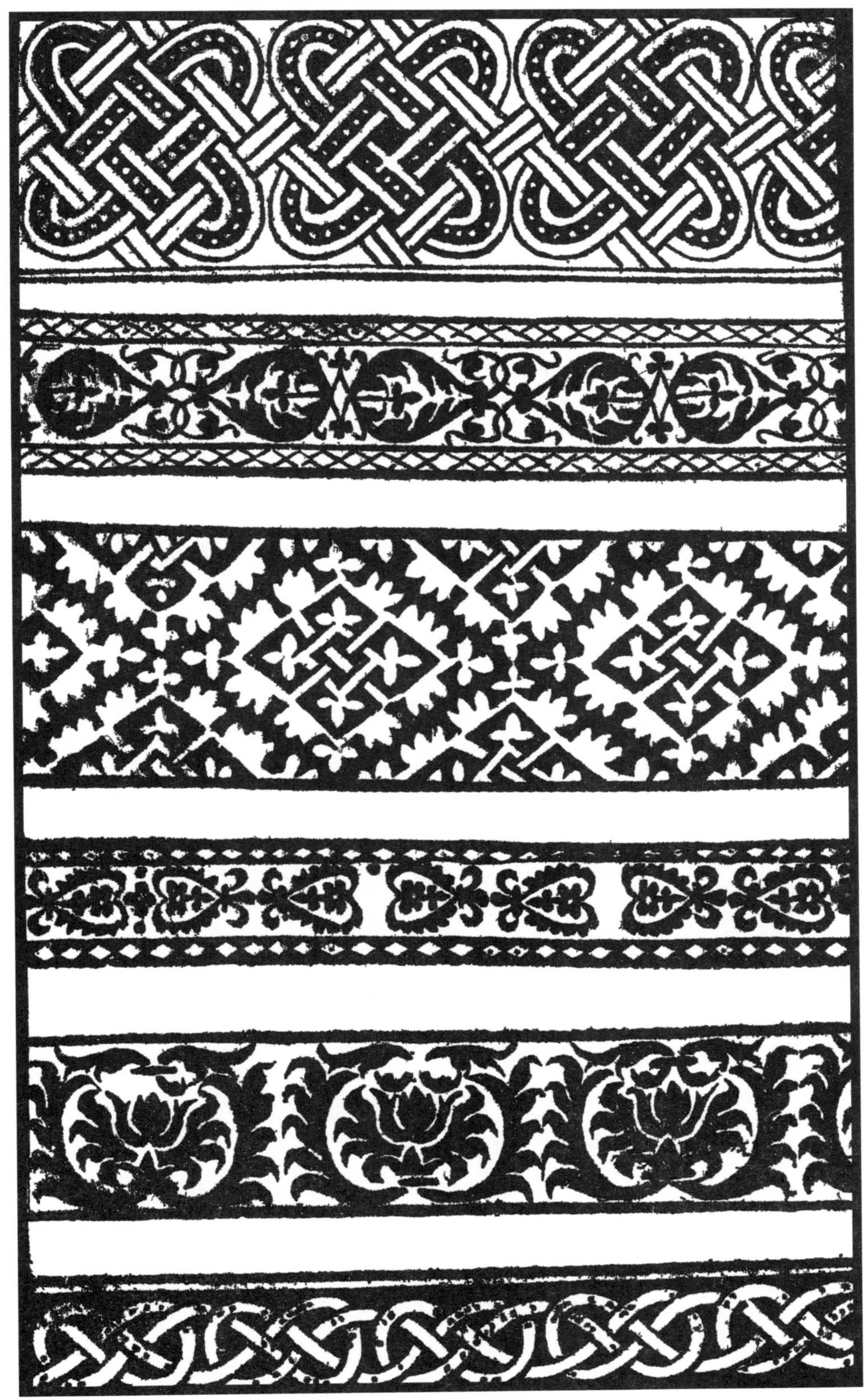

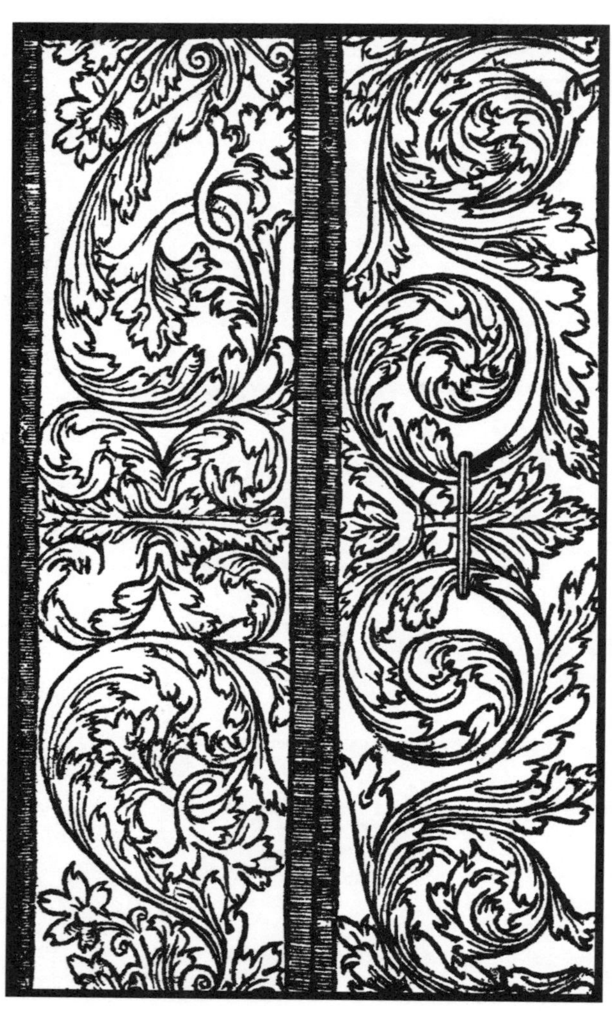 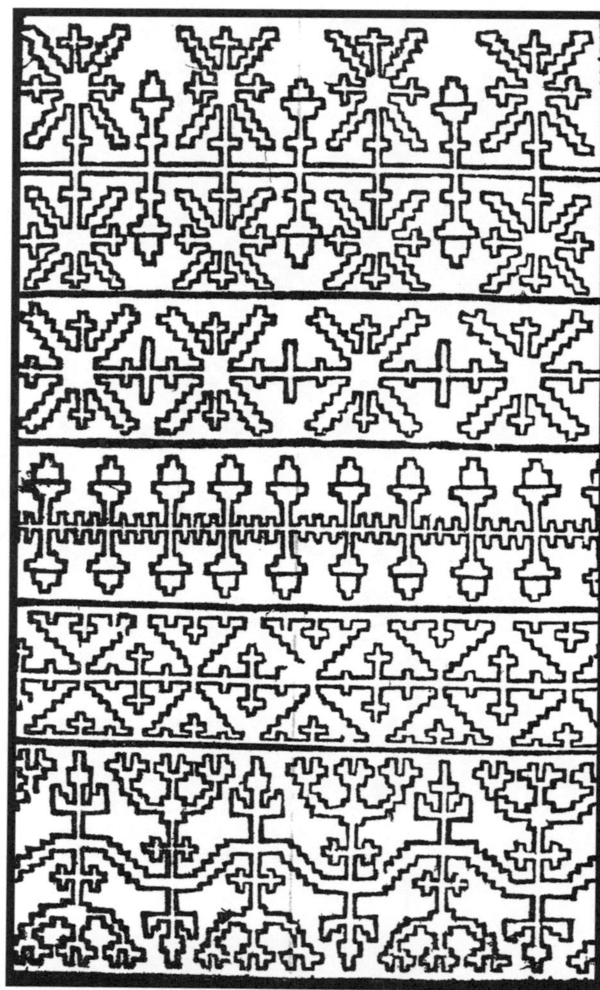

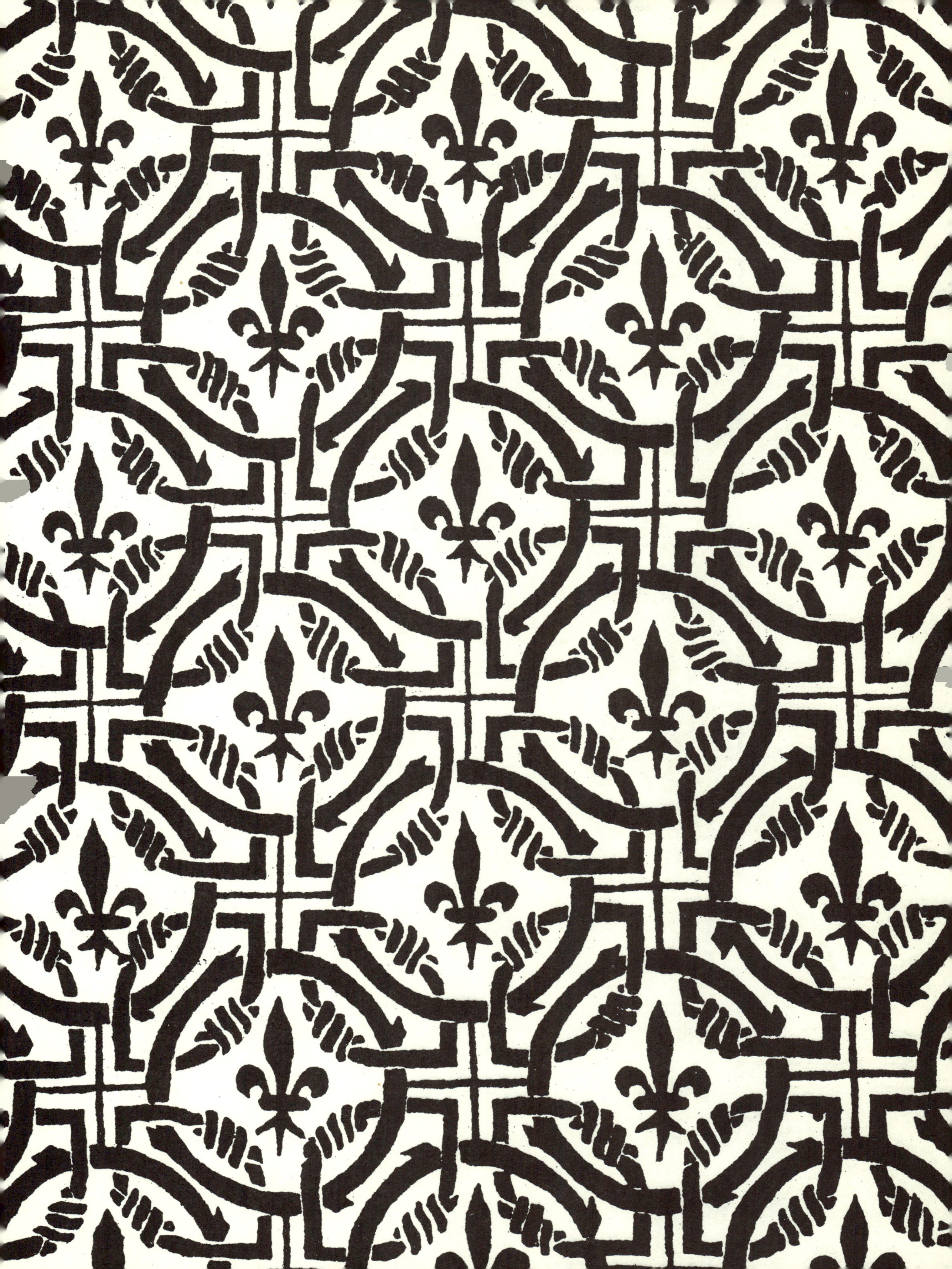

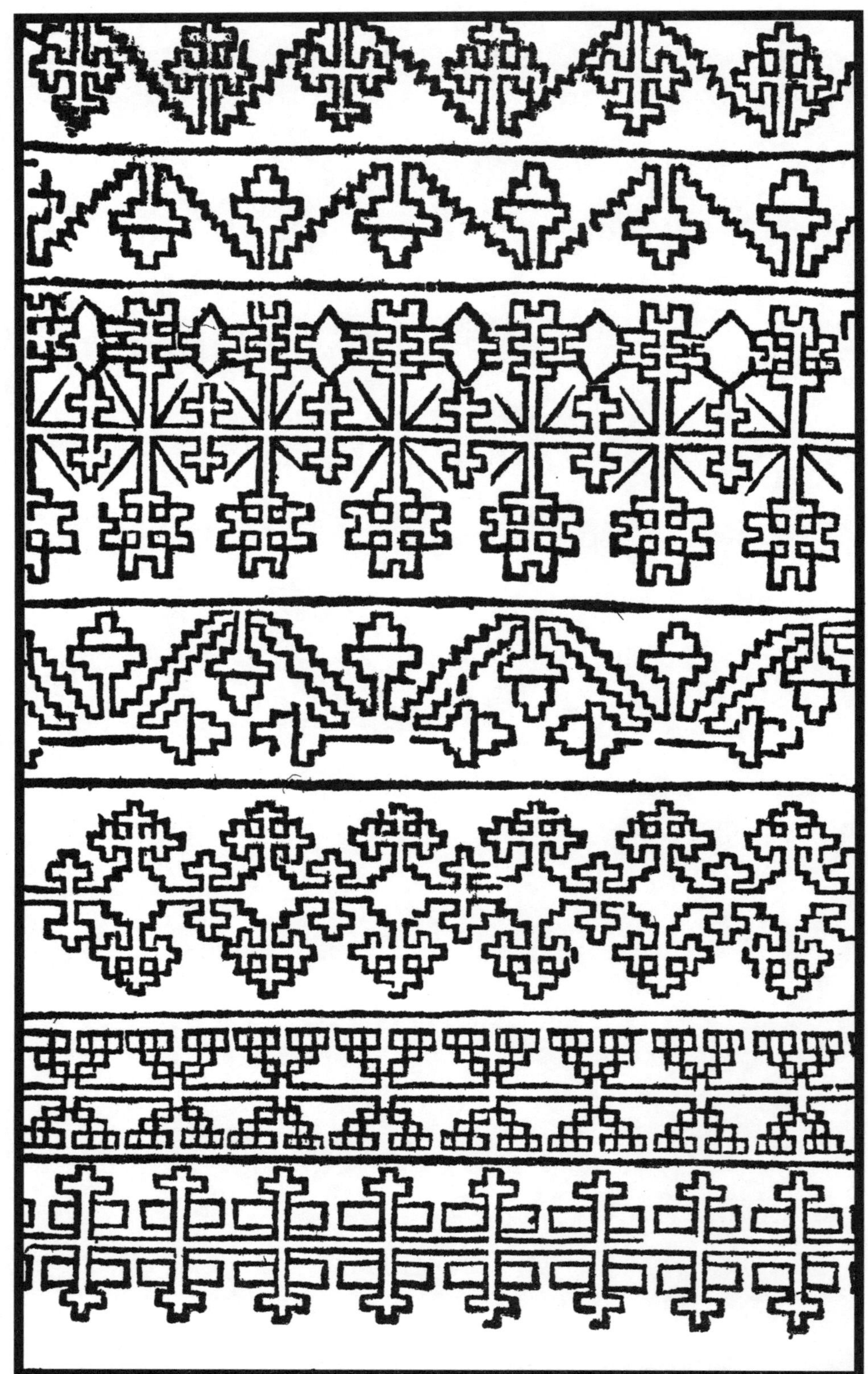

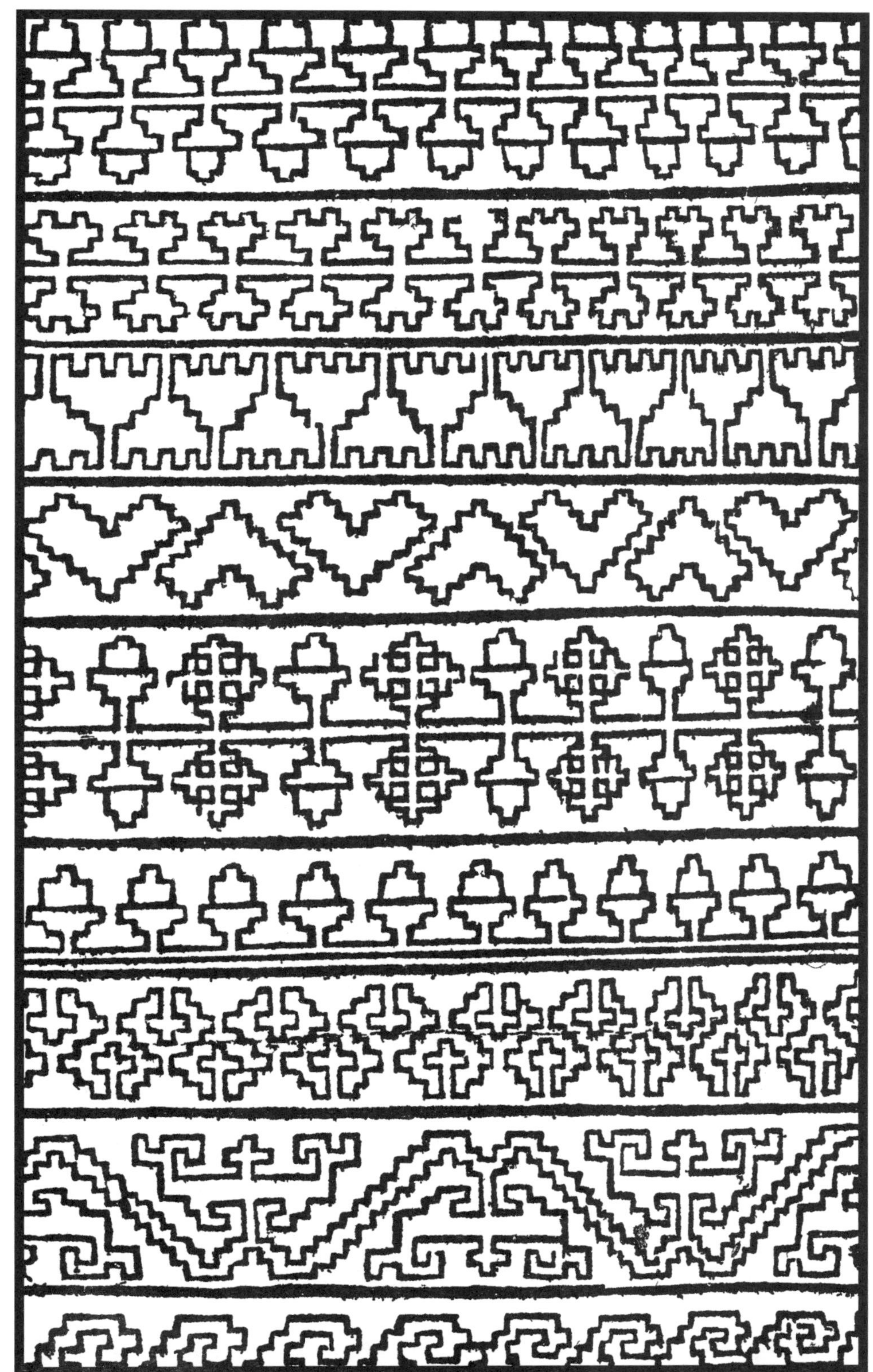

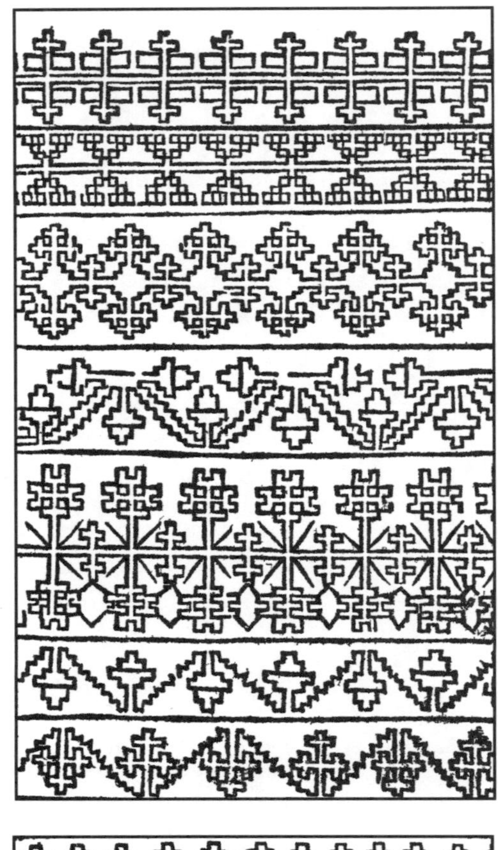

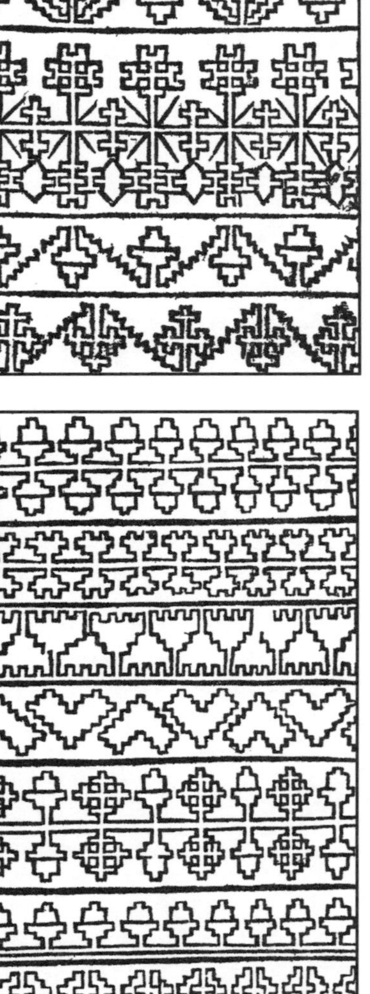

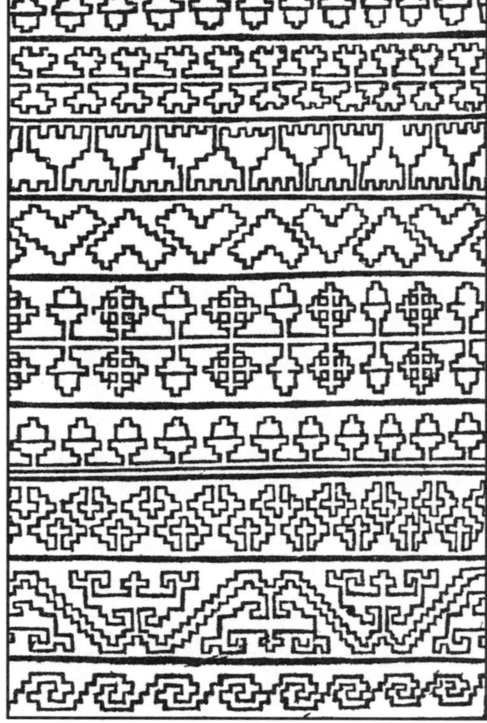

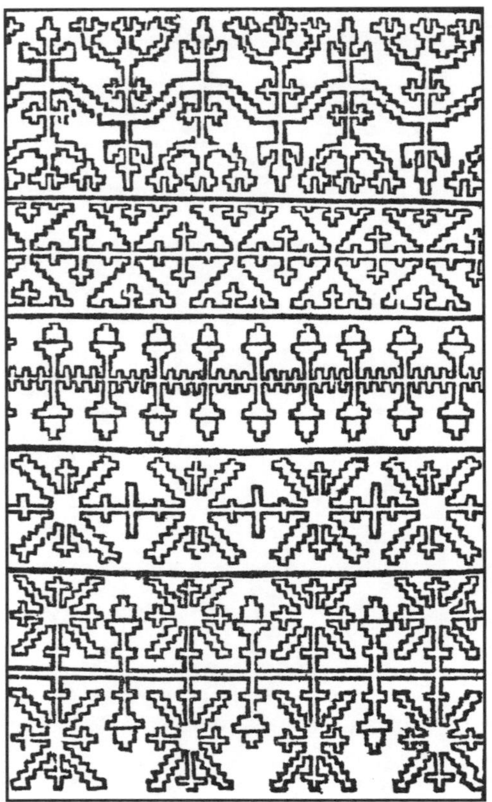

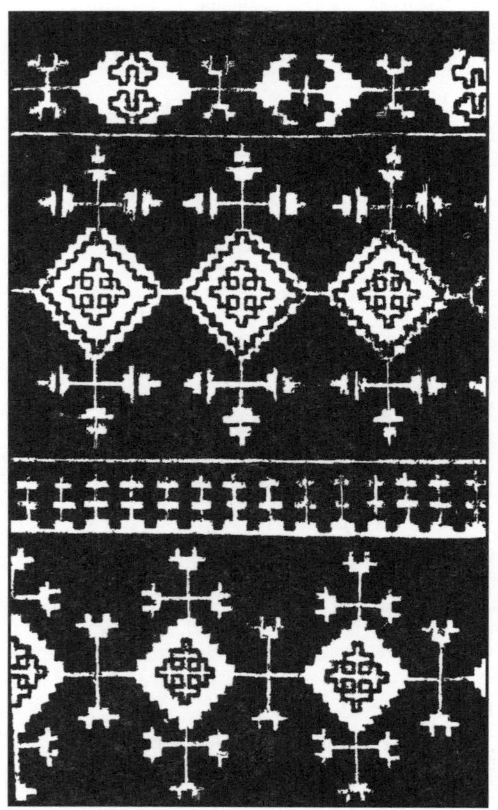

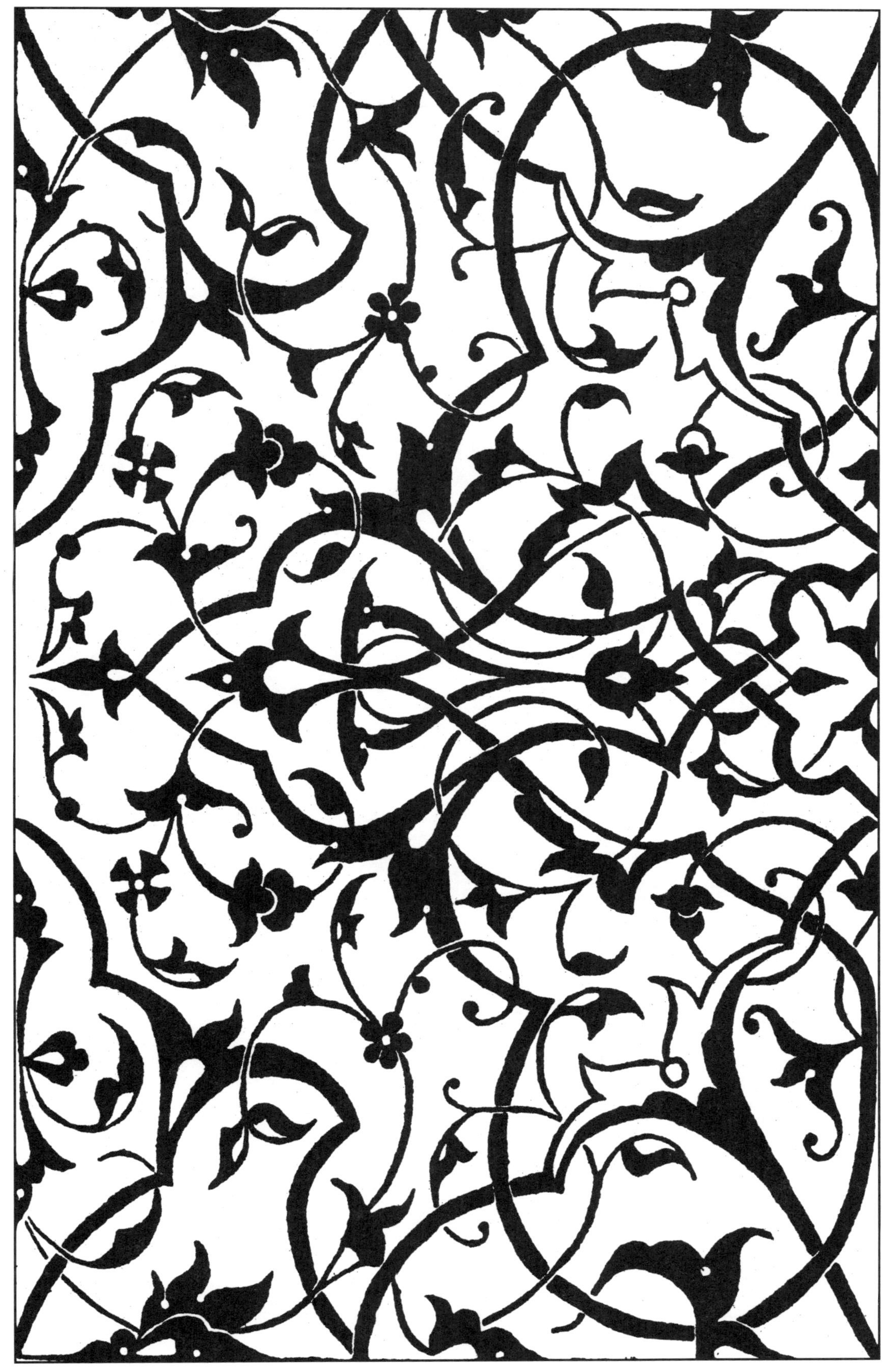

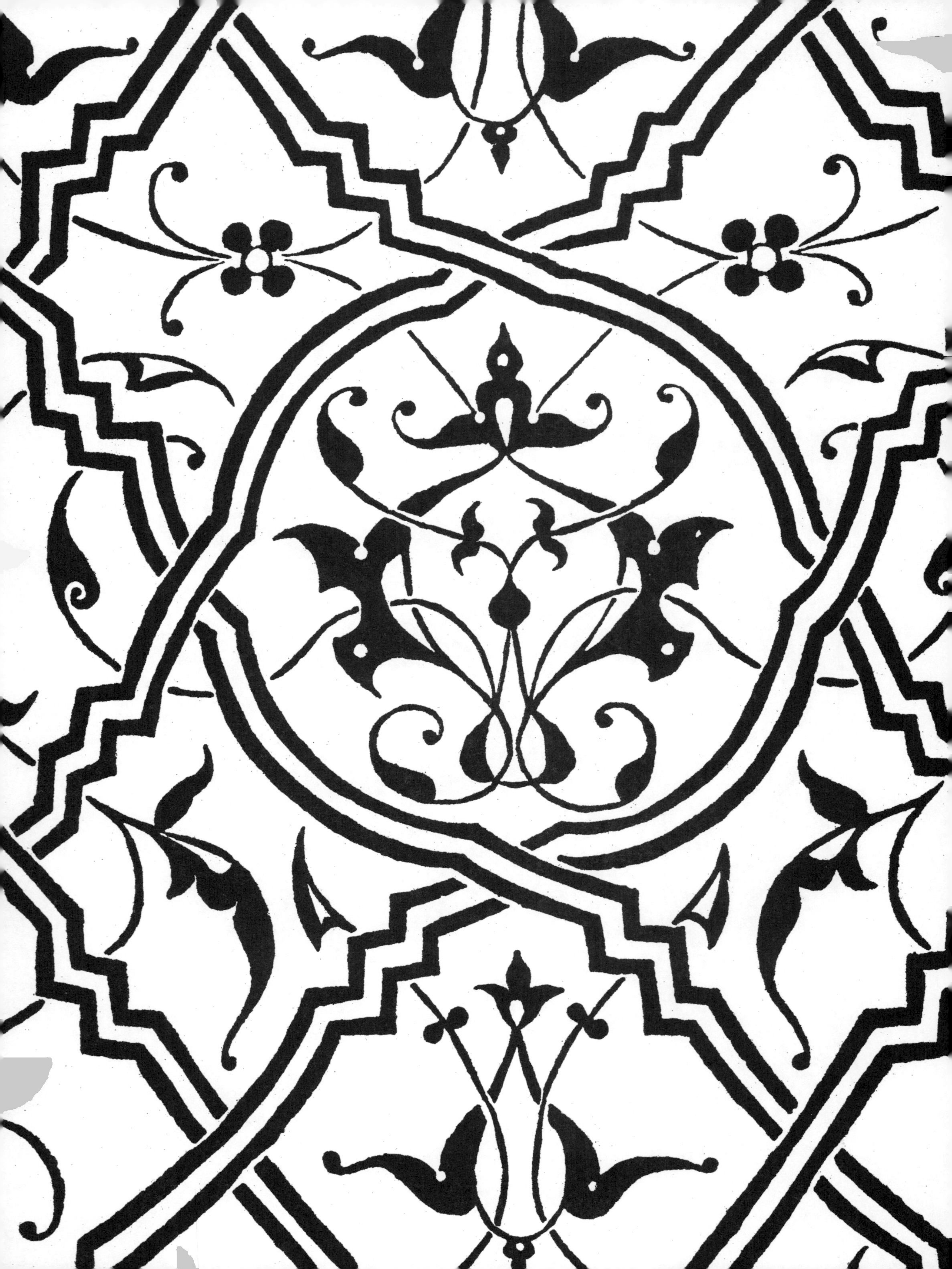

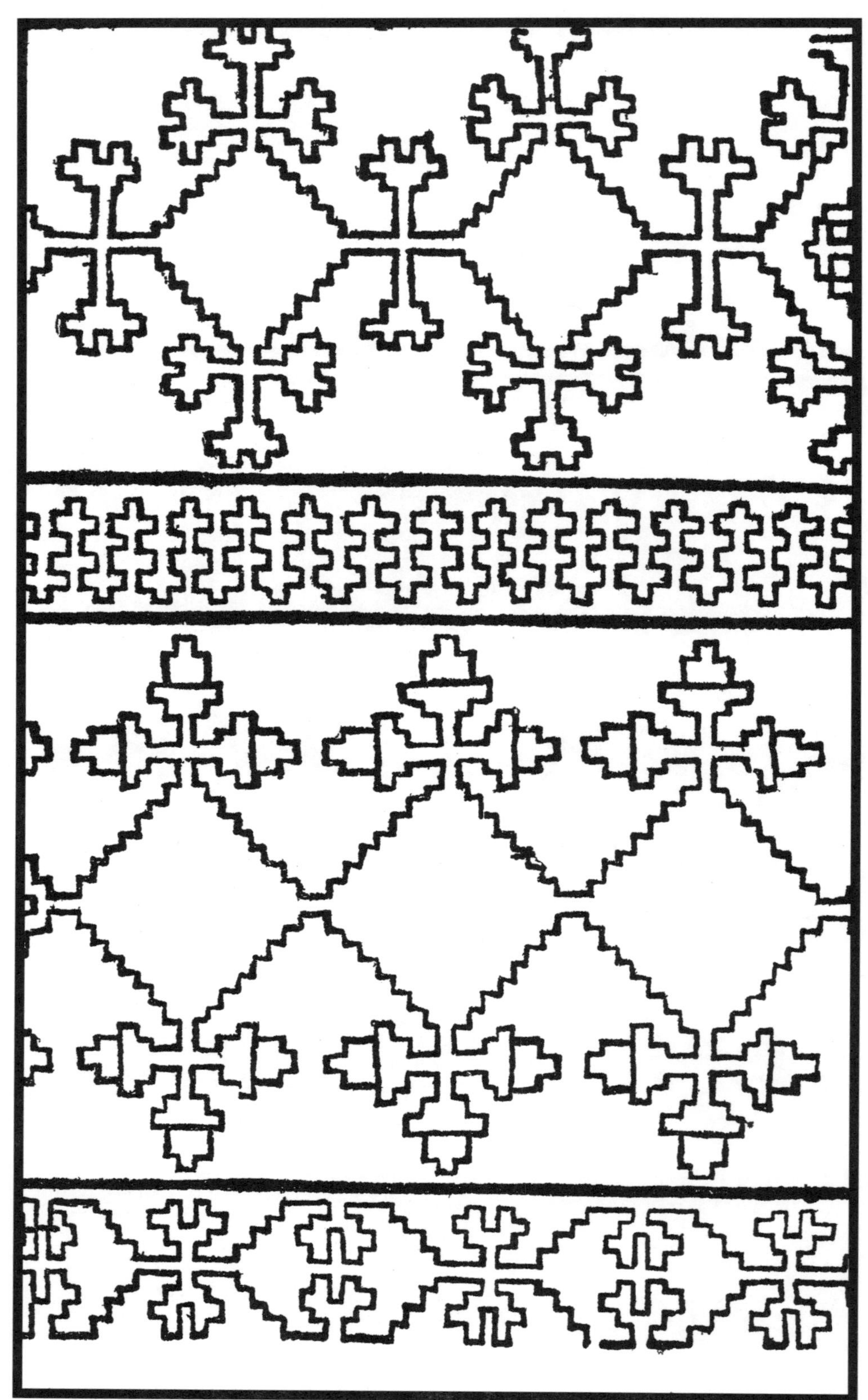

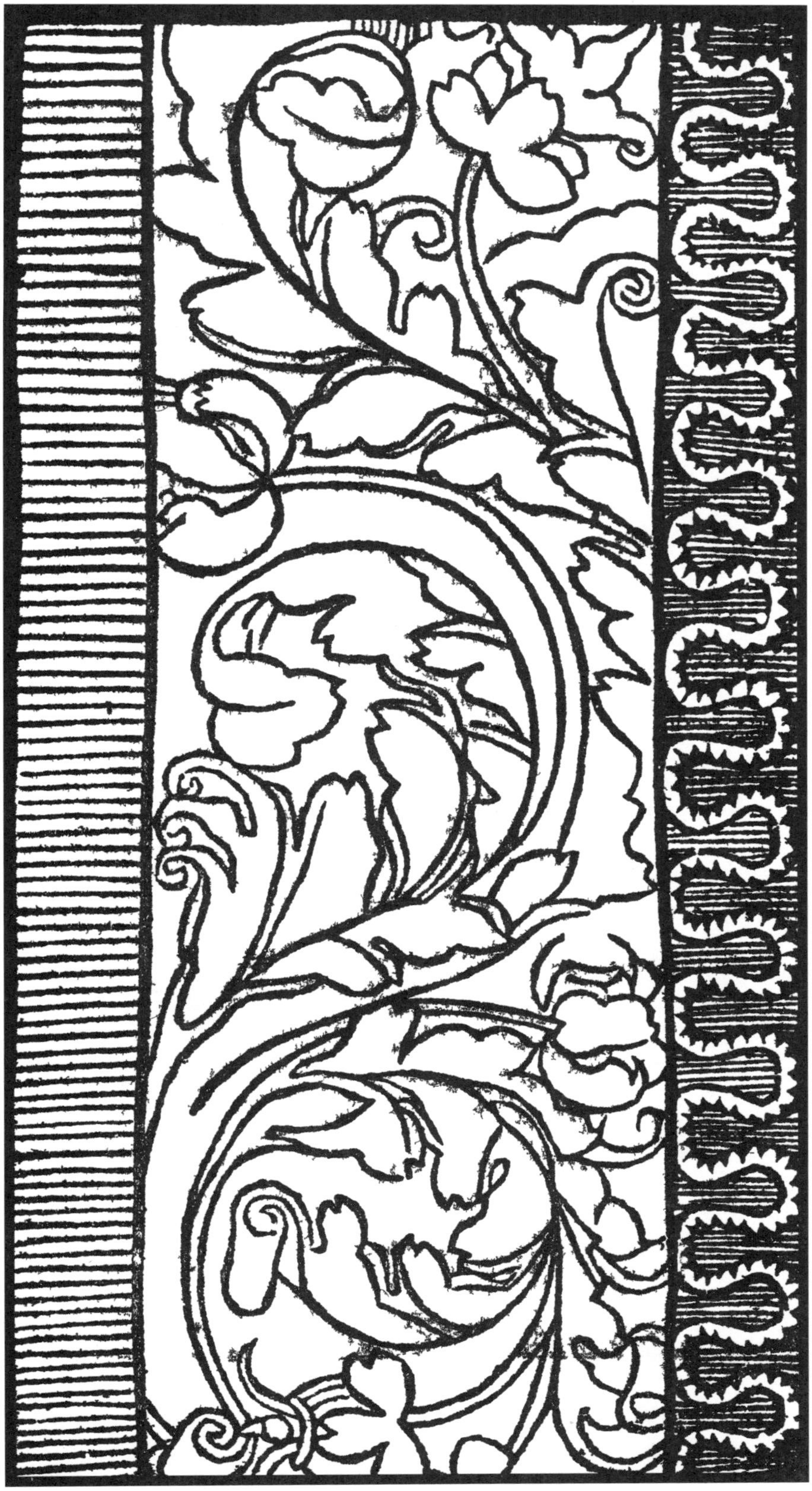

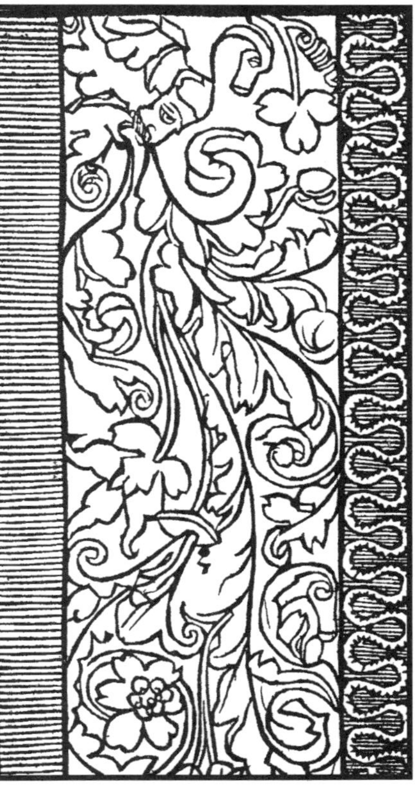

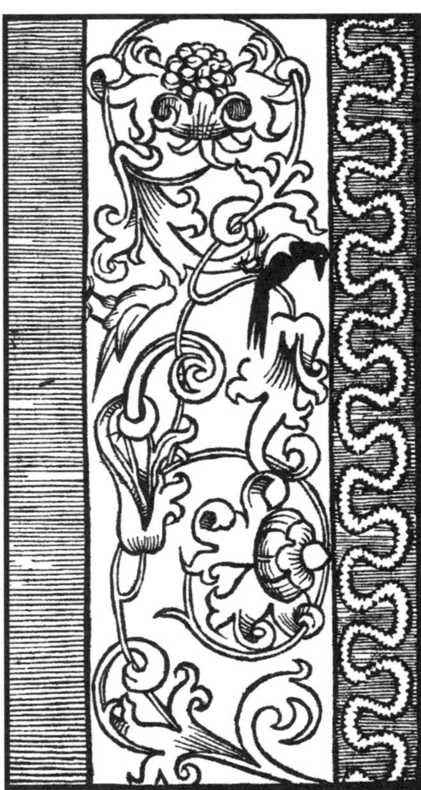

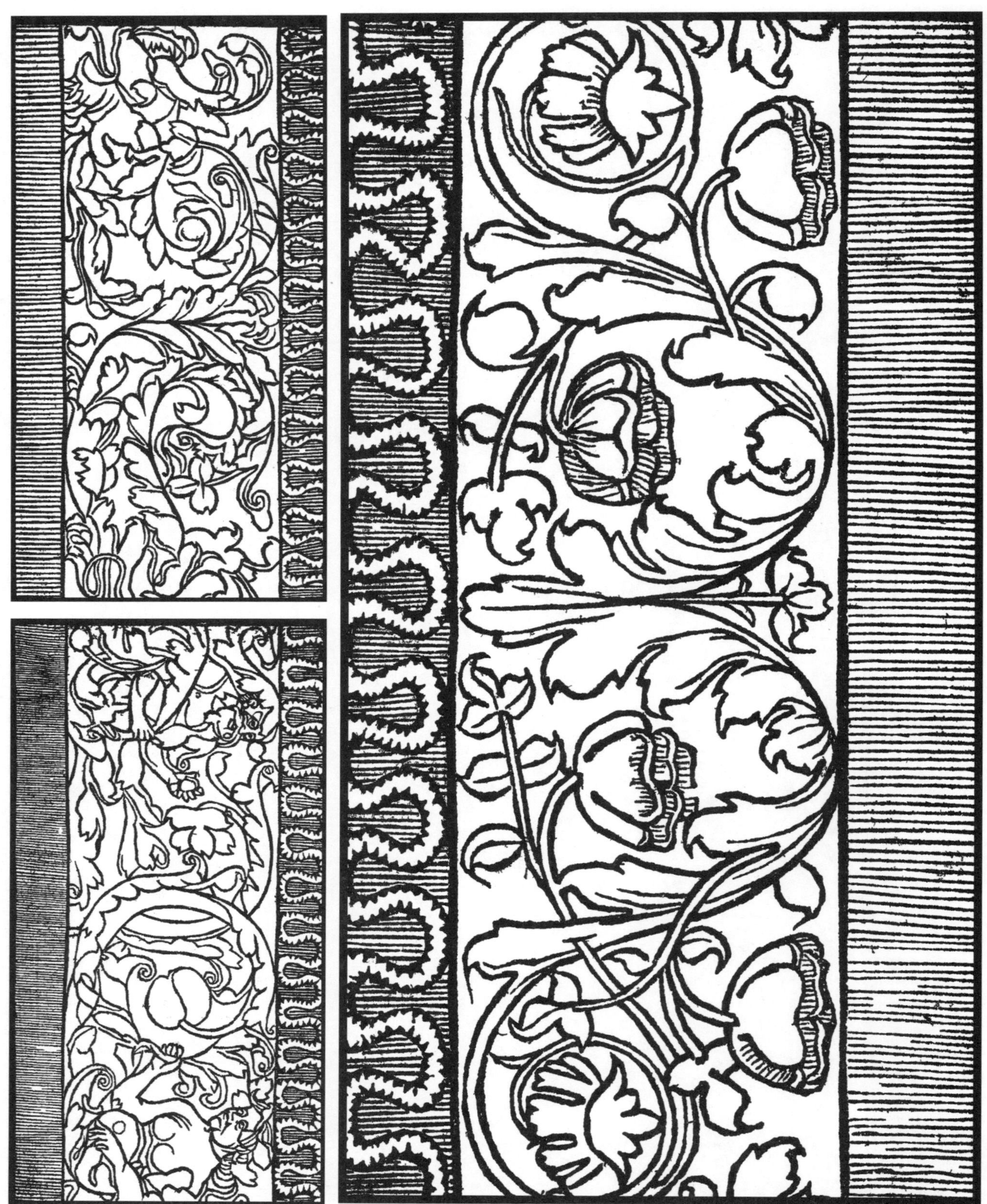

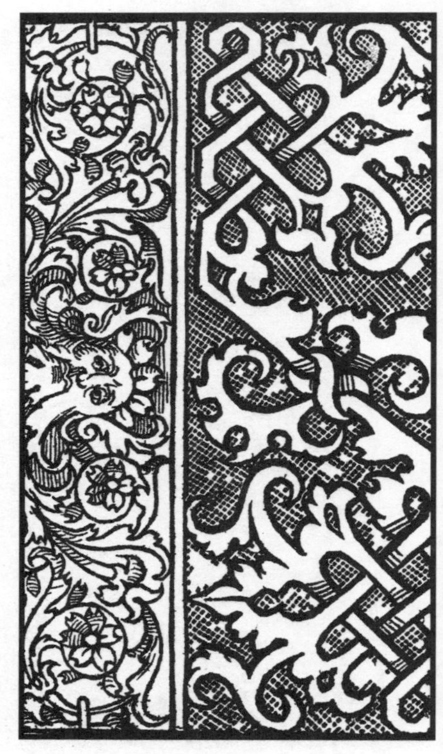

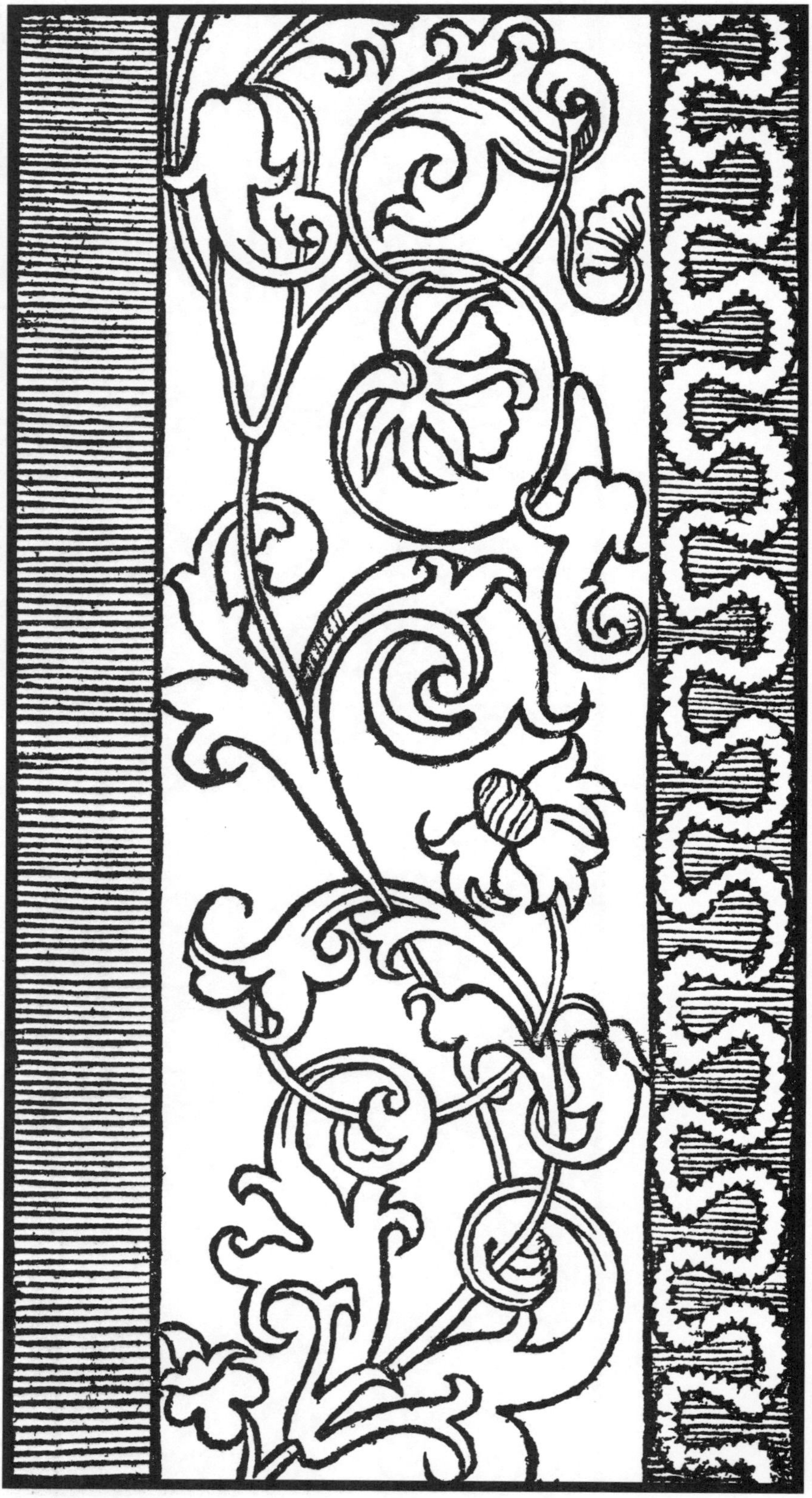

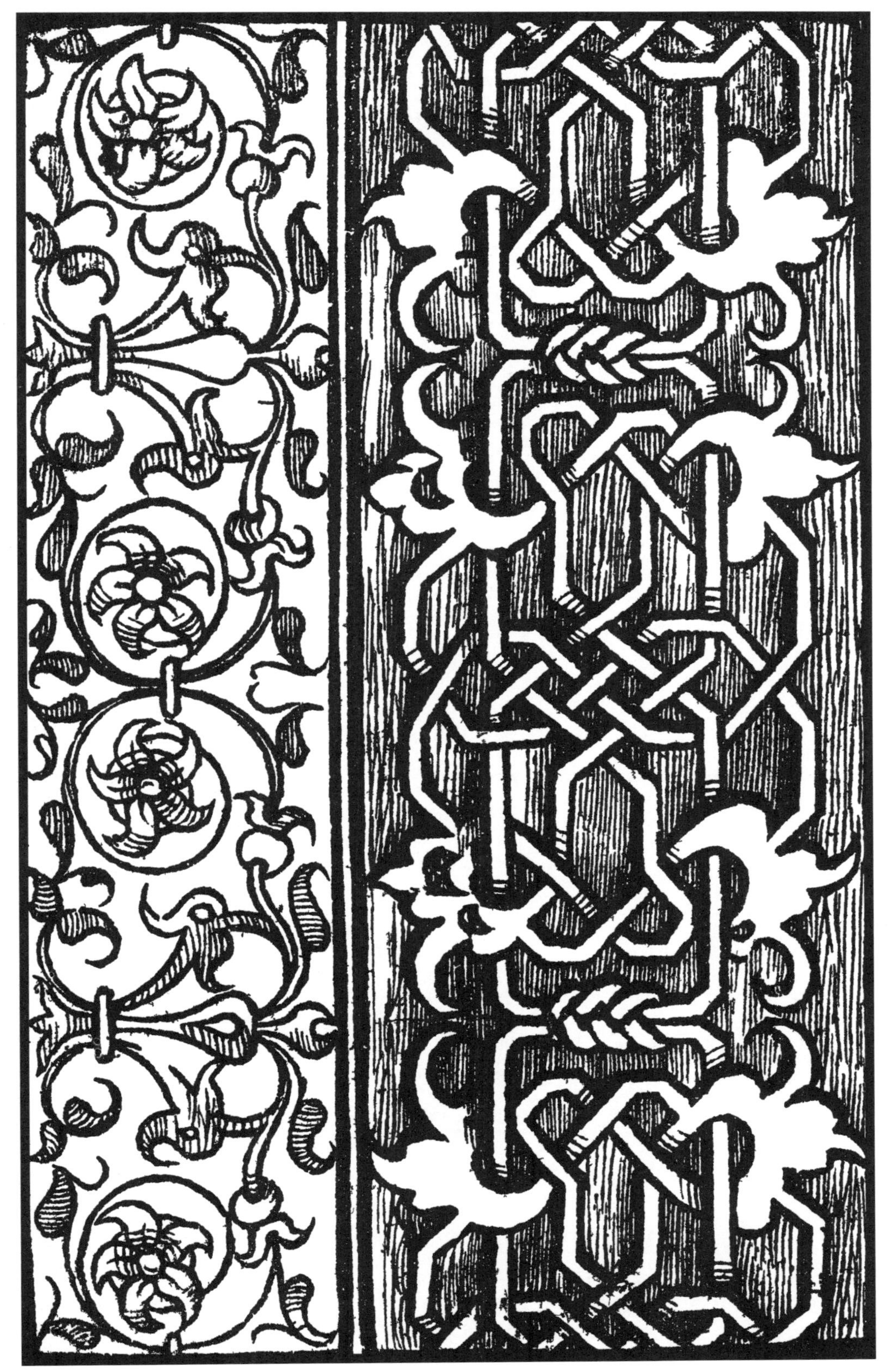

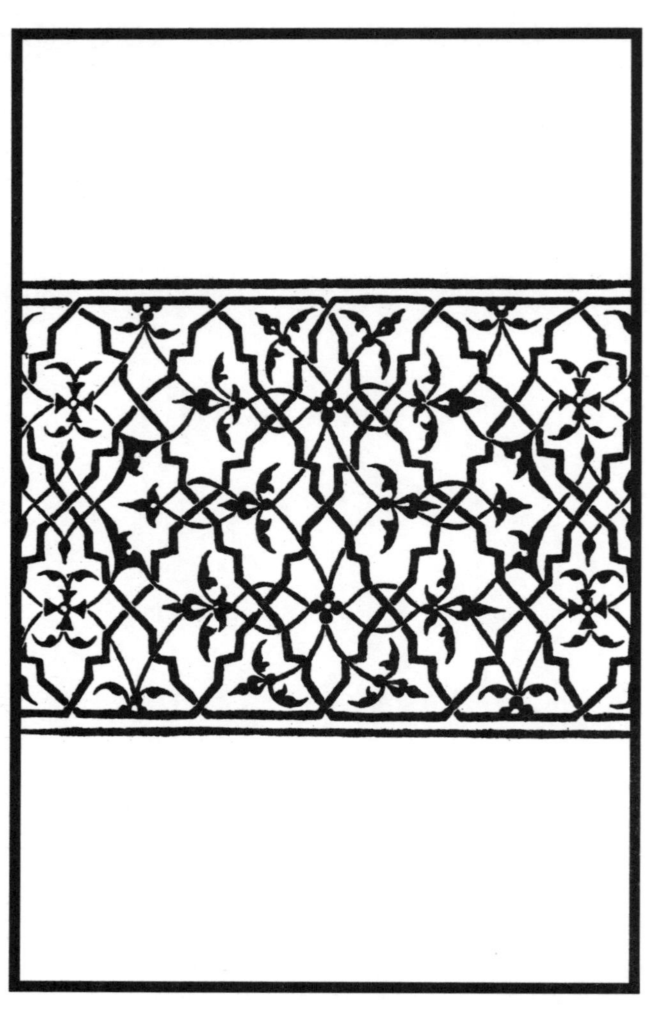

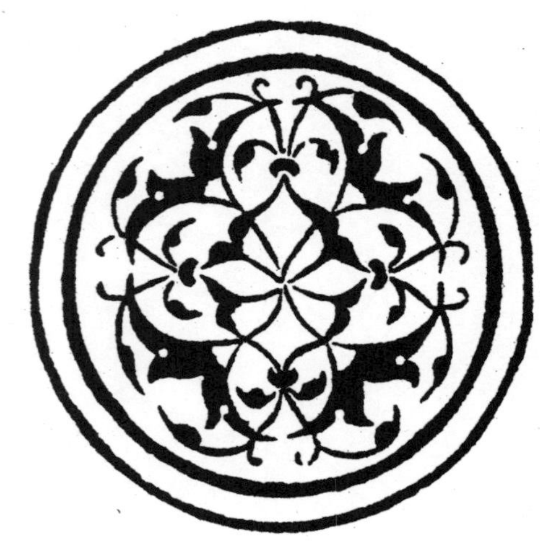

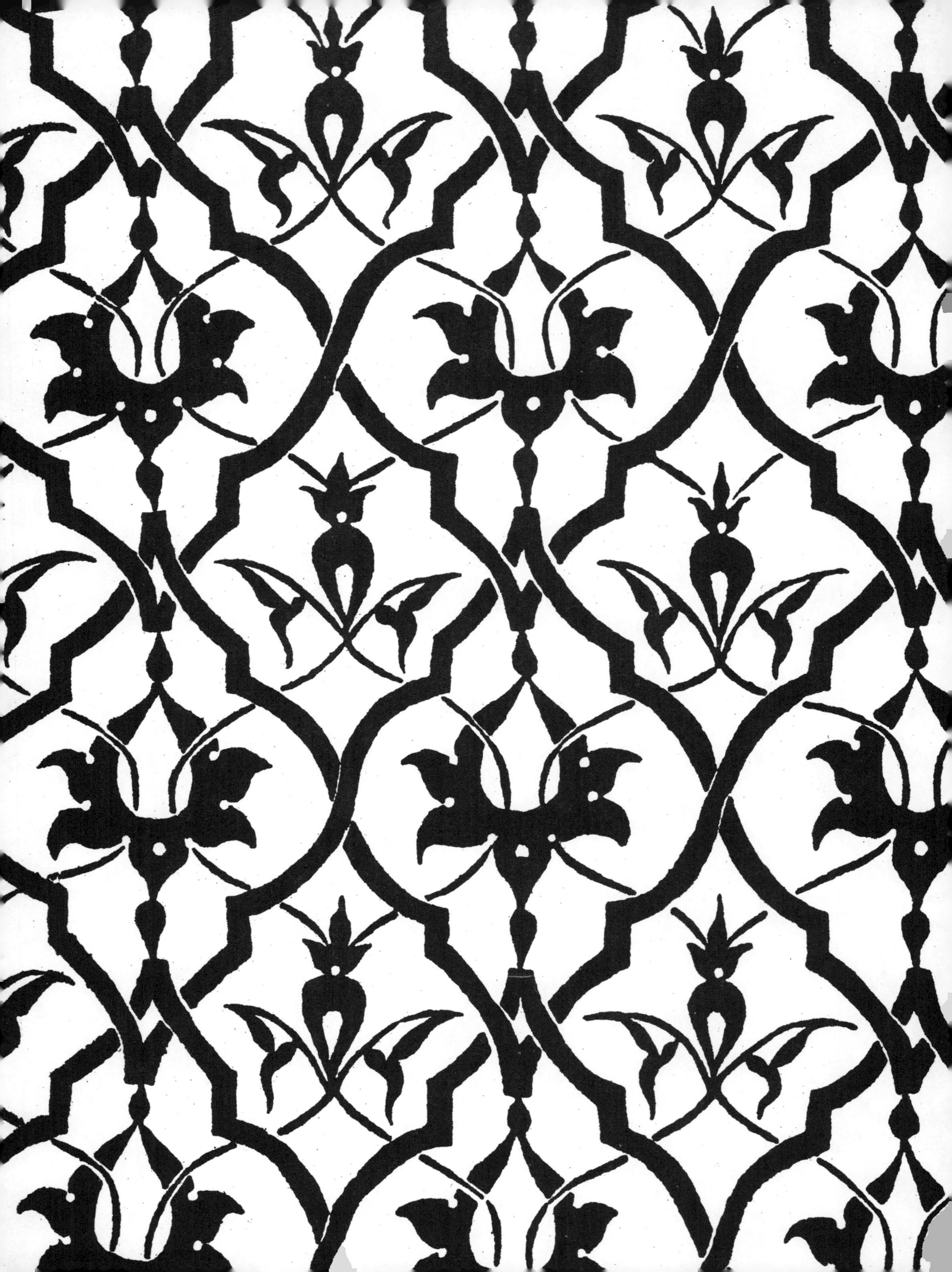

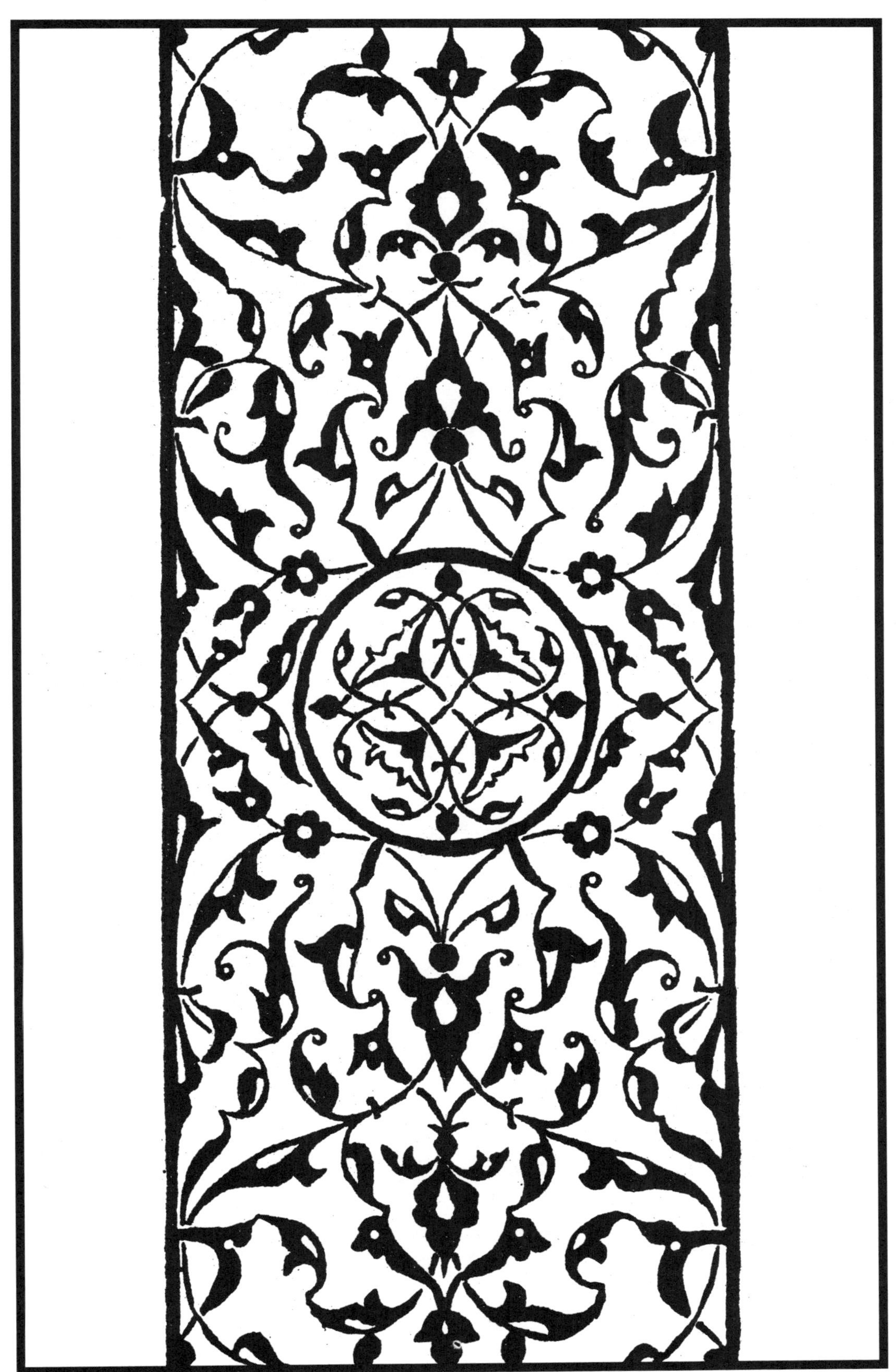

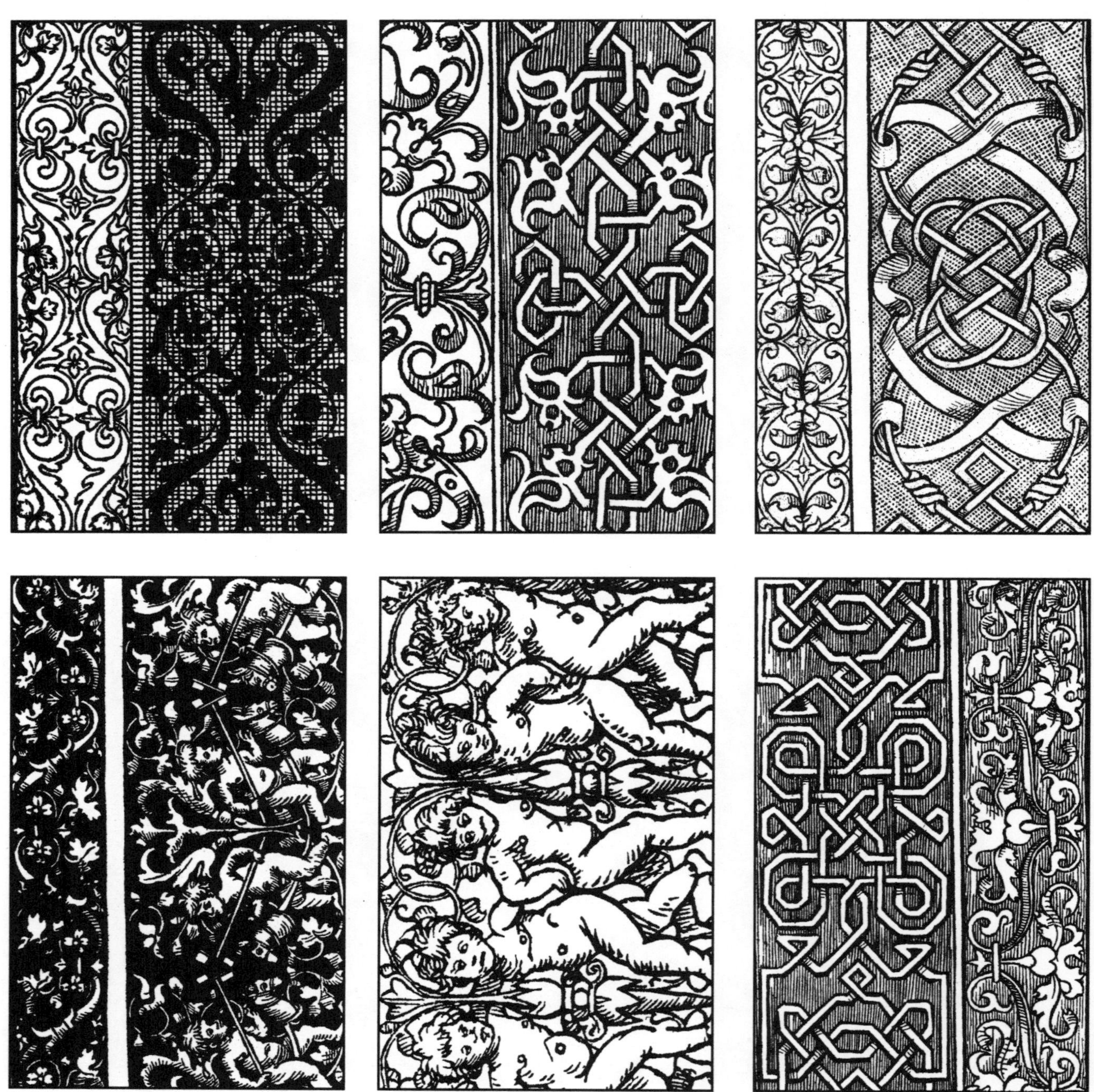

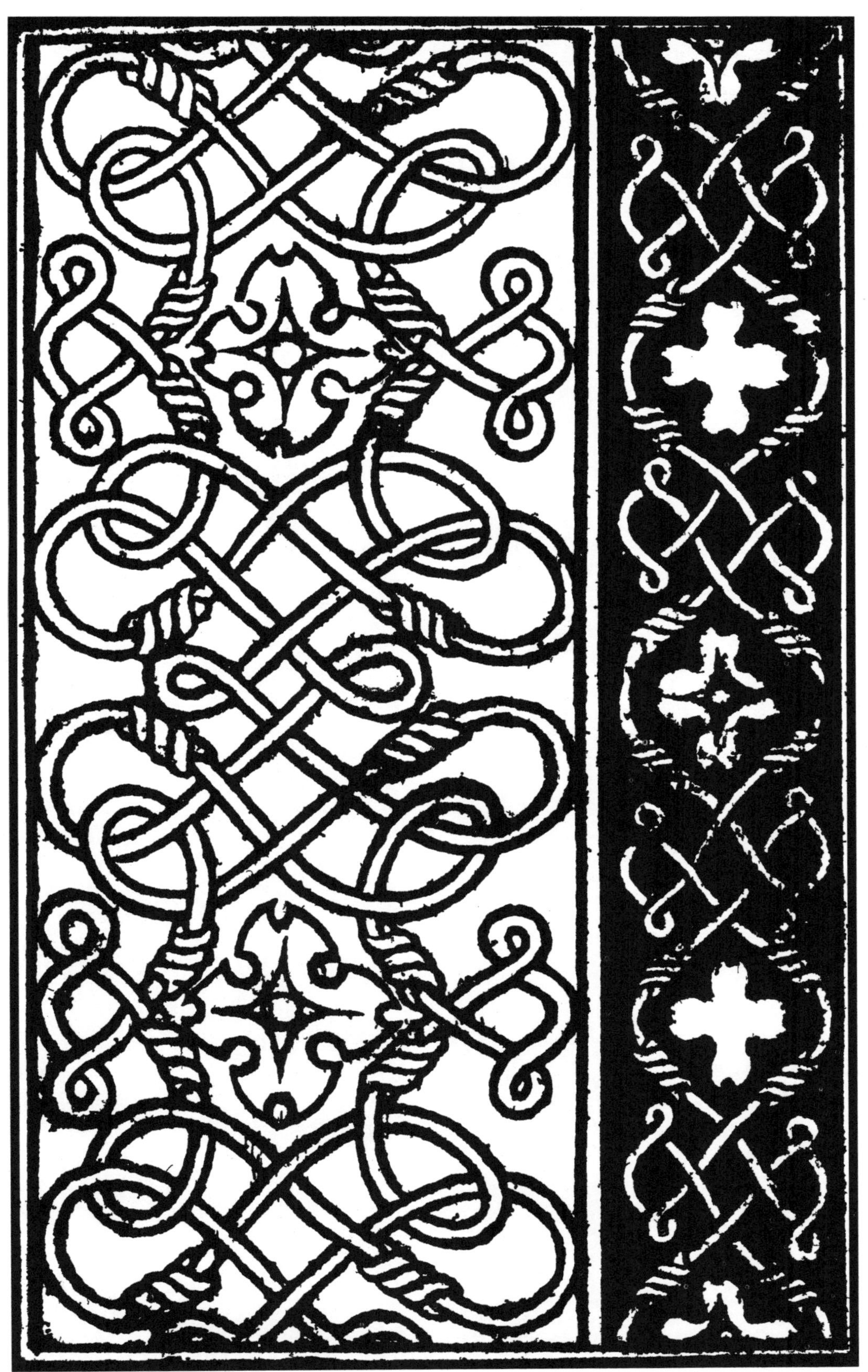

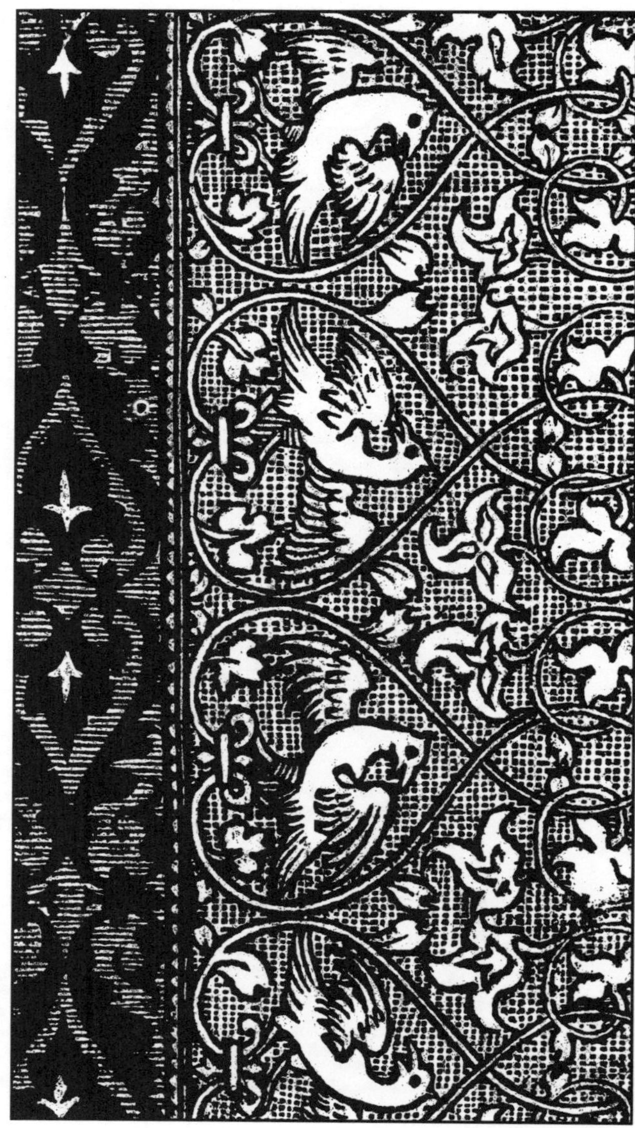

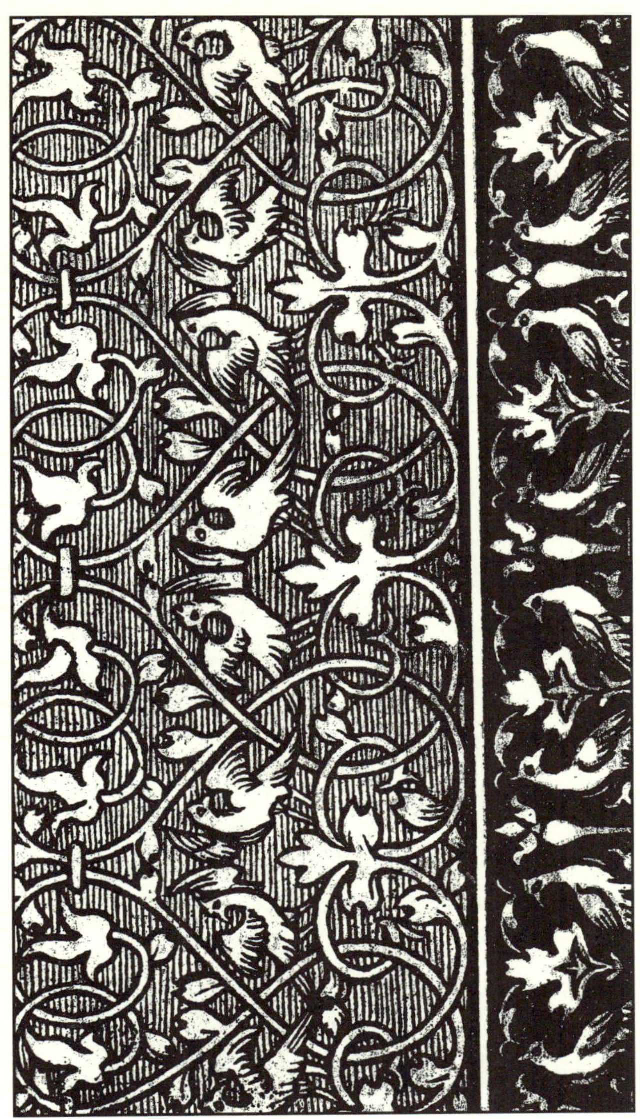

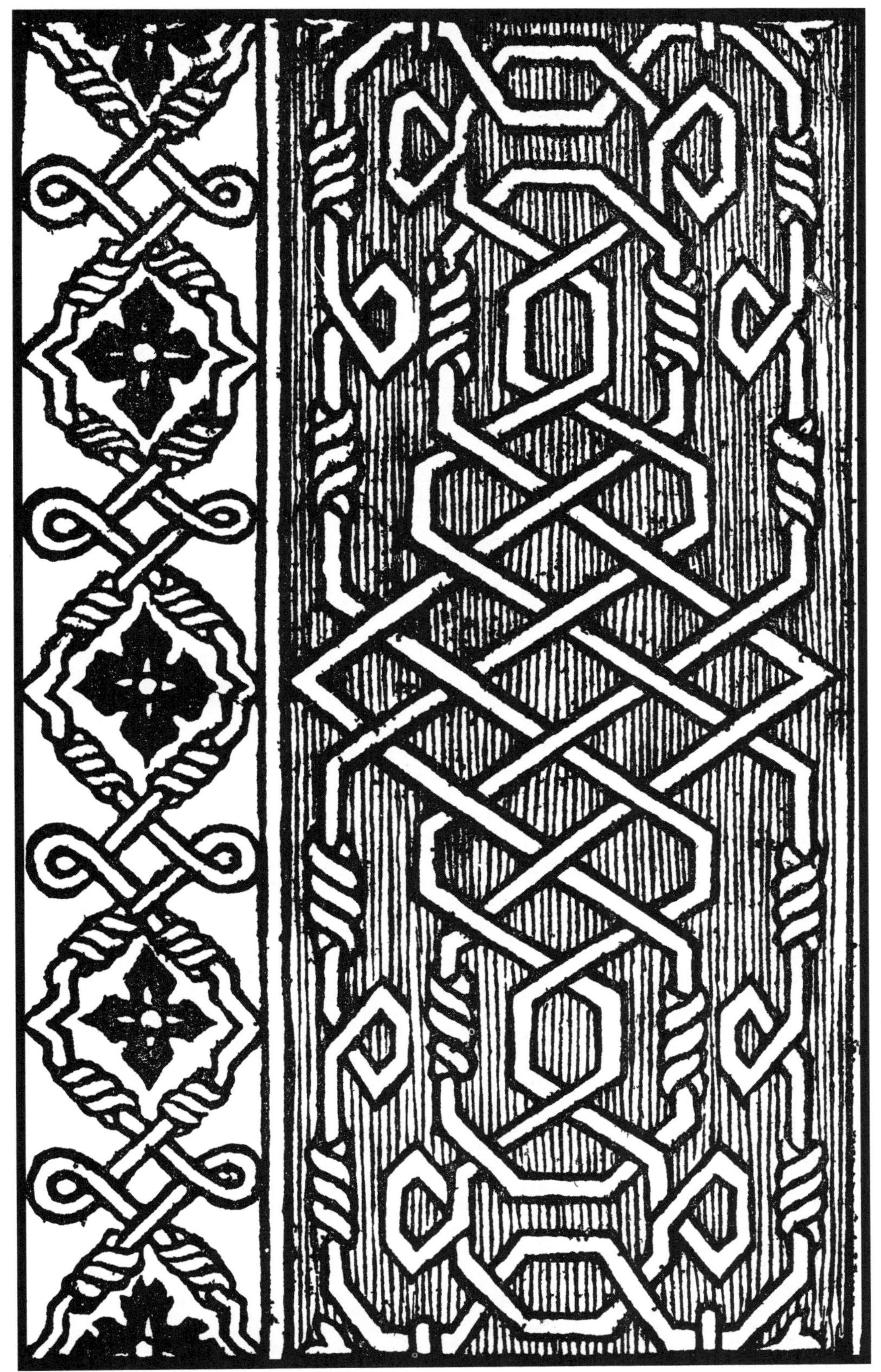

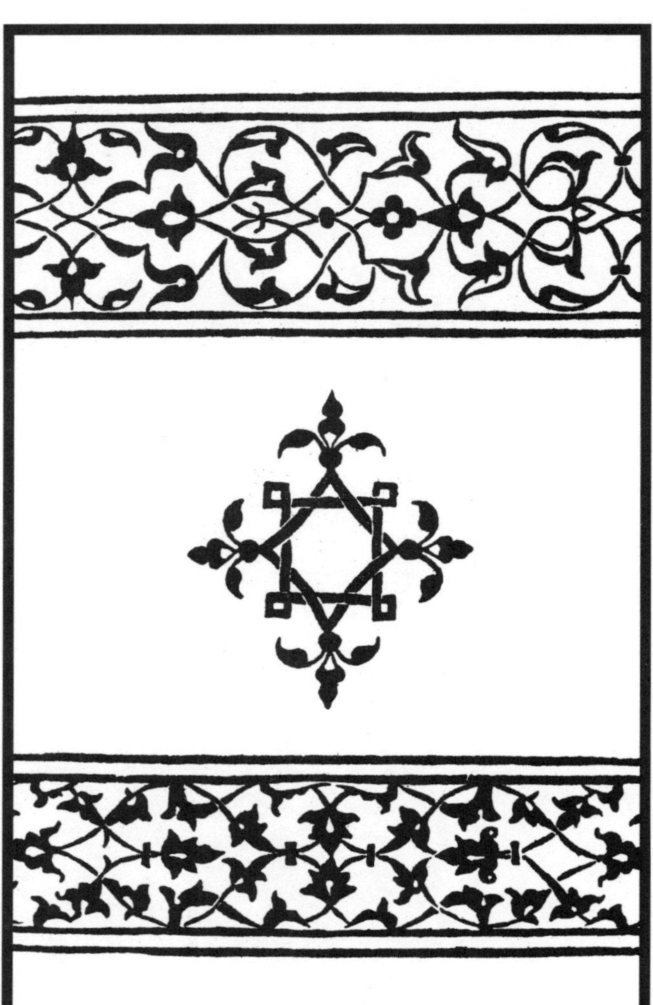

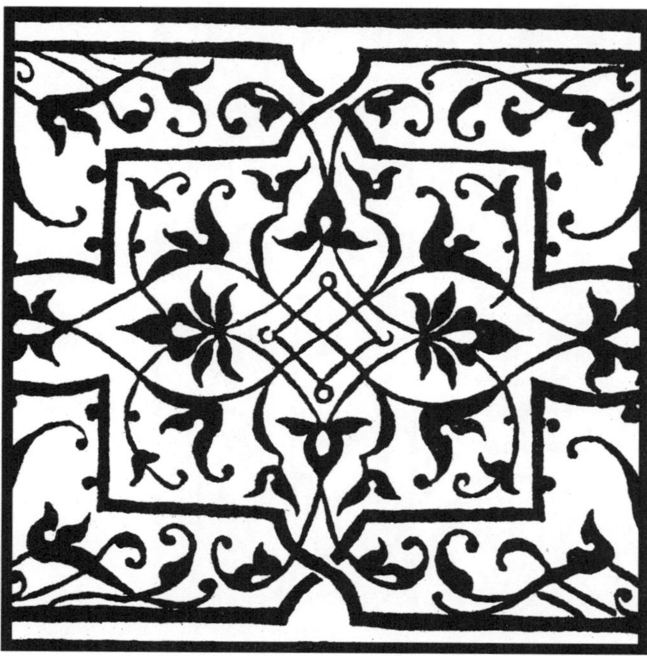

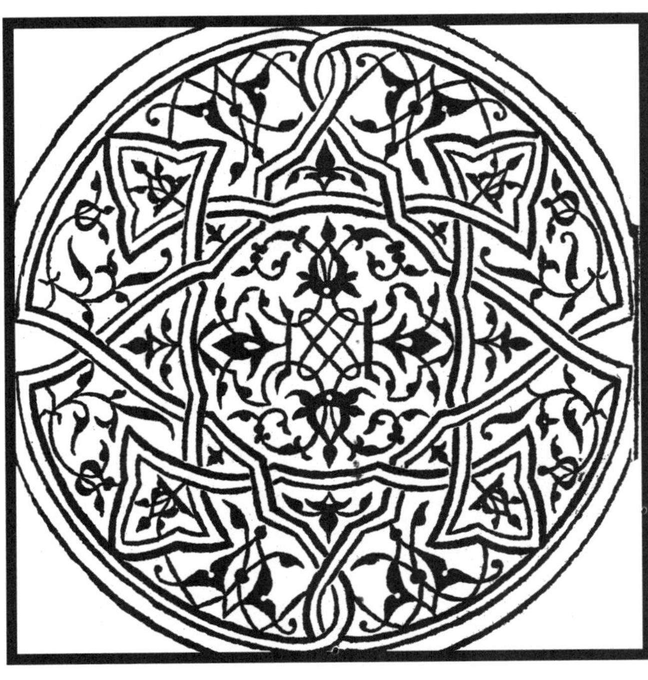

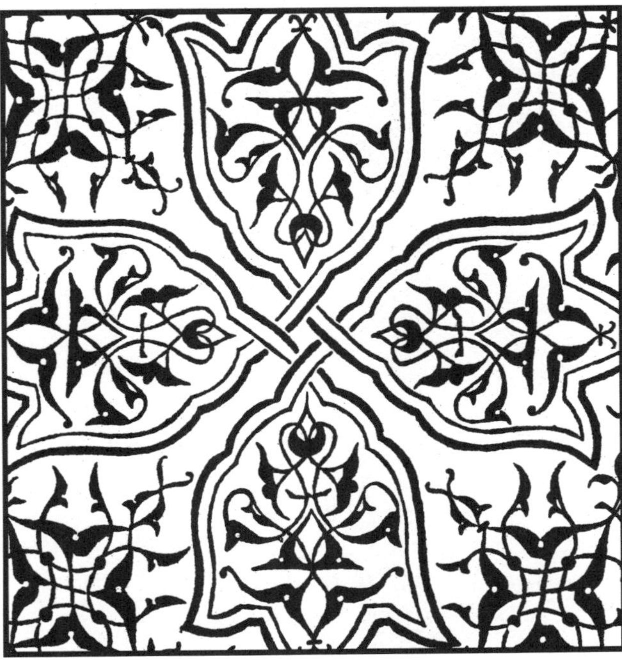

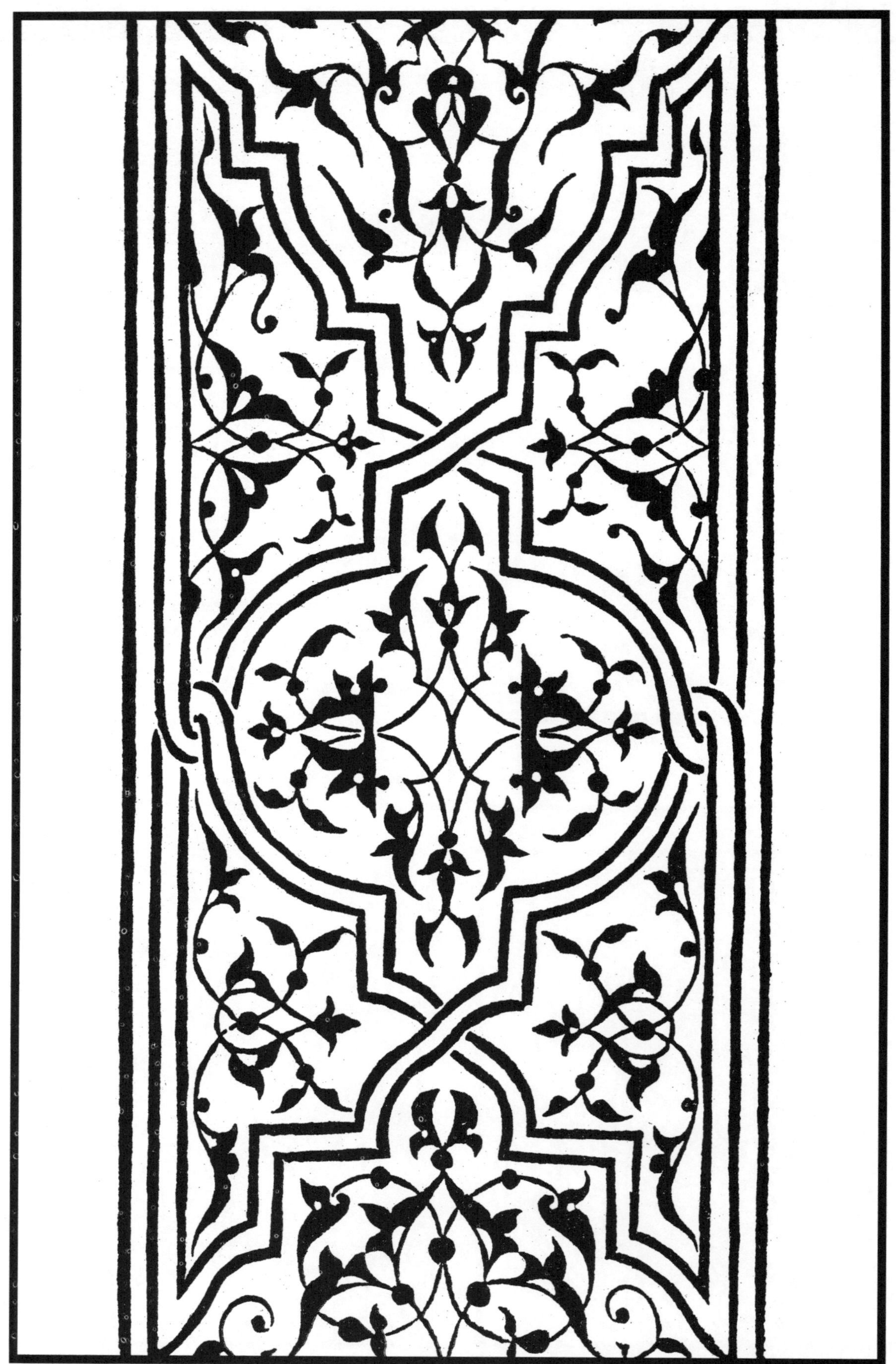

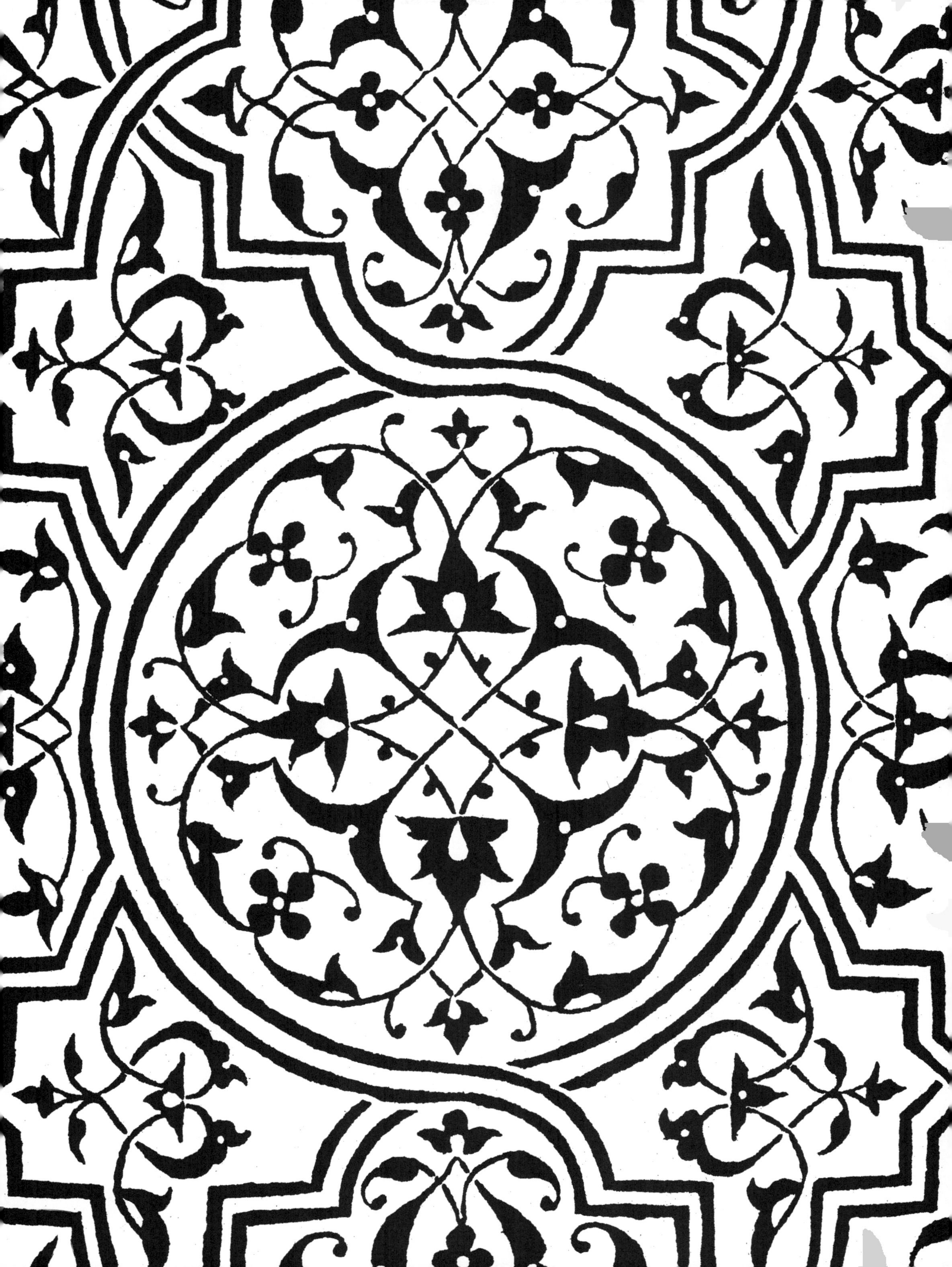

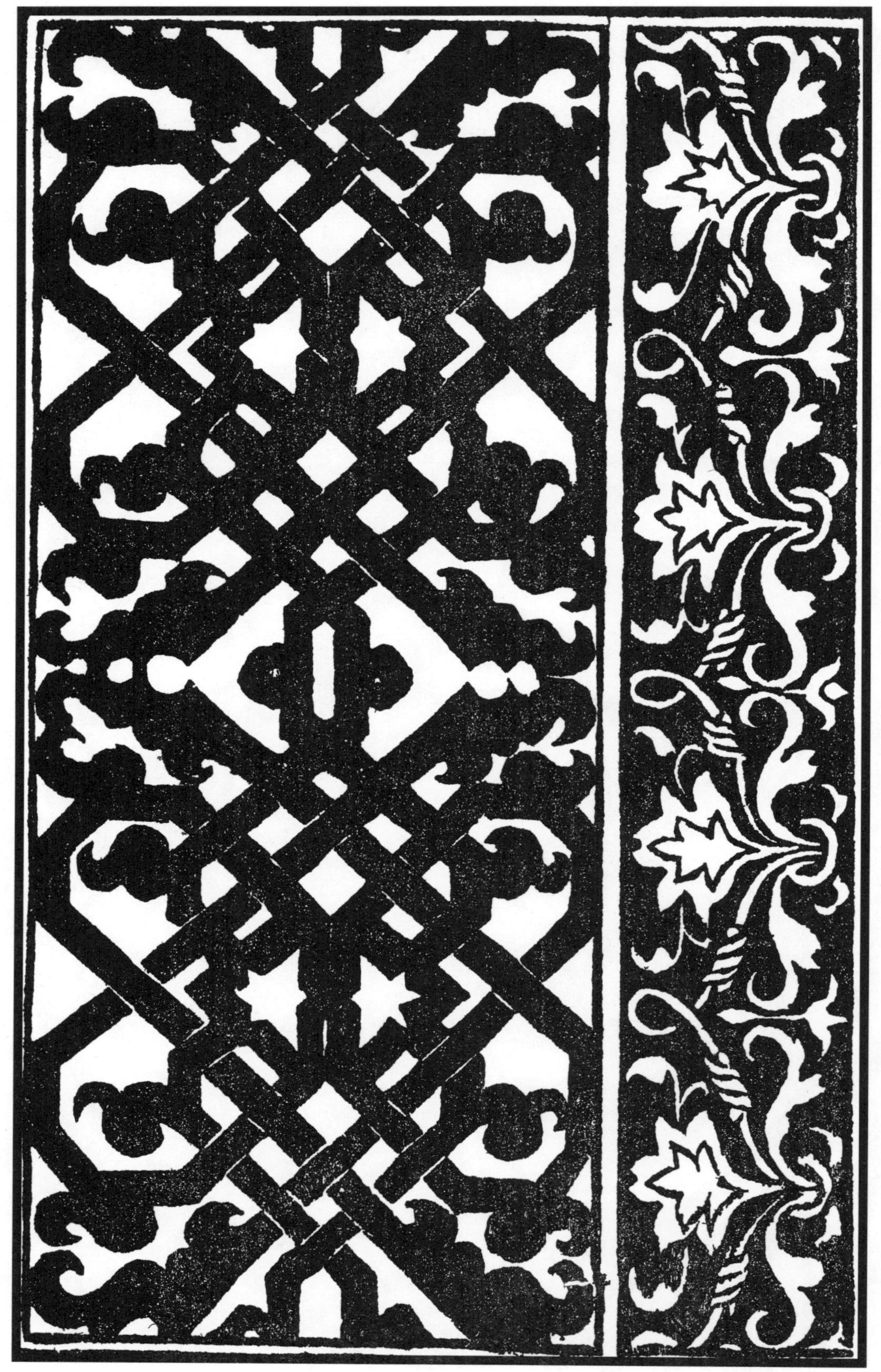

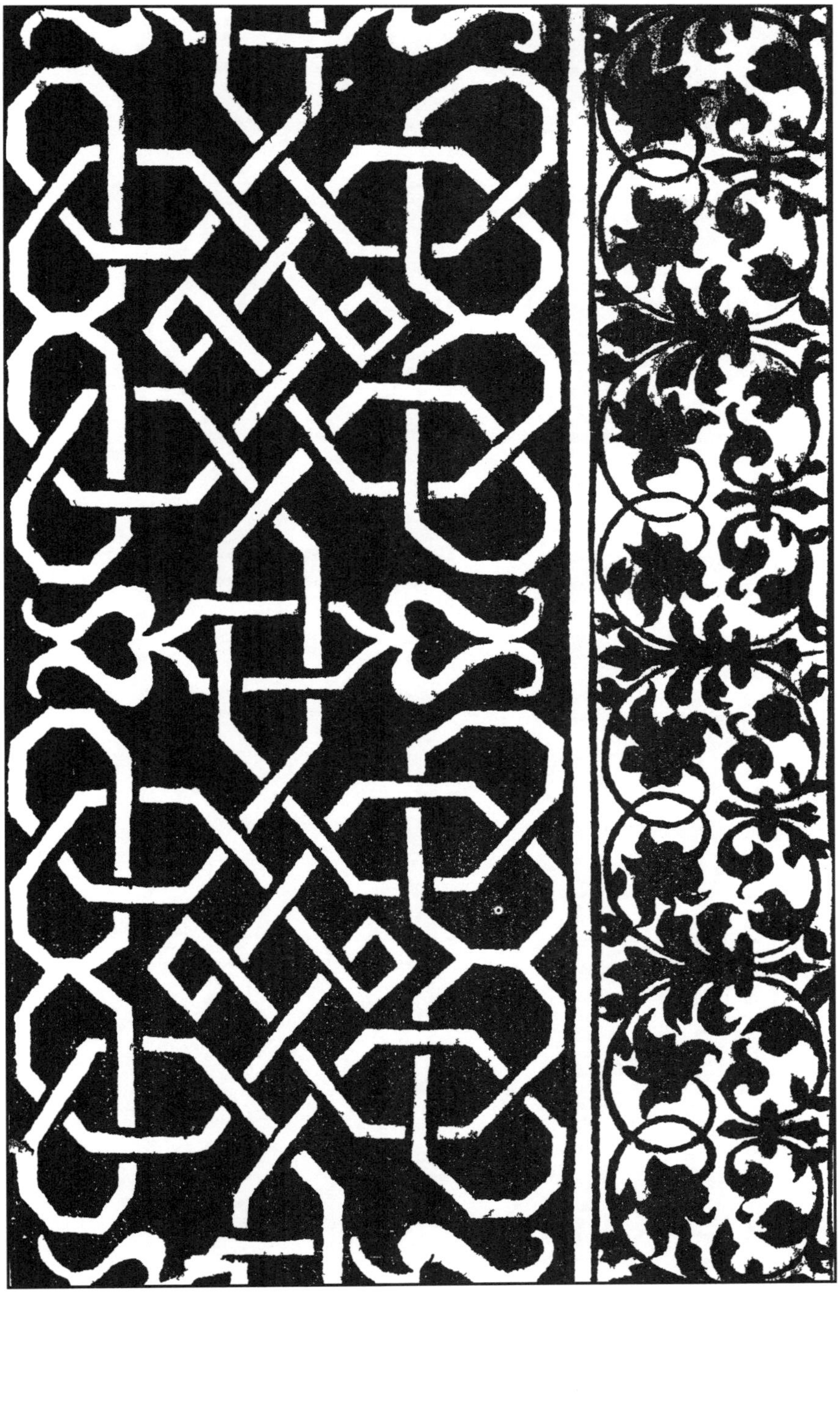

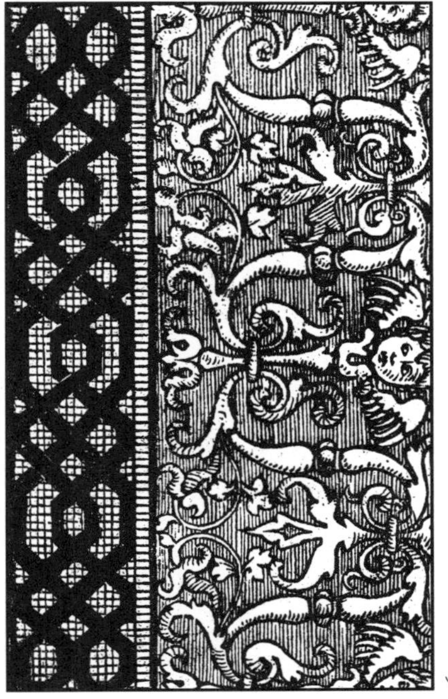

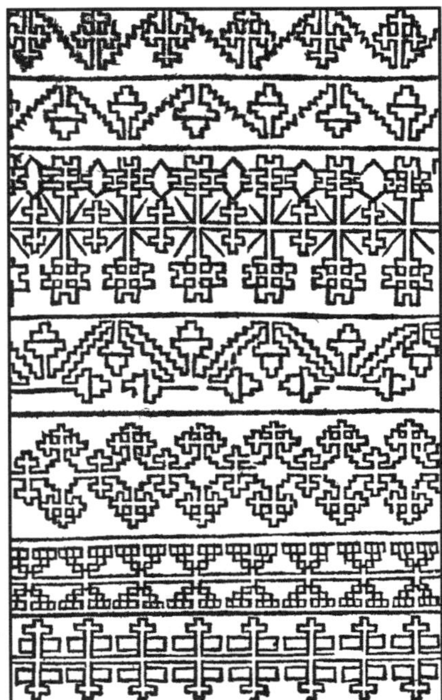

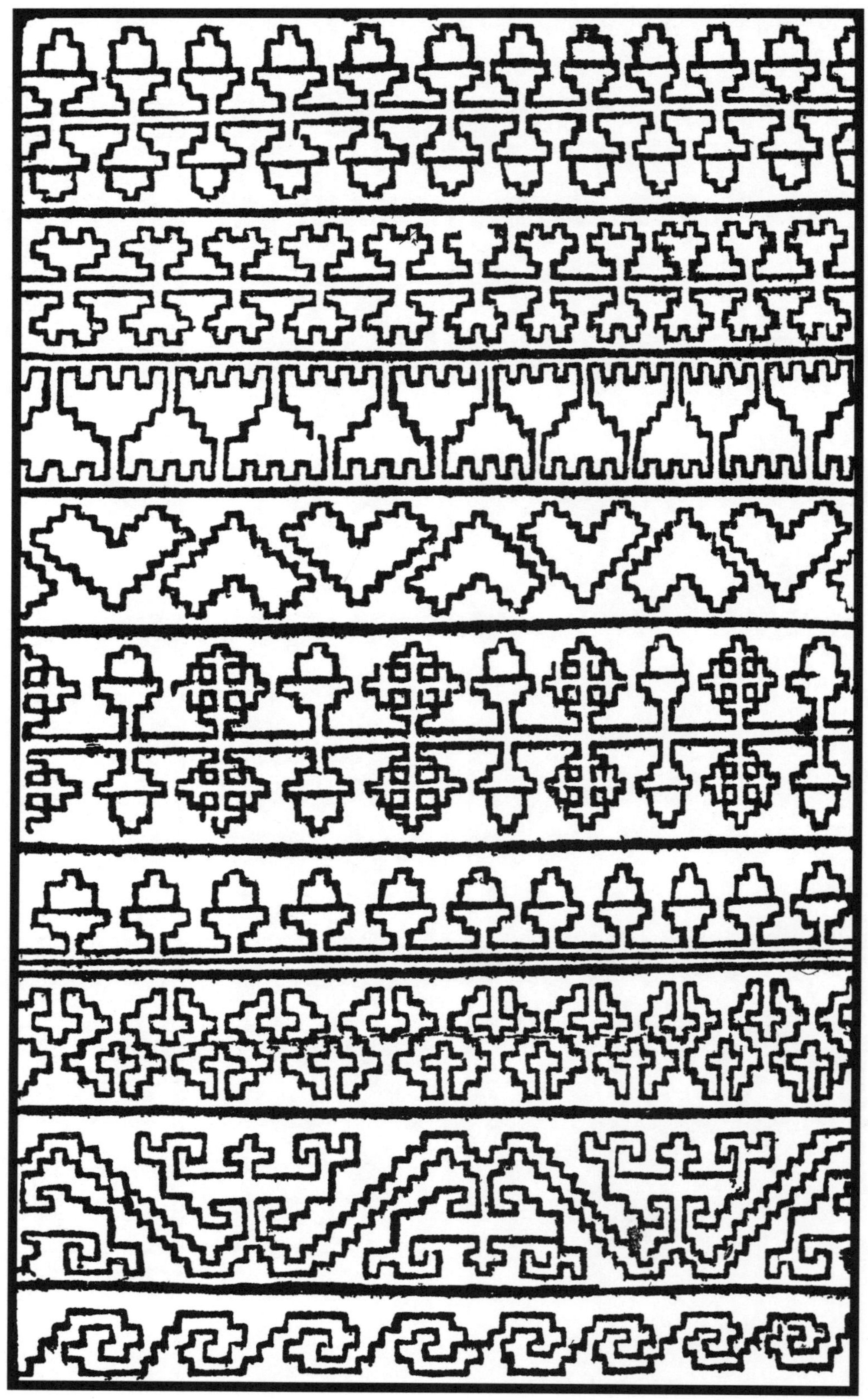

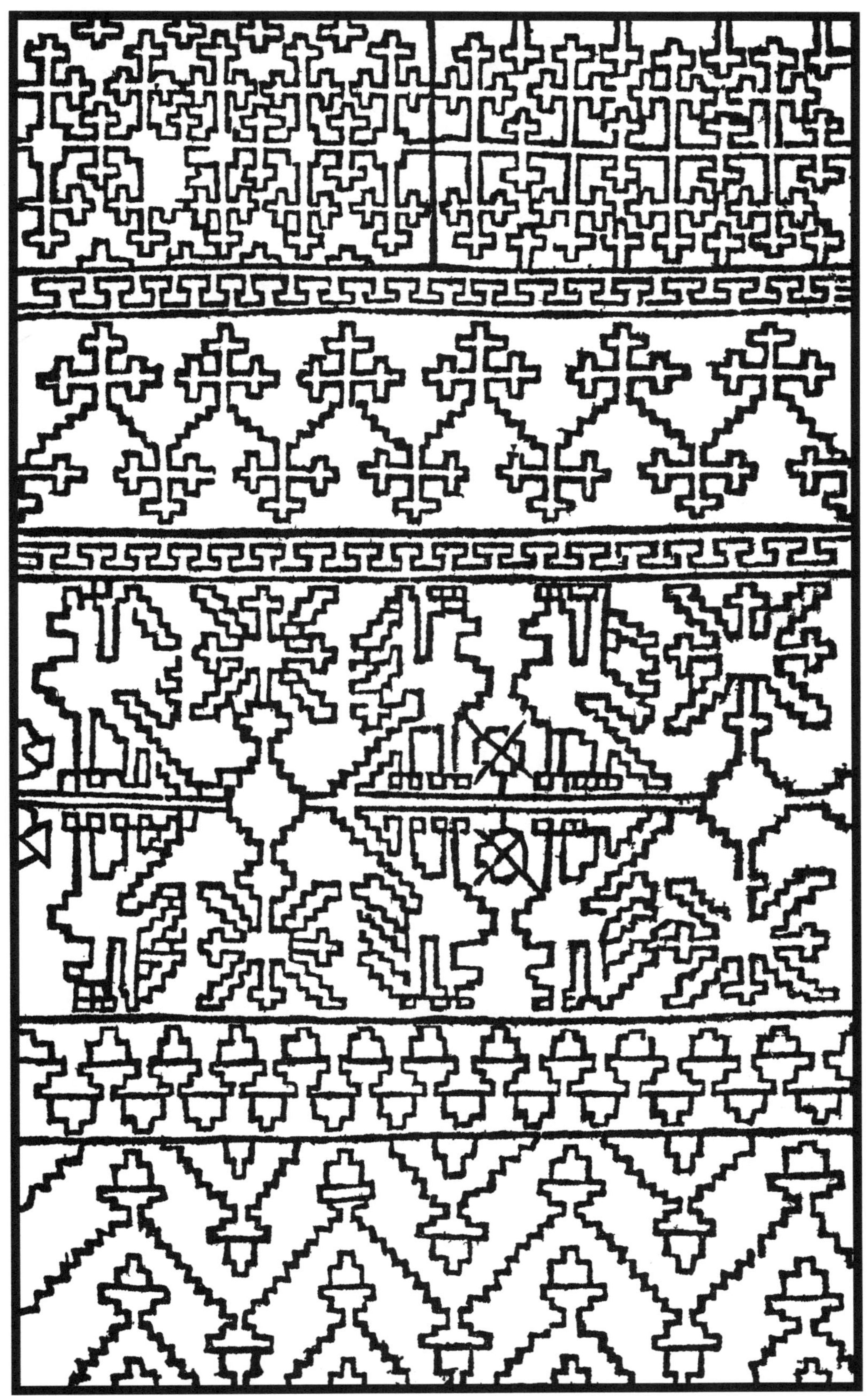

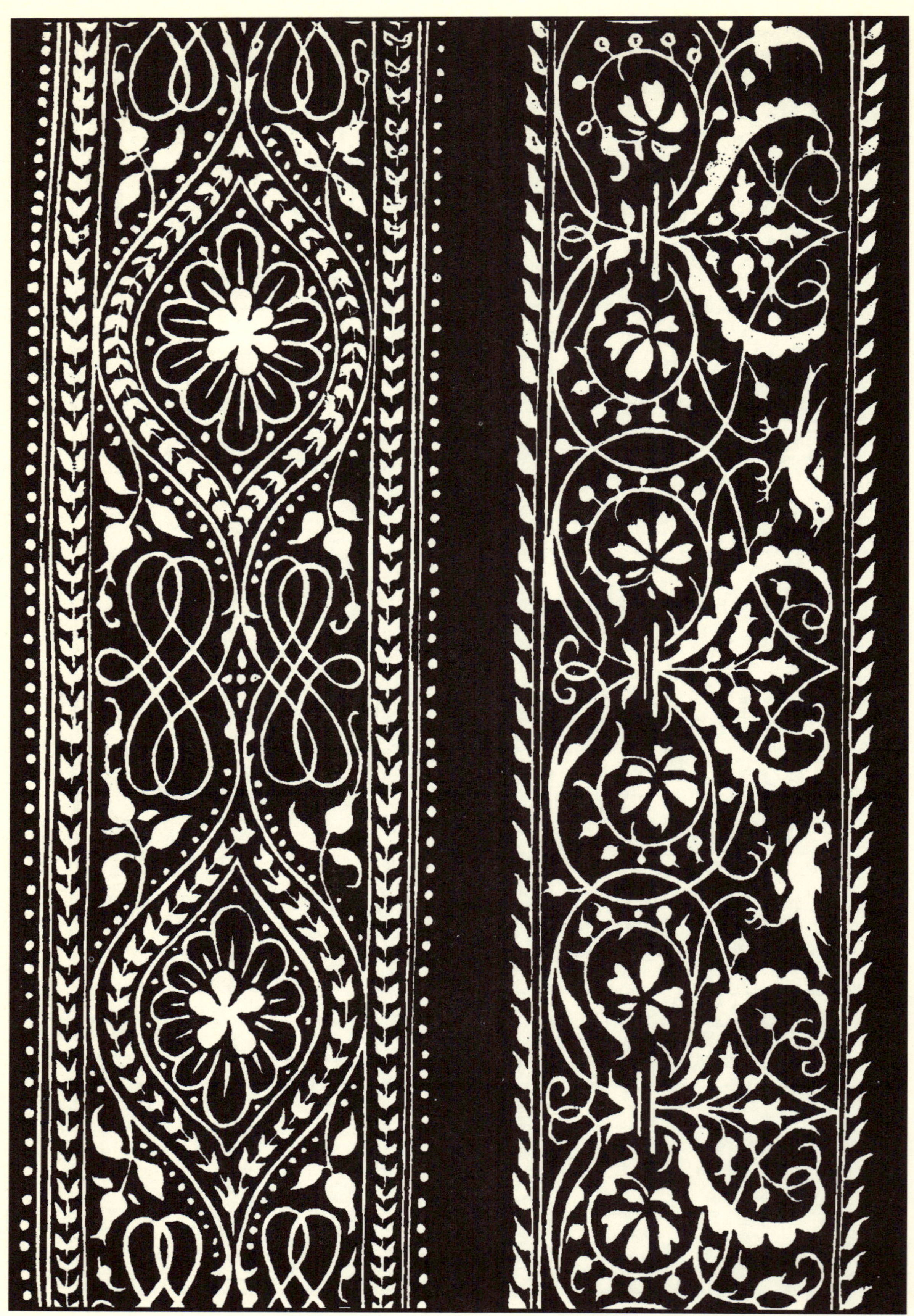

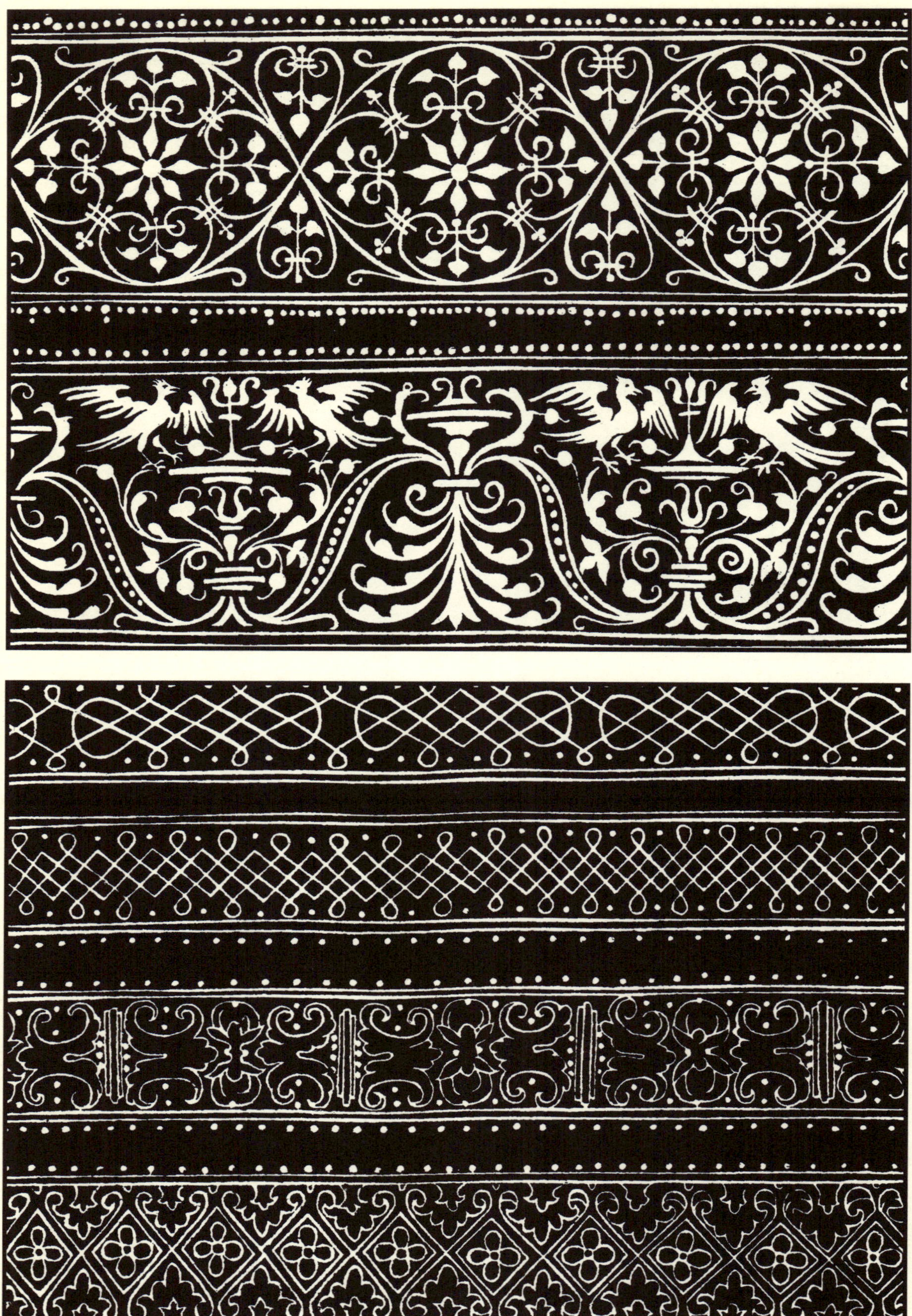

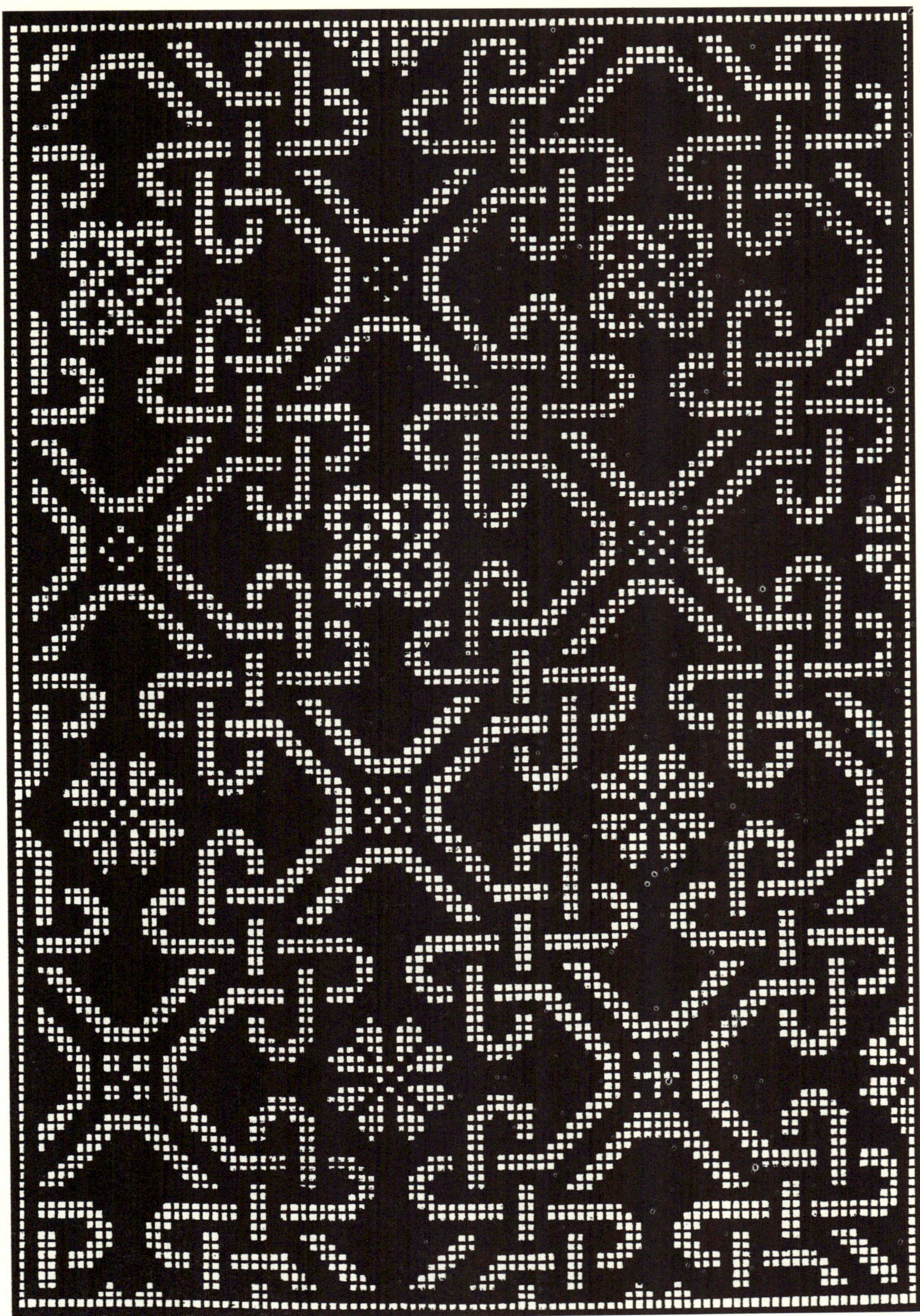

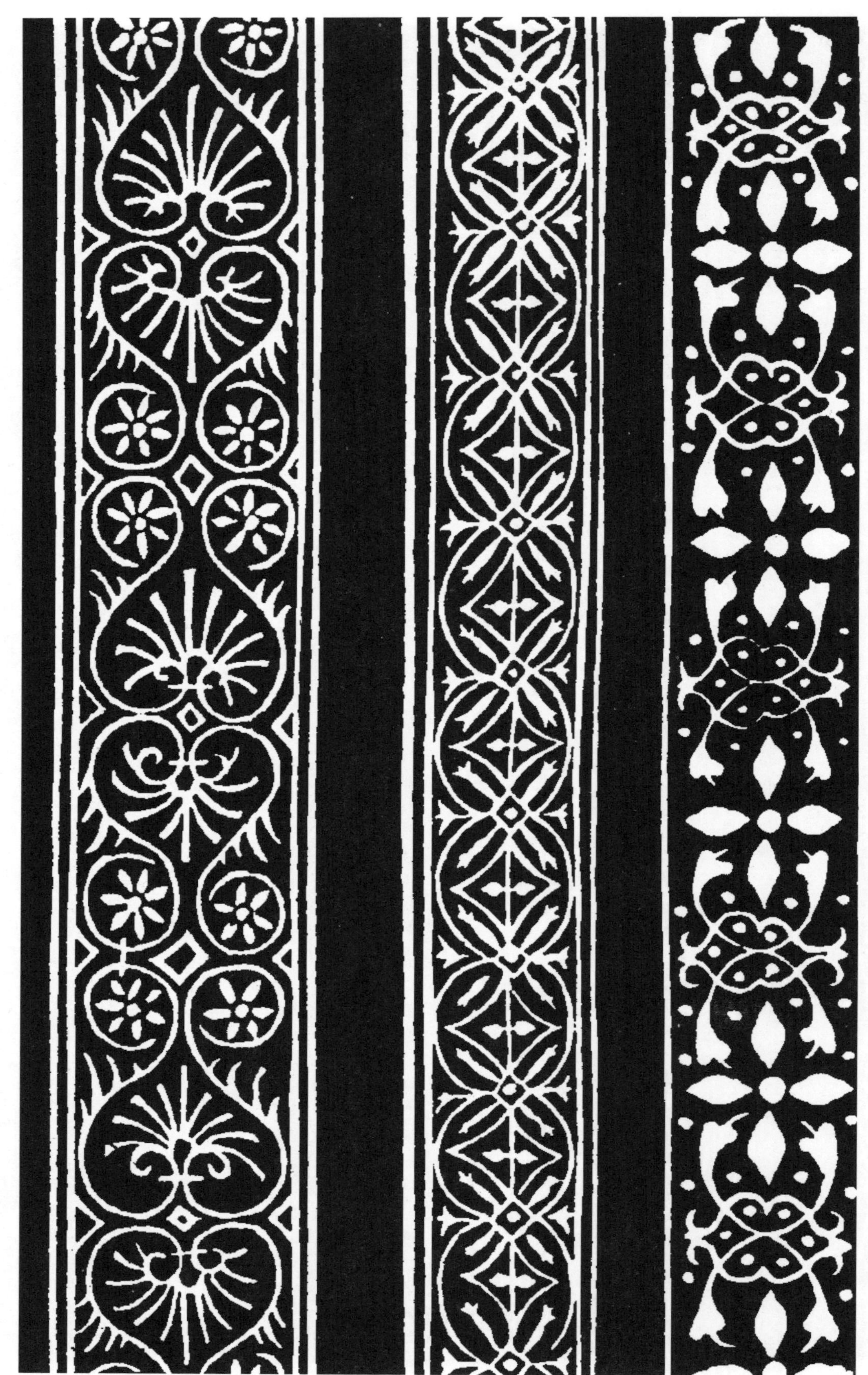

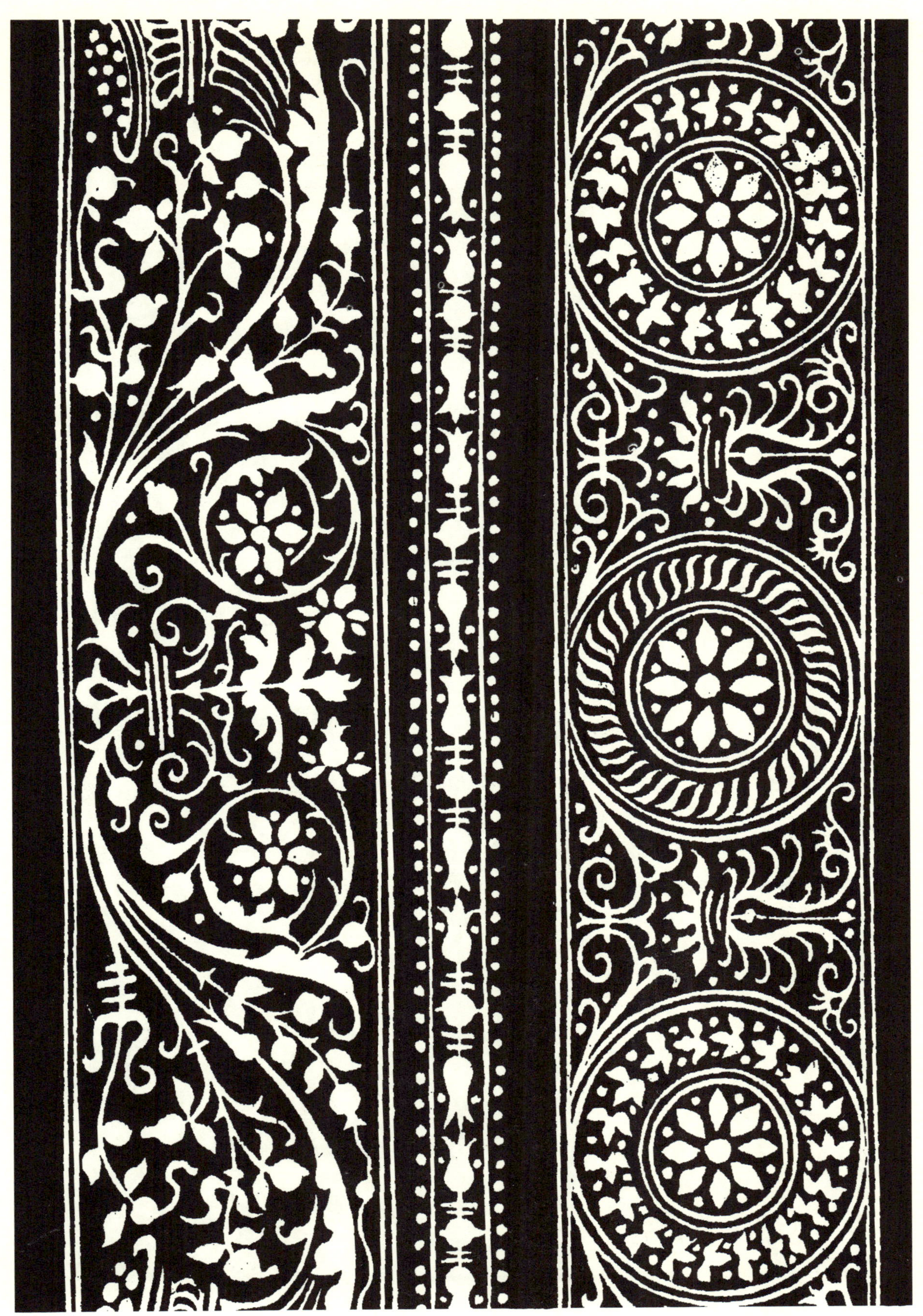

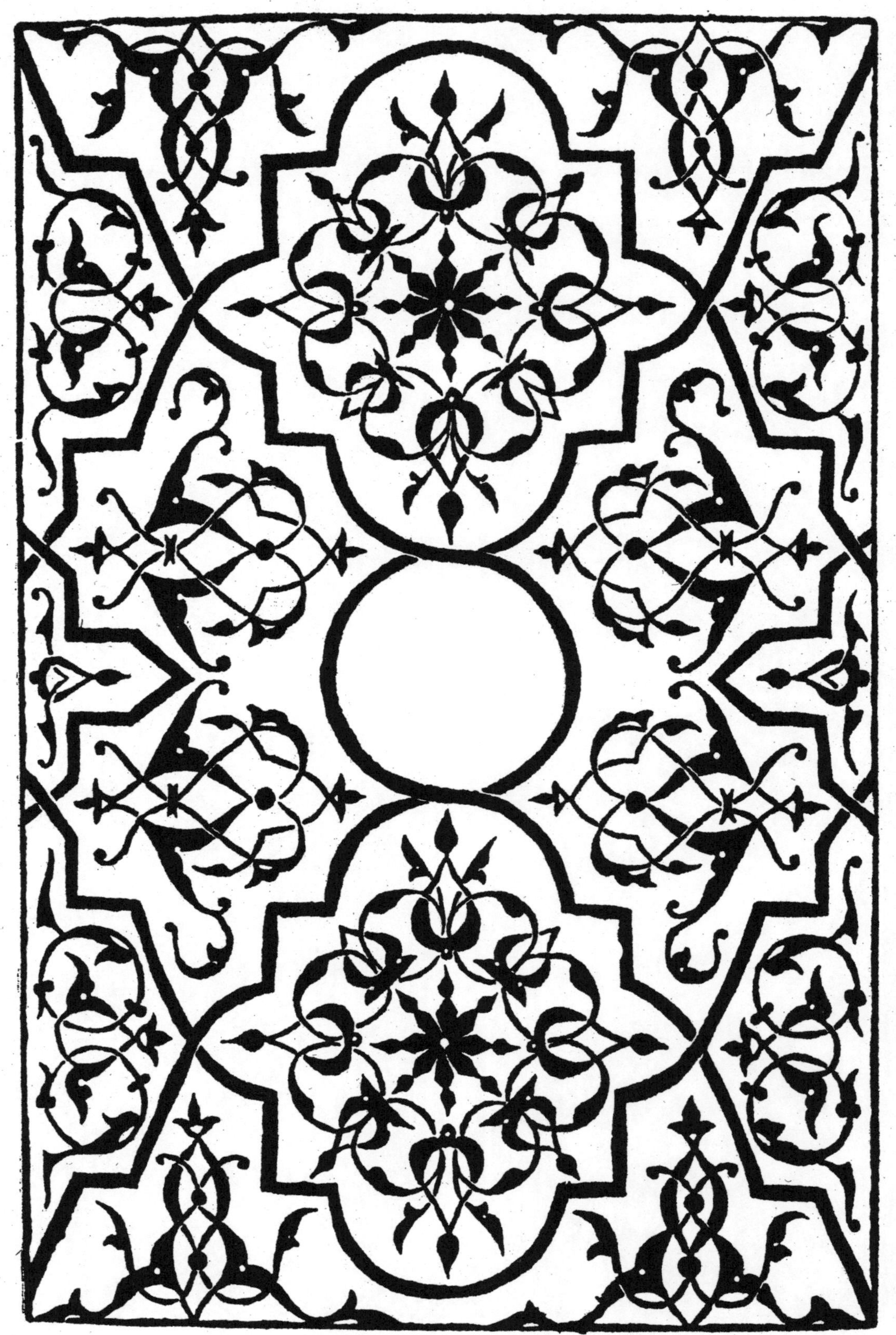

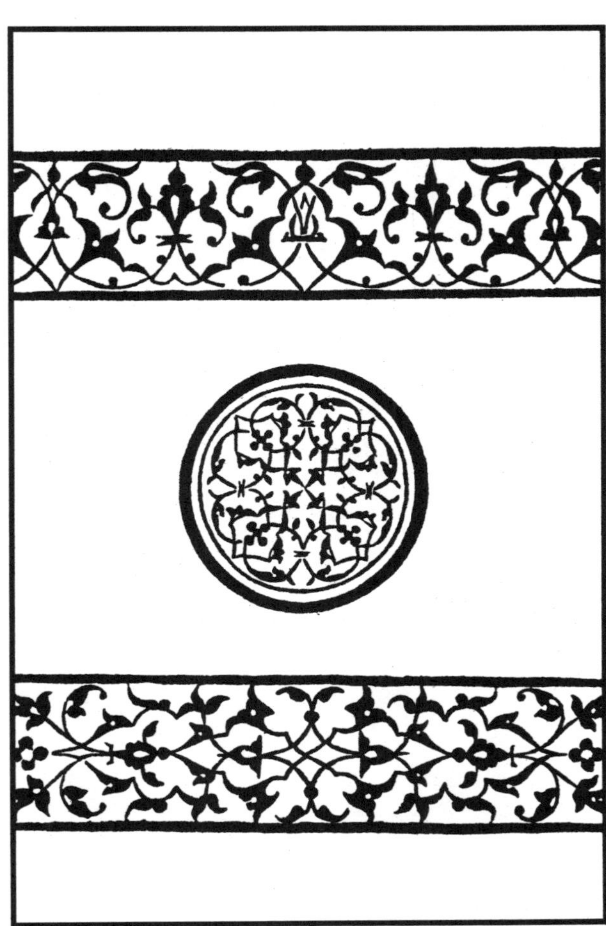

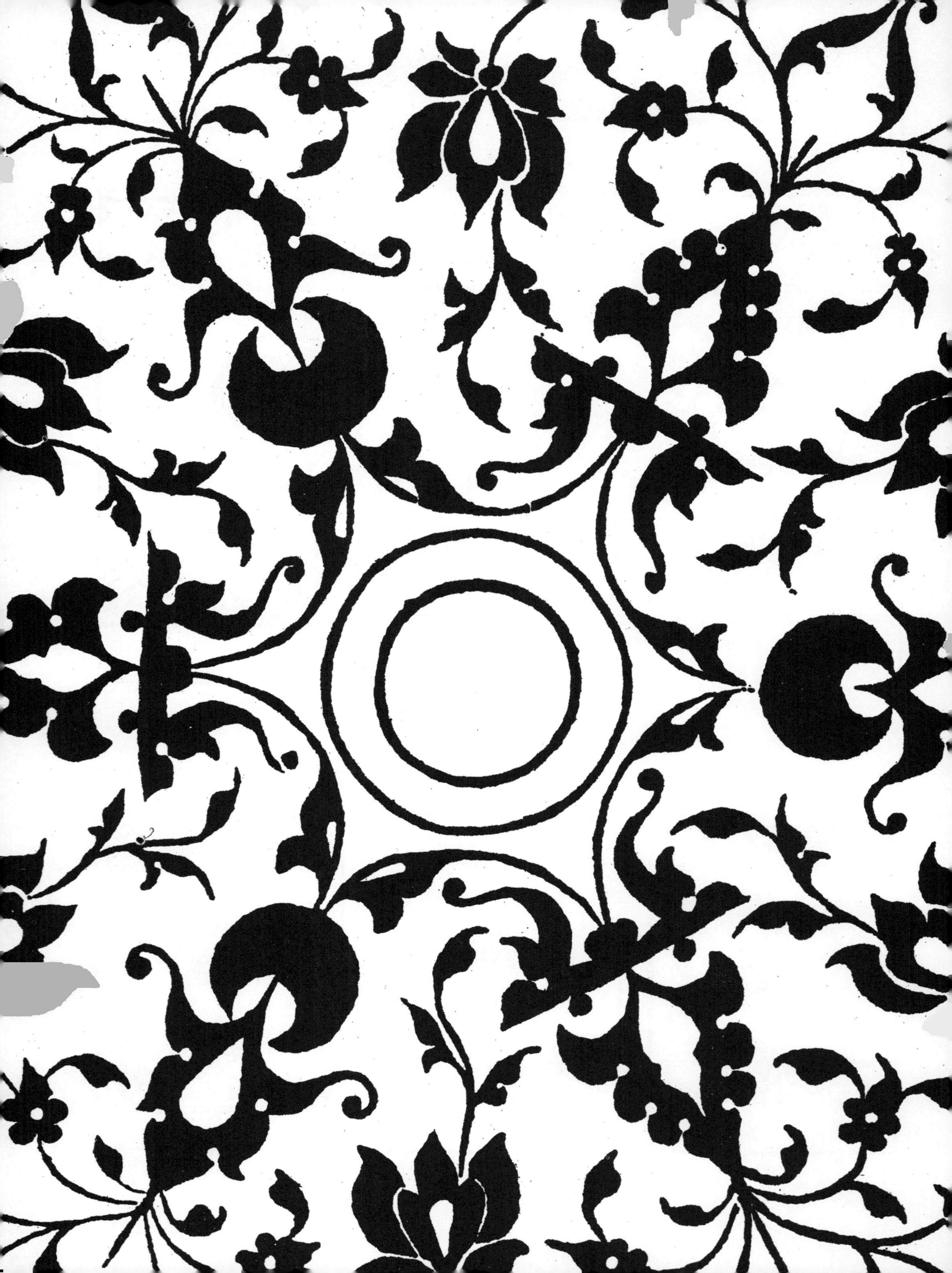

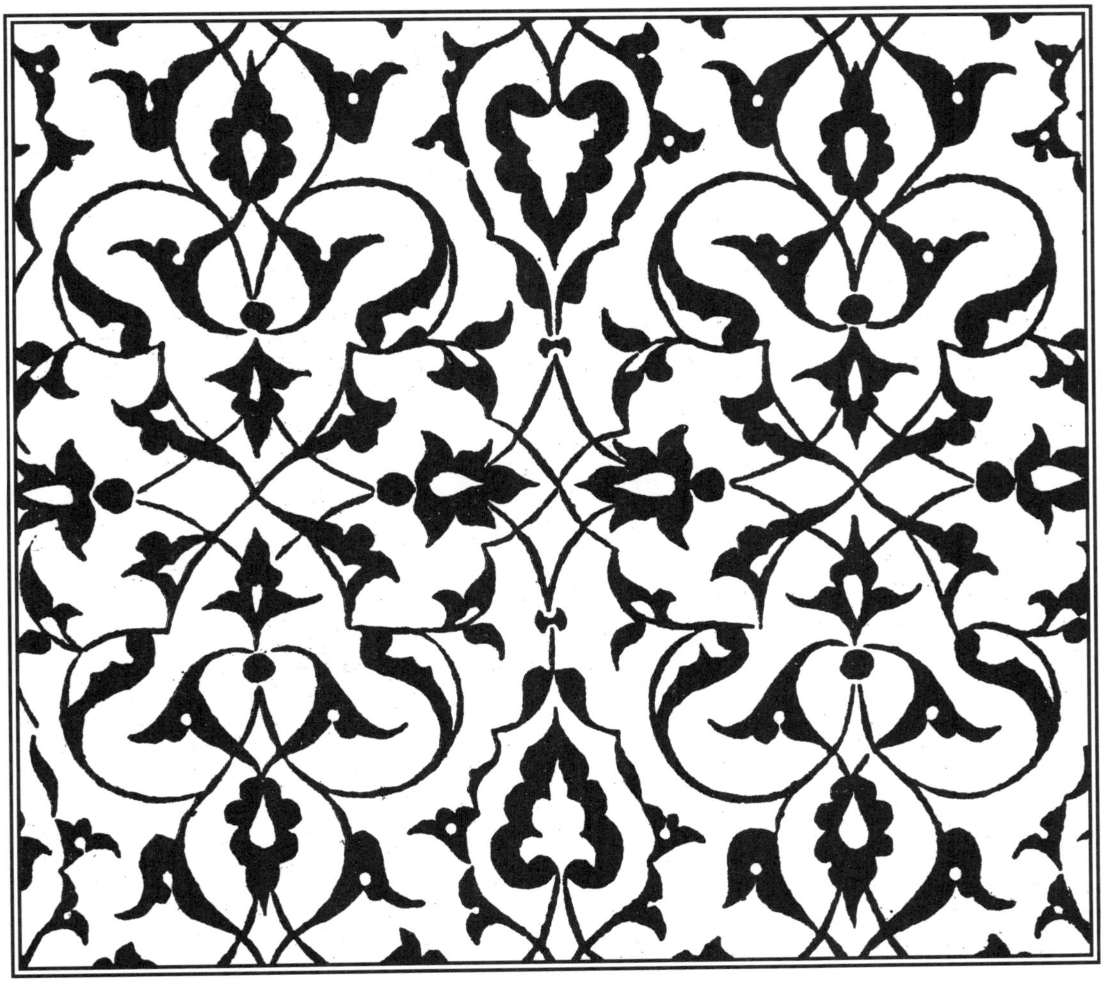

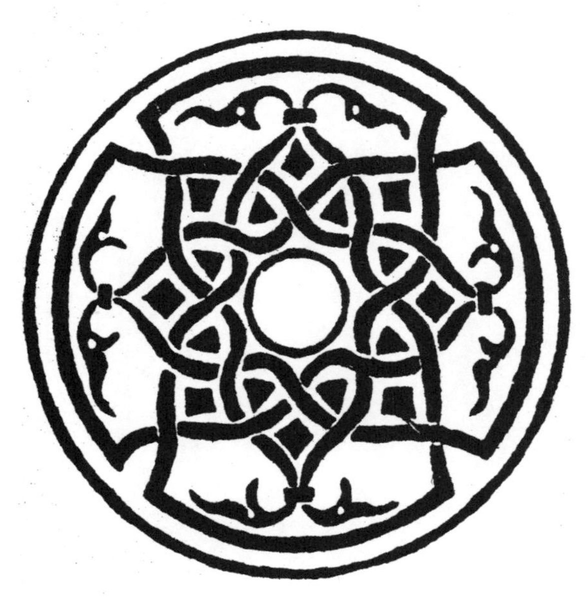

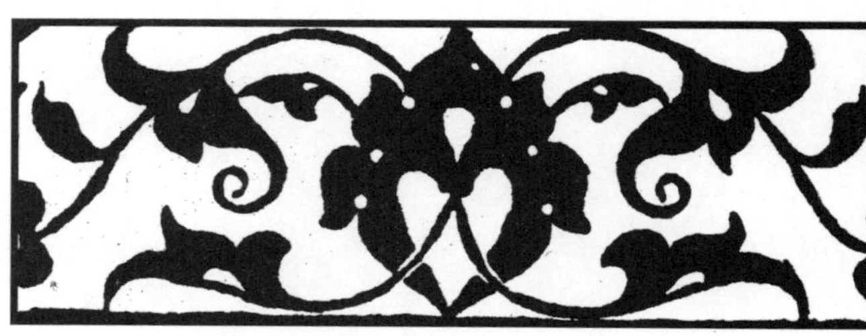

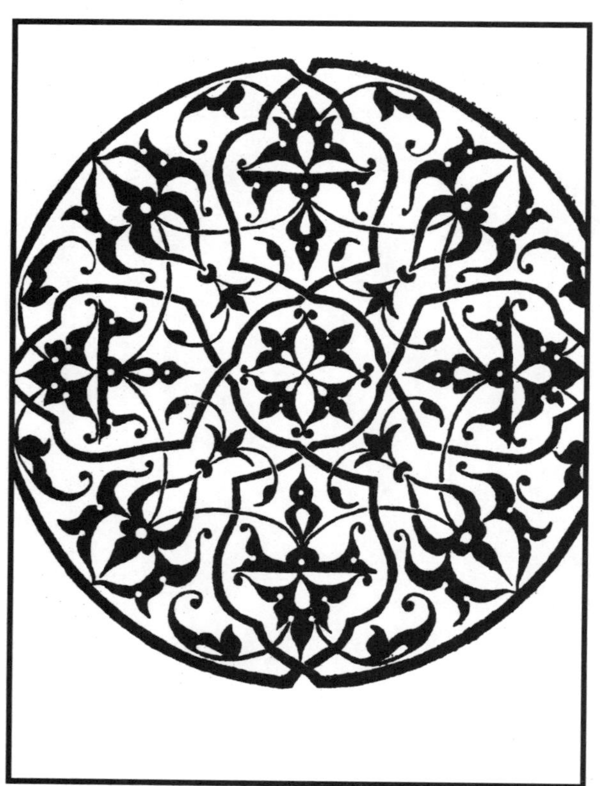

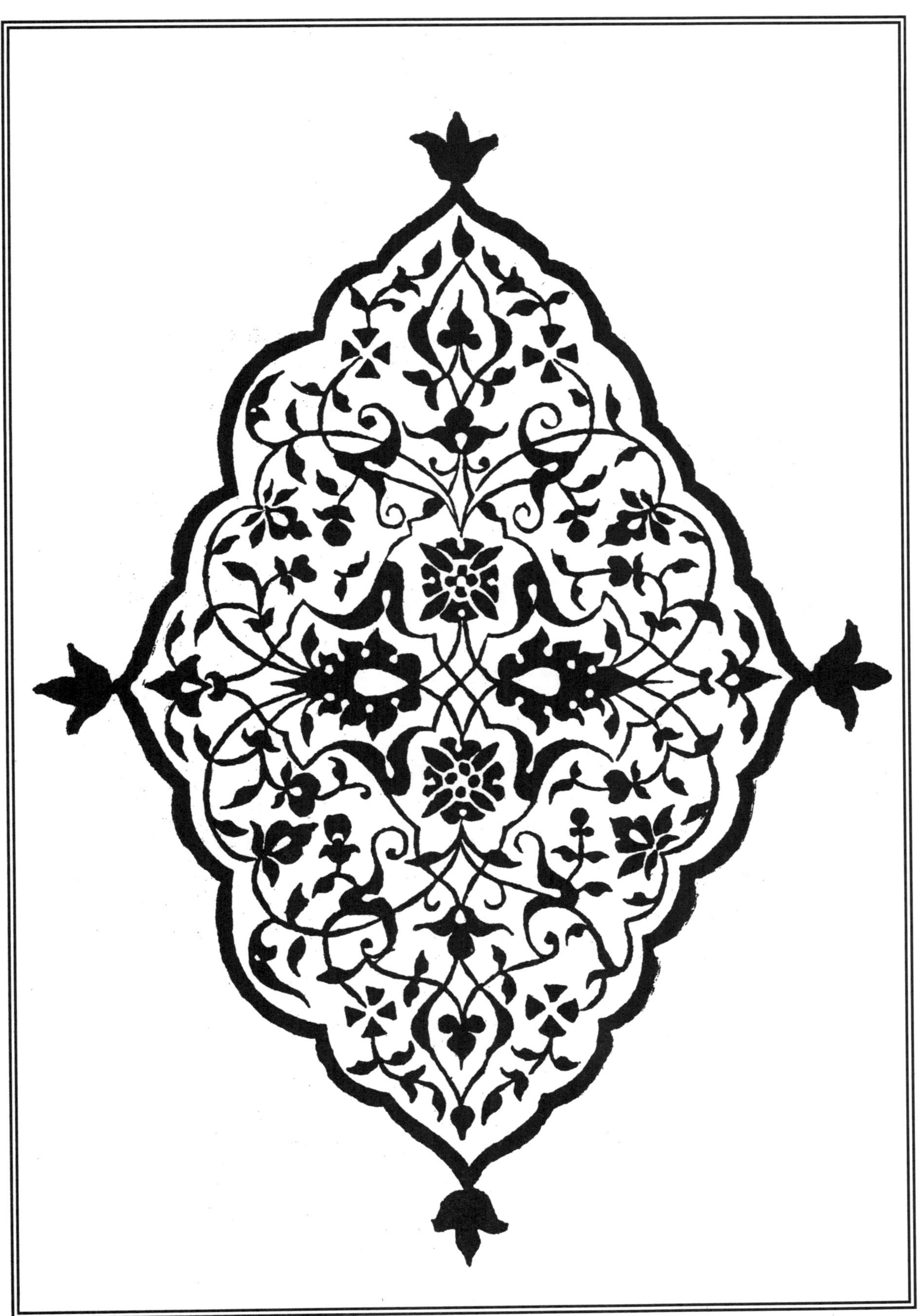

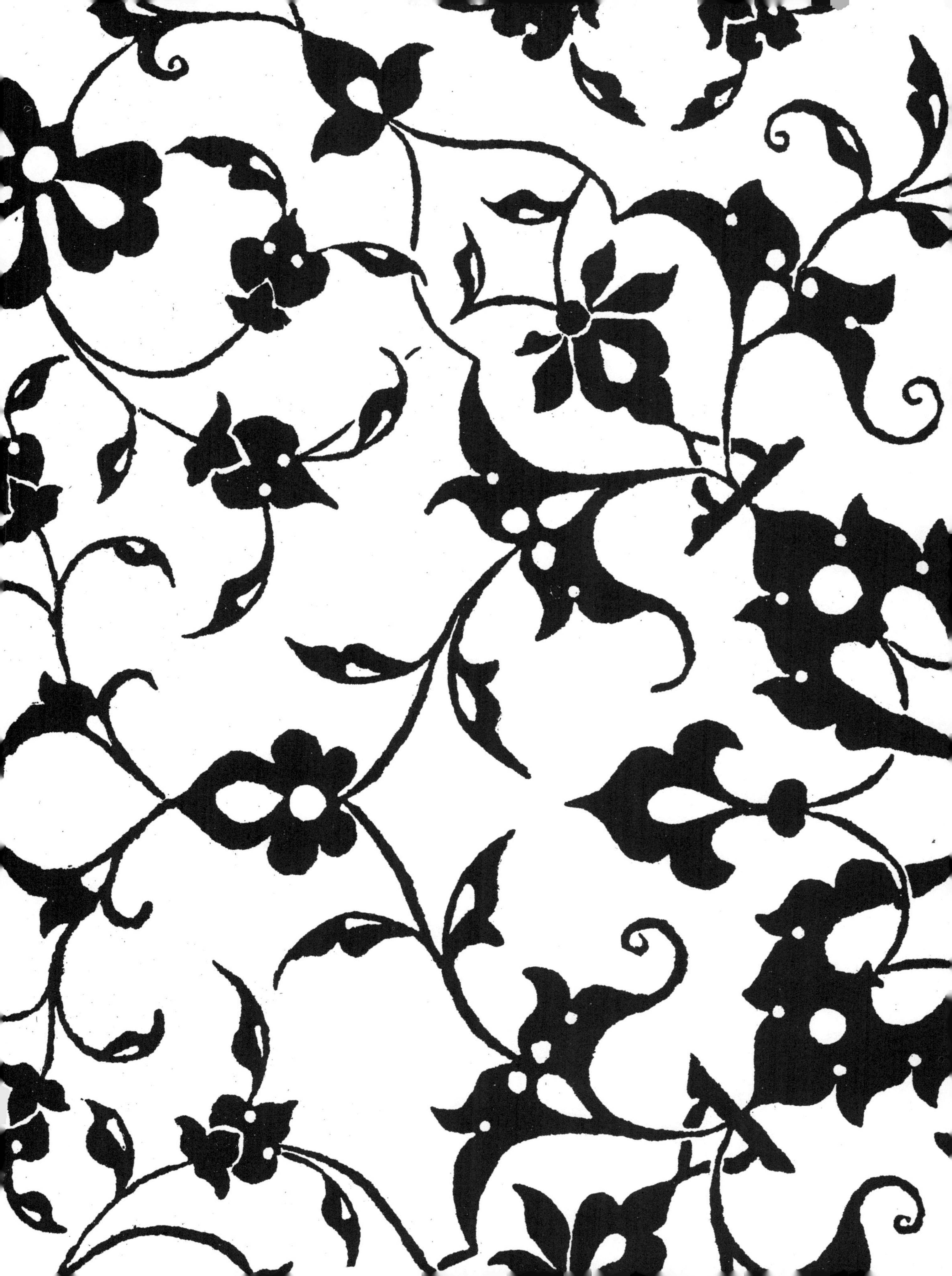

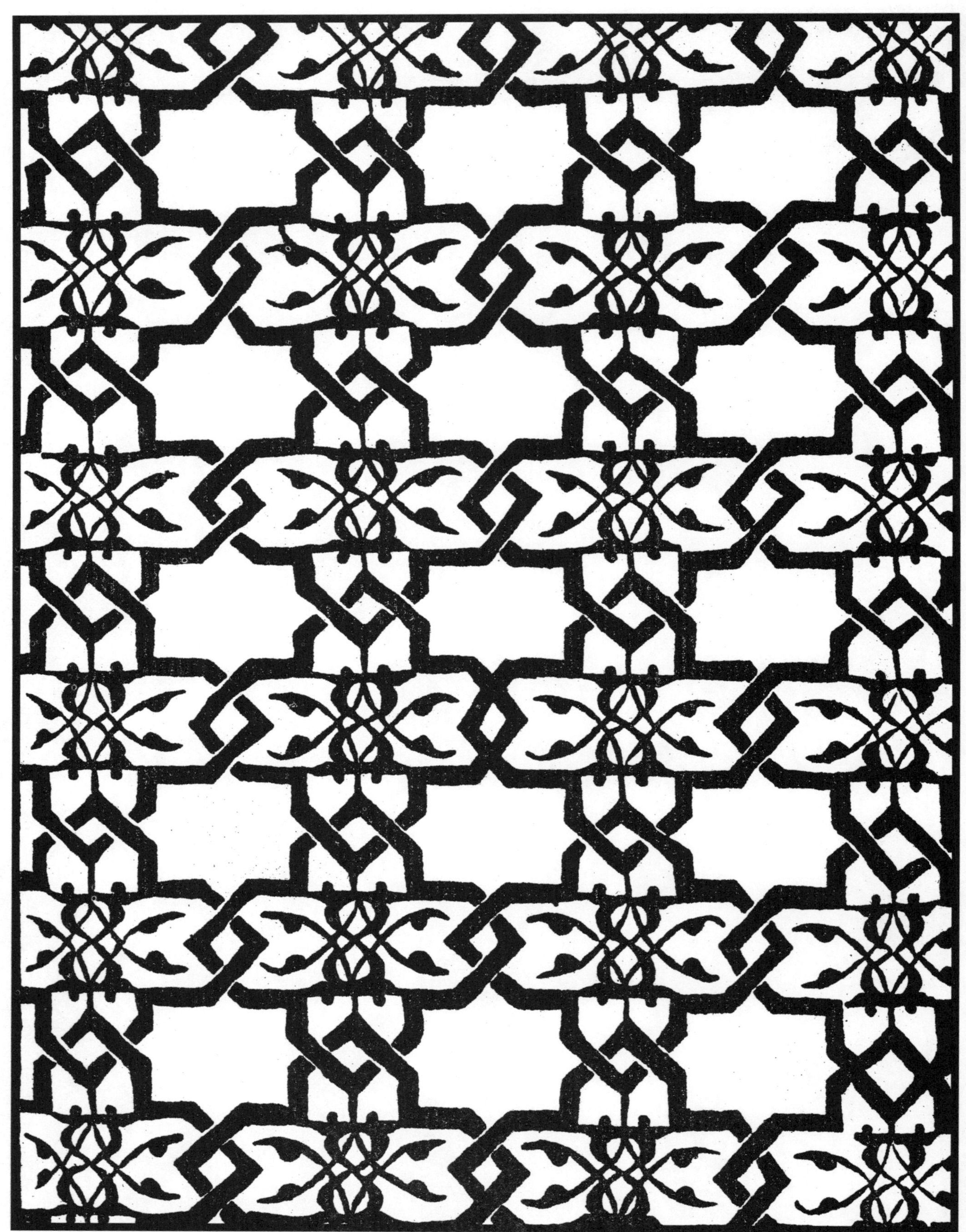

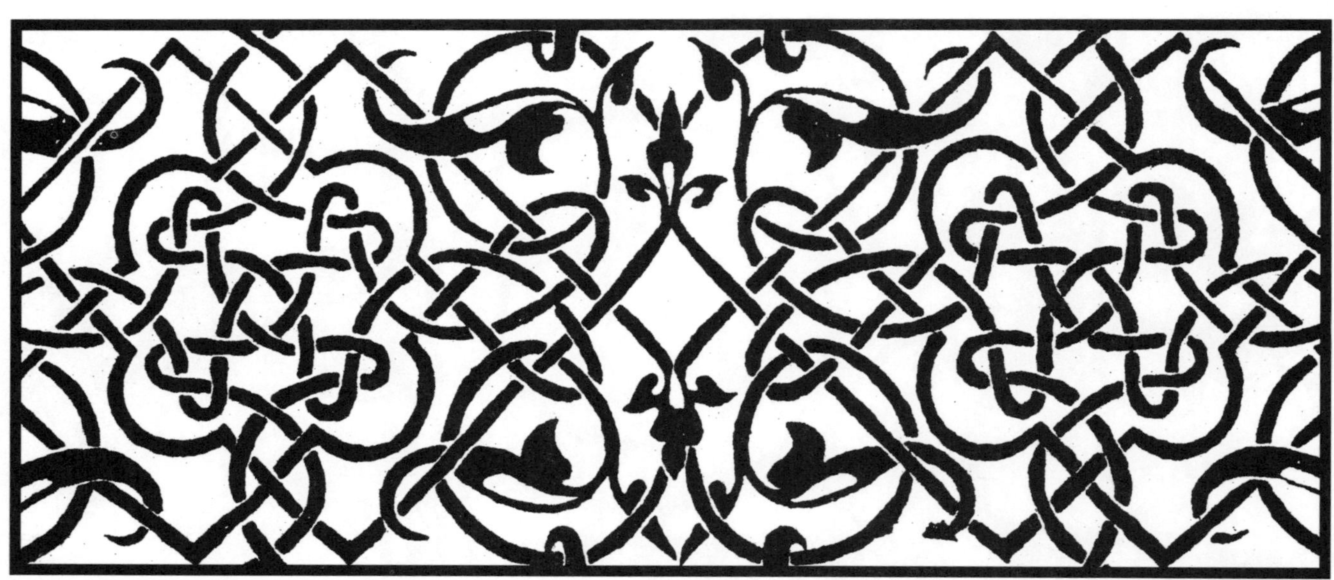

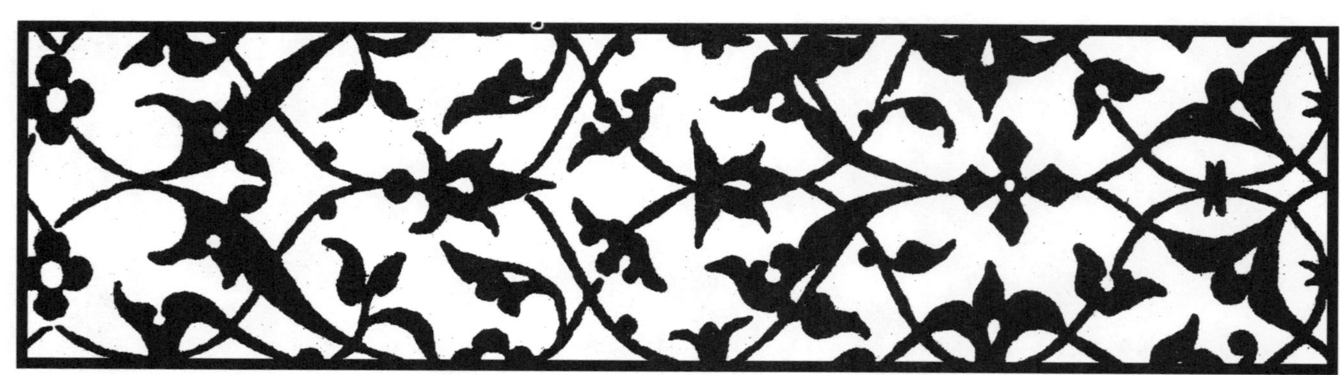

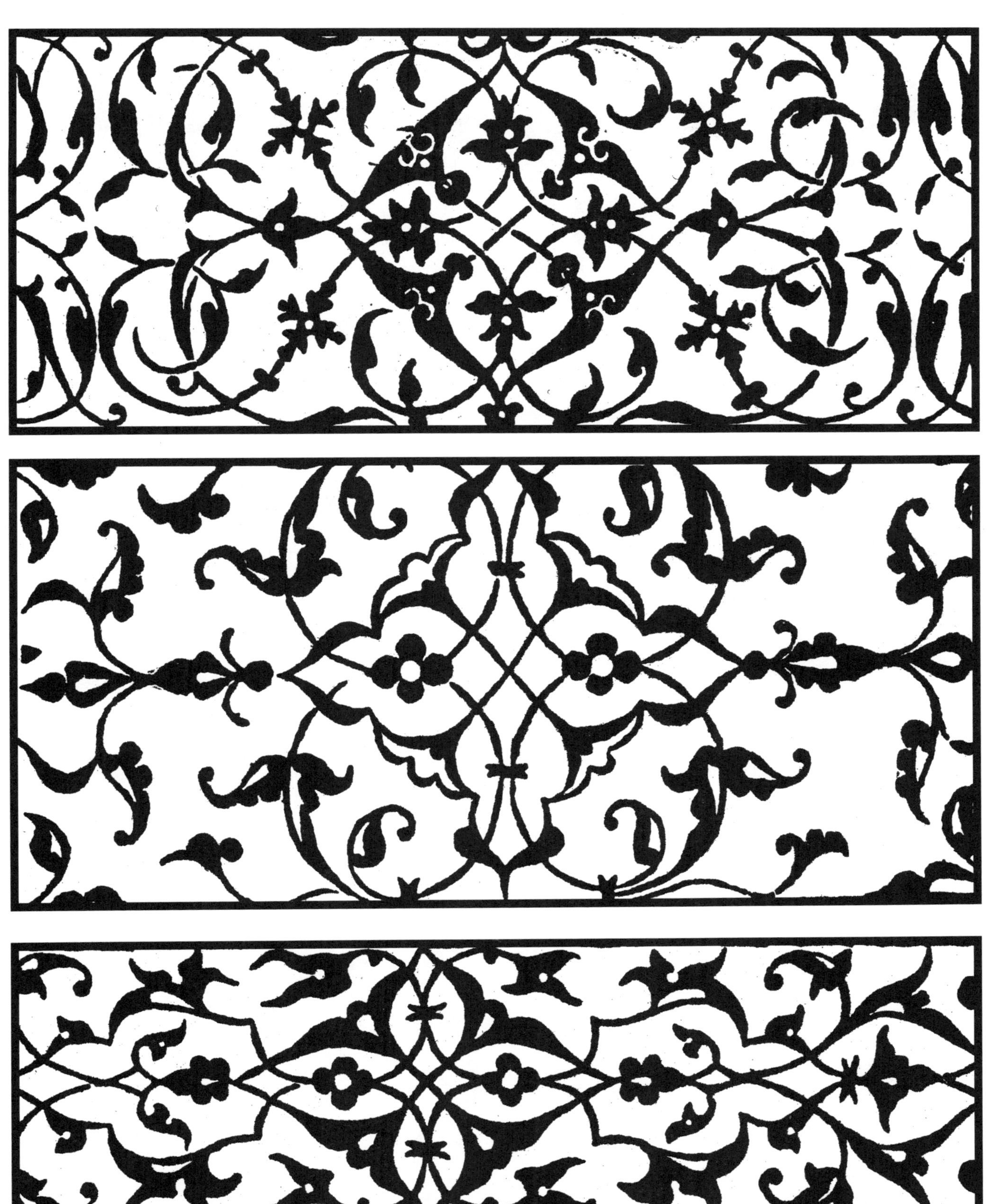

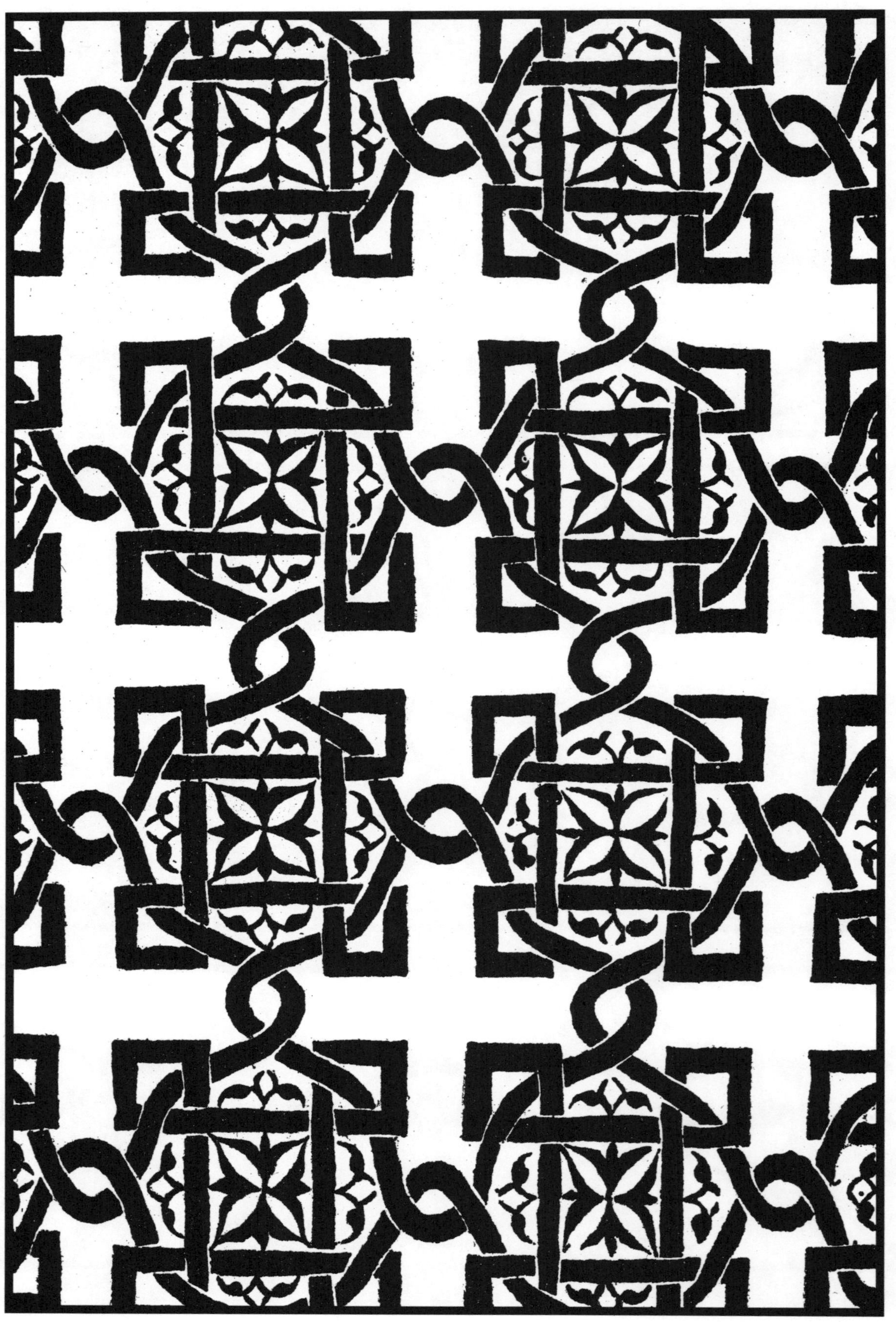

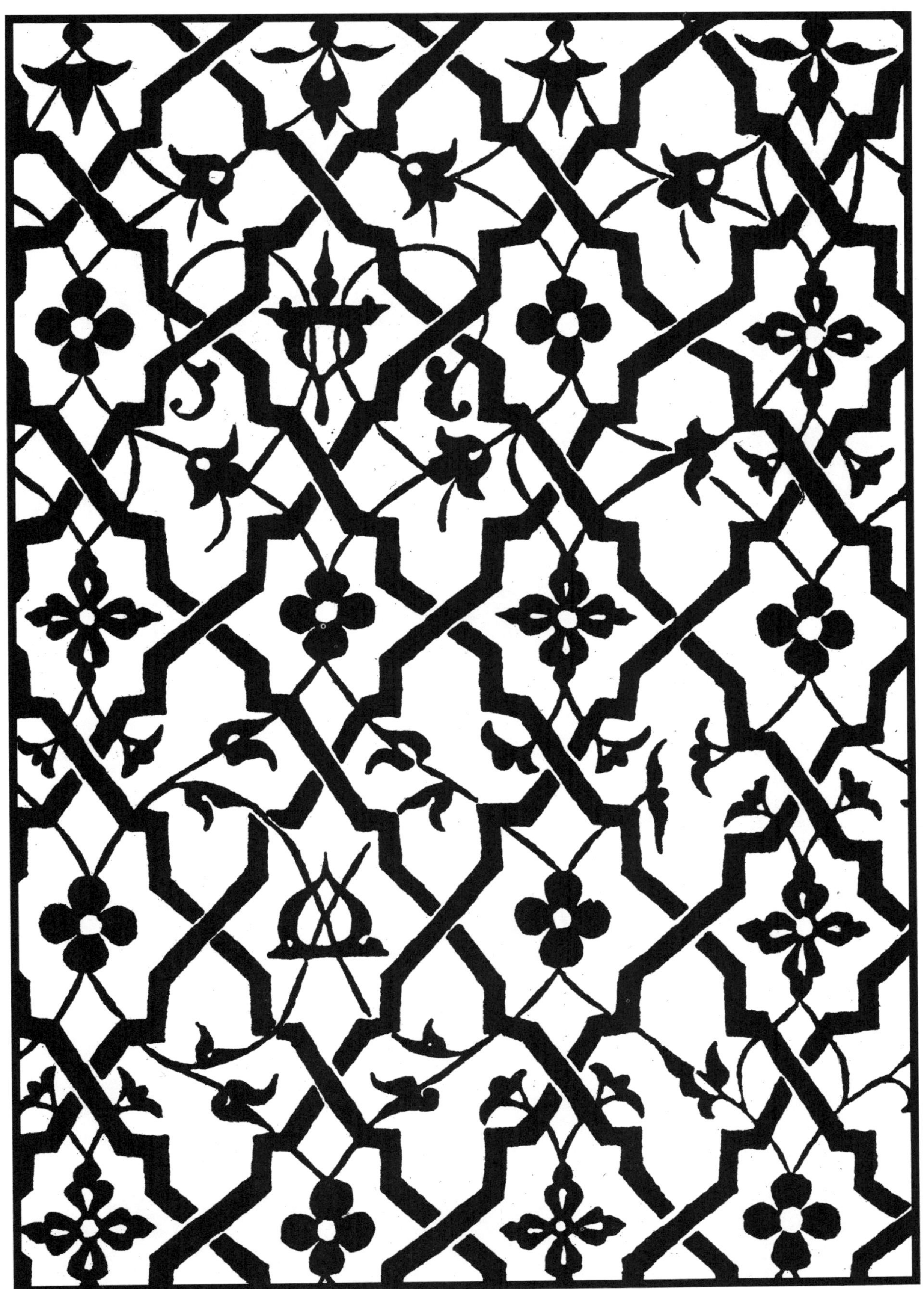

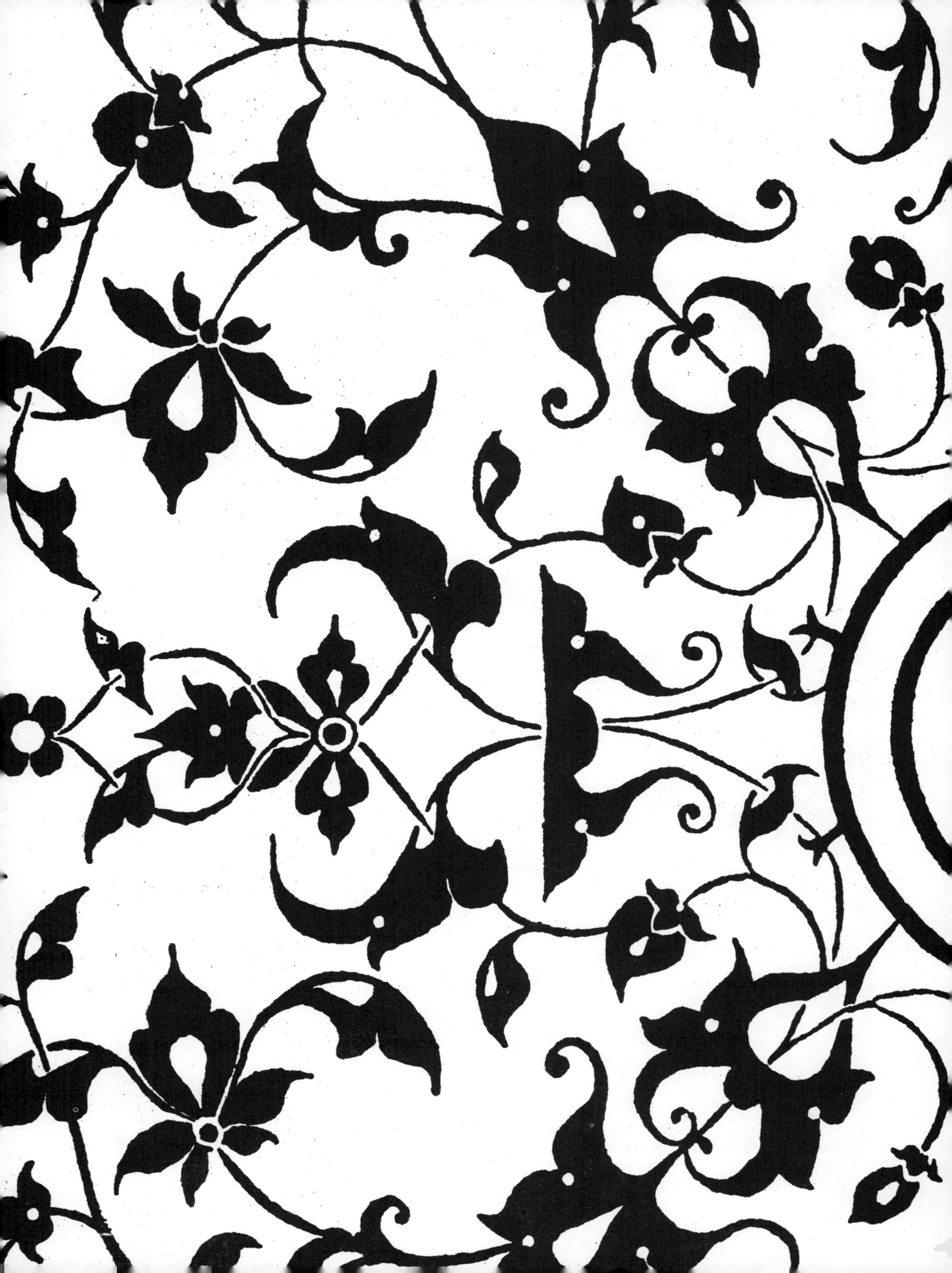

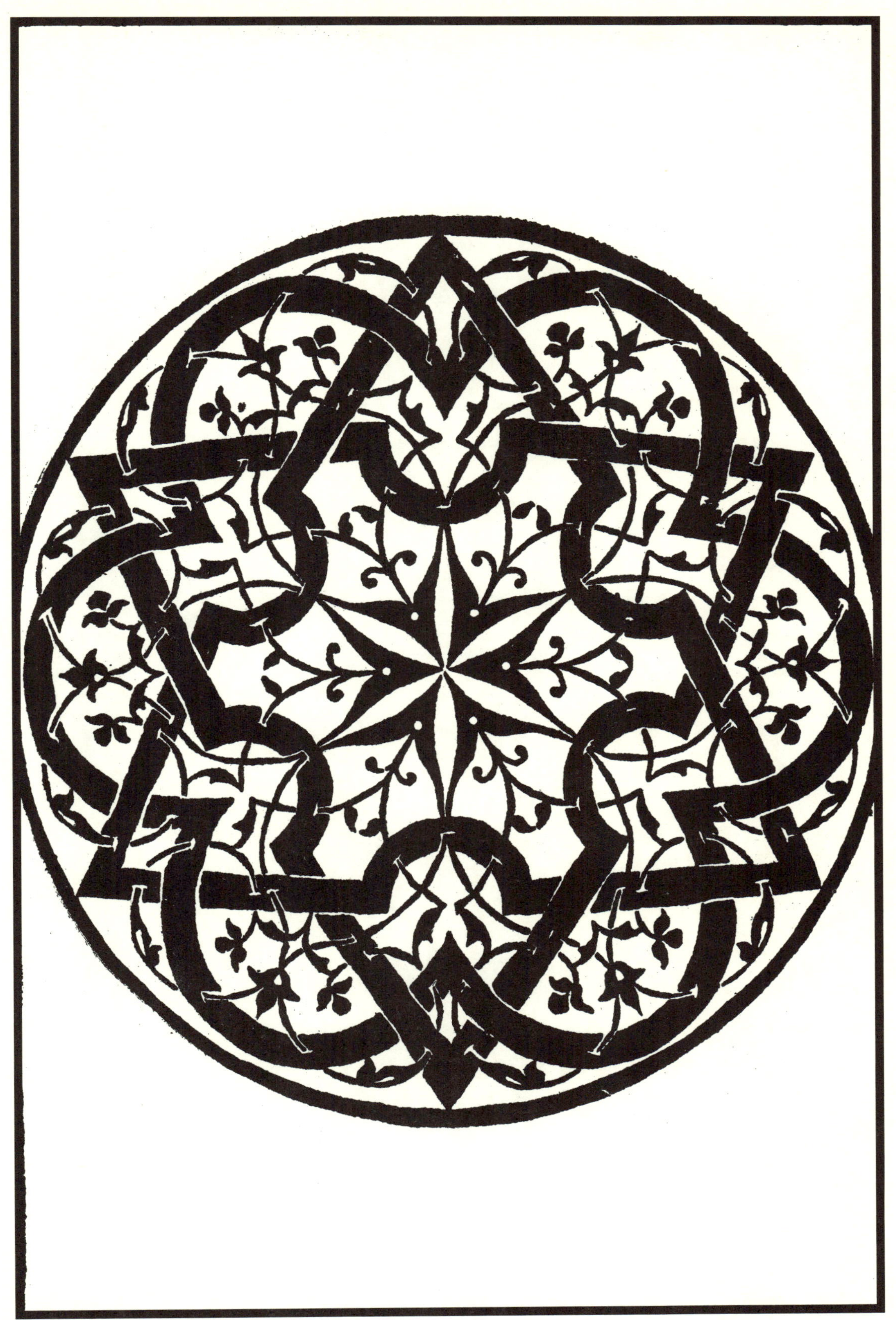

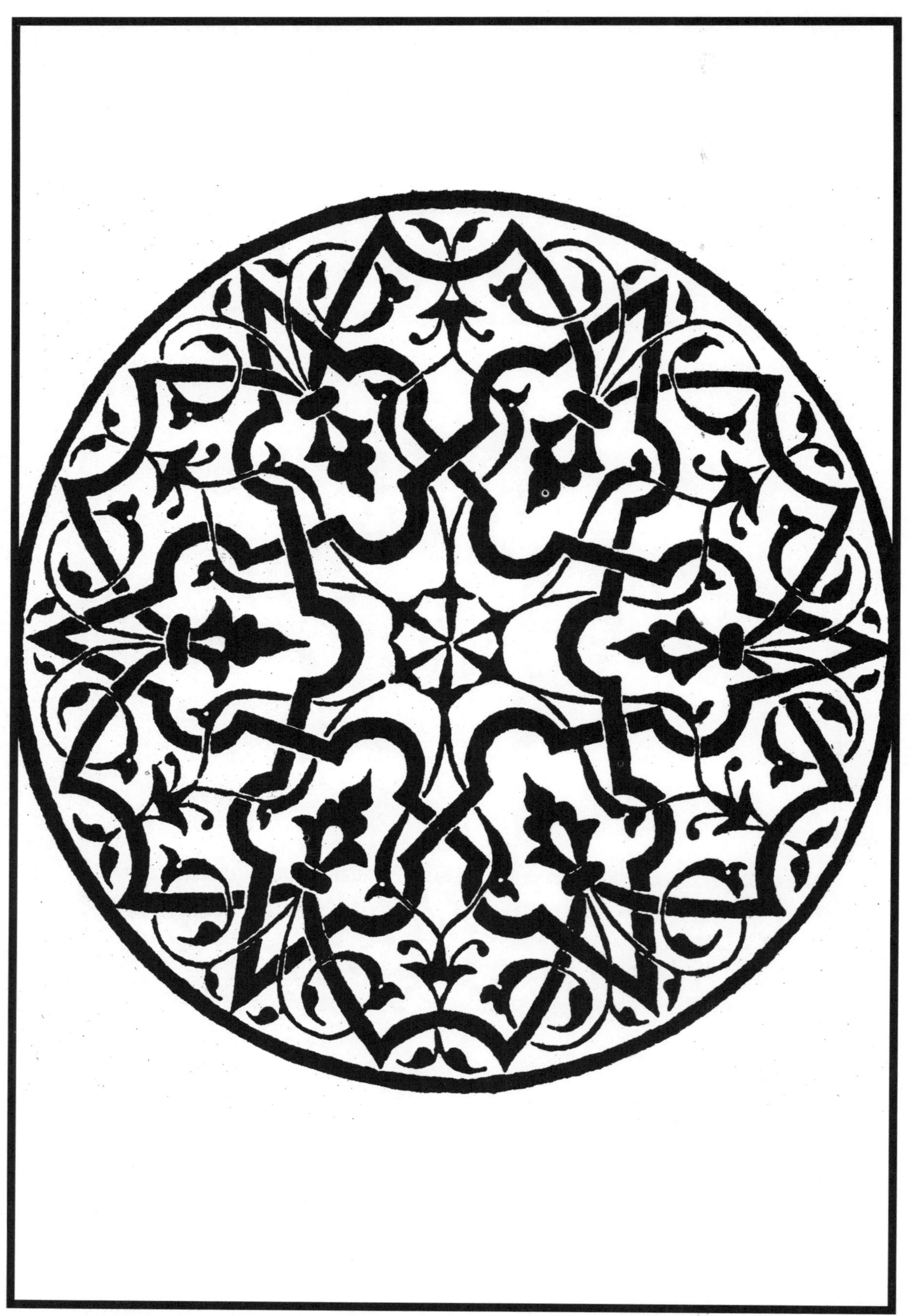

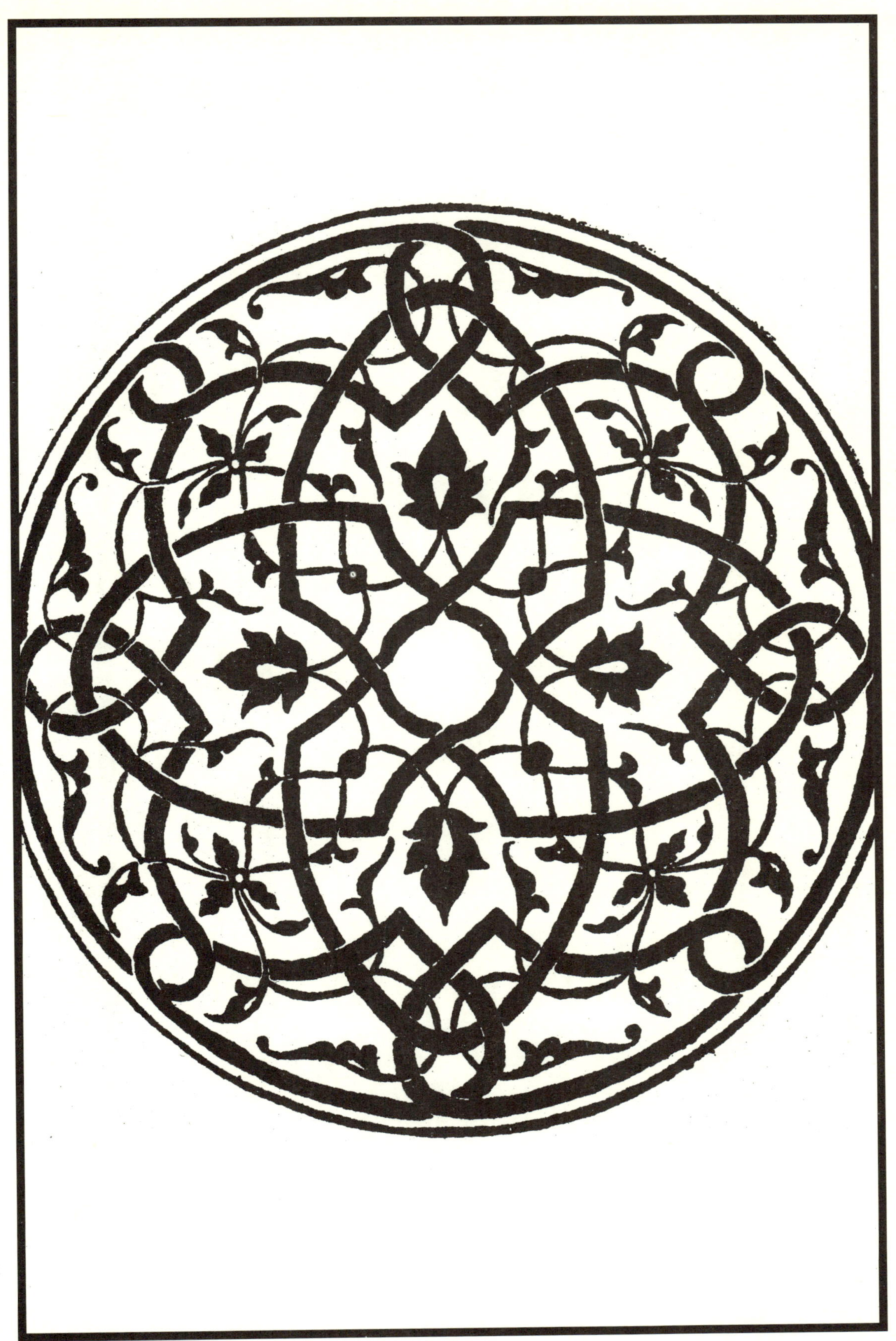

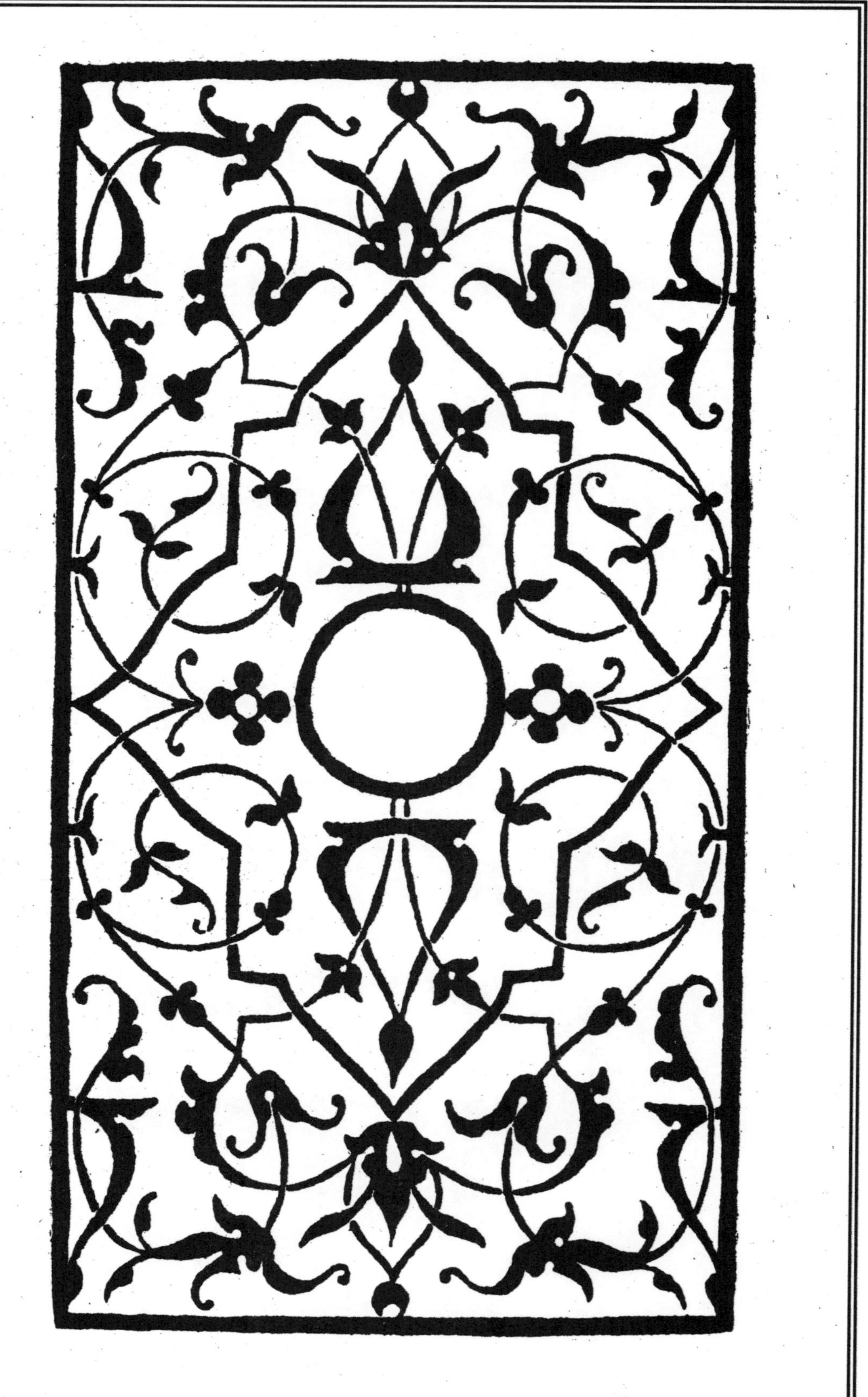

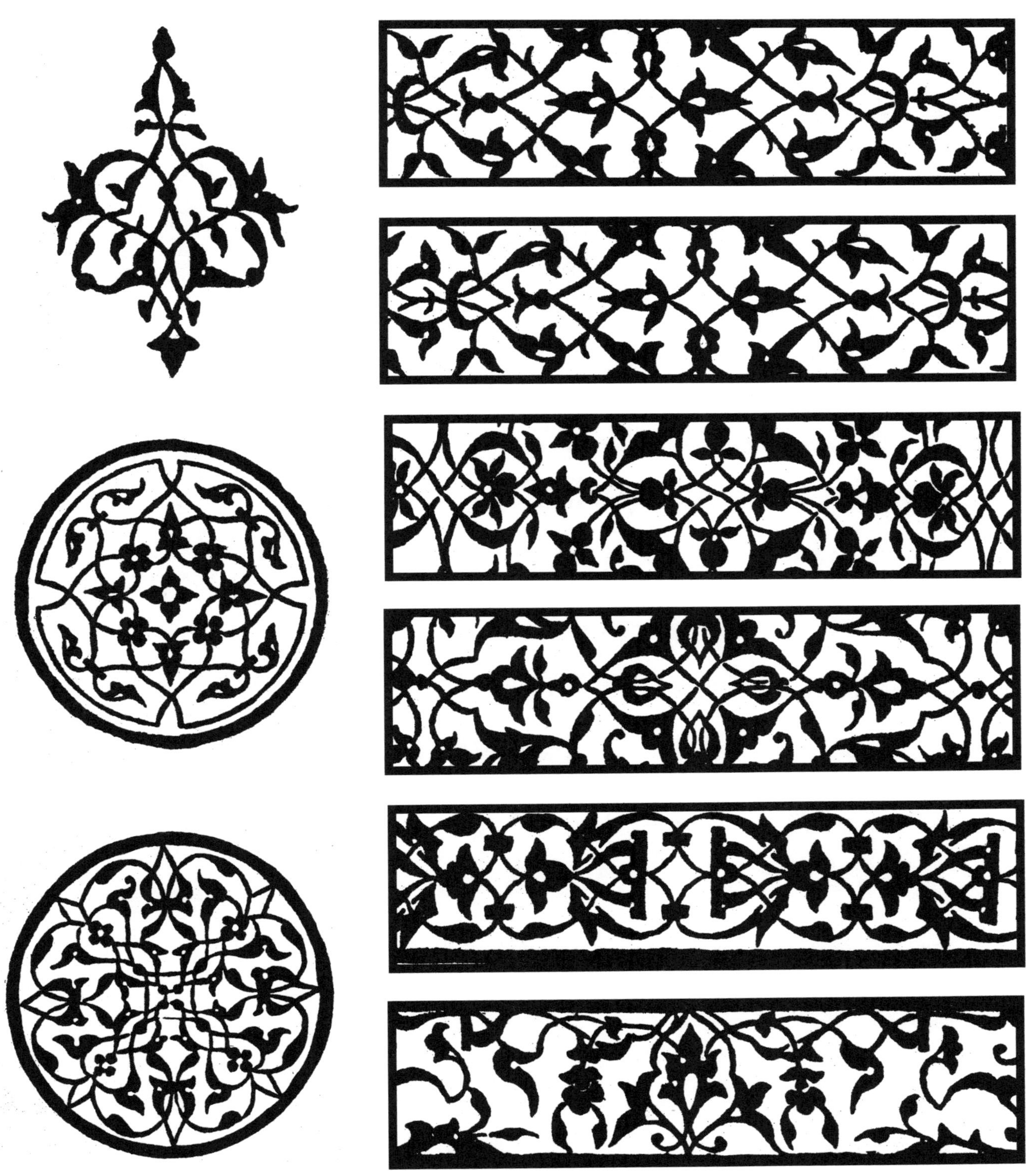

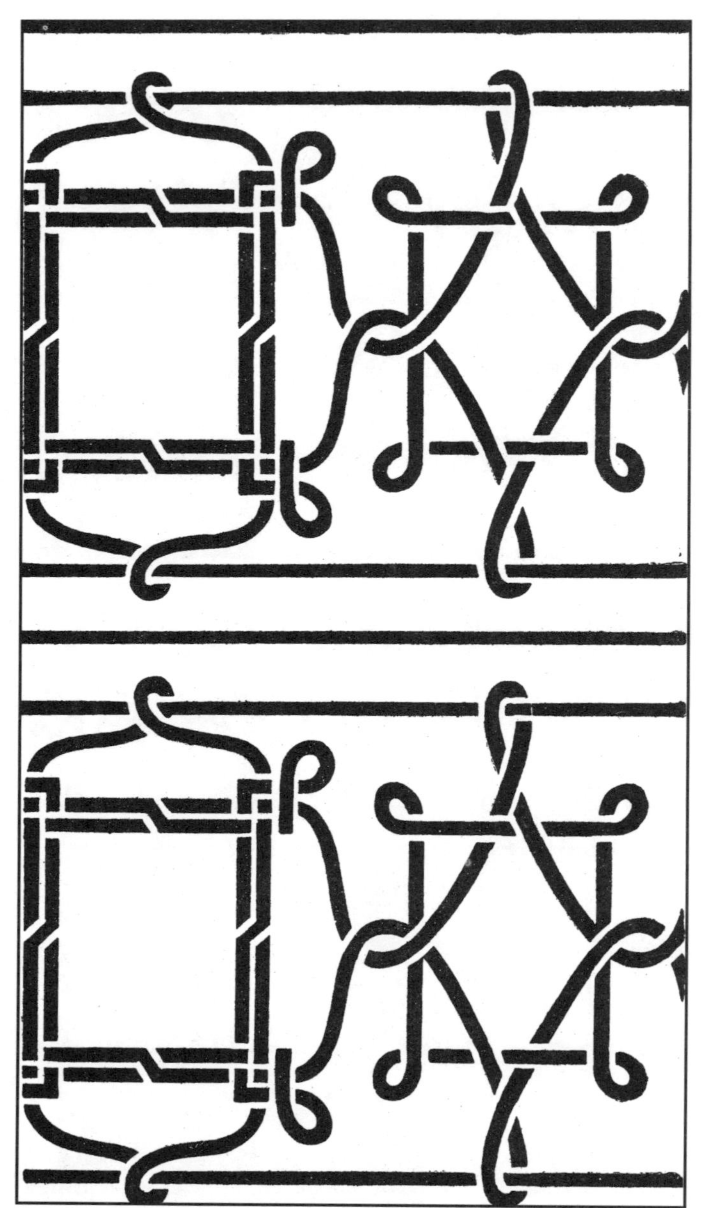

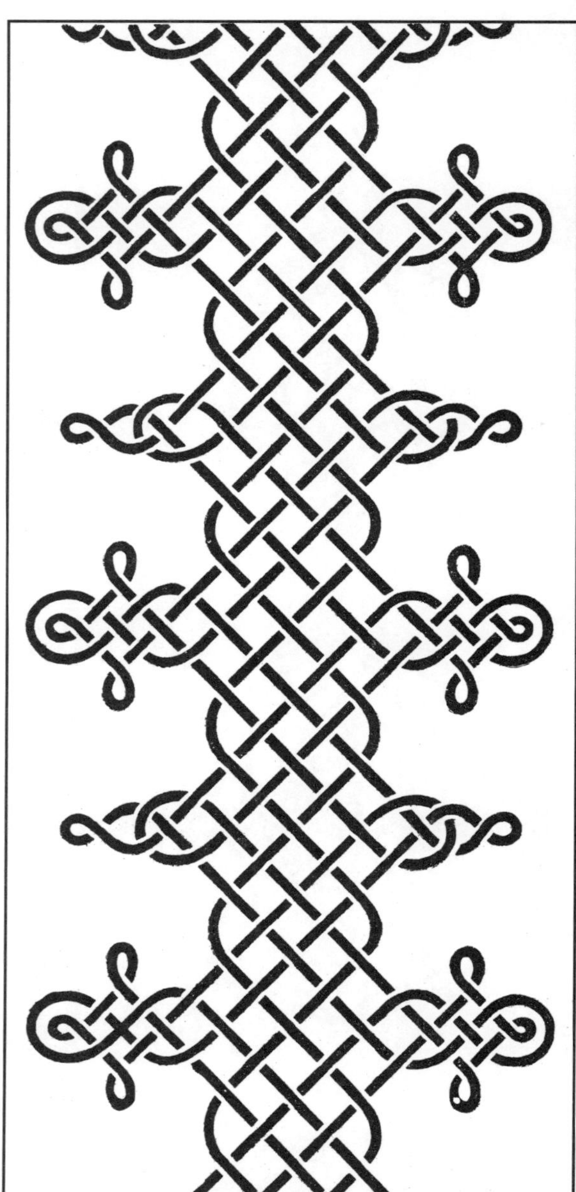

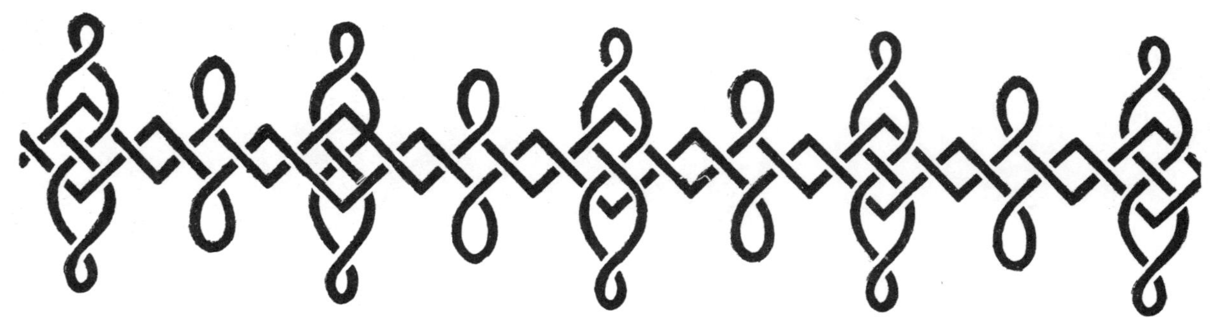

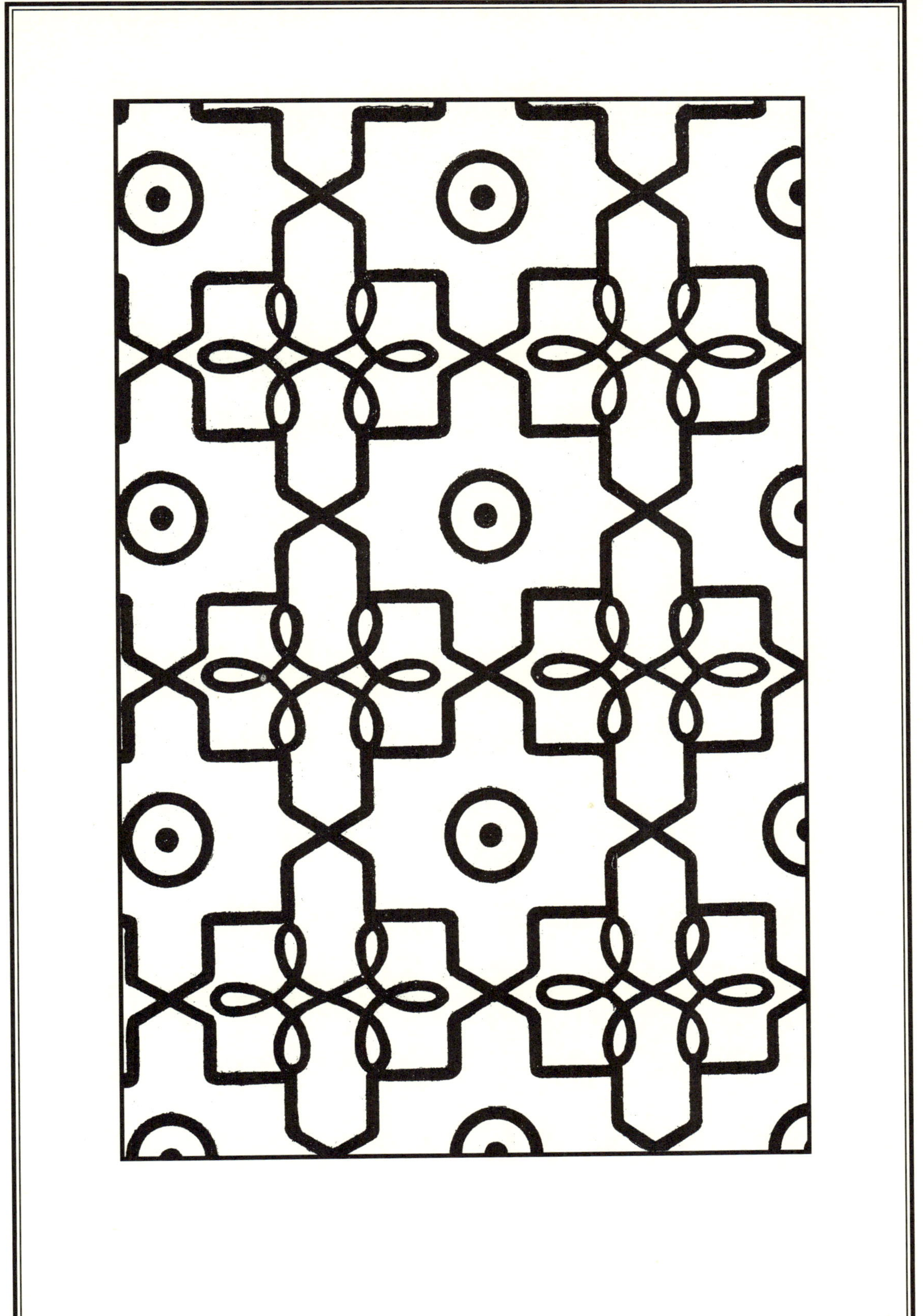

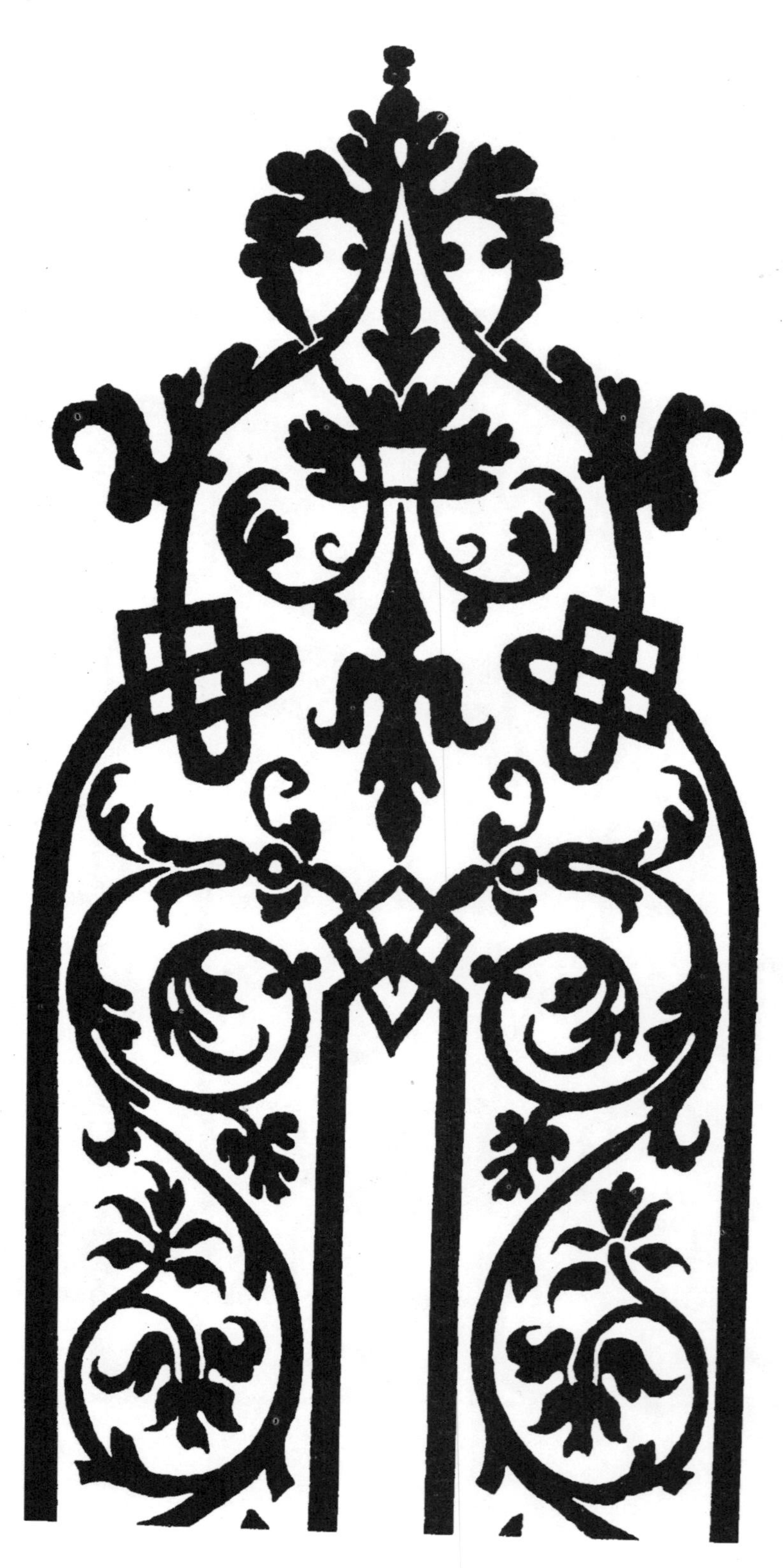

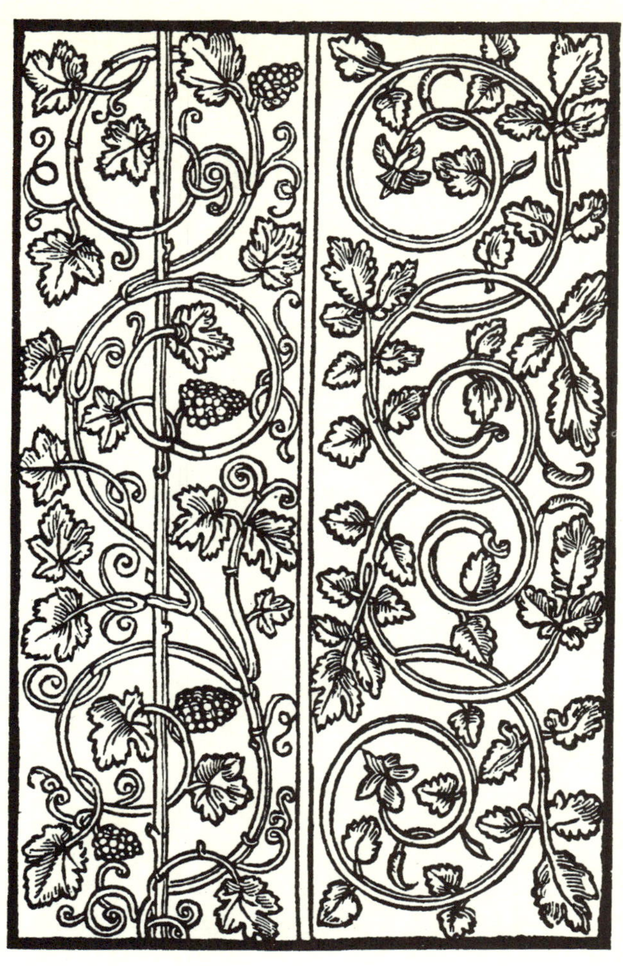

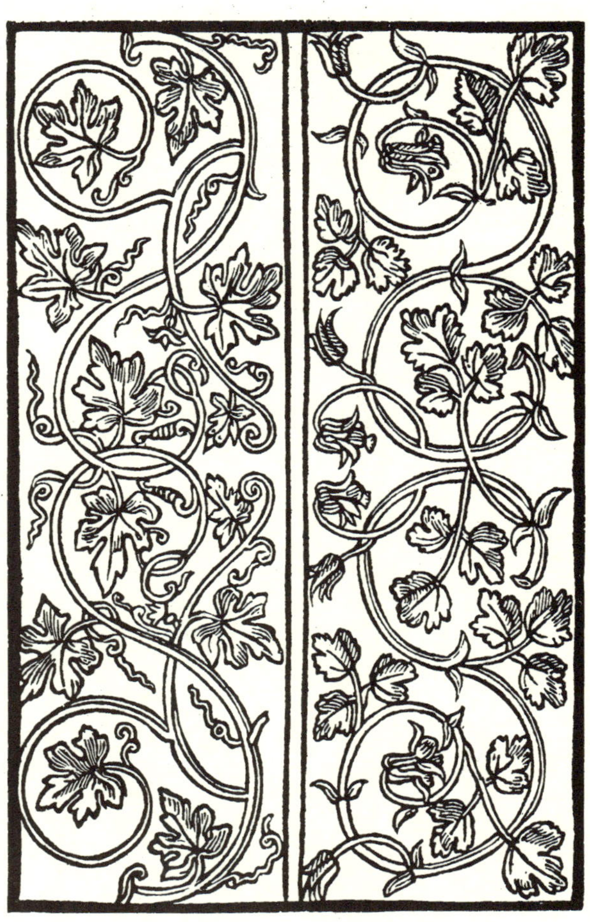

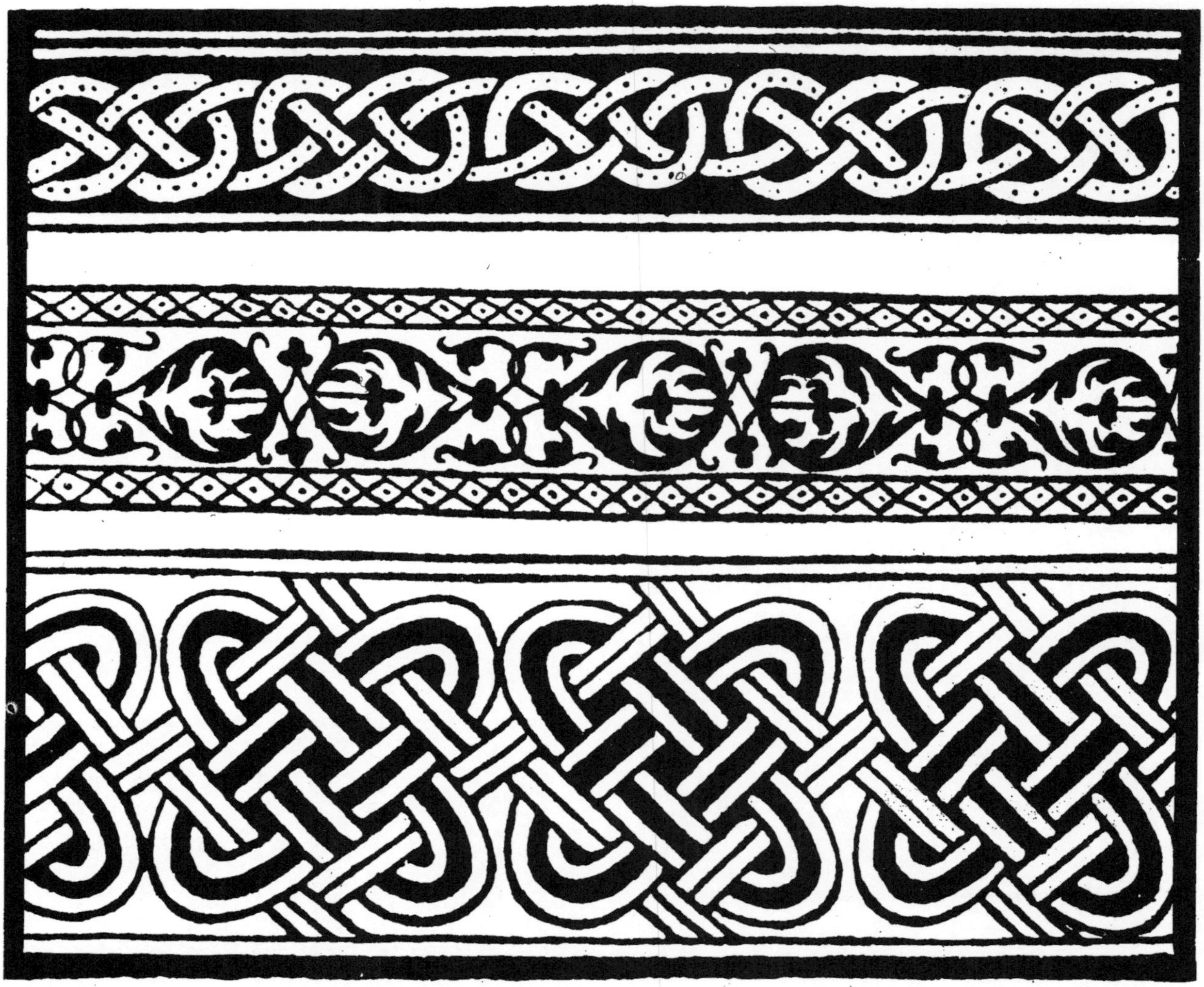

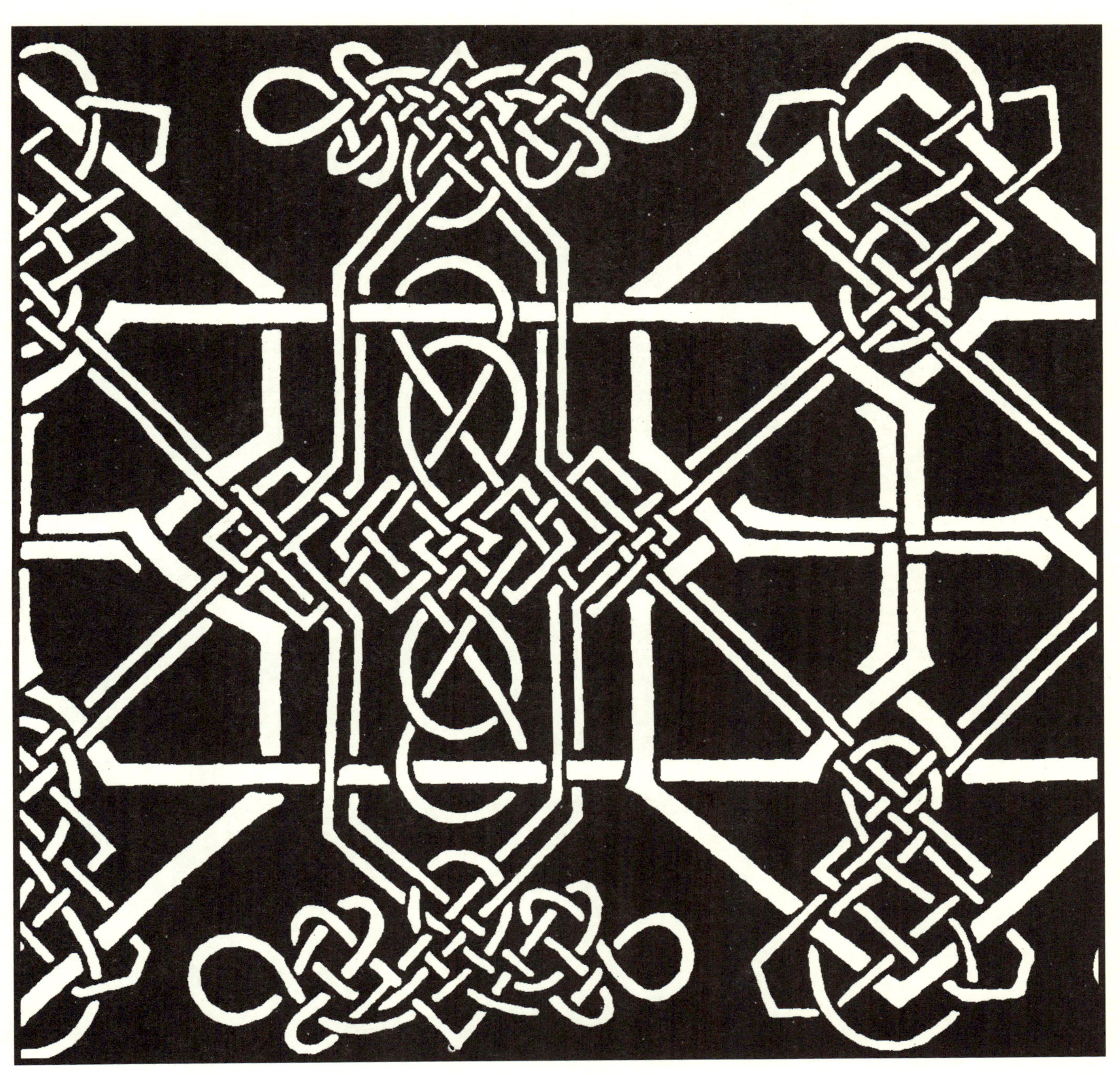

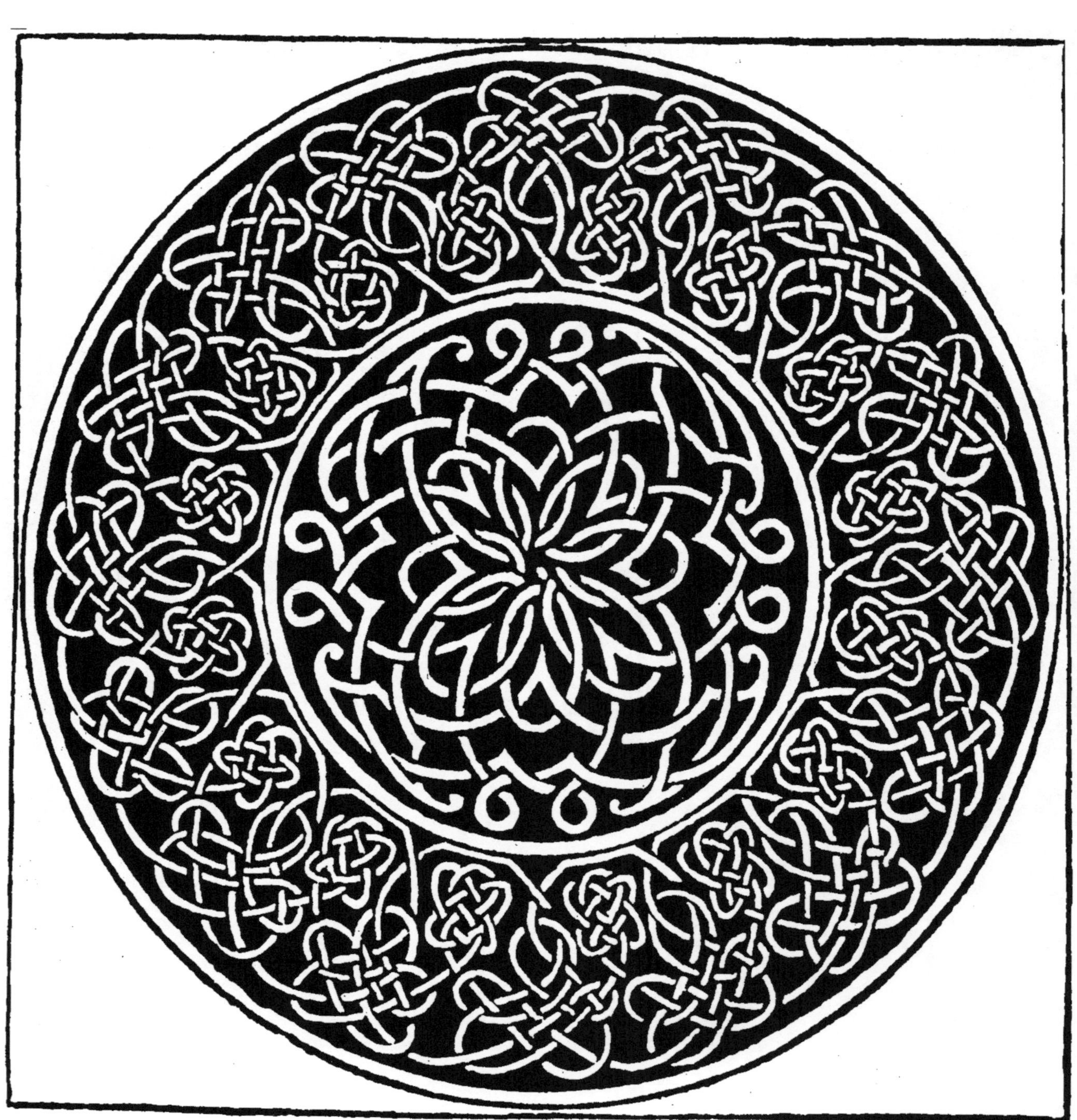

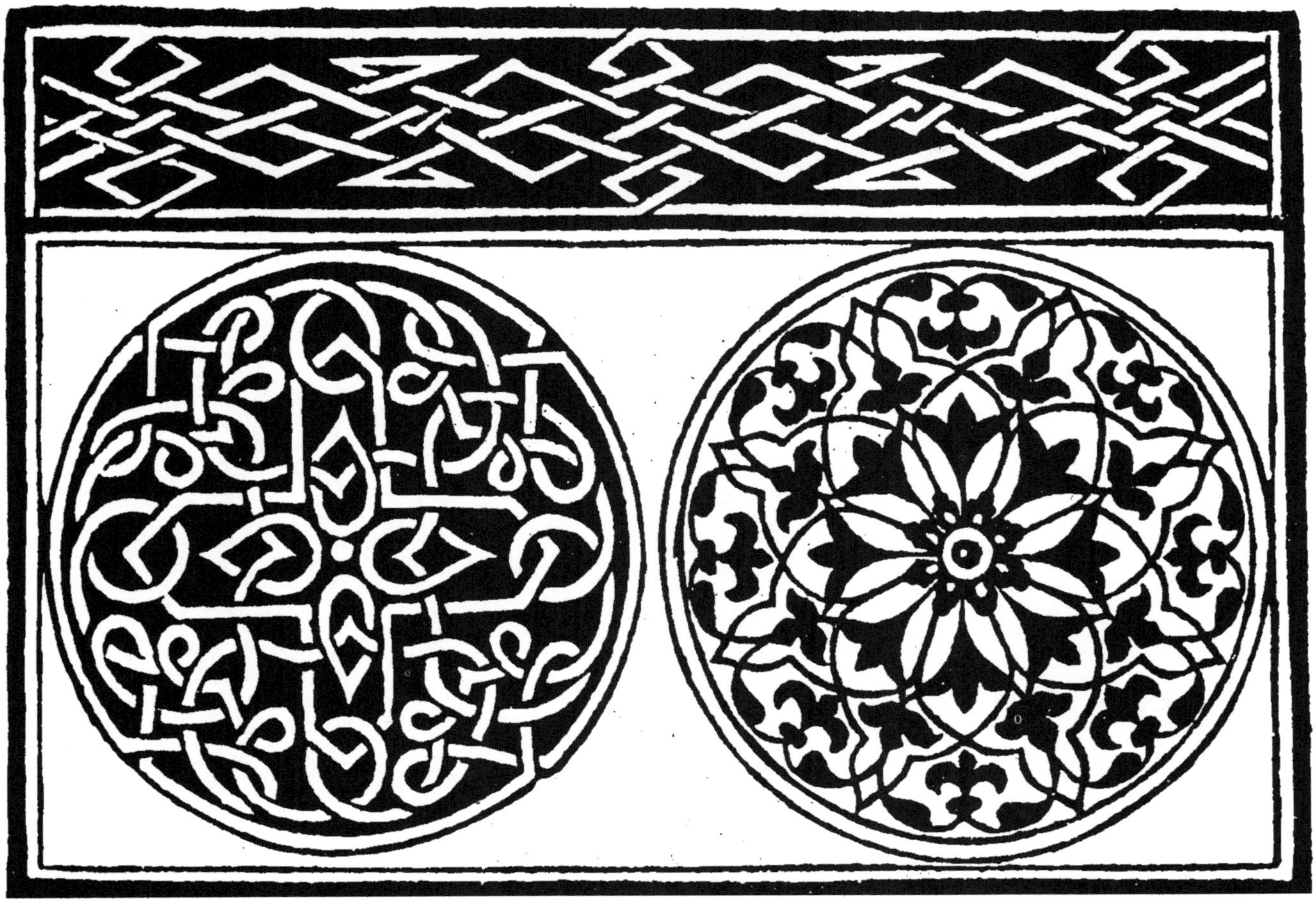

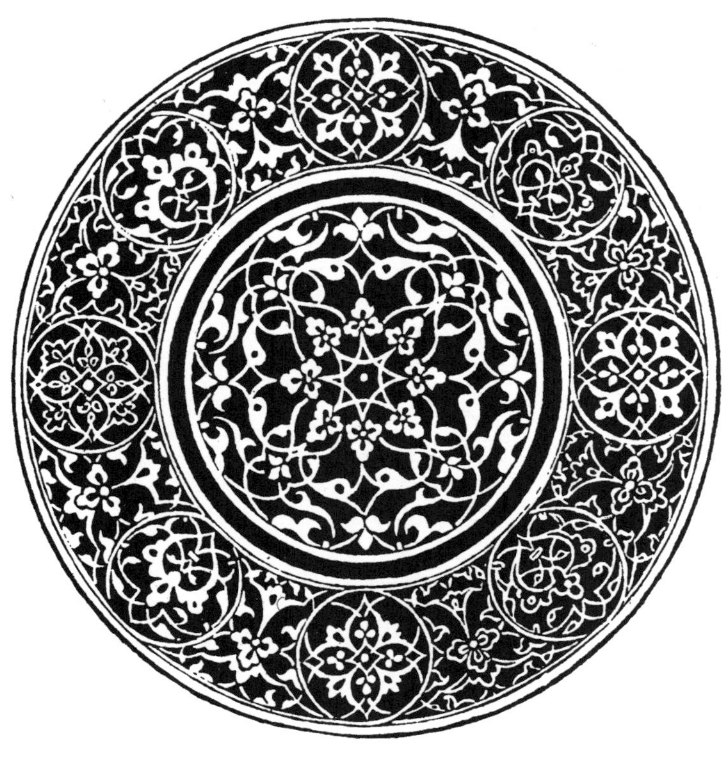

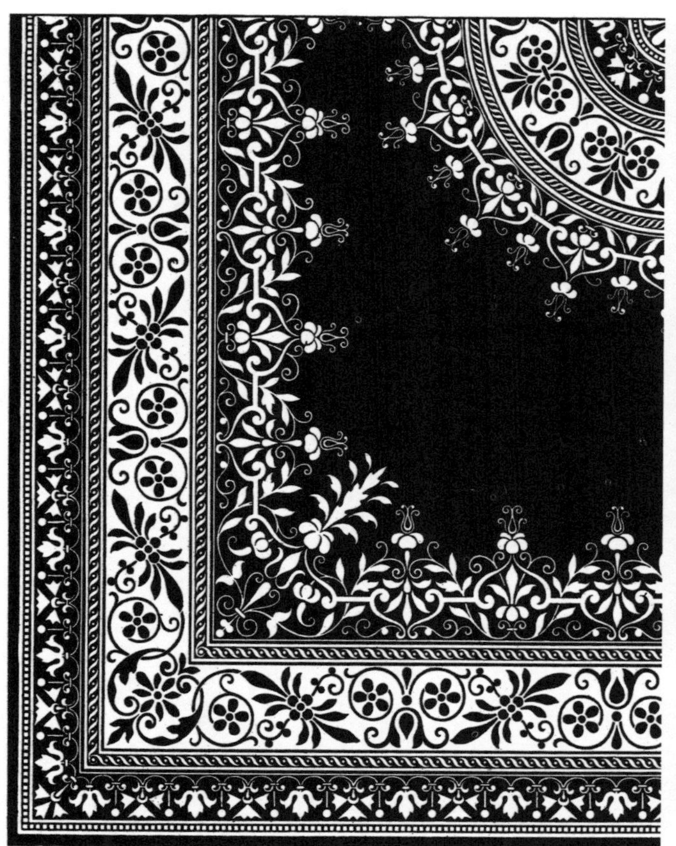 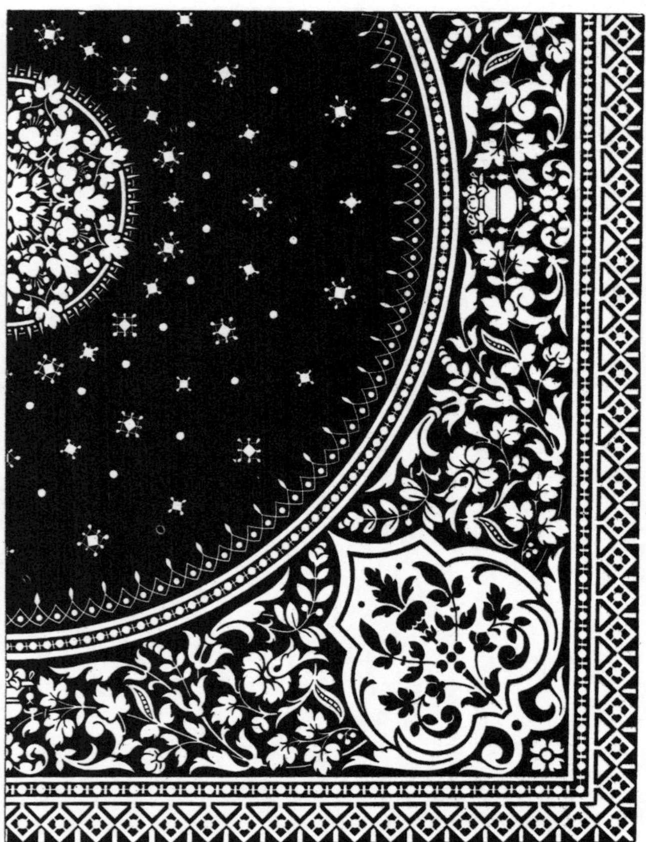

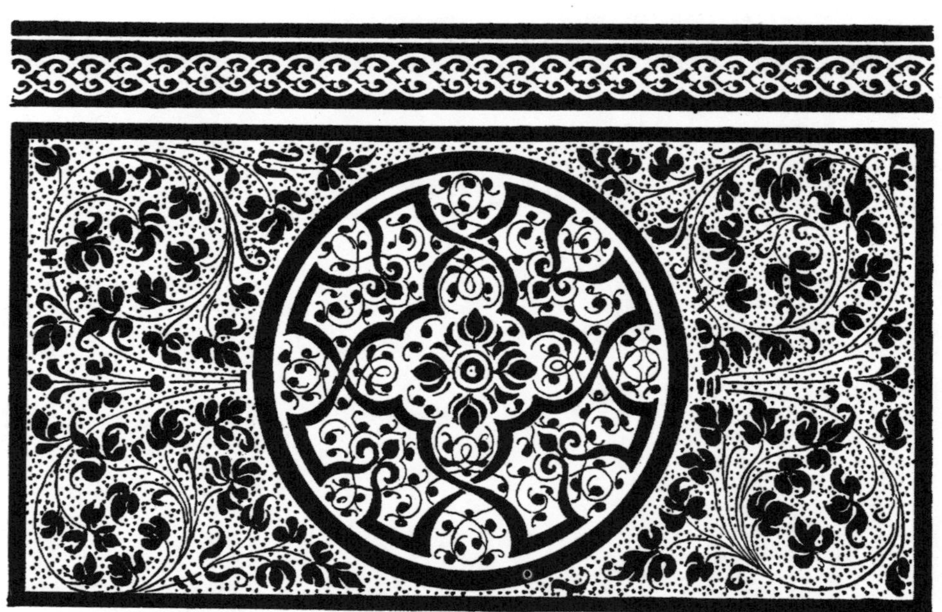

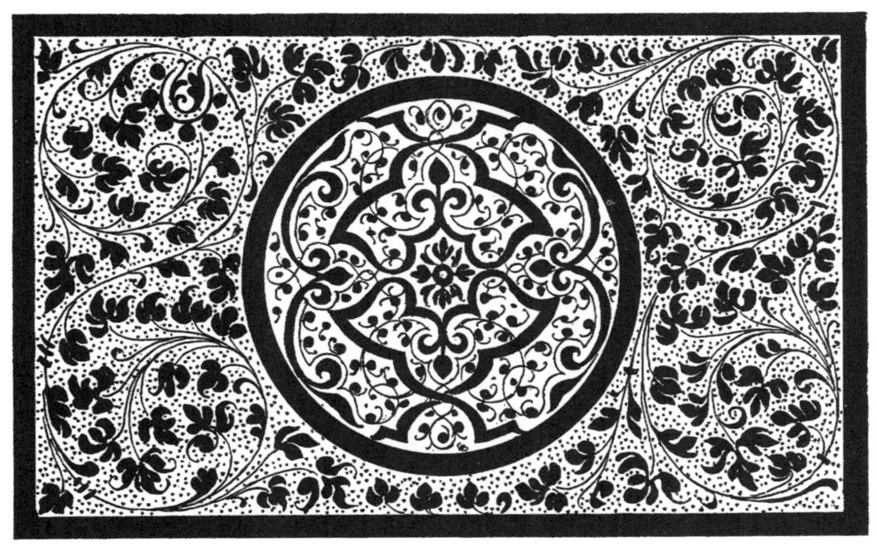

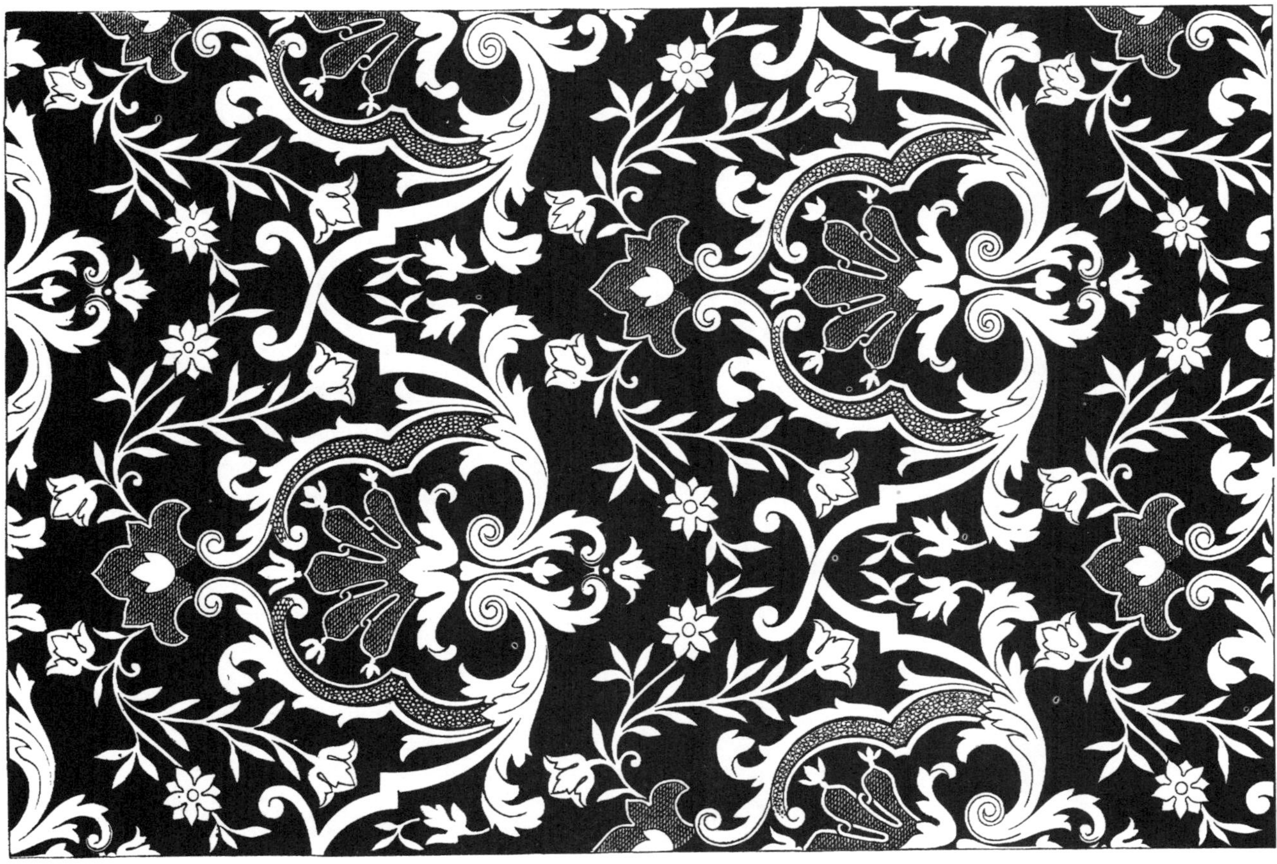

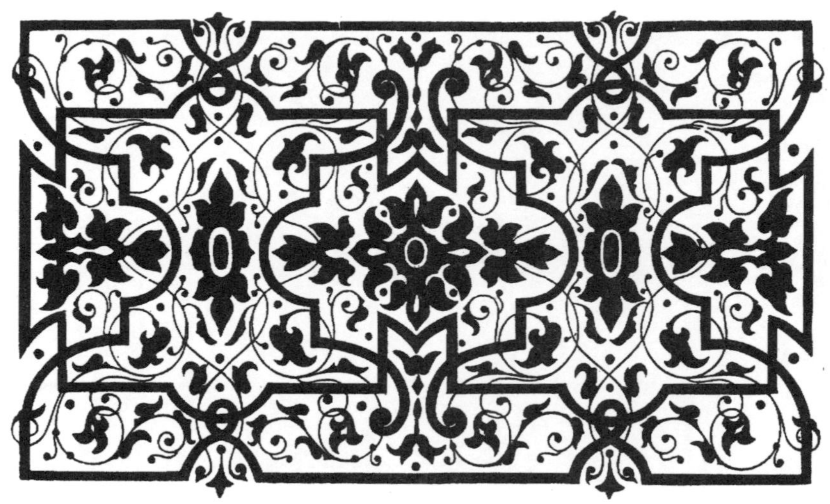

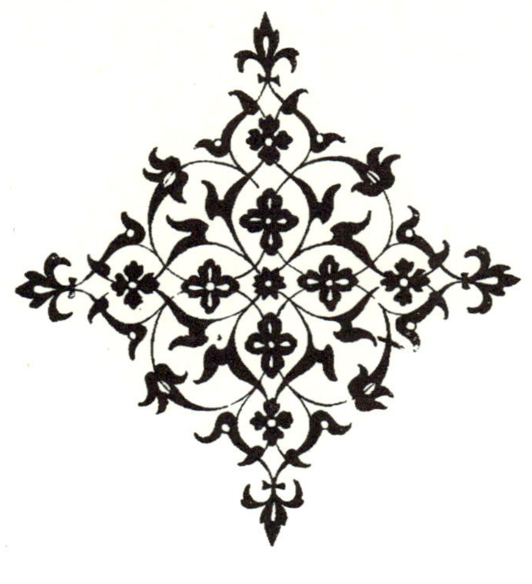

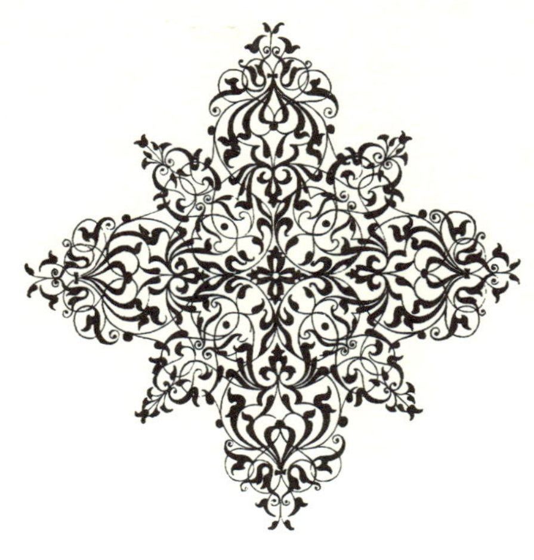

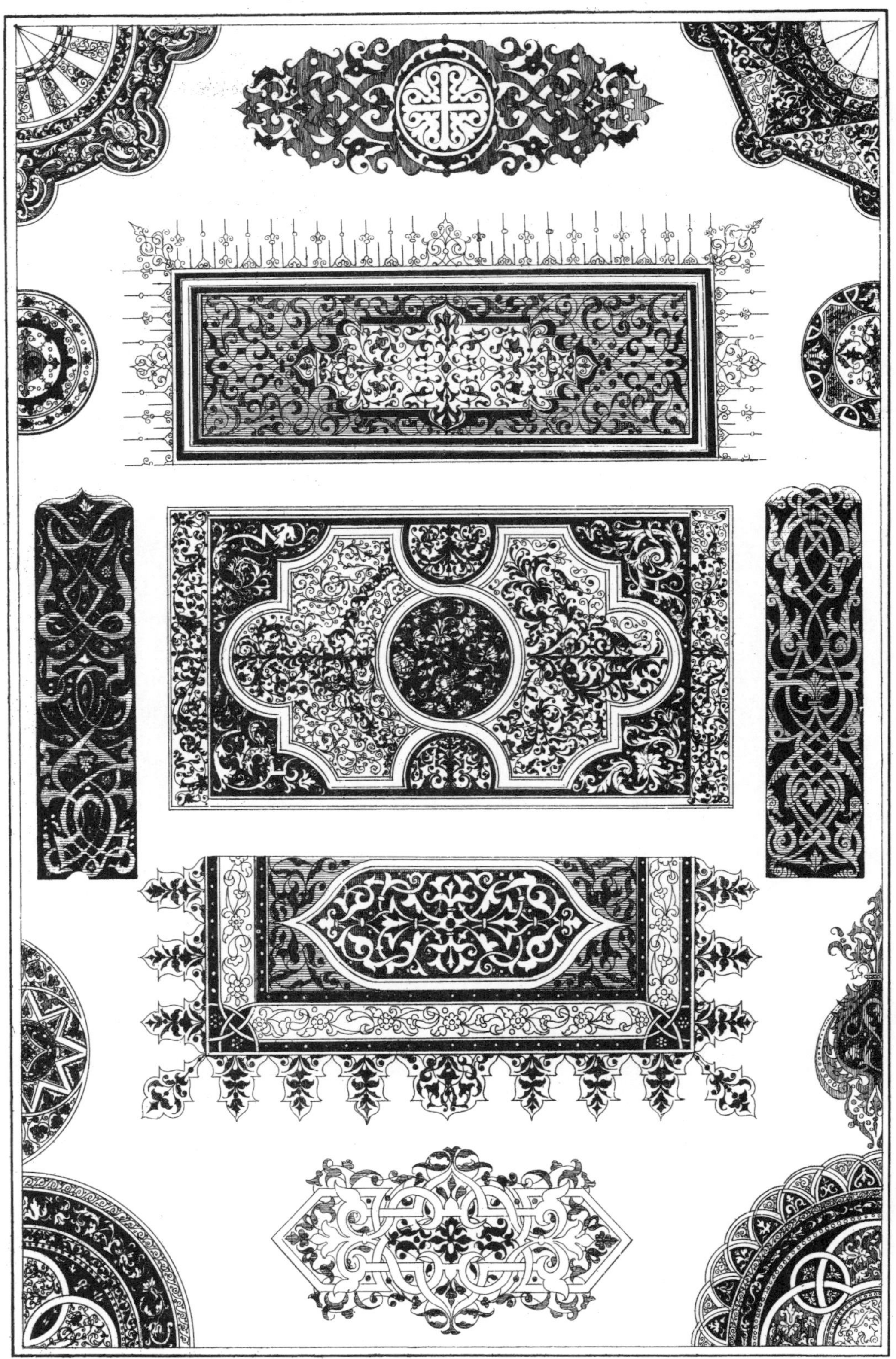

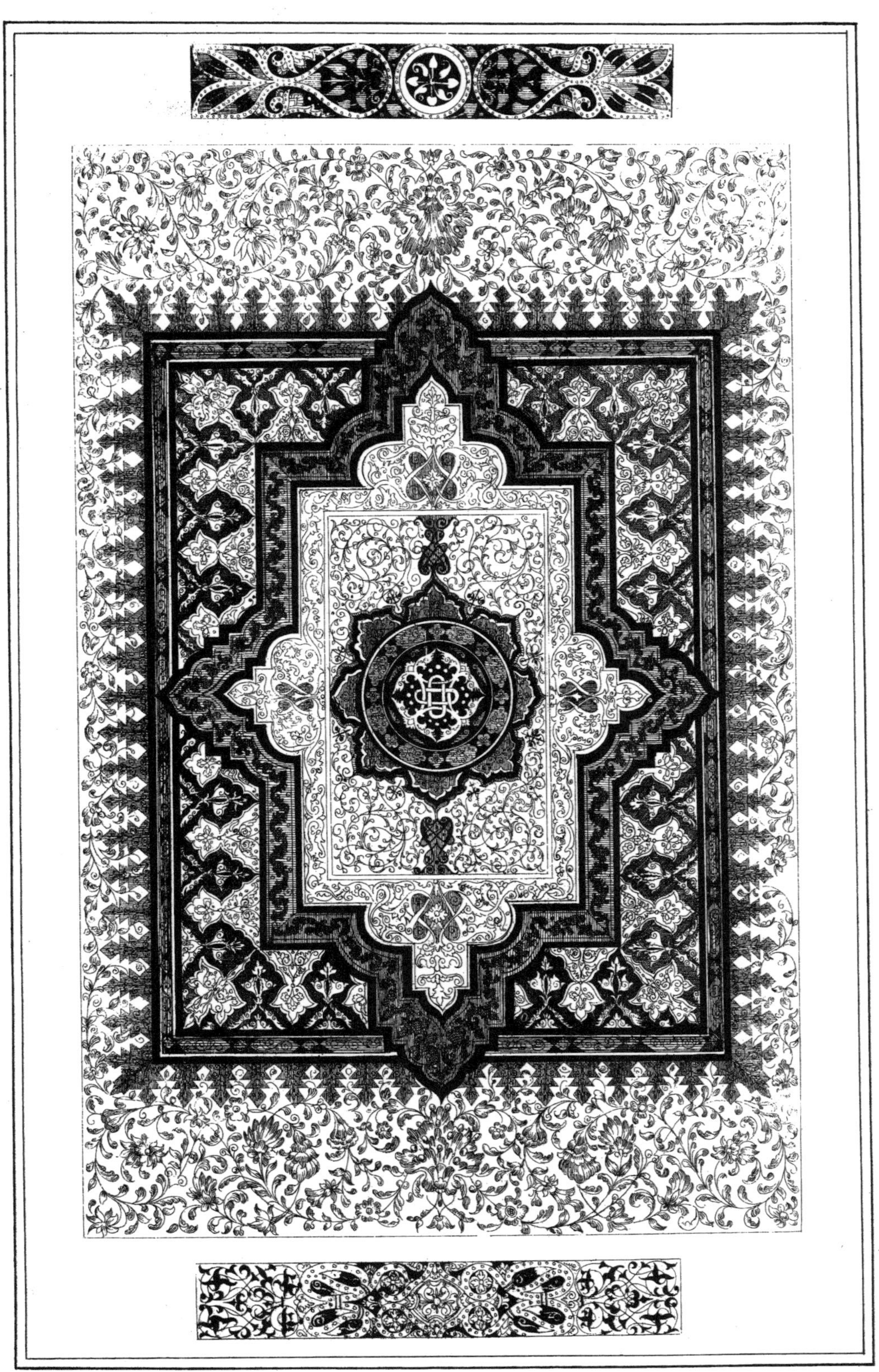

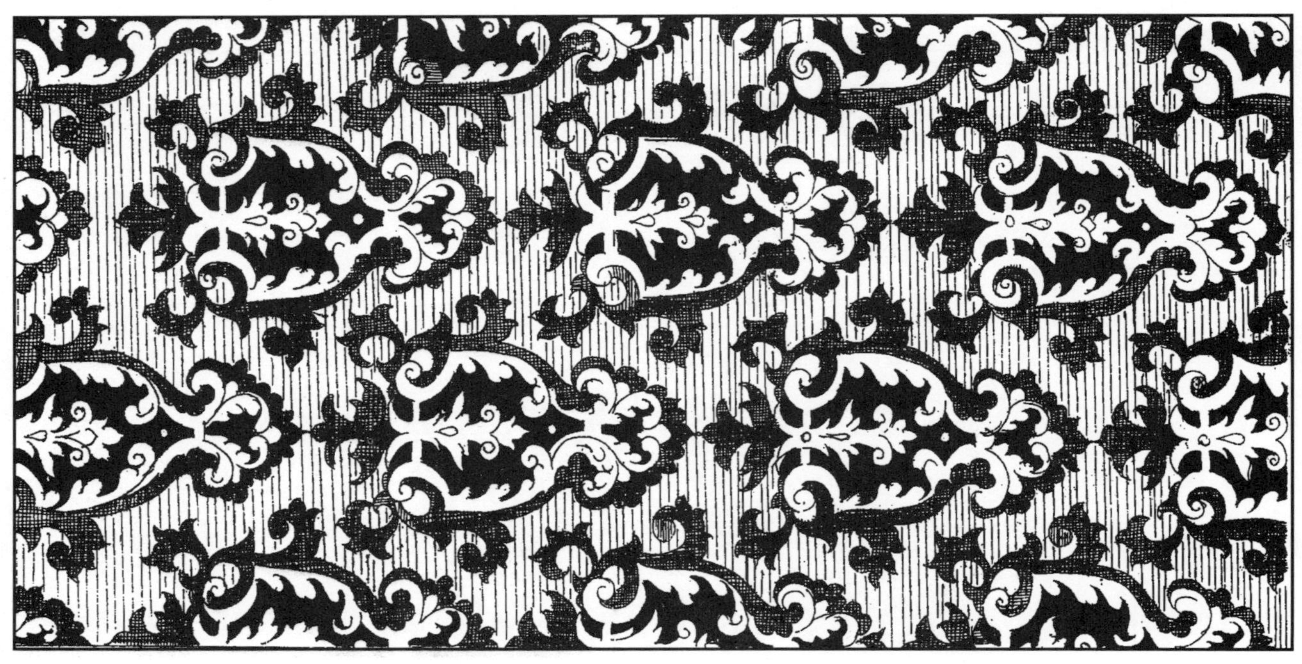

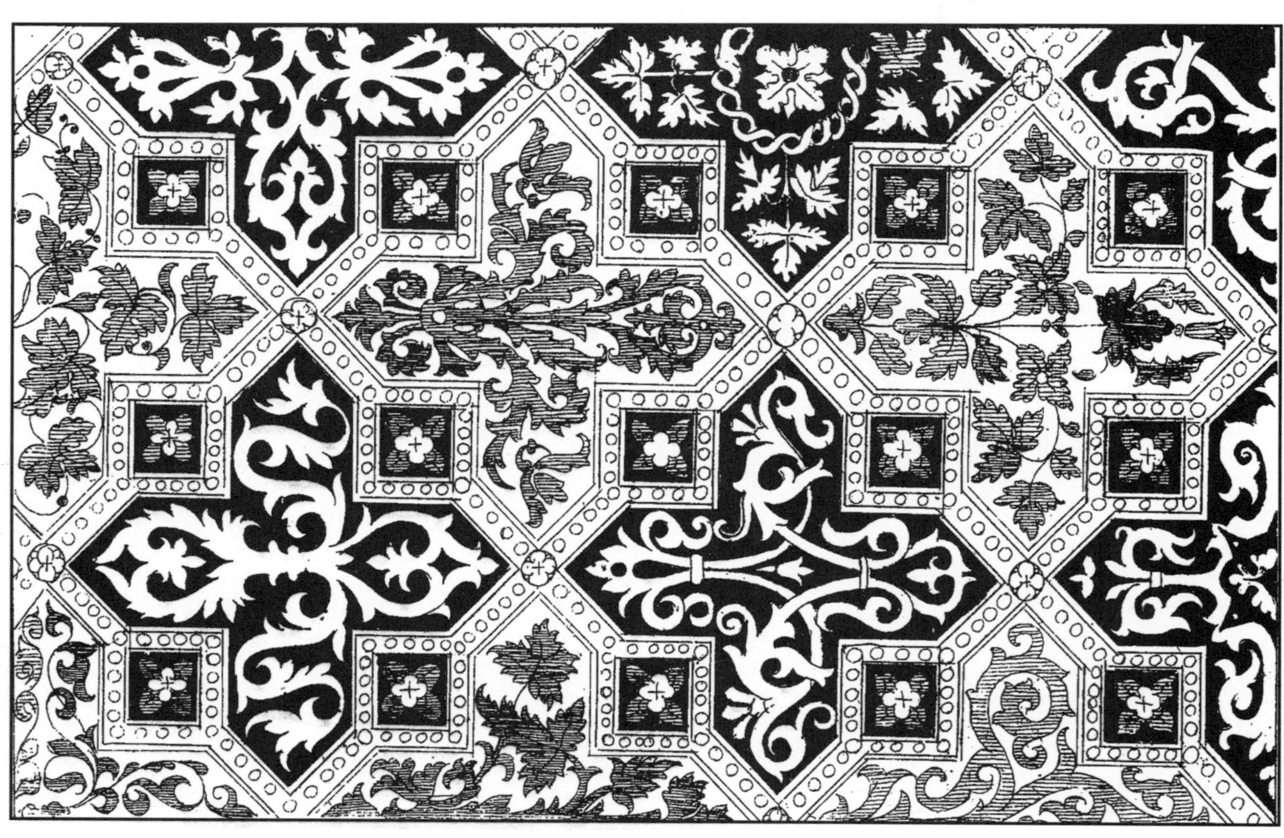

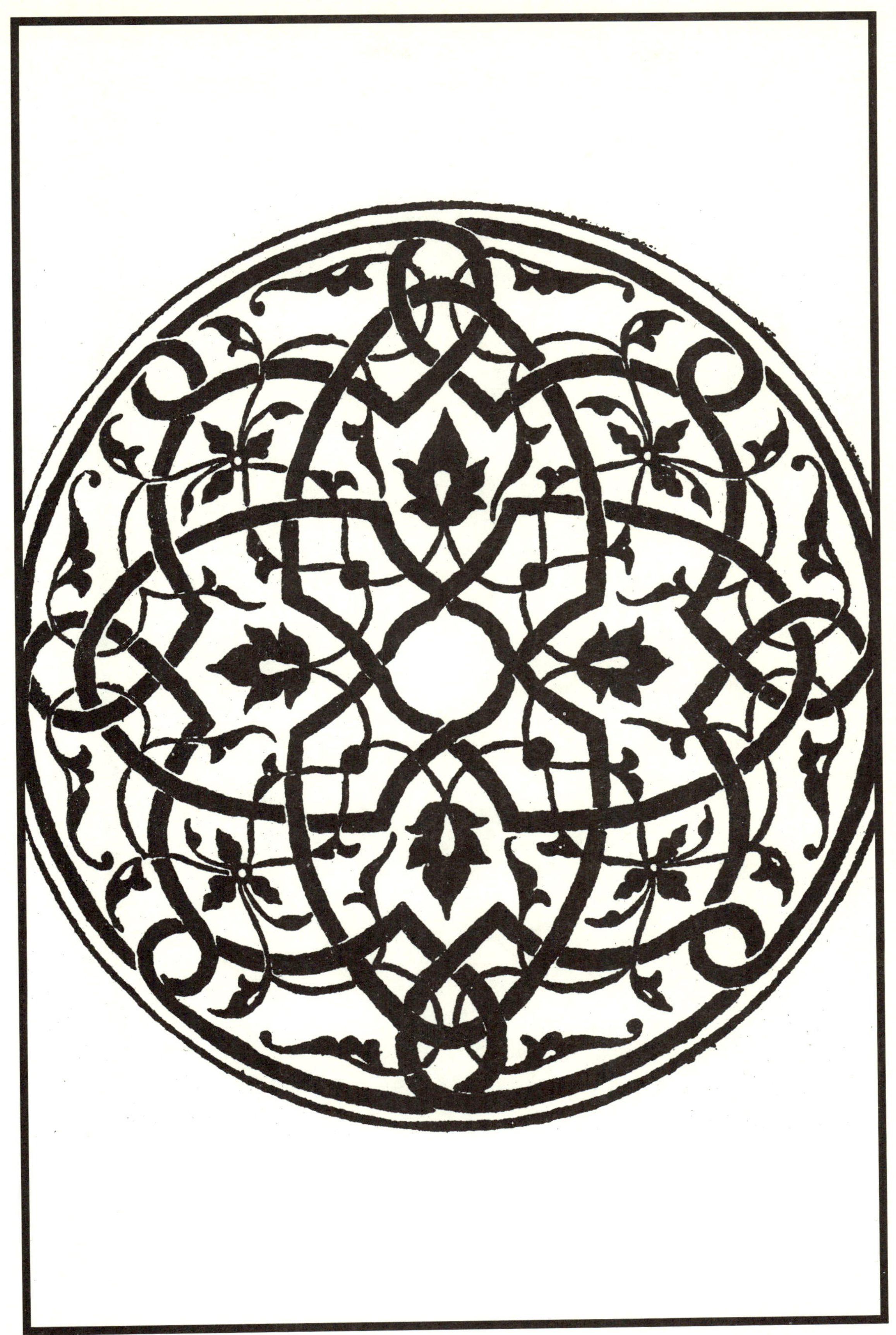

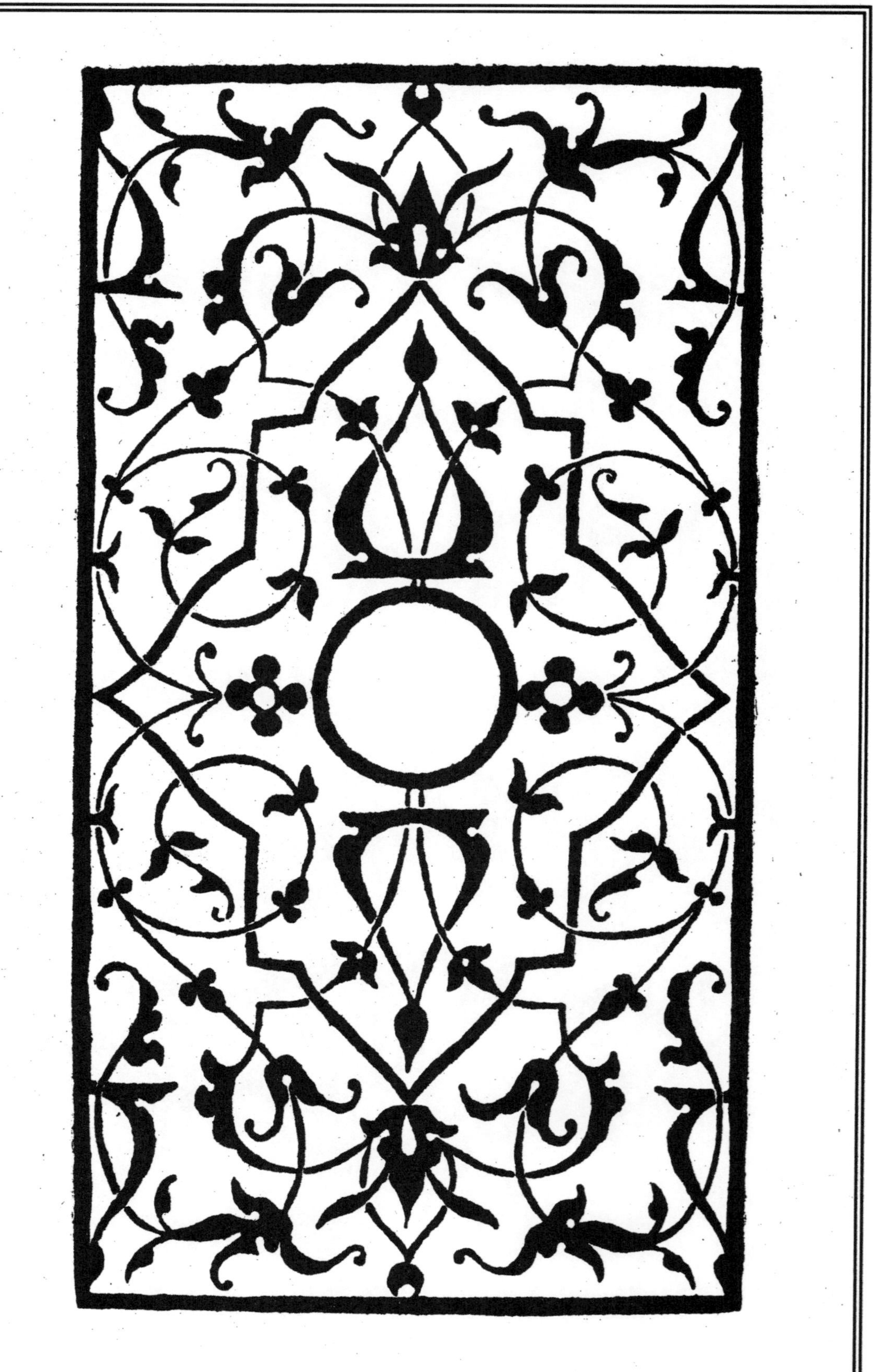

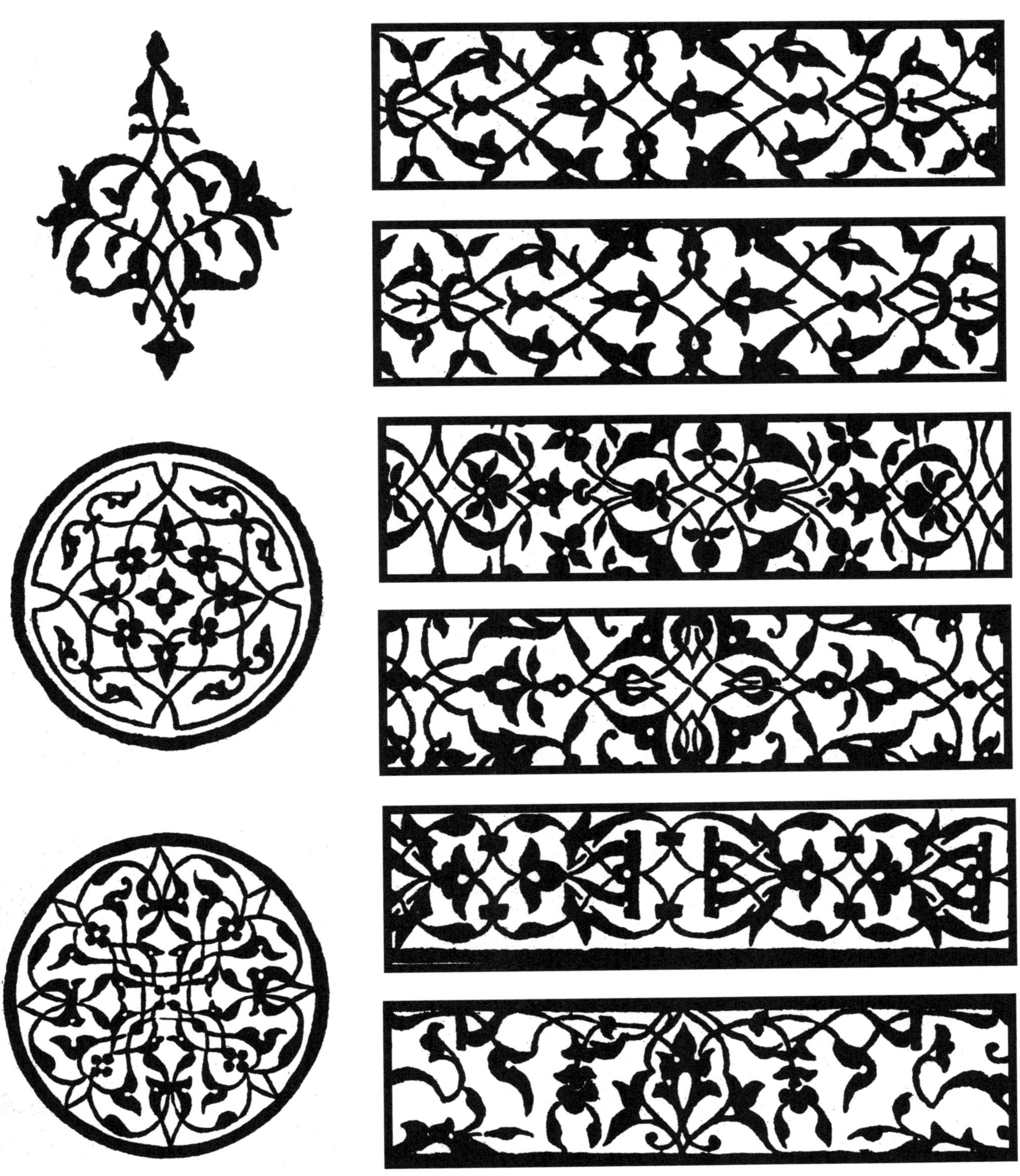

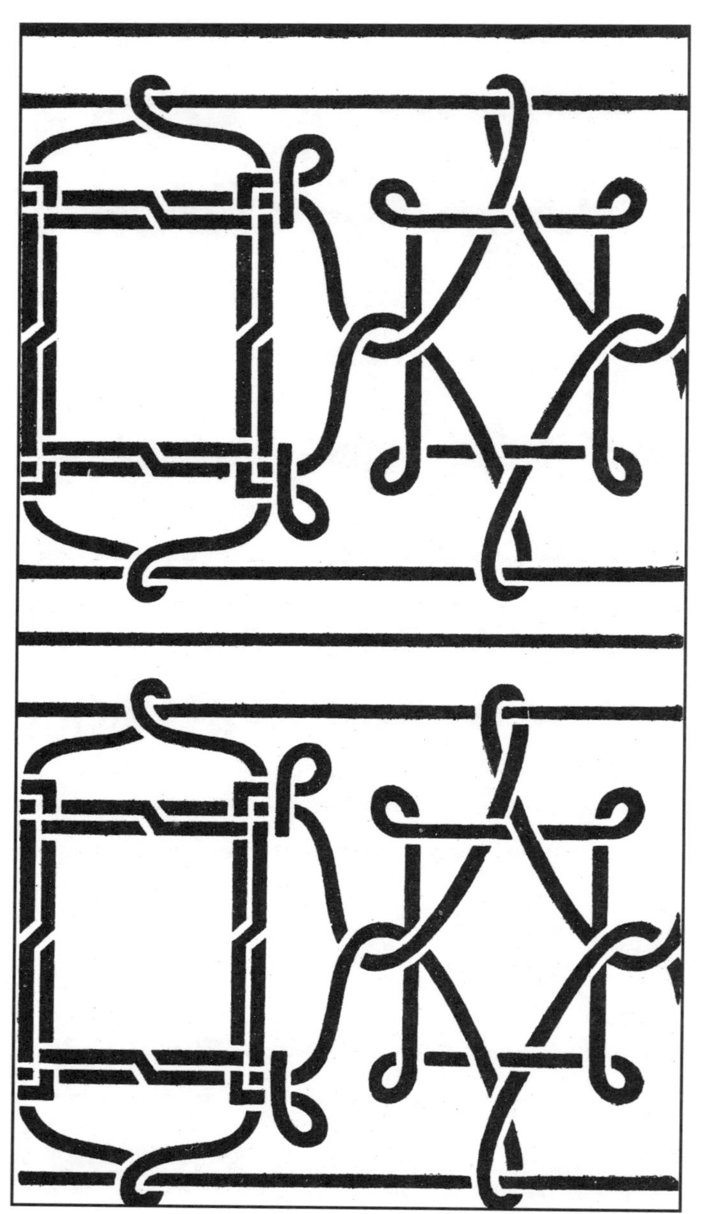

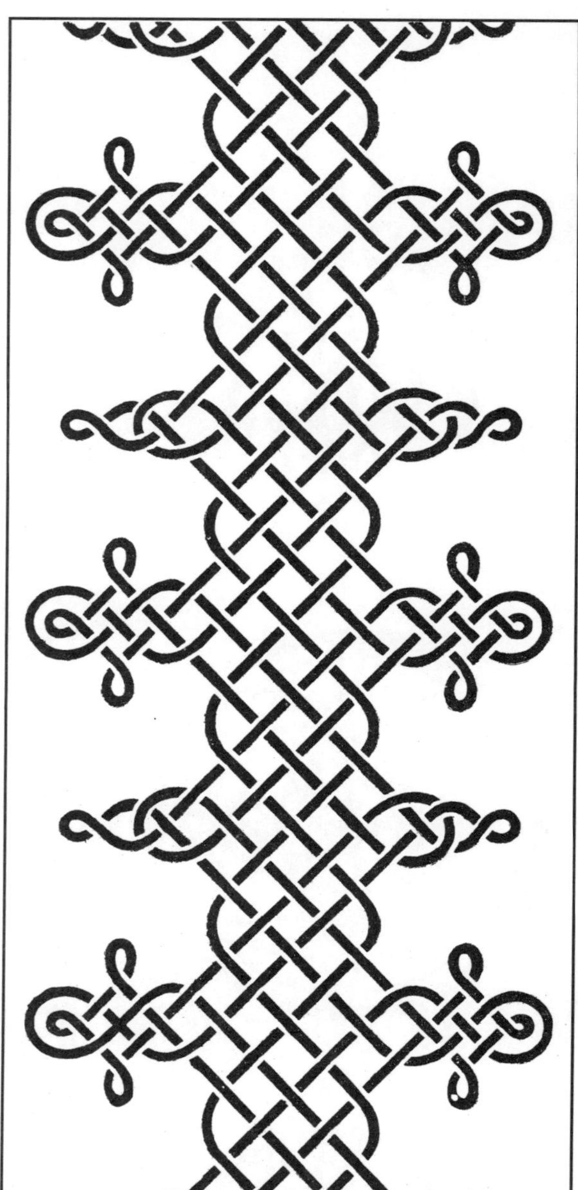

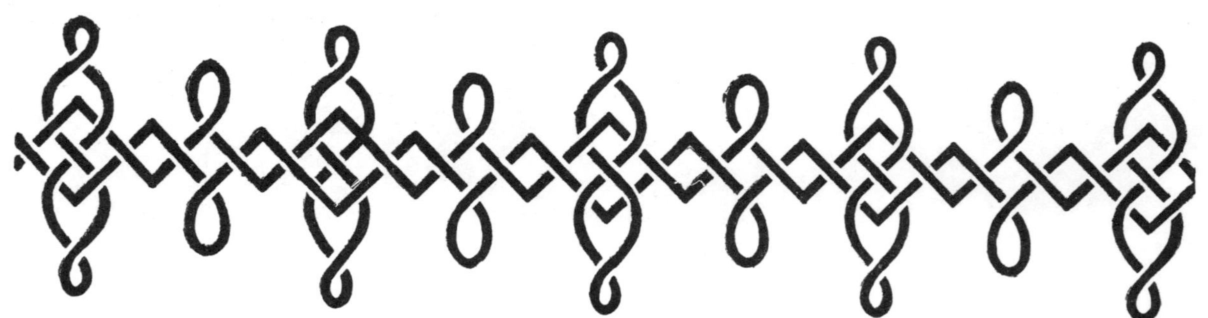

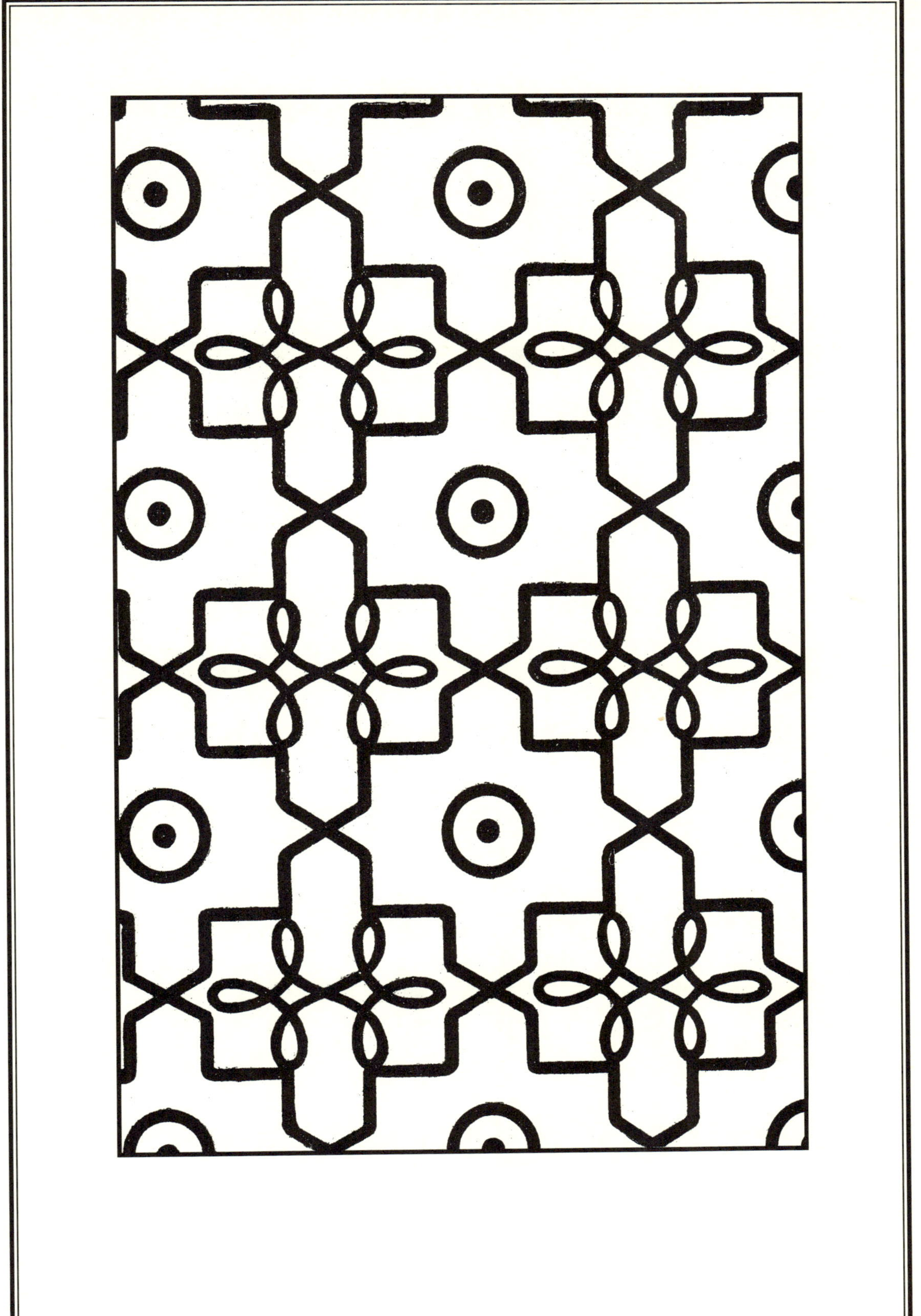

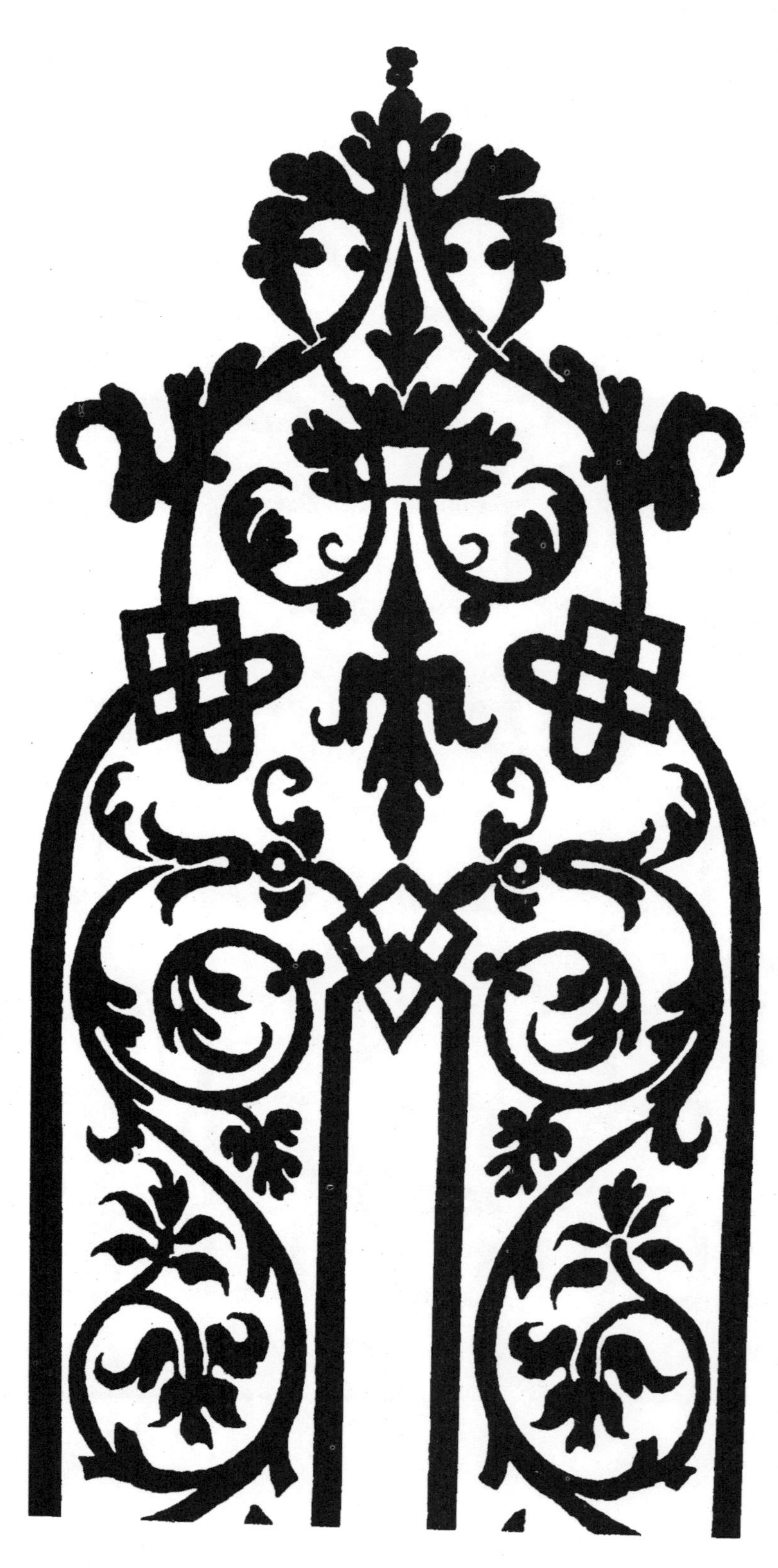

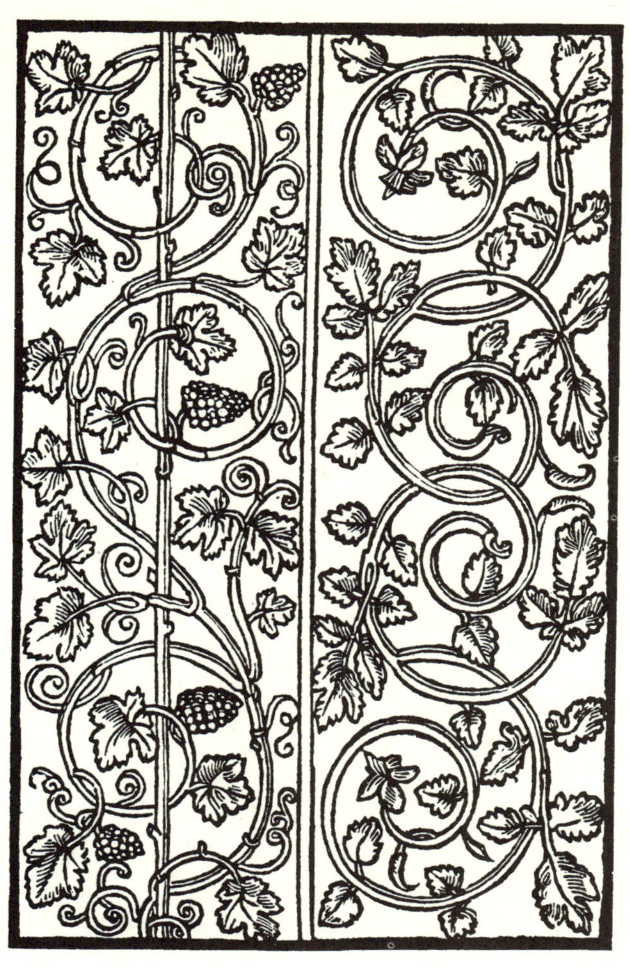

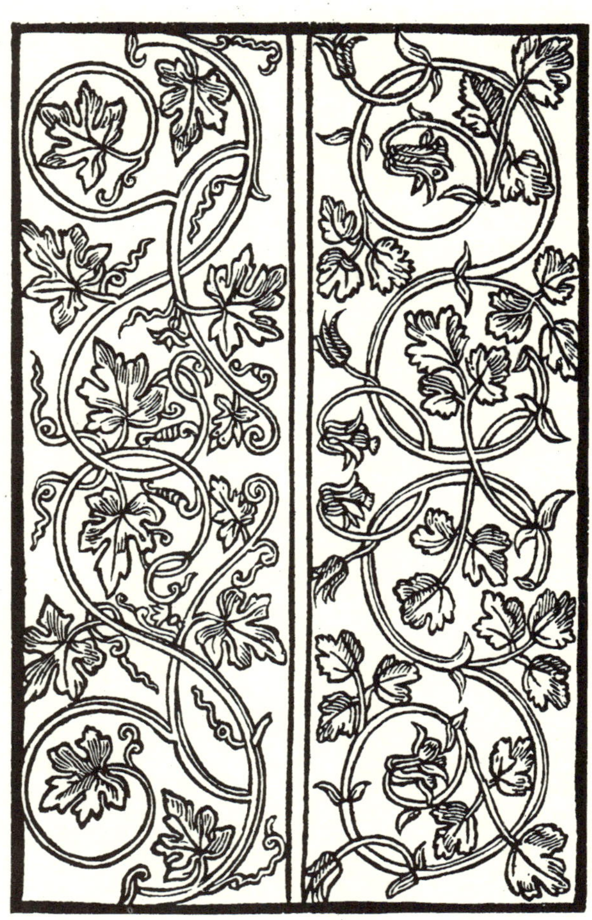

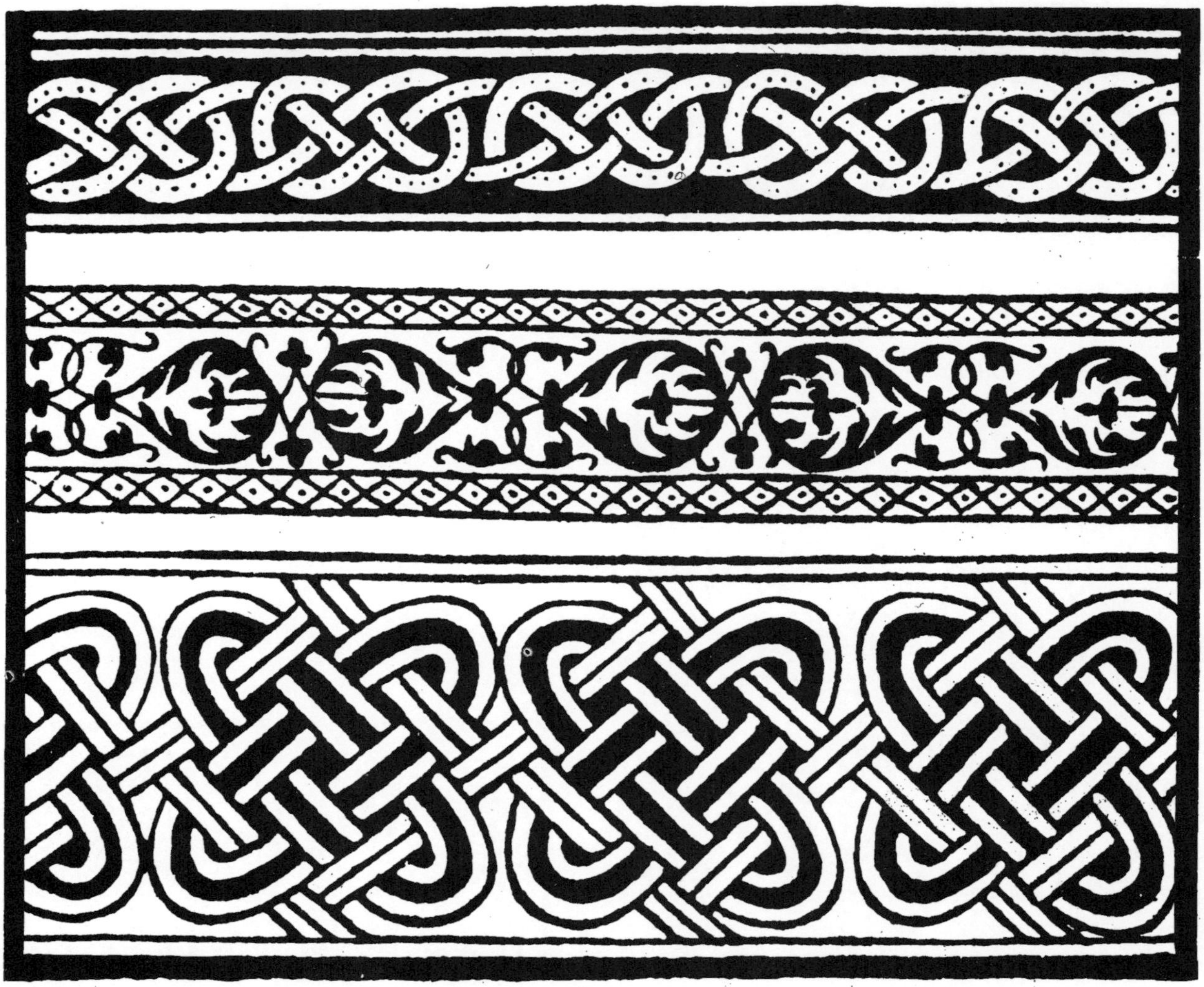

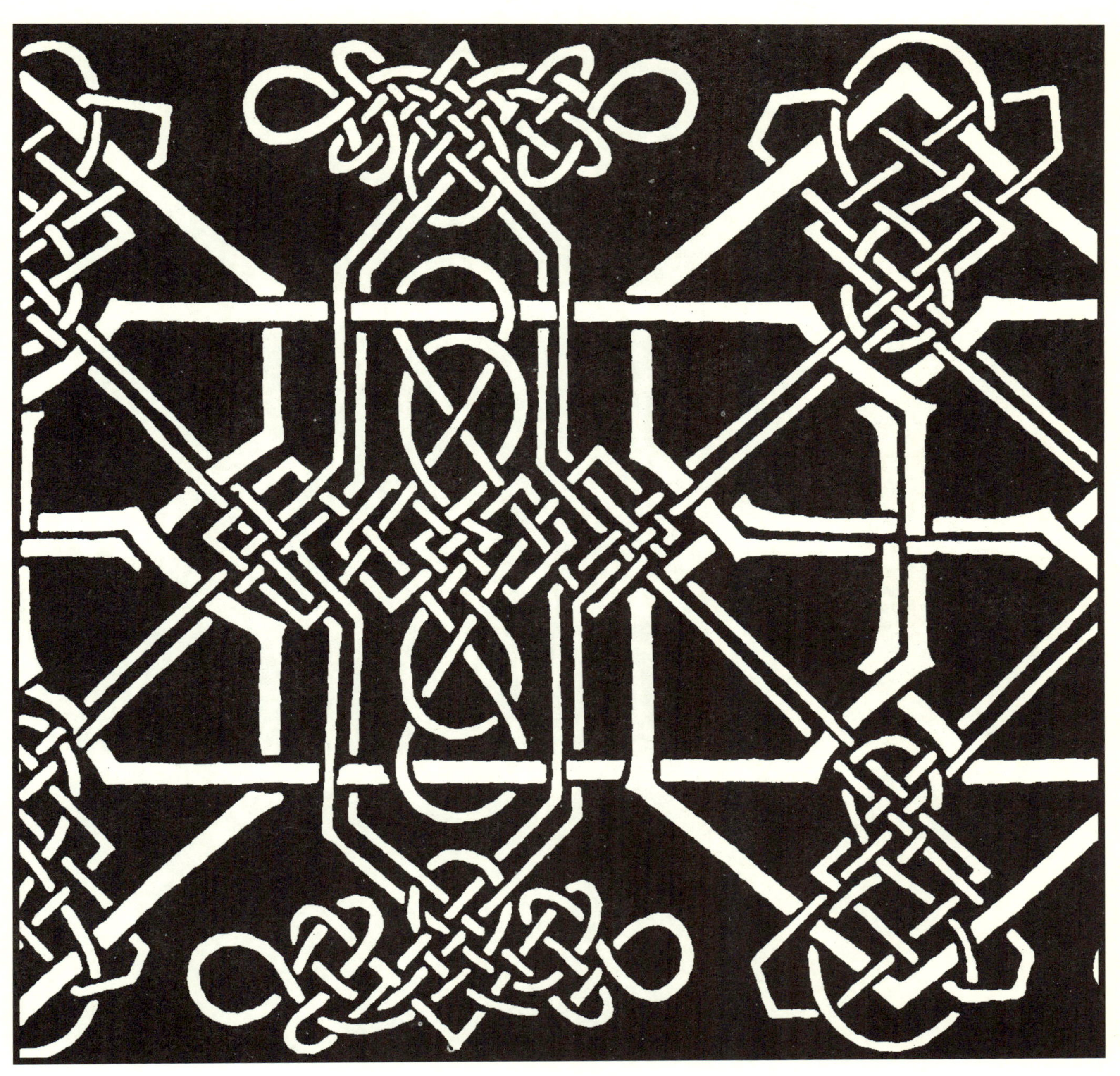

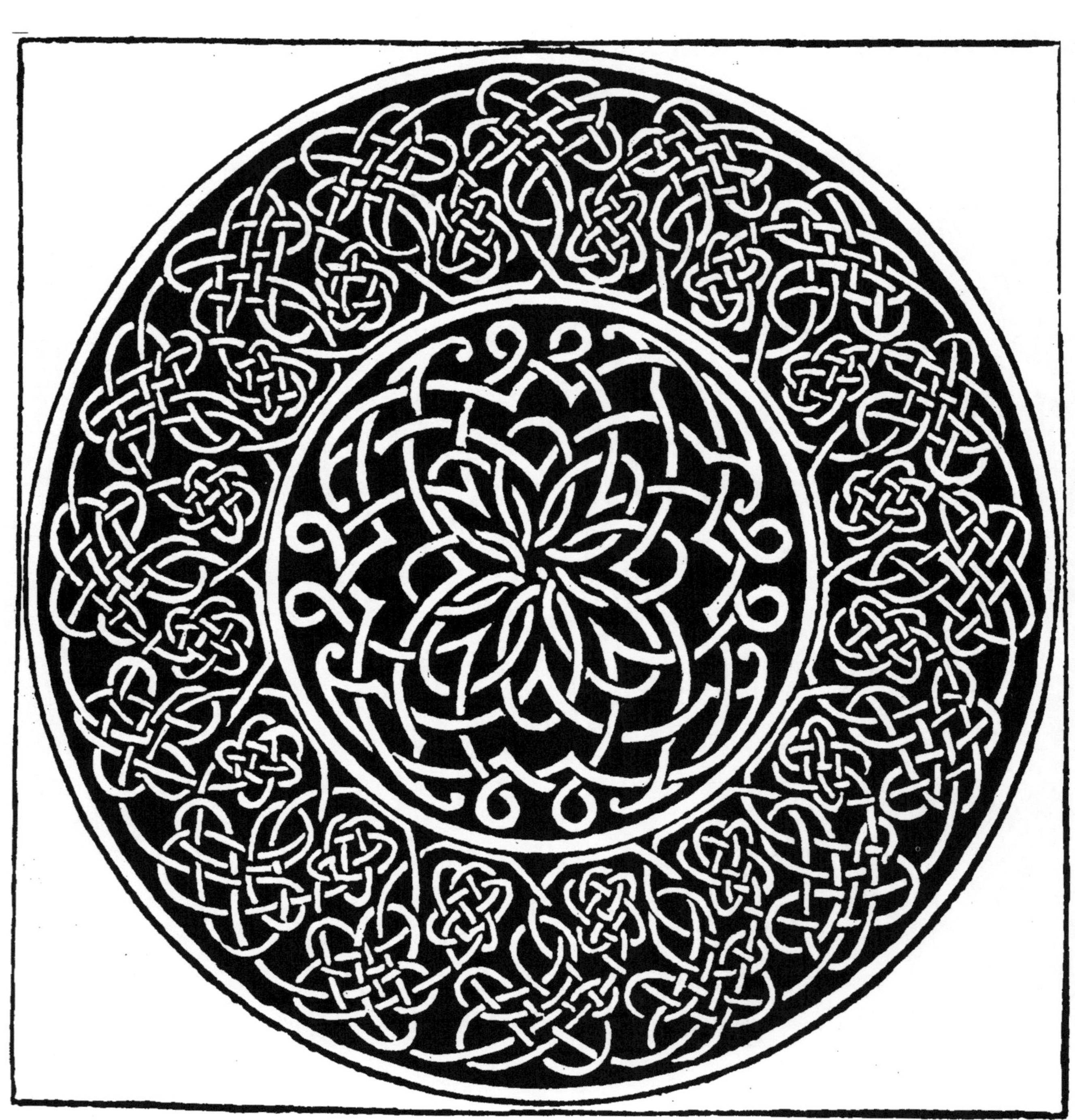

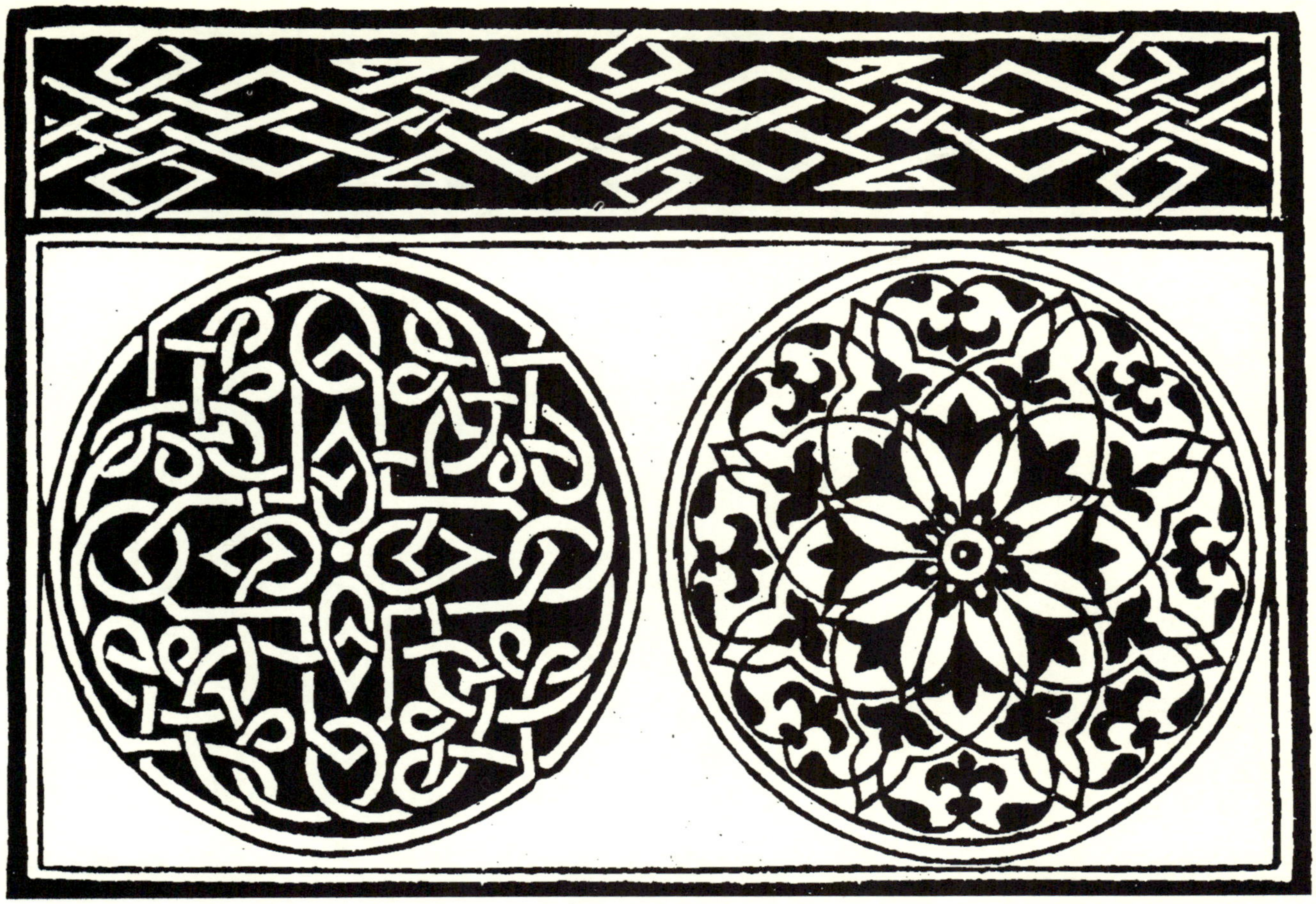

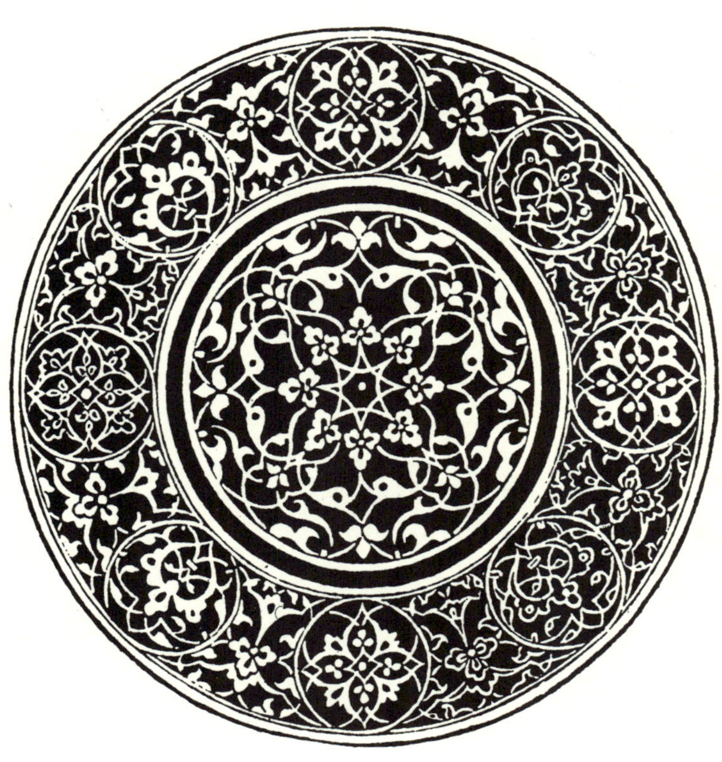

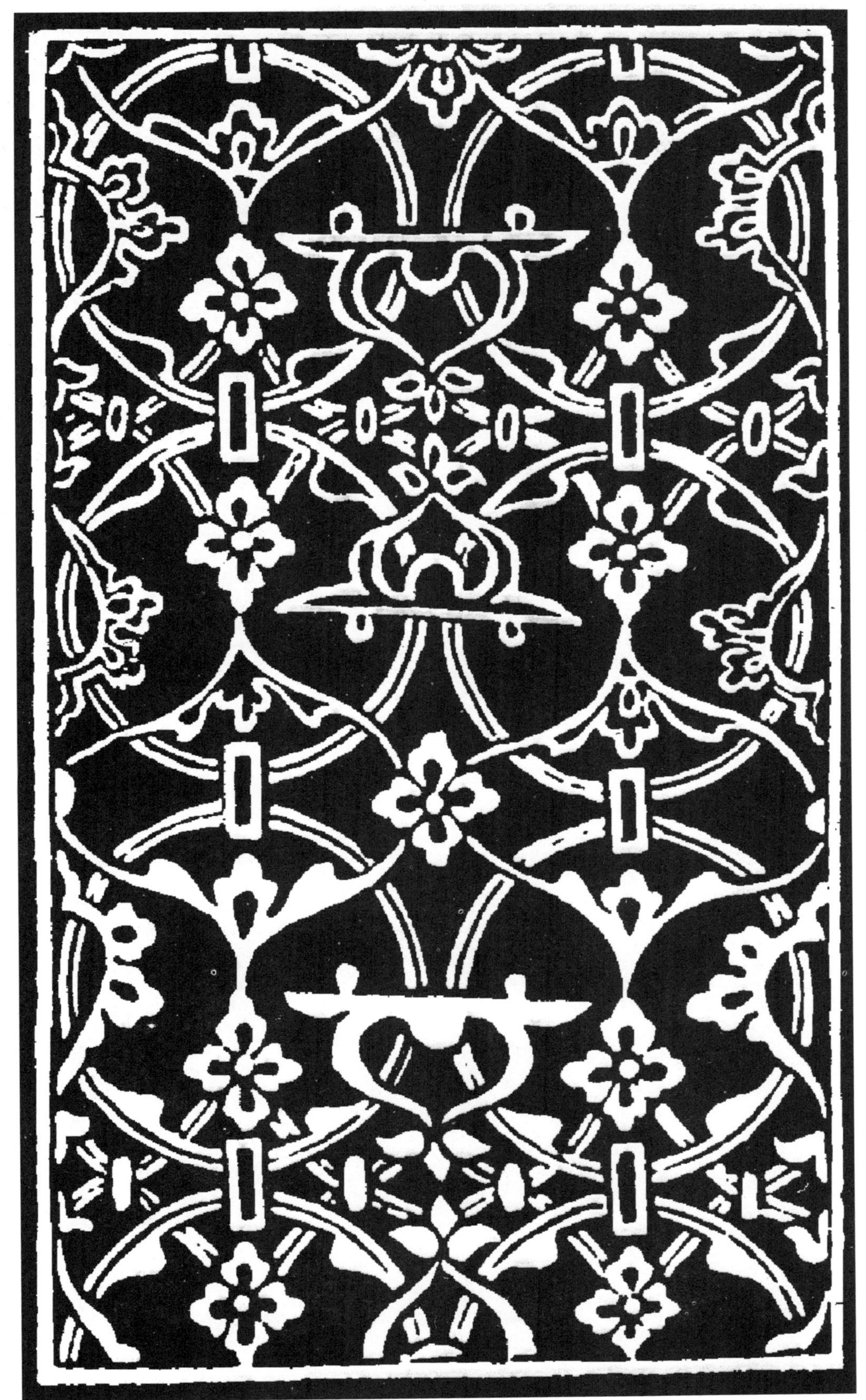

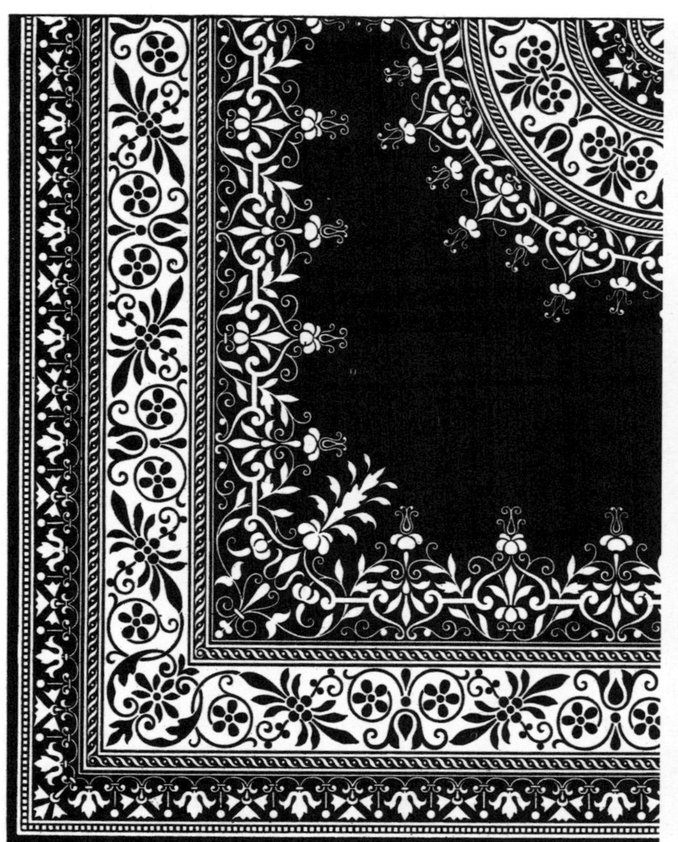
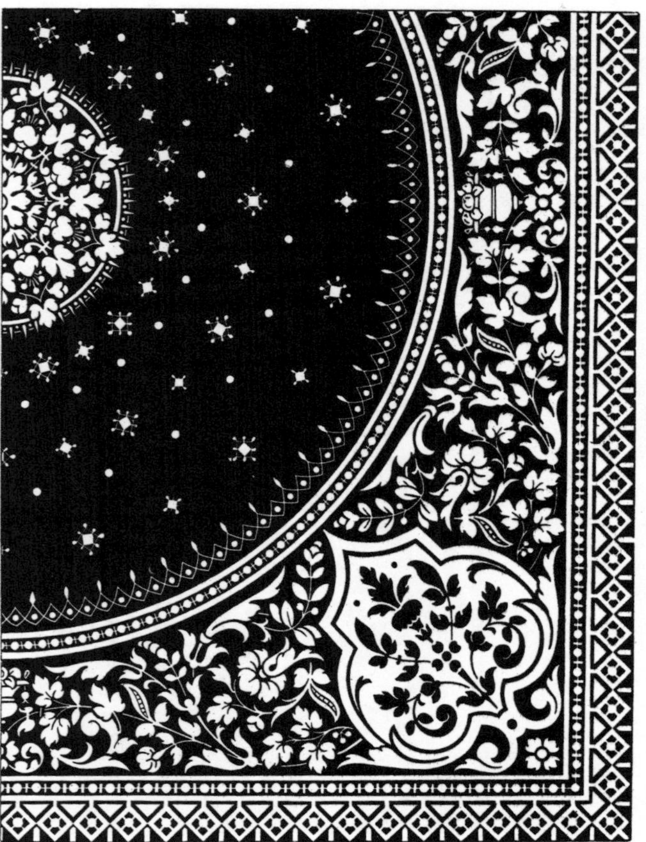
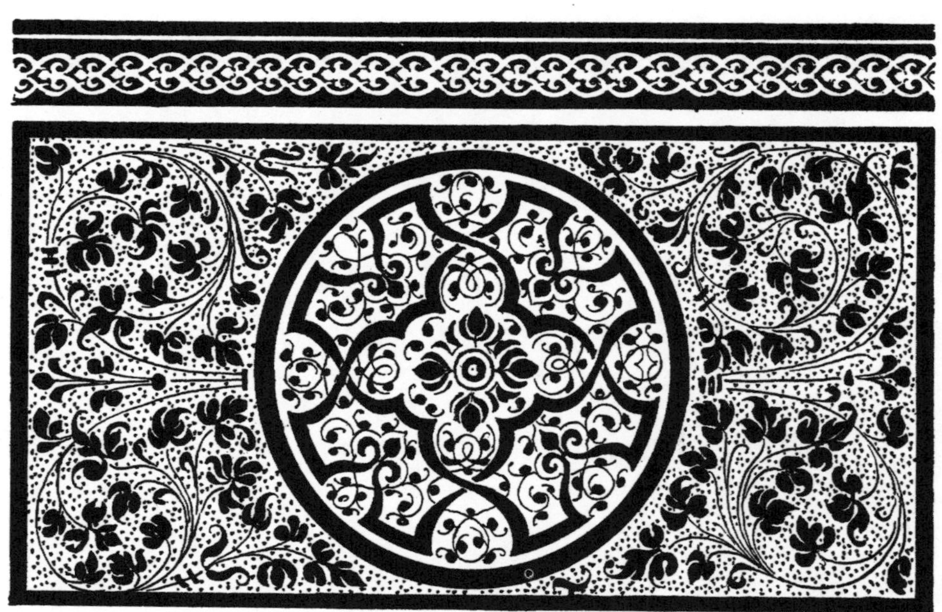

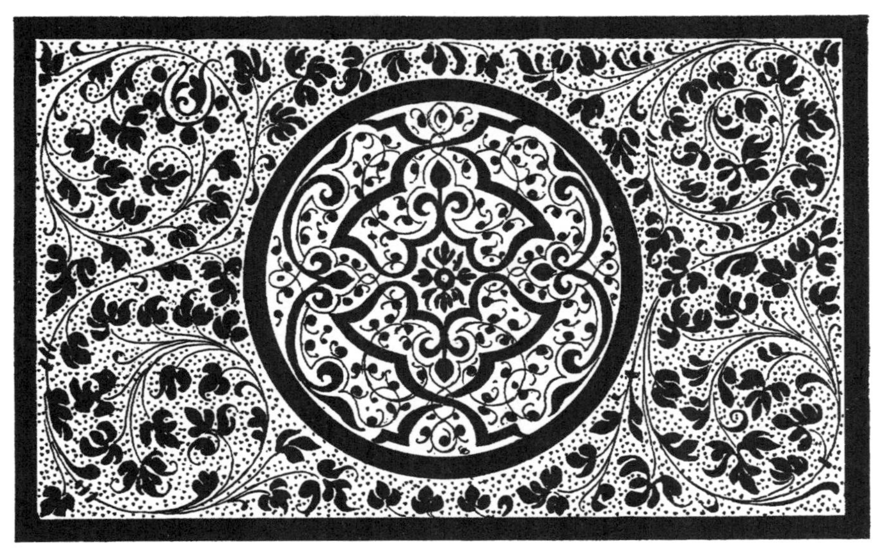

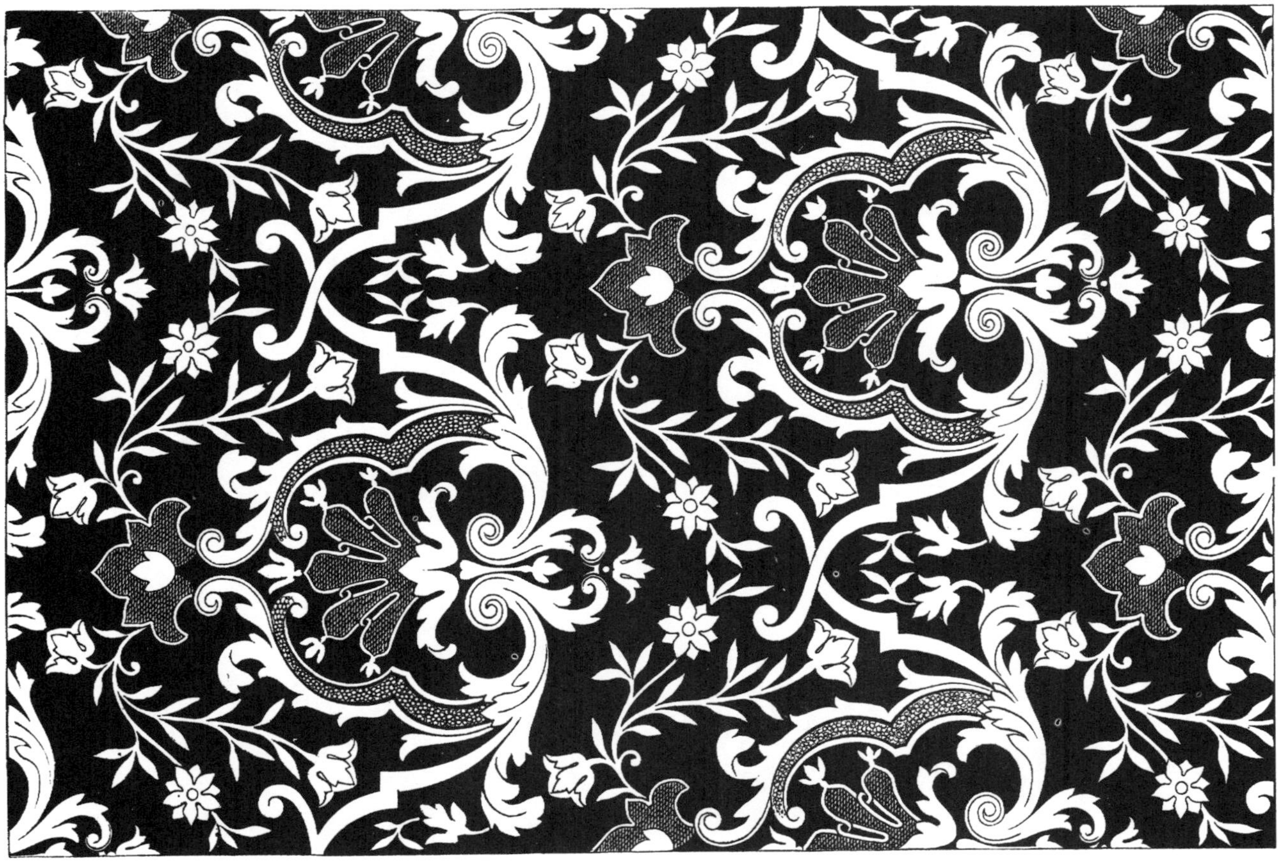

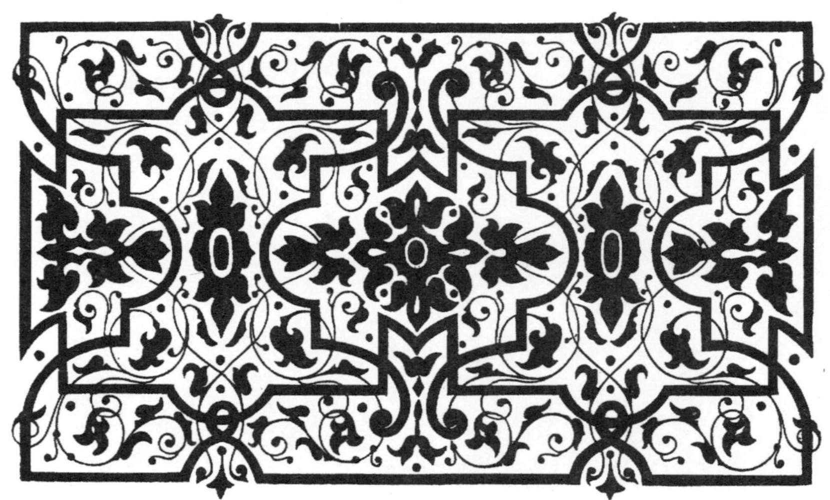

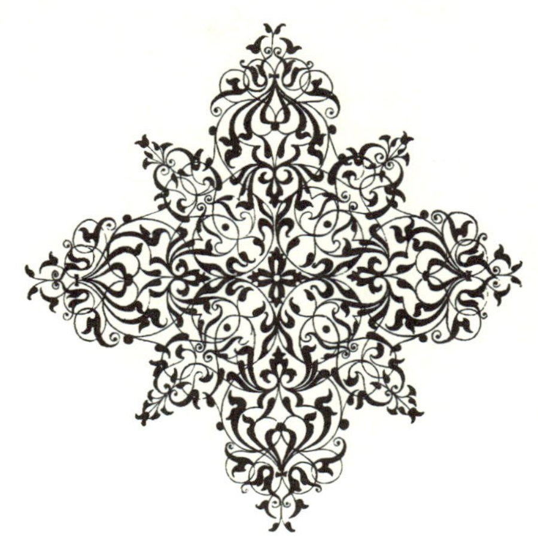

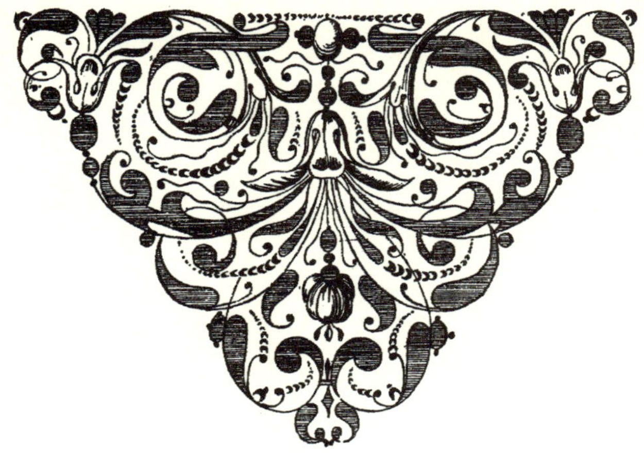

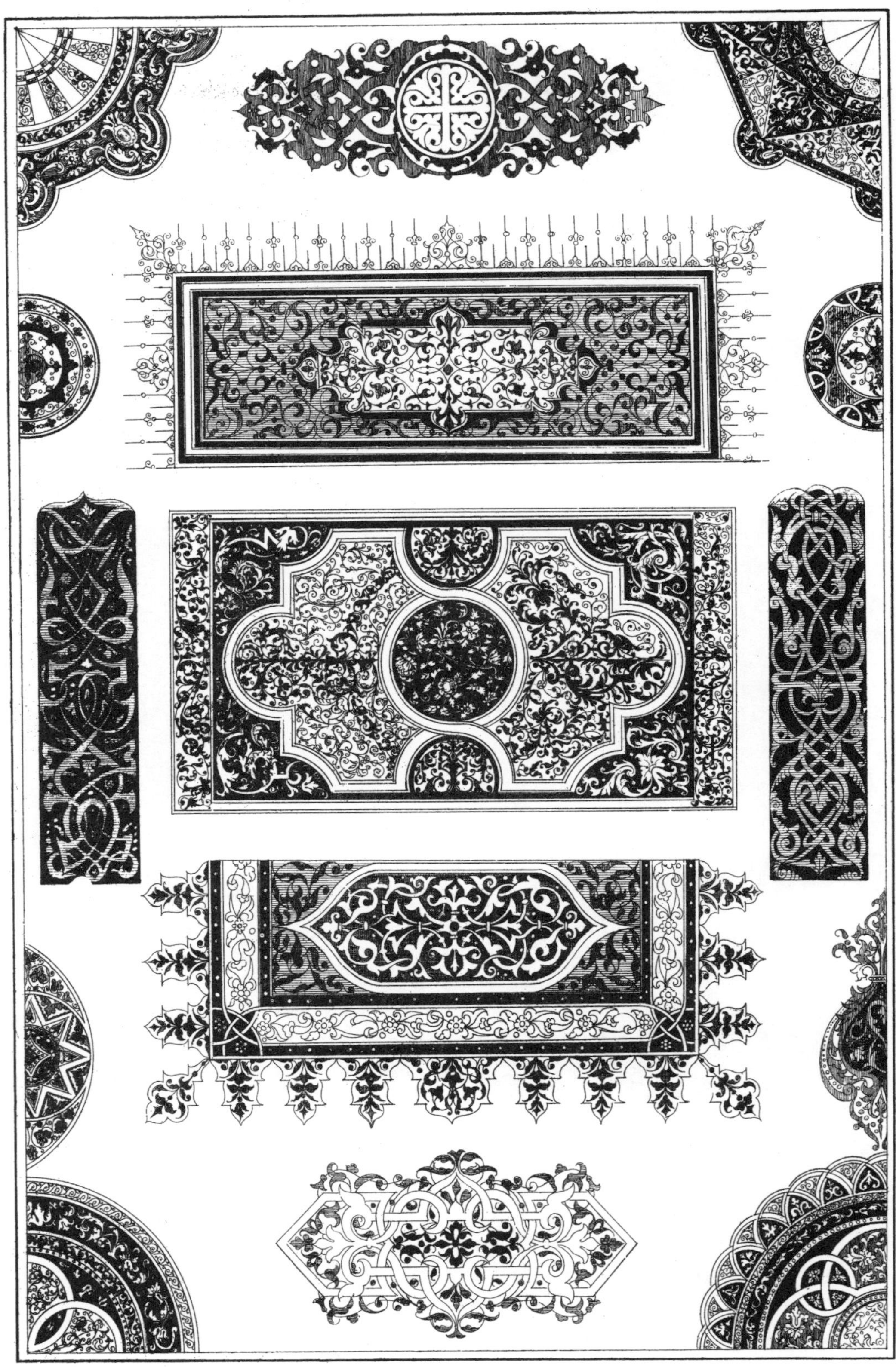

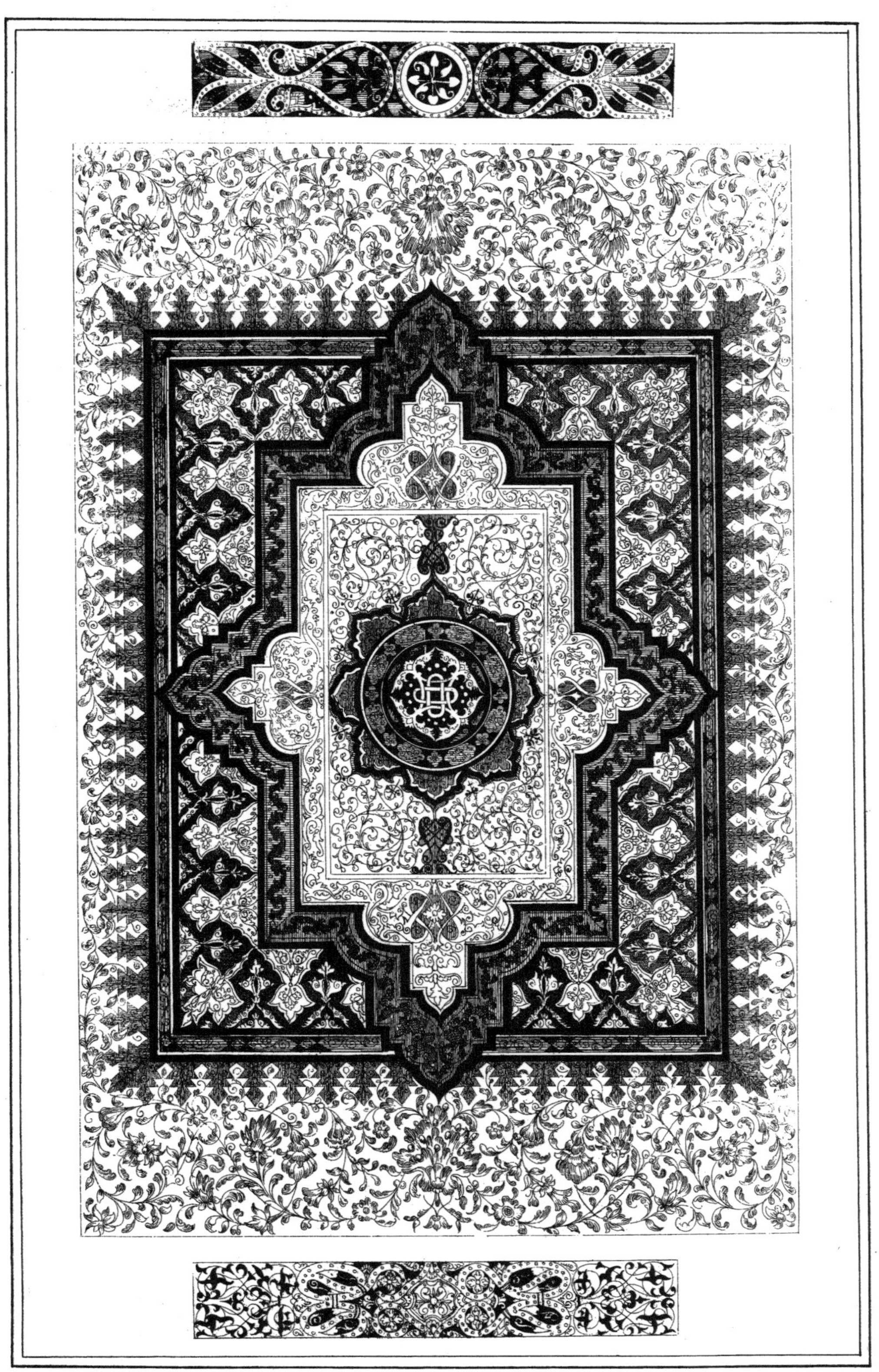

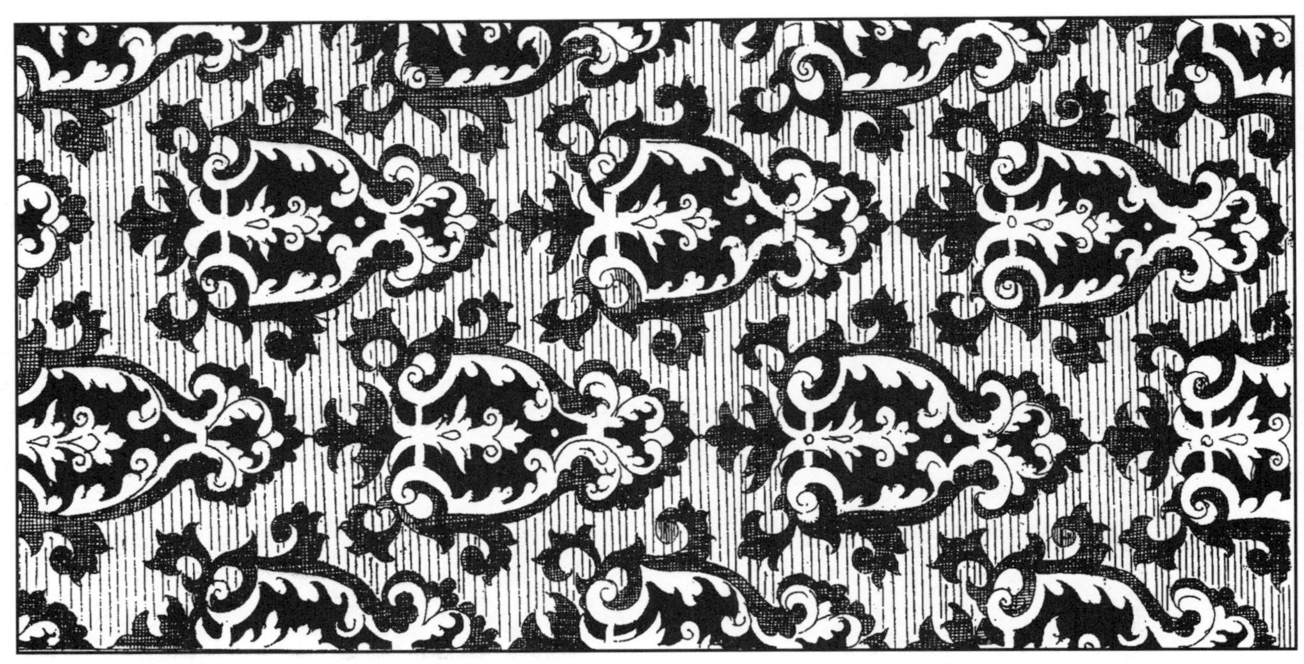

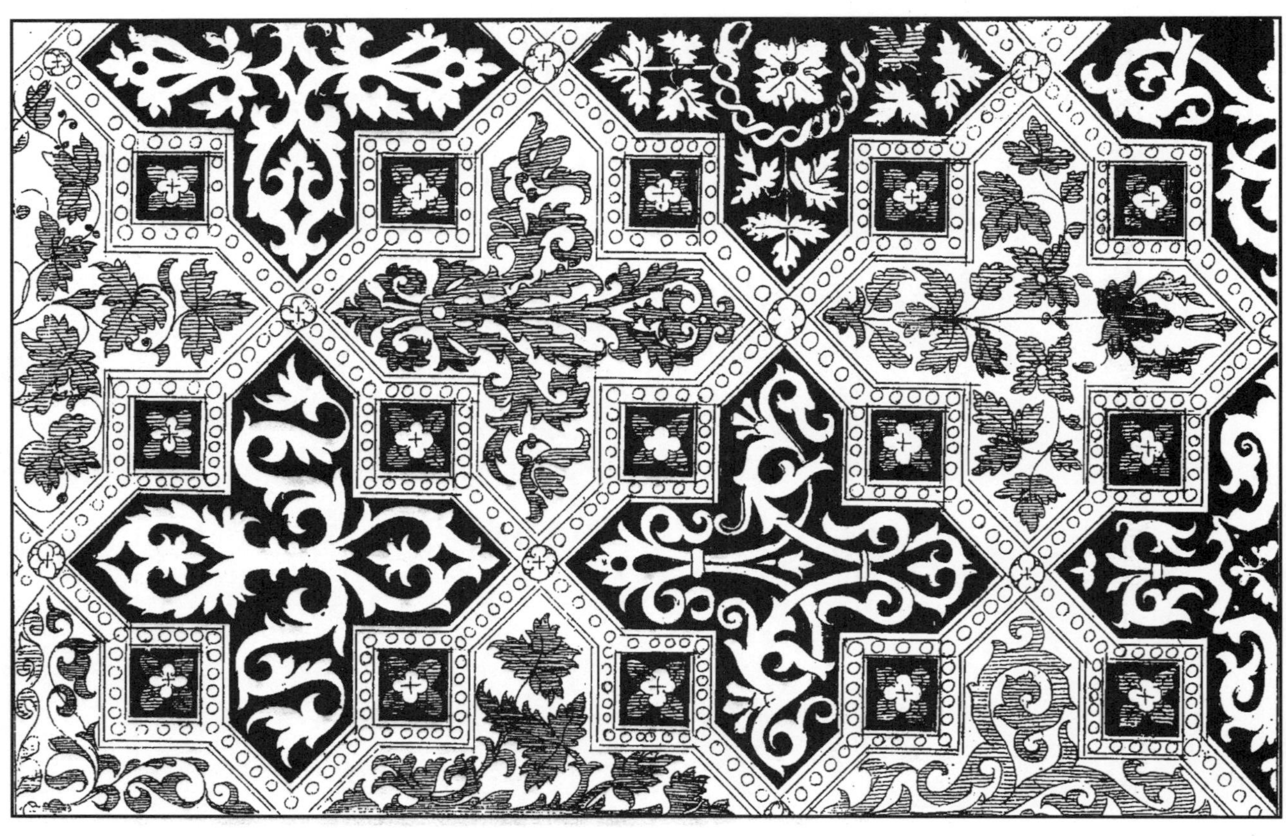

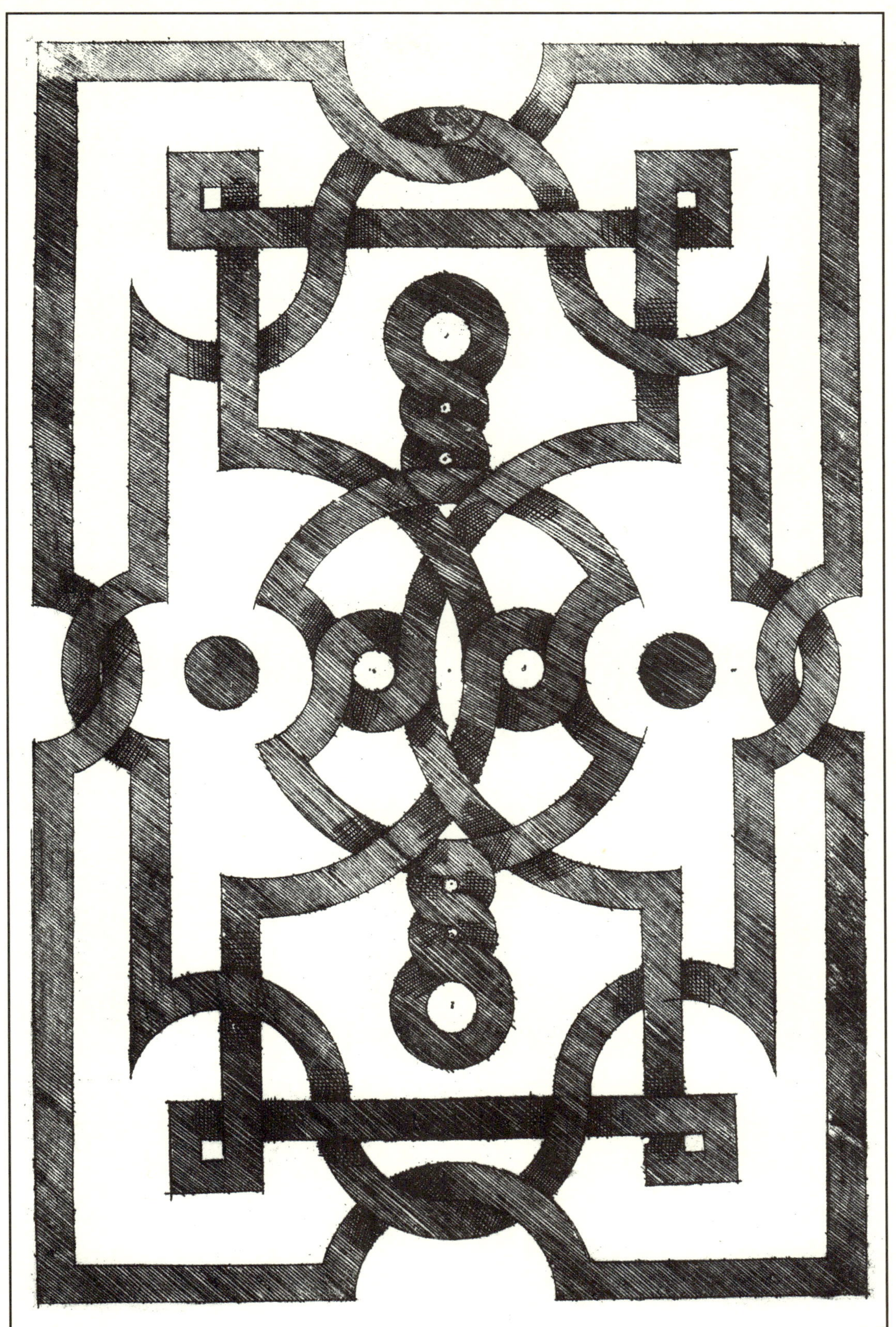

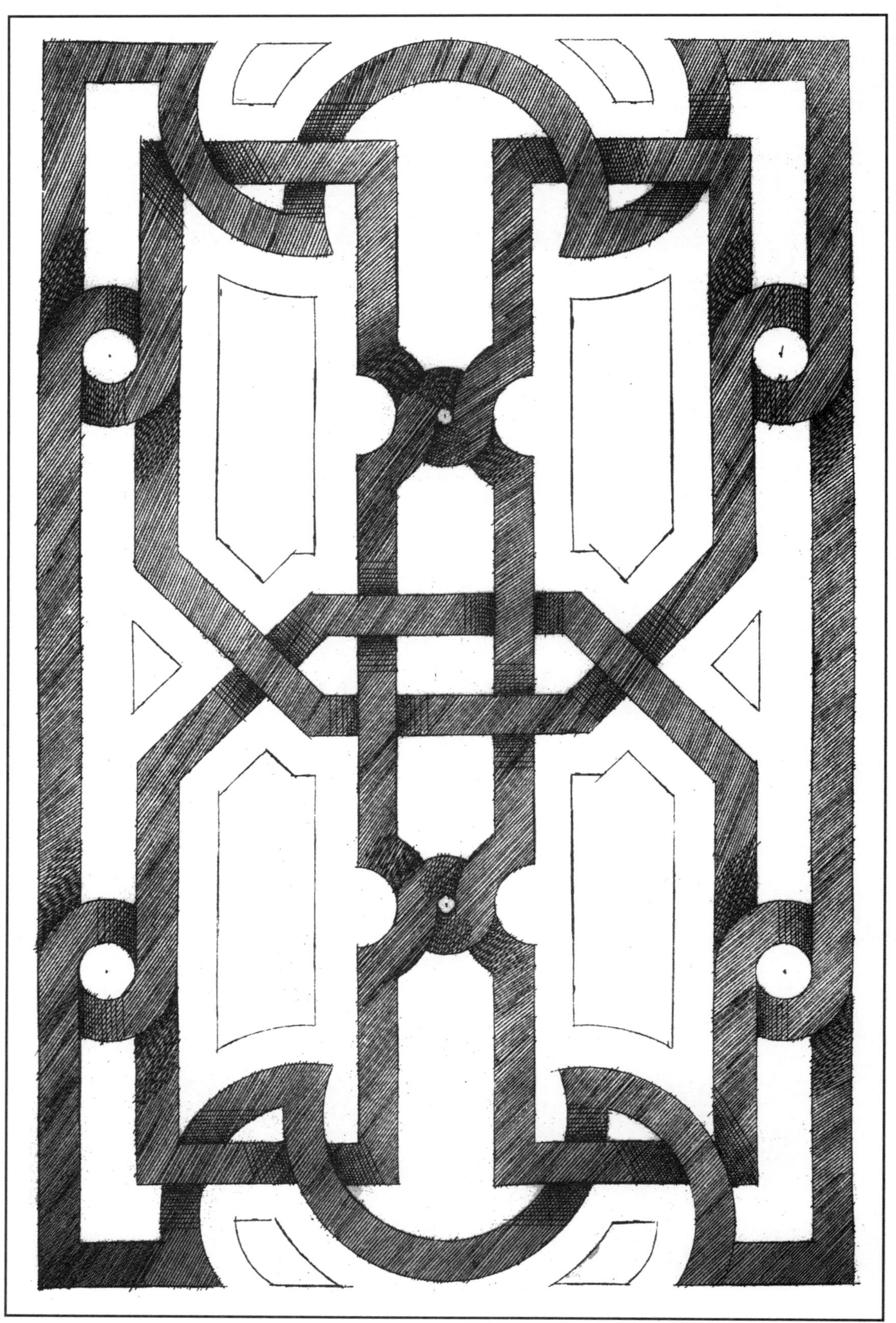

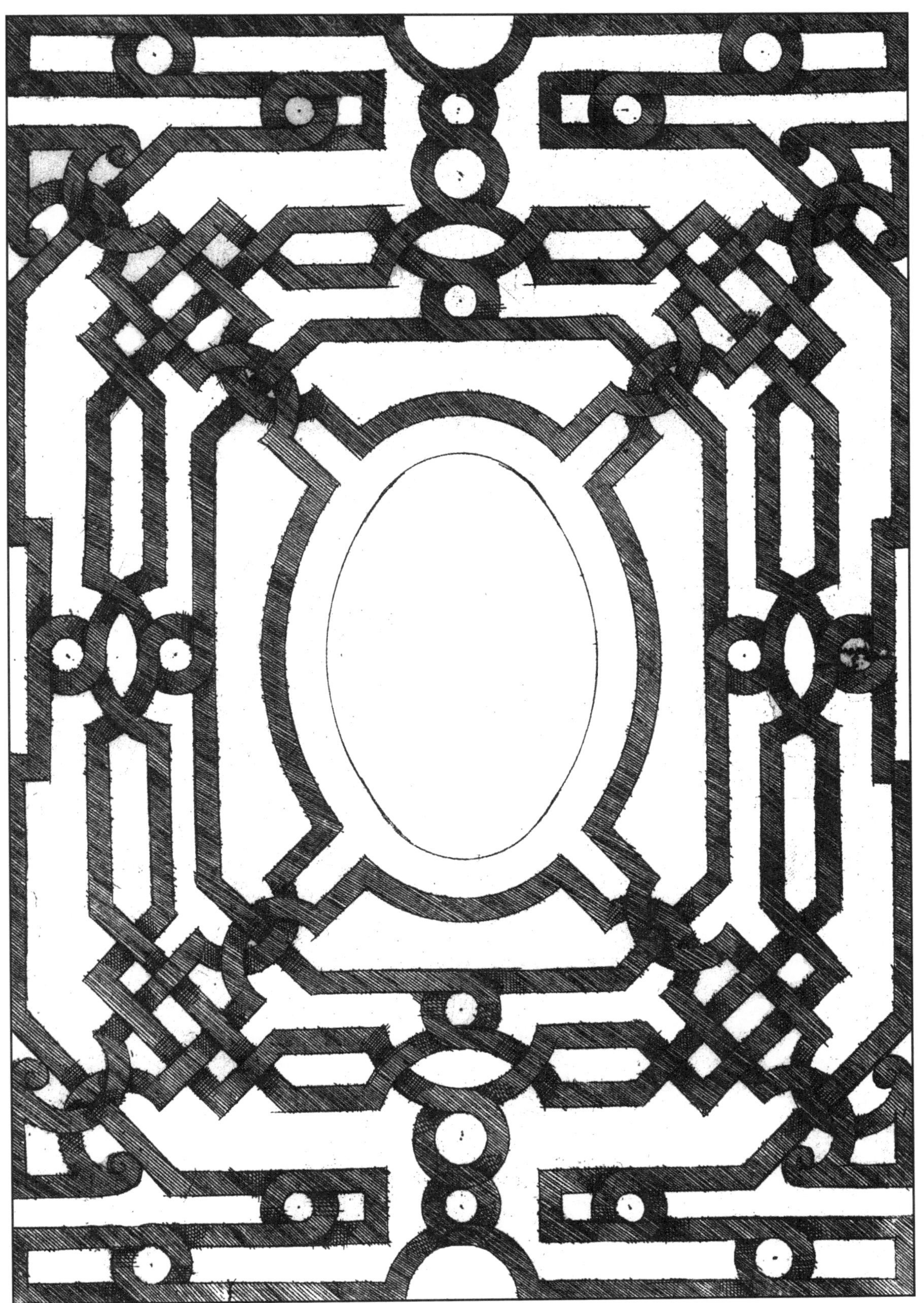

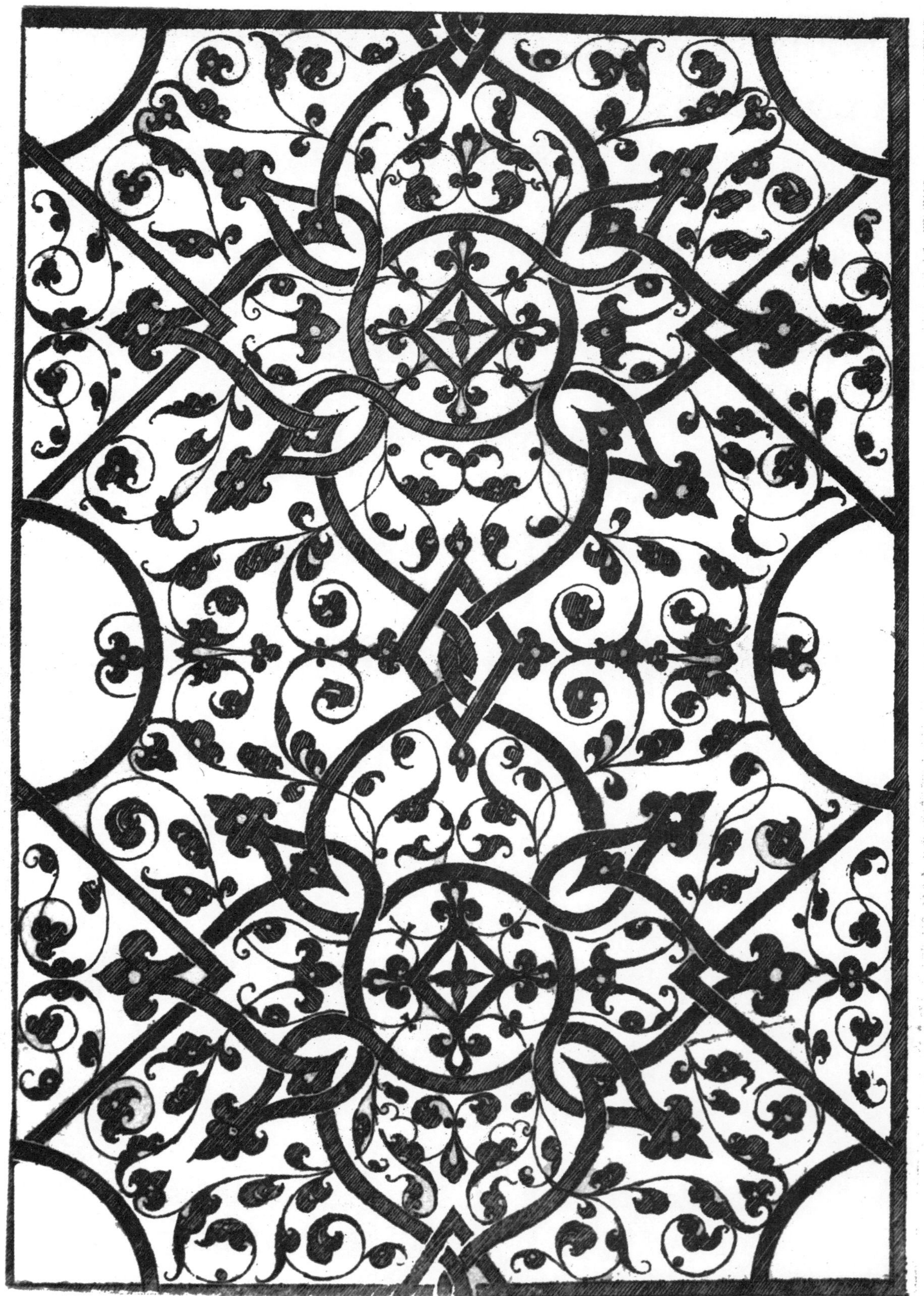

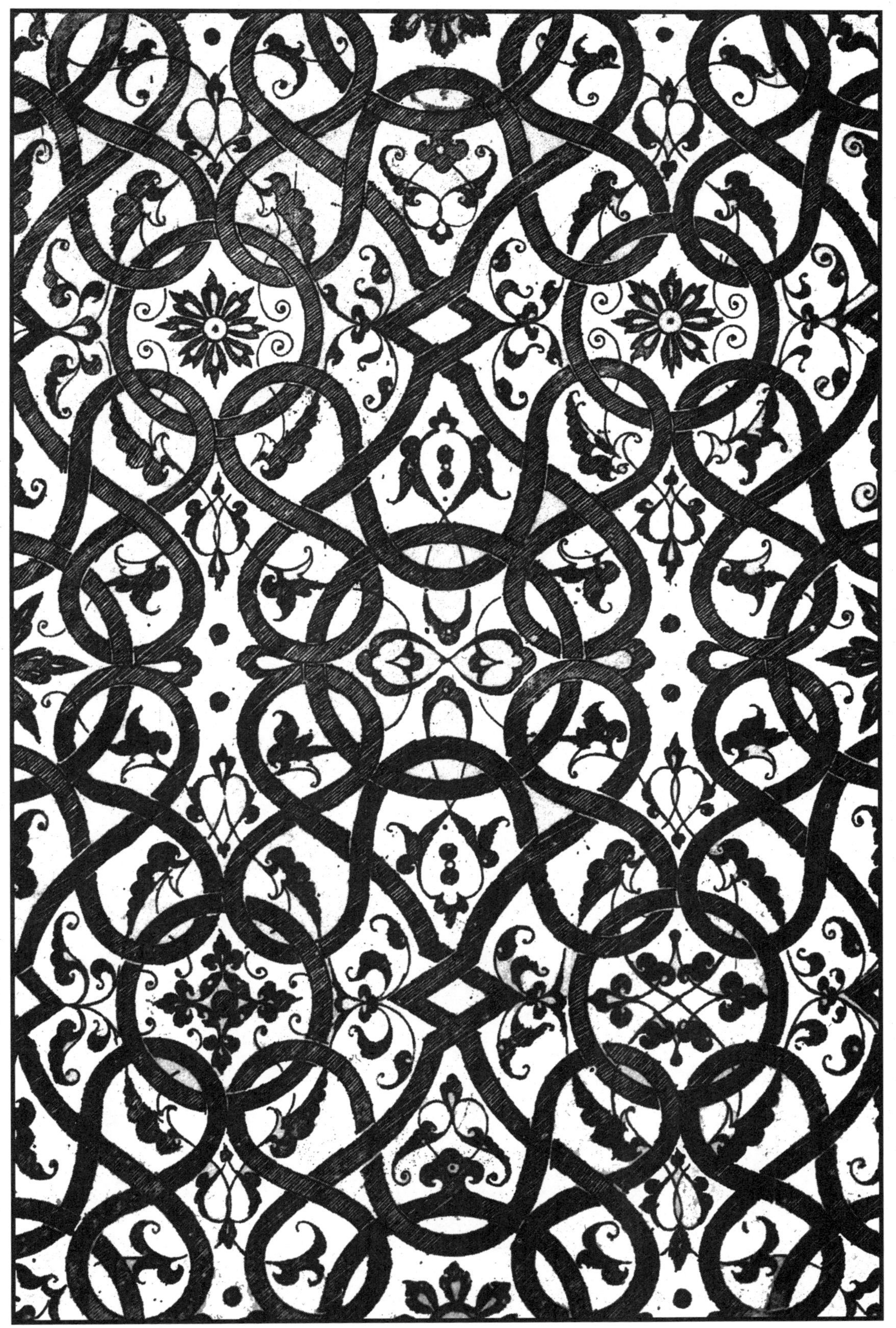

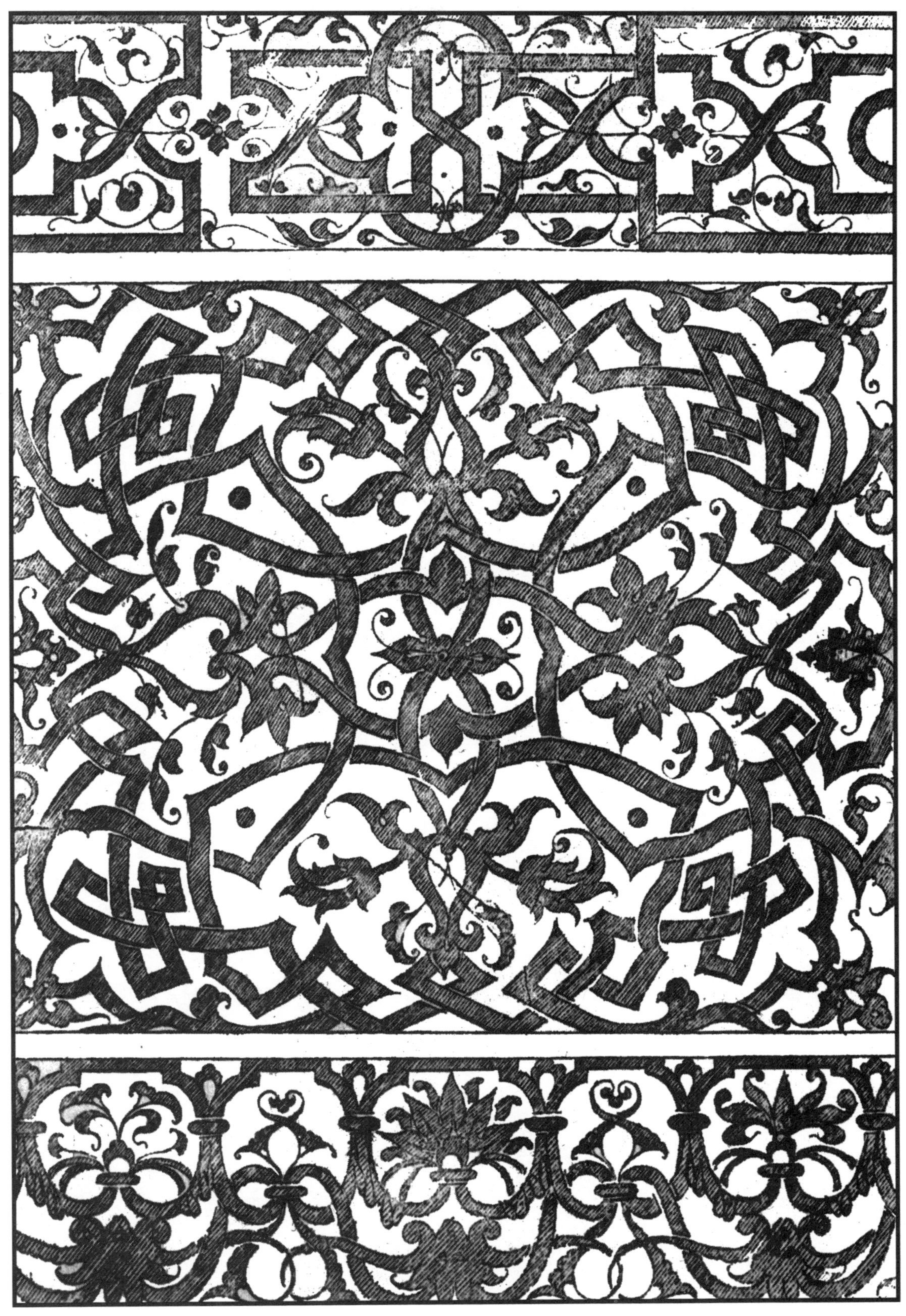

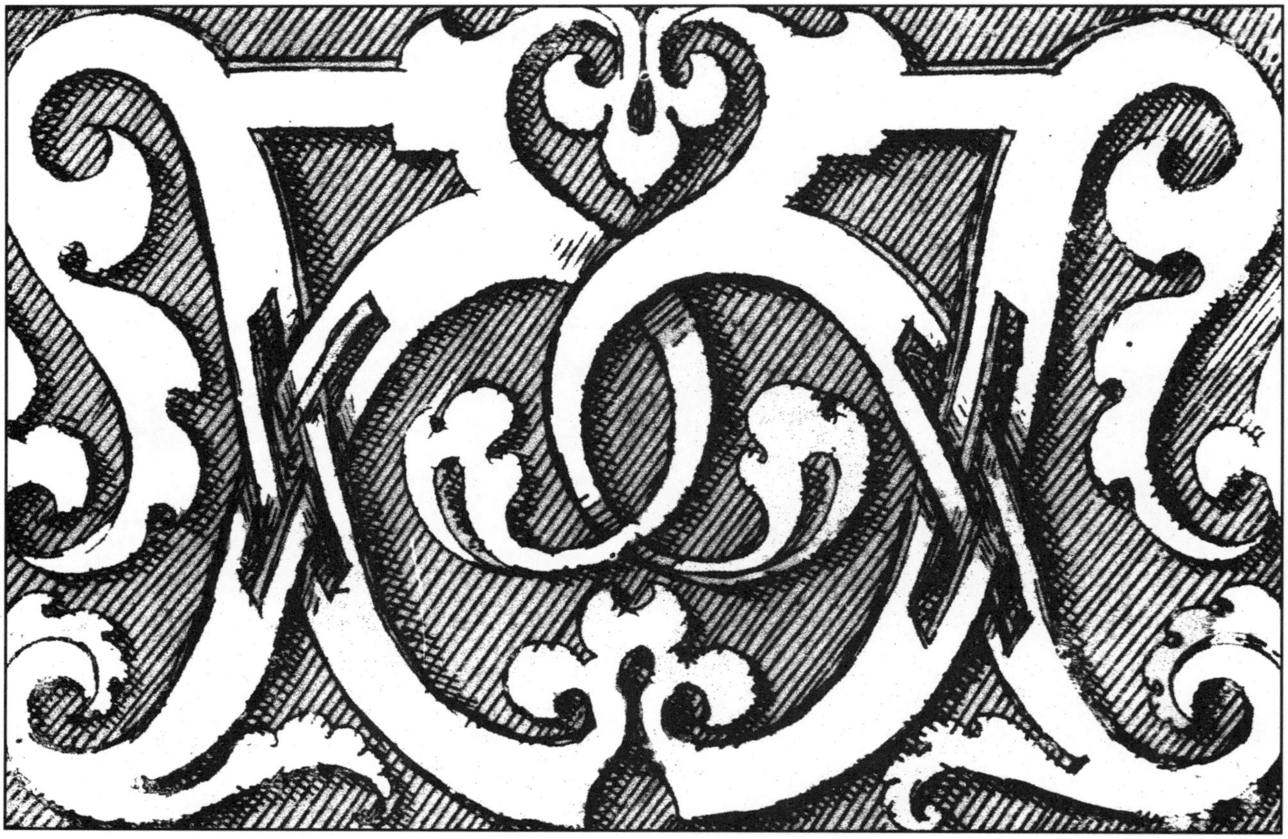

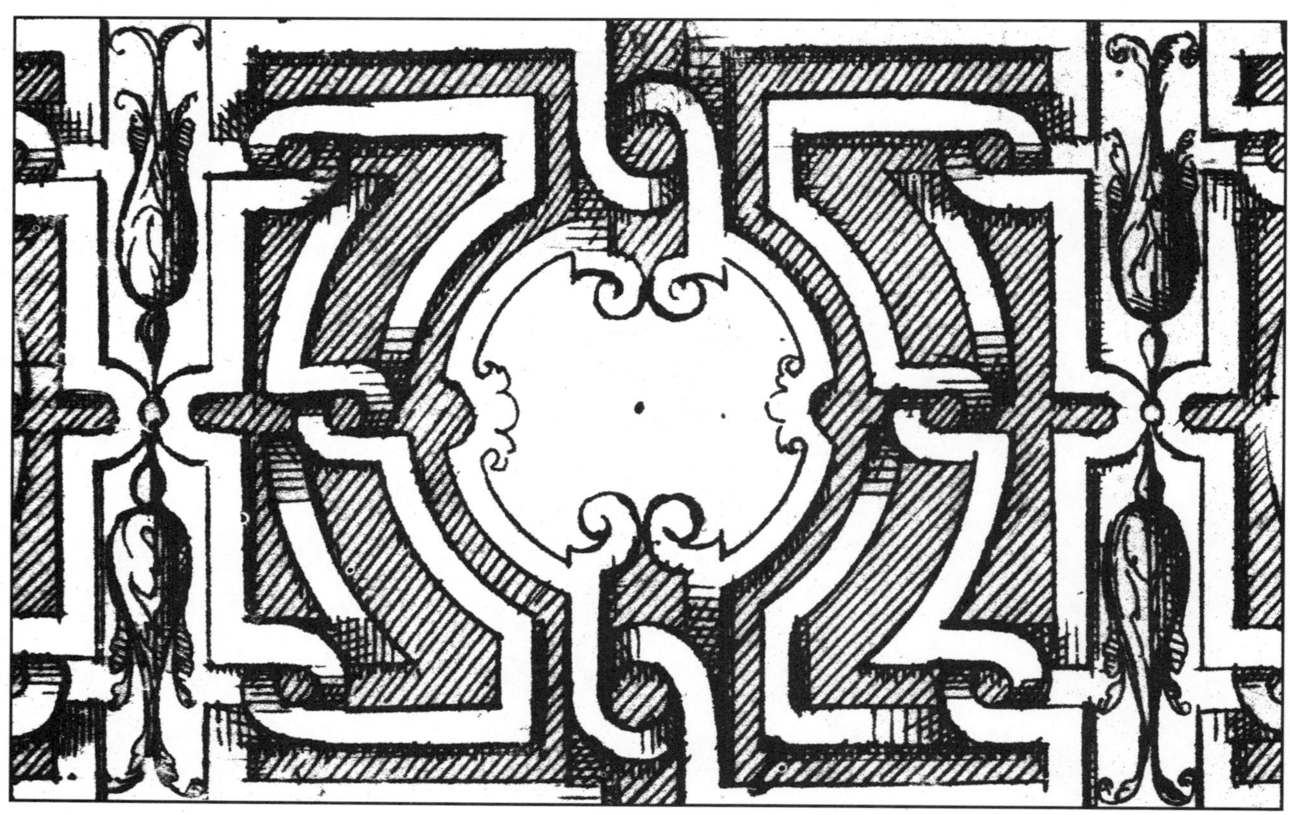

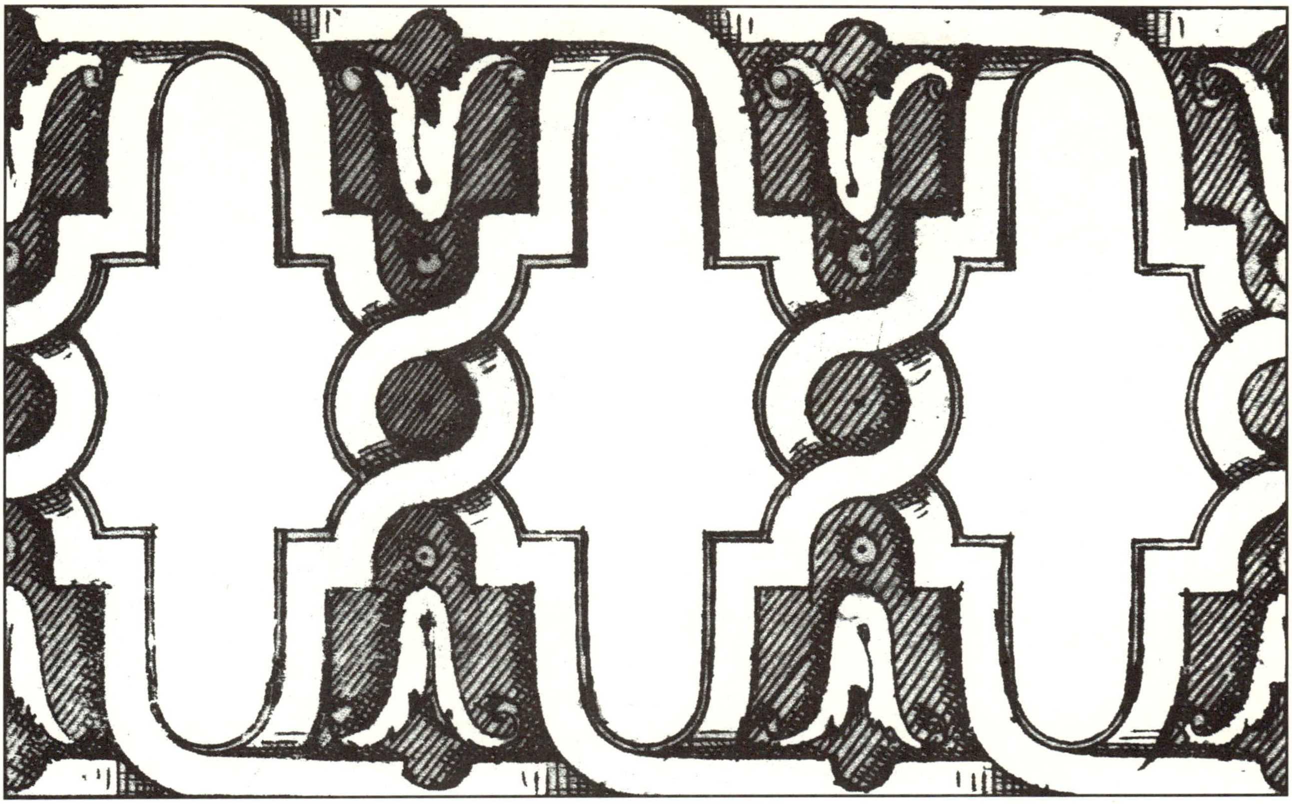

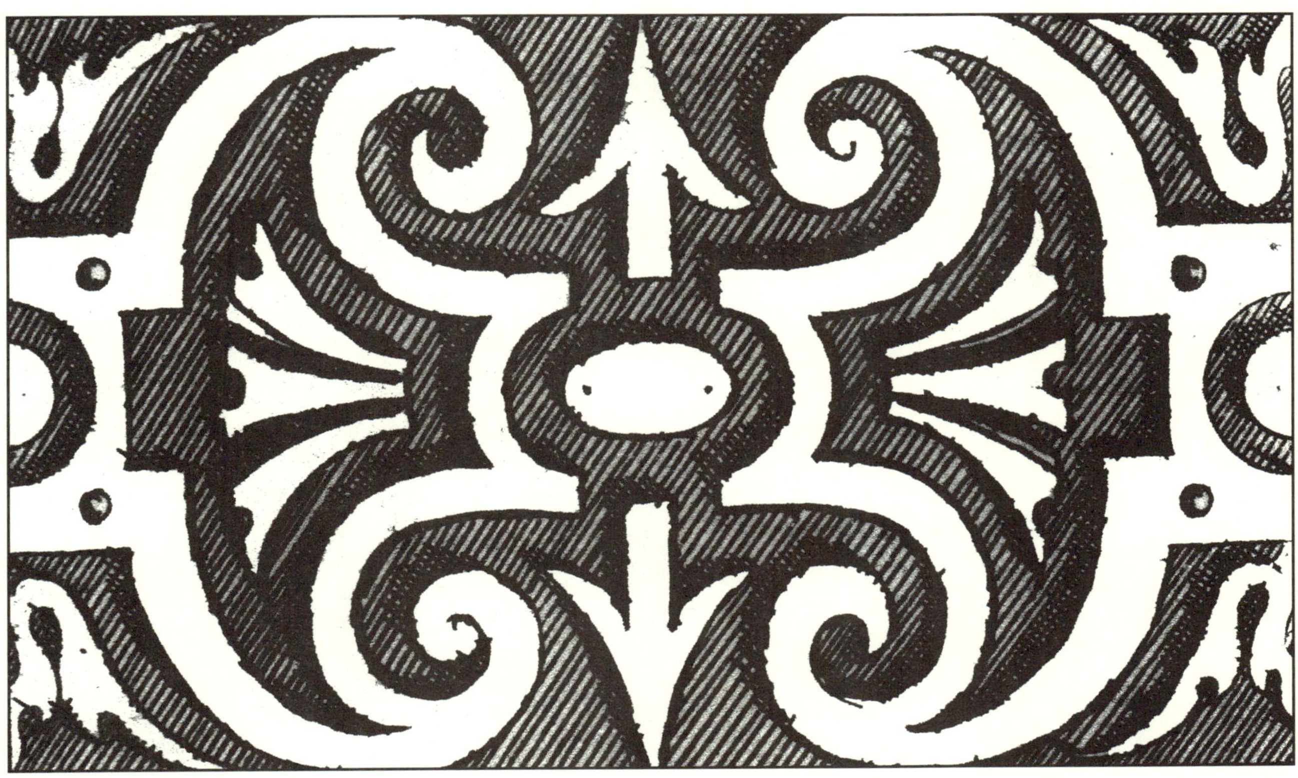

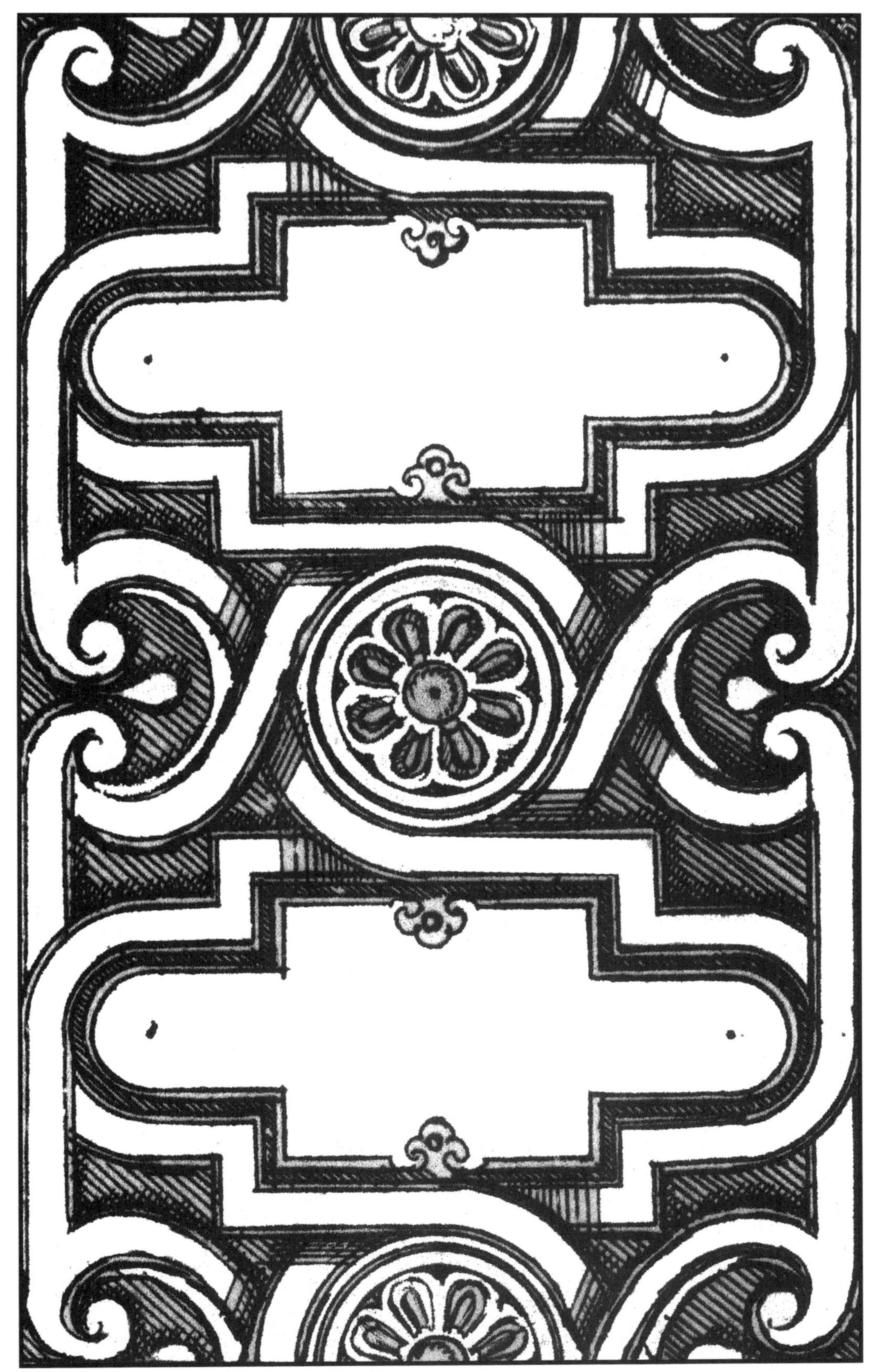

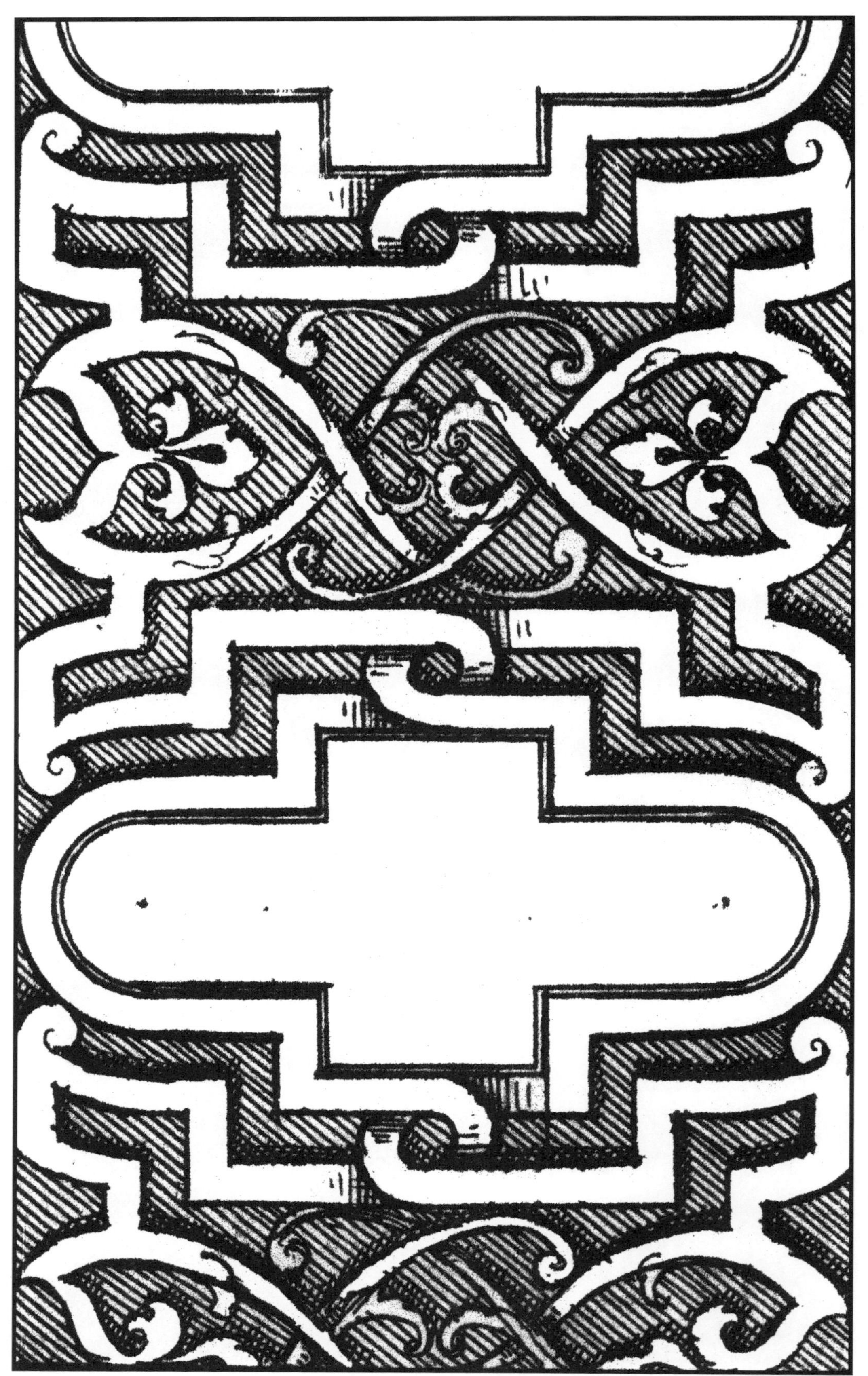

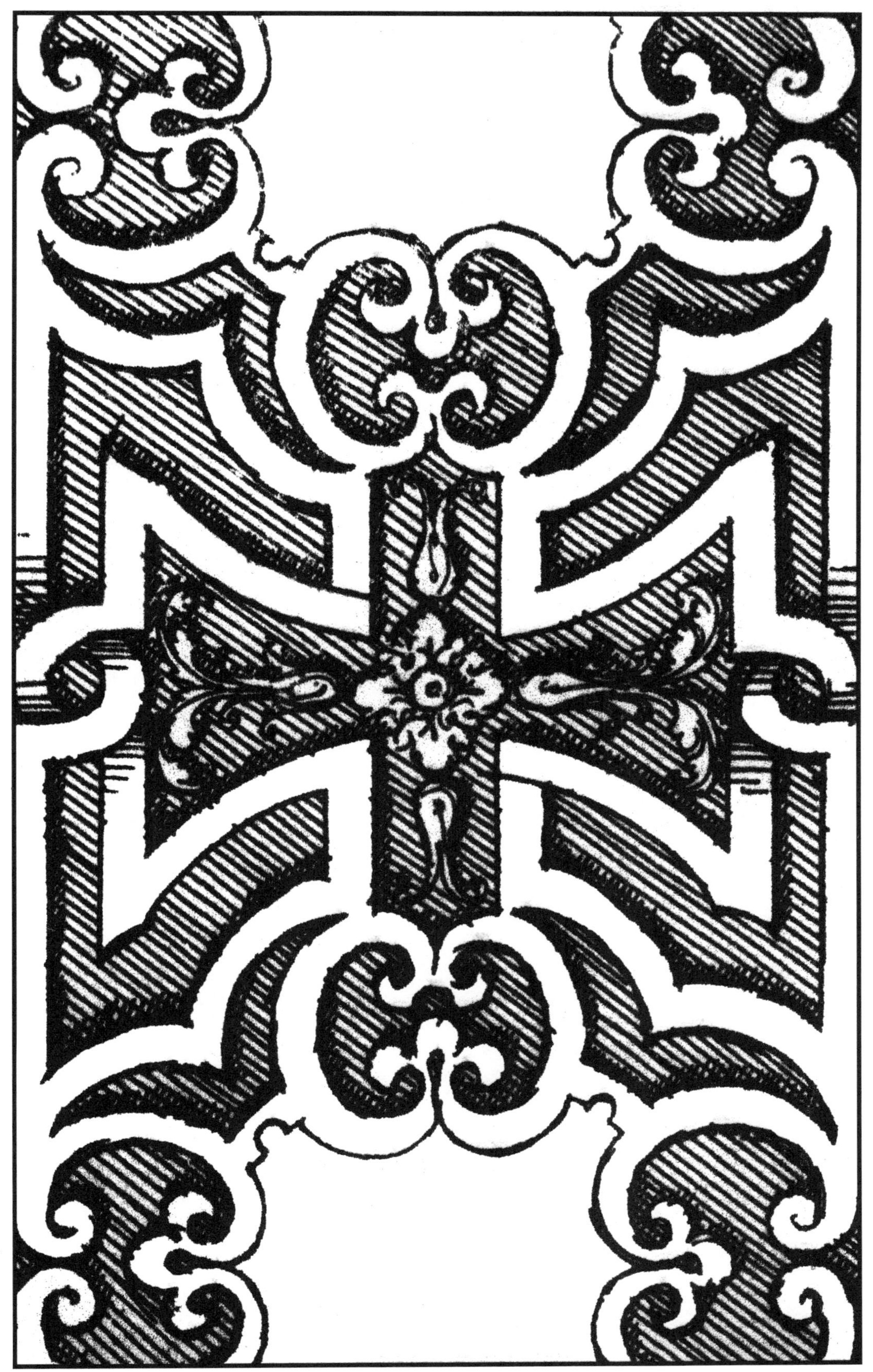

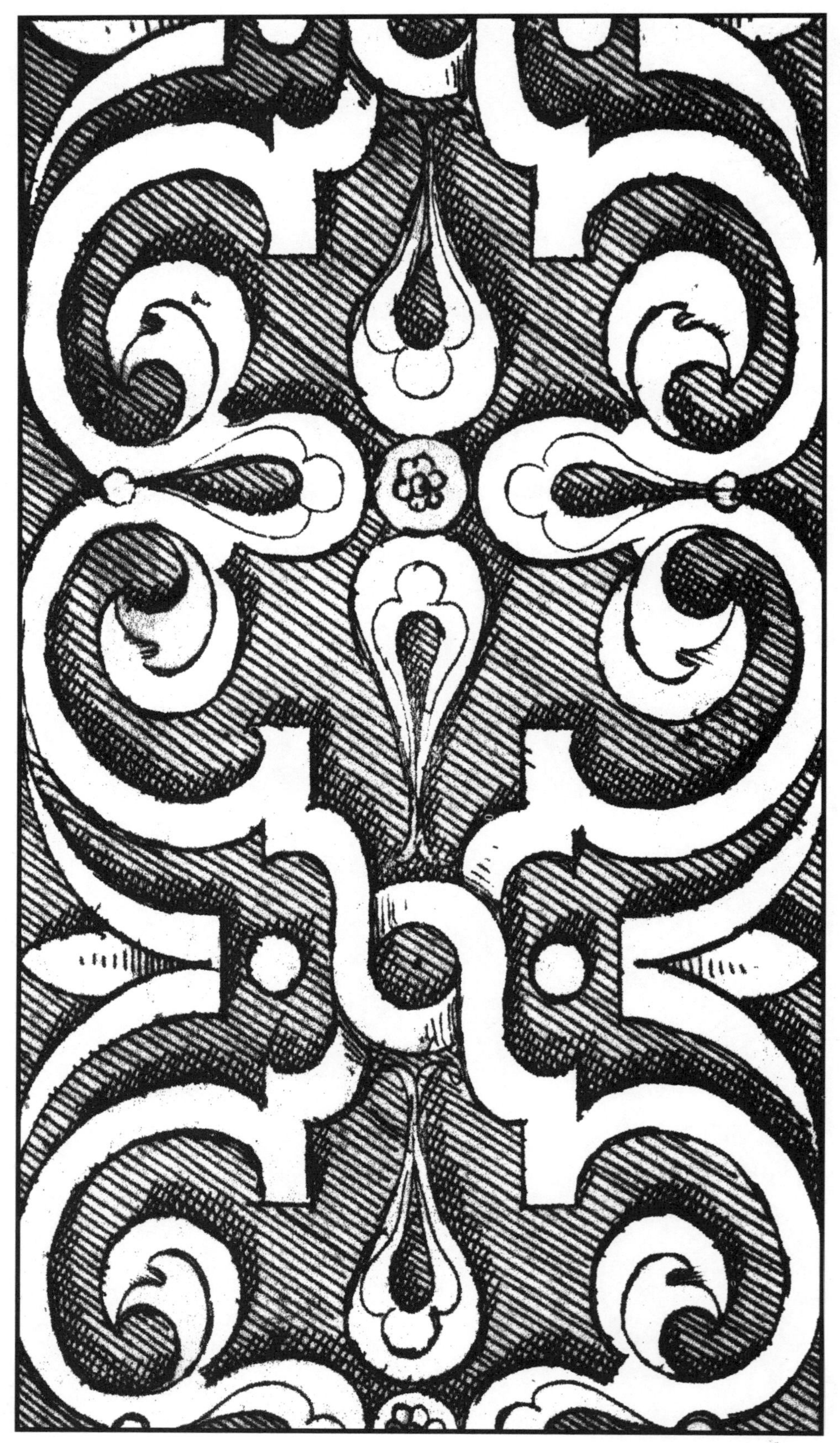

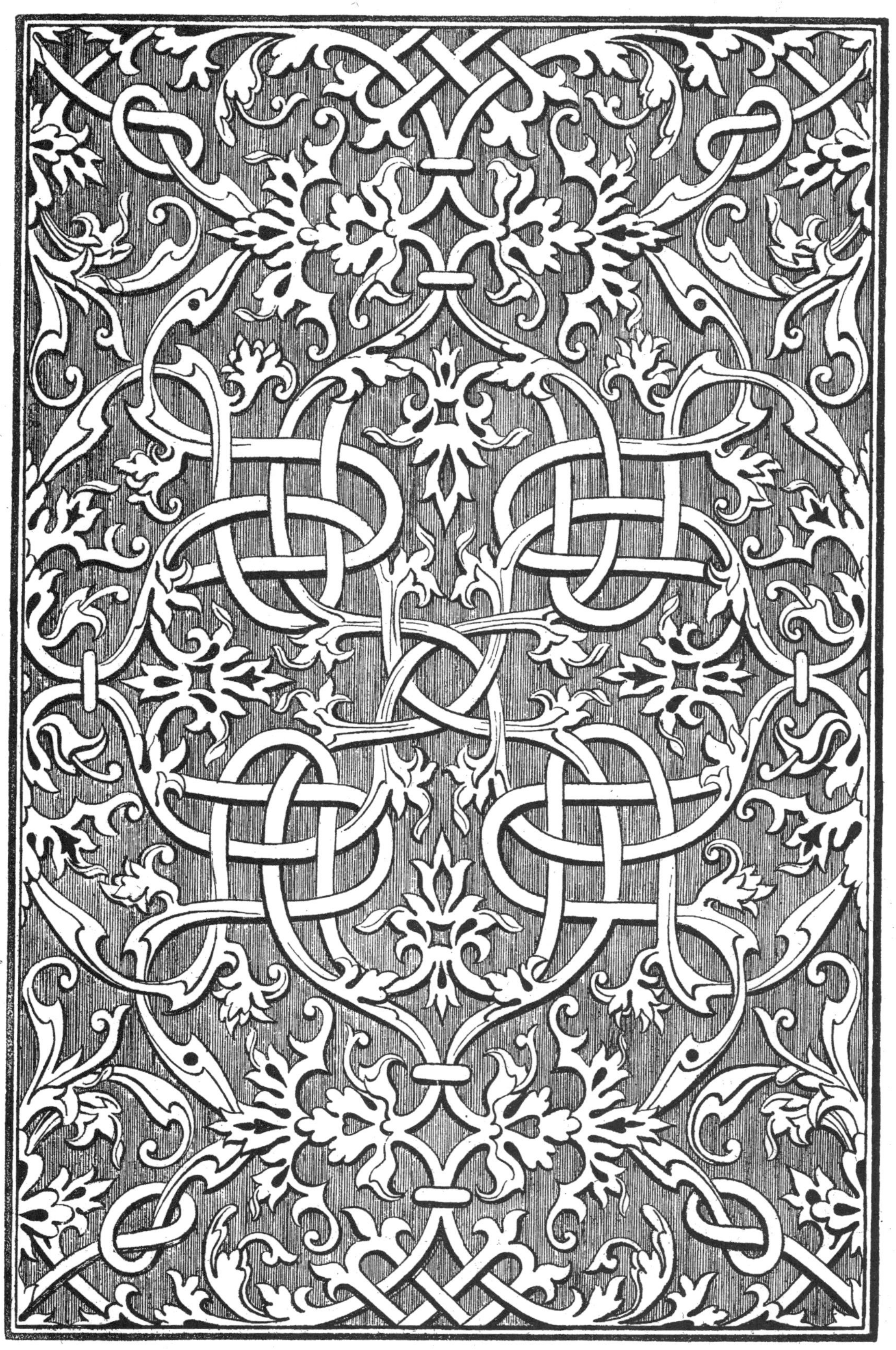

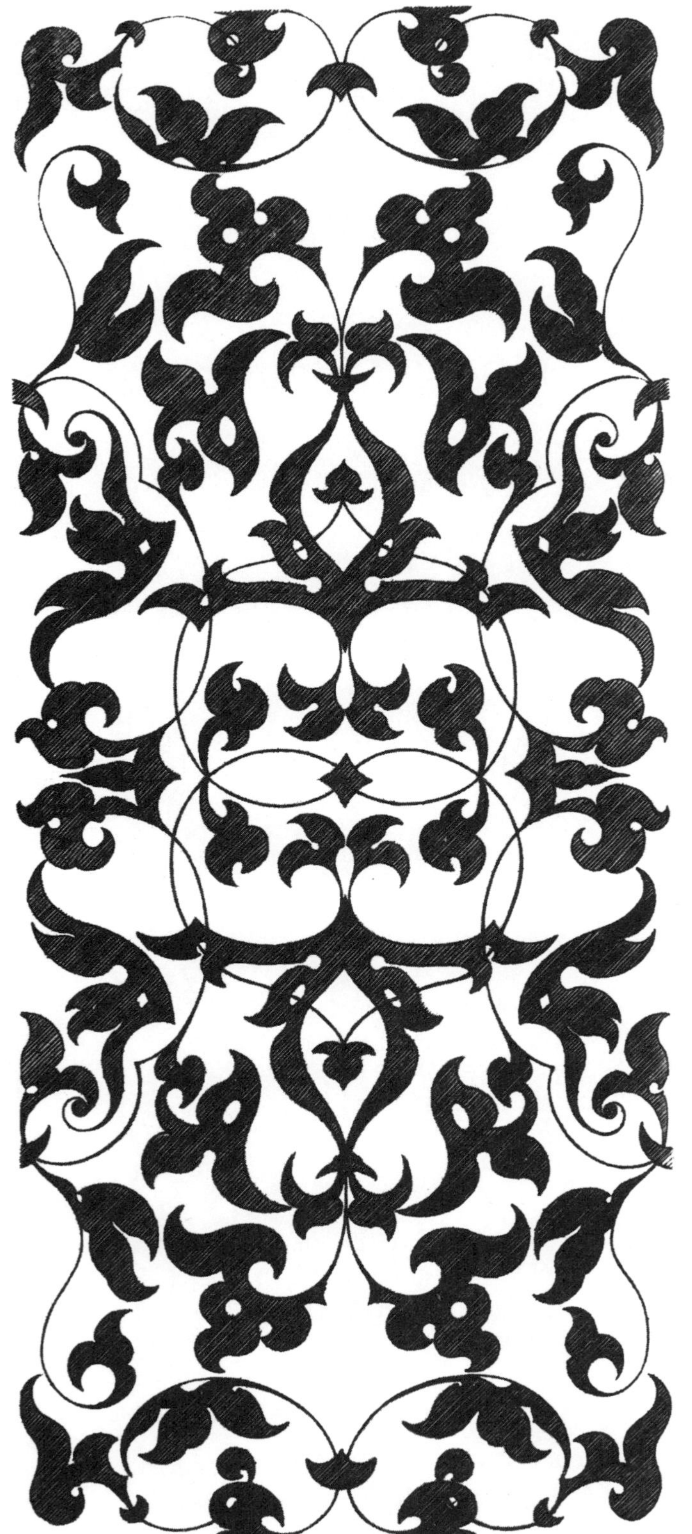

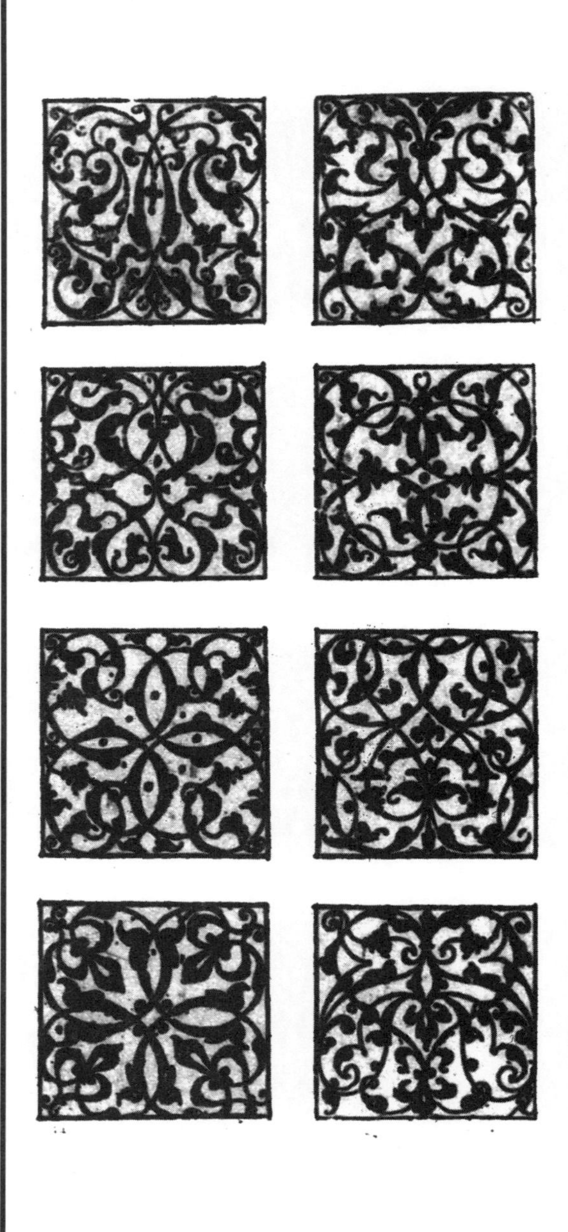

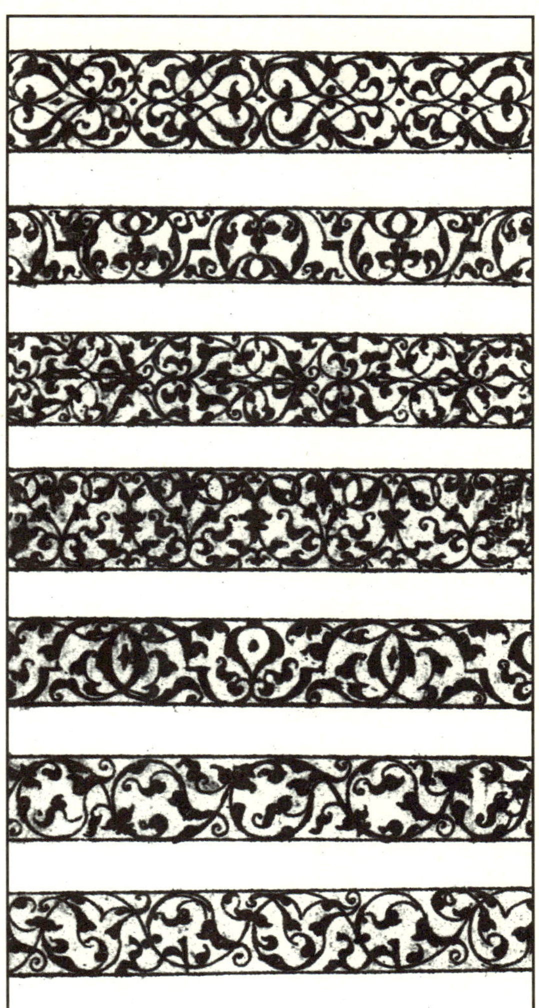

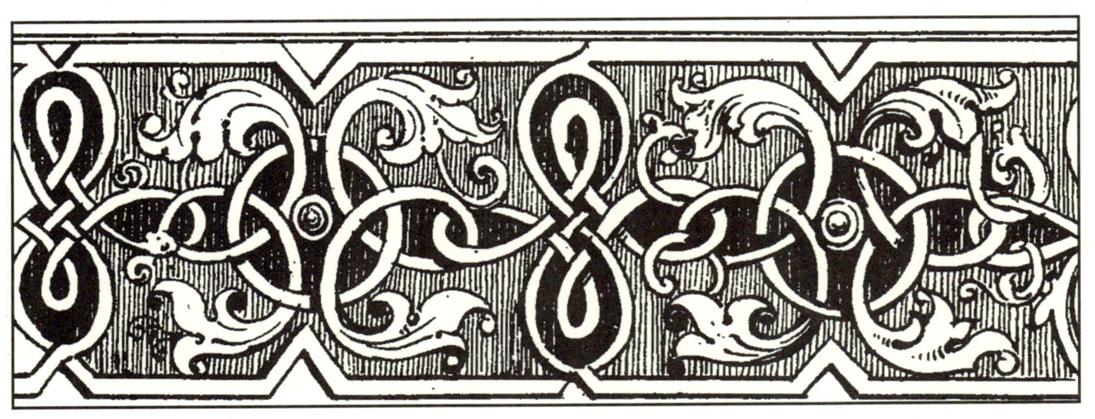

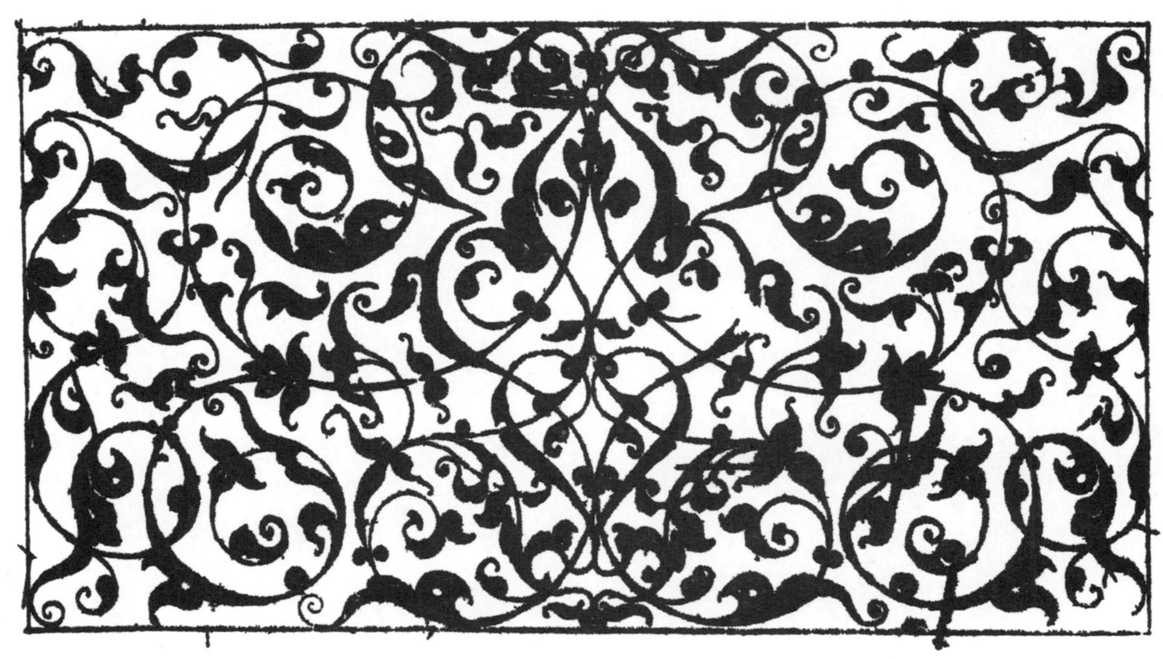

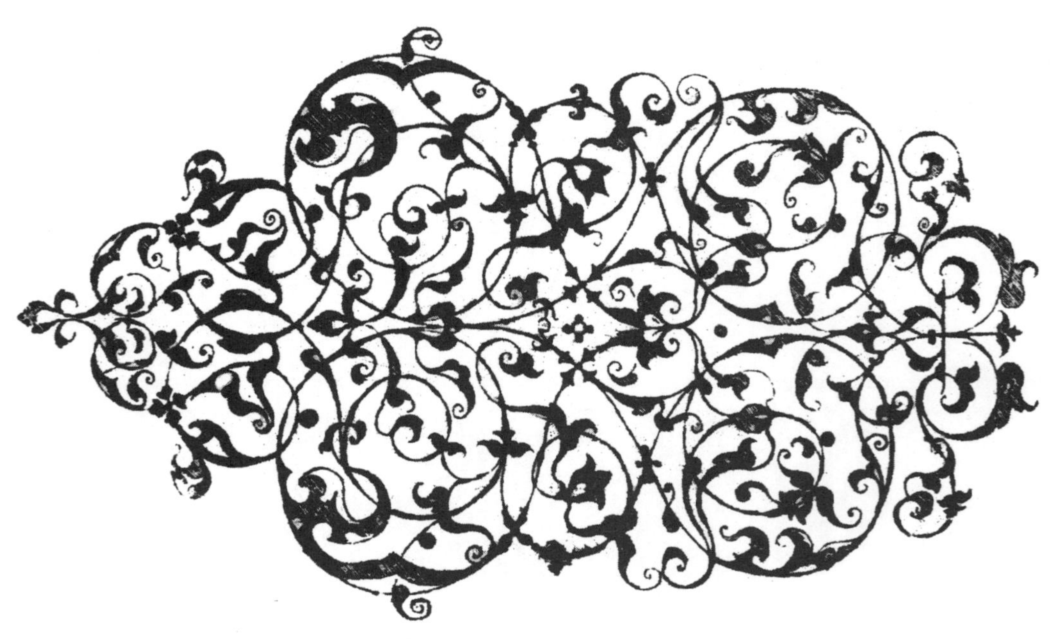

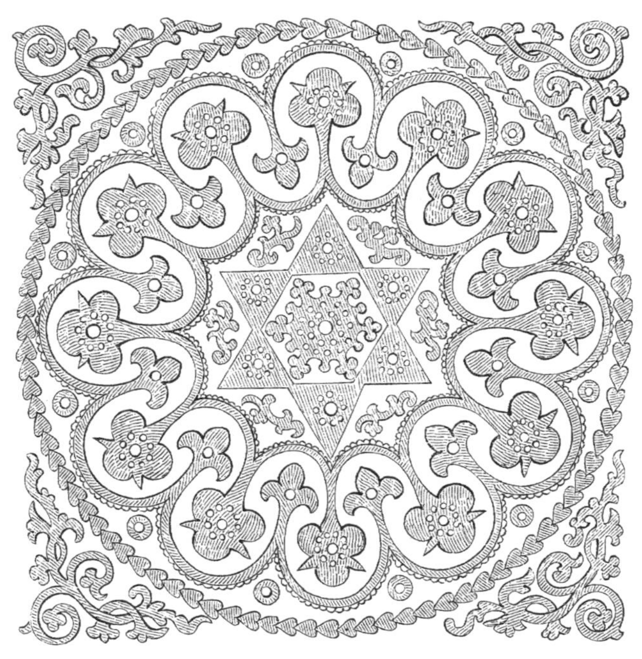

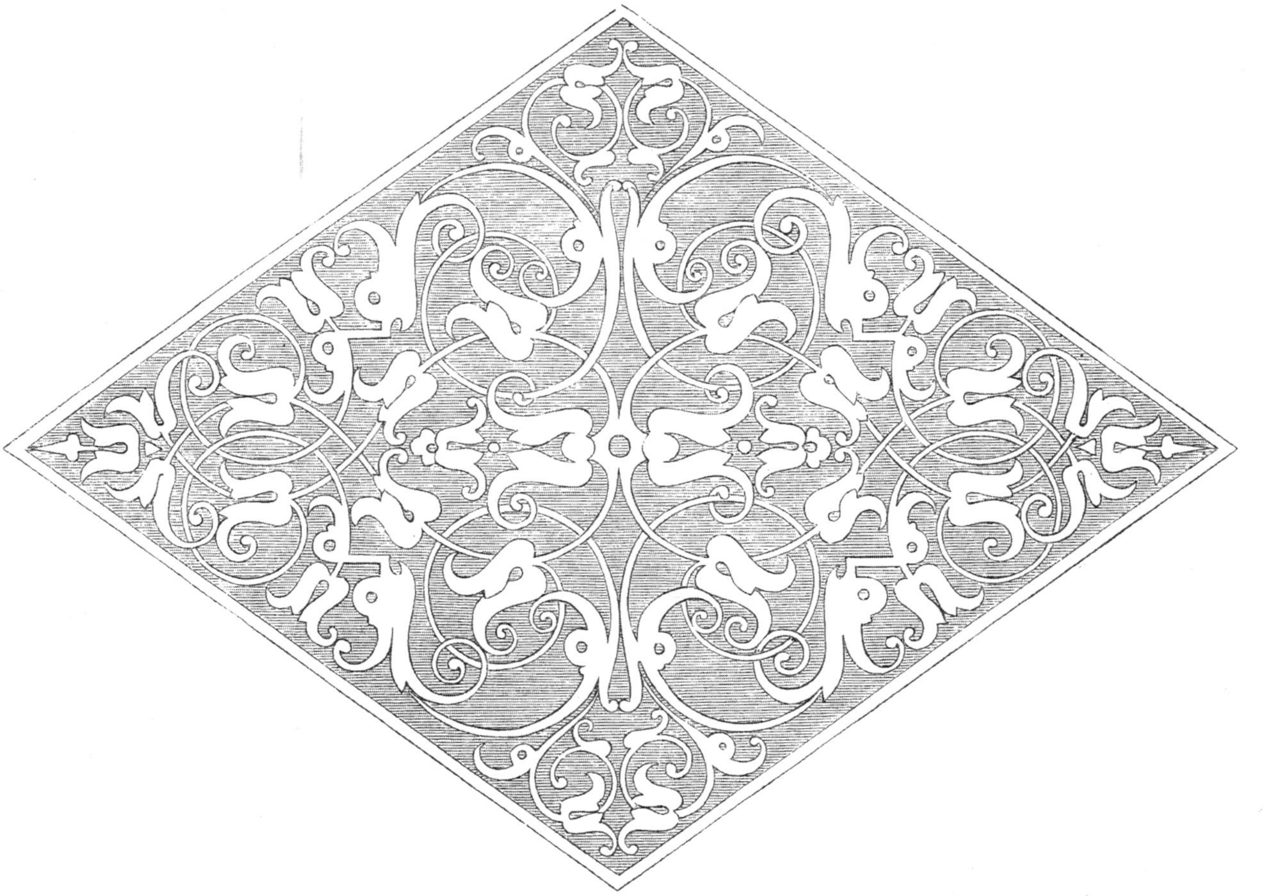

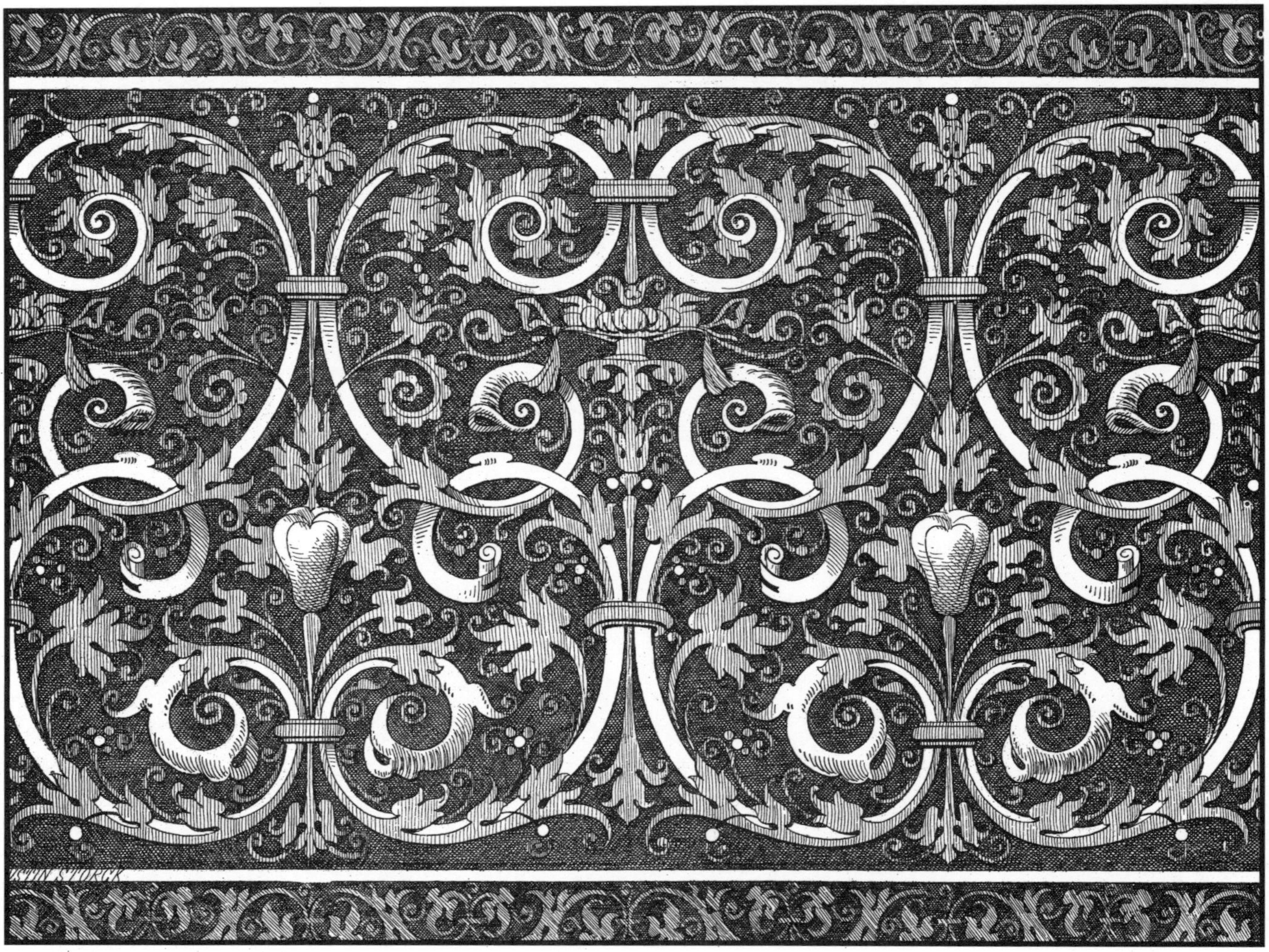

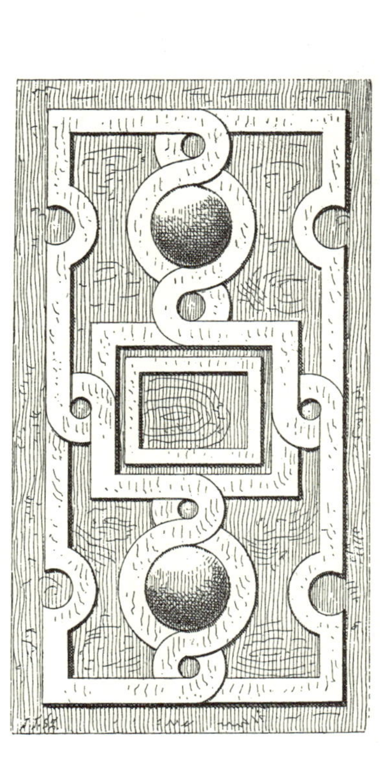

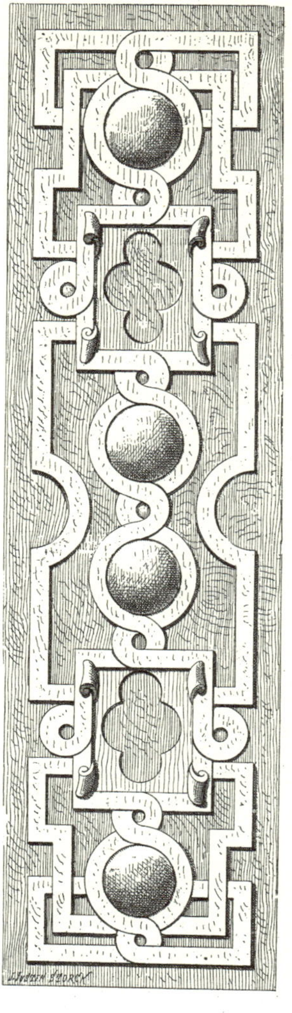

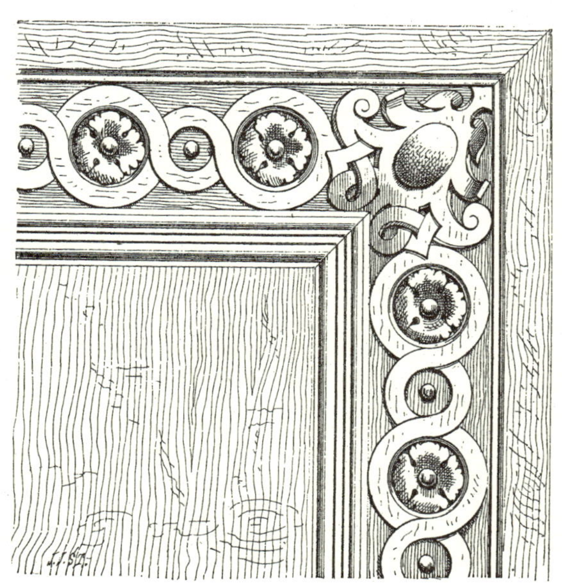

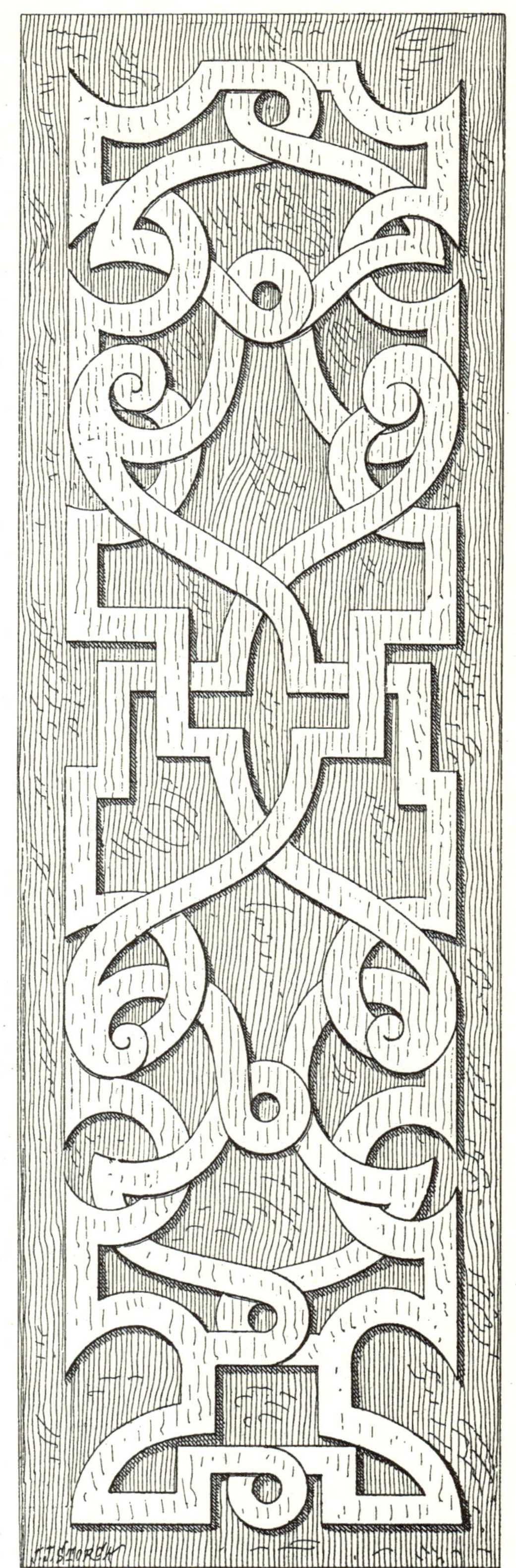

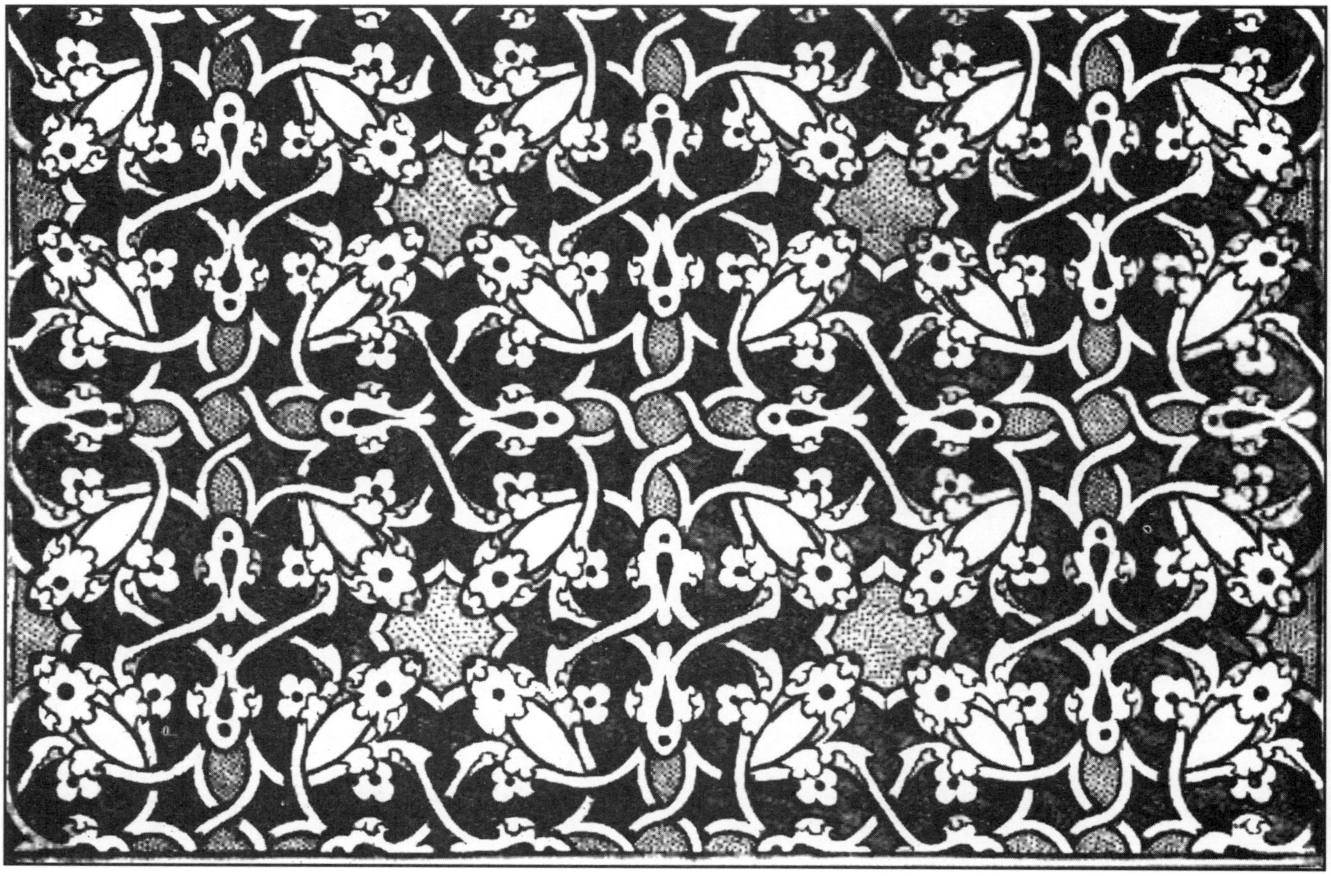

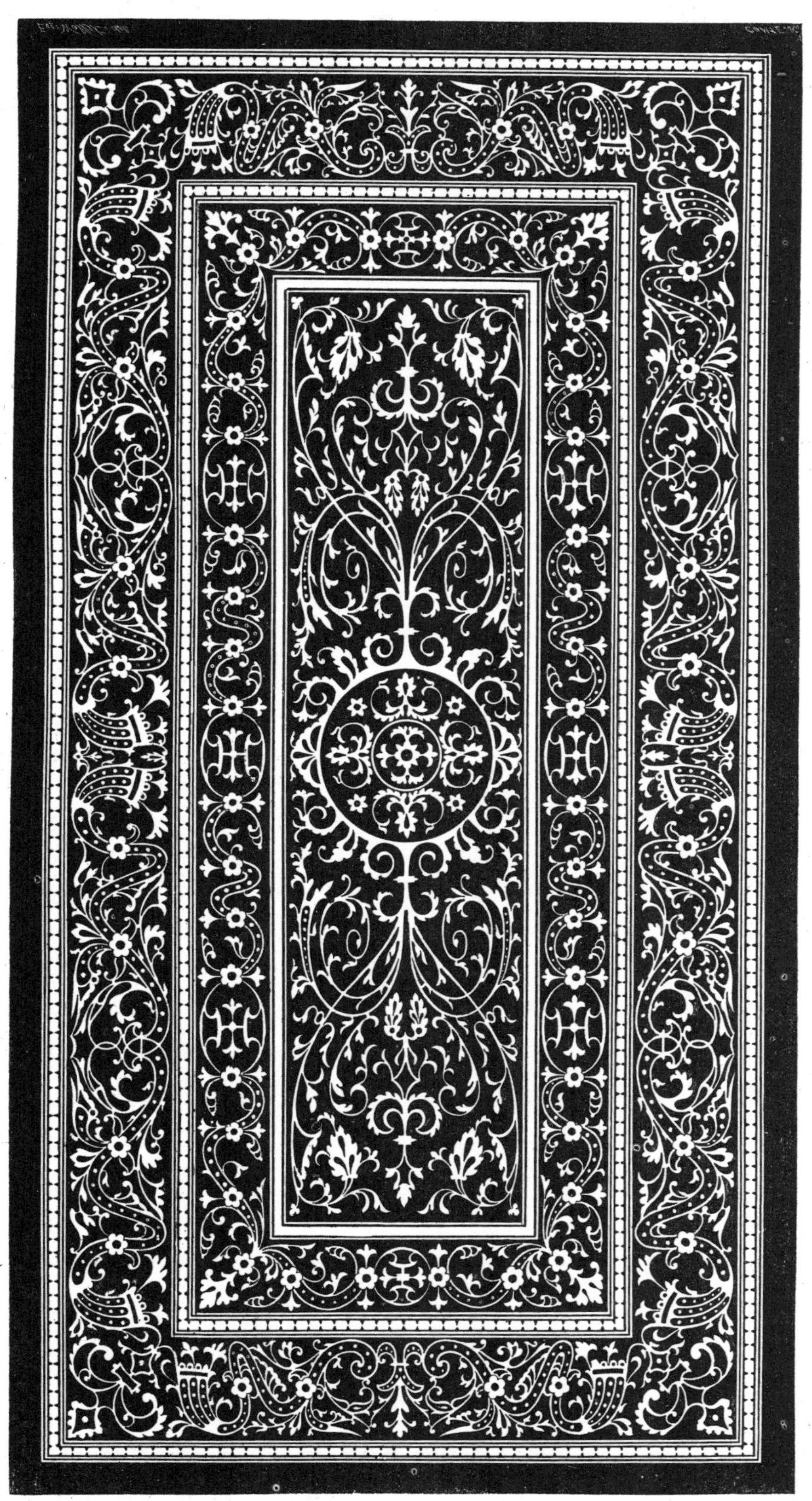

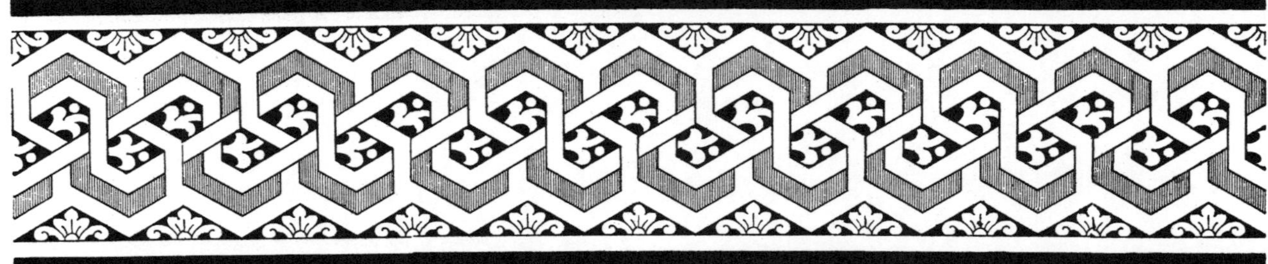

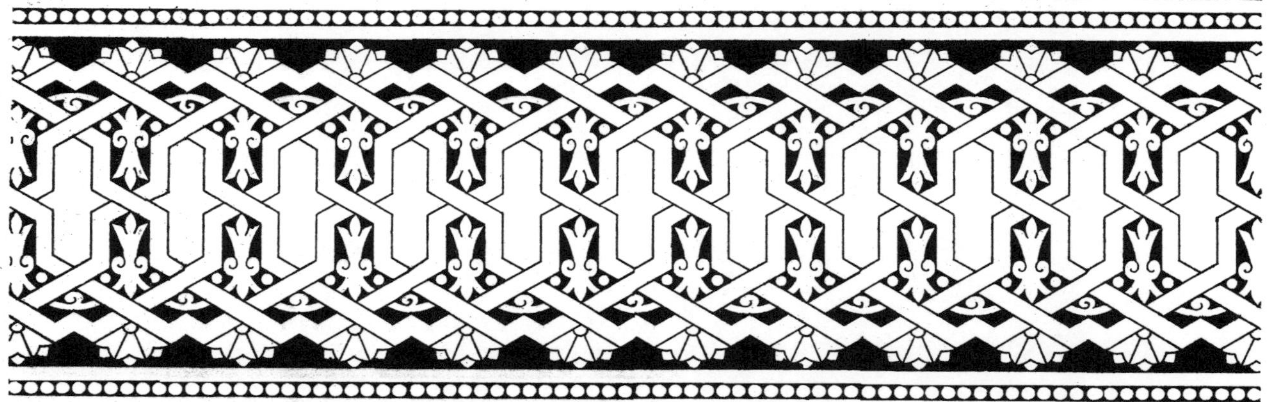

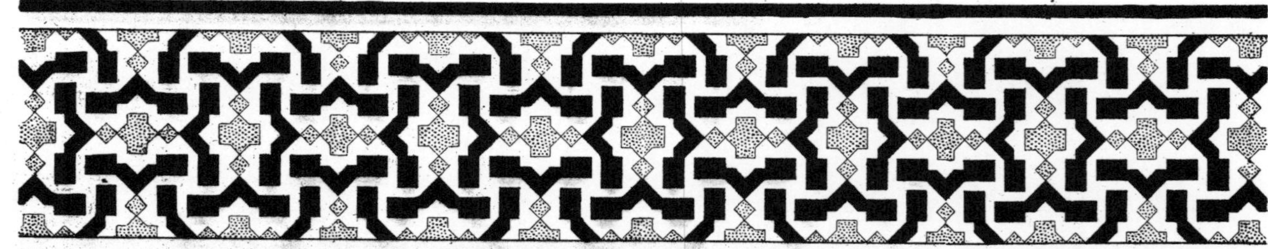

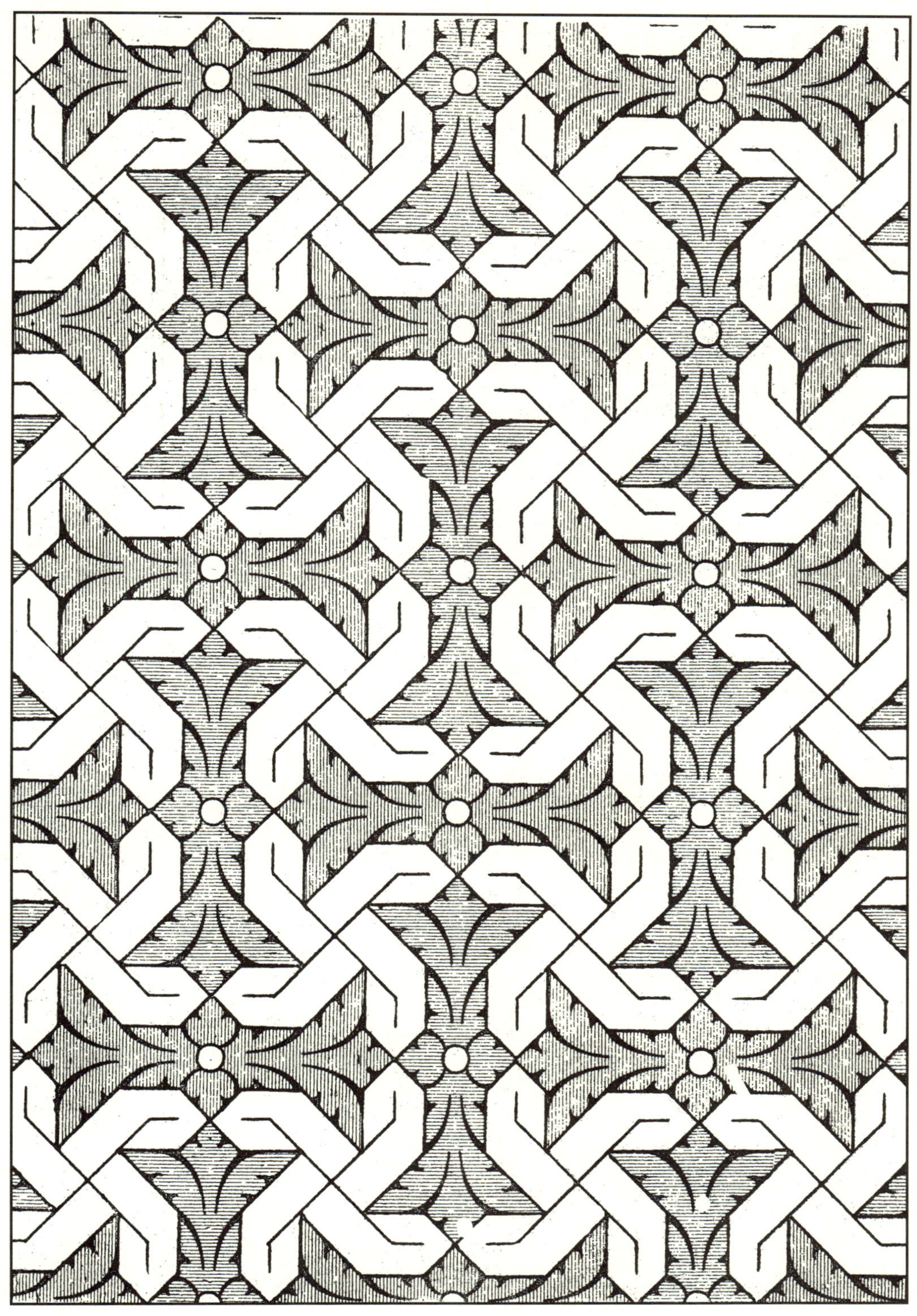

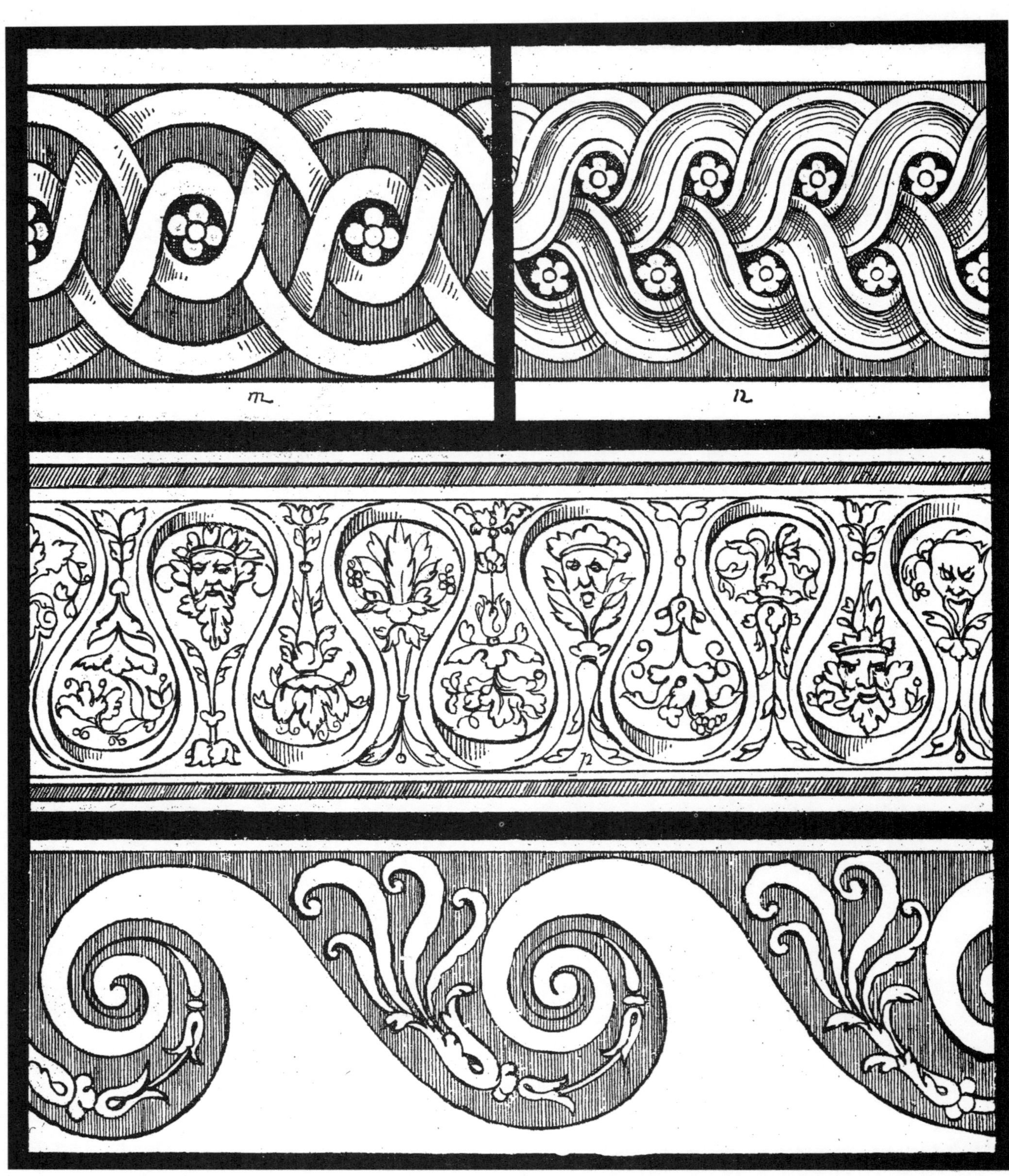

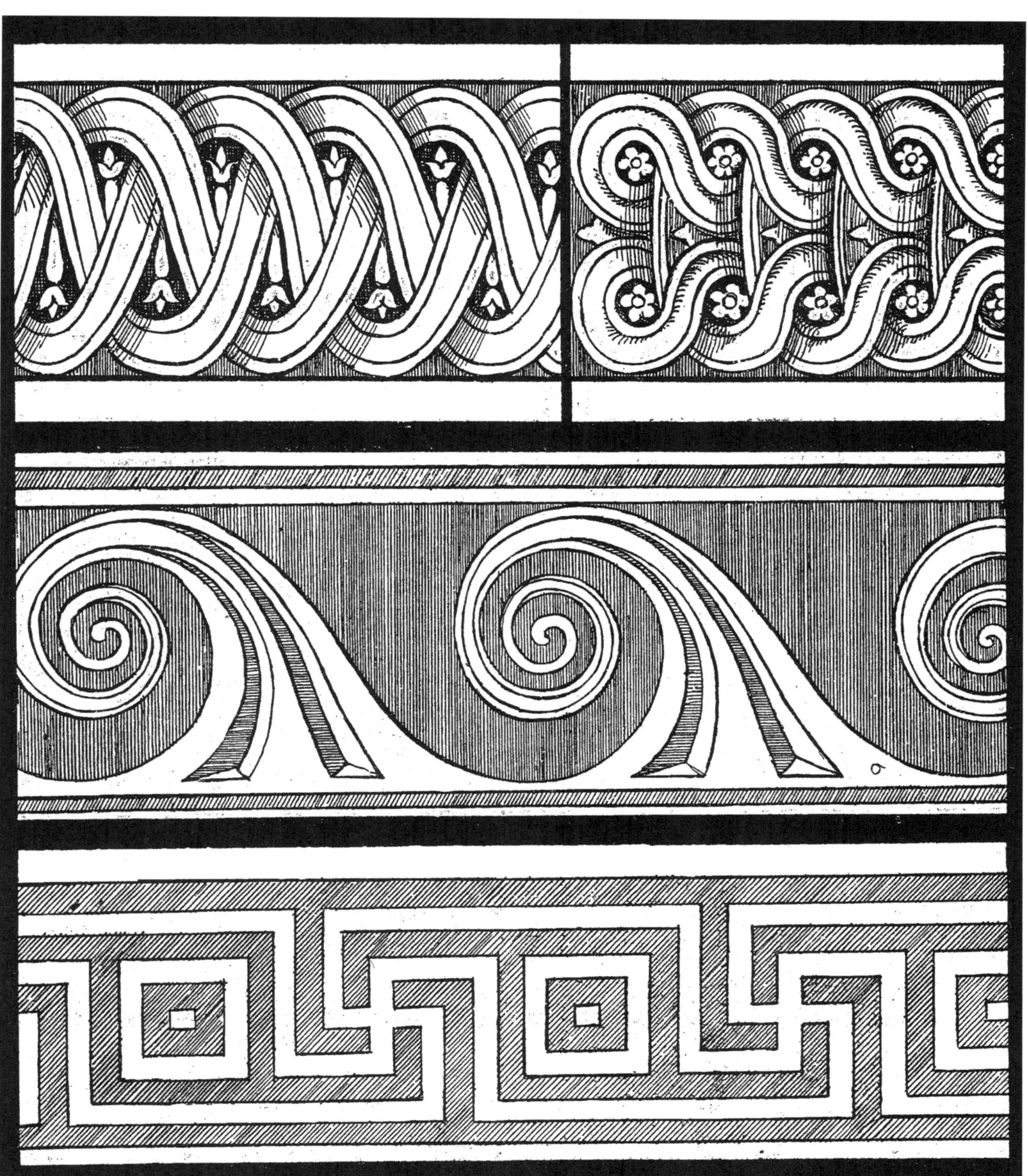

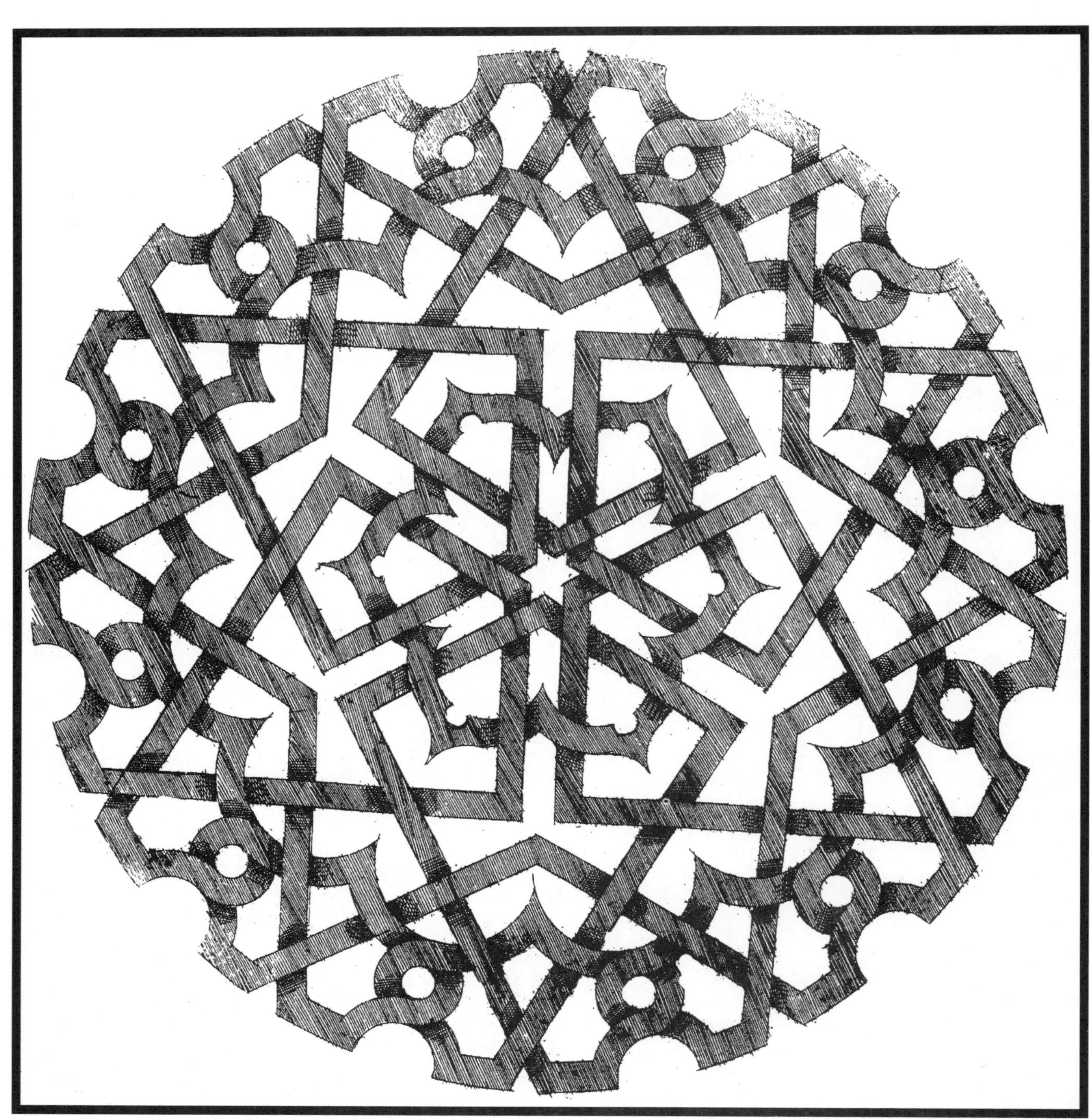

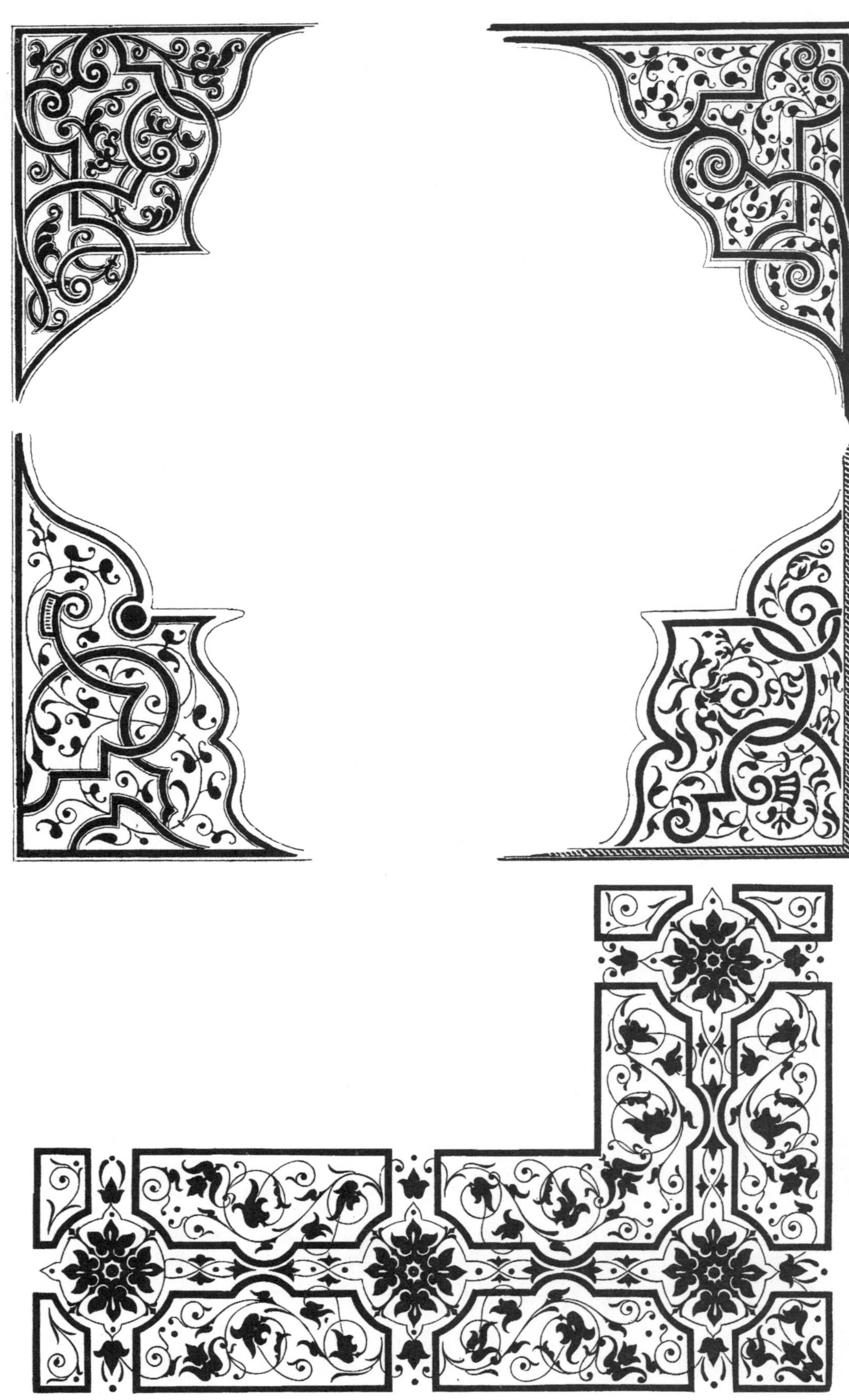

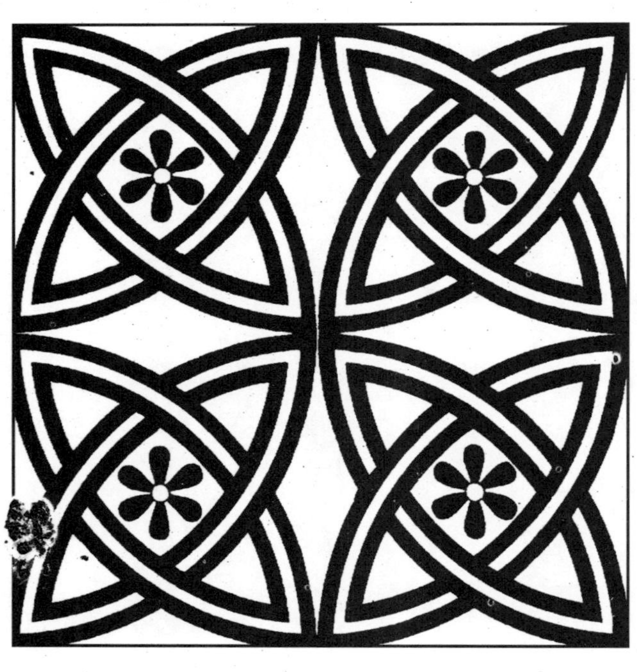
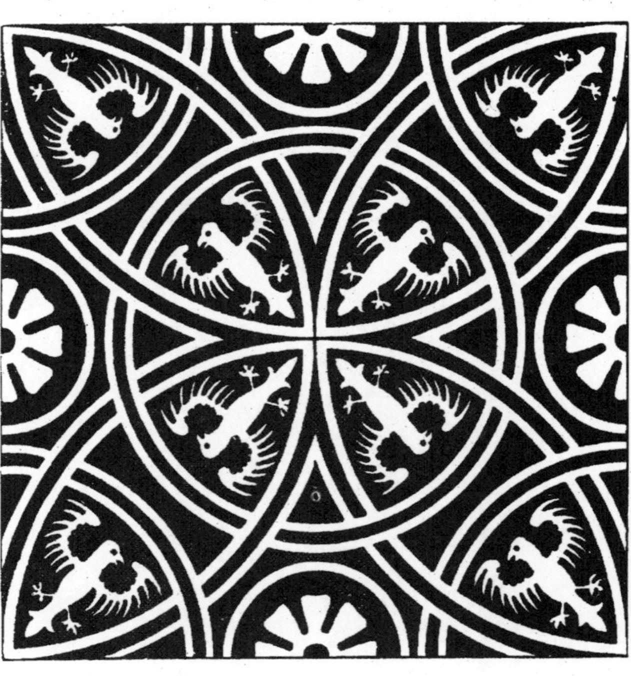

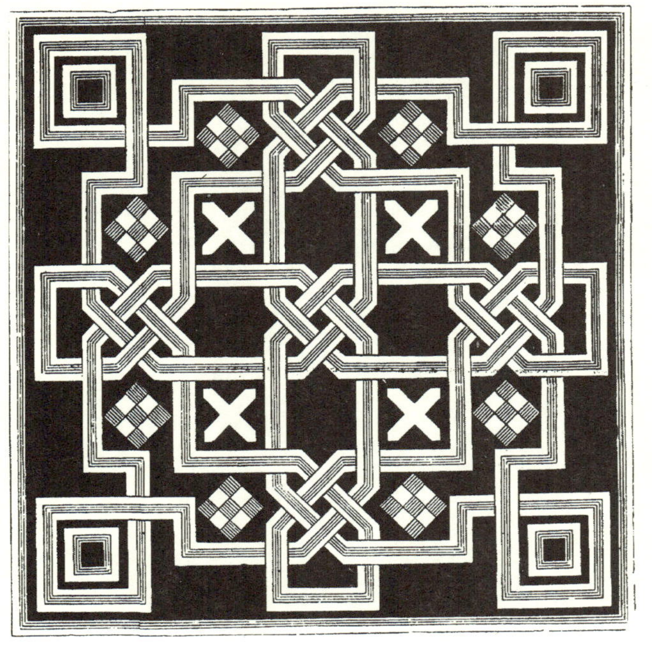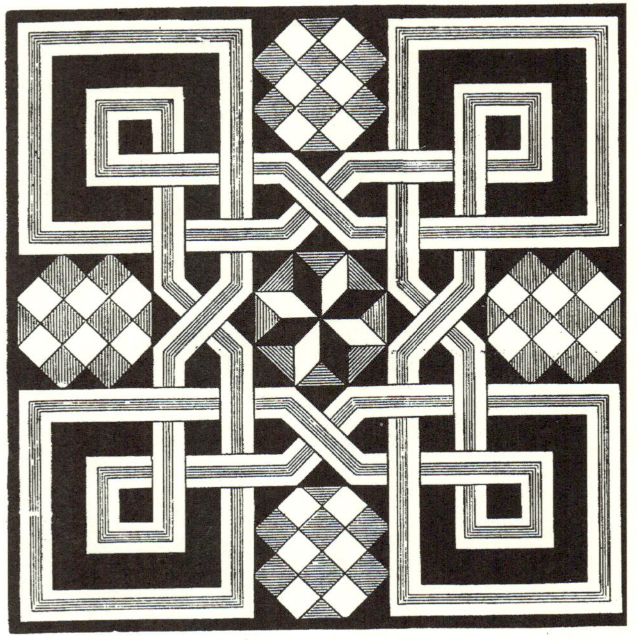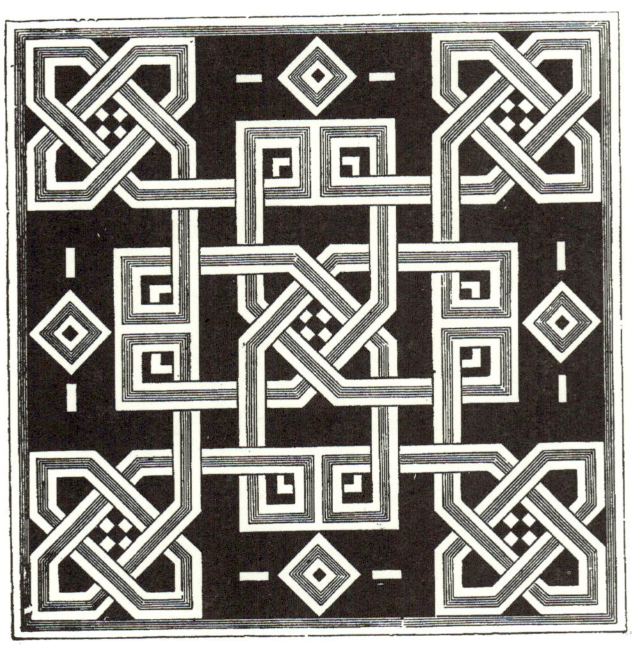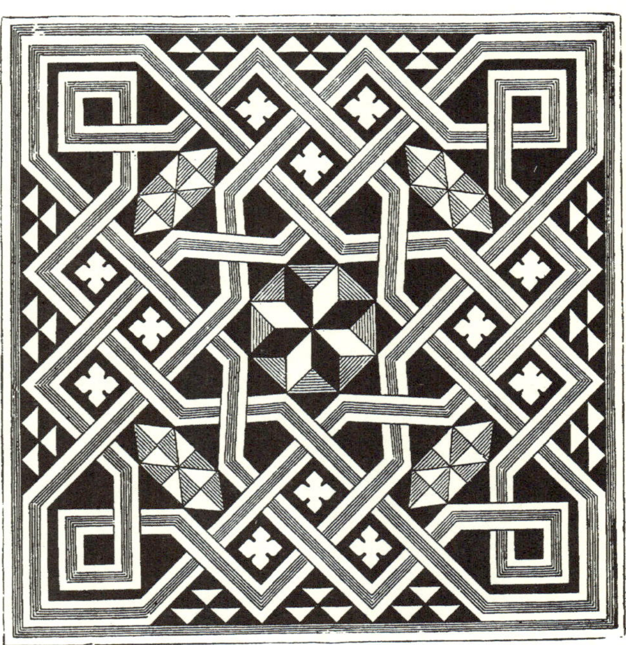

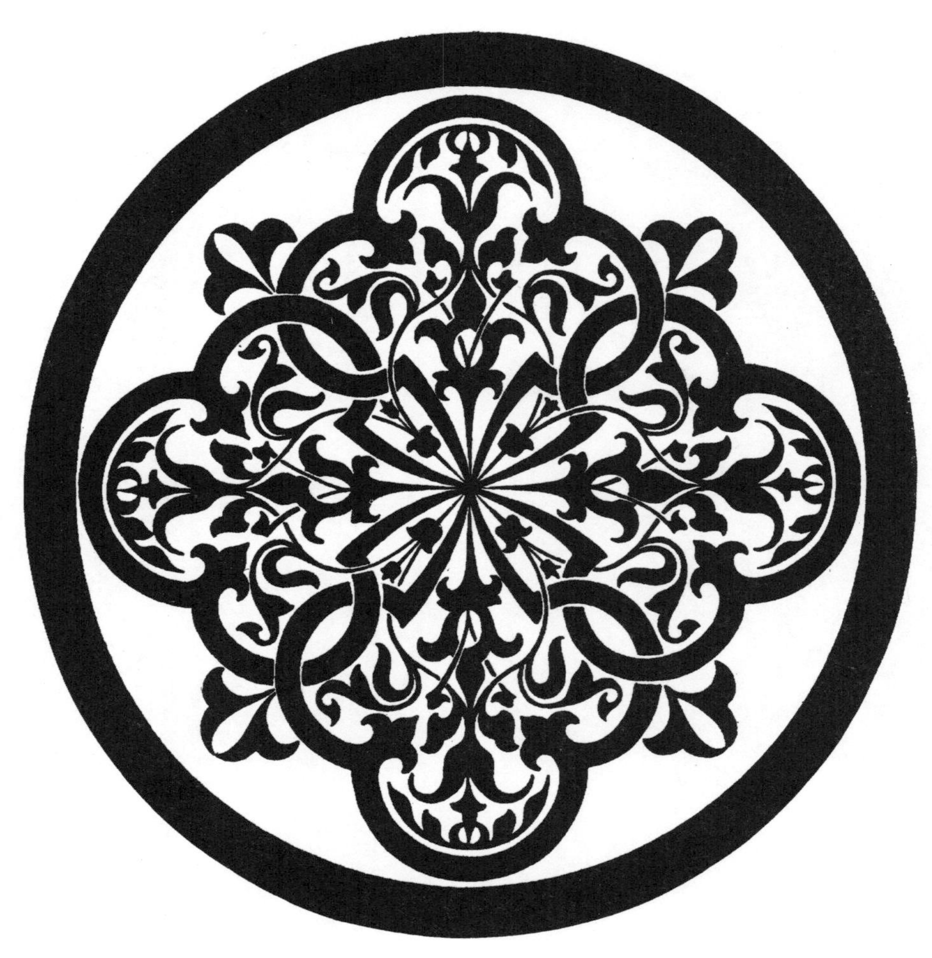

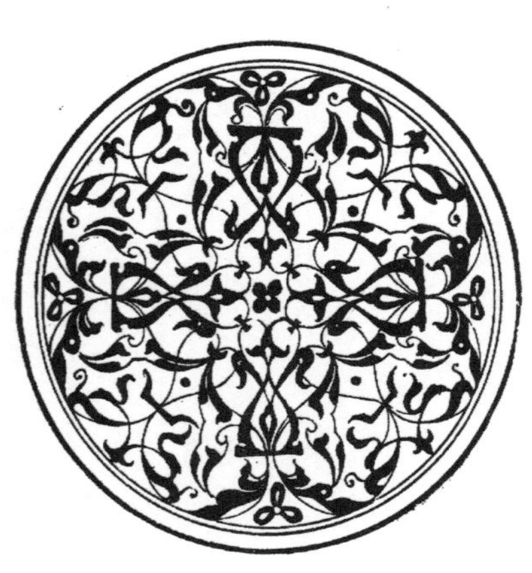

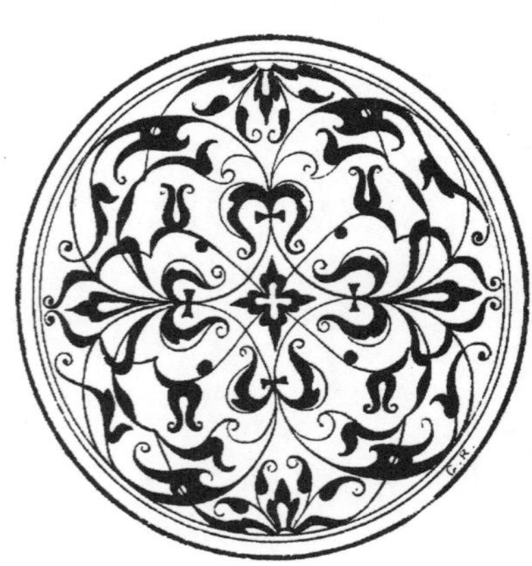

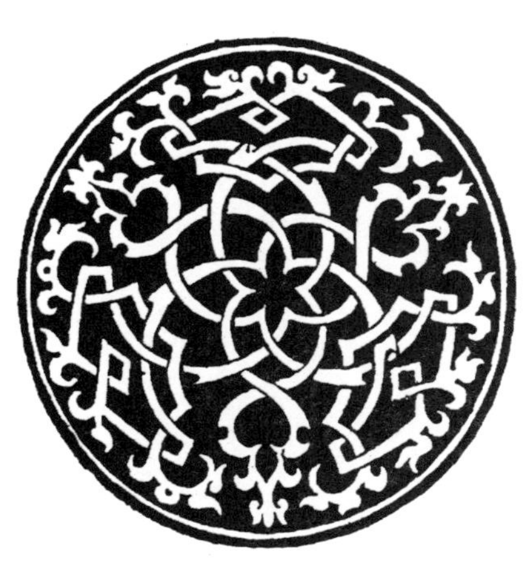

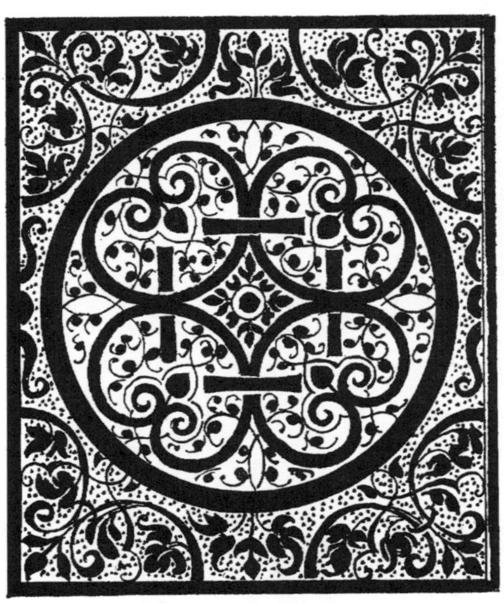

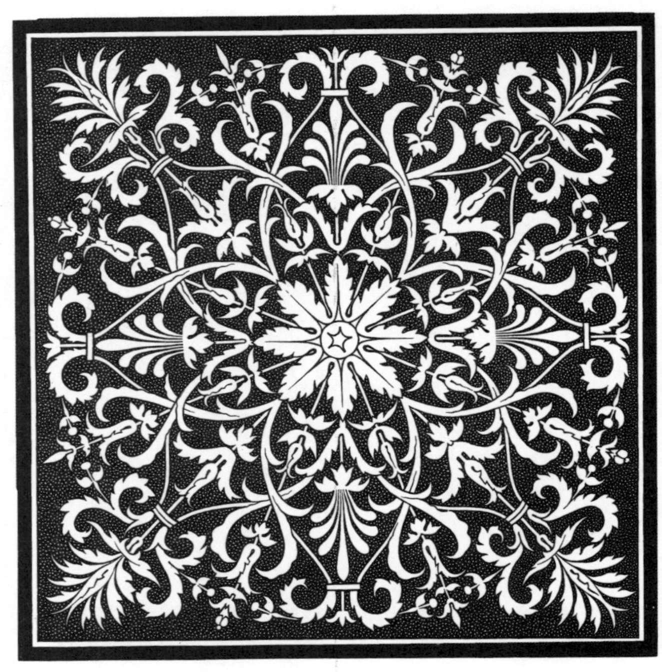

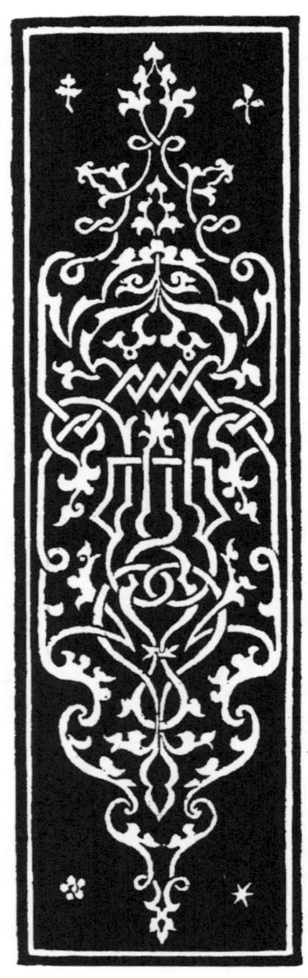

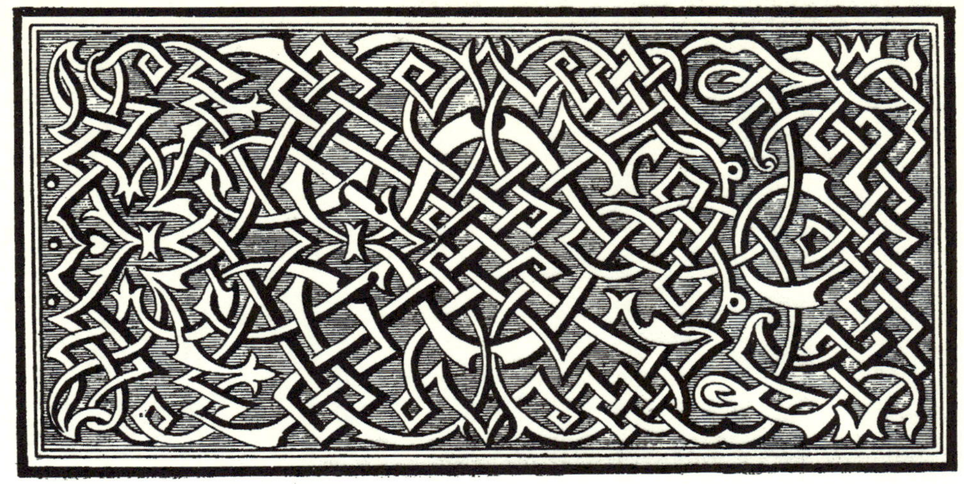

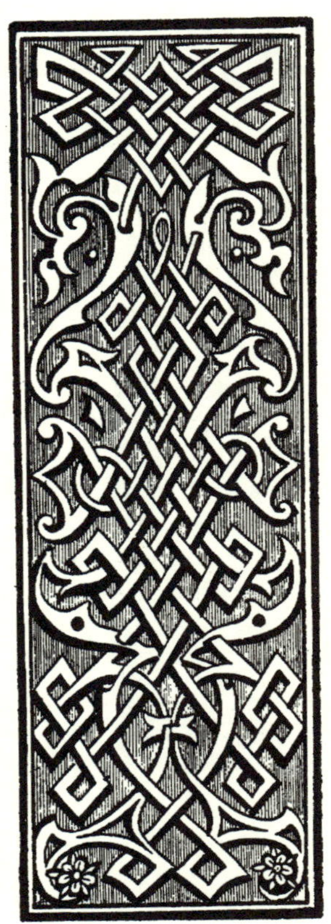

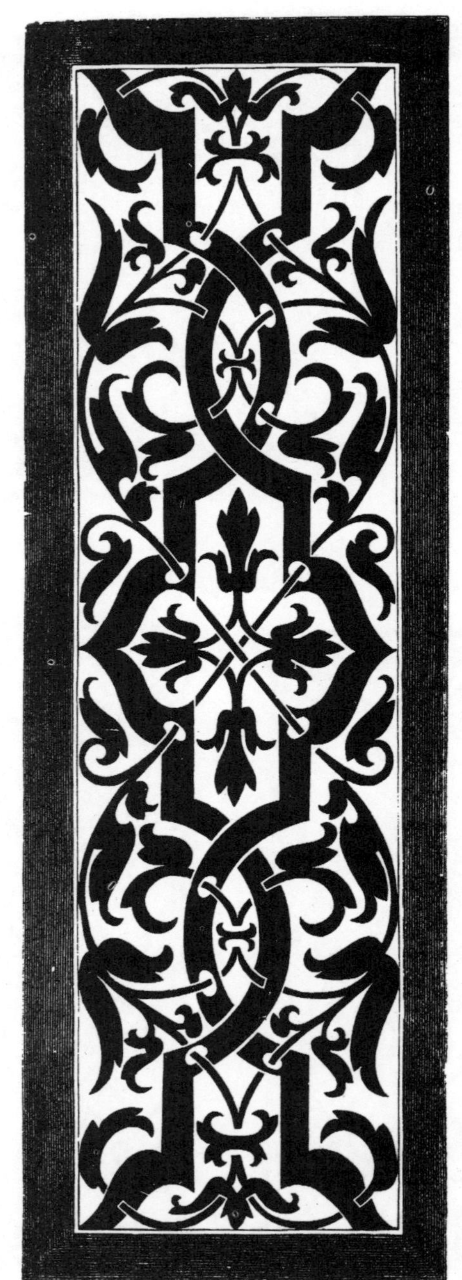

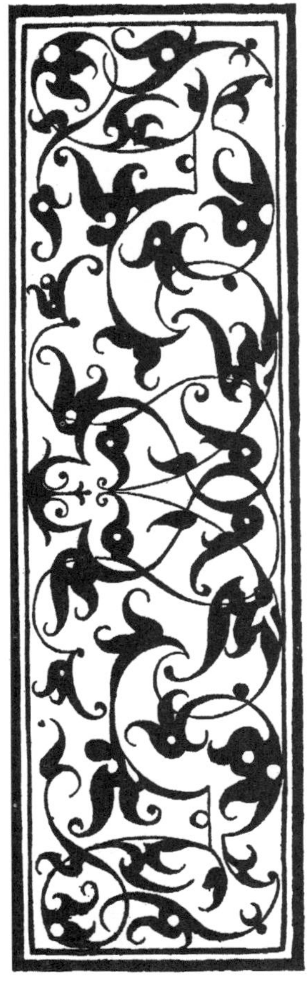

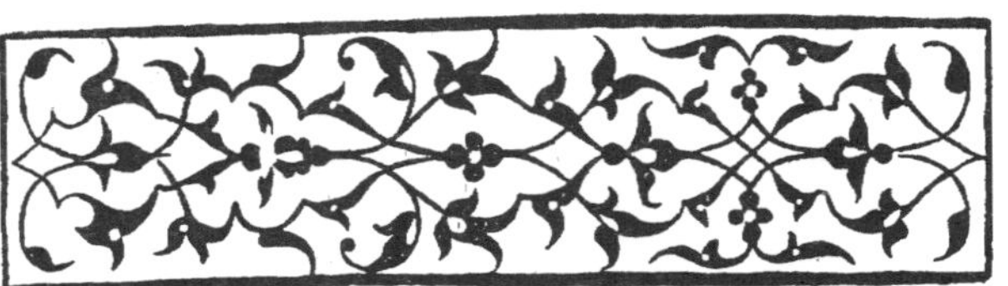

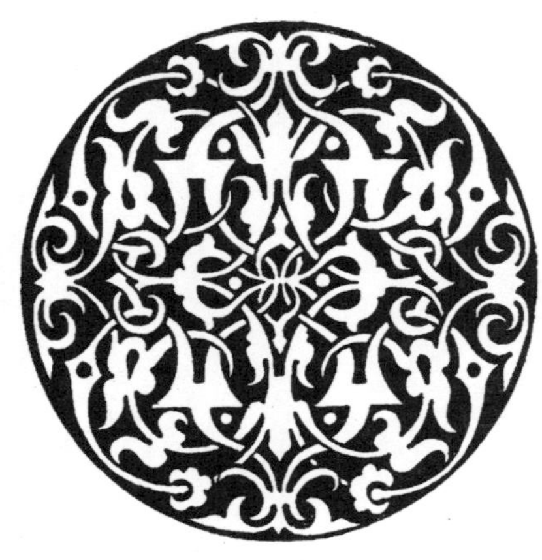

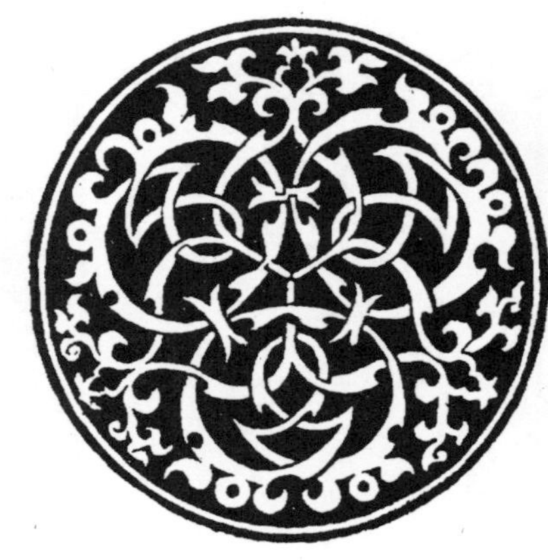
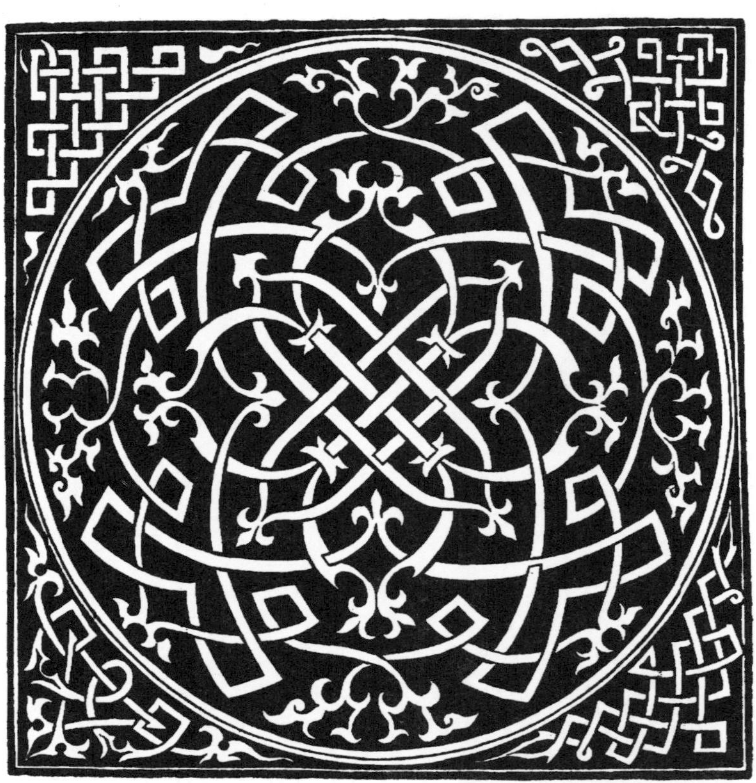

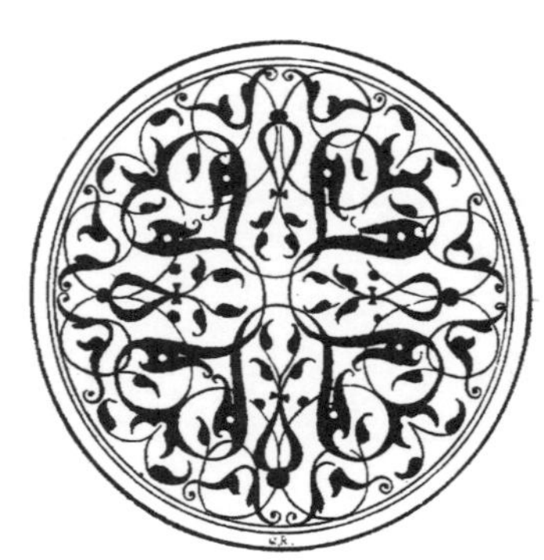

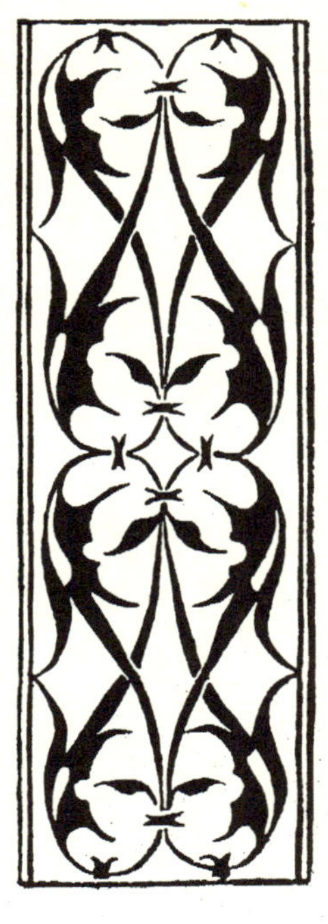
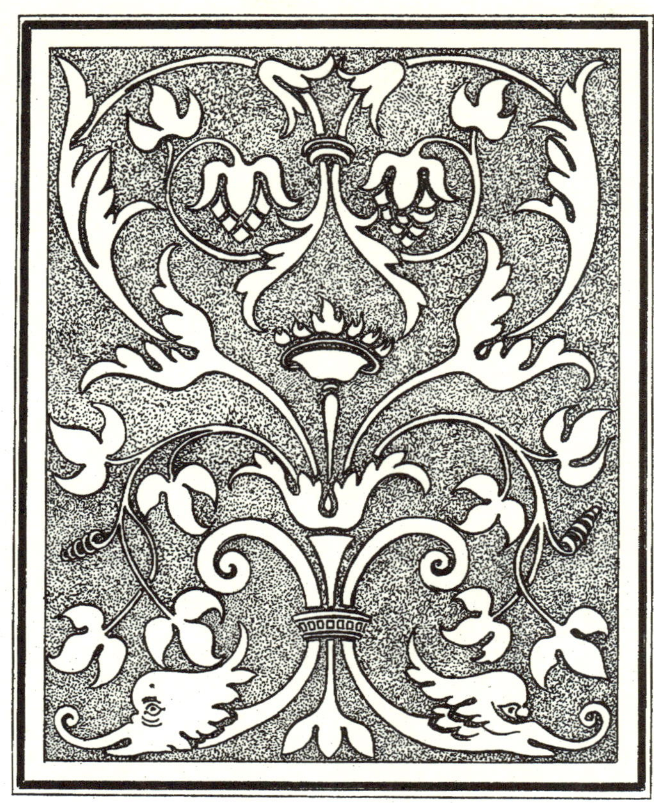

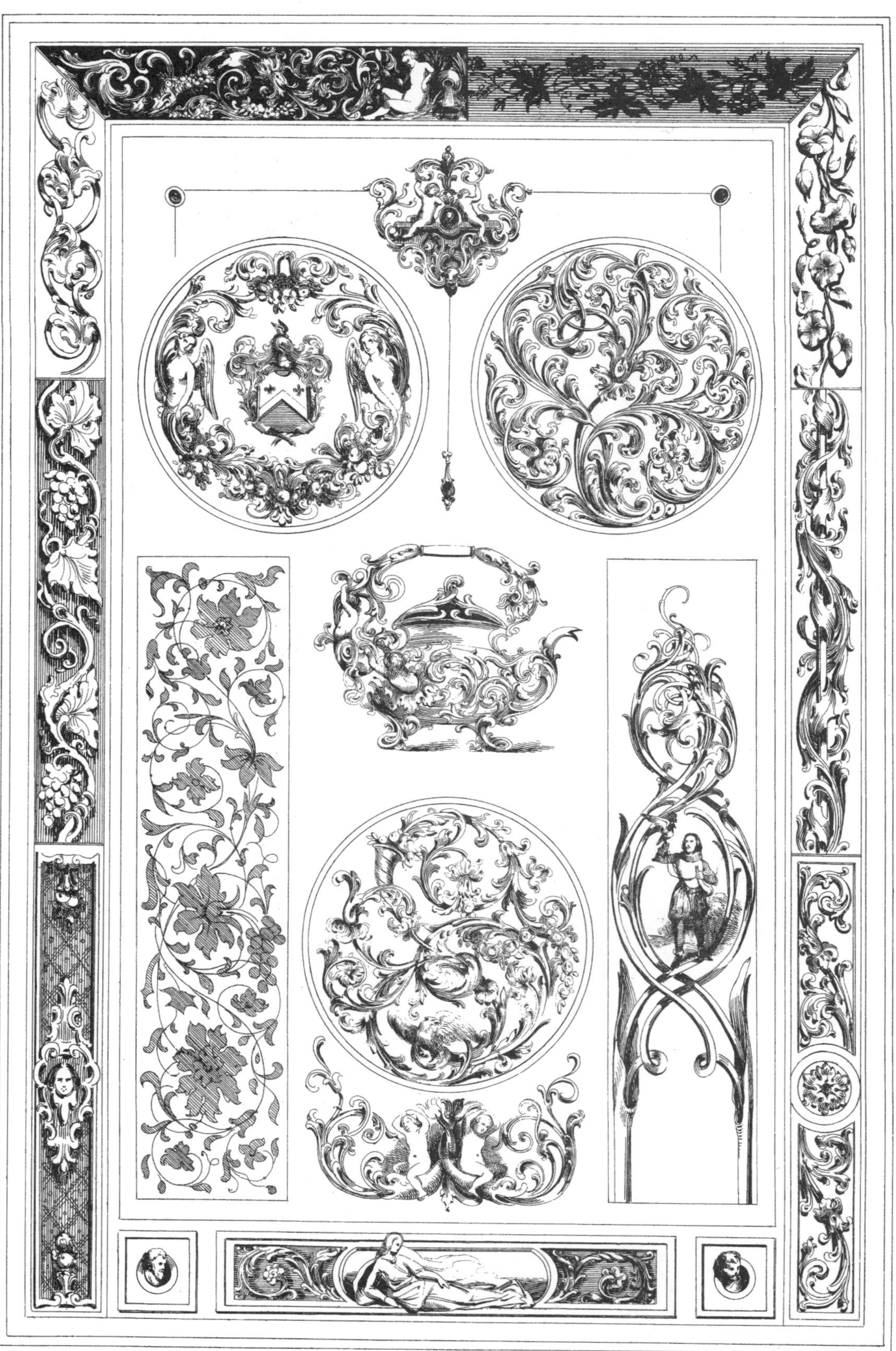

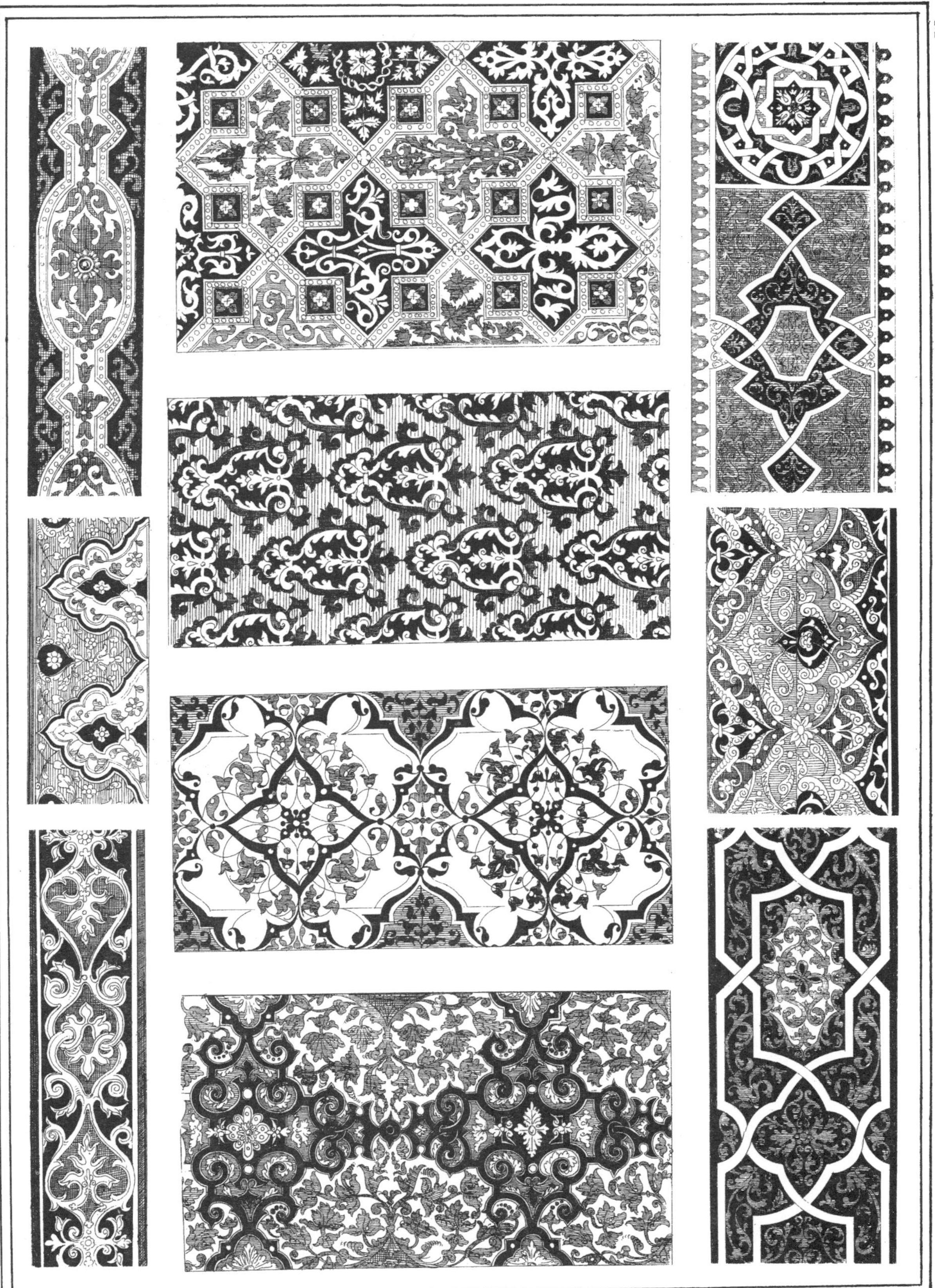

Lithog.

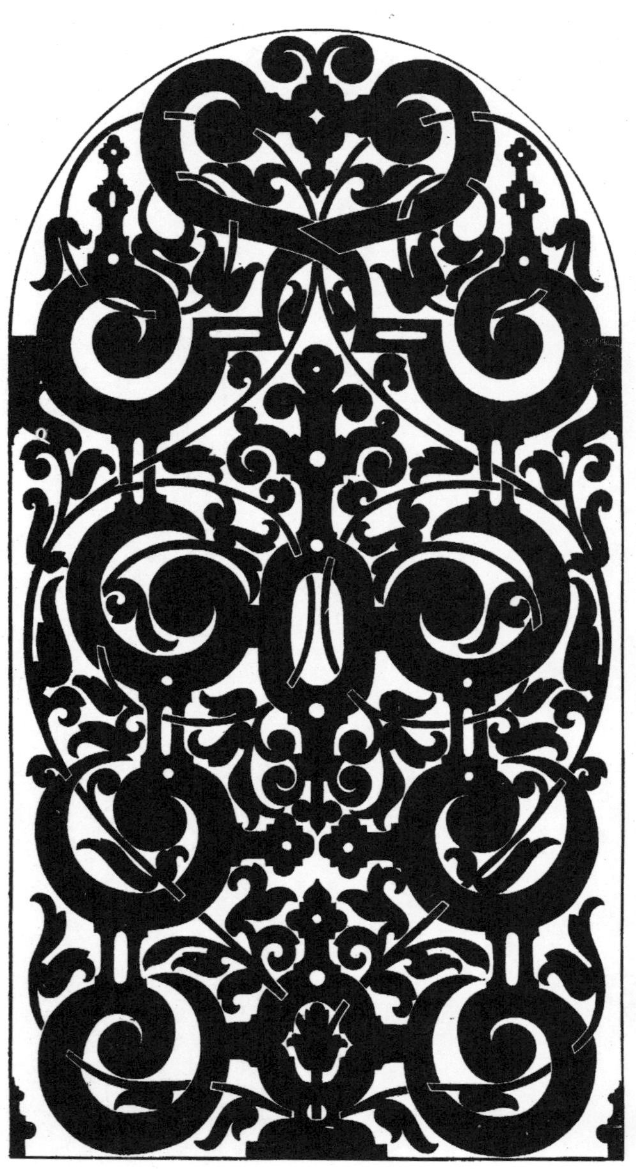 

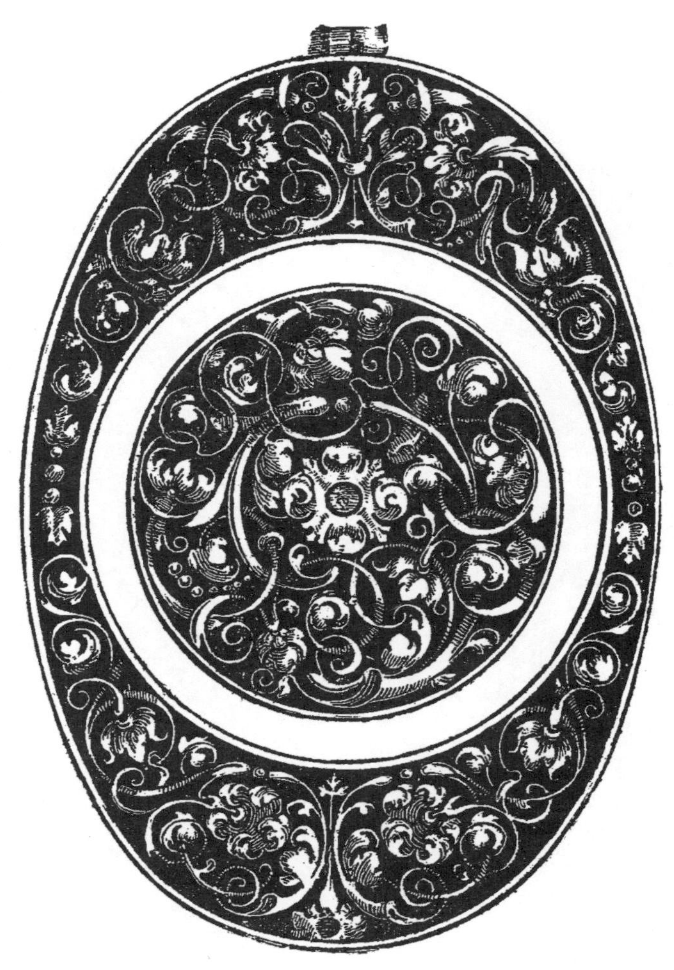

• Objects •
• Les Objets •
• Gegenstände •
• Los objetos •

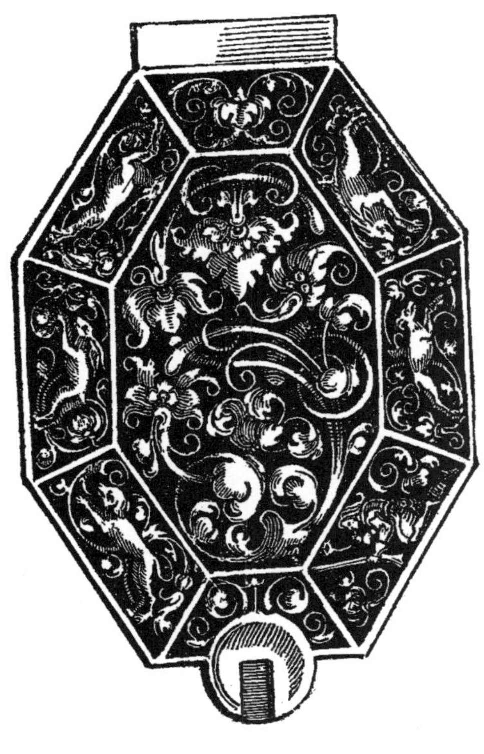

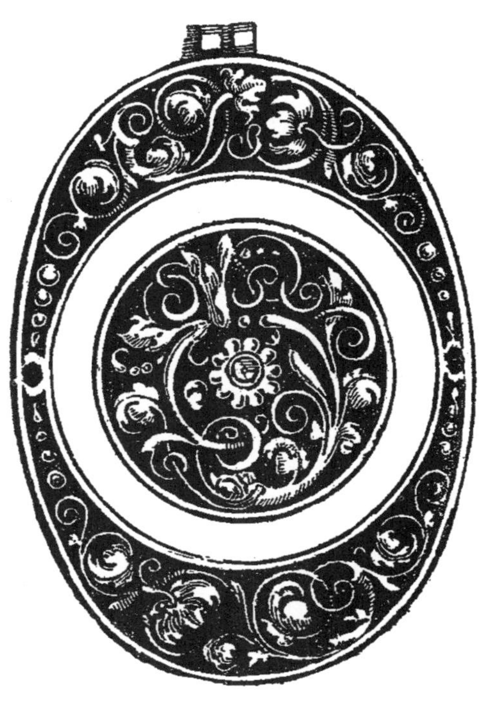

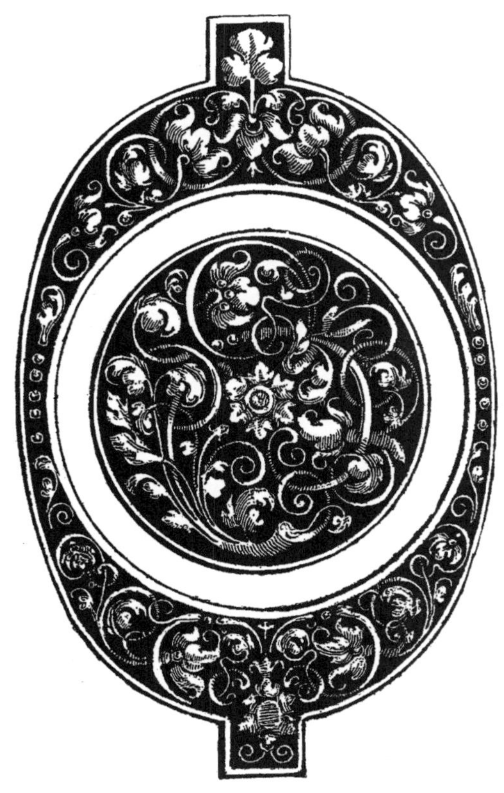

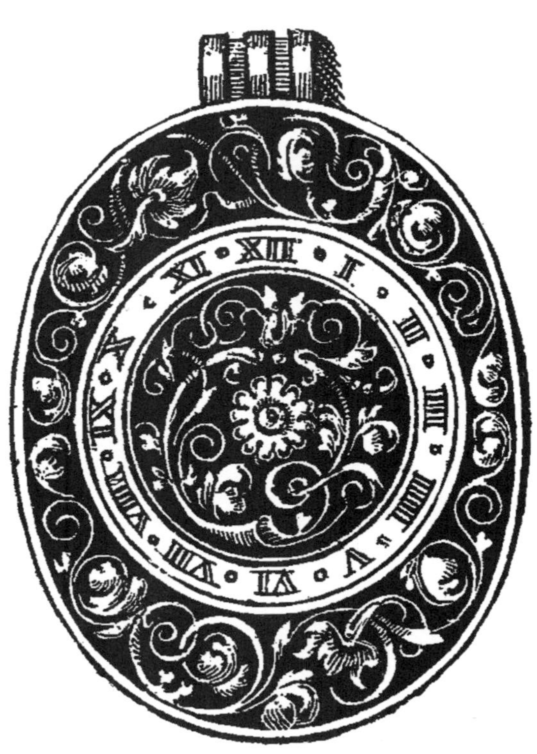

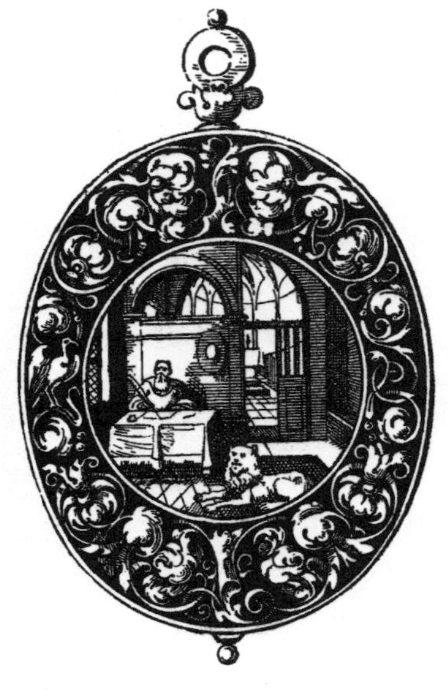
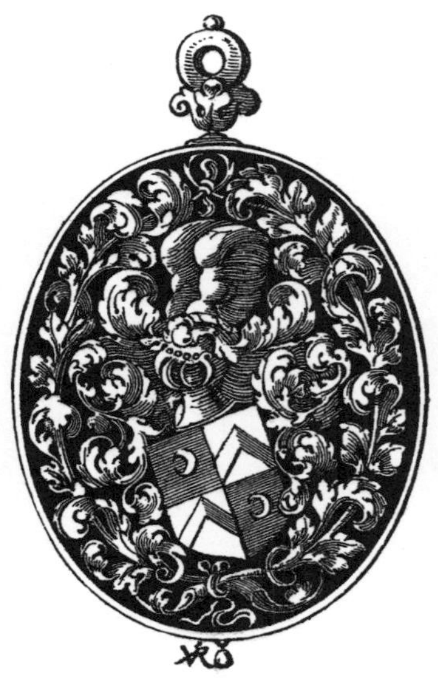
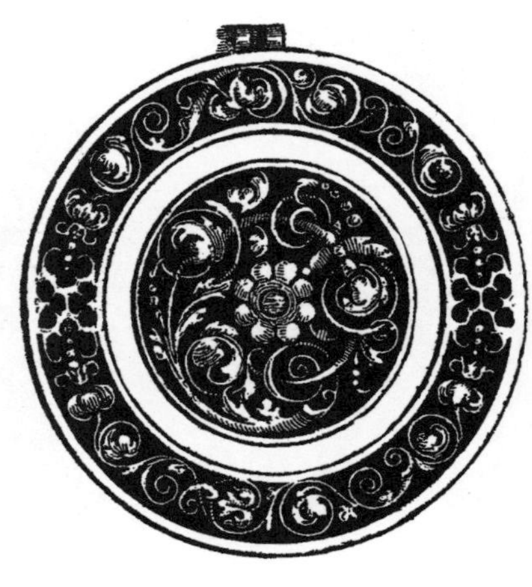
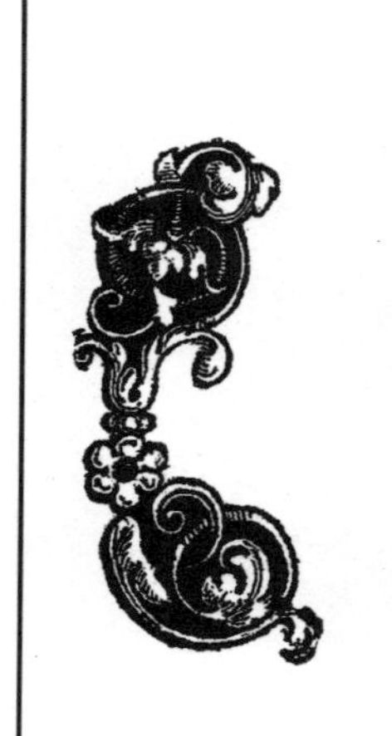
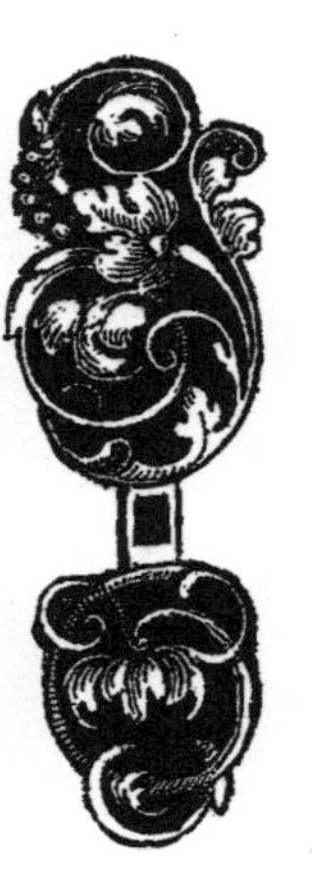
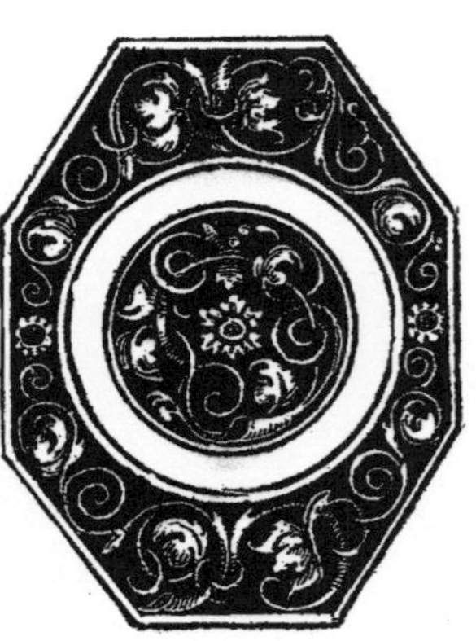
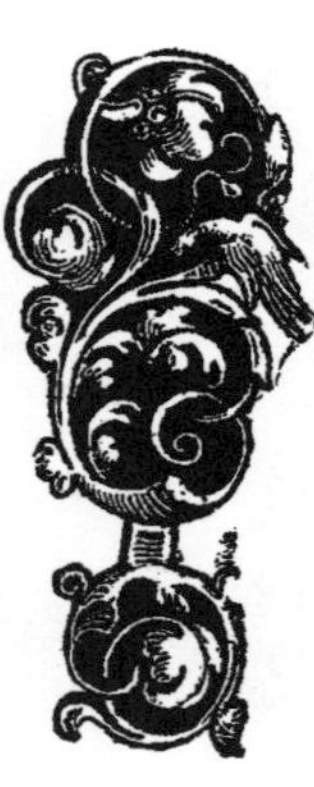
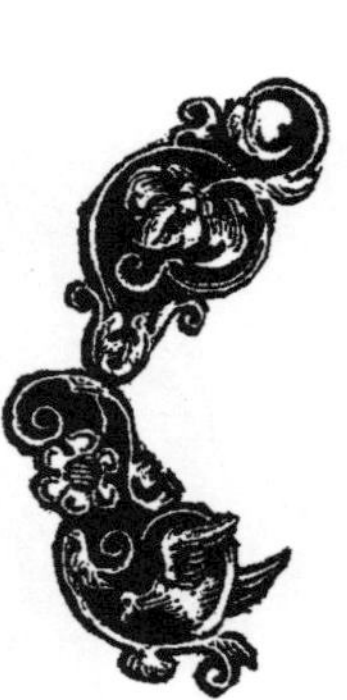

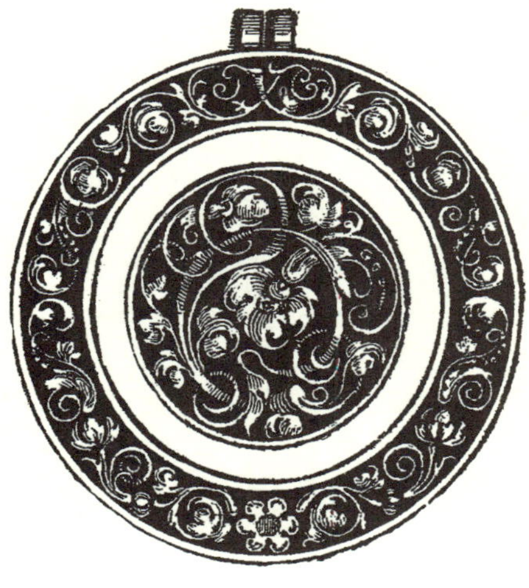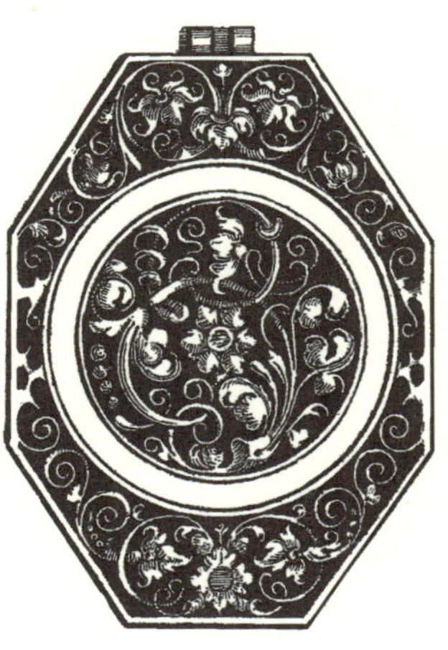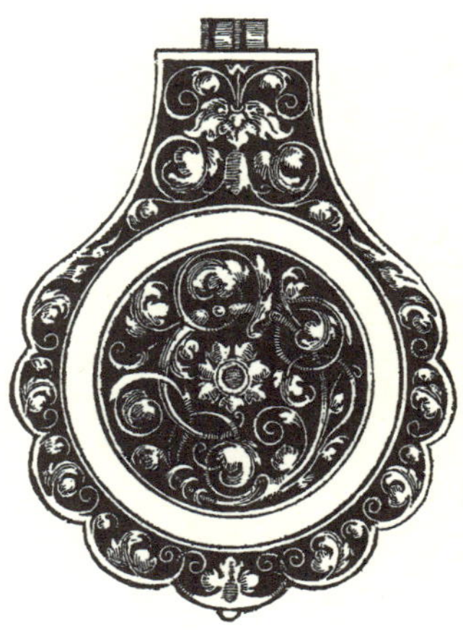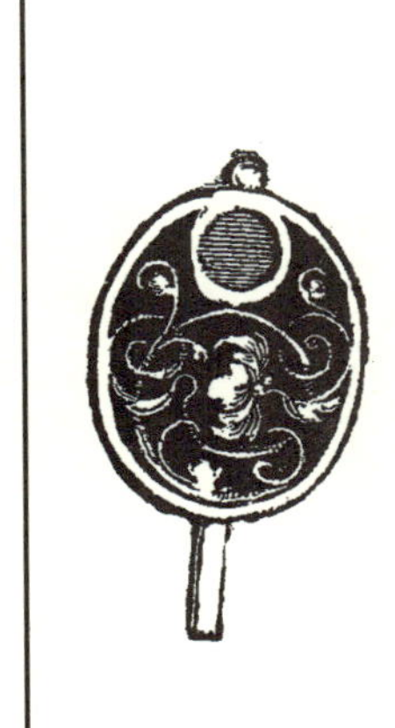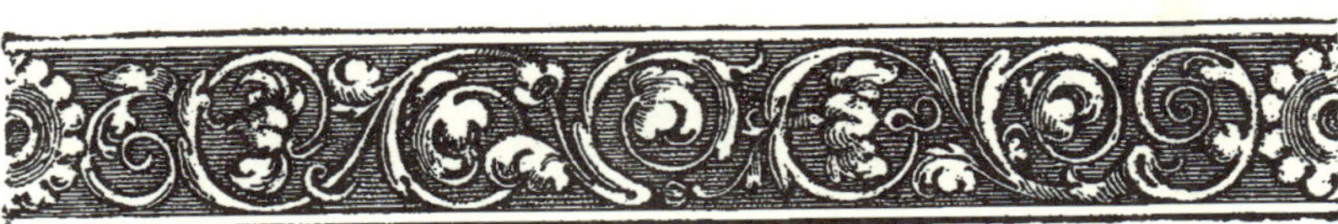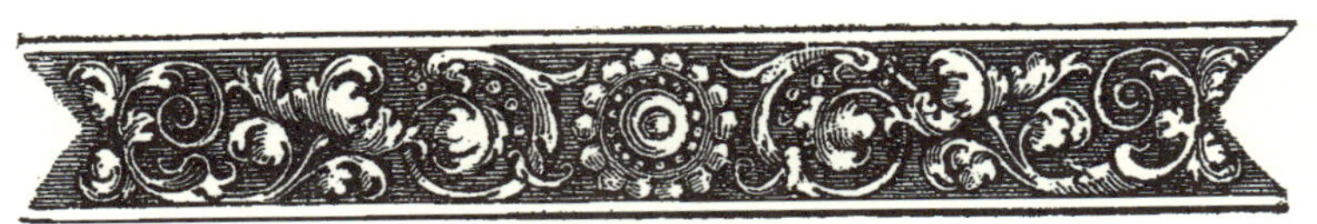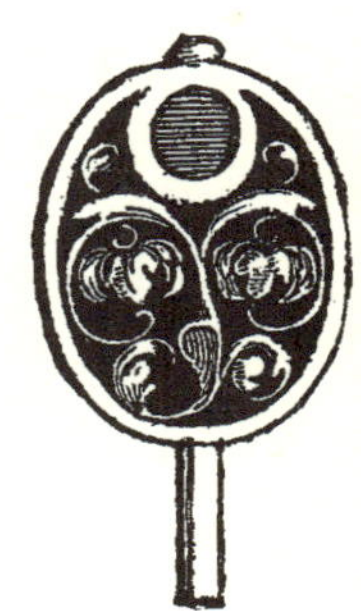

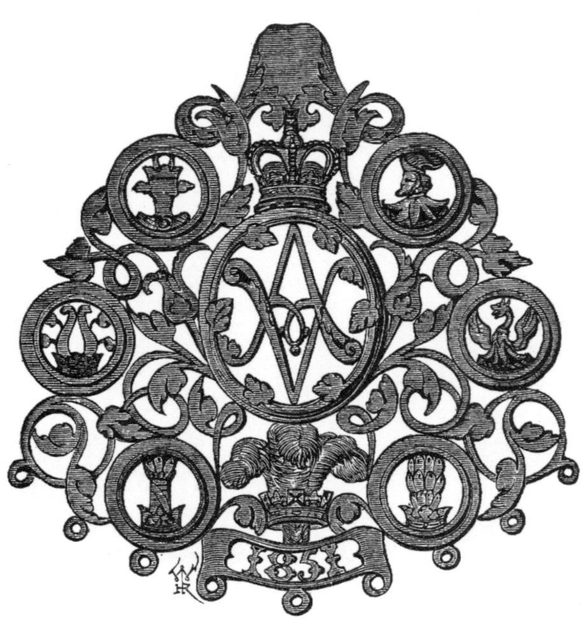

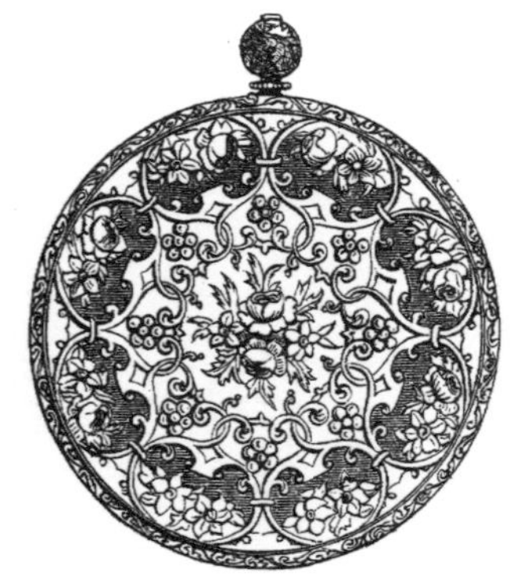

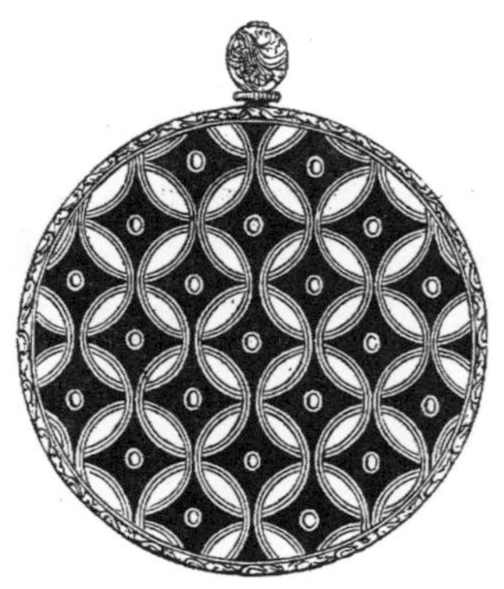

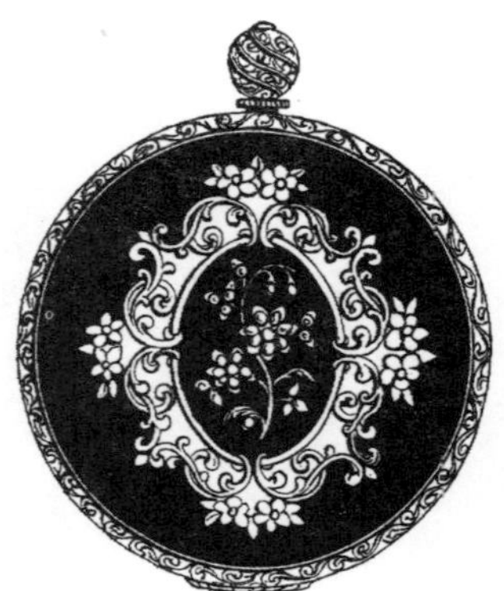

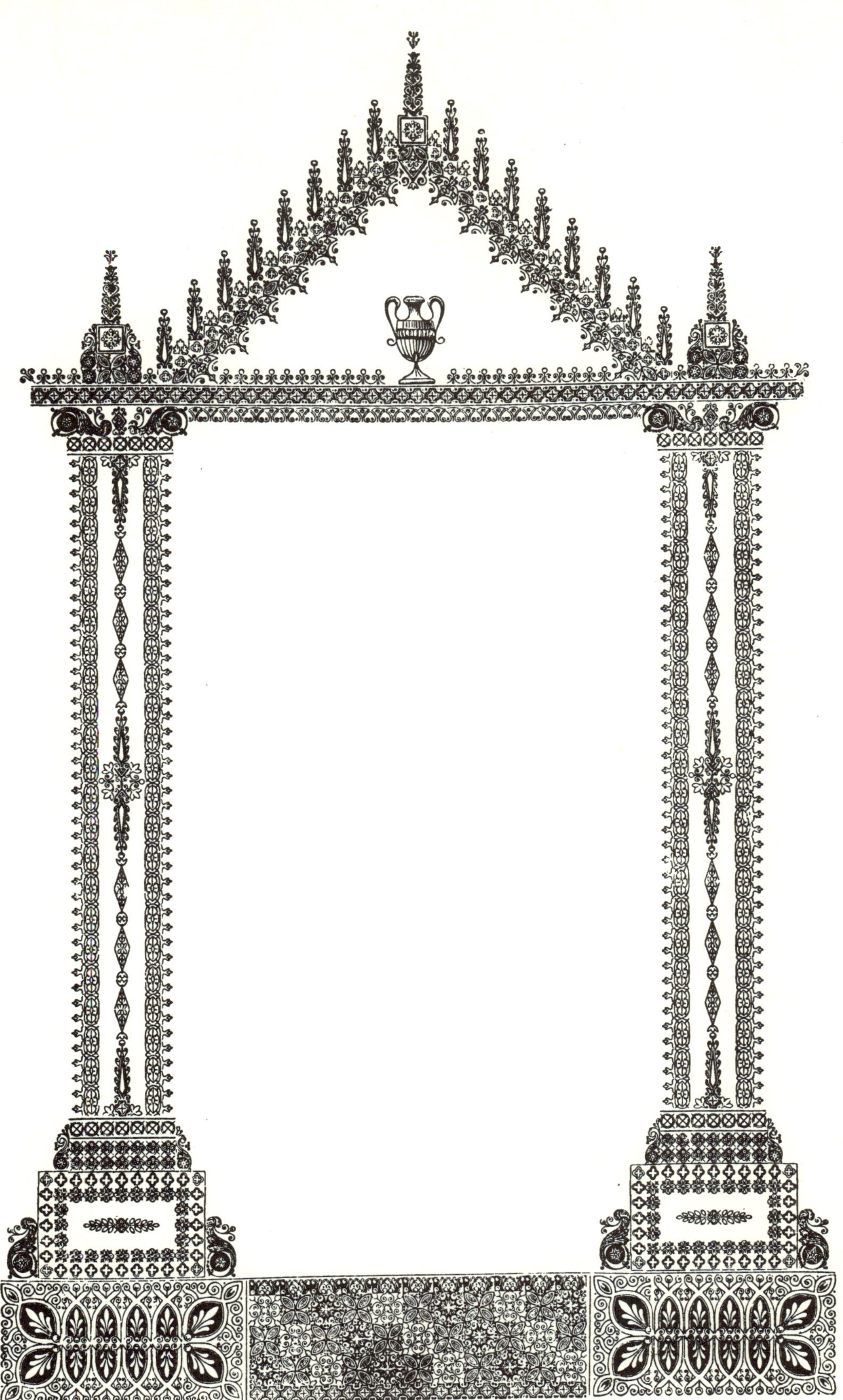

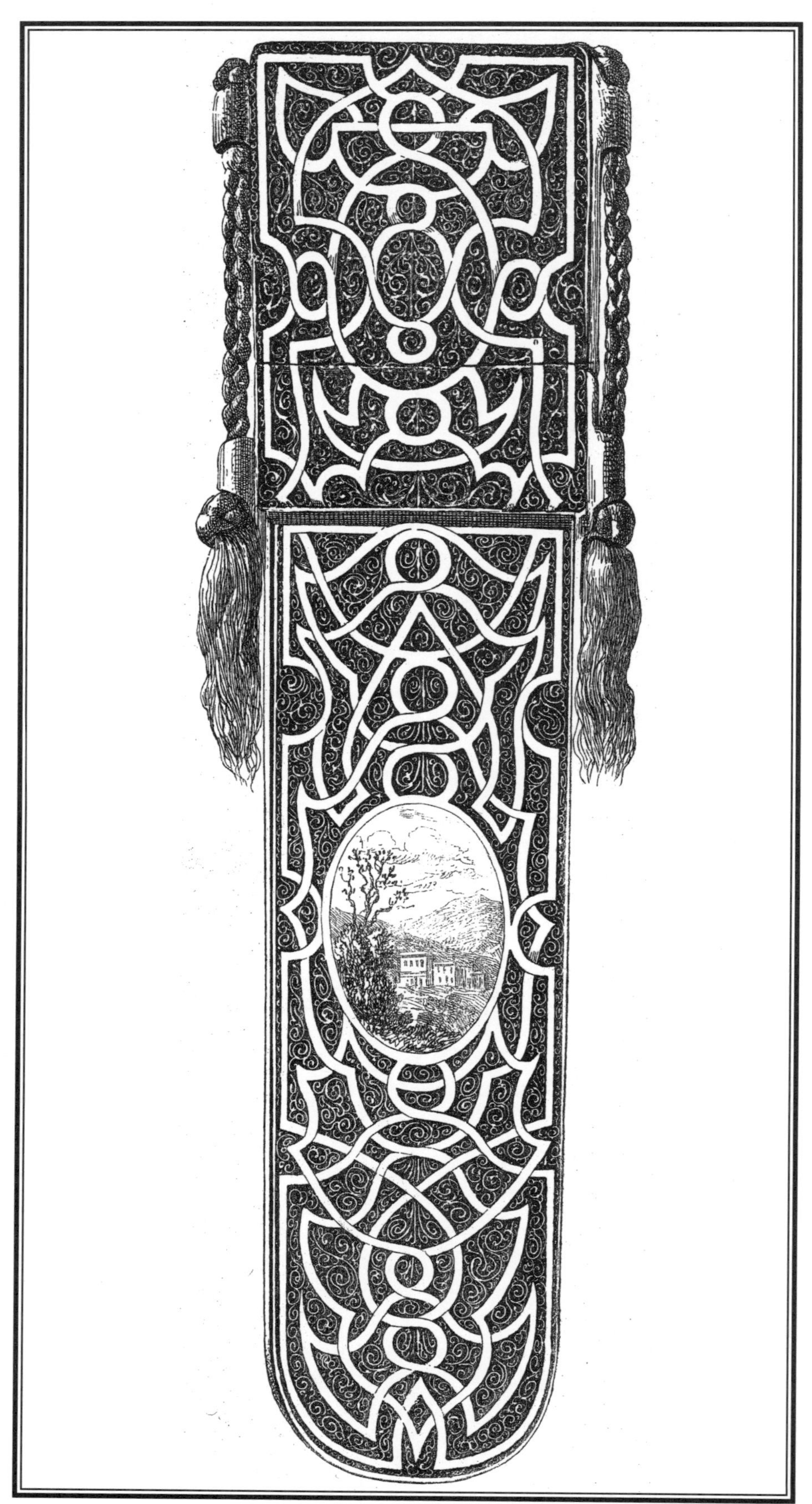

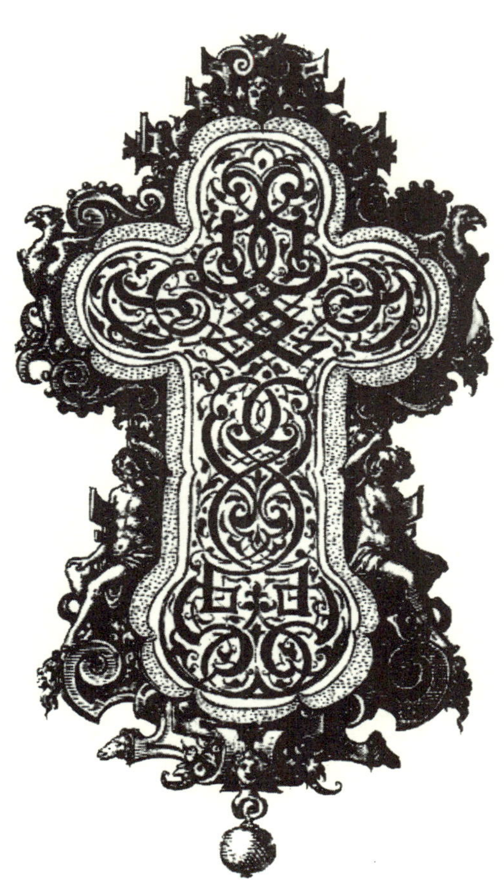

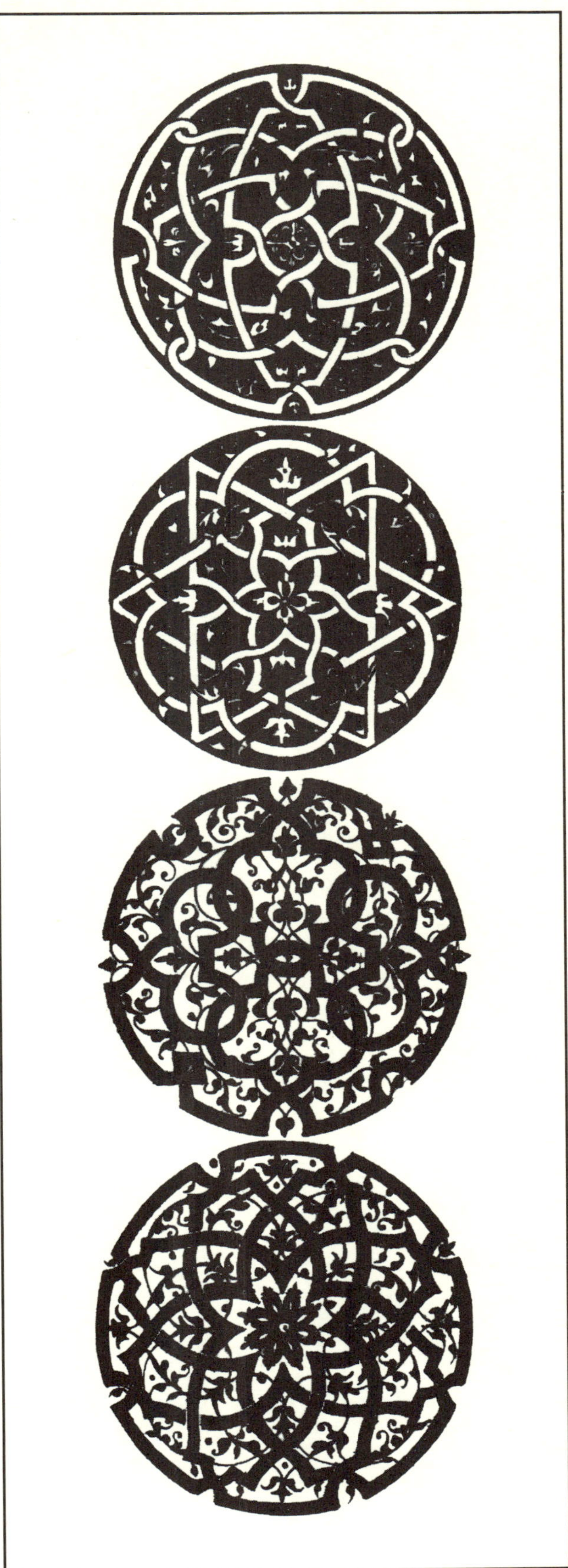

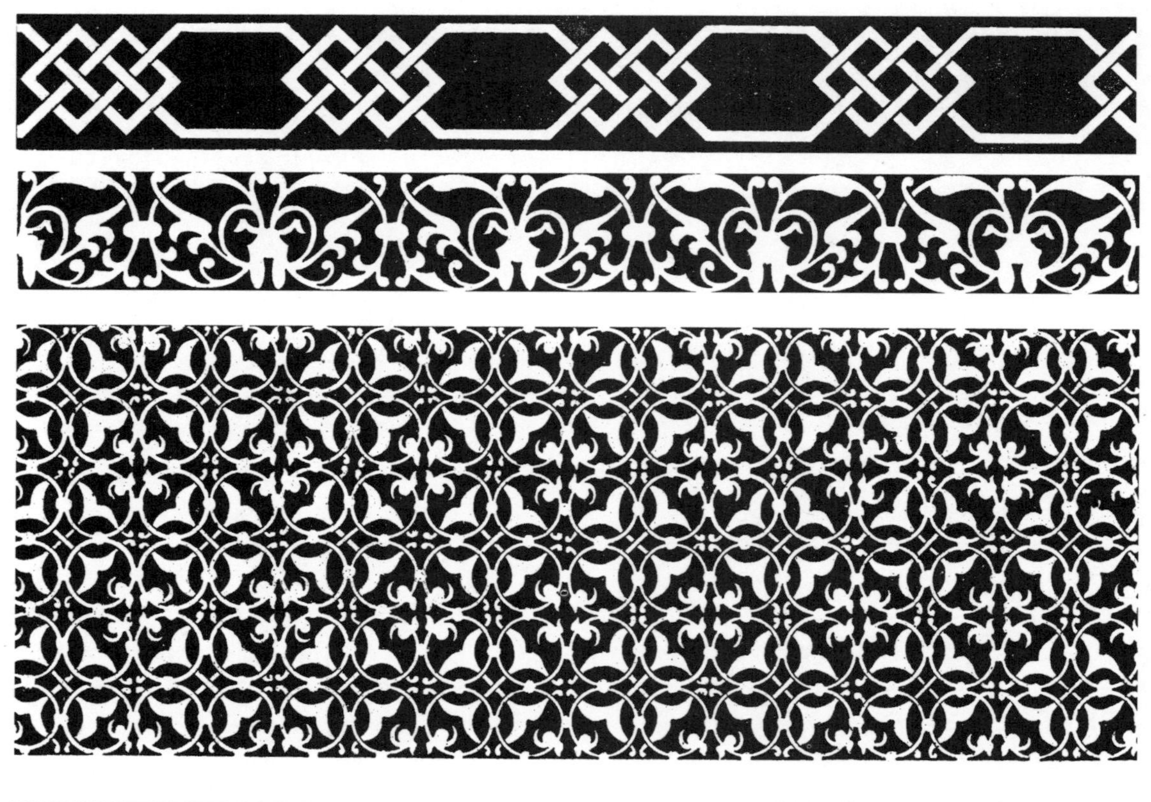

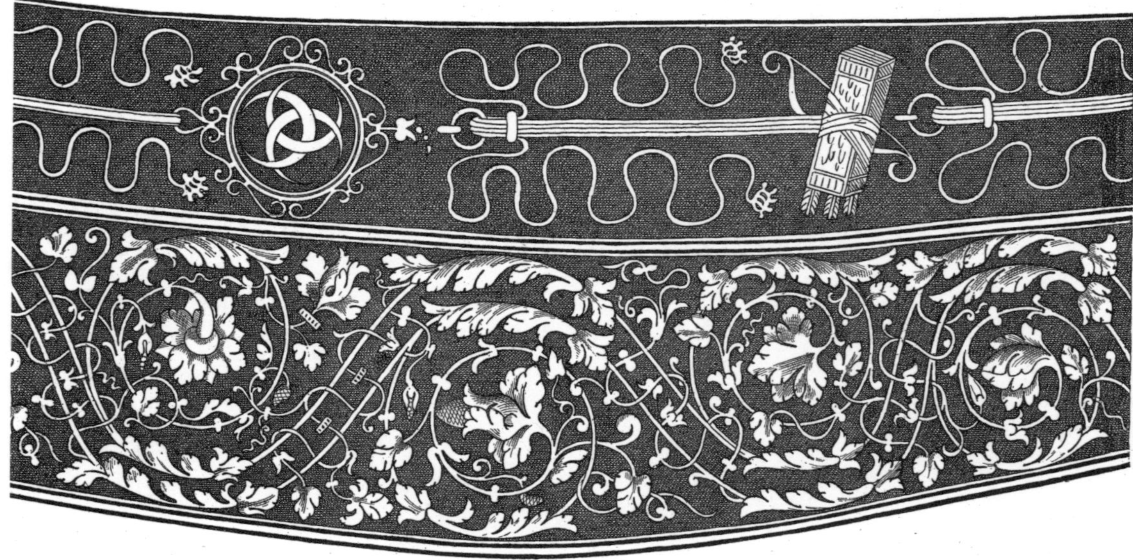

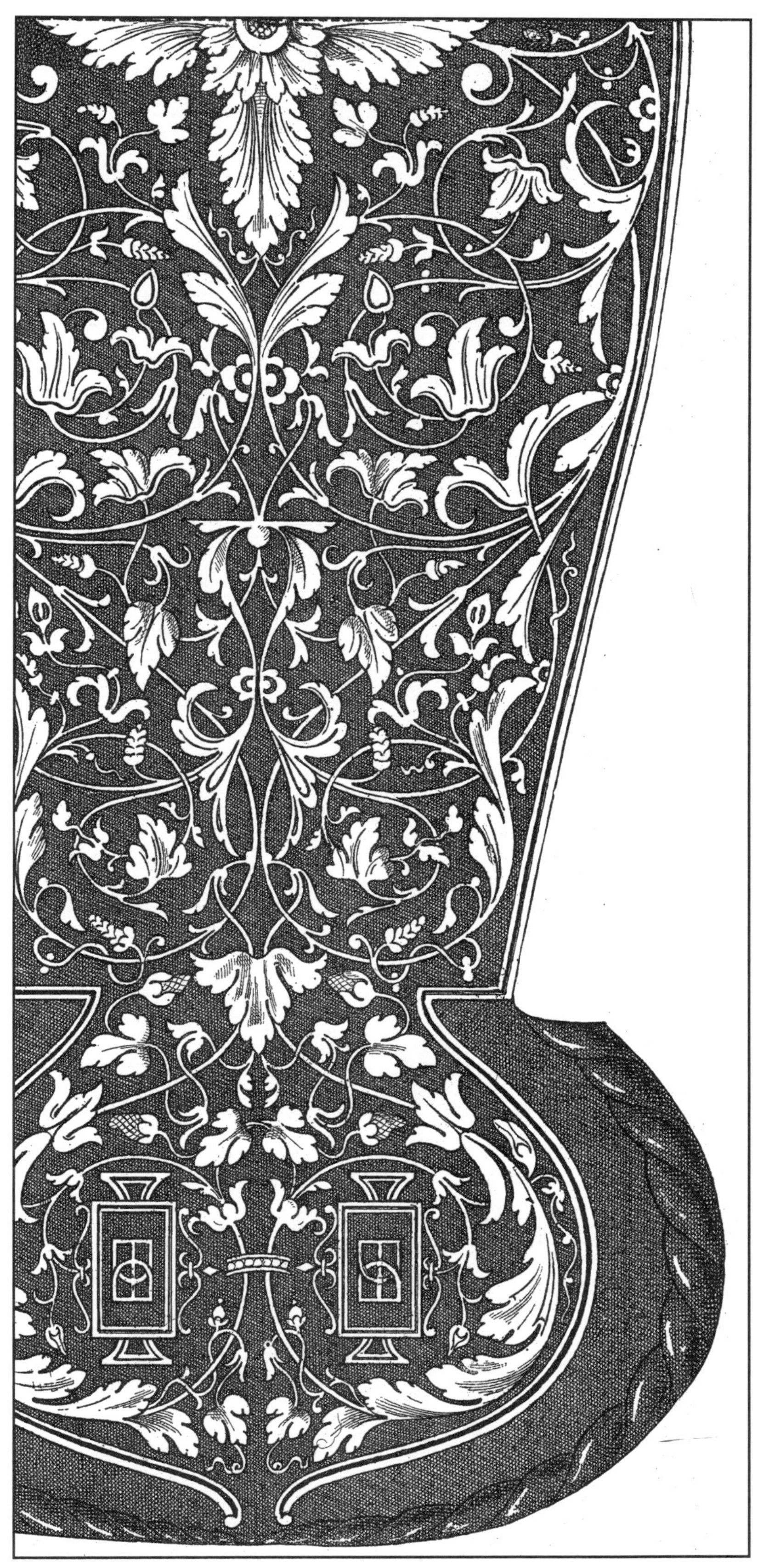

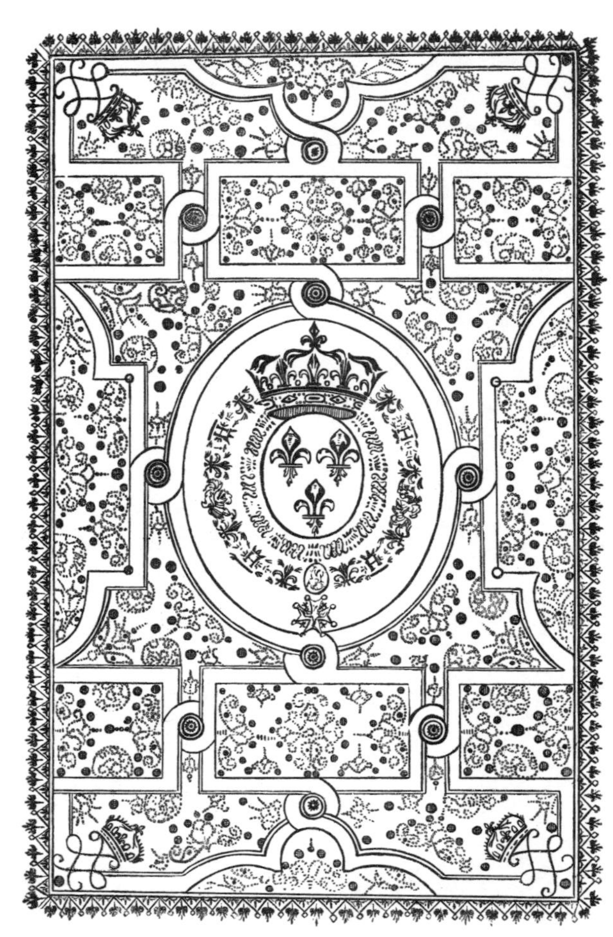 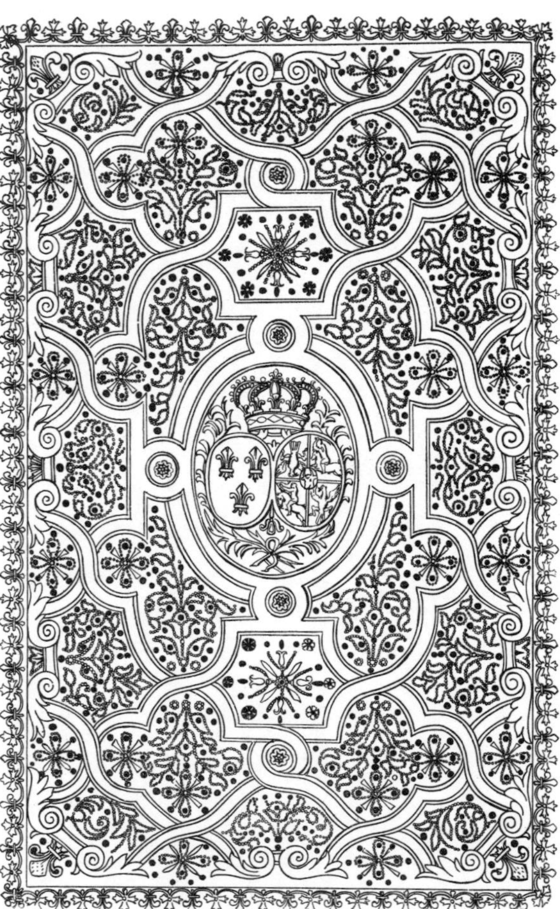

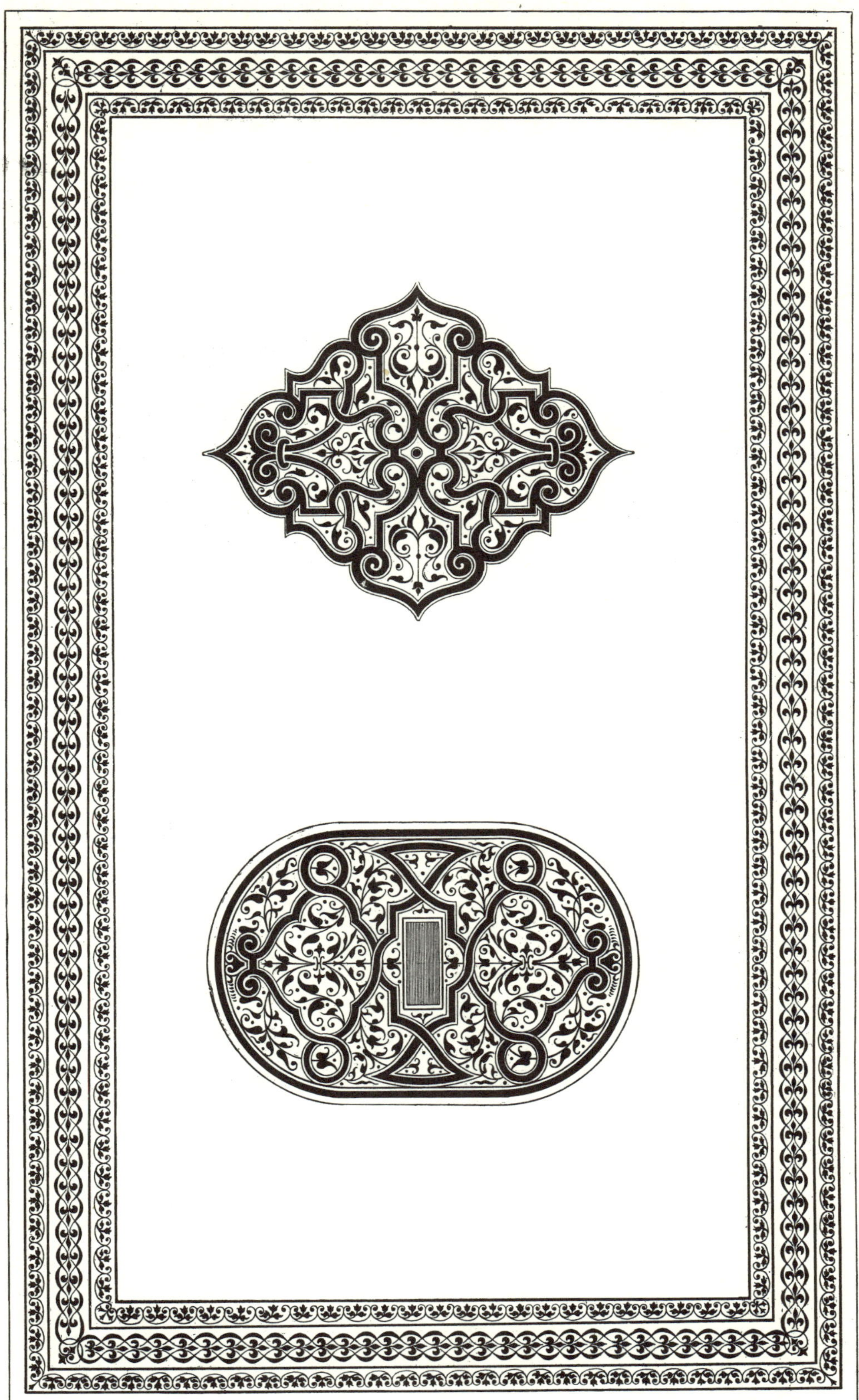

Pratt
CONTI. SC

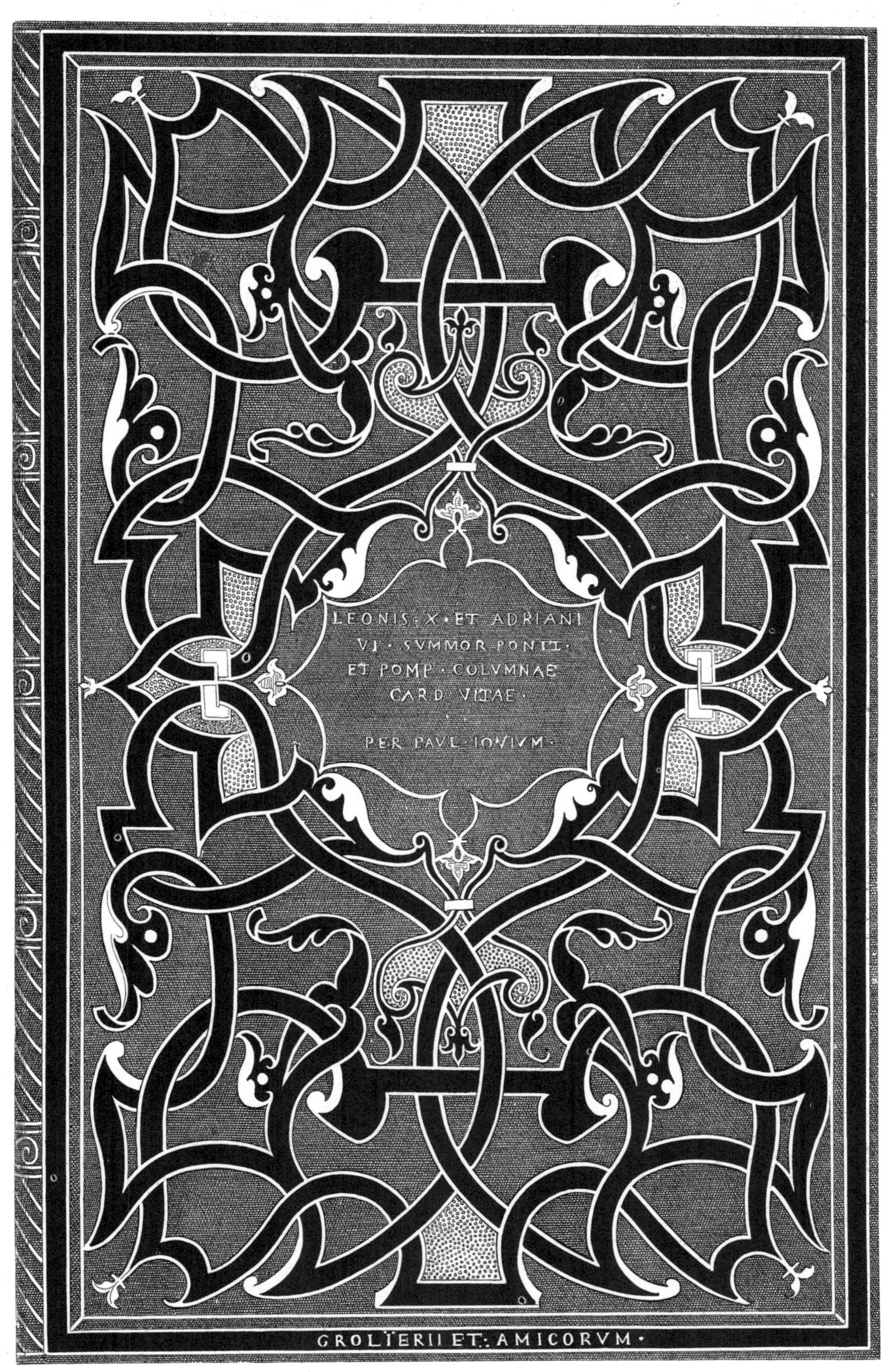

LEONIS · X · ET ADRIANI
VI · SVMMOR PONTI ·
ET POMP · COLVMNAE
CARD · VITAE ·

PER PAVL · IOVIVM ·

GROLIERII ET · AMICORVM ·

PROCOPIVS
DE · BELLO
PERSICO
TH · MAIOLI · ET · AMICORVM

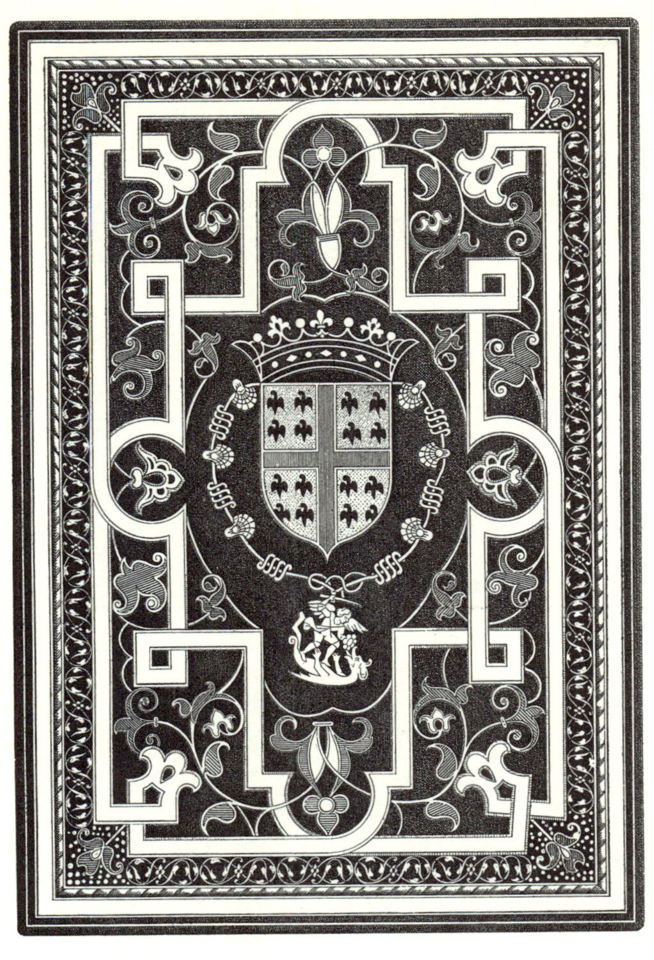

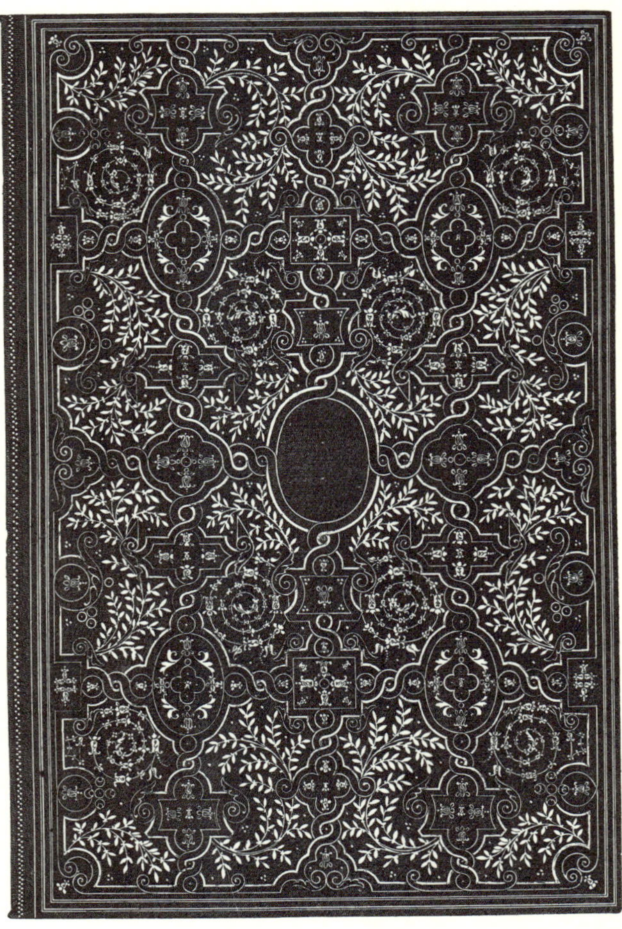

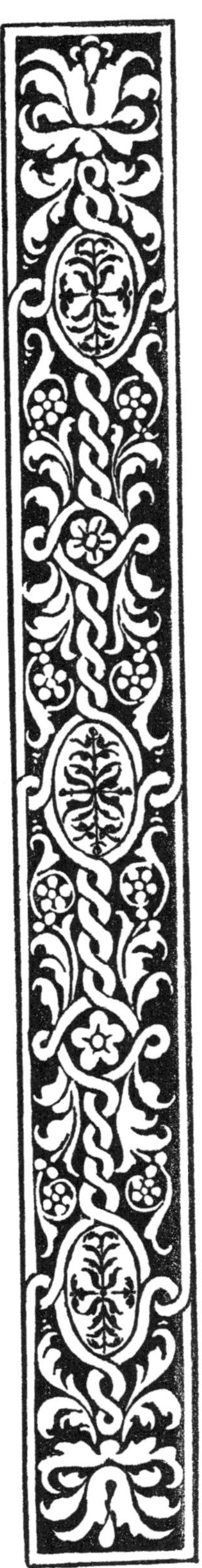

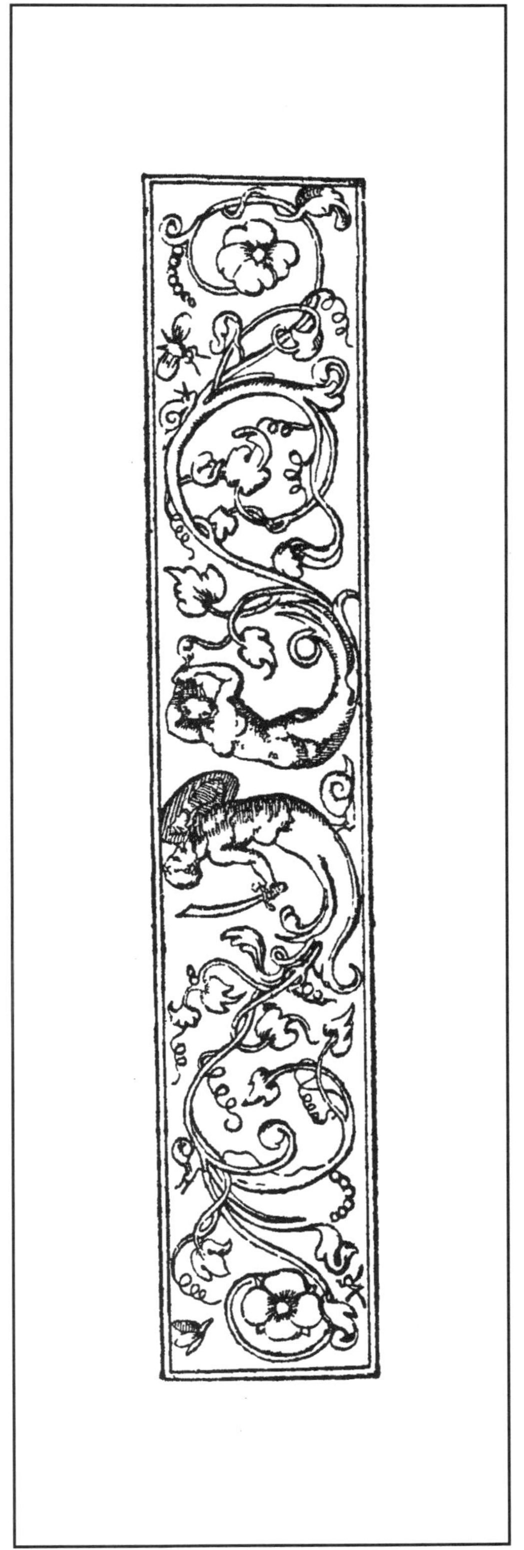

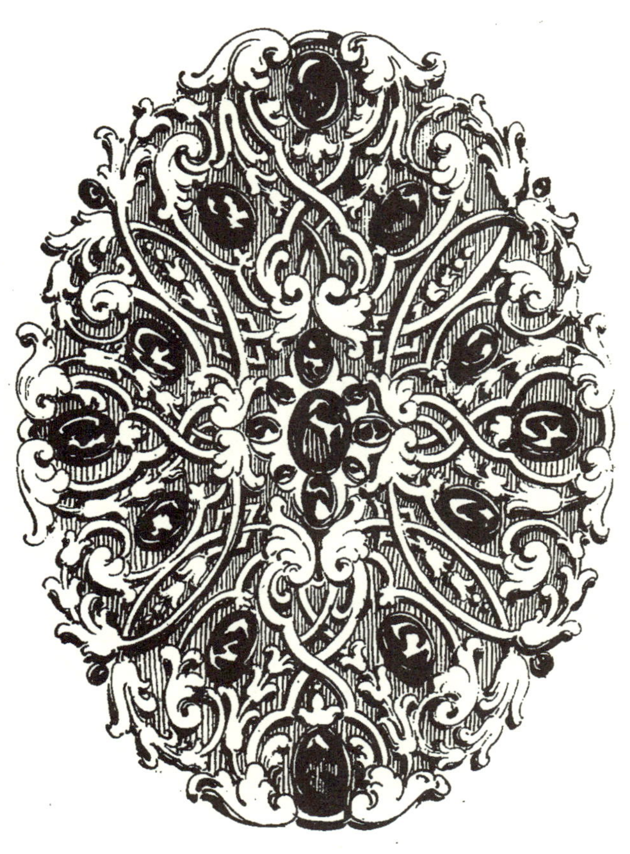

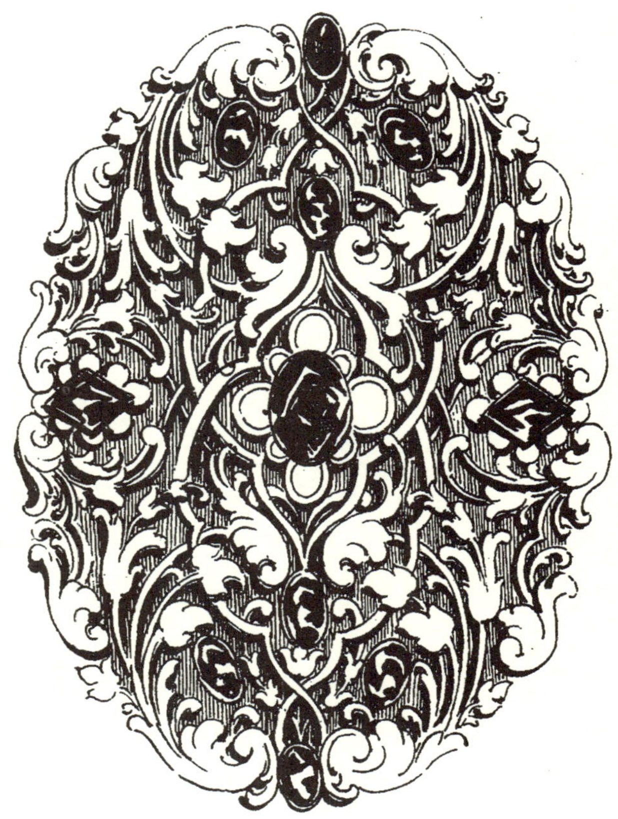

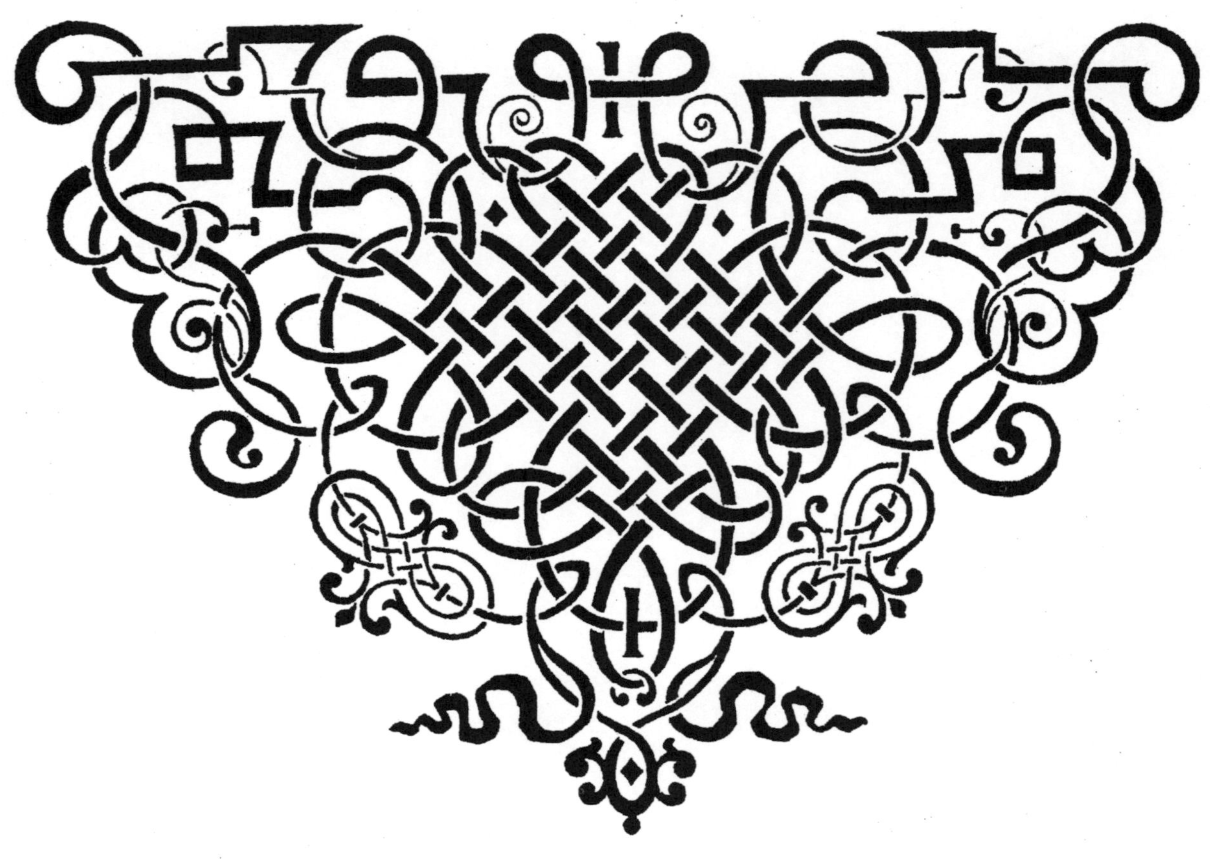

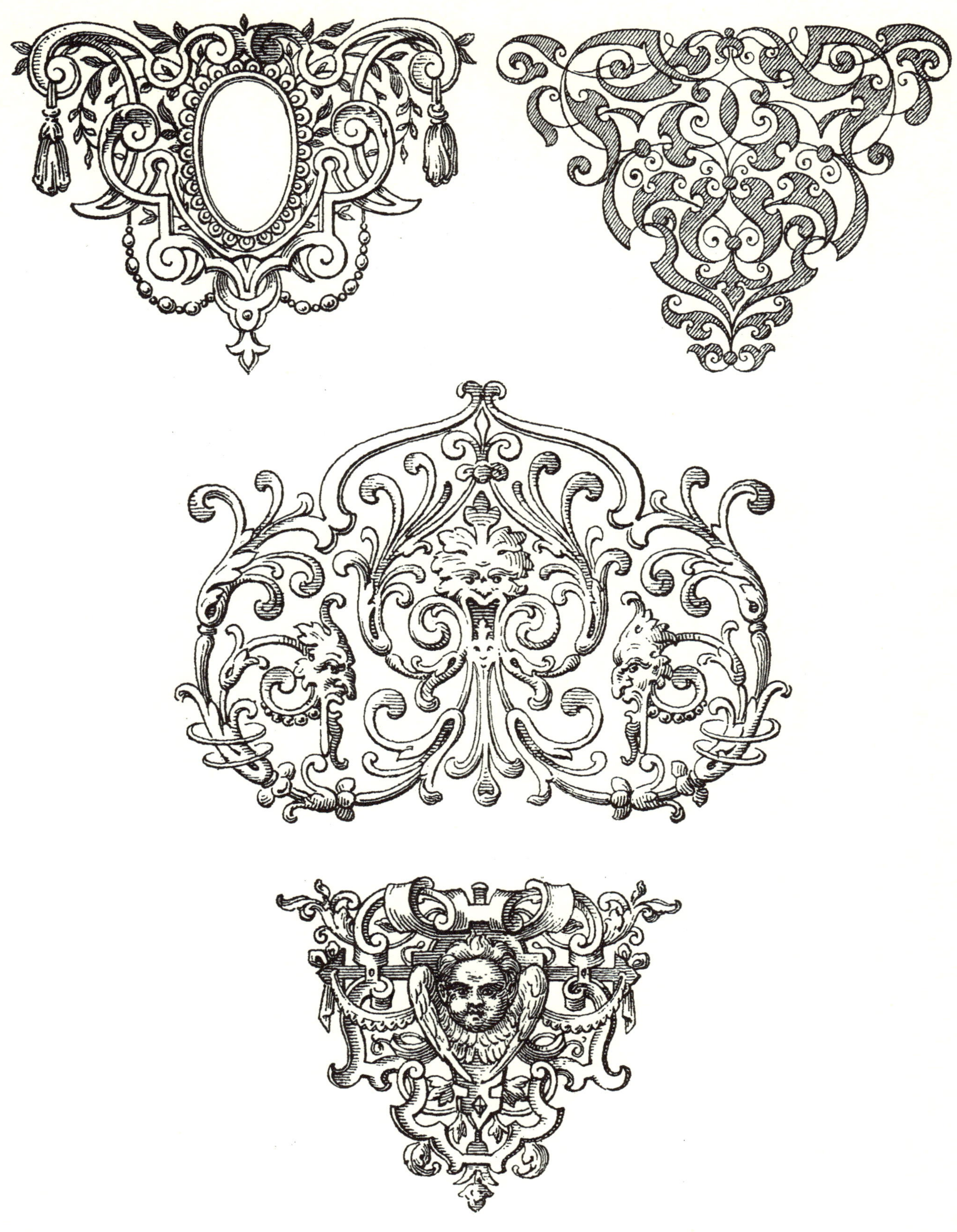

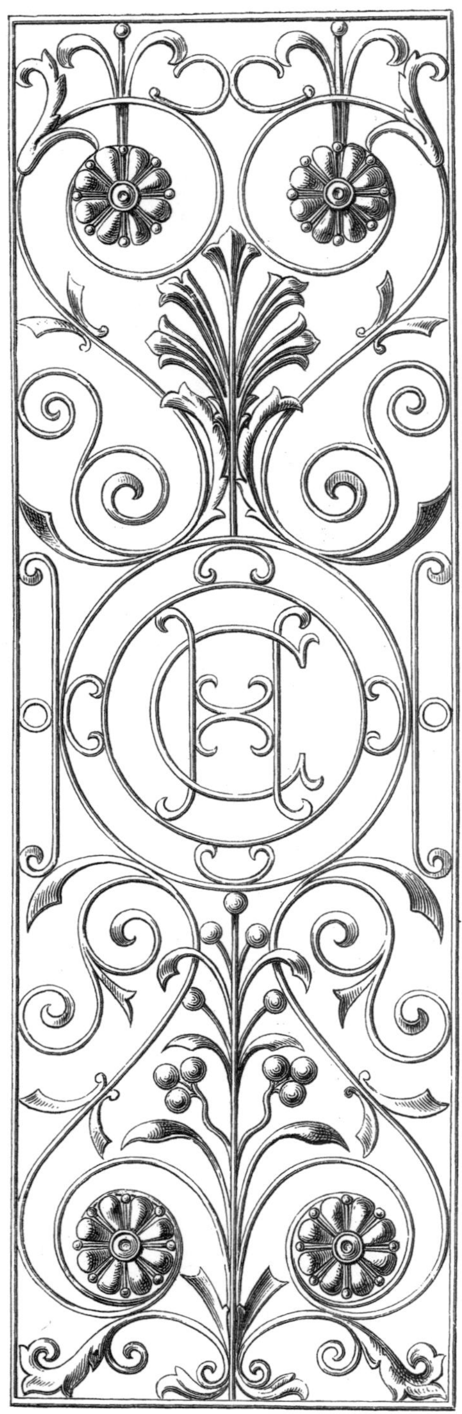
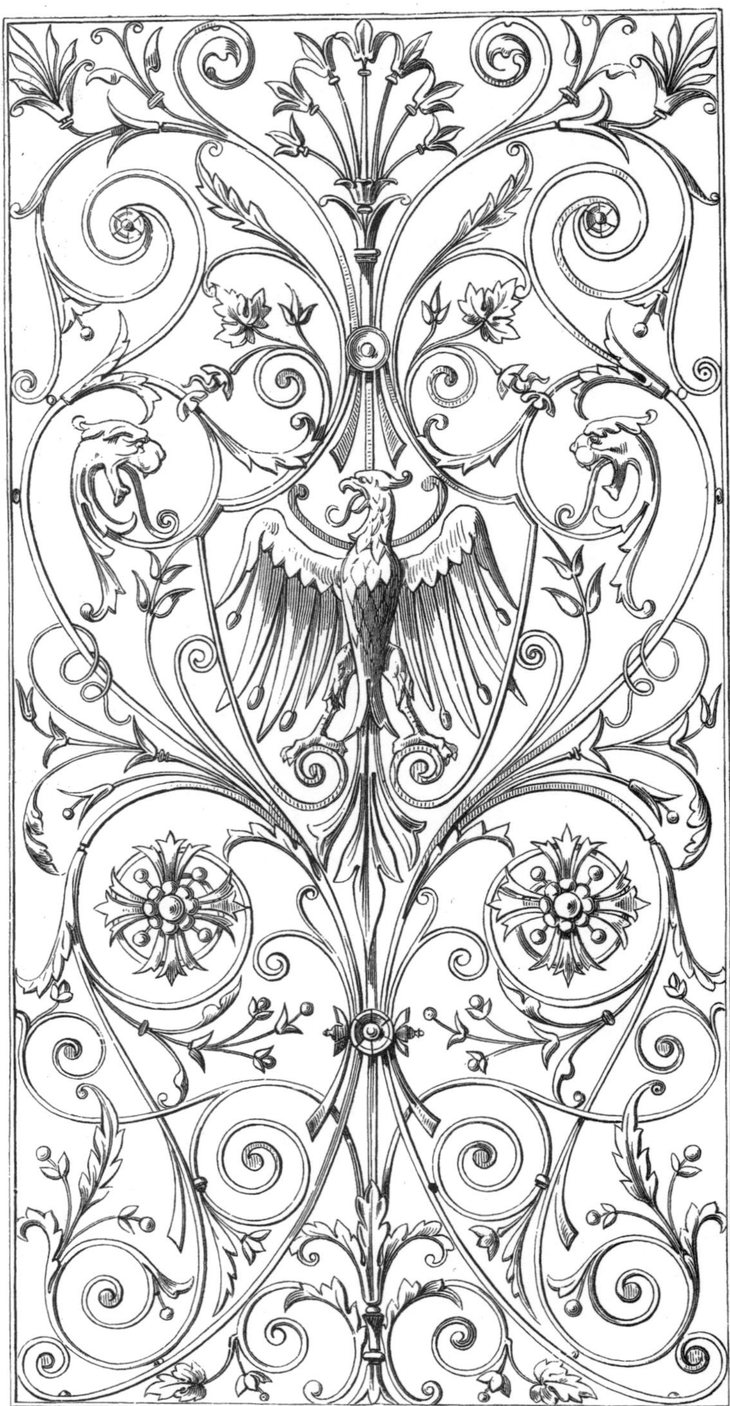

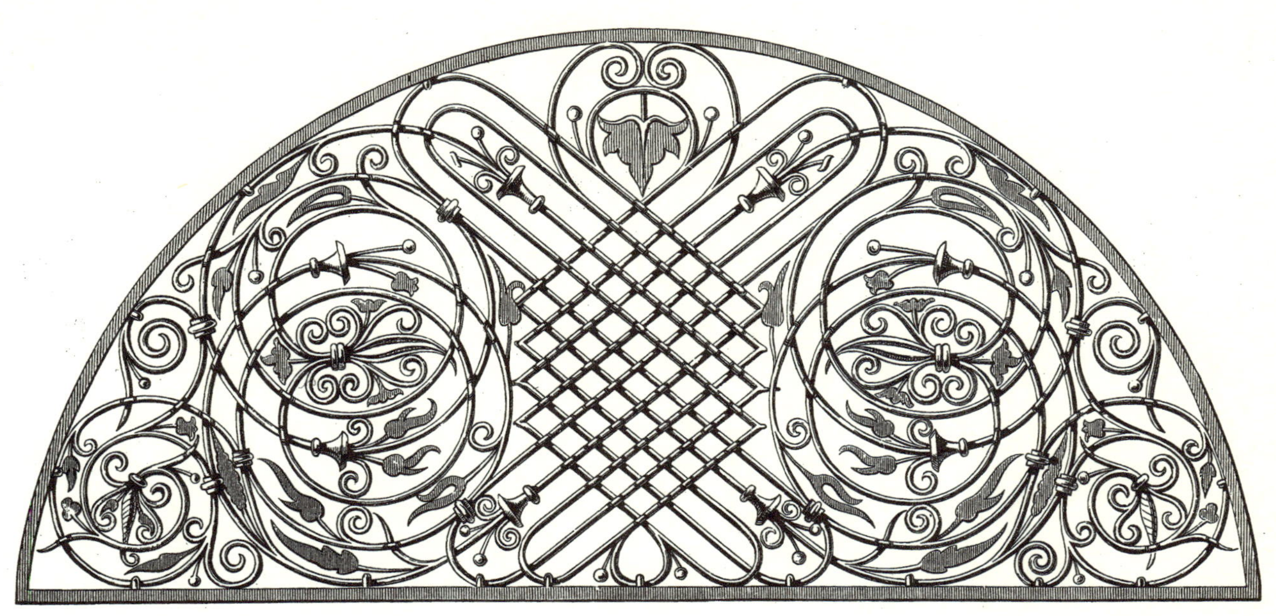

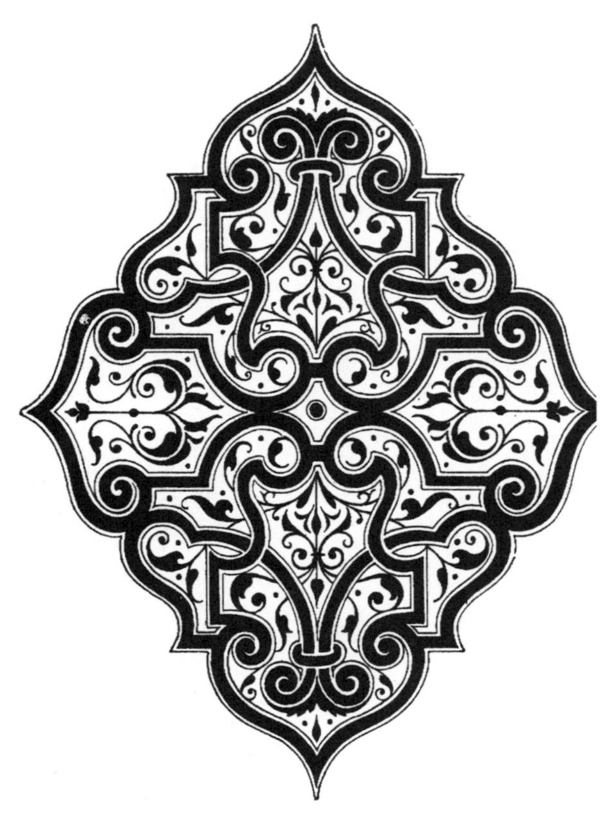

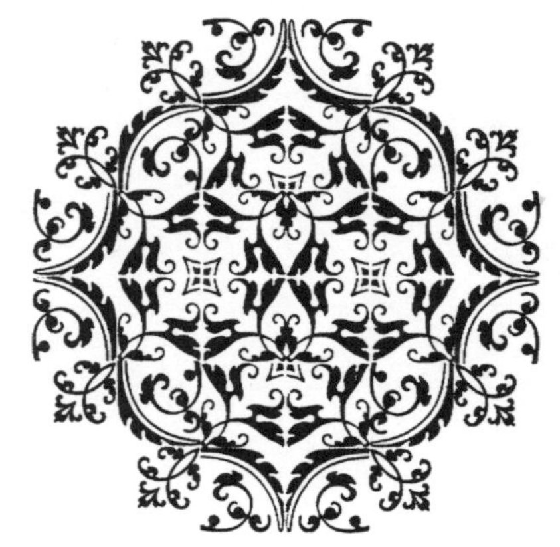

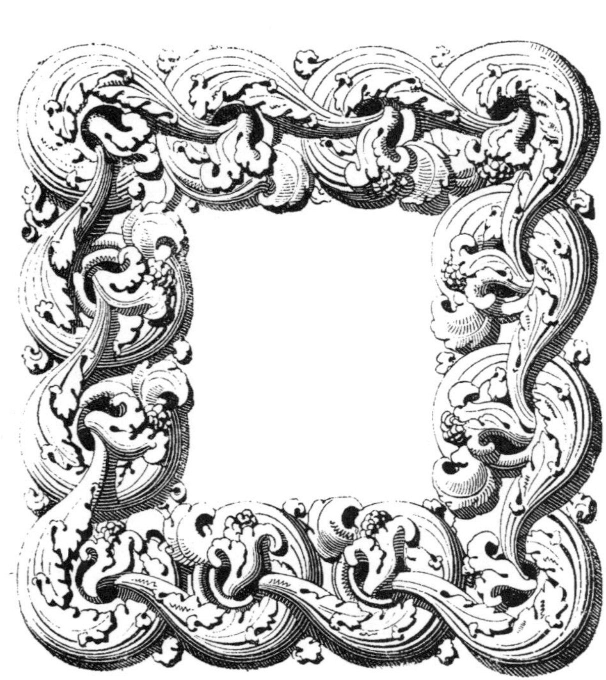

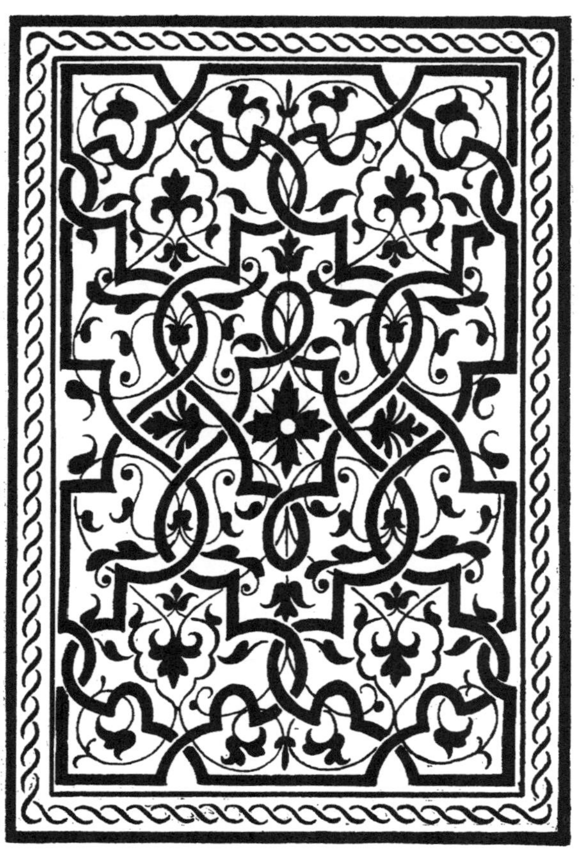

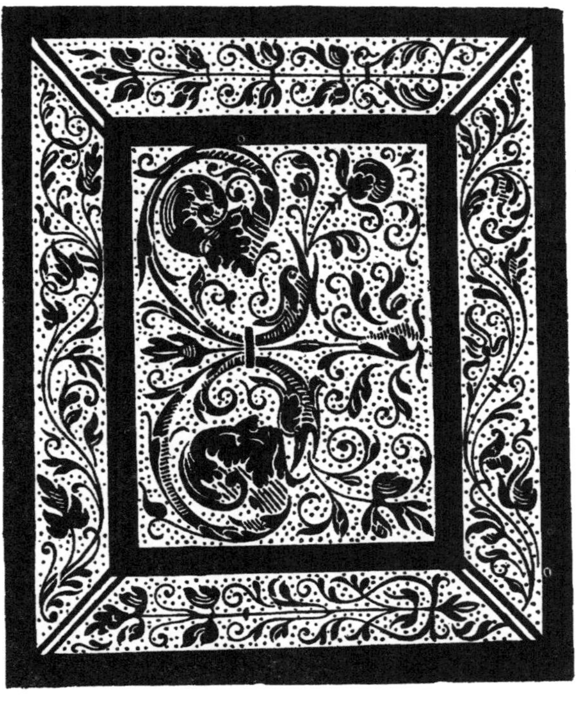

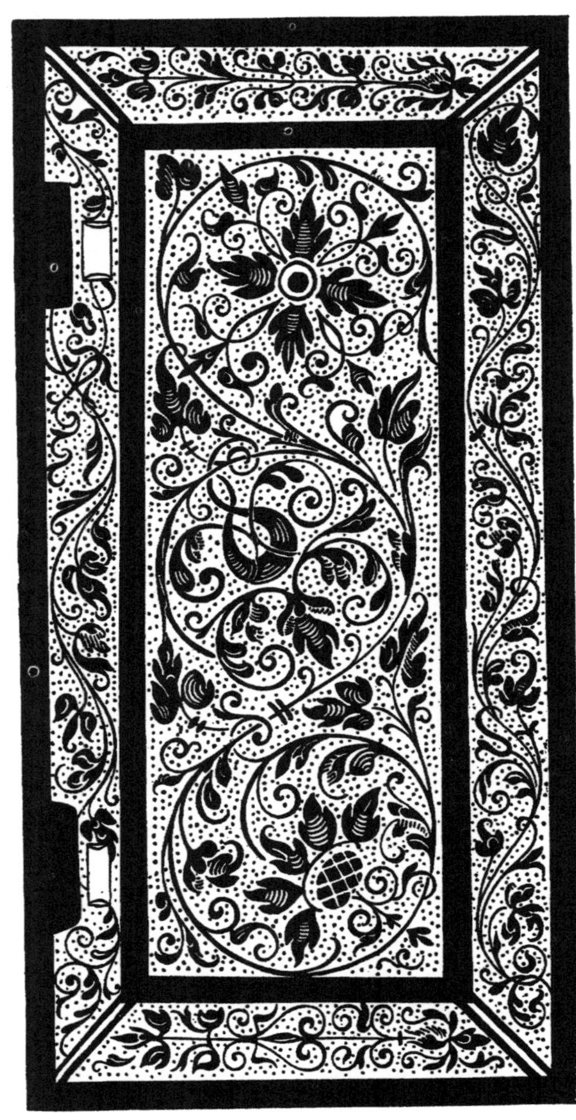

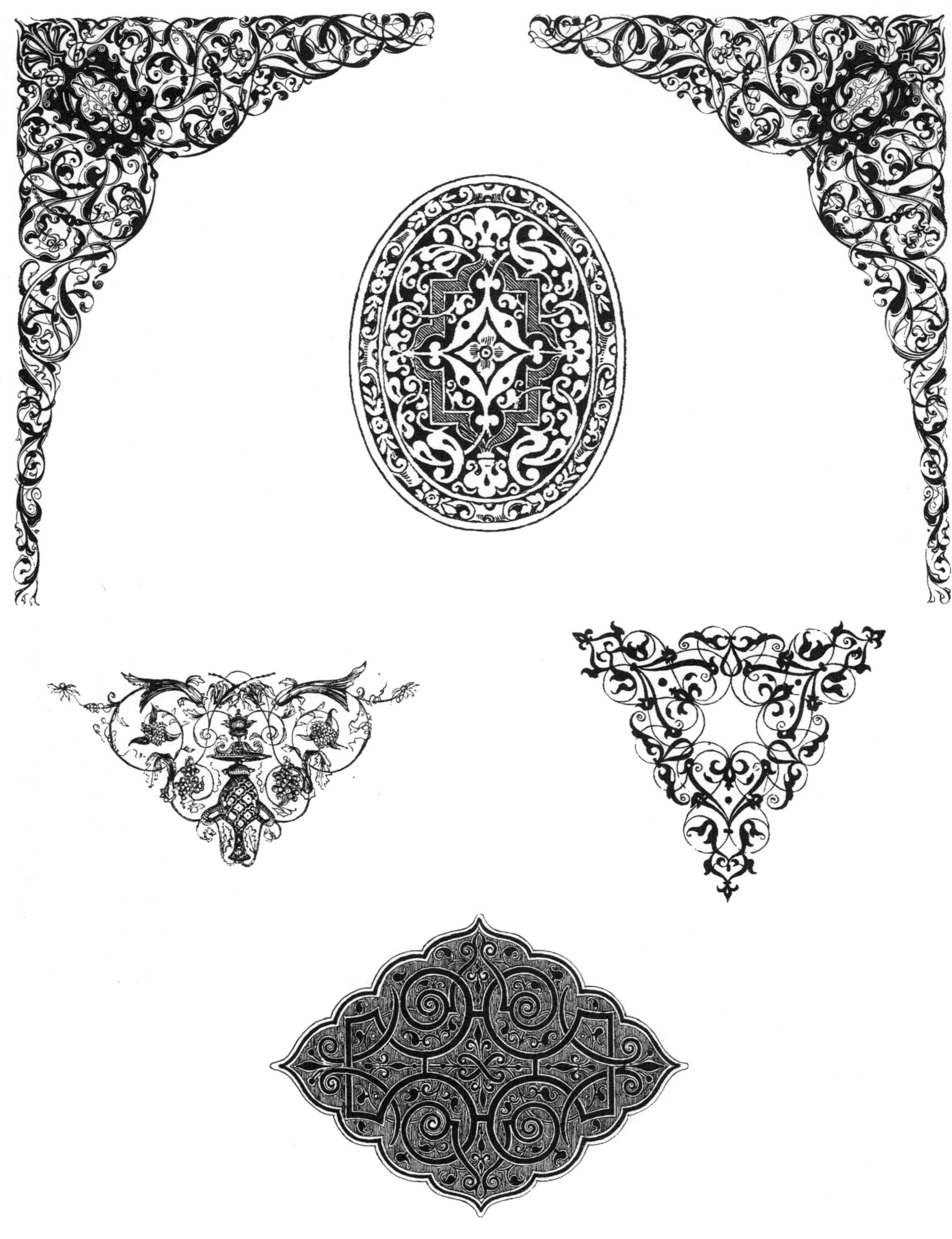

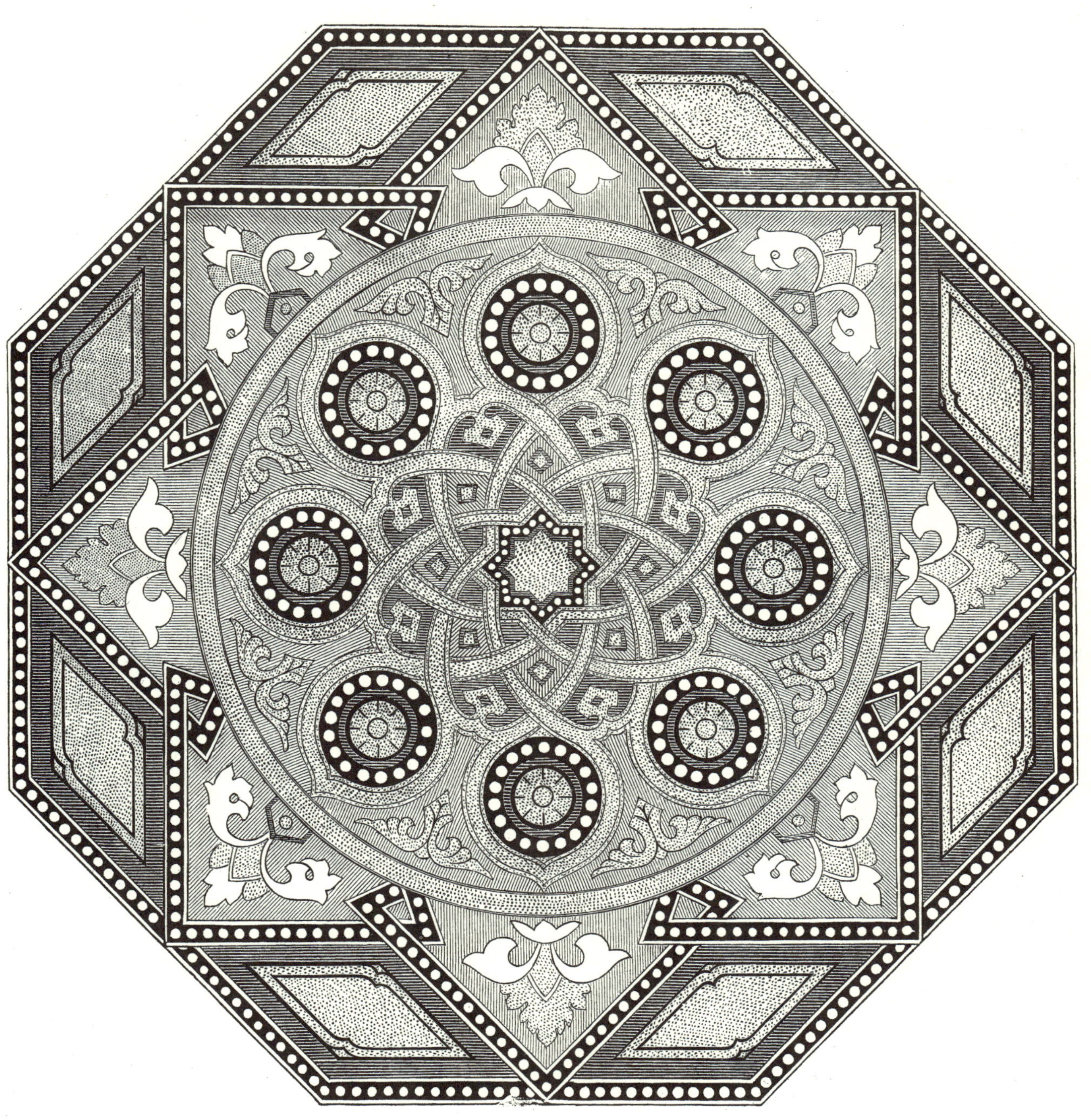

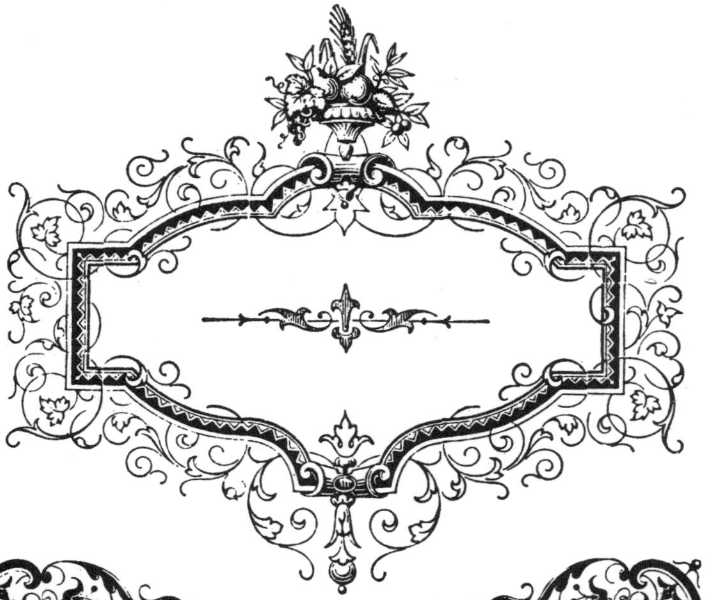

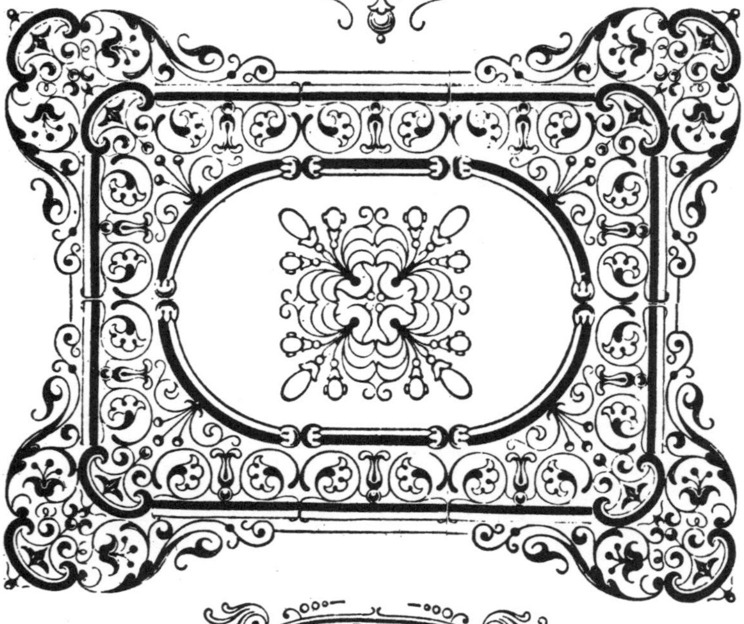

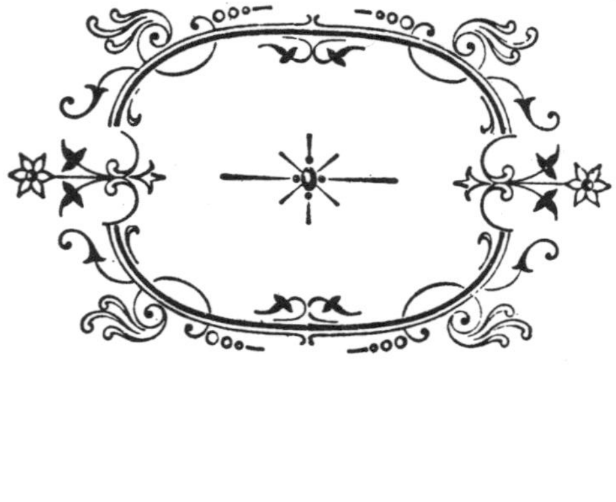

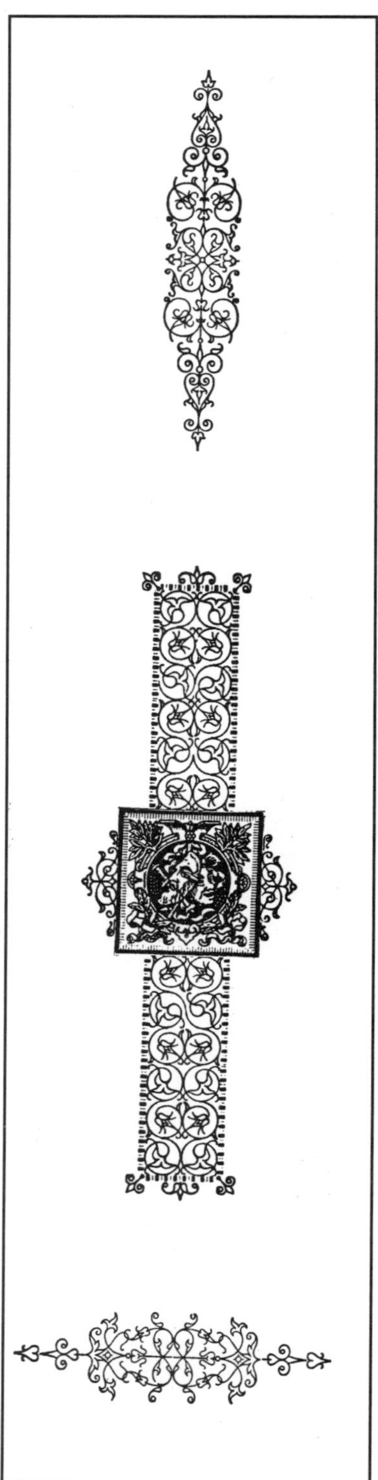

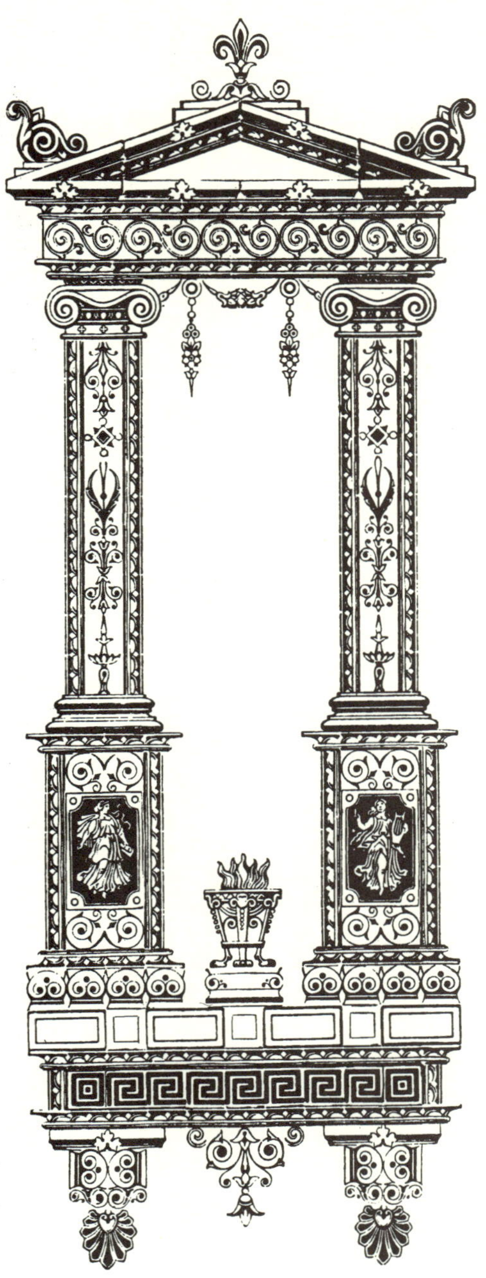

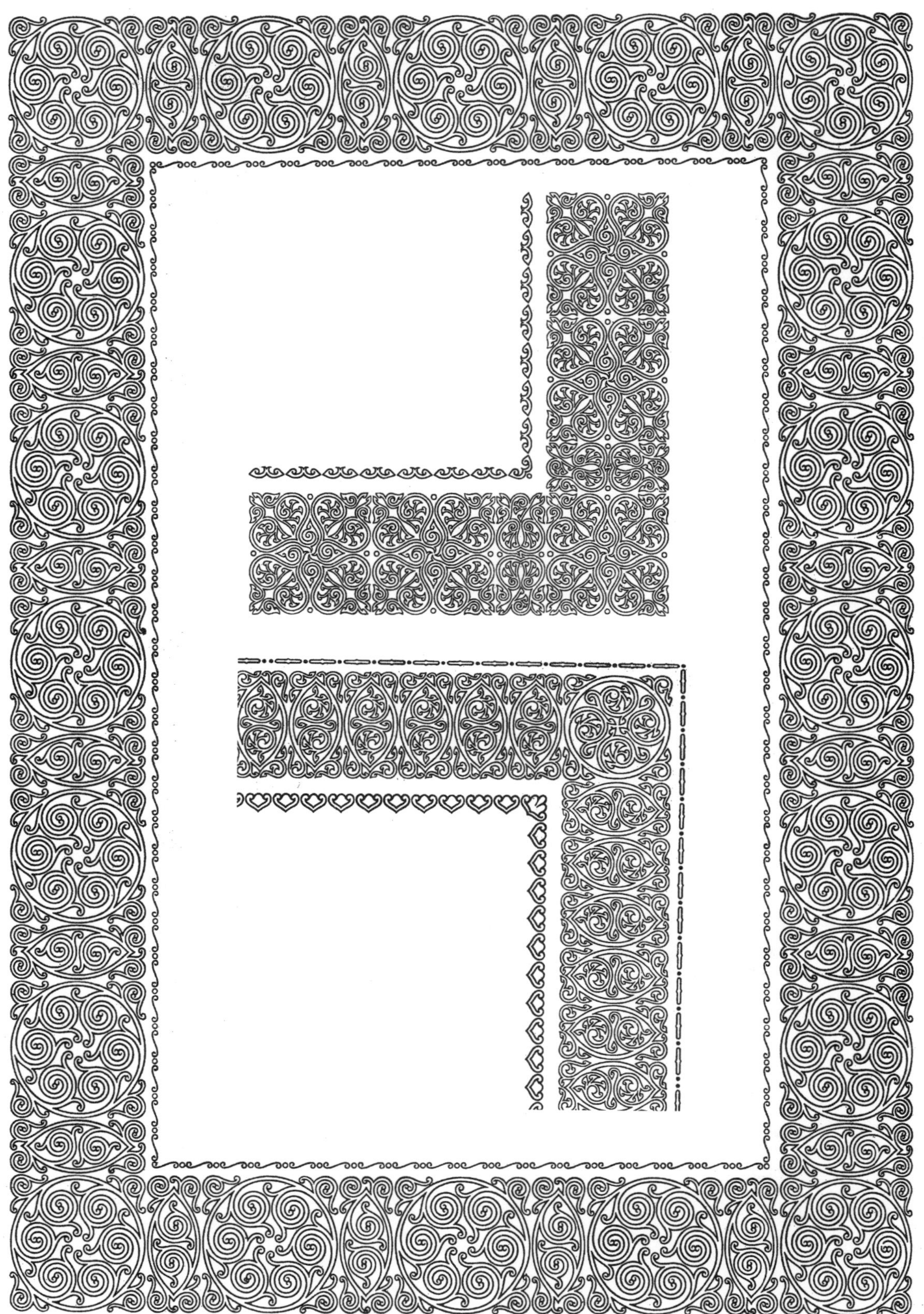

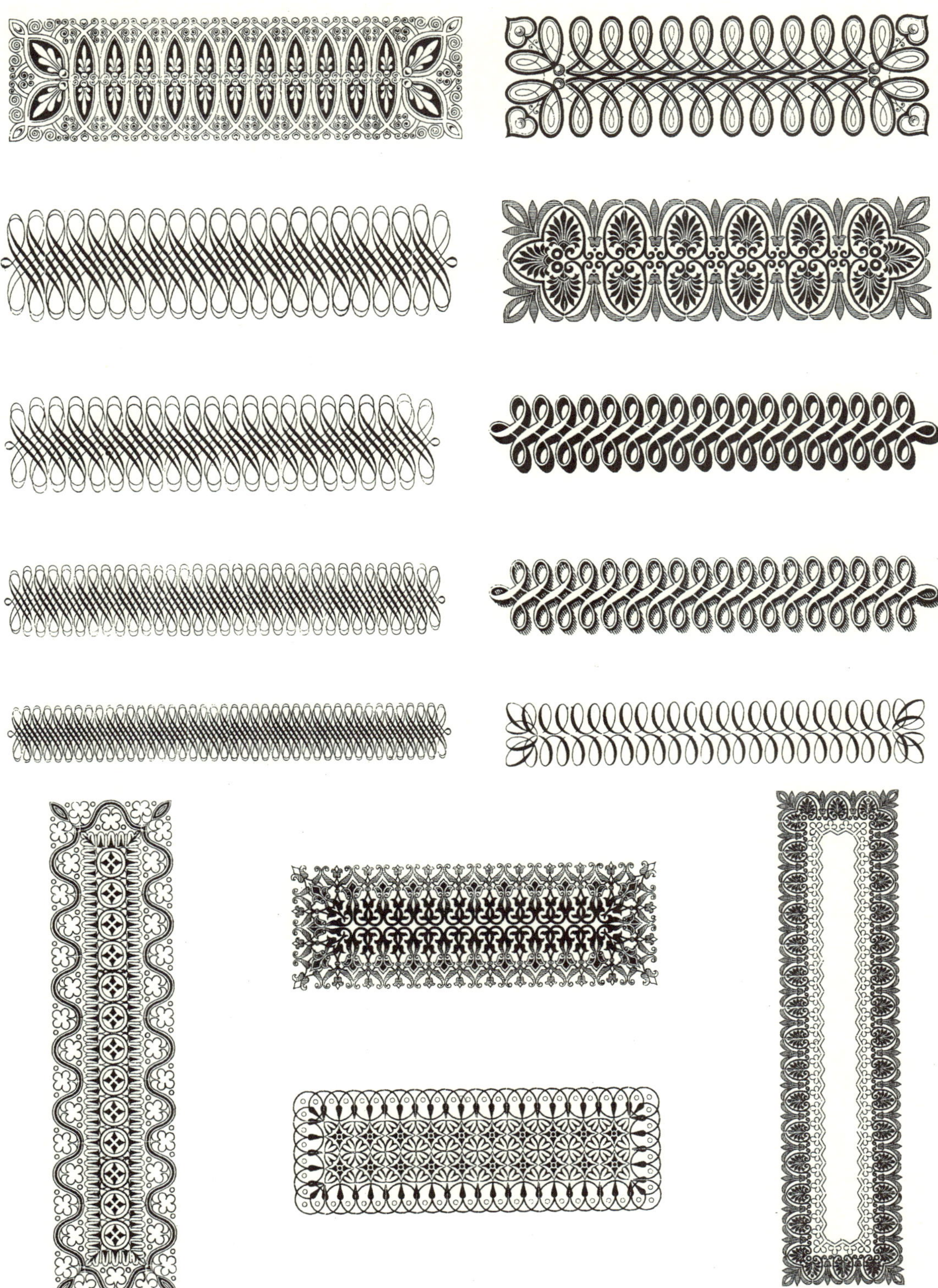

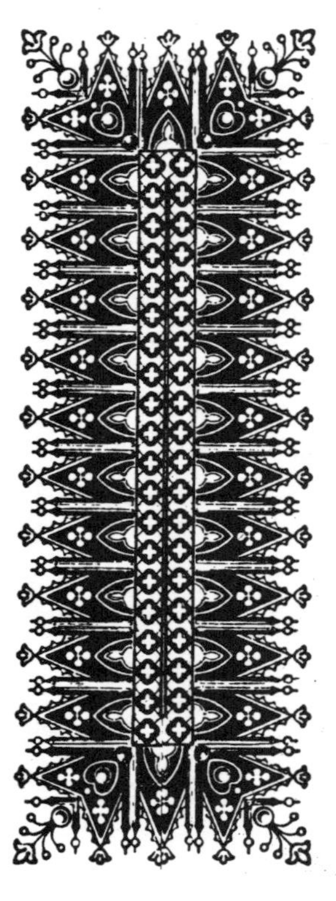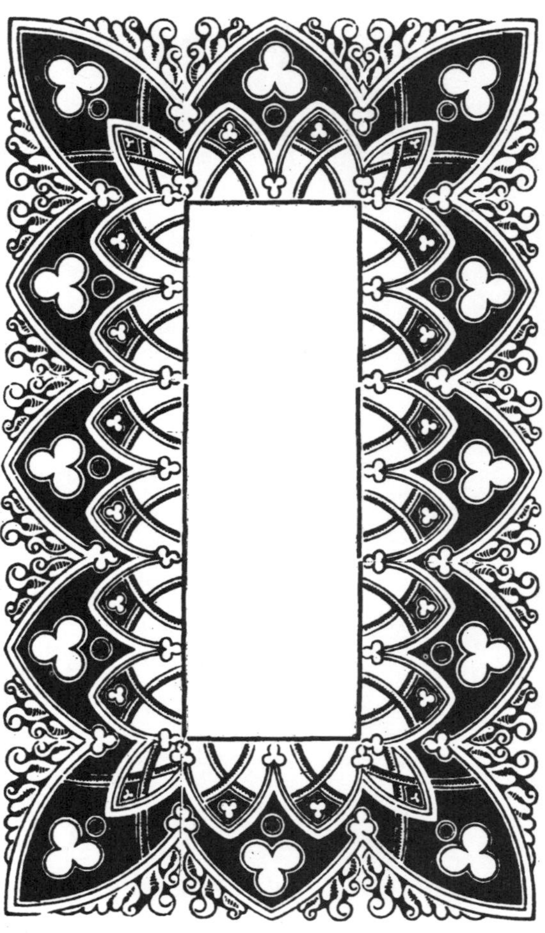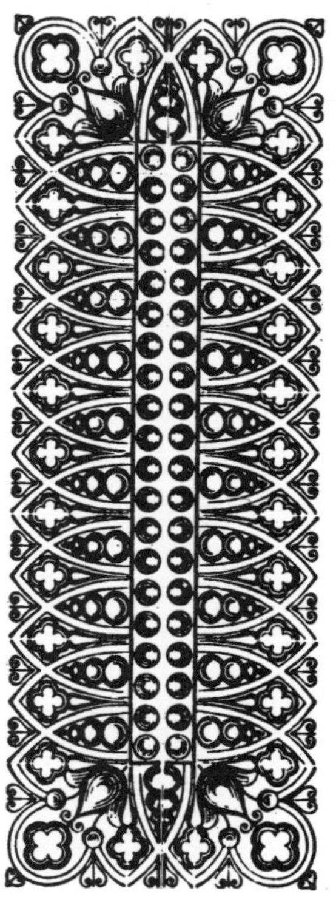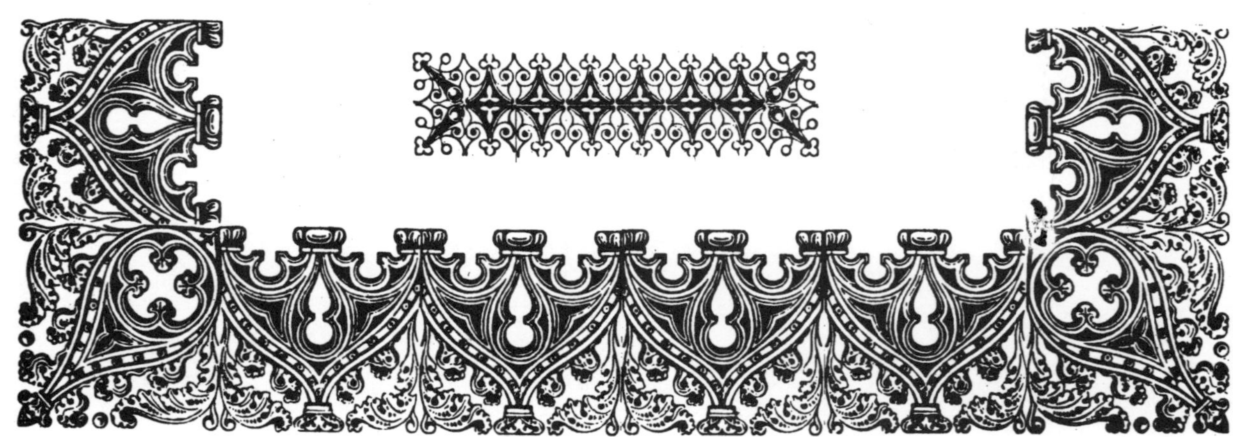

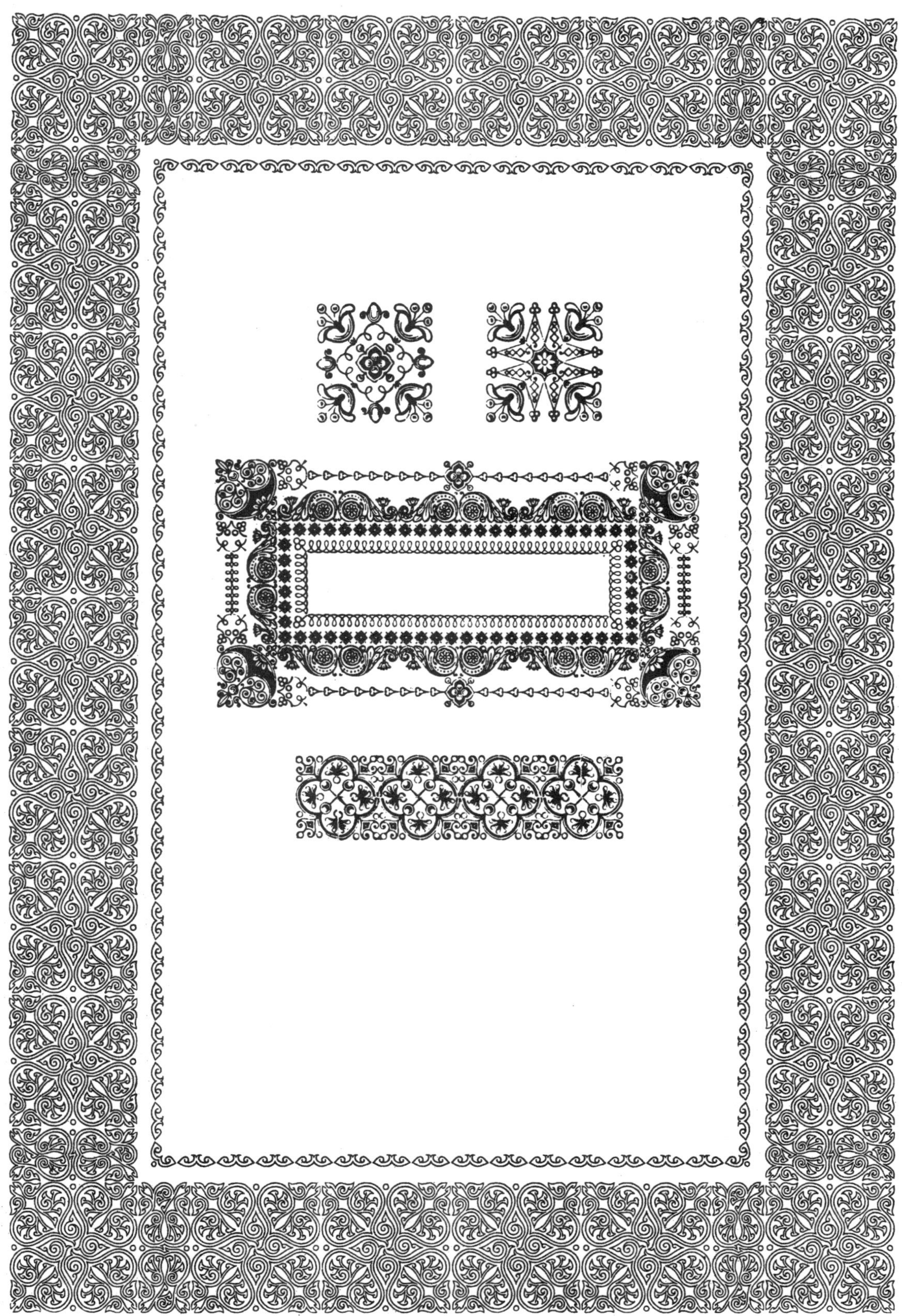

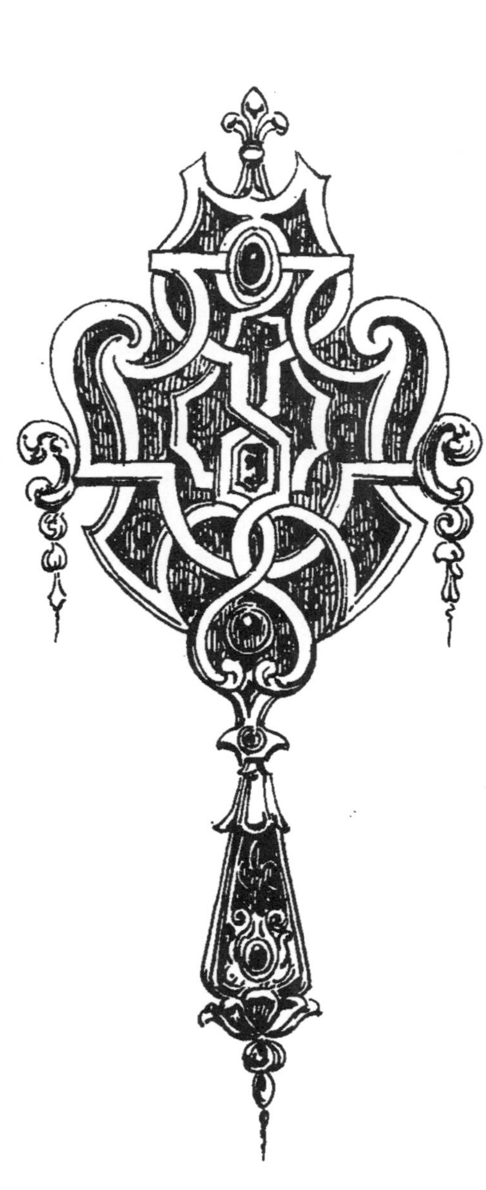

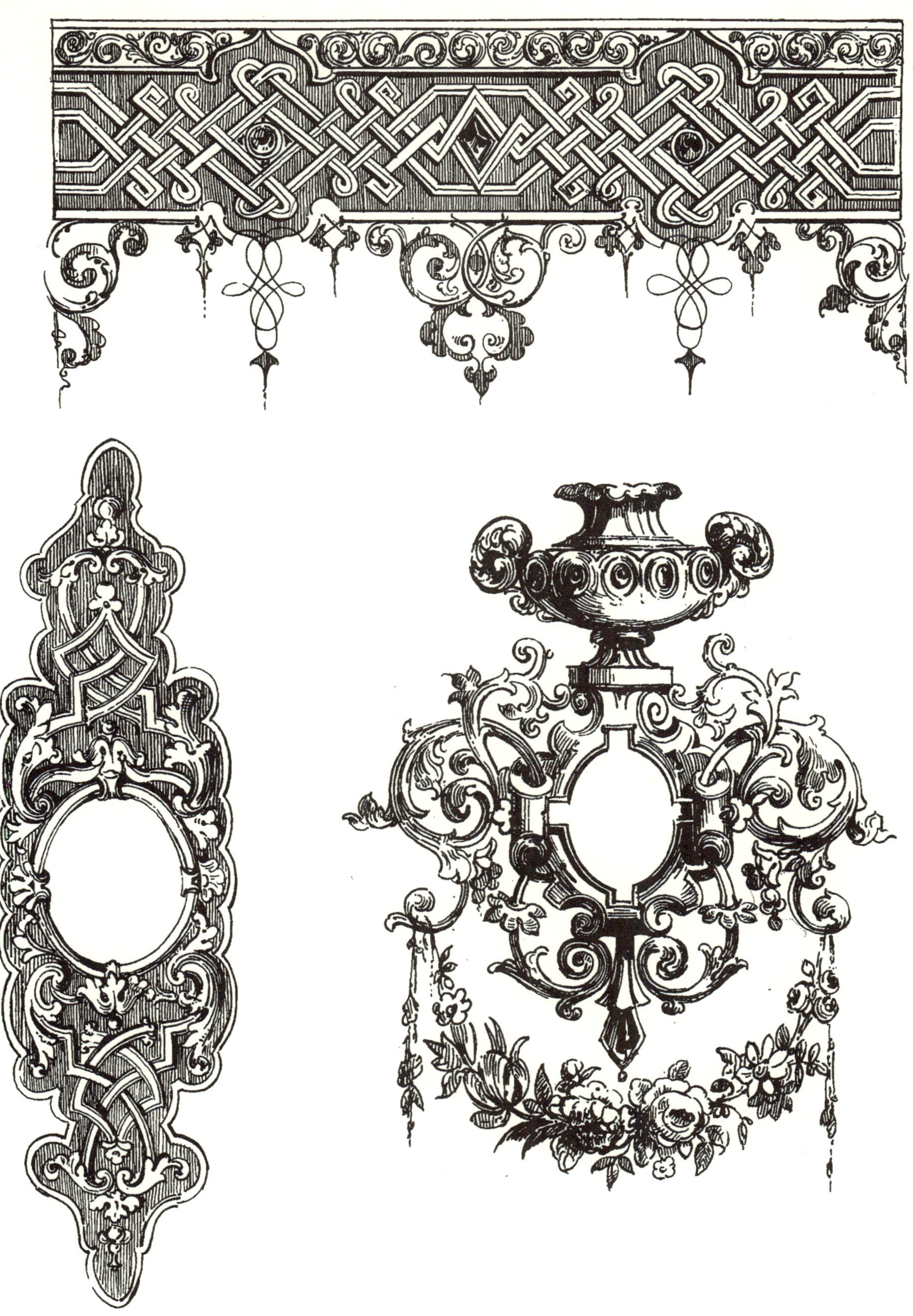

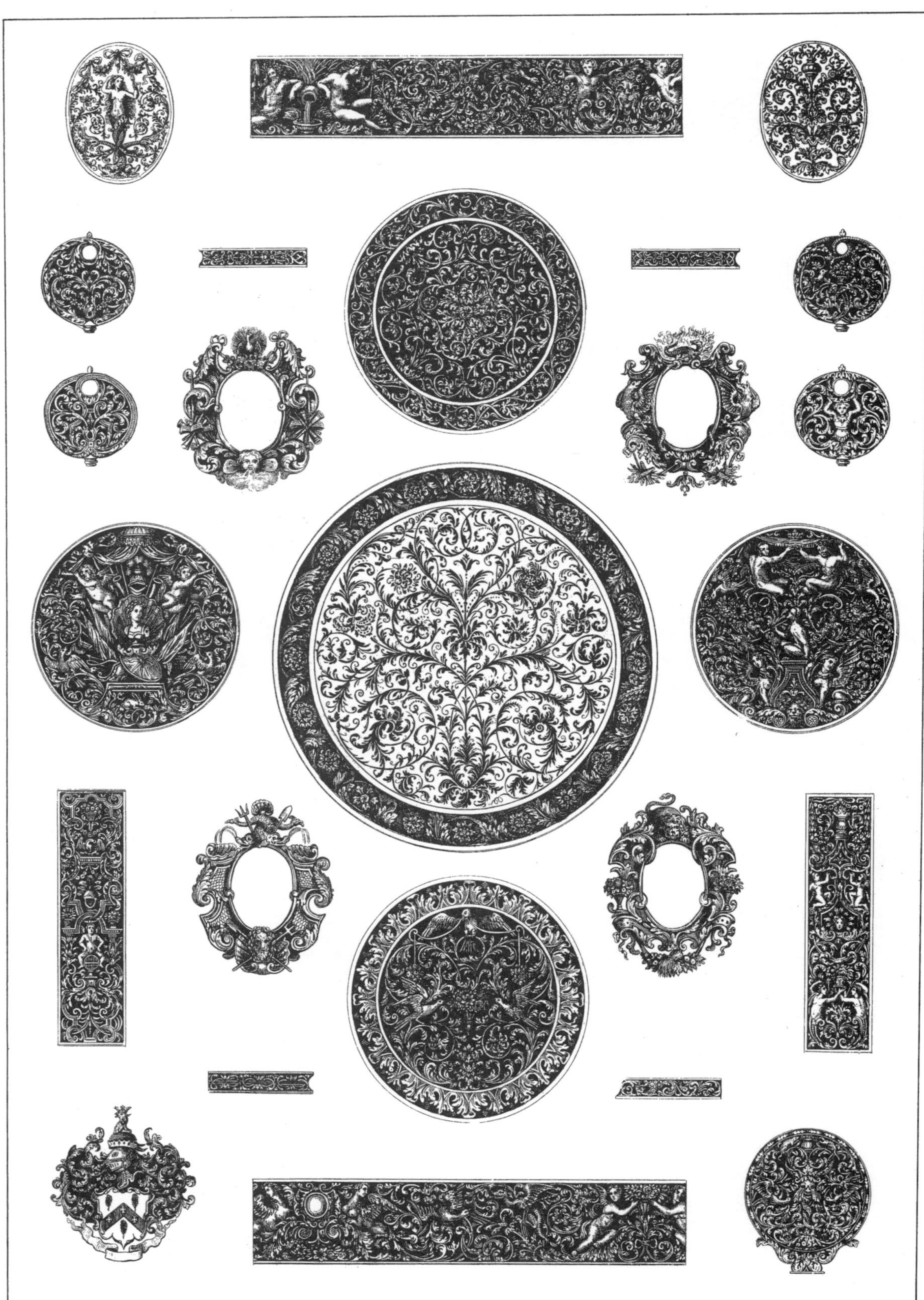

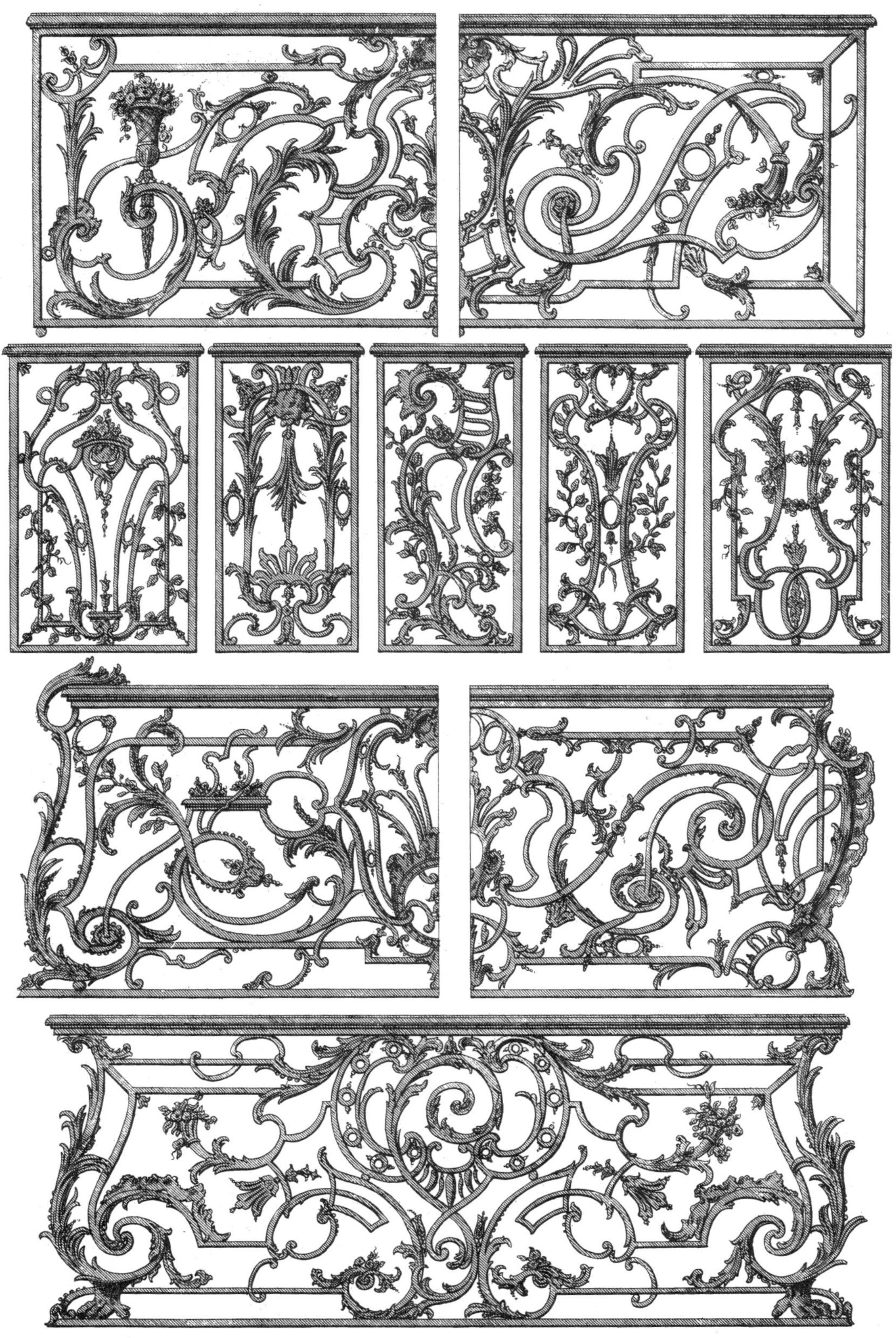

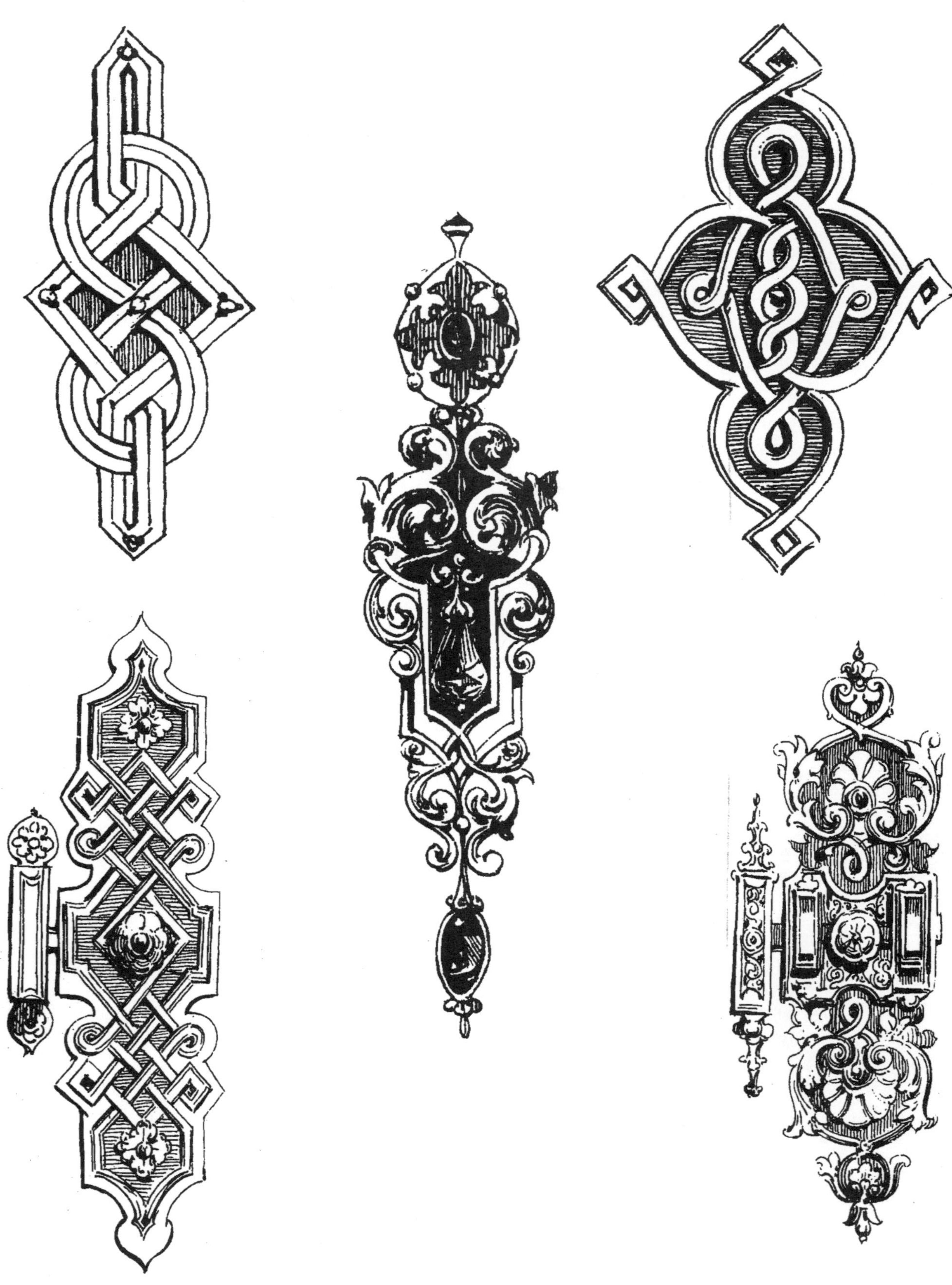

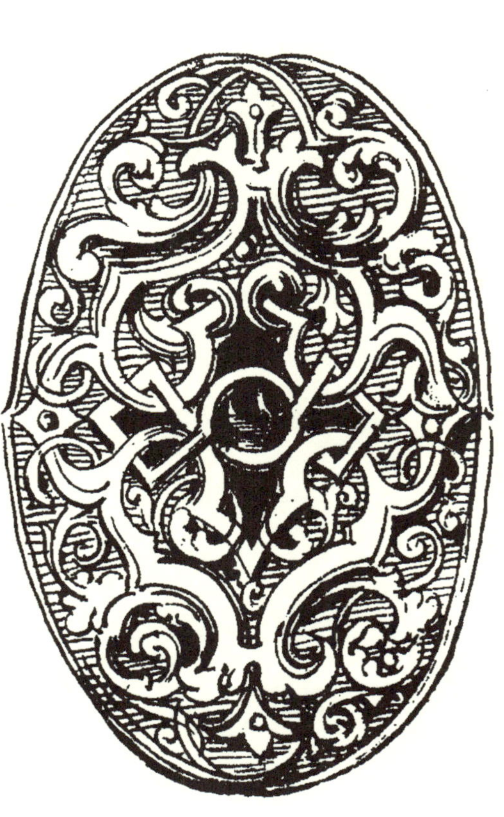

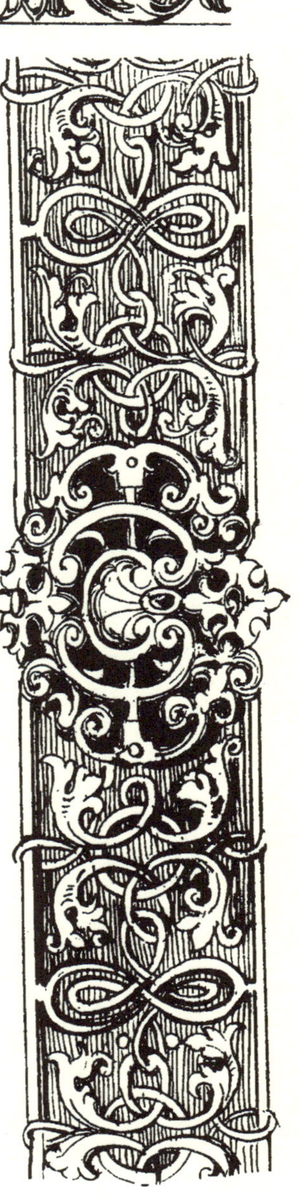

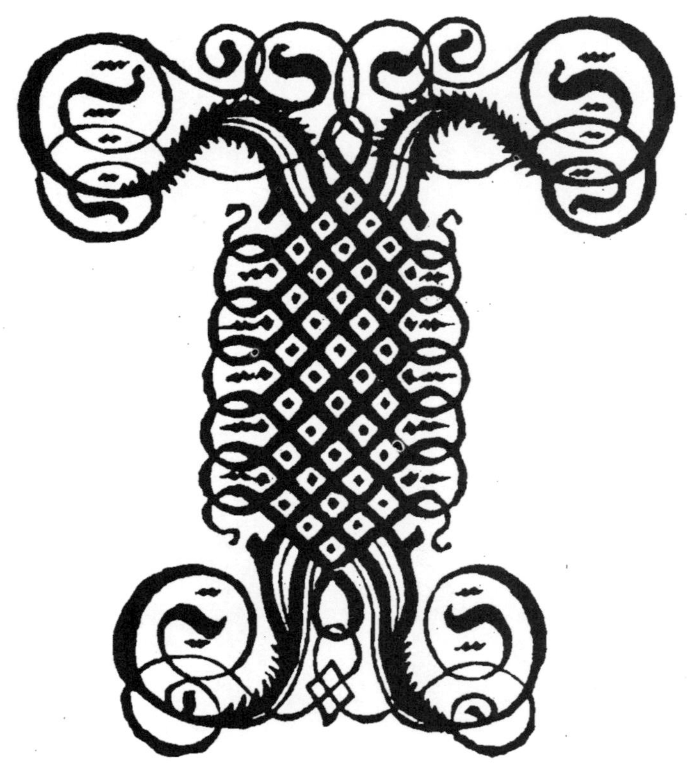

• Calligraphy •
• La calligraphie •
• Kalligraphie •
• La caligrafía •

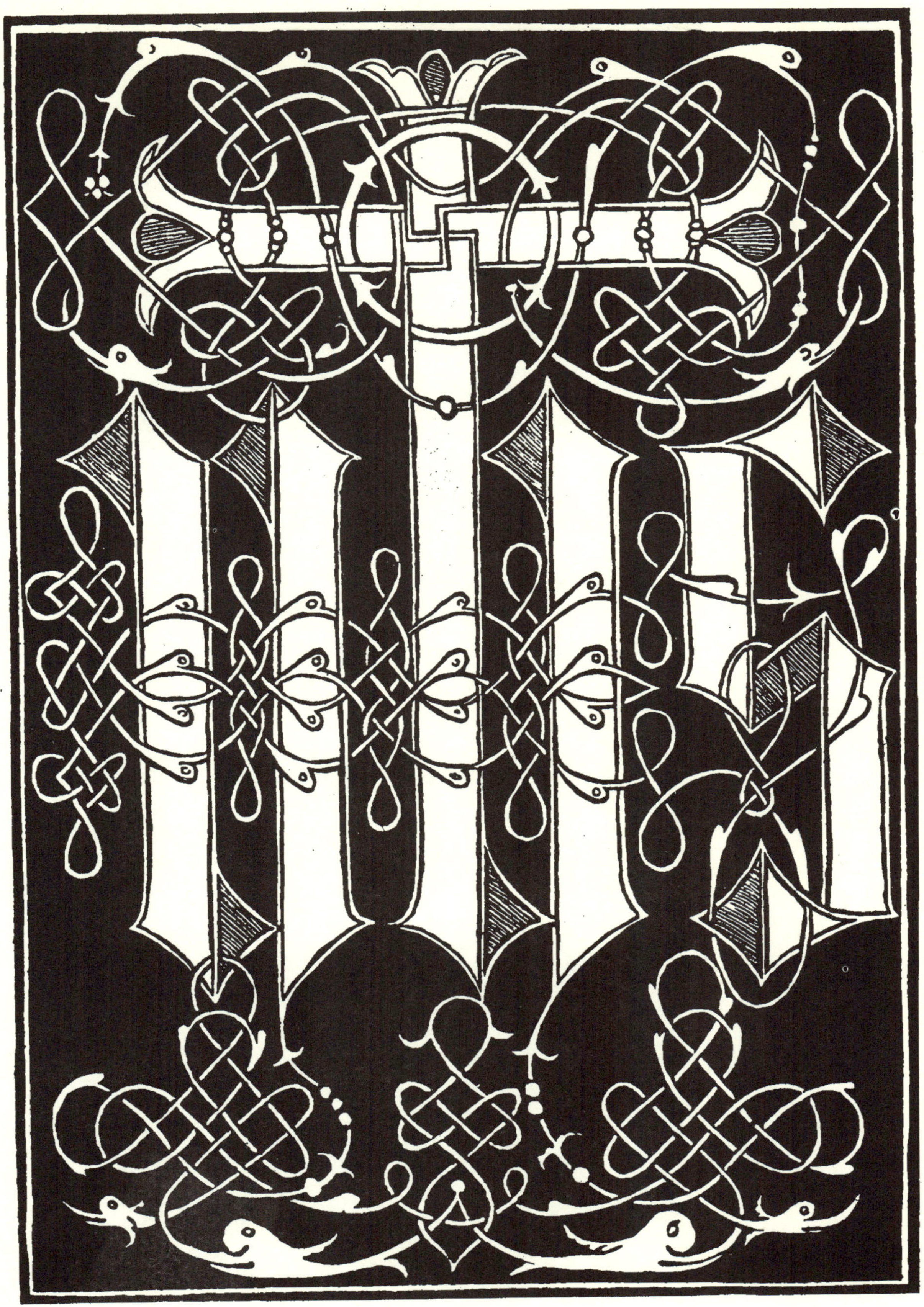

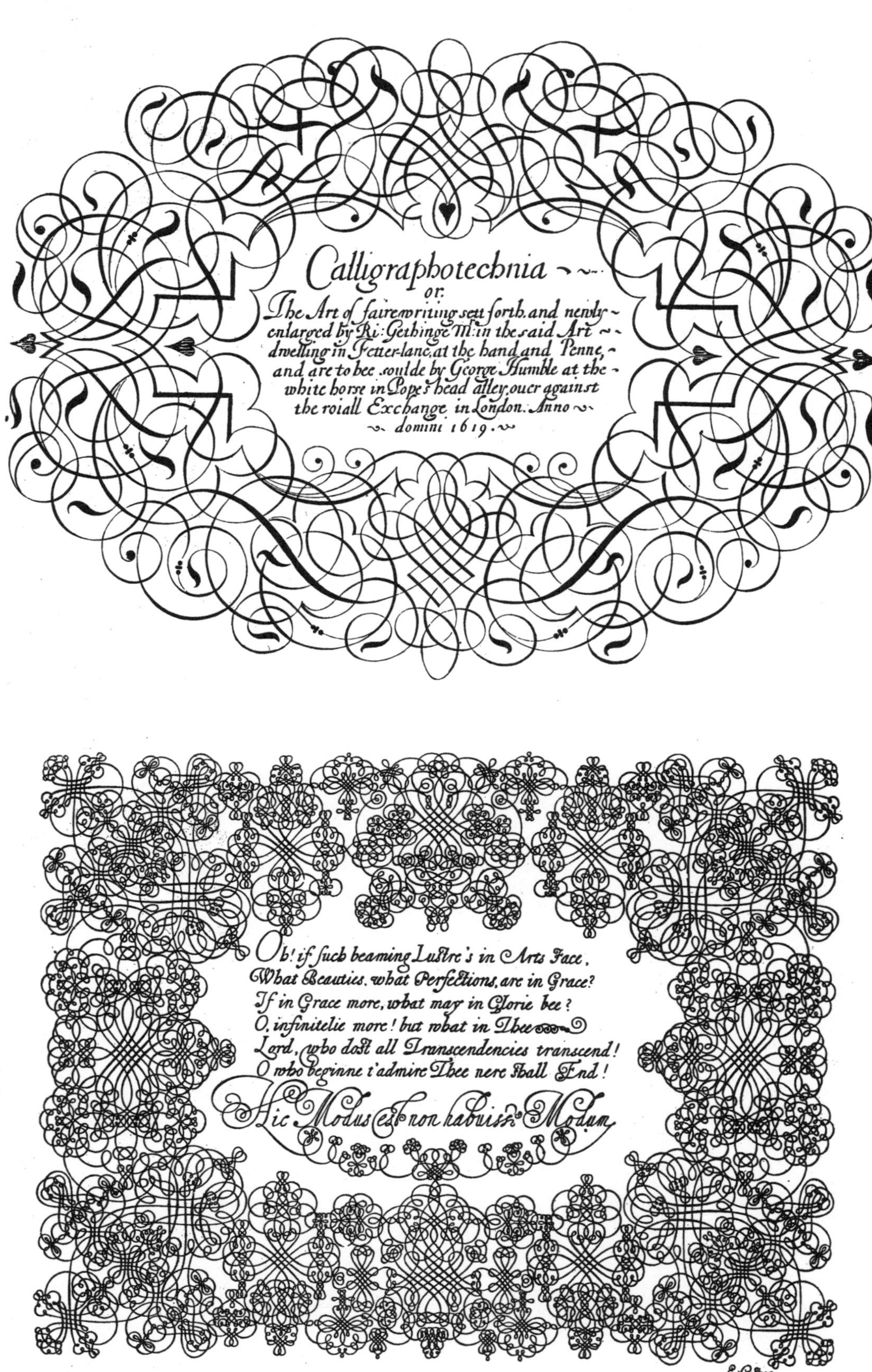
Calligraphotechnia
or.
The Art of faire writing sett forth. and newly
enlarged by Ri: Gethinge M: in the said Art
dwelling in Fetter-lane, at the hand and Penne,
and are to bee soulde by George Humble at the
white horse in Popes head alley, ouer against
the roiall Exchange in London. Anno
domini 1619.

Oh! if such beaming Lustre's in Arts Face,
What Beauties, what Perfections, are in Grace?
If in Grace more, what may in Glorie bee?
O, infinitelie more! but what in Thee
Lord, who dost all Transcendencies transcend!
O who beginne t'admire Thee nere shall End!
Hic Modus est non habuisse Modum

E. Gether.

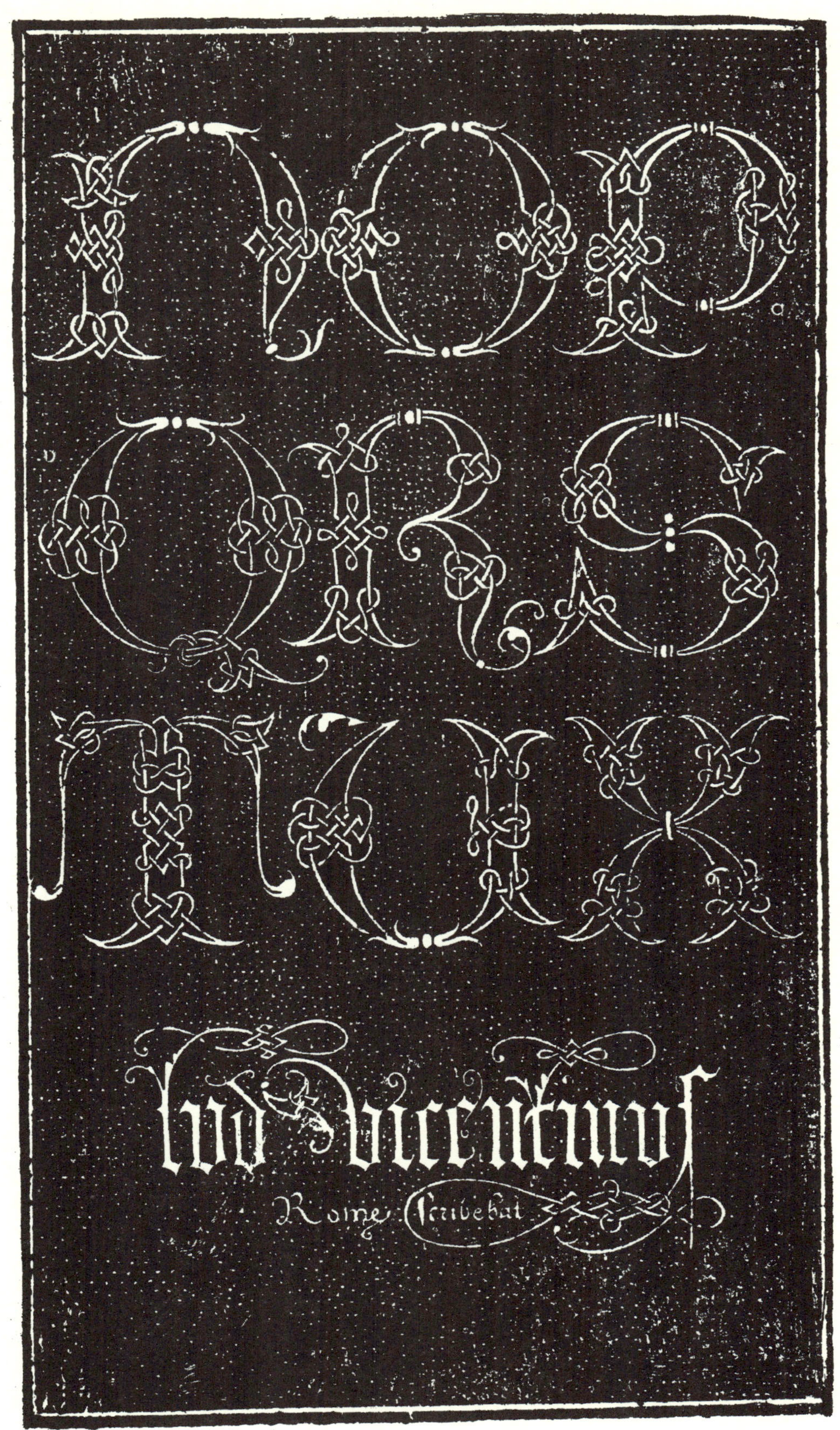
lud Vicentinus
Rome Scribebat

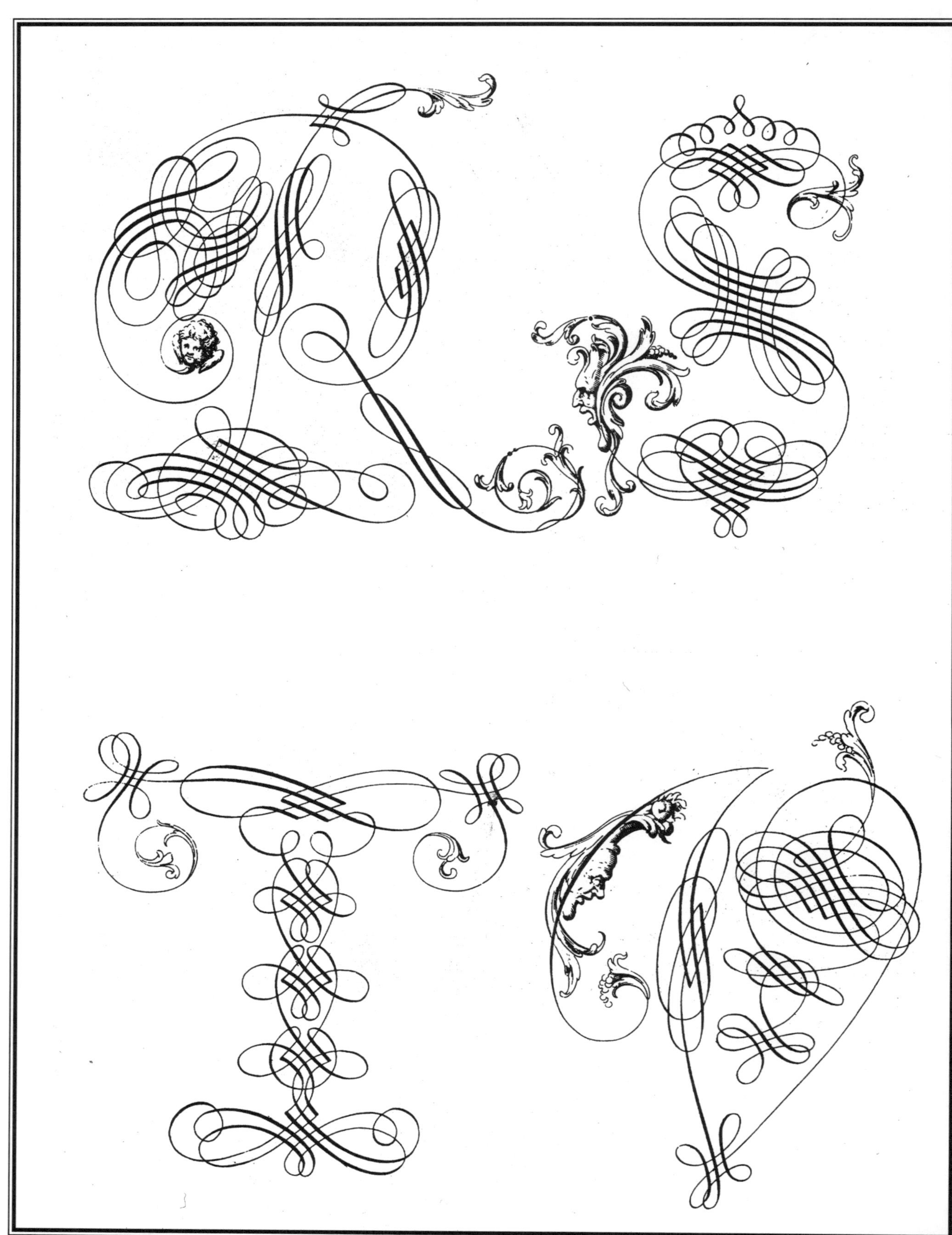

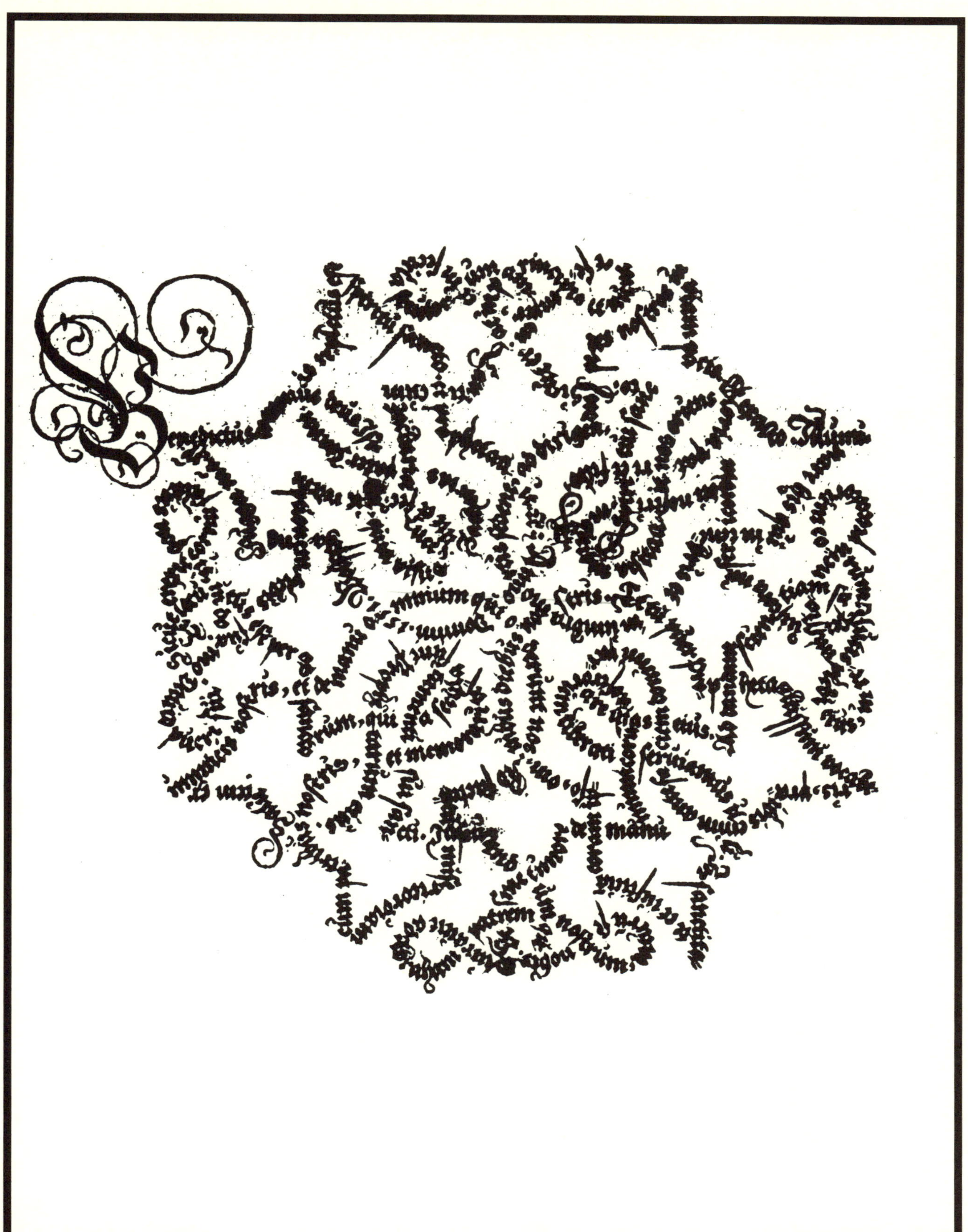

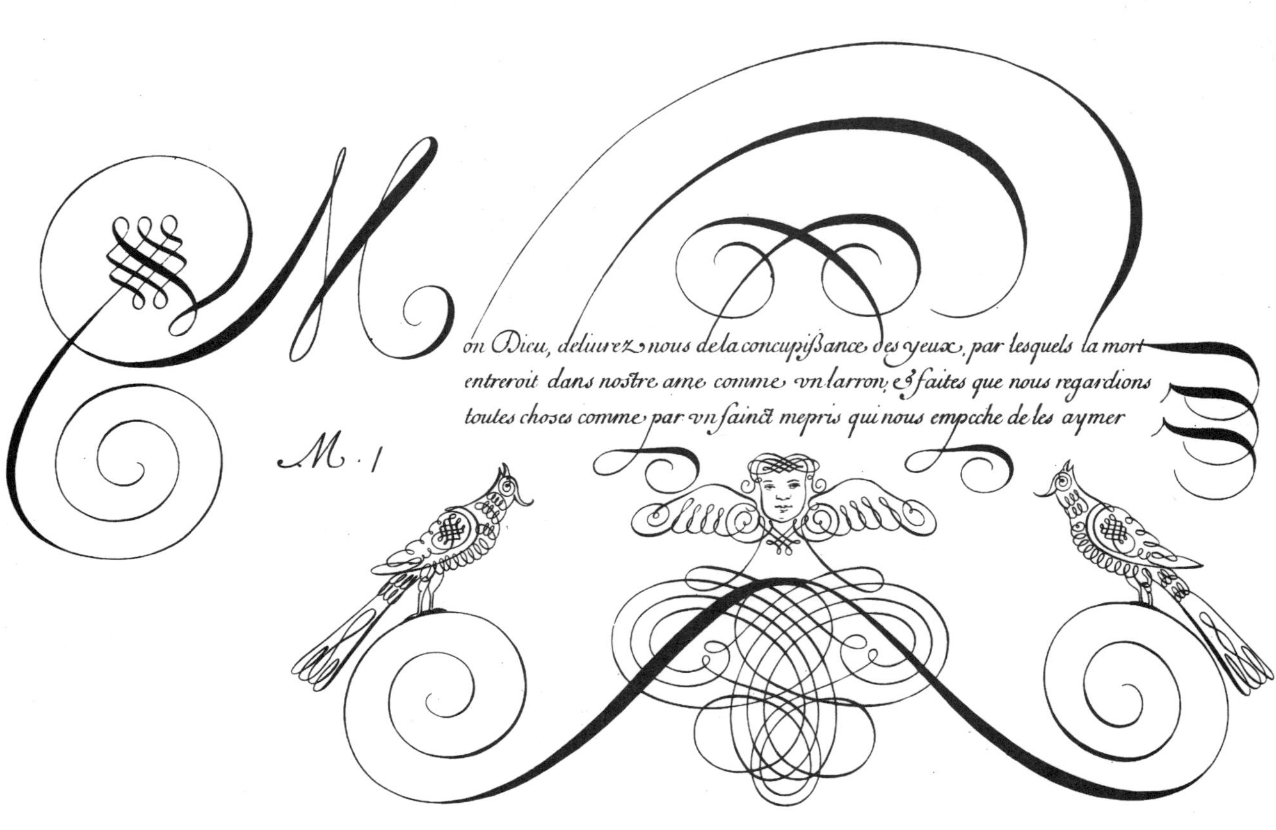

M
M · 1
on Dieu, deliurez nous de la concupißance des yeux, par lesquels la mort
entreroit dans nostre ame comme vn larron, & faites que nous regardions
toutes choses comme par vn sainct mepris qui nous empeche de les aymer

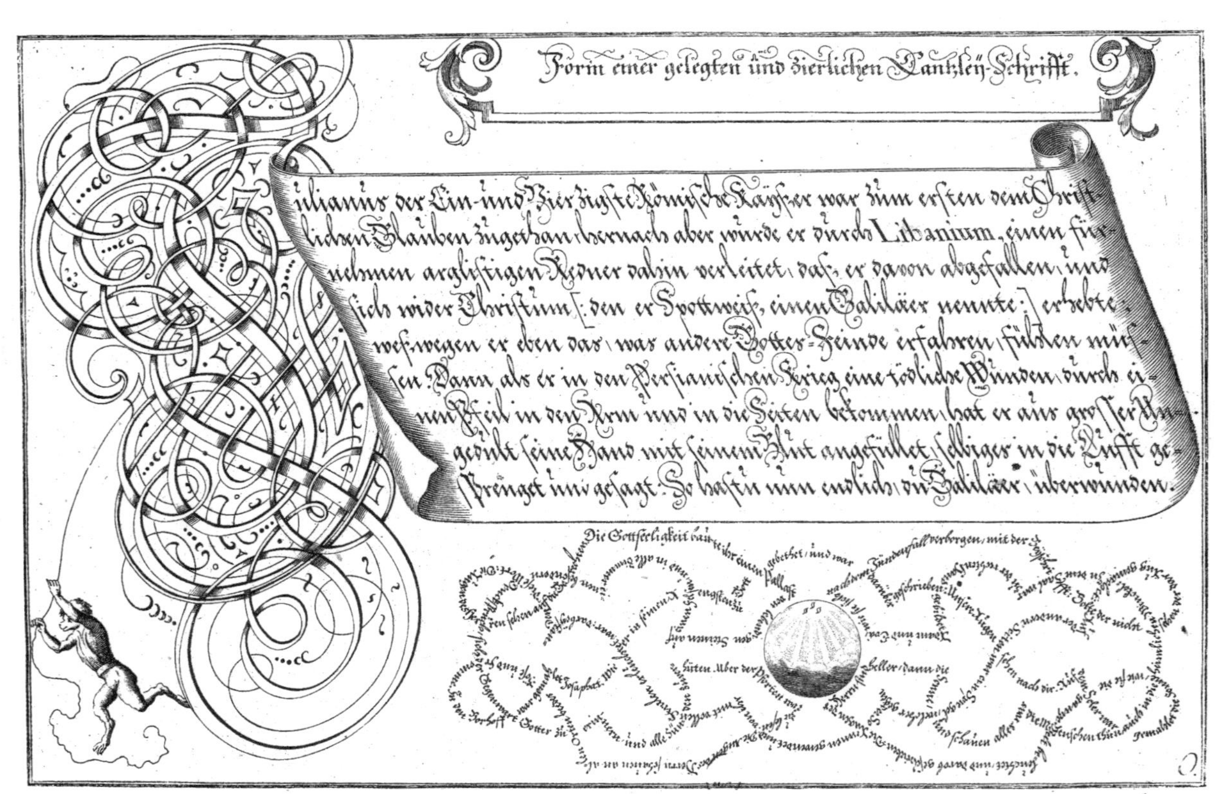

Form einer gelegten und zierlichen Cantzley-Schrifft.

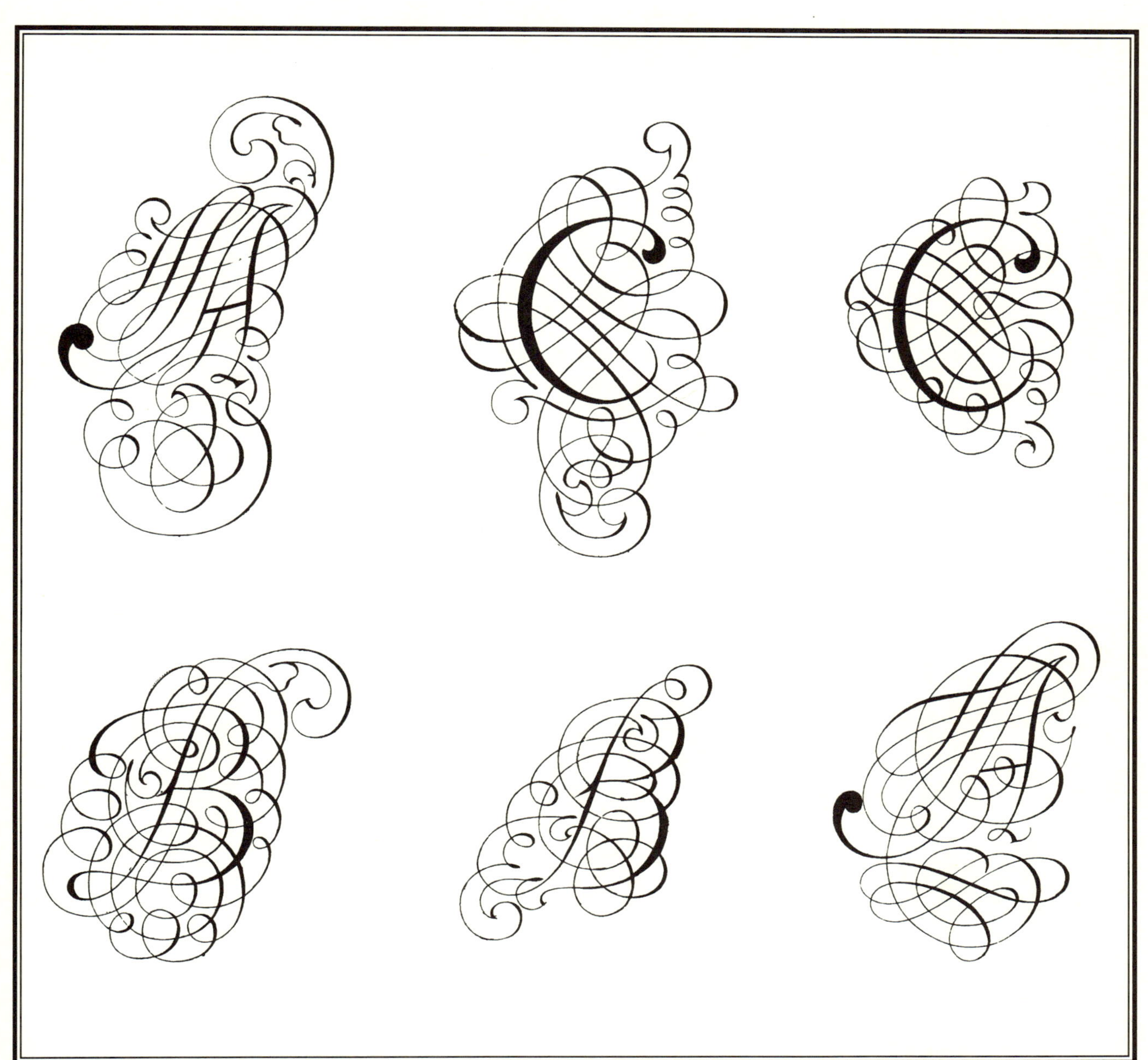

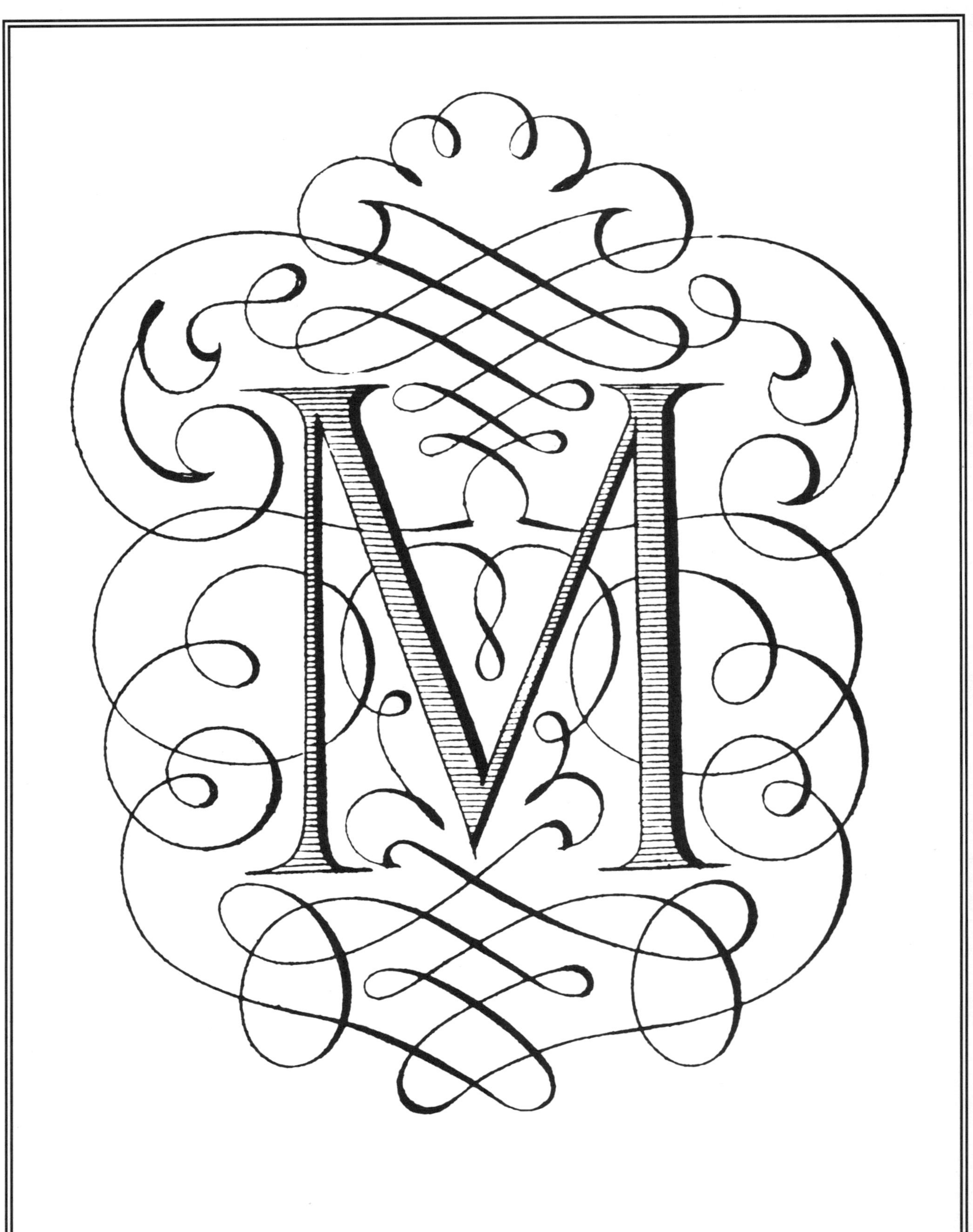

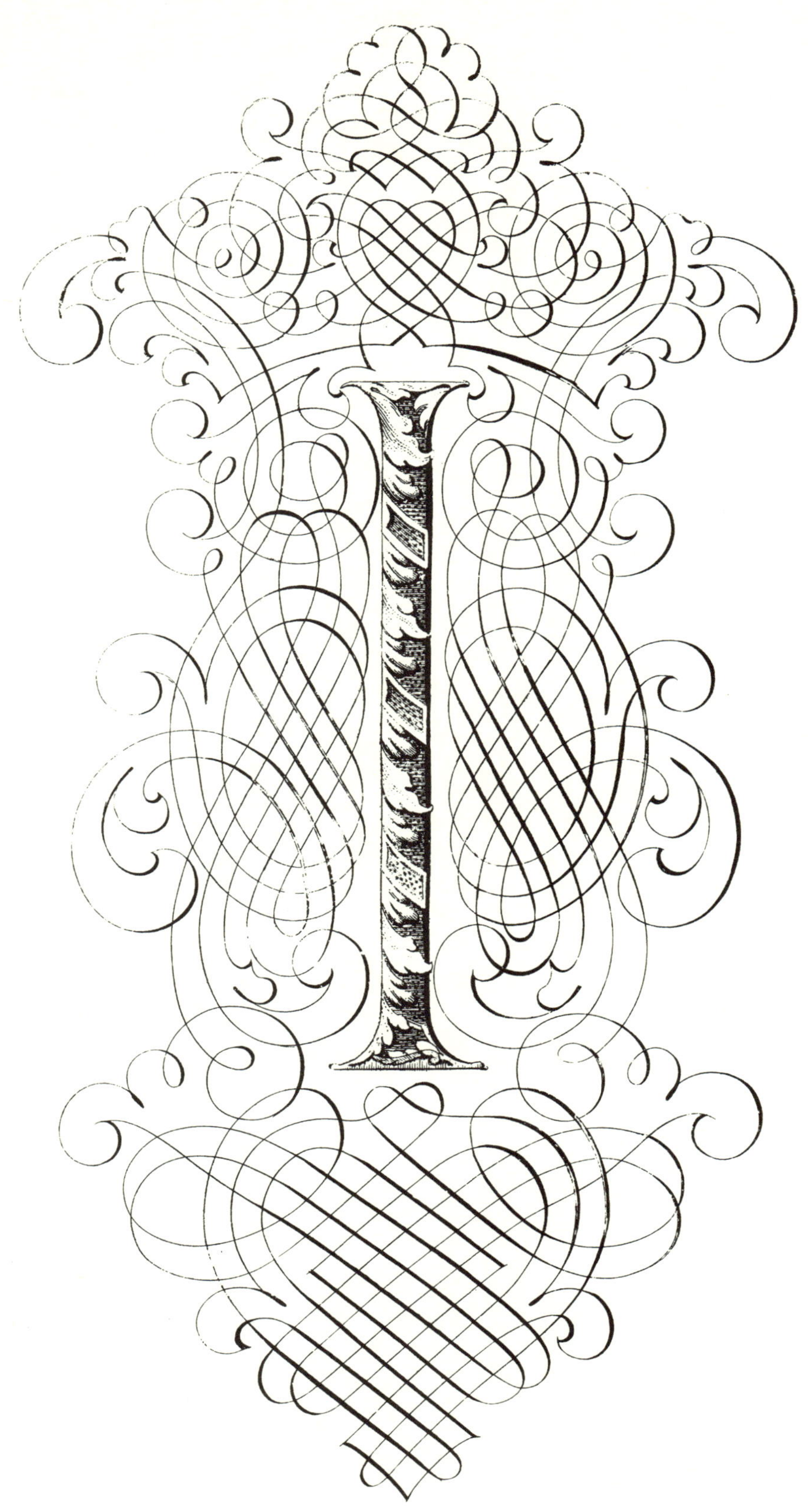

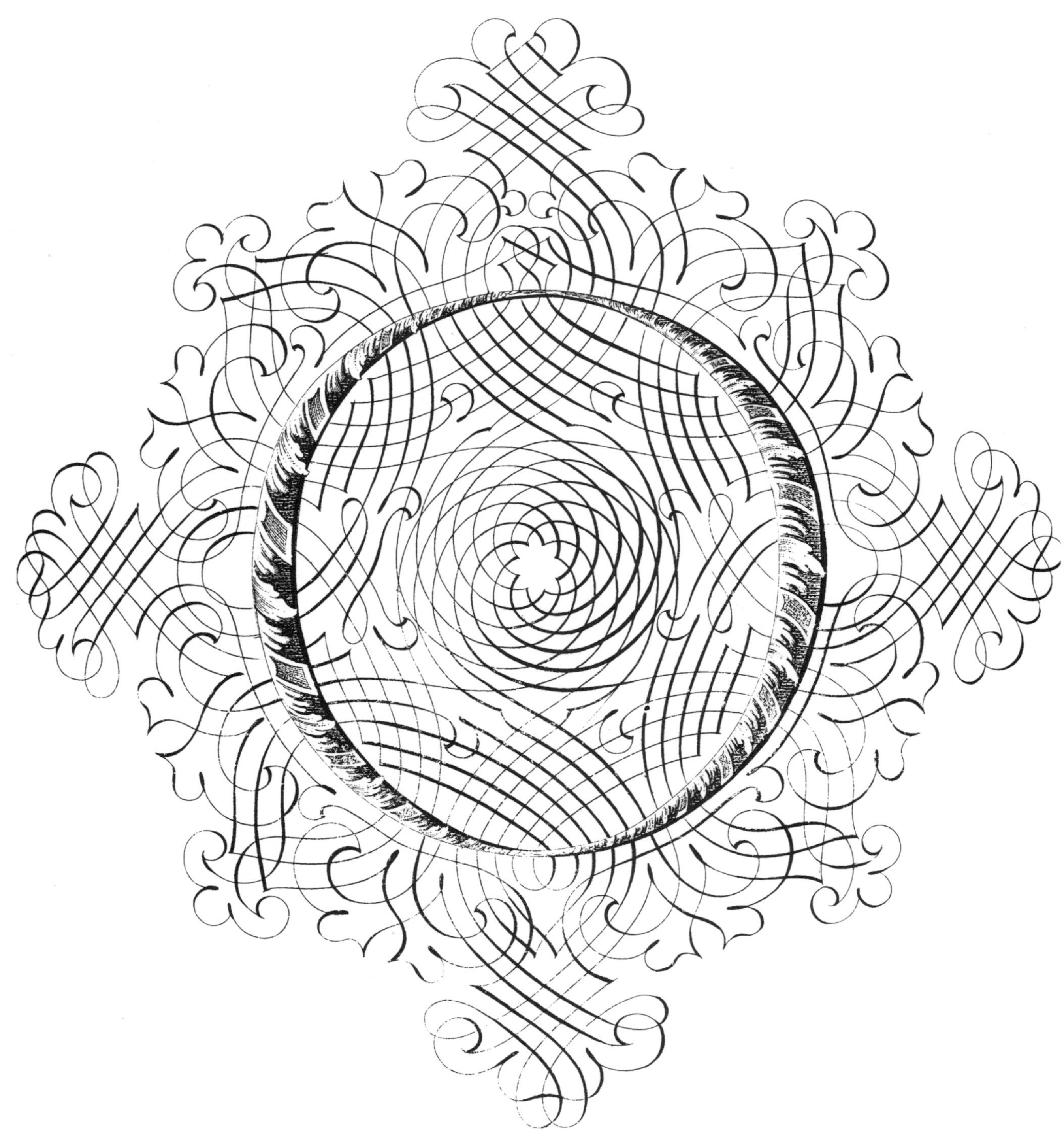

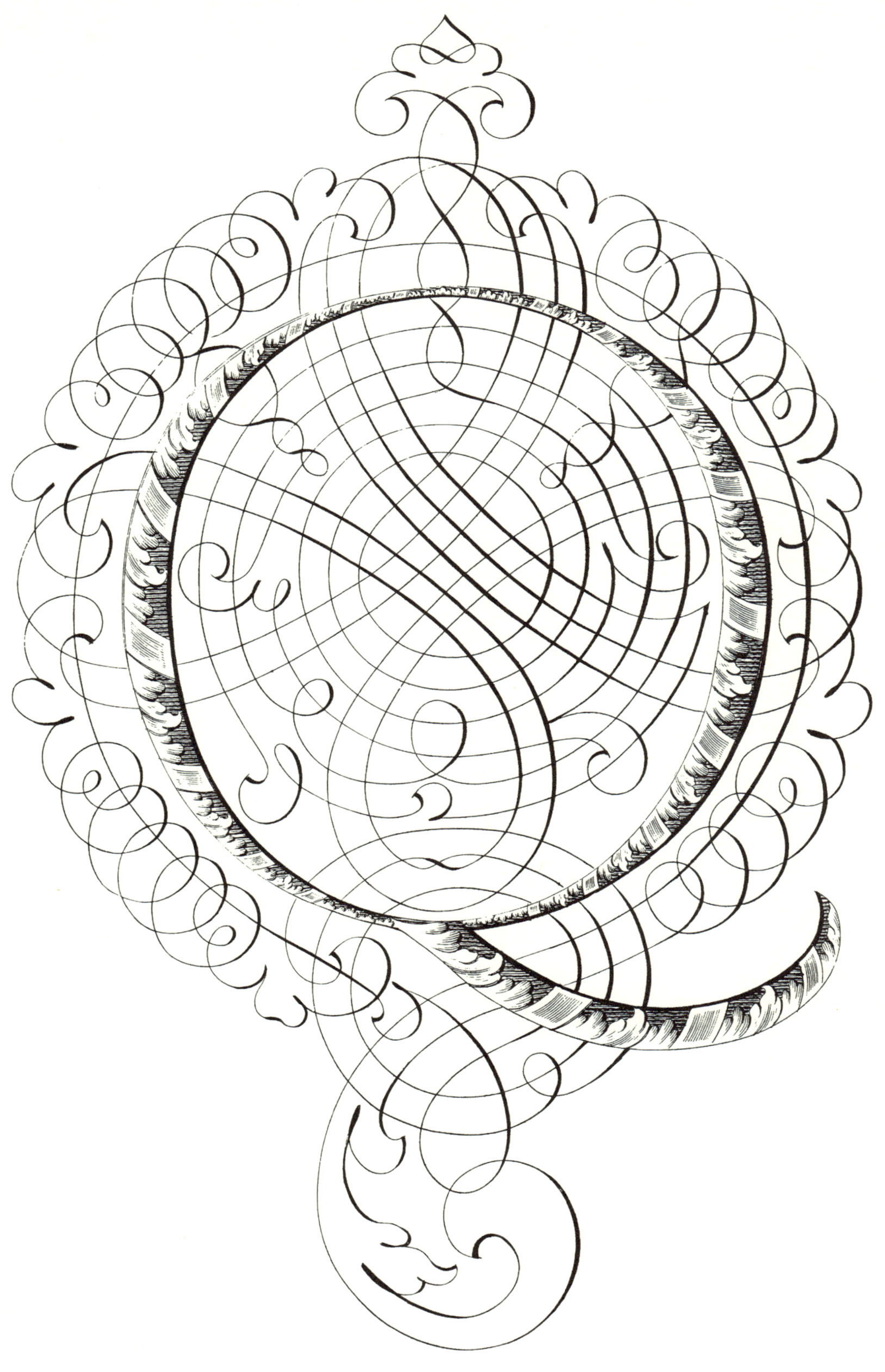

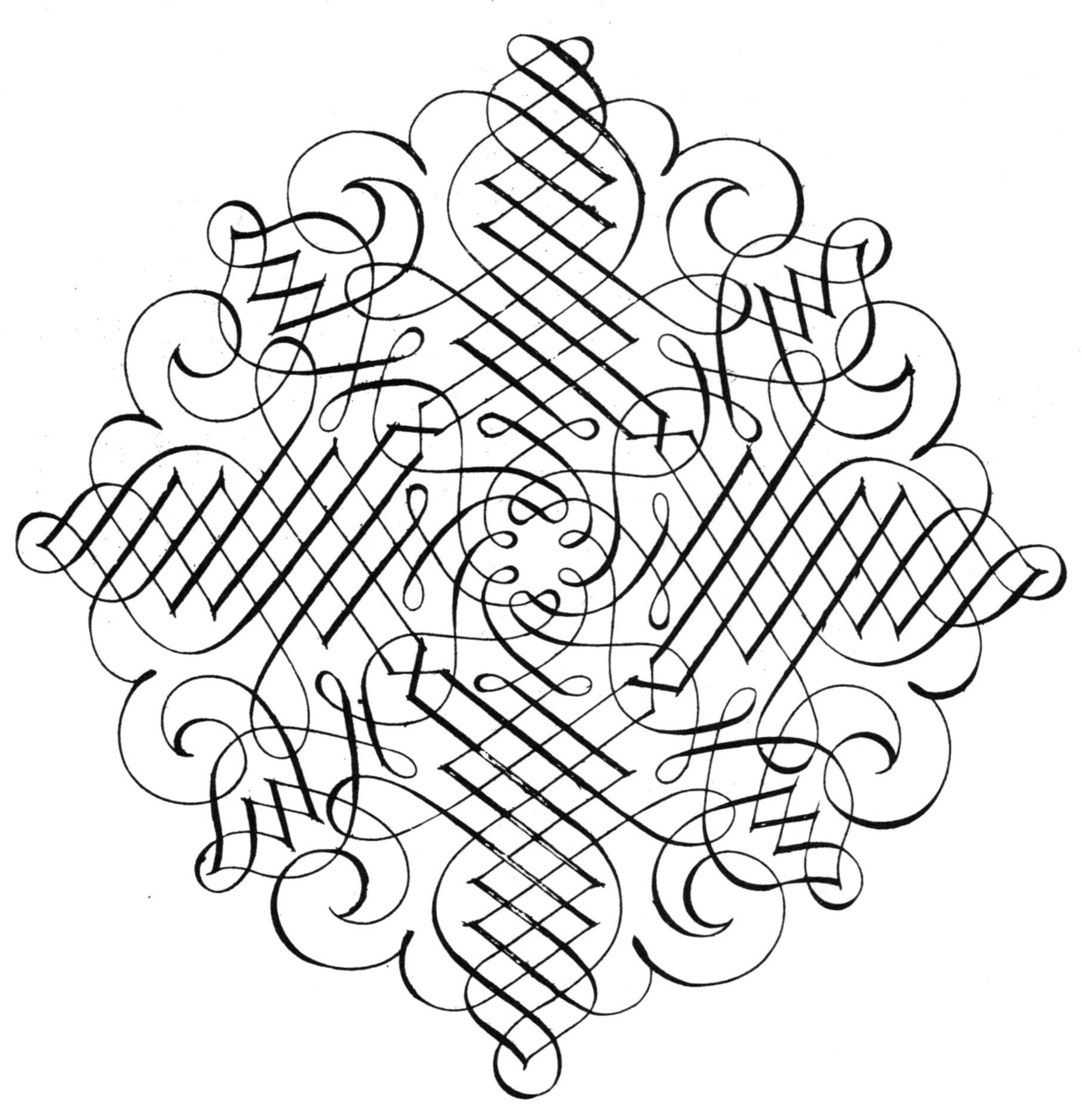

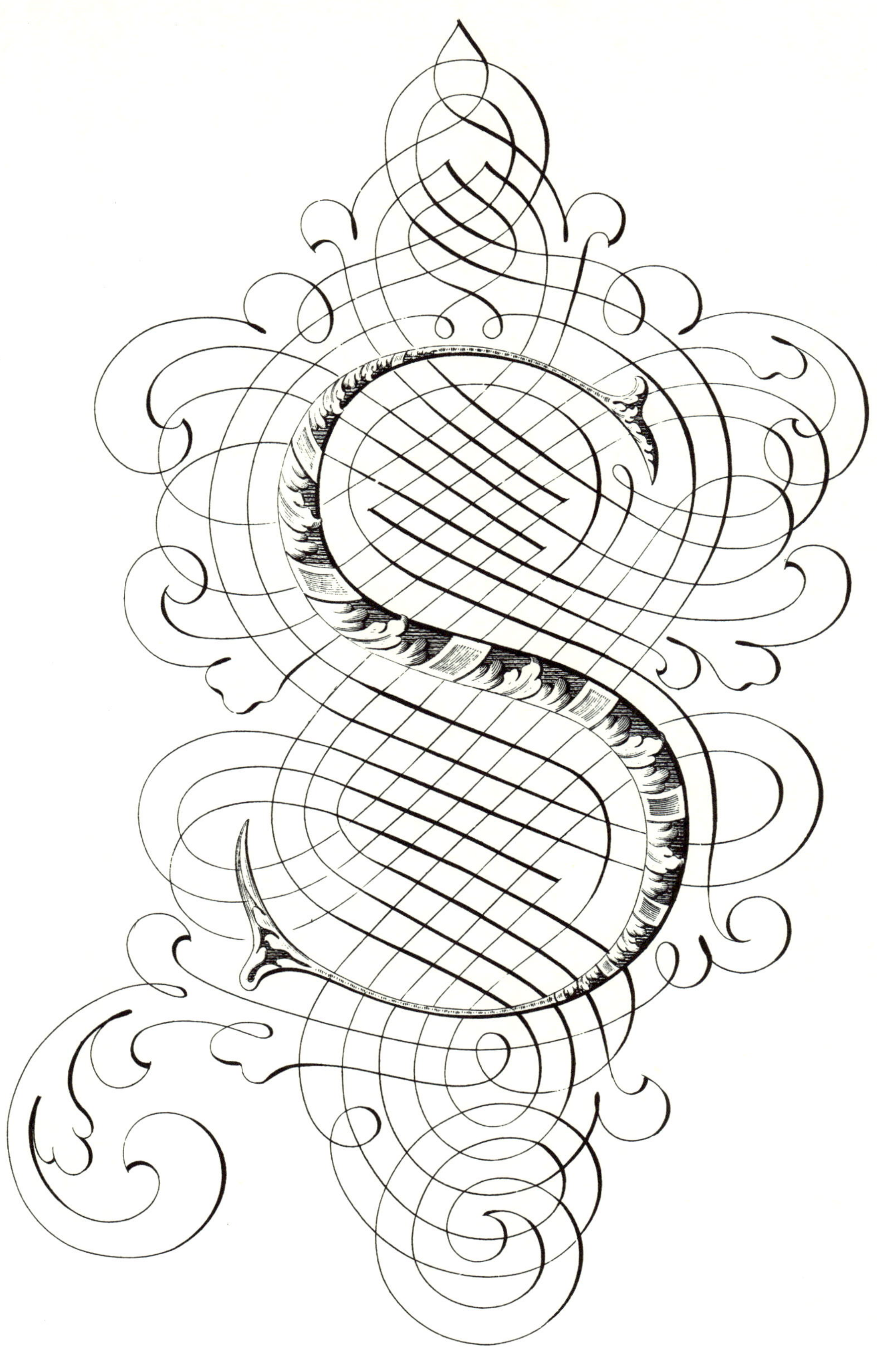

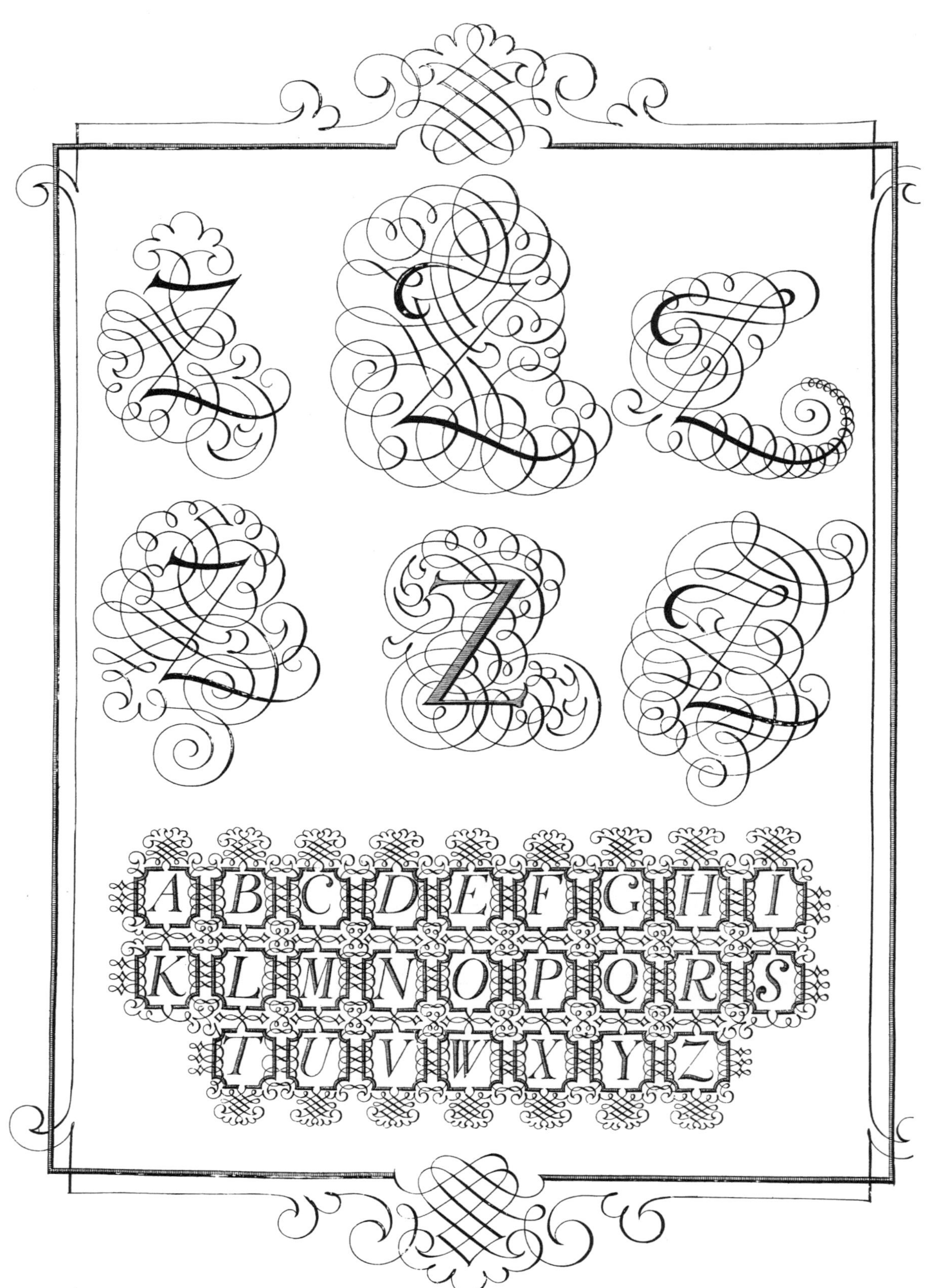

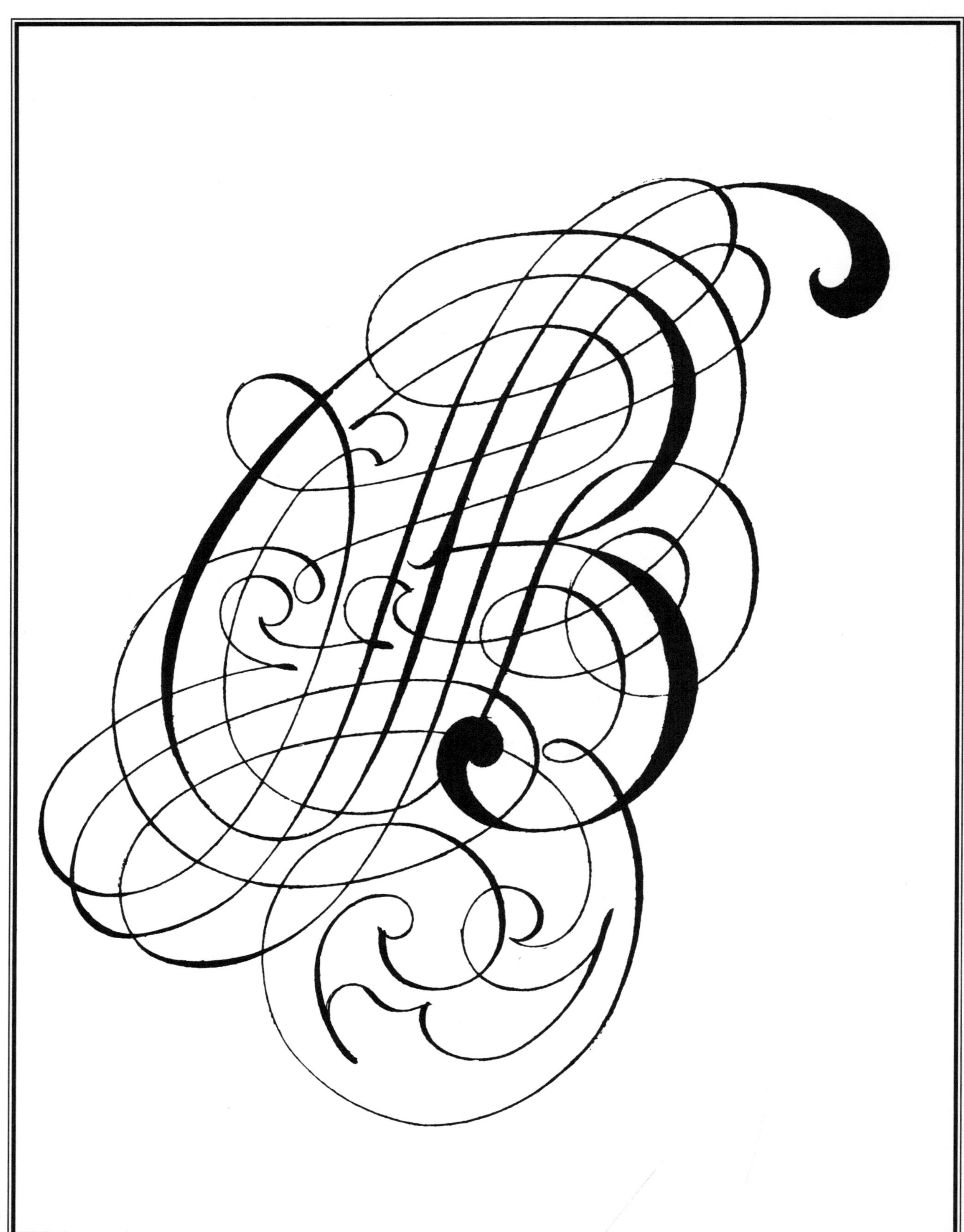

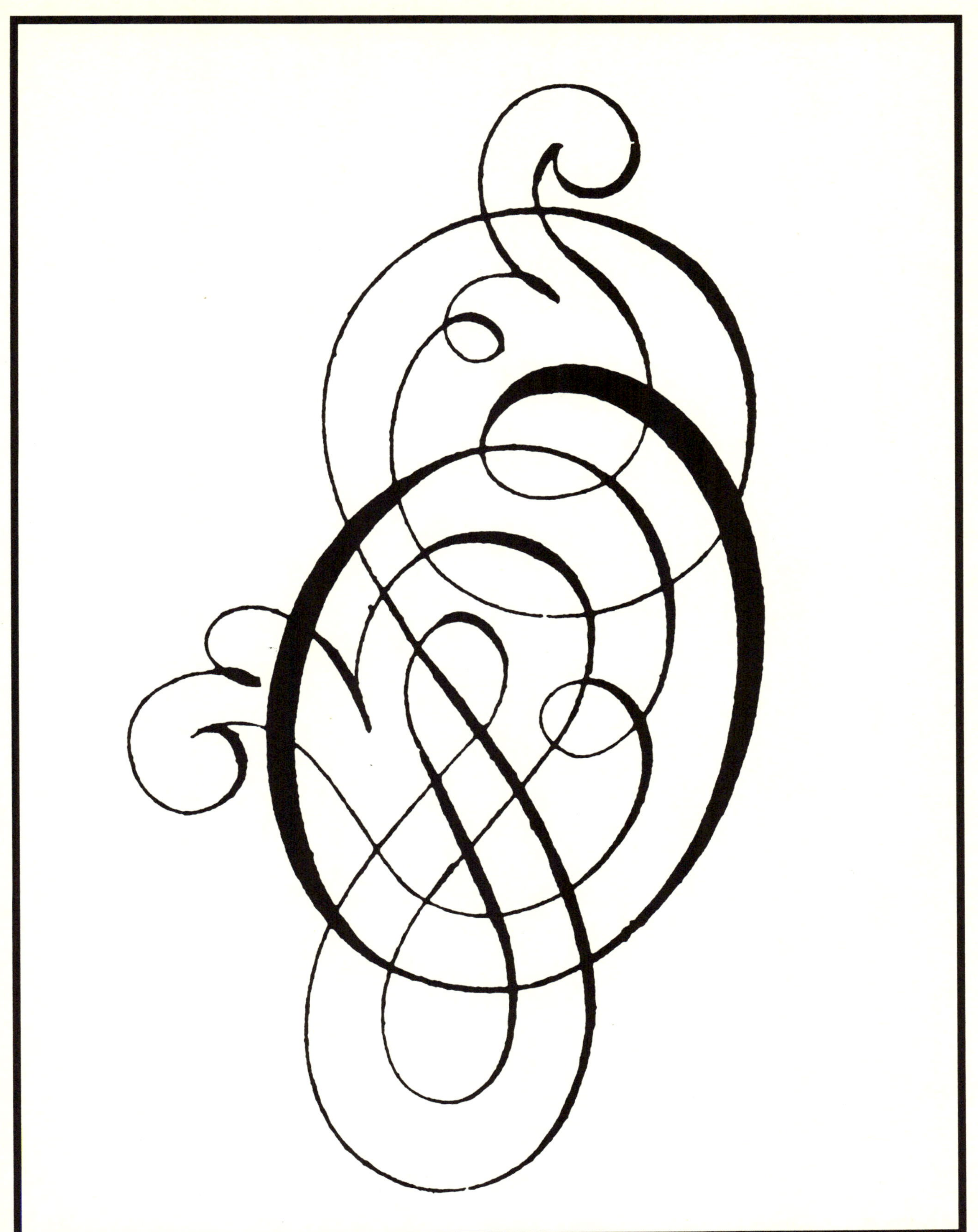

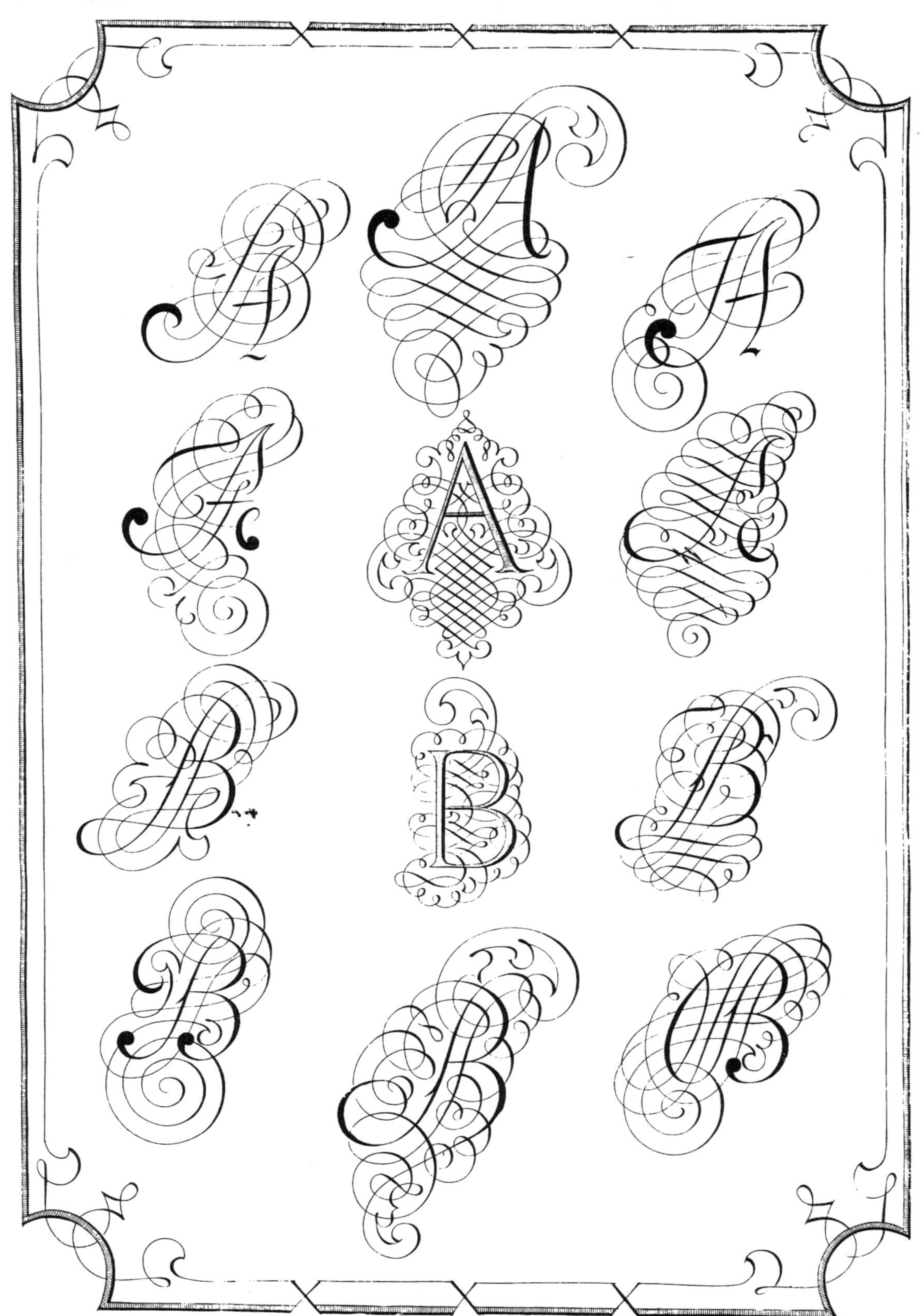

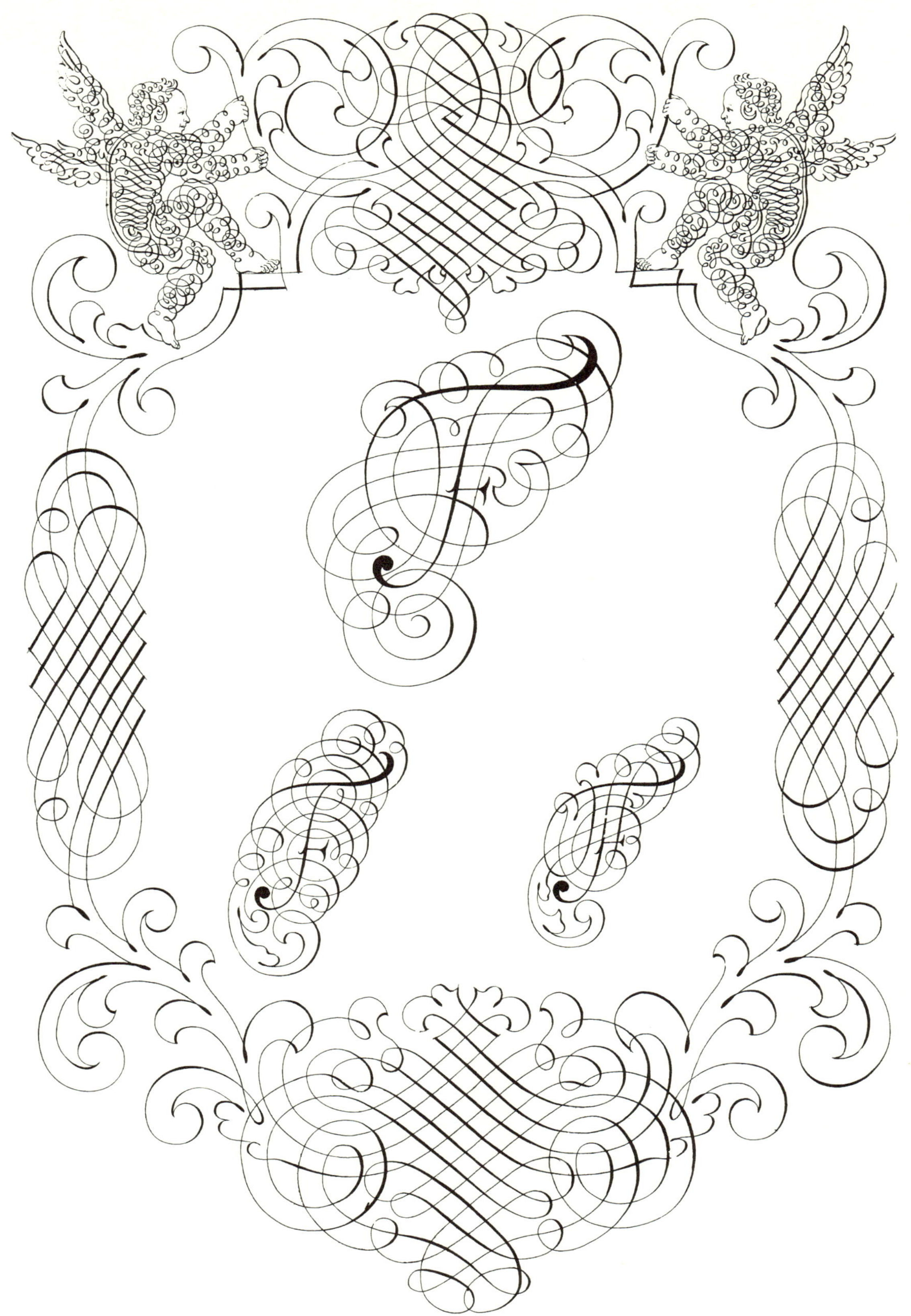

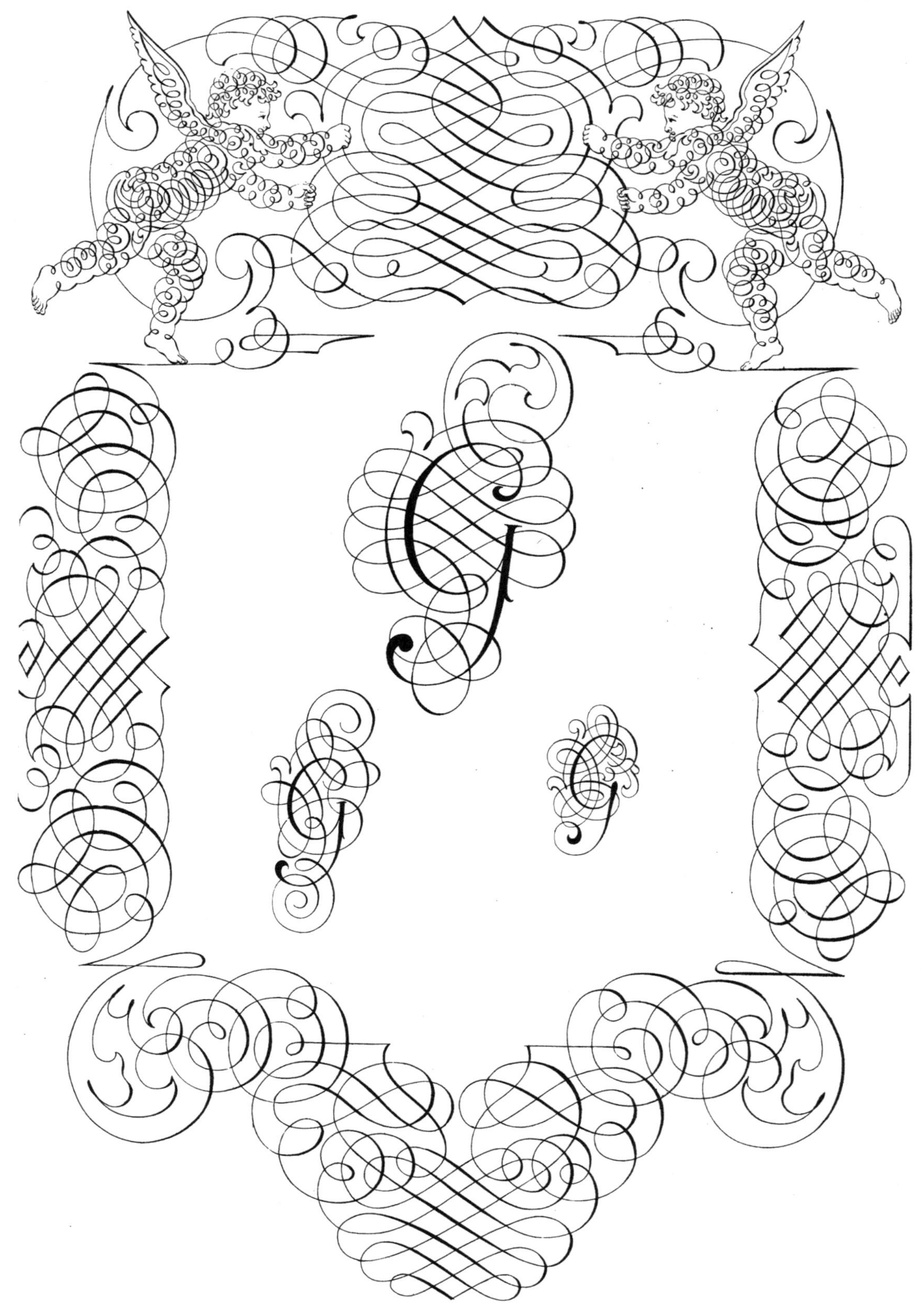

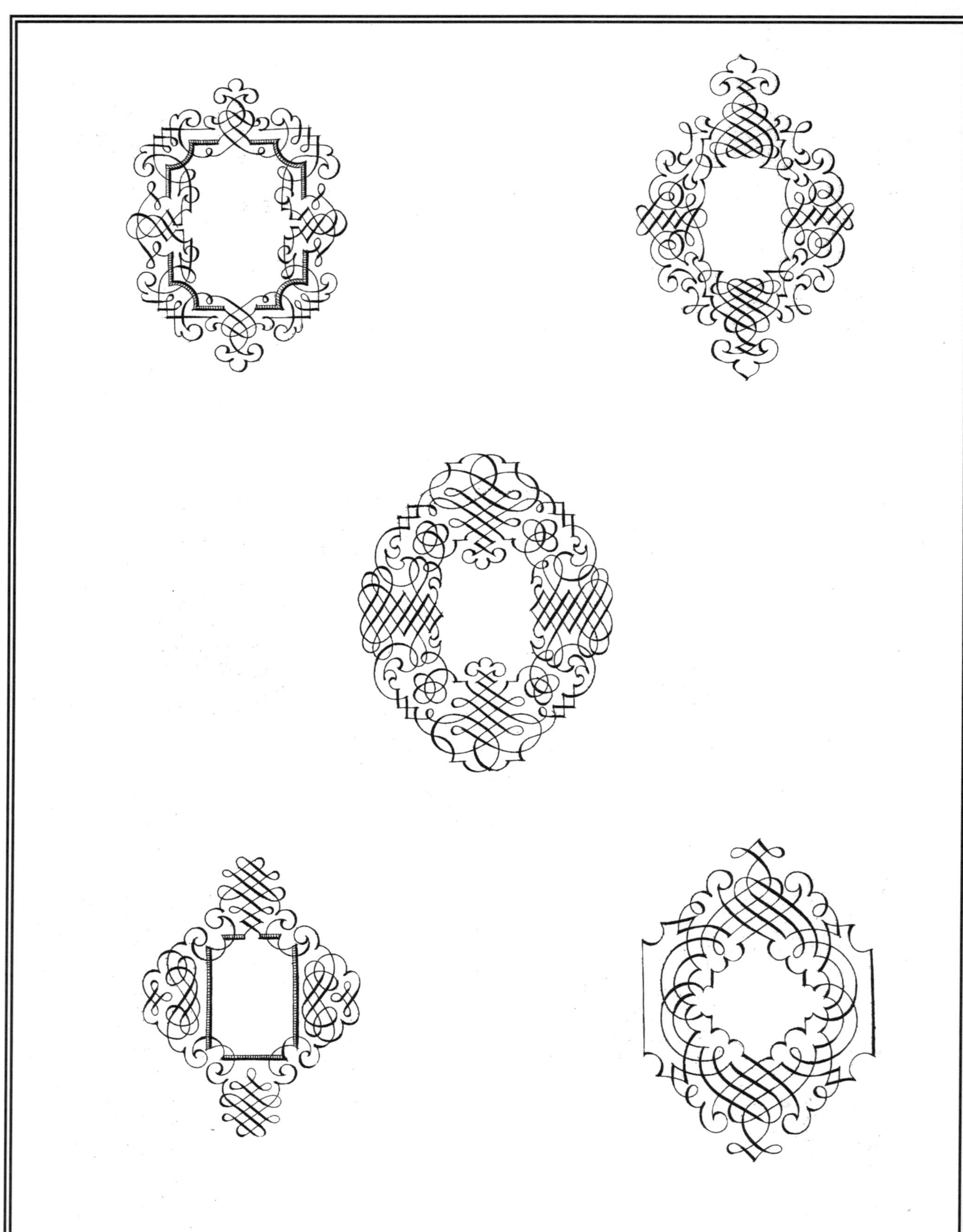

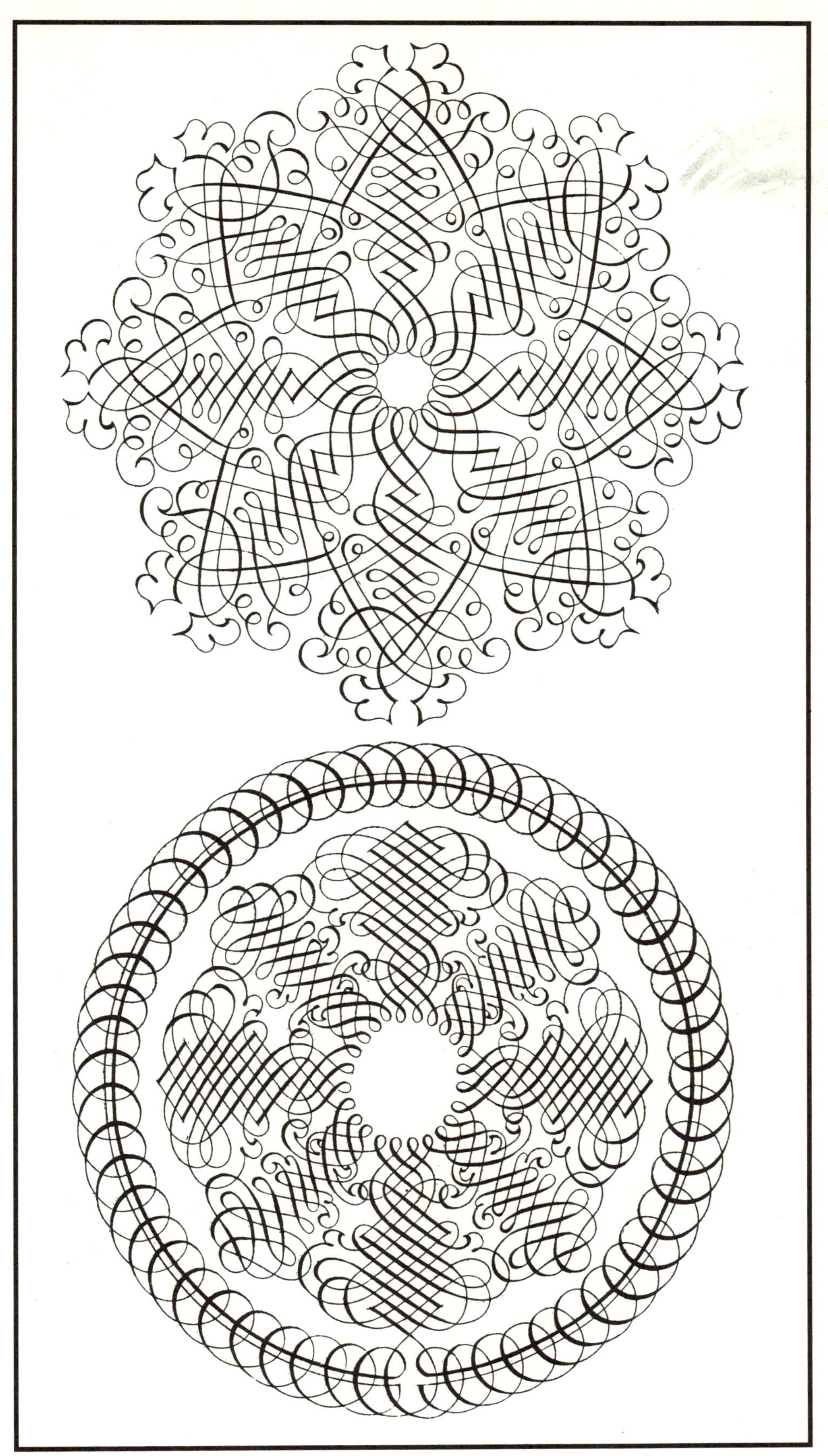

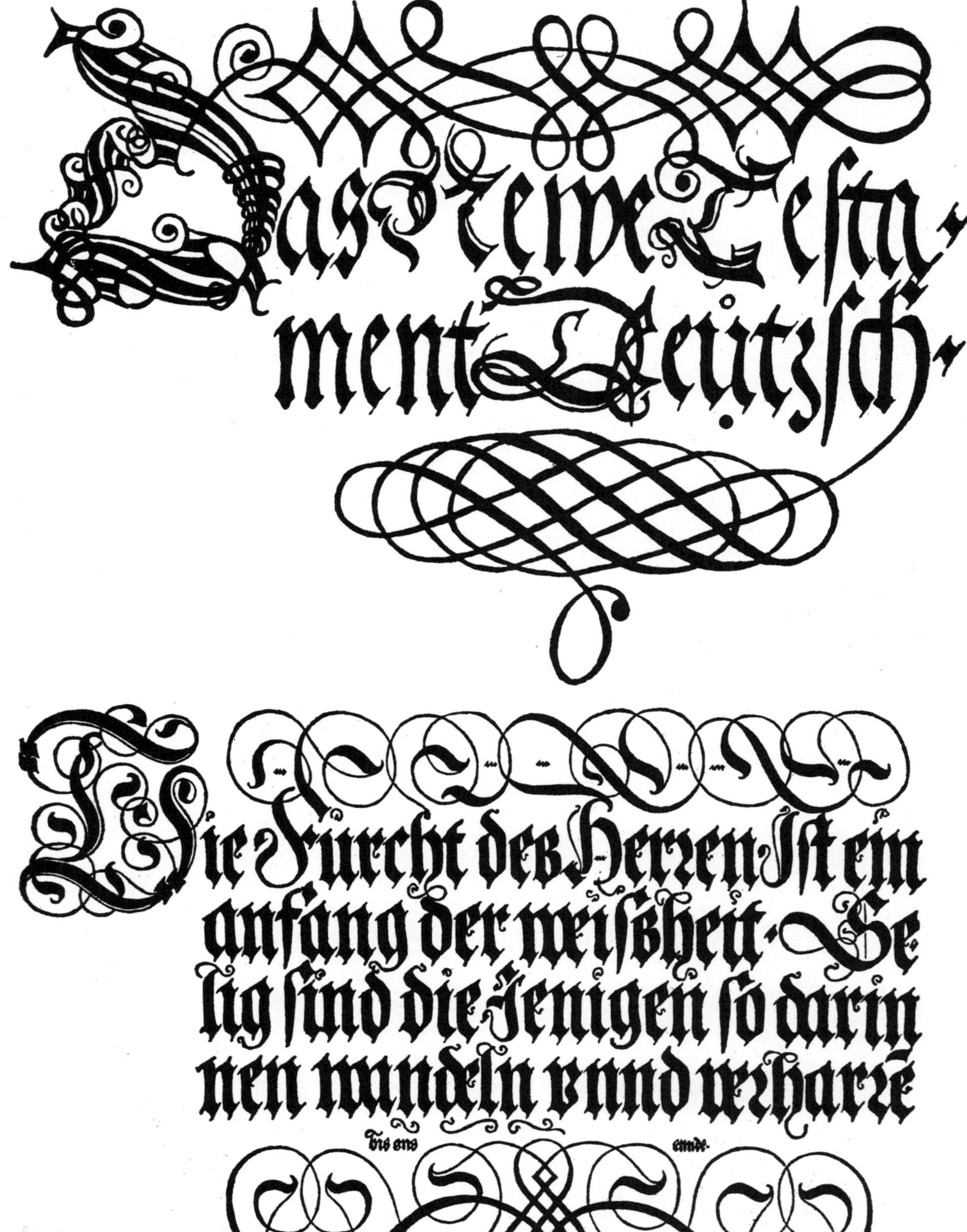
Das newe Testa-
ment Teutzsch

Die Furcht des Herren Ist ein
anfang der weißheit. Se-
lig sind die jenigen so darin
nen wandeln vnnd verharre

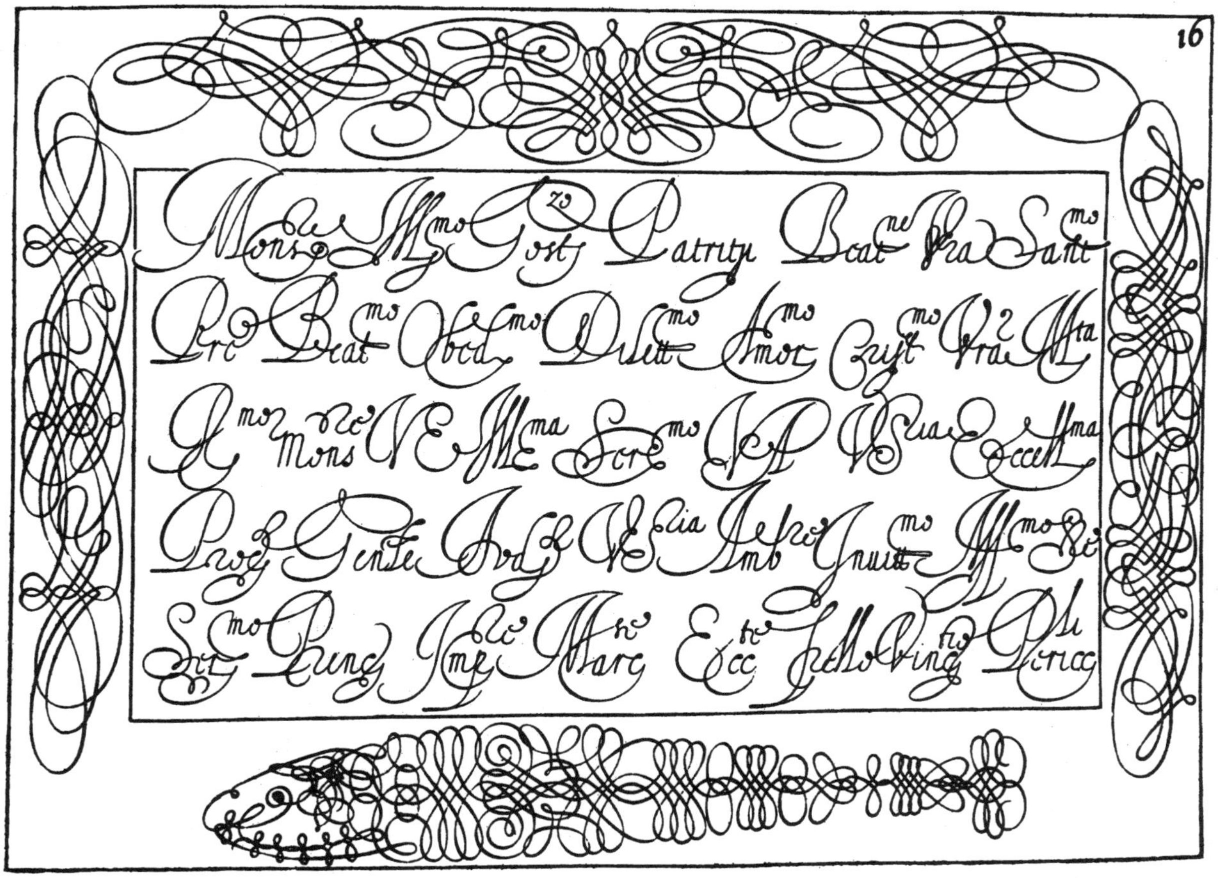

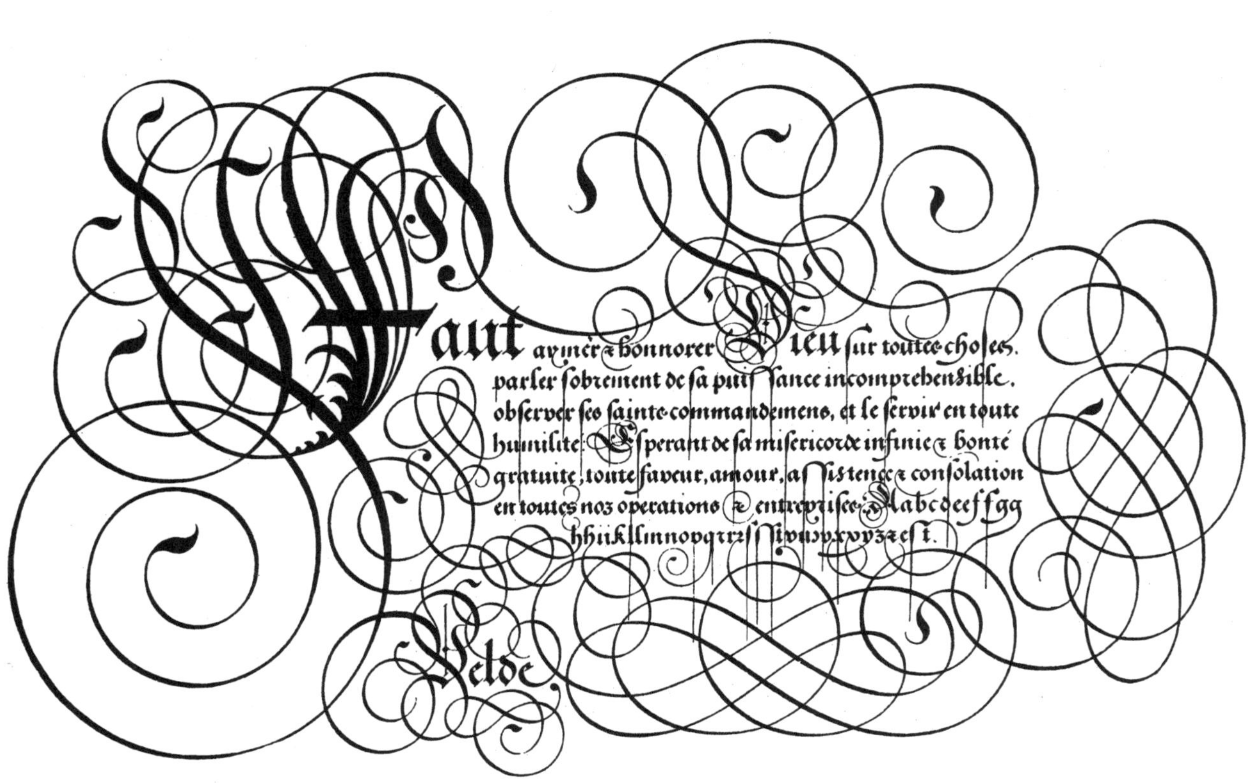
Il faut aymer & honnorer DIEU sur toutes choses.
parler sobrement de sa puissance incomprehensible.
observer ses sainte commandemens, et le servir en toute
humilité. Esperant de sa misericorde infinie & bonté
gratuite, toute faveur, amour, assistence & consolation
en toutes nos operations & entreprises. Aabcdeeffgg
hhiikllmnnopqrrsstuvuxyyzz et &.
Velde

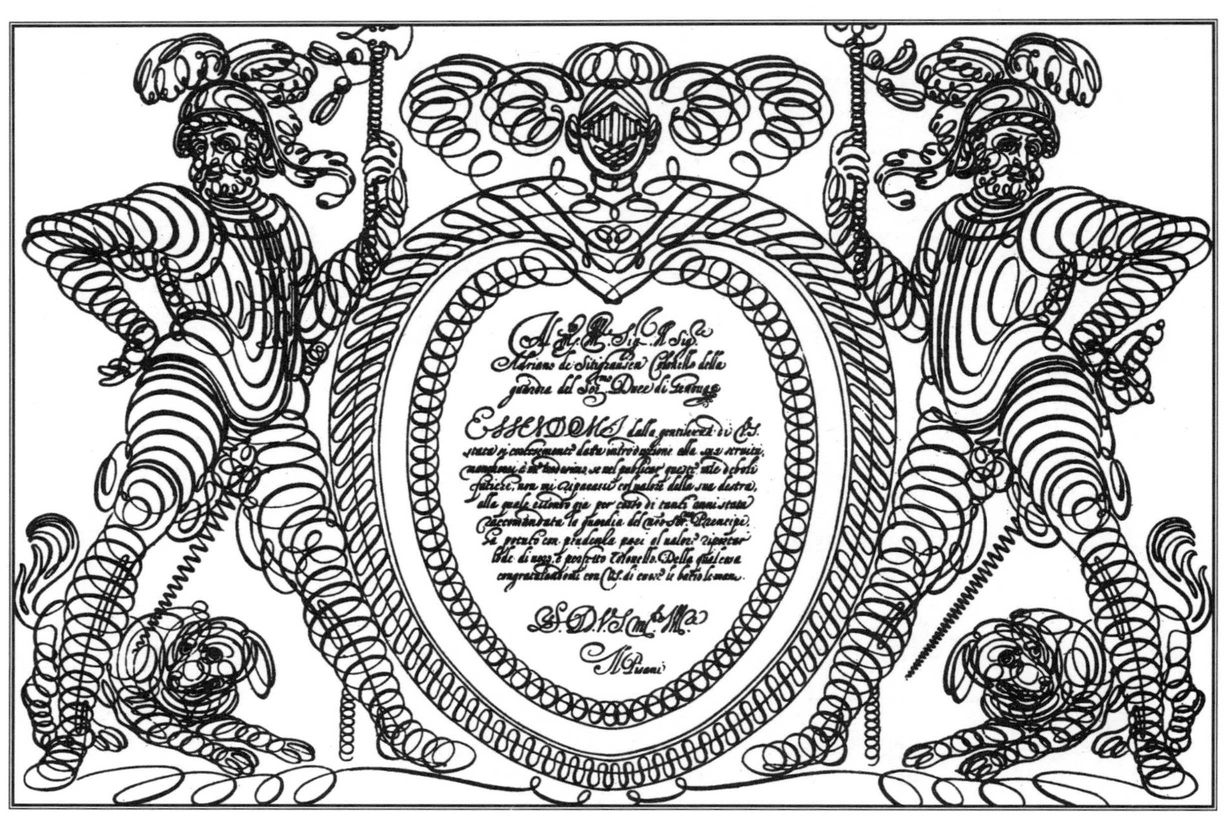

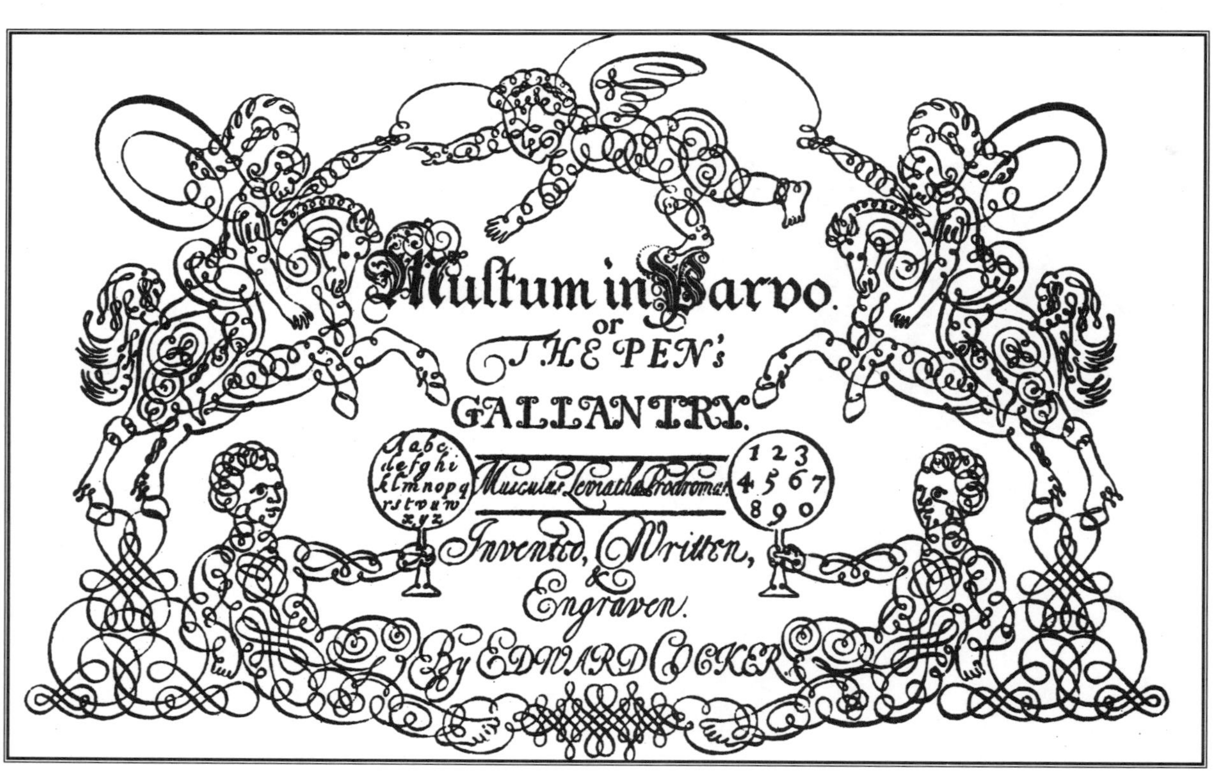
Multum in Parvo.
or
THE PEN's
GALLANTRY.
Musculus Leviathae Prodromus
Invented, Written, & Engraven.
By EDWARD COCKER

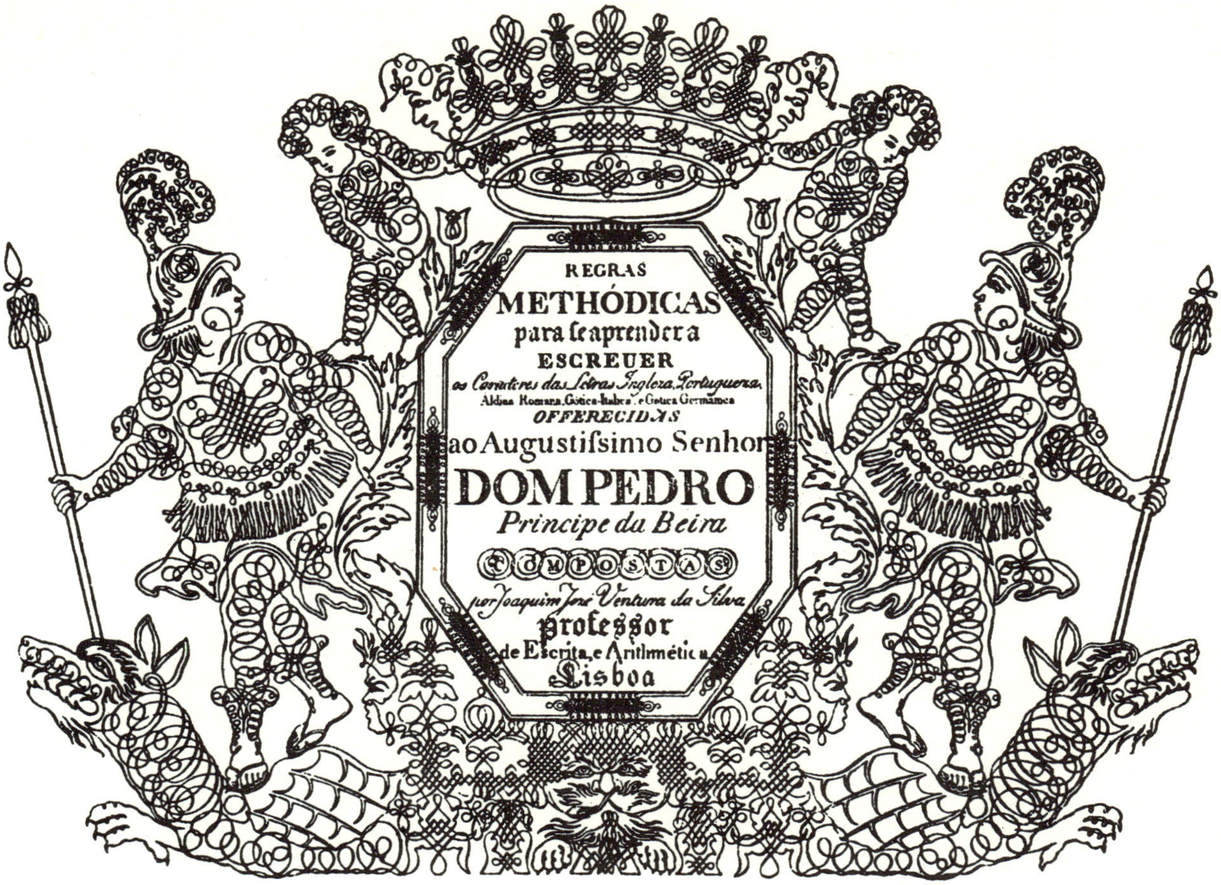

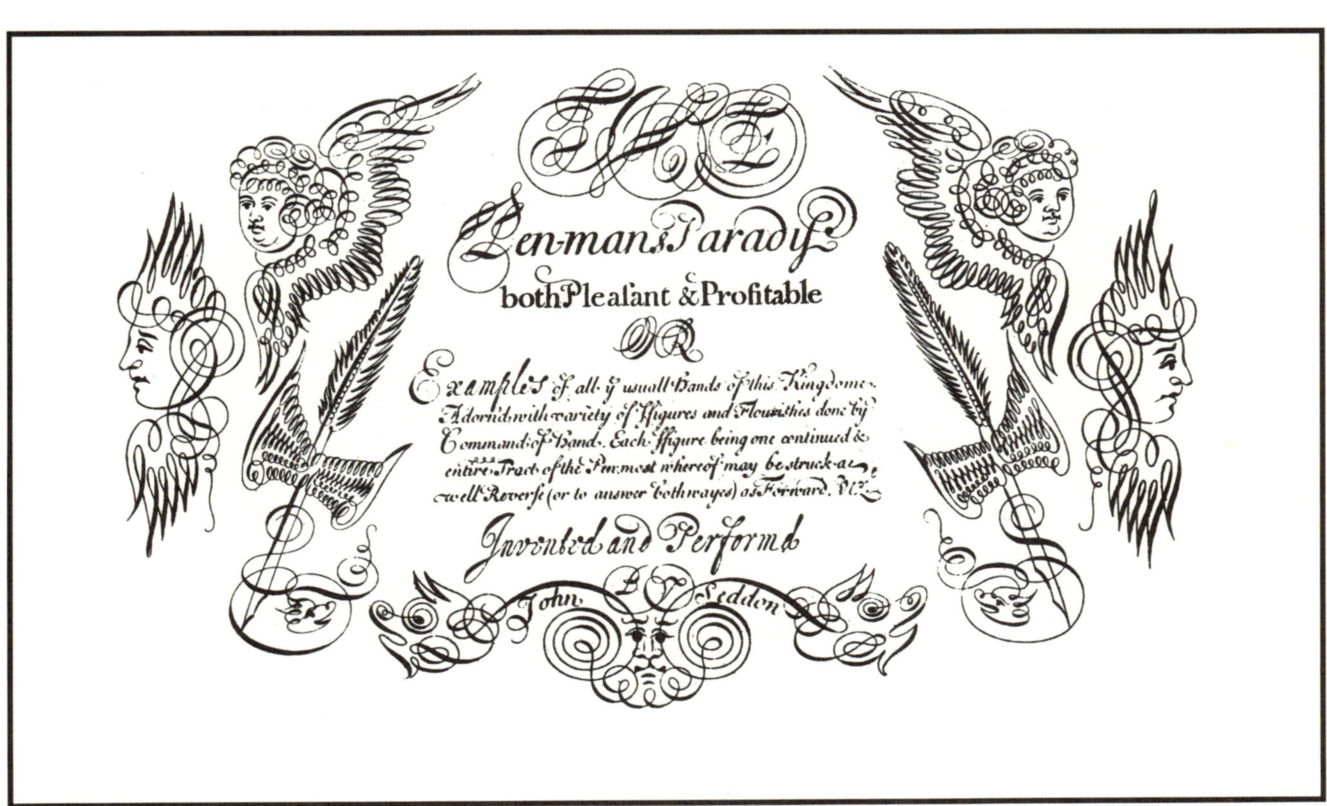

REGRAS
METHÓDICAS
para se aprender a
ESCREUER
os Caratères das Letras Ingleza, Portugueza,
Aldina, Romana, Gotica-Italica, e Gotica Germanica
OFFERECIDAS
ao Augustissimo Senhor
DOM PEDRO
Principe da Beira
COMPOSTAS
por Joaquim José Ventura da Silva
professor
de Escrita, e Arithmética
Lisboa

The
Pen-mans Paradis
both Pleasant & Profitable
OR
Examples of all ye usuall Hands of this Kingdome.
Adorn'd with variety of Ffigures and Flourishes done by
Command of Hand. Each Ffigure being one continued &
entire Tract of the Pen: most whereof may be struck as
well Reverse (or to answer bothwayes) as Forward. Viz:
Invented and Perform'd
John Seddon

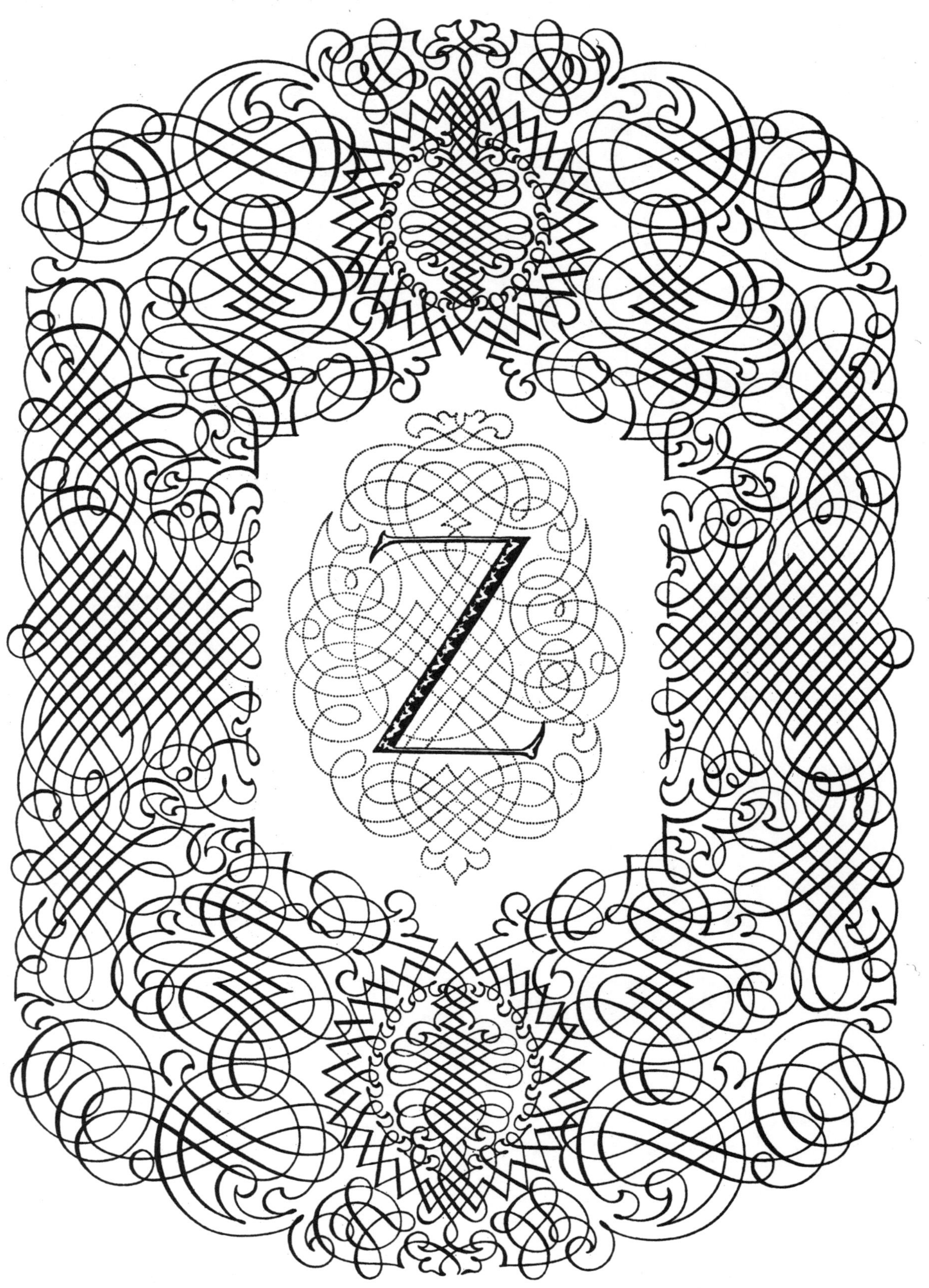

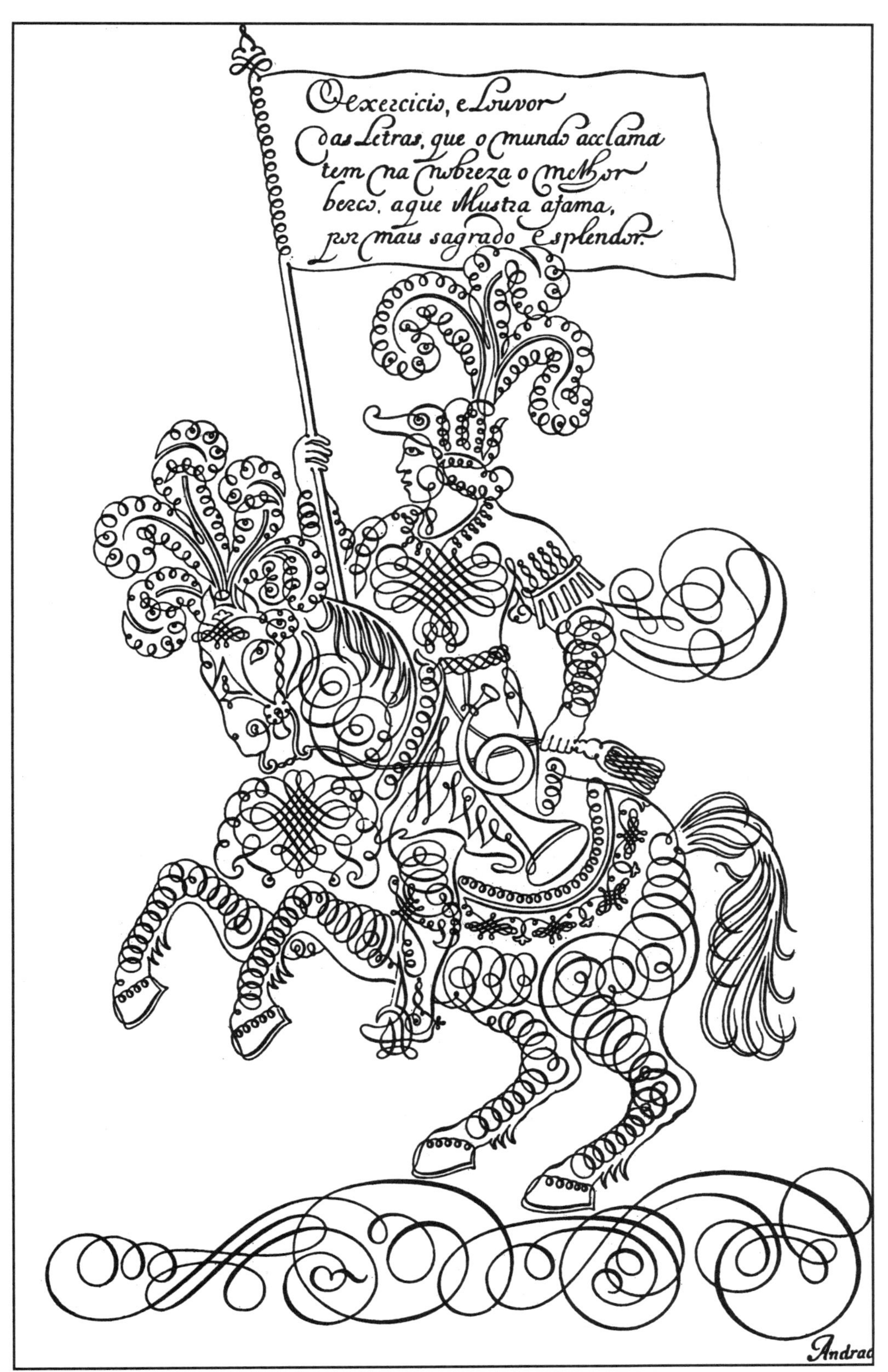

O exercicio, e Louvor
das Letras, que o mundo acclama
tem na nobreza o melhor
berço, a que Illustra a fama,
por mais sagrado esplendor.
Andrade

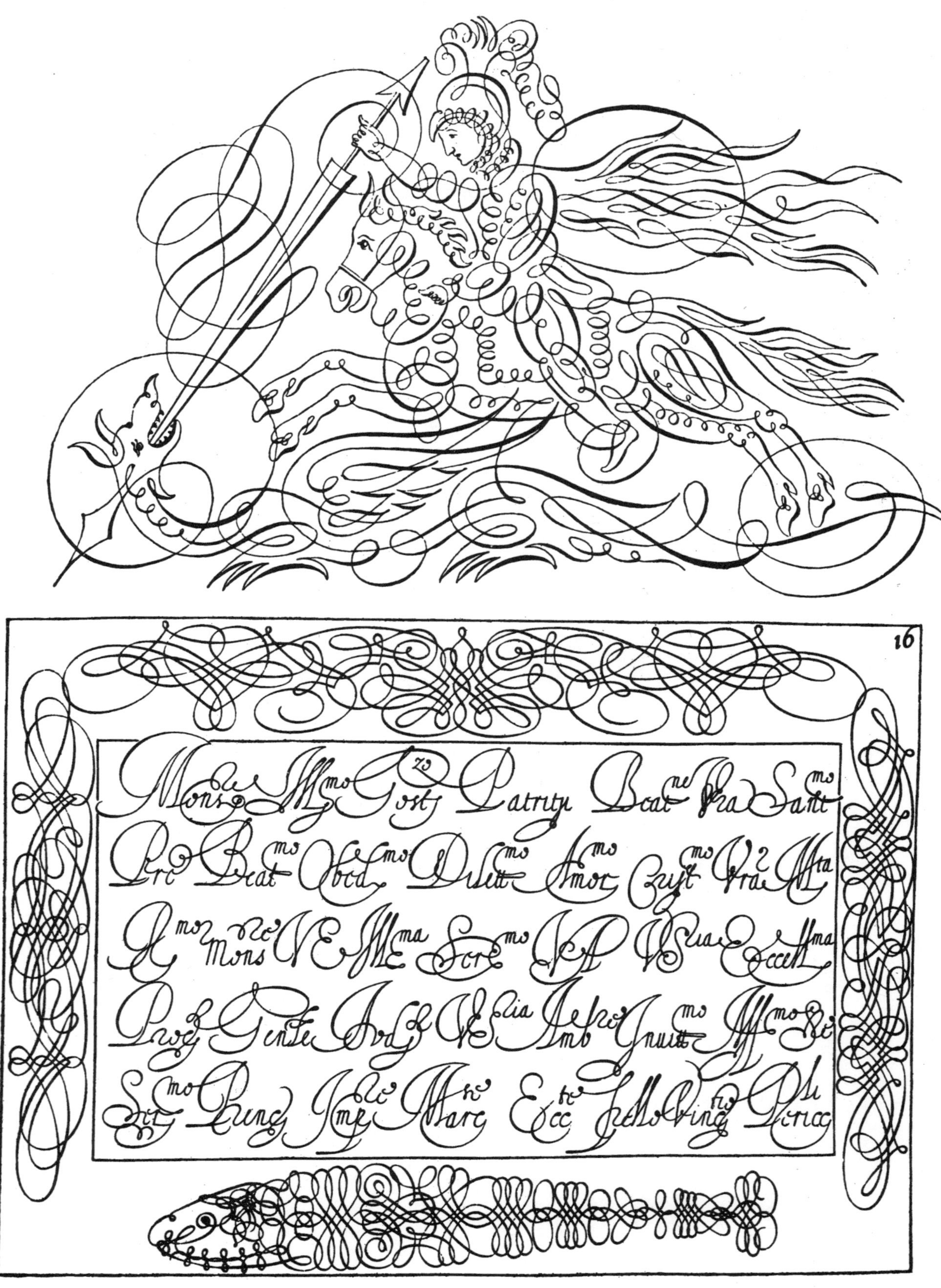

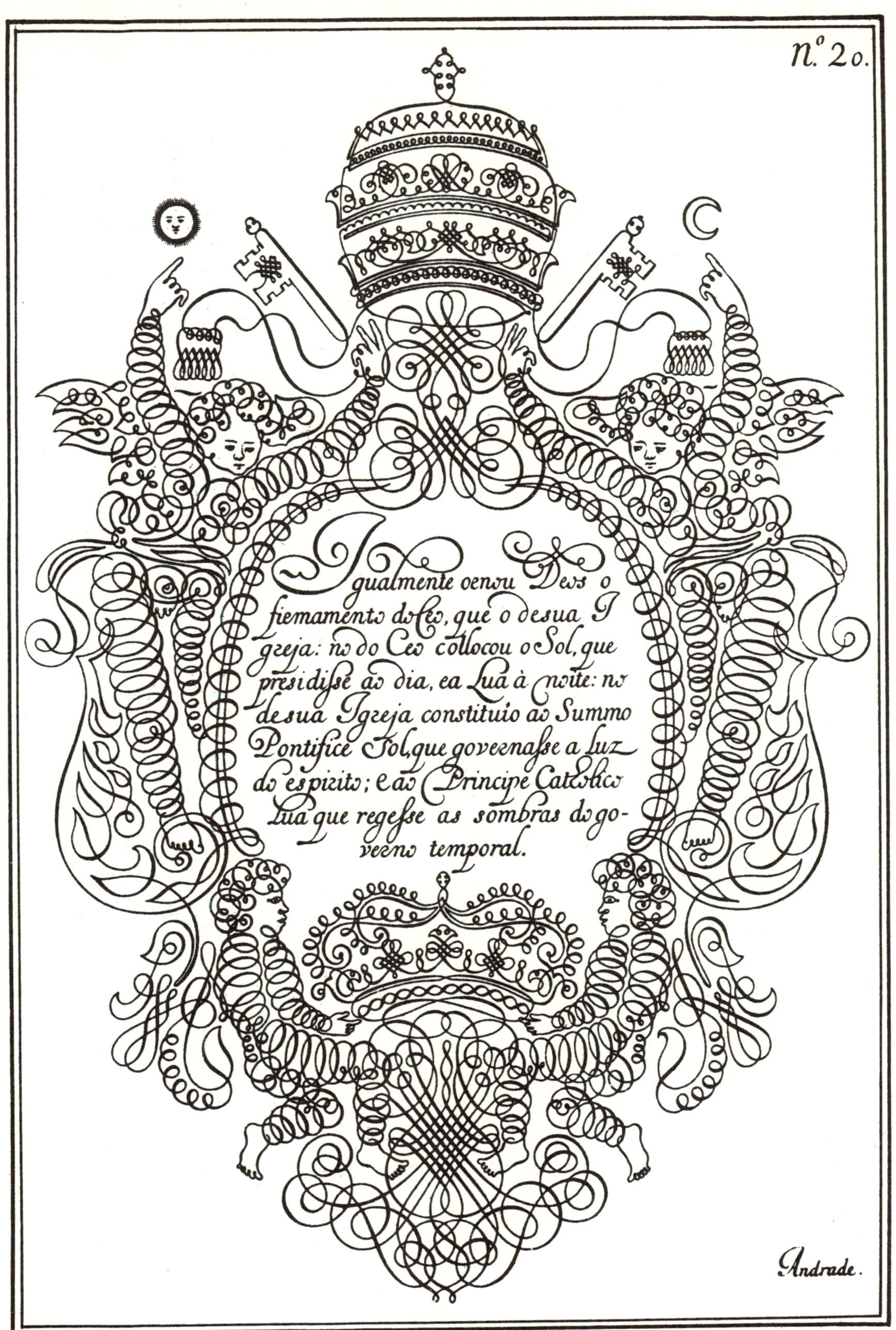
Igualmente ornou Deos o
firmamento do Ceo, que o de sua I
greja: no do Ceo collocou o Sol, que
presidisse ao dia, ea Lua à noite: no
de sua Igreja constituio ao Summo
Pontifice Sol, que governasse a luz
do espirito; e ao Principe Catholico
Lua que regesse as sombras do go-
verno temporal.

Andrade.

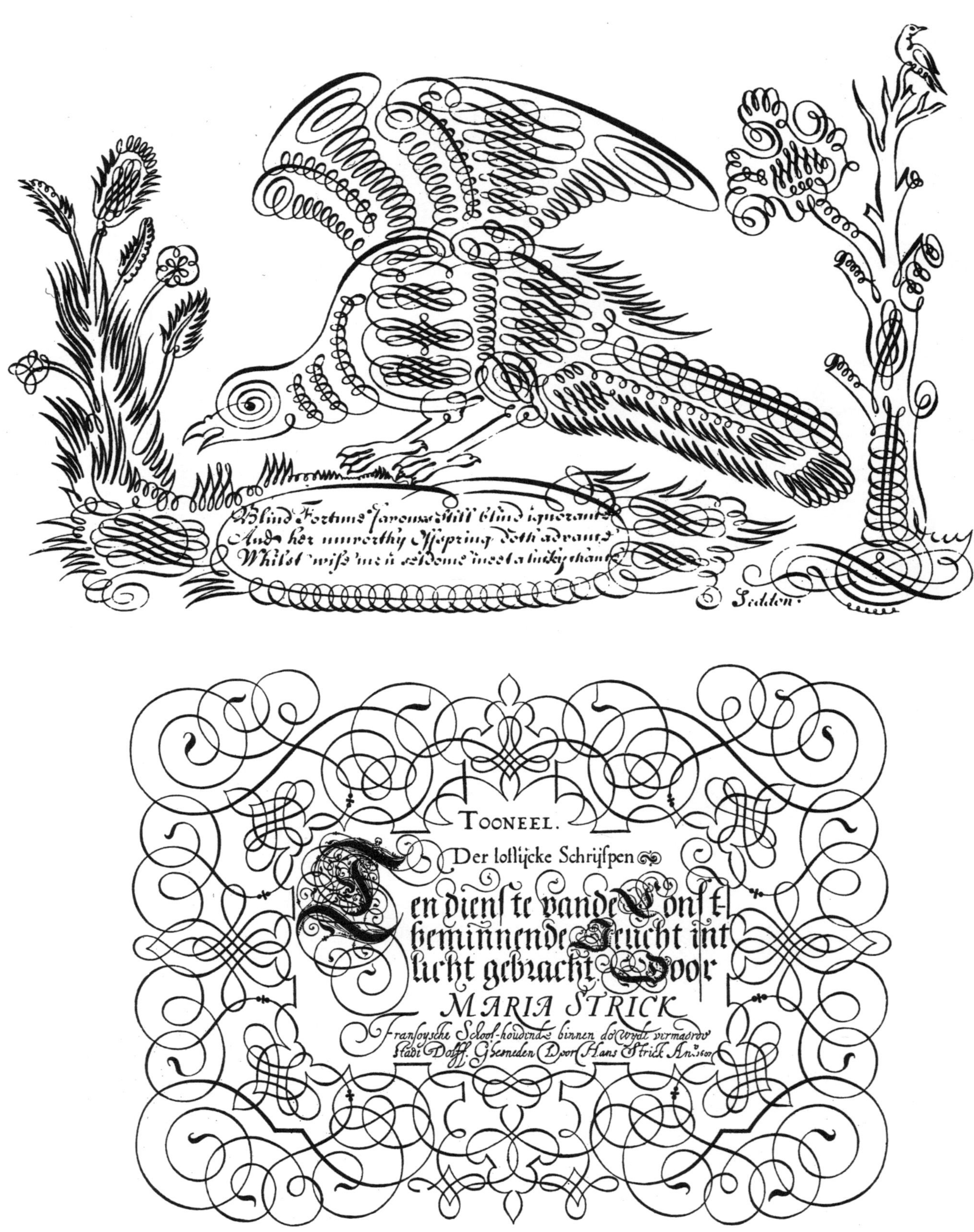

Blind Fortune favours still blind ignorance
And her unworthy Offspring doth advance
Whilst wiss men seldome meet a lucky chance
Seddon

TOONEEL.
Der loflijcke Schrijfpen
Ten dienste vande Const-
beminnende Ieucht int
licht gebracht. Door
MARIA STRICK
Fransoysche School-houdende binnen dò wydt vermaerdo
stadt Dolff: Ghesneden Door Hans Strick An. 1607

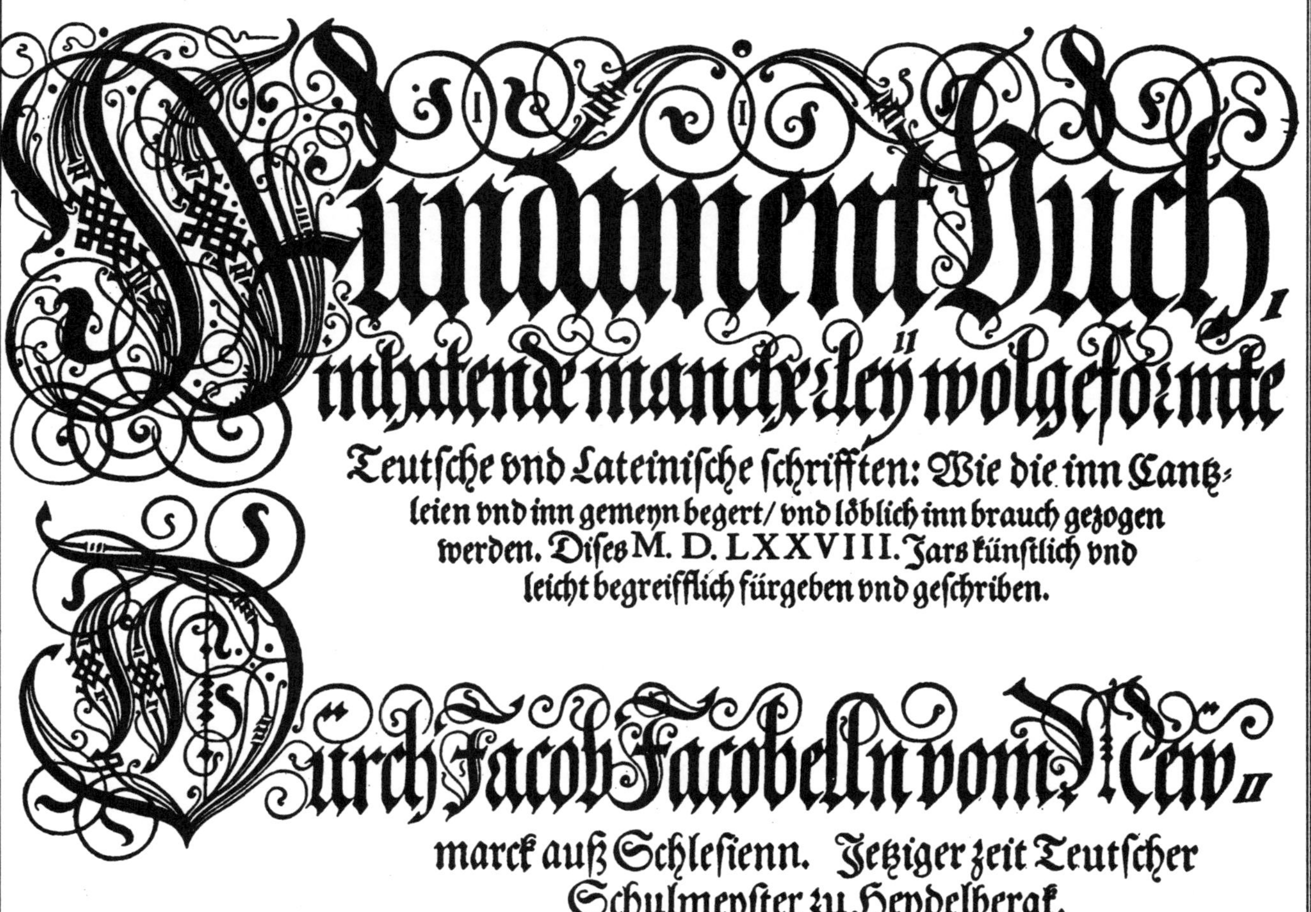

Fundament Buch,
inhaltende mancherley wolgeformte
Teutsche vnd Lateinische schrifften: Wie die inn Cantz-
leien vnd inn gemeyn begert/ vnd löblich inn brauch gezogen
werden. Dises M. D. LXXVIII. Jars künstlich vnd
leicht begreifflich fürgeben vnd geschriben.
Durch Jacob Jacobelln vom New-
marck auß Schlesienn. Jetziger zeit Teutscher
Schulmeyster zu Heydelbergk.
Getruckt zu Straßburg/bei Bernhard Jobin. Anno 1579.

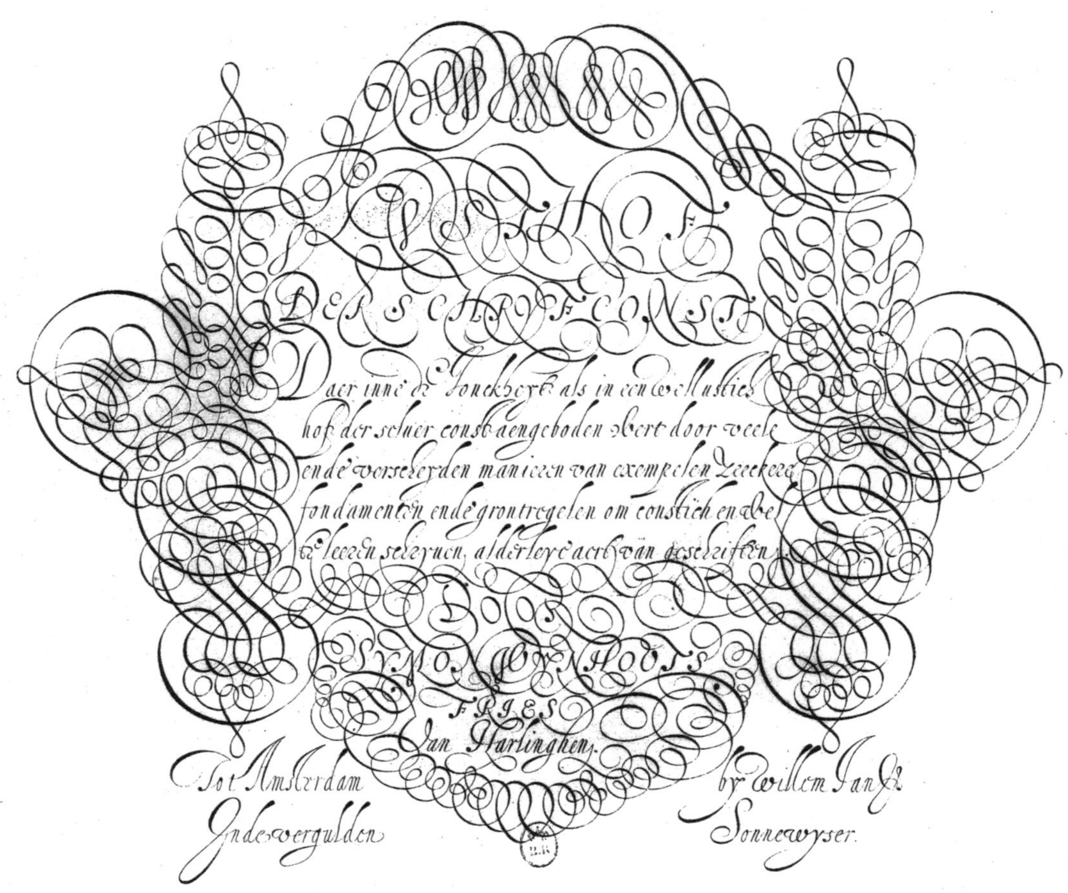

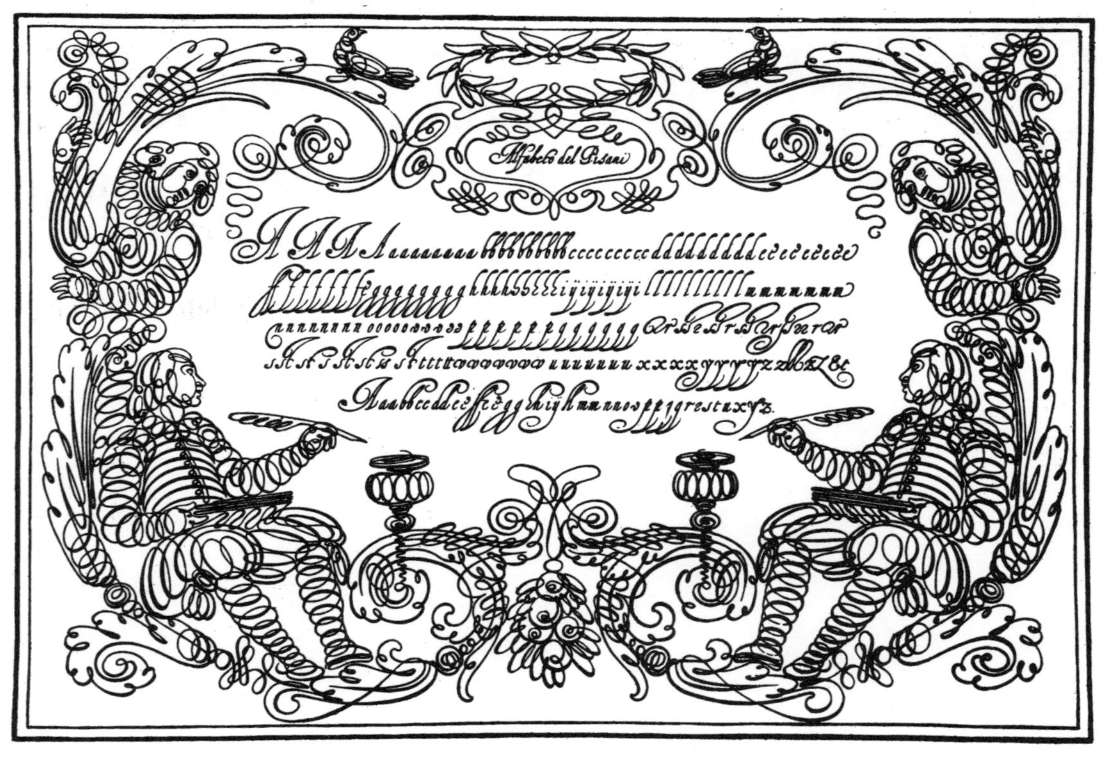

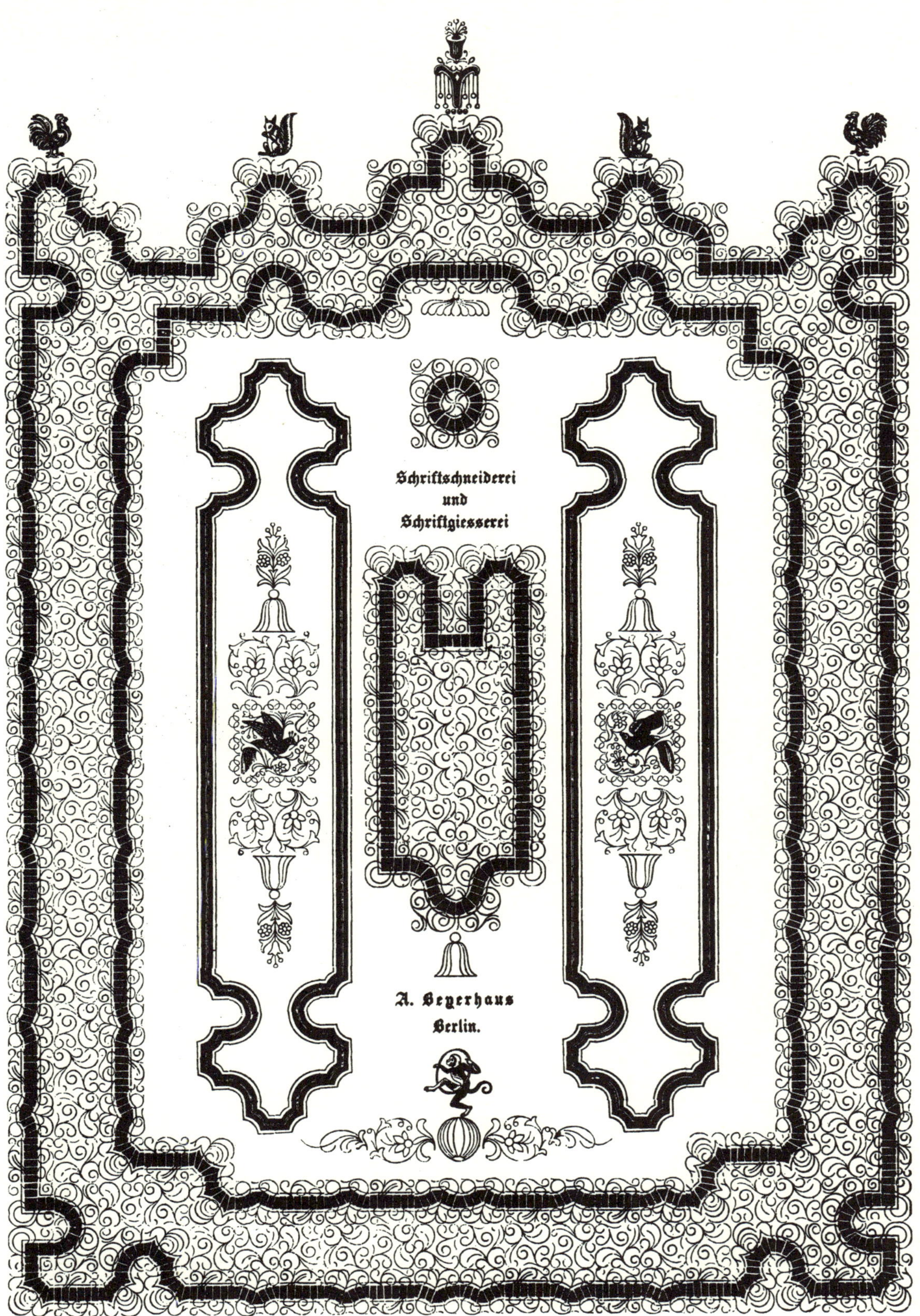

Schriftschneiderei
und
Schriftgiesserei

A. Beyerhaus
Berlin.

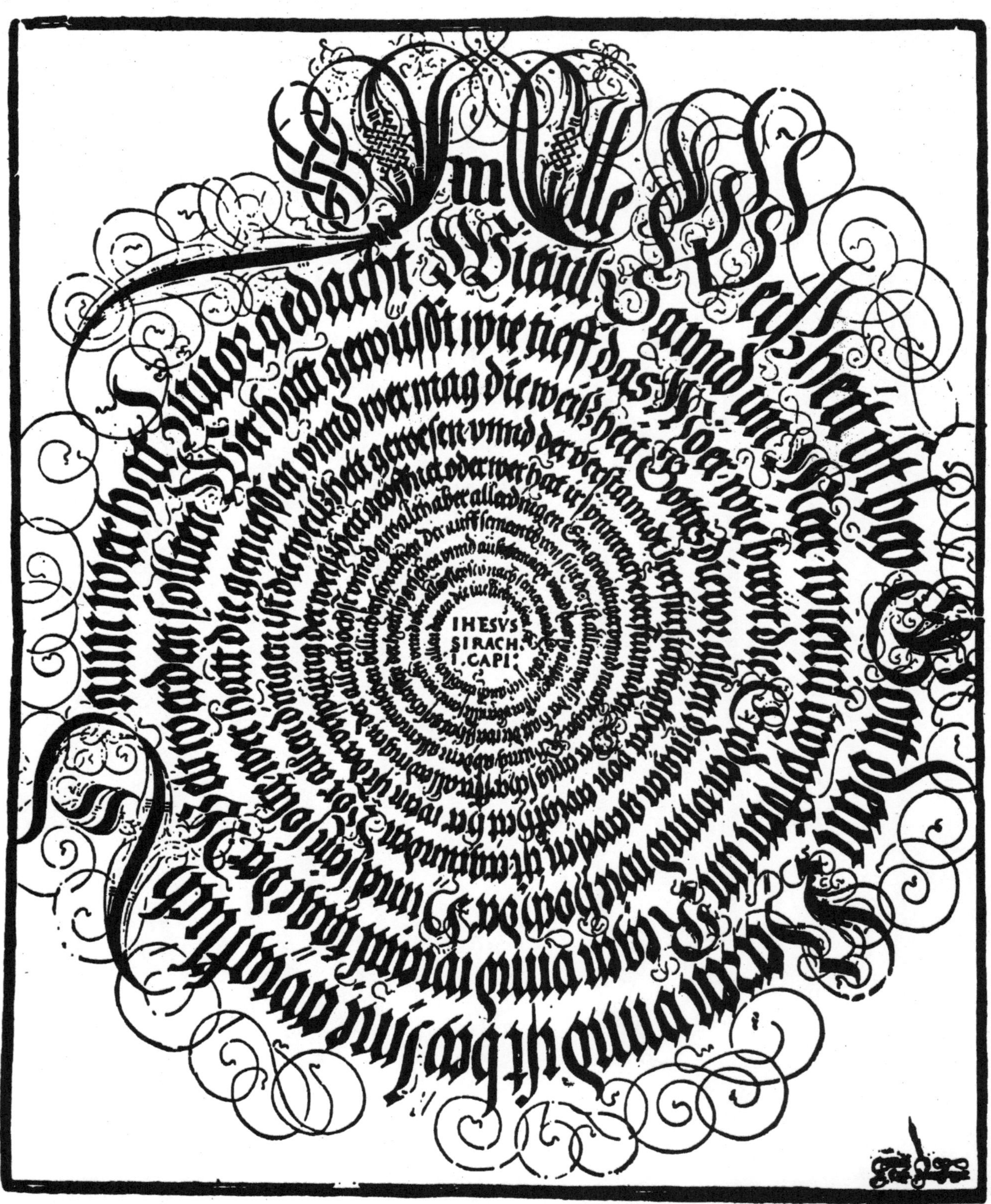

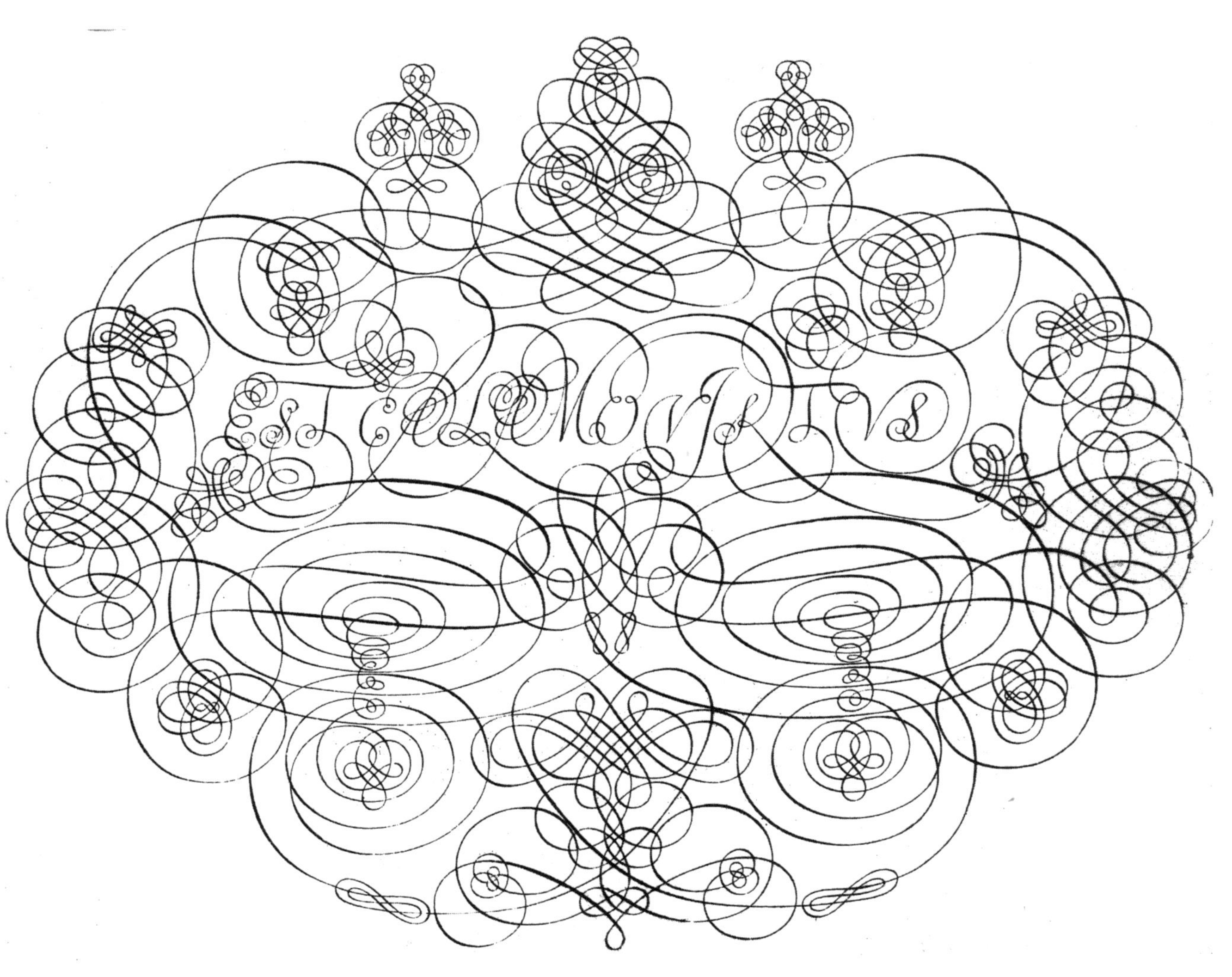

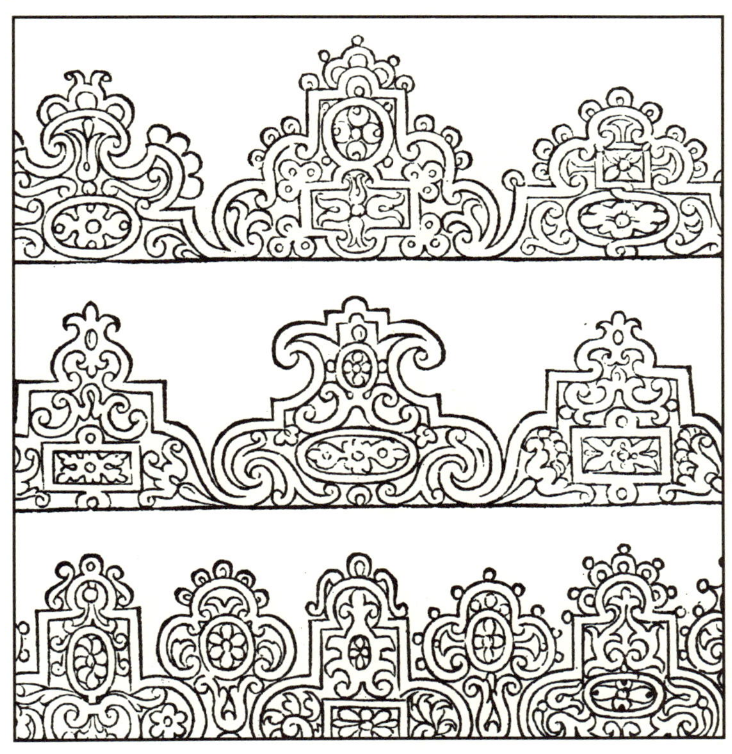

• Captions •

• Légendes •

• Legenden •

• Leyendas •

365

Page 38: *Foliated scrolls,* in *La Composition décorative arabe,* by Collin, Paris, n.d.
Page 39: *Foliated scrolls,* in *La Composition décorative arabe,* by Collin, Paris, n.d.
Pages 40 to 41: *Foliated scrolls,* in *La Composition décorative arabe,* by Collin, Paris, n.d.
Page 42: *Fixed rectangles,* in *La Composition décorative arabe,* by Collin, Paris, n.d.
Page 43: *Curvilinear triangles and circles,* in *La Composition décorative arabe,* by Collin, Paris, n.d.
Page 44: *Polygons, circles and shields,* in *La Composition décorative arabe,* by Collin, Paris, n.d.
Page 45: *Circles,* in *La Composition décorative arabe,* by Collin, Paris, n.d.
Page 46: *Shields,* in *La Composition décorative arabe,* by Collin, Paris, n.d.
Pages 47 to 51: *Borders,* in *La Composition décorative arabe,* by Collin, Paris, n.d.
Pages 52 to 56: *Counterparts,* in *La Composition décorative arabe,* by Collin, Paris, n.d.
Page 57, top: William Dyce. *Drawing Book of the Government School of Design,* 1842-1843. **Bottom:** H. Stevens. *The Art Journal illustrated Catalogue. The Industry of all Nations,* 1851.
Pages 58 to 59: *Interlacing and geometrical designs,* French school, 19th century.
Page 60: Leonardo Da Vinci. *Interlaced designs,* 16th century.
Page 61 to 69: Virgile Solis. *Plates of moresques,* German school, 16th century.
Pages 70 to 74: Pierre Flœtner. *Niellos and arabesques,* German school, 16th century.
Pages 75 to 76: Jacques Androuet du Cerceau. *Livre contenant passements de moresques très utile à toutes gens exerçant ledit art,* France, 16th century.
Page 77: Pierre Flœtner. *Niellos and arabesques,* German school, 16th century.
Page 78: Leonardo Da Vinci. *Knot with heart-shaped shield,* Italy, 1490-1500.
Page 79: Leonardo Da Vinci. *Knot forming seven rosaces,* Italy, 1490-1500.
Page 80 to 85: Albrecht Dürer. *The Six Knots,* Germany, 1506-1507.
Pages 86 to 87: Nicolo Zoppino. *Motifs de broderies et dentelles,* Venice, 1529.
Pages 88 to 96: Pierre Flœtner. *Niellos and arabesques,* Germany, 16th century.
Page 97: Jacques Androuet du Cerceau. *Livre contenant passements de moresques très utile à toutes gens exerçant ledit art,* France, 16th century.

Page 38 : *Rinceaux,* in : Collin. *La Composition décorative arabe,* Paris, s.d.
Page 39 : *Rinceaux, habillage,* in : Collin. *La Composition décorative arabe,* Paris, s.d.
Page 40 à 41 : *Rinceaux,* in : Collin. *La Composition décorative arabe,* Paris, s.d.
Page 42 : *Rectangles fixes,* in : Collin. *La Composition décorative arabe,* Paris, s.d.
Page 43 : *Triangle curviligne et cercles,* in : Collin. *La Composition décorative arabe,* Paris, s.d.
Page 44 : *Polygone, cercle et écussons,* in : Collin. *La Composition décorative arabe,* Paris, s.d.
Page 45 : *Cercles,* in : Collin. *La Composition décorative arabe,* Paris, s.d.
Page 46 : *Écusson,* in : Collin. *La Composition décorative arabe,* Paris, s.d.
Pages 47 à 51 : *Bordures,* in : Collin. *La Composition décorative arabe,* Paris, s.d.
Pages 52 à 56 : *Contrepartie,* in : Collin. *La Composition décorative arabe,* Paris, s.d.
Page 57, en haut : William Dyce. *Drawing Book of the Government School of Design,* 1842-1843. **En bas :** H. Stevens. *The Art Journal illustrated Catalogue. The Industry of all Nations,* 1851.
Pages 58 à 59 : *Entrelacs et dessins géométriques,* école française, XIXe siècle.
Page 60 : Leonardo Da Vinci. *Dessin à entrelacs,* XVIe siècle.
Pages 61 à 69 : Virgile Solis. *Planches de mauresques,* école allemande, XVIe siècle.
Page 70 à 74 : Pierre Flœtner. *Nielles, arabesques,* école allemande, XVIe siècle.
Pages 75 à 76 : Jacques Androuet du Cerceau. *Livre contenant passements de moresques très utile à toutes gens exerçant ledit art,* France, XVIe siècle.
Page 77 : Pierre Flœtner. *Nielles, arabesques,* école allemande, XVIe siècle.
Page 78 : Leonardo Da Vinci. *Nœud avec un écusson en forme de cœur,* Italie, 1490-1500.
Page 79 : Leonardo Da Vinci. *Nœud formant sept rosaces,* Italie, 1490-1500.
Pages 80 à 85 : Albrecht Dürer. *Les Six Nœuds,* Allemagne, 1506-1507.
Pages 86 à 87 : Nicolo Zoppino. *Motifs de broderies et dentelles,* Venise, 1529.
Pages 88 à 96 : Pierre Flœtner. *Arabesques, nielles,* Allemagne, XVIe siècle.
Page 97 : Jacques Androuet du Cerceau. *Livre contenant passements de moresques très utile à toutes gens exerçant ledit art,* France, XVIe siècle.

Pages 98 to 102: Virgile Solis. *Plates of ornaments*, Germany, 16th century.

Pages 103 to 104: Jacques Androuet du Cerceau. *Livre contenant passements de moresques très utile à toutes gens exerçant ledit art*, France, 16th century.

Page 105: Peter Flötner. *Kunstbuch*, Germany, 16th century.

Page 106: Jacques Androuet du Cerceau. *Livre contenant passements de moresques très utile à toutes gens exerçant ledit art*, France, 16th century.

Page 107: Peter Flötner. *Kunstbuch*, Germany, 16th century.

Page 108, top: Balthazar Sylvius. *Variarum protactionum quas vulgo maurusias vocant*, Germany, 16th century; **bottom:** Virgile Solis. *Plates of ornaments*, 16th century.

Pages 109 to 110: Virgile Solis. *Plates of ornaments*, Germany, 16th century.

Page 111: Balthazar Sylvius. *Variarum protactionum quas vulgo maurusias vocant*, Germany, 16th century.

Page 112: Peter Flöttner. *Metal engraving designs*, Germany, 16th century.

Page 113: Matteo Pagan. *Lace designs*, Italie, 16th century.

Pages 114 to 115: Jacques Androuet du Cerceau. *Livre contenant passements de moresques très utile à toutes gens exerçant ledit art*, France, 16th century.

Pages 116 to 117: Virgile Solis. *Plates of ornaments*, Germany, 16th century.

Pages 118 to 128: Jacques Androuet du Cerceau. *Livre contenant passements de moresques très utile à toutes gens exerçant ledit art*, France, 16th century.

Page 129: Balthazar Sylvius. *Variarum protactionum quas vulgo maurusias vocant*, Germany, 16th century.

Pages 130 to 132: Claude Nourry. *La Fleur des patrons de lingerie*, France, 1501-1533.

Page 133: Francisque Pellegrin. *La Fleur de la science de pourtraicture, patrons de broderie, façon arabique et ytalique*, France, 1530.

Pages 134 to 135: Claude Nourry. *La Fleur des patrons de lingerie*, France, 1501-1533.

Page 136: Pierre de Sainte-Lucie. *Livre nouveau, dict patron de lingerie*, France, 1530-1533.

Pages 137 to 139: Francisque Pellegrin. *La Fleur de la science de pourtraicture, patrons de broderie, façon arabique et ytalique*, France, 1530.

Pages 140 to 144: Pierre de Sainte-Lucie. *Livre nouveau, dict patron de lingerie*, France, 1530-1533.

Page 145: Pierre de Sainte-Lucie. *Patrons de diverses manières…*, France, vers 1533.

Pages 98 à 102 : Virgile Solis. *Planches d'ornements*, Allemagne, XVIᵉ siècle.

Pages 103 à 104 : Jacques Androuet du Cerceau. *Livre contenant passements de moresques très utile à toutes gens exerçant ledit art*, France, XVIᵉ siècle.

Page 105 : Peter Flötner. *Kunstbuch*, Allemagne, XVIᵉ siècle.

Page 106 : Jacques Androuet du Cerceau. *Livre contenant passements de moresques très utile à toutes gens exerçant ledit art*, France, XVIᵉ siècle.

Page 107 : Peter Flötner. *Kunstbuch*, Allemagne, XVIᵉ siècle.

Page 108, en haut : Balthazar Sylvius. *Variarum protactionum quas vulgo maurusias vocant*, Allemagne, XVIᵉ siècle. **en bas :** Virgile Solis. *Planches d'ornements*, Allemagne, XVIᵉ siècle.

Pages 109 à 110 : Virgile Solis. *Planches d'ornements*, Allemagne, XVIᵉ siècle.

Page 111 : Balthazar Sylvius. *Variarum protactionum quas vulgo maurusias vocant*, Allemagne, XVIᵉ siècle.

Page 112 : Peter Flöttner. *Motifs de gravure sur métal*, Allemagne, XVIᵉ siècle.

Page 113 : Matteo Pagan. *Motifs de dentelles*, Italie, XVIᵉ siècle.

Pages 114 à 115 : Jacques Androuet du Cerceau. *Livre contenant passements de moresques très utile à toutes gens exerçant ledit art*, France, XVIᵉ siècle.

Pages 116 à 117 : Virgile Solis. *Planches d'ornements*, Allemagne, XVIᵉ siècle.

Pages 118 à 128 : Jacques Androuet du Cerceau. *Livre contenant passements de moresques très utile à toutes gens exerçant ledit art*, France, XVIᵉ siècle.

Page 129 : Balthazar Sylvius. *Variarum protactionum quas vulgo maurusias vocant*, Allemagne, XVIᵉ siècle.

Pages 130 à 132 : Claude Nourry. *La Fleur des patrons de lingerie*, France, 1501-1533.

Page 133 : Francisque Pellegrin. *La Fleur de la science de pourtraicture, patrons de broderie, façon arabique et ytalique*, France, 1530.

Pages 134 à 135 : Claude Nourry. *La Fleur des patrons de lingerie*, France, 1501-1533.

Page 136 : Pierre de Sainte-Lucie. *Livre nouveau, dict patron de lingerie*, France, 1530-1533.

Pages 137 à 139 : Francisque Pellegrin. *La Fleur de la science de pourtraicture, patrons de broderie, façon arabique et ytalique*, France, 1530.

Page 140 à 144 : Pierre de Sainte-Lucie. *Livre nouveau, dict patron de lingerie*, France, 1530-1533.

Page 145 : Pierre de Sainte-Lucie. *Patrons de diverses manières…*, France, vers 1533.

Pages 146 to 149: Francisque Pellegrin. *La Fleur de la science de pourtraicture, patrons de broderie, façon arabique et ytalique*, France, 1530.
Pages 150 to 155: Pierre de Sainte-Lucie. *Patrons de diverses manières…*, France, vers 1533.
Pages 156 to 159: Francisque Pellegrin. *La Fleur de la science de pourtraicture, patrons de broderie, façon arabique et ytalique*, France, 1530.
Pages 160 to 163: Pierre de Sainte-Lucie. *Patrons de diverses manières…*, France, vers 1533.
Pages 164 to 173: *Livre à dentelles et dessins d'ornements*, Germany, 16th century.
Pages 174 to 195: Francisque Pellegrin. *La Fleur de la science de pourtraicture, patrons de broderie, façon arabique et ytalique*, France, 1530.
Pages 196 to 197: *Marquetry designs and various interlacings*, 16th century.
Pages 198 to 199: Alessandro Paganino. *Motifs de dentelles*, Venice, 1518.
Pages 200 to 205: Nicolo Zoppino. *Patterns for embroidery and lace*, Venice, 1529.
Pages 206 to 210: *Textile designs*, 16th-17th centuries.
Page 211: *Endpieces and typographic decorations*, France, 17th century.
Pages 212 to 213: *Textile designs*, 16th century.
Pages 214 to 219: *Textile designs*, in: *The Ornamentist, or Artisan's Manual in the various branches of Ornamental Art*, London, 1853.
Pages 220 to 227: Jacques Androuet du Cerceau. *Les Plans et parterres des jardins de propreté*, France, 16th century.
Pages 228 to 229: Gervase Markham, *The English husbandman*, London, 16th century.
Page 230: Francesco Colonna. *Knot garden designs*, Italy, 1499.
Pages 231 to 247: Jacques Androuet du Cerceau. *Livre contenant passements de moresques très utile à toutes gens exerçant ledit art*, France, 16th century.
Page 248 to 254: Jacques Androuet du Cerceau. *Parquets and mosaic patterns*, France, 16th century.
Pages 255: Pierre Flötner. *Niellos and arabesques*, Germany, 16th century.
Pages 256 to 258: Jacques Androuet du Cerceau. *Livre contenant passements de moresques très utile à toutes gens exerçant ledit art*, France, 16th century.
Page 259: *Mosaic and textile designs*, 19th century.
Page 260: *Part of a pelmet*, 16th century.
Page 261: *Carved wood interlacing on the doors of Saint Maclou Church*, Rouen, France, 16th century.

Pages 146 à 149 : Francisque Pellegrin. *La Fleur de la science de pourtraicture, patrons de broderie, façon arabique et ytalique*, France, 1530.
Pages 150 à 155 : Pierre de Sainte-Lucie. *Patrons de diverses manières…*, France, vers 1533.
Pages 156 à 159 : Francisque Pellegrin. *La Fleur de la science de pourtraicture, patrons de broderie, façon arabique et ytalique*, France, 1530.
Pages 160 à 163 : Pierre de Sainte-Lucie. *Patrons de diverses manières…*, France, vers 1533.
Pages 164 à 173 : *Livre à dentelles et dessins d'ornements*, Allemagne, XVIe siècle.
Pages 174 à 195 : Francisque Pellegrin. *La Fleur de la science de pourtraicture, patrons de broderie, façon arabique et ytalique*, France, 1530.
Pages 196 à 197 : *Marqueterie, entrelacs divers*, XVe siècle.
Pages 198 à 199 : Alessandro Paganino. *Motifs de dentelles*, Venise, 1518.
Pages 200 à 205 : Nicolo Zoppino. *Motifs de broderies et dentelles*, Venise, 1529.
Pages 206 à 210 : *Motifs pour textile*, XVIe-XVIIe siècles.
Page 211 : *Culs de lampe, ornements typographiques*, France, XVIIe siècle.
Pages 212 à 213 : *Motifs pour textiles*, XVIe siècle.
Pages 214 à 219 : *Motifs pour textiles*, in : *The Ornamentist, or Artisan's Manual in the various branches of Ornamental Art*, Londres, 1853.
Pages 220 à 227 : Jacques Androuet du Cerceau. *Les Plans et parterres des jardins de propreté*, France, XVIe siècle.
Pages 228 à 229 : Gervase Markham, *The English husbansman*, Londres, XVIe siècle.
Page 230 : Francesco Colonna. *Plans de parterres de jardins*, Italie, 1499.
Pages 231 à 247 : Jacques Androuet du Cerceau. *Livre contenant passements de moresques très utile à toutes gens exerçant ledit art*, France, XVIe siècle.
Pages 248 à 254 : Jacques Androuet du Cerceau. *Parquets mosaïques*, France, XVIe siècle.
Page 255 : Pierre Flötner. *Arabesques, nielles*, Allemagne, XVIe siècle.
Pages 256 à 258 : Jacques Androuet du Cerceau. *Livre contenant passements de moresques très utile à toutes gens exerçant ledit art*, France, XVIe siècle.
Page 259 : *Décors pour mosaïque et textile*, XIXe siècle.
Page 260 : *Fragments d'un lambrequin*, XVIe siècle.
Page 261 : Portes de l'église Saint-Maclou, Rouen, *entrelacs sculptés sur bois*, France, XVIe siècle.

Pages 314 to 319: *Typographic ornaments,* 19th century.
Pages 320 to 321: *Jewelery designs,* in: *The Ornamentist, or Artisan's Manual in the various branches of Ornamental Art,* London, 1853.
Page 322: *Metal engraving designs,* in: *The Ornamentist, or Artisan's Manual in the various branches of Ornamental Art,* London, 1853.
Page 322: *Ironwork designs,* in: *The Ornamentist, or Artisan's Manual in the various branches of Ornamental Art,* London, 1853.
Pages 323 to 325: *Jewelery designs,* in: *The Ornamentist, or Artisan's Manual in the various branches of Ornamental Art,* London, 1853.
Page 326: Caspar Neff. *Initial,* Cologne, 1549.
Page 327: Antonio Tagliente. *Ornamental page,* Venice, 1524.
Page 328, top: Richard Gething. *Calligraphic title,* London, 1619; **bottom:** Edward Cocker. *Scrolls,* London, 1657.
Page 329: Ludovico degli Arrighi. *La operina da Imparare di scrivere littera Cancellaresca,* Italy, 1522.
Page 330: Giorgio Sellari. *Ornamental capitals,* Italy, 16th century.
Page 331: Wolfgang Fugger. *Labyrinth,* Nuremberg, 1553.
Page 332, top: *Calligraphy,* France, 17th century; **bottom:** *Calligraphy,* France, 16th century.
Pages 333 to 349: Johann Georg Schwandner. *Calligraphia latina,* Vienna, 1756.
Page 350, bottom: Melchior Lotter. *Calligraphic title,* Wittenberg, 1522. **top:** Caspar Neff. *Calligraphic title,* Cologne, 1549.
Page 351, top: Jan Van den Velde. *Calligraphic page,* Rotterdam, 1605; **bottom:** Periccioli. *Calligraphic page,* Sienna, 1619.
Page 352: Geobattista Pisani. *Scrolls,* Genoa, 1640.
Page 353, top: Joaquin José Ventura da Silva. *Scrolls,* Lisbon, 1803; **bottom:** Edward Cocker. *Scrolls,* London, 1672.
Page 354: Johann Georg Schwandner. *Calligraphia latina,* Vienna, 1756.
Page 355: Manoel Andrade de Figueiredo. *Scrolls,* Lisbon, 1722.
Page 356: Jean L'Évangéliste Mettenleiter. *Scrolls,* Munich, 1850.
Page 357: Manoel Andrade de Figueiredo. *Pen stroke exercises,* Lisbon, 1722.
Page 358, Top: John Seddon. *Scrolls,* London, 1695; **bottom:** Maria Strick. *Calligraphic page,* Delft, 1607.

Pages 314 à 319 : *Ornements typographiques,* XIXe siècle.
Pages 320 à 321 : *Motifs pour joaillerie,* in : *The Ornamentist, or Artisan's Manual in the various branches of Ornamental Art,* Londres, 1853.
Page 322 : *Motifs pour gravure sur métal,* in : *The Ornamentist, or Artisan's Manual in the various branches of Ornamental Art,* Londres, 1853.
Page 322 : *Motifs pour ferronerie,* in : *The Ornamentist, or Artisan's Manual in the various branches of Ornamental Art,* Londres, 1853.
Pages 323 à 325 : *Motifs pour joaillerie,* in : *The Ornamentist, or Artisan's Manual in the various branches of Ornamental Art,* Londres, 1853.
Page 326 : Caspar Neff. *Initiale,* Cologne, 1549.
Page 327 : Antonio Tagliente. *Pages ornées,* Venise, 1524.
Page 328, en haut : Richard Gething. *Titre calligraphié,* Londres, 1619. **En bas :** Edward Cocker. *Volutes,* Londres, 1657.
Page 329 : Ludovico degli Arrighi. *La operina da Imparare di scrivere littera Cancellaresca,* Italie, 1522.
Page 330 : Giorgio Sellari. *Majuscules calligraphiées,* Italie, XVIe siècle.
Page 331 : Wolfgang Fugger. *Labyrinthe,* Nuremberg, 1553.
Page 332, en haut : *Pièce d'écriture,* France, XVIIe siècle. **En bas :** *Pièce d'écriture,* France, XVIe siècle.
Pages 333 à 349 : Johann Georg Schwandner. *Calligraphia latina,* Vienne, 1756.
Page 350, en bas : Melchior Lotter. *Titre calligraphié,* Wittenberg, 1522. **En haut :** Caspar Neff. *Titre calligraphié,* Cologne, 1549.
Page 351 en haut : Jan Van den Velde. *Page calligraphiée,* Rotterdam, 1605. **En bas :** Periccioli. *Page calligraphiée,* Sienne, 1619.
Page 352 : Geobattista Pisani. *Volutes,* Gênes, 1640.
Page 353 en haut : Joaquin José Ventura da Silva. *Volutes,* Lisbonne, 1803. **En bas :** Edward Cocker. *Volutes,* Londres, 1672.
Page 354 : Johann Georg Schwandner. *Calligraphia latina,* Vienne, 1756.
Page 355 : Manoel Andrade de Figueiredo. *Volutes,* Lisbonne, 1722.
Page 356 : Jean L'Évangéliste Mettenleiter. *Volutes,* Munich, 1850.
Page 357 : Manoel Andrade de Figueiredo. *Exercices de traits de plume,* Lisbonne, 1722.
Page 358, en haut : John Seddon. *Volutes,*

Seite 310 bis 312 : *Typographische Ornamente,* 17. Jahrhundert.

Seite 313 : *Mosaik- und Marketeriemotive,* 19. Jahrhundert.

Seite 314 bis 319 : *Typographische Ornamente,* 19. Jahrhundert.

Seite 320 bis 321 : *Juwelierkunstmotive,* aus : *The Ornamentist, or Artisan's Manual in the various branches of Ornamental Art,* London, 1853.

Seite 322 : *Metallstichmotive,* aus : *The Ornamentist, or Artisan's Manual in the various branches of Ornamental Art,* London, 1853.

Seite 322 : *Kunstschmiedmotive,* aus : *The Ornamentist, or Artisan's Manual in the various branches of Ornamental Art,* London, 1853.

Seite 323 bis 325 : *Juwelierkunstmotive,* aus : *The Ornamentist, or Artisan's Manual in the various branches of Ornamental Art,* London, 1853.

Seite 326 : Caspar Neff. *Initialen,* Köln, 1549.

Seite 327 : Antonio Tagliente. *Verzierte Seiten,* Venedig, 1524.

Seite 328, oben : Richard Gething. *Kalligraphierte Titel,* London, 1619. **Unten :** Edward Cocker. *Voluten,* London, 1657.

Seite 329 : Ludovico degli Arrighi. *La operina da Imparare di scrivere littera Cancellaresca,* Italien, 1522.

Seite 330 : Giorgio Sellari. *Kalligraphierte Großbuchstaben,* Italien, 16. Jahrhundert.

Seite 331 : Wolfgang Fugger. *Labyrinth,* Nürnberg, 1553.

Seite 332, oben : *Schreibstücke,* Frankreich, 17. Jahrhundert. **Unten :** *Schreibstücke,* Frankreich, 16. Jahrhundert.

Seite 333 bis 349 : Johann Georg Schwandner. *Calligraphia latina,* Wien, 1756.

Seite 350, unten : Melchior Lotter. *Kalligraphierte Titel,* Wittenberg, 1522. **Oben :** Caspar Neff. *Kalligraphierte Titel,* Köln, 1549.

Seite 351 oben : Jan Van den Velde. *Kalligraphierte Seite,* Rotterdam, 1605. **Unten :** Periccioli. *Kalligraphierte Seite,* Siena, 1619.

Seite 352 : Geobattista Pisani. *Voluten,* Genua, 1640.

Seite 353 oben : Joaquin José Ventura da Silva. *Voluten,* Lissabon, 1803. **Unten :** Edward Cocker. *Voluten,* London, 1672.

Seite 354 : Johann Georg Schwandner. *Calligraphia latina,* Wien, 1756.

Seite 355 : Manoel Andrade de Figueiredo. *Voluten,* Lissabon, 1722.

Seite 356 : Johannes der Evangelist Mettenleiter. *Voluten,* München, 1850.

Páginas 310 hasta 312 : *Adornos tipograficos,* siglo XVII.

Página 313 : *Motivo para mosaico o marquetería,* siglo XIX.

Páginas 314 hasta 319 : *Adornos tipográficos,* siglo XIX.

Páginas 320 hasta 321 : *Motivos para la joyería,* in : *The Ornamentist, or Artisan's Manual in the various branches of Ornamental Art,* Londra, 1853.

Página 322 : *Motivos para ferretería,* in : *The Ornamentist, or Artisan's Manual in the various branches of Ornamental Art,* Londra, 1853.

Páginas 323 hasta 325 : *Motivos para la joyería,* in : *The Ornamentist, or Artisan's Manual in the various branches of Ornamental Art,* Londra, 1853.

Página 326 : Caspar Neff. *Inicial,* Colonia, 1549.

Página 327 : Antonio Tagliente. *Páginas adornadas,* Venecia, 1524.

Página 328, alto : Richard Gething. *Título caligrafico,* Londra, 1619. **Bajo :** Edward Cocker. *Volutas,* Londra, 1657.

Página 329 : Ludovico degli Arrighi. *La operina da Imparare di scrivere littera Cancellaresca,* Italia, 1522.

Página 330 : Giorgio Sellari. *Mayúsculas caligráficas,* Italia, siglo XVI.

Página 331 : Wolfgang Fugger. *Laberinto,* **Nuremberg,** 1553.

Página 332, alto : *Pieza de escritura,* Francia, siglo XVII. **Bajo :** *Pieza de escritura,* Francia, siglo XVI.

Página 333 hasta 349 : Johann Georg Schwandner. *Calligraphia latina,* Vienna, 1756.

Página 350, bajo : Melchior Lotter. *Título caligrafico,* Wittenberg, 1522. **Alto :** Caspar Neff. *Título caligrafico,* Cologne, 1549.

Página 351 alto : Jan Van den Velde. *Página caligrafica,* Rotterdam, 1605. **Bajo :** Periccioli. *Página caligrafica,* Sienne, 1619.

Página 352 : Geobattista Pisani. *Volutas,* Génova, 1640.

Página 353 alto : Joaquin José Ventura da Silva. *Volutas,* Lisbonne, 1803. **Bajo :** Edward Cocker. *Volutas,* Londres, 1672.

Página 354 : Johann Georg Schwandner. *Calligraphia latina,* Vienna, 1756.

Página 355 : Manoel Andrade de Figueiredo. *Volutas,* Lisboa, 1722.

Página 356 : Jean L'Évangéliste Mettenleiter. *Volutas,* **Munich,** 1850.

Página 357 : Manoel Andrade de Figueiredo. *Ejercicios de trazo de pluma,* Lisboa, 1722.

Page 359: Jacob Jacobelln. *Title page,* Strasburg, 1579.
Page 360 Top: Marolles. *Examples of calligraphy by various masters,* Paris, n.d. ; **bottom:** Geobattista Pisani. *Pen strokes,* Genoa, 1640.
Page 361: *Borders,* London, 1840.
Page 362: *Calligraphy,* 16th century.
Page 363: Marolles. *Examples of calligraphy by various masters,* Paris, n.d.

Londres, 1695. **En bas :** Maria Strick. *Page calligraphiée,* Delft, 1607.
Page 359 : Jacob Jacobelln. *Page de titre,* Strasbourg, 1579.
Page 360 en haut : Marolles. *Pièces d'écriture des différents maîtres,* Paris, s.d. **En bas :** Geobattista Pisani. *Traits de plume,* Gênes, 1640.
Page 361 : *Bordures,* Londres, 1840.
Page 362 : *Calligraphie,* XVIᵉ siècle.
Page 363 : Marolles. *Pièces d'écriture des différents maîtres,* Paris, s.d.

Seite 357 : Manoel Andrade de Figueiredo. *Federstrichübungen,* Lissabon, 1722.
Seite 358, oben : John Seddon. *Voluten,* London, 1695. **Unten :** Maria Strick. *Kalligraphierte Seiten,* Delft, 1607.
Seite 359 : Jacob Jacobelln. *Titelseite,* Straßburg, 1579.
Seite 360 oben : Marolles. *Pièces d'écriture des différents maîtres,* Paris, undatiert. **Unten :** Geobattista Pisani. *Federstriche,* Genua, 1640.
Seite 361 : *Bordüren,* London, 1840.
Seite 362 : *Kalligraphie,* 16. Jahrhundert.
Seite 363 : Marolles. *Pièces d'écriture des différents maîtres,* Paris, undatiert.

Página 358, alto : John Seddon. *Volutas,* Londres, 1695. **Bajo :** Maria Strick. *Página caligrafica,* Delft, 1607.
Página 359 : Jacob Jacobelln. *Página de titulo,* Strasbourg, 1579.
Página 360 alto : Marolles. *Pièces d'écriture des différents maîtres,* Paris, s.d. **Bajo :** Geobattista Pisani. *Trazos de pluma,* Genoa, 1640.
Página 361 : *Bordillos,* Londra, 1840.
Página 362 : *Calligrafia,* siglo XVI.
Página 363 : Marolles. *Pièces d'écriture des différents maîtres,* Paris, s.d.

Bibliography • Bibliographie
Literaturnachweis • Bibliografía

Berliner (R.). *Ornamentale Vorlagebläter des 15. bis 19. Jhs,* Leipzig, 1925-1926.
Chastel (A.). *Mythe de la Renaissance,* Genève, 1966.
Chastel (A.). *Crise de la Renaissance,* Genève, 1966.
Chastel (A.). *La Grottesque,* Paris, 1988.
Geymuller de. *Les Du Cerceau, leur vie, leur œuvre,* Paris, 1887.
Gruber (A.). *L'Art décoratif en Europe,* Paris, 1993.
Guilmard (D.). *Les Maîtres ornemanistes,* Paris, 1880-1882.
Migeon (G.). *Francisque Pellegrin, la fleur de la science de pourtraicture,* Paris, 1908.
Reynard. *L'Ornement des anciens maîtres,* Paris, 1845.

Achevé d'imprimer
en avril 2000 sur les presses
de l'imprimerie Grafedit à Azzano San Paolo – Italie
Dépôt légal 2e trimestre 2000